POLICY STUDIES IN CAN
The State of the Art

The study of public policy in Canada is well rooted in traditional legal-
historical analysis of Canadian government and political economy.
However, the current emphasis among political and other social scientists
on policy issues, and the proliferation of theoretical concepts that such an
emphasis has generated, are relatively recent developments. In fact, it is
only since the 1970s that a separate field of policy studies has emerged in
Canada. In *Policy Studies in Canada* twenty-one leading scholars in the
field of Canadian public policy trace the progress of a quarter century of
research and publication in the fields of policy studies and policy
analysis.

The essays in Part I, 'Policy Studies in Canada: A Thirty-Year Retrospect,' and in Part II, 'Policy Studies in Practice: The Rise of Policy
Analysis in Canada,' examine the formative influences and theoretical
underpinnings of policy studies, and the penetration of policy analysis
into governmental and non-governmental organizations. Part III,
'Contemporary Approaches to Canadian Policy Studies,' describes and
assesses the four major methodological approaches used in contemporary
Canadian policy studies: rational choice, network analysis, discourse
analysis, and comparative studies. Part IV, 'Prospects for the Near
Future,' provides observations on future directions of policy studies in
Canada, presenting fresh approaches suited to the unique character of the
Canadian social and political environments, and a reminder of the
importance of empirical research and theory construction.

LAURENT DOBUZINSKIS is an associate professor in the Department of
Political Science, Simon Fraser University. He is author of *The Self-
Organizing Polity: An Epistemological Analysis of Political Life*.
MICHAEL HOWLETT is an associate professor in the Department of Political
Science, Simon Fraser University. His most recent work, co-authored
with M. Ramesh, is *Studying Public Policy*.
DAVID LAYCOCK is an associate professor in the Department of Political
Science, Simon Fraser University. He is author of *Populism and Democratic
Thought in the Canadian Prairies, 1910–1945*; and co-editor, with Michael
Howlett, of *The Puzzles of Power*.

Policy Studies in Canada:
The State of the Art

EDITED BY LAURENT DOBUZINSKIS,
MICHAEL HOWLETT, DAVID LAYCOCK

UNIVERSITY OF TORONTO PRESS
Toronto Buffalo London

© University of Toronto Press Incorporated 1996
Toronto   Buffalo   London
Printed in Canada

ISBN 0-8020-0528-4 (cloth)
ISBN 0-8020-6966-5 (paper)

Printed on acid-free paper

Canadian Cataloguing in Publication Data

Main entry under title:

Policy studies in Canada

Includes bibliographical references.
ISBN 0-8020-0528-4 (bound)
ISBN 0-8020-6966-5 (pbk.)

1. Policy sciences. 2. Policy sciences – Methodology. 3. Political planning – Canada.
I. Dobuzinskis, Laurent, 1947–   . II. Howlett, Michael Patrick, 1955–
III. Laycock, David H. (David Howard), 1954–

JL75.P65 1996   320'.6'0971   C96-930355-6

University of Toronto Press acknowledges the financial assistance to its
publishing program of the Canada Council and the Ontario Arts Council.

Contents

Acknowledgments

This book originated in a series of papers presented to an extended workshop at the annual general meeting of the Canadian Political Science Association in June 1993. Several participants in that Ottawa workshop contributed to the development of these essays, including especially Patrick Smith of Simon Fraser University, Robert Campbell of Trent University, and Rainer-Olaf Schultze of the University of Augsburg, Germany. A follow-up workshop held in Vancouver under the auspices of the Institute of Public Administration of Canada and the Governance Research Group at Simon Fraser University contributed further valuable components to this volume. We would like to thank Luc Bernier, Myrna Hall, and Norm Cook for their help in organizing that second workshop. The Dean of Arts at Simon Fraser University provided financial aid in support of this latter workshop, for which we are grateful. To complete the theoretically diverse canvas which we have hoped from the outset would be one of the volume's major virtues, we invited a group of recognized specialists to contribute additional chapters. Once the collection was complete, several anonymous reviewers from the University of Toronto Press provided helpful commentaries.

On the production side, the book was typeset by Anita Mahoney of the Dean of Arts Office at Simon Fraser University. Her professional expertise and judgment made joint editorship a relative ease.

Finally, our thanks to Virgil Duff of the University of Toronto Press for his early encouragement of, and continuing support for, this project. Virgil's editorial support for innovative Canadian public policy scholarship goes back as far as any of our contributors' own research history. Students of Canadian public policy all owe him a collective debt of gratitude.

1

Introduction

LAURENT DOBUZINSKIS, MICHAEL HOWLETT, DAVID LAYCOCK

This book surveys the past, present, and future of Canadian political scientists' contributions to policy studies in Canada. Retrospective chapters examine the beginnings of these policy studies, including formative influences and theoretical departures, in the works of students of Canadian government, public administration, and political economy. Early chapters are devoted to the evolution of the profession and outline the penetration of policy analysis into governmental and nongovernmental organizations. The main section of the book outlines the principal elements of, and critical concerns with, the four major methodological approaches found in contemporary Canadian policy studies: rational choice, network analysis, discourse analysis, and comparative studies. These methodological chapters present the principal elements of contemporary approaches, describe the research agendas followed by their adherents, and illustrate strengths and weaknesses with reference to Canadian policy experience. Concluding chapters present views of likely directions for policy studies within Canadian political science. These chapters illustrate the promise of current work but also underline the need for careful conceptualization and empirical referents if that promise is to be realized.

The study of public policy is by no means a new focus of research in Canadian political science. It is well rooted in traditional Canadian legal-historical and staples analysis of Canadian government and economy.[1] However, the current emphasis among political and other social scientists on policy issues and the rich assortment of theoretical concepts that such an emphasis has generated are relatively recent developments. In fact, it is only since the early 1970s that one can properly speak of a separate field of policy studies in Canada. Prior to this, researchers saw little need to critically assess their methods or findings within the context of a disciplinary canon. But this situation has changed, and students of policy making in Canada now face an evolving and complex range of approaches to the subject. Interested observers in related areas such as public administration or Canadian politics also need a map to guide them through this newly charted terrain. The purpose of this volume is to offer such a map.

We have tried to represent most established and new perspectives on Canadian policy studies, and to divide the field in a manner that allows authors to offer clear, distinctive interpretations of the major features in both the more familiar territory and in recently colonized analytical regions. A related concern structuring the volume is to facilitate comparisons between policy studies and other areas of interest to Canadian political scientists. For example, the fact that rational choice models constitute a newly important direction of research in policy studies invites comparisons with other subfields, such as the study of parties and elections, to determine the extent to which the use of these models can be generalized across various political phenomena. The same is true of recent emphases on policy networks and communities, or on discourse analysis, both of which beg comparisons with more general pluralist and post-modern analyses of political life.

This volume has been organized to provide a basis for assessing aspects of distinctiveness and increasing tensions within Canadian policy studies, and aspects of convergence and future expansion. The development of political studies in Canada since the 1960s generally parallels that in the United States, with a conscious or unconscious emphasis on Eastonian 'outputs.'[2] However, Canadian students of public policy have been influenced by a different set of antecedent historical studies, which compete with the American imports in establishing research interests and designs. The neo-Marxist school of political economy, for example, has occupied a more influential place within the Canadian policy studies community than their equivalents south of the border who have tended to emphasize groups rather than class in the policy process. We also notice in the Canadian literature less emphasis on rights issues such as abortion, biomedical choices, crime, and law and order. Canadian students of public policy making have tended to focus on neither the high-level ethical issues nor on the micro-level pressure group issues which have attracted scholars in other countries, notably the United States. To the extent that they have made theoretical contributions to policy studies, it has been in the middle-level range of theorizing about aspects of the policy process, including especially policy subsystems and implementation.[3]

When political scientists become too preoccupied with the study of the policy process, however, they tend to have less and less to say about the content and impact of policies. They run the risk of appearing to ignore the practical concerns of policy makers and the attentive public. In Canada this problem has manifested itself in a tendency for studies of public administration and public policy to diverge substantially in form and content. It is only recently that this impasse has begun to be addressed, as Part II of this volume indeed attempts to do.

This is not to say, however, that the most significant aspect of policy studies in Canada is the extent to which they are pulled in different directions. There have been several encouraging developments pointing toward examples of convergence in the goals and methods of research. One obvious new departure from past practice in Canada (although the extent of the departure is challenged by Colin Bennett in his contribution to this volume) is the emphasis on a comparative approach. Almost all authors in this volume use a comparative approach, more or less systematically, and more or less explicitly, but always in some significant measure. This is partly due to what Bruce Doern identifies as the trend toward growing interdependence between domestic and international issues. But the choice of comparative approaches is also a response to what scholars now perceive as the need to test and refine competing models of policy making derived from careful empirical examinations of Canadian circumstances.

At a more theoretical level, one also notices a deeper appreciation in Canadian studies of the complexity, fluidity, and contingent nature of most policy problems. Authors vary in the degree to which they believe that policy problems are constructed by actors whose very involvement in, or exclusion from, debates and decision-making processes changes the nature of the problem at hand and opens up or restricts possible options. Nonetheless, most authors in this volume comment on related themes, using the language of 'context,' 'learning,' 'complex relationships,' 'mutual dependence,' to describe important elements of Canadian policy making. All contributors to this volume demonstrate a clear awareness that policy problems can be framed at different levels of analysis, from a variety of perspectives leading to divergent hypotheses, and that policy issues involve open-ended sets of shifting variables and parameters.

This book has grown out of attempts to chart this shifting terrain. Beginning with a series of workshops held in conjunction with the 1993 Canadian Political Science Association annual general meeting, leading students of the policy process in Canada were asked to reflect on where policy studies in Canada have been, and where they are headed. This book brings together papers presented at these and other forums to survey the policy studies landscape in Canada in the mid-1990s – or, at any rate, the place of political science contributions within it.

Our eighteen substantive chapters are divided into four Parts. Part I includes four chapters that examine the origins of policy studies in Canada, identify important formative influences, and underline some significant departures from original premises. In Chapter 2, G. Bruce Doern offers a retrospective view of thirty years of research on public policy in Canada through the prism of his own significant contributions to the field. He argues that policy studies are often inspired by scientific concerns but also reflect values that are more commonly associated with the practice of an art, and draw upon the experience of practitioners in ways that describe a craft.[4] Doern sees these qualities and dimensions in all five evolutionary stages he analyses. The first stage represents the beginning of contemporary efforts to study public policy as a specific dimension of political life; it was primarily concerned with the 'structures and processes of the inner state,' that is, cabinet, central agencies, regulatory agencies, and so on. The growing influence of neo-Marxist political economy, on the one hand, and public choice, on the other, corresponds to the second stage. It was followed by attempts to 'bring the state back in,' which were prompted, in part, by the society-centred quality of studies in the neo-Marxist political economy tradition. The development of comparative policy analysis could be viewed as a fourth stage. With the 1990s, and the recognition that domestic policy formation and international relations overlap in many ways, we have entered into a fifth stage. Doern presents these stages not as completely distinct and isolated categories but rather as heuristic tools for making sense of some significant trends.

Chapter 3 briefly highlights the many relationships that have always existed between public administration and policy studies in Canada, even if in recent years these two approaches seem to have diverged somewhat. Richard W. Phidd argues that the focus on institutions which is noticeable in the recent literature on policy making can continue to serve as a bridge between the two disciplines. While at its core public administration appears to be limited to the study of administrative and legal structures, and policy studies to be particularly concerned with the influence of groups and other actors external to the state, implementation studies, the importance of which is now widely acknowledged, draw interesting insights from both these sources. The approach that is best suited to undertake this kind of research, according to Phidd, is one that is concerned with organizational behaviour and dynamics.

In Chapter 4 A. Paul Pross contends that the emphasis on government institutions cannot altogether hide the fact that Canadian politics and Canadian policy studies have been profoundly influenced by the American minimalist view of the state. (Dobuzinskis provides additional evidence of this influence in Chapter 7.) The problem, in his view, is how to 'address the tension between our understanding of the proper role of the state in Canada and our wish to incorporate into our political life those features of pluralism we find attractive and beneficial.' But even if one wishes to denounce the pervasive impact of American values, Pross claims pluralism ought not to be the principal target of these attacks. Critics of pluralism, who reject its individualist presuppositions and think that it denigrates the notion of public interest, overlook the relevance of pluralism to an analysis of the dynamic aspects of political life. Significant political changes often result from a conjunction of the kind of incremental adjustments described by pluralist models. Besides, Pross argues, Canadian authors working within the pluralist tradition never lost sight of the state; what they have done is to draw attention to the relationships that develop between organized interests and the state.

In Chapter 5 Stephen McBride provides a historical account of the development and impact of studies of Canadian political economy upon Canadian policy studies. This uniquely Canadian school of thought has been and continues to be an important academic tradition within Canadian social science. Canadian political economy has focused on the relationships between the state and markets, and examines how power structures are shaped by these relationships. Early political economists led by Harold Innis and W.A. Mackintosh formulated a theory that accounted for the activism of the Canadian state as well as for Canada's dependence on international trade (and disadvantaged position within the international economy). This theory underlined the dominant character of the staples-producing sector in the Canadian economy. What characterized that sector – and still does – is an almost exclusive orientation toward exports, requiring massive infrastructural investments that only the state could finance. Once the Canadian economy got stuck in this developmental path, it became very difficult to follow a different course. At various points in Canadian history, this analysis informed not only theoretical studies but also the practice of Canadian public policy making. Hence during the Trudeau years, for example, and especially between 1980 and 1984, a number of important policy initiatives that were designed to achieve greater domestic control over foreign-dominated industrial sectors were inspired at least in part by ideas originally put forward by political economists. Of course, the shift toward a neoconservative agenda under Prime Minister Brian Mulroney, which continues under Prime Minister Jean Chrétien, has meant that political economists have become policy critics rather than influential policy advocates. They nonetheless continue to have some influence on social movements and coalitions defending the welfare state.

While policy studies tend to be carried out by academic researchers interested in *explaining* how the policy process is shaped by a combination of macro and micro variables, policy analysis tends to be more oriented toward the *evaluation* of policy outcomes. But these two research strategies are not mutually exclusive and sometimes overlap in interesting ways. Therefore, it is important to keep both approaches in perspective, and more generally to reflect upon the respective roles of academic observers, professional analysts, and public servants. Part II includes three chapters. The first two discuss the rise of policy analysis in Canada during the last two or three decades and assess its political significance. The third one deals more specifically with the dilemmas faced by public servants

In Chapter 6 Stephen Brooks shows how policy analysis has become the principal activity of a growing numbers of professional experts. The rise of experts has complex implications. Not only do experts intervene more frequently and openly in the policy-making process, but their presence affects the dynamics of power relations. Moreover, their specialized discourse, which often contains 'plastic' words that sound authoritative but mean very little, has become an integral part of our cultural environment. Brooks argues that while experts may not have a great deal of autonomous power, their indirect influence is pervasive; speaking the language of experts and projecting an image of professional competence have become prerequisites for effective group participation in the policy process.

In Chapter 7 Laurent Dobuzinskis describes the formation of a marketplace of policy ideas in which a variety of actors intervene, paying particular attention to the relative displacement in recent years of public policy research organizations such as the now defunct Economic Council of Canada by privately financed 'think-tanks.' While the policy debates to which these policy institutes contribute vary considerably from year to year and from one institution to another, Dobuzinskis identifies two dominant trends that have generated far more discussions and policy proposals than other concerns. These are, on the one hand, a gradual shift from the paradigm of market failure to the idea of government failure and, on the other hand, a growing interest in institutional reform prompted by demands from a variety of sources for more democratic and participatory practices. Dobuzinskis argues that professional policy analysts have done little more than echo themes and demands already voiced by a variety of groups or individuals in academia, the business world, or social movements. Their record in responding to these developments with innovative proposals is not very impressive, albeit with several interesting exceptions.

Chapter 8 offers a challenging account of the evolution of both the theory and practice of public administration and of its relationship with policy analysis. Public policy and public administration complement each other in many ways. Nevertheless, the concepts and methods, as well as the practical skills, that define public administration remain distinct from the tools used in policy studies. Donald J. Savoie argues that one of the consequences of the expansion of the scope of government responsibilities in the postwar years, and especially in the 1960s and 1970s, was that the rules of the bureaucratic game changed during these years. A new generation of public servants made of the mastery of policy analysis techniques a means toward rapid promotion and career success. At the same time, Savoie also notes, the study of the policy process and the evaluation of policy outcomes displaced more traditional concerns with public administration and public law in the academic world; he points to the evolution of the curriculum of several Canadian graduate programs in public administration as a telling example of this trend. More recently, however, the administrative state has had to deal with increasingly severe financial constraints, and the public service has lost the confidence of the Canadian public. In an attempt to address these problems, government officials, often on the advice of consultants and of academics specializing in business administration, have shown considerable interest in management practices borrowed from the private sector. Savoie contends that public administration is reducible neither to policy analysis nor to management studies. In order to understand what governments do best – a question that is obviously relevant to the concerns of students of the policy process – a detour through public administration, as it has traditionally been taught, researched, and practised, continues to be unavoidable.

Part III contains nine chapters that critically evaluate the respective merits and limitations of four methodological approaches to the study of public policy now contending for popularity among political scientists. These approaches have been chosen either because they already are widely used or because they seem to offer interesting potentials.

Chapters 9 and 10 focus on rational (or public) choice, a relatively new paradigm in Canadian policy studies that is already a major current in the United States and elsewhere. In Chapter 9 Mark Sproule-Jones uses epistemological analysis to make sense of what he sees as the fracturing of the field into two schools of public choice, whose differences revolve around varying definitions of public goods. While earlier models of public choice were concerned primarily with deciding how public goods should be produced and distributed, some of the more recent models claim to rest on principles (i.e., the analysis of rules) that are meant to be applied to any political problem – whether or not they involve public goods or even policy concerns. This is unfortunate, according to Sproule-Jones, because significant variations in the nature of the goods at stake in policy problems, and in the 'situational variables' that describe the time and place of the occurrence of such problems, can no longer be taken into account. Sproule-Jones argues in favour of models that continue to pay more attention to situational variables and their effects on policy issues by proposing a 'perspectivist' epistemology that allows sufficient attention to the nature of goods about which policy choices are made.

In Chapter 10 Réjean Landry provides an overview and an assessment of the three methodological options open to researchers who wish to apply the principles of rational choice to policy analysis. In his view, the least satisfactory is the 'rational actor model,' which examines the choices supposedly made by an individual strictly on the basis of his or her preferences and without any reference to the actions of other members of society. Game theoretical models, on the other hand, take into account the mutual adjustments to their strategies made by 'players' engaged in various 'games'; the most interesting of these games are those in which cooperation between the players can evolve over time, even though there are also strong incentives to 'defect' (e.g., the prisoner's dilemma). But Landry argues that policy analysts should find models of 'institutional rational choice' more advantageous because they more realistically reflect the complex context in which policy decisions are made. The task of the analyst then becomes one of identifying the most beneficial institutional arrangements. Interestingly, Landry suggests that these do not have to be defined only in terms of a choice between markets and hierarchical organizational structures.

Chapters 11 and 12 examine aspects of a network approach to understanding the policy process, which focuses on the key role played by policy subsystems in the policy process. In Chapter 11 Michael M. Atkinson and William D. Coleman discuss the merits of the overall network approach, and of one particular variant that divides a subsystem into a policy community and a policy network. They see this approach as capable of reconciling the fact that public policy processes unite both ideas and interests or knowledge and power in producing authoritative government decisions on complex, subjectively defined social problems. They see this particular approach as useful not only in aiding the understanding of discrete policy decisions, but also in helping to explain the dynamic elements of policy change and development.

In Chapter 12 Evert A. Lindquist also addresses the strengths and weaknesses of this approach. His chapter, however, contains a plea for more empirical tests of any theoretical models against the realities of the Canadian administrative state. Such studies, he argues, have the potential not only to refine and improve theory, but also to aid the practice of public policy making in Canada.

In Chapters 13 and 14 Susan D. Phillips and Douglas Torgerson outline elements of the new post-modern perspectives on public policy making. Each author focuses on how policy making is affected by the social discourses and discursive practices that surround any complex social problem.

In Chapter 13 Phillips examines the impact of feminist analysis on the 'grammar' of policy making in Canada. She contends that debates over epistemology and the notion of 'difference' within feminist theory have led to three major contributions to policy studies. The first identifies socially constructed discourse as a terrain within which dramatically different effects of policy design are experienced by women and other nonhegemonic constituencies as a consequence of battles over strategic conceptual and linguistic ground. The second contribution invites a reconsideration of the unequal and limiting impacts of policy – especially social welfare policy – on various social categories, utilizing feminist notions of group 'difference' and identity. The third contribution examines how concerted action based on identity develops women's self-consciously active and participatory 'voice,' and hence democratic intervention in the public sphere/policy processes. As Phillips notes, these contributions lead toward a serious critique of our relatively closed policy communities, addressing a commitment of social responsibility to both researchers and the policy process itself.

In Chapter 14 Torgerson starts from the observation that three post-positivist approaches – hermeneutics, critical theory, and deconstructionism – have successfully challenged conventional empirical methods in the social sciences. From a post-positivist standpoint, questions of meaning must be placed at the centre of the process of inquiry. Consequently, that process is refocused on issues attendant to problem definition; the analyst's role is to investigate how problems are socially constructed rather than to formulate optimal solutions to given problems. Technocratic practices that dominated two or three decades ago have proven to be unsatisfactory in a number of policy areas. Torgerson argues that several recent policy initiatives in Canada developed through participatory processes which hold out the promise of overcoming narrowly defined political or bureaucratic discourses and their negative effects on policy making. However, according to Torgerson, further progress in that direction may depend on a deeper appreciation of the subtle differences that exist between the three elements of the new post-positivist discourse.

In Chapters 15 to 17 the state of comparative studies of public policy making in Canada is examined. Colin Bennet explains in Chapter 15 why and how a comparative approach holds much potential for enriching the field of policy studies. He laments, however, the fact that too few comparisons are attempted with countries other than the United States, and argues that comparative policy studies in Canada have failed to keep pace with those carried out in the United States, Europe, and elsewhere. Unfortunately, comparativists in other countries have so far tended not to include Canada in their case studies.

In Chapter 16 Carolyn Hughes Tuohy starts from the observation that 'a fundamental ambivalence about the role of the state versus the role of the market, about the level of primary identification with the political community (national versus regional), and about the right and responsibilities of the individual versus those of the collectivity, has been incorporated into the institutions of the Canadian state.' After examining various dimensions of this ambivalence (e.g., the different ways in which Québécois and 'English' Canadians relate to federal institutions), Tuohy turns to three policy arenas that exemplify the interplay between Canada's ambivalent institutions and different organized interests. These examples assist her outline of specific characteristics of the Canadian 'policy style,' in an account that facilitates the comparisons with other countries she sees as essential to Canadian policy studies.

In Chapter 17 Mildred A. Schwartz notes the Canadian tendency to focus intentionally or otherwise on comparisons with our southern neighbour. She argues that there is much to be learned from Canada–U.S. comparisons. For example, an institutionalist approach can explain interesting differences as well as some similarities. Many contemporary studies are indeed premised on institutionalist assumptions. However, Schwartz suggests that such an approach should not be allowed to completely brush aside the role of individual actors and groups in promoting new policy goals. The search for significant cultural differences and their impact on policy making is another perspective that has yielded valuable insights. But Schwartz warns that these insights may turn out to be meaningless if attention is not also paid to the process of cultural change.

Finally, in Part IV, Leslie A. Pal and Richard Simeon offer several observations on future directions of policy studies in Canada. In Chapter 18 Pal takes note of the emergence of five 'fresh orientations' that happen to be particularly well suited to the unique character of the Canadian academic, social, and political environments: 'the rise of post-modern/post-positivist approaches to policy analysis; the increasing attention to the noninstrumental dimensions of public policy; the renewed attention to institutions as key factors in explaining the policy process; the internalization of domestic policy processes; and the question of public policy and the political community' (this last point refers to issues such as the definition of citizenship in a multicultural and bilingual nation-state). Confident that researchers will continue to explore the problems posed by these orientations as well as other interesting questions, Pal paints an optimistic picture of a relevant, activist-driven, post-positivist form of policy analysis. In Chapter 19 Simeon reminds us, however, that we should not lose sight of the link between methodologies and the subject matter to which they are applied – that is, the policies to be explained – if we want to sort out the most relevant factors. Simeon is also less sanguine than Pal about the staying power of many recent approaches, suggesting that there is little substitute for time-consuming empirical research and careful, painstaking efforts at theory construction.

Notes

1 See Dawson, *The Government of Canada*; Innis, *Essays in Canadian Economic History*; Macpherson, 'By Innis out of Marx.'
2 On the evolution of policy studies in the American context see Dunn and Kelly, eds., *Advances in Policy Studies since 1950*.
3 It is in the area of identification or configuration of policy instruments, and the rationale for their selection, that Canadian scholarship in the 1970s and early 1980s is most often cited. See Doern and Phidd, *Canadian Public Policy*, Linder and Peters, 'Instruments of Government,' and Howlett, 'Policy Instruments, Policy Styles, and Policy Implementation.' Since the mid-1980s, the most often cited Canadian contributions have concerned the identification and categorization of policy communities and networks; here see Chapter 11 by Atkinson and Coleman in this volume, Linquist, 'Public Managers and Policy Communities,' and references to these and other works in van Waarden, 'Dimensions and Types of Policy Networks.'
4 A similar argument with respect to policy studies in the United States can be found in Wildavsky, *Speaking Truth to Power*.

PART ONE

Policy Studies in Canada:
A Thirty-Year Retrospect

2

The Evolution of Canadian Policy Studies as Art, Craft, and Science

G. BRUCE DOERN

The purpose of this chapter is to offer a personal view of the broad evolution of Canadian policy studies over the past thirty years paying attention to its history as art, craft, and science. It must be stressed from the outset that my views are those of a political scientist who is a beaverish interdisciplinary Canadian policy animal.[1] Some of my work has been undertaken alone, but most of it has been stimulatingly collaborative. My eclecticism also emerges from having carried out research in several policy fields (industrial, energy, trade, environment, occupational health, and macroeconomic) and on the main policy instruments (spending, taxation, regulation). A continuous involvement in the research for *How Ottawa Spends*, the School of Public Administration's annual review of national priorities and spending, has involved a perpetual appreciation of, and often dismay about, the underbelly of the state.

This experience, coupled with close involvement in developing a PhD program in public policy and an MA program in public administration at Carleton's School of Public Administration, is what prompts, indeed compels me, to title this chapter the 'art, craft, and science' of Canadian policy studies. But the reason why the evolution of Canadian policy studies must in part be seen as embracing the art, craft, and science of policy studies is in one sense self-evident. It is an art in the primary sense that the making of policy involves the purposeful pursuit of ideas, beliefs, and goals that are valued by interests and citizens in a democracy but that are not easily, or perhaps even properly, reducible to scientific study.[2] It is an art because the evidence about ideas and their causal importance is highly judgmental. Our common sense tells us that policy ideas are important, but our science often does not know what to do with them or how to weight them as a decisive causal variable.

Canadian policy studies is secondly a craft-like activity because it must involve, and account for, the actions of both practitioners and policy advocates. It must factor in both the role of analysis and the nature of advocacy.[3] It is craft-like precisely because there are competing departments, royal commissions, think-tanks, media gurus, scientists, academic and bureaucratic notables, and interest group pressures to contend with, deflect, and accommodate.

And last but not least, Canadian policy studies is part science. The scientific aspects and aspirations have emerged at several levels and in several ways: in elementary efforts at classification[4] in comparative study among countries and among provinces, and in efforts to integrate the politics and economics of public policy within and among countries.[5]

For each of the periods or stages in the development of Canadian policy studies examined below, I seek to show why the art, craft, and science of public policy each have a necessary and compelling presence. The evolutionary journey itself, however, is cast somewhat differently. My assessment of the art, craft, and science of Canadian policy studies portrays the existence of five broad stages of evolution. While I think there are discernible features to each stage, I naturally caution against viewing them as watertight periods. Intellectual and practical developments rarely are. But as a practising public policy academic they mean something to me because I know that they have influenced my fellow academics in how and what we were thinking about and researching as the years went by.

Other cautionary points are needed about such efforts at classification. First, phases do not so much replace each other as build new emphases on to each other. Second, the key phases cannot help but be influenced by the larger political economic forces that influence all of our lives and thoughts. These forces include: the pro-statist preferences of the post–World War II to 1960s period; the pro-market urges of the 1980s; periodic energy crises and wars, especially in the 1970s; and the end of the Cold War in the 1990s. Third, stylized labels of 'neo-this' or 'neo-that' that are coined to capture new periods or insights are often only half right and too often engage academics in a mass-media-style stereotyping of the phases that preceded them … a kind of academic equivalent to the one-minute television news byte. Fourth, clearly these phases are not peculiarly Canadian since they reflect increasingly broad developments in the study of public policy in other OECD countries. But some of the Canadian experience is different in detail and needs to be appreciated.

Canadian Public Policy and the Inner State

The contemporary effort to study Canadian public policy in a concerted way begins, in my view, with an effort in the late 1960s and early 1970s to understand the inner state and how policy was formulated. I recall quite concretely the frustration I had with my own PhD studies where I felt strongly that politics (understood to be mainly parties, elections, interest groups, and federalism) was well examined but 'government' and governing and policy making were not. This frustration is partly what prompted Peter Aucoin and I to produce our initial edited book, *The Structures of Policy Making*. This frustration also influenced the early work of colleagues then studying at Queen's, such as Richard Phidd, Vince Wilson, Michael Whittington, and Richard Van Loon.[6]

If recent terminology were in vogue then, our focus on structures and processes would be viewed as 'neo-institutional' and 'state-centred.' It was earlier neo-institutionalism because it was a reaction against what we regarded as the excesses of *formal* institutionalism. Formal institutionalism was said to involve too descriptive and formal a view of institutions such as cabinet, Parliament, and so-called 'traditional' public administration;[7] hence, we labelled this policy studies work as having a focus on 'structures and processes.' It is helpful to remind ourselves, however, that one was reacting against the *excesses* of formal institutional political science. As with all efforts to break some new ground, in short to become a 'neo,' one must be careful not to throw the baby out with the bathwater. The old institutionalism from Dawson, Corry, and Hodgetts, to name only three exemplars, was always rooted in a set of realities that are as compelling for any student of modern public policy today as they were then. First, at the root of all basic policy institutions are powerful ideas and norms that affect policy formation. Second, it remains the case that core political institutions do not exist, in the first instance, to make policy. In short, they were not established as policy-making machines. Rather their first purpose is the larger democratic one of ensuring representation, preventing tyranny, and ensuring accountable and peaceful transitions in power.

This initial focus on the structures and processes of the inner state, particularly cabinet and executive dynamics, was essential to the early stages of Canadian policy studies. It helped build a base that fleshed out the meaning of what policy institutions more fully were and how they functioned both within the state and outside it. Thus several authors shed light on the actual dynamics of central agencies, departmental policy processes, regulatory agencies, state enterprises, and advisory bodies.[8] Initial work on the classification of policy instruments during this stage also helped bring more subtlety to how policy was forged and to the complex means-ends struggles that went on inside the Canadian political-bureaucratic executive. This incidentally was clearly a work divided between economists and political scientists.[9]

Canadian Policy Studies and the Two Political Economies

If the initial inner state phase can be said to have occurred roughly from the mid- to late-1960s to the mid-1970s, the next phase is clearly dominated by the emergence of the two political economies, Marxist political economy on the one hand, and public choice theory on the other. But coincident with these influences were the contributions of those who simply but strongly cautioned against too much of a 'structures' approach. Hence, Richard Simeon's 1976 review article quite properly reasserted the need to reincorporate institutions and ideas in the study of Canadian public policy.[10]

But it was the two political economies that most forced a change of emphasis, a change of terminology and discourse and, in many respects, a polarization of thought. Above all, the two approaches made the field, in my view, more interesting and stimulating. Marxist or class-based views were hardly new to the study of politics, but they were new in the study of policy formation. The work of Panitch and many others forced a focus on the presence and nature of inequality both in policy outputs and in policy representation and power inside the state.[11] Though largely and broadly society-centred in its focus, the Marxist literature turned some specific policy terminology on its head. Liberal policy theorists and analysts did not know quite what to do with terms such as the coercive, legitimizing, and capital accumulation functions of the state in policy formation, let alone with how 'fractions' of capital are represented in the state. Nonetheless, Marxist theory helped reclassify policy terminology and elicited a subsequent counteraction that was partly a rejection and partly an acceptance of some of these insights. As always, these initial insights and reactions to them are themselves governed by, and screened through, the core values of the authors engaged in the analysis.

The other political economy to emerge in Canadian policy studies centred on the economics discipline's already well tilled concepts of public choice theory.[12] This theory, with its reductionist approach to the behaviour of decision makers and policy institutions, was also jolting to conventional policy study, not only because new terminology had to be absorbed and digested but also because it largely assumed away the existence of concepts such as the public interest and seemed, at times, simply to mark an unwelcome invasion of economists into a domain that seemed comfortably to belong to political scientists and practitioners.

But while public choice was then new to Canadian policy studies, it could hardly be claimed even then that economists were new to the field of policy studies. After all, economists were clearly the dominant knowledge profession behind the whole intellectual architecture of the post–World War II Keynesian macroeconomic policy.[13] They were the dominant profession in the Department of Finance, the Bank of Canada, and in other economic policy departments of government.[14]

What was different about public choice theory was that it did offer insights about policy institutions and processes in part by focusing on the incentive systems of institutional leaders and players.[15] It was also associated with attacks on the efficacy of the state and on the progressive assumptions about the entire liberal democratic social welfare consensus that had emerged after World War II. Interestingly, the more strident and ideological of these attacks came not from academic policy economists but rather from policy think-tanks such as the Fraser Institute.

A particularly interesting feature of Canadian academic economists who broadly used these economic approaches is that, for the most part, they have been much more subtle than their American counterparts in the assumptions they made about real institutions. They are still largely reductionist in their approach, but a virtual Canadian school of public choice can be said to exist in that several Canadian economists showed that institutions and their incentives were quite complex, interactive, and multidimensional.[16]

Refilling the Gaps in the State-Centred Versus Society-Centred Debate on Policy Studies

One of the unfortunate outcomes of the two political economies phase is that the focus on class-based approaches in particular led to the polar labelling of society- versus state-centred schools of thought about policy. My immediate reaction to titles such as Skocpol's 'bringing the state back in' was 'when did it ever leave?'[17] In any event, the brief 'society versus state' polarity was almost instantly succeeded by constructive efforts to refill the gaps with important new layers of subtlety.[18]

One of these efforts was the emergence of conceptual ideas and research about policy communities and networks.[19] Largely these insights can be seen as moving directionally from society or larger polity-based realms to relationships inside the state. Thus what was tracked more clearly were the relationships between components of an interacting community (interest groups, key departments and agencies of government, knowledge groups inside and outside of the state) each armed with similar but not necessarily identical ideas and forms of discourse and rhetoric. Authors such as Paul Pross, Michael Atkinson, Bill Coleman, and Grace Skogstad have made important contributions in seeing these realities. The notion of policy communities emerged, in a sense, from efforts to be more sophisticated about exactly how society-centred interests interacted both outside the state and, to some extent, within the structure of the state as policy was made and brokered.

Moving in the other direction – from internal state structures out to groups, interests, and communities – is recent work on the concept of 'policy sectors.' There are several strands to this work. One is Tom Conway's approach used in his recent study of Environment Canada.[20] It focuses on whether or not lead policy bureaucracies such as the Department of the Environment possess the specific array of organizational resources needed to function and succeed politically and substantively.

A policy sector is a matrix or cluster of government organizations that regularly interact and compete in an effort to defend or promote their policy interests, and that gain access to the policy sector on the basis of their control over organizational resources that are critical for policy sector activities. These government organizations are influenced by, and often closely associated with, nongovernmental interests that may also control organizational resources critical for the policy sector.

Organizations that are active within a policy sector are always to one degree or another dependent upon other organizations within the sector. This is because no one organization can ever control all the resources necessary to achieve a policy objective. In this sense concrete resource dependencies are at the root of power relationships within a sector. These resources are: a workable set of policy ideas; political and organizational leadership; money and financial resources; legal jurisdiction and statutory capacity; and scientific and technical knowledge.[21]

Another earlier strand to this kind of increased subtlety is found in Richard Phidd's and my second edition of *Canadian Public Policy: Ideas, Structure, Process*. The policy interplay framework, elaborated on considerably from the first edition in 1983, seeks to require that the student of any policy field look quite concretely at what kinds of ideas, structures, and processes are present in a policy field, with each of the three components further broken down into their potential component subparts. Thus ideas as a variable involves looking at the role of paradigms in certain policy fields as well as at the particular and actual meanings of norms and values such as efficiency, equality, stability, equity, nationalism, and regionalism. Processes refers to the need to understand the independent influence of the regular rhythms of policy cycles centred around priority-setting, regulation, spending, taxation, and exhortation.

Much of the above gap-filling occurred throughout the past decade and gradually took on the label of neo-institutionalism.[22] However, for the reasons set out above, I prefer to see the stage just described as state-society gap-filling since institutions per se had always been central to Canadian policy studies.

Comparative Policy Studies

As each stage is portrayed it is not difficult to see that the whole notion of stages as an accurate concept becomes more difficult. If metaphors were used, we would be seeing instead a huge policy studies layercake being constructed. This is certainly true of comparative policy studies. Some element of comparison is inevitable in almost any nominal single-country study of a policy field. But clearly the impetus for comparative study was that there could not be a science of public policy until one had systematic comparison across countries.[23] The stages and iterations of such comparative work can be noted briefly.

First, there was an initial wave of simplistic 'input-output' analysis that came close to saying that 'politics,' or political variables, defined in certain ways, 'did not matter' in explaining comparative general policy outputs such as social welfare policy.[24] This immediately generated a search for more sophisticated variables, and how to measure them, on both the dependent variable and independent variable sides of the cause and effect equation. Second, problems of comparison varied greatly when one moved from mass public spending areas to policies or aspects of policies that were delivered through regulatory instruments.[25] The data in the latter areas were simply not as well tilled but also cause and effect relations seemed to have even more intermediary carriers as policy outputs led (perhaps) to later observed effects.

A third problem for comparative policy analysis is how many countries to study, at what depth, and over what time frames. For an author, or even teams of authors, knowing one's own country was often challenge enough. Knowing a second or a third country at a policy-relevant level is daunting, not only on hard scientific empirical grounds but also precisely because policy analysis *is* part art and craft as well.

I have no trouble in concluding that comparative policy analysis has improved greatly and that one can understand Canada's policies better through such comparison. But I also caution against two realities of both carrying out and reading comparative work. First, for such work to be credible it must deal concretely with difficult and often impossible to quantify variables such as the influence of ideas and structural/institutional entities, policy communities, and political cultures. But the more that such variables are seriously treated, the more 'dense' the book or analysis inevitably becomes. In short, it ceases to be a stylish or easy 'read.' Clearly, the number of countries also affects this equation of reader tolerance and stamina. Most of the good analyses in this realm are also 'tough reads.' They are unlikely to be candidates for future movie rights!

The Internationalization of Domestic Policy Formation

The last area of classification is one that is, in one sense, only emerging as the 1990s evolve.[26] The internationalization of domestic policy formation refers to the growing number of ways in which international pressures, policy agencies, ideas, and interest coalitions are penetrating the structure of the Canadian state.

In short, policy analysis now needs to examine how such forces are affecting the concrete functioning of domestic or national governmental institutions, especially in heretofore relatively 'domestic' policy fields. The analytical concerns here are numerous but they include: understanding concretely any changes in the way policy is made; the changed (diminishing?) room for policy manoeuvre; and the way domestic policy institutions and policy communities think and act, and reshape their policy discourse.[27]

It is of course true that foreign policy and international relations have always exercised influence on domestic policy.[28] Moreover, domestic policy makers have always learned and adapted policies borrowed from abroad. But even Canadian foreign policy, international political economy, and integration scholars have tended to focus on state-to-state relations, rather than following policy formation through into the entrails of the state and into domestic politics in detail. Similarly, domestic policy specialists, while recognizing the general influence of international forces, tend to stop at the border. They may compare other countries, but they do not often 'internationalize.' And the two, comparison and examining internationalizing dynamics, are not the same thing. The internationalization of policy formation seems to me to involve a different kind of slice through both comparative and Canadian public policy. Clearly, many different aspects are a part of the work needed here, including: issues of sovereignty and pooled sovereignty and the rhetorical and real politics they create; the actual extent to which national policy capacity is being enhanced or weakened by internationalizing agreements and regimes;[29] the role of various international organizations and the bureaucratic politics within them;[30] international priority-setting through the G-7 and other forms of summitry;[31] and the use of international events and agreements to 'discipline' domestic interests.

My recent work in this field via studies of the Canada–U.S. free trade decision, environmental protocol-setting, and competition policy regimes makes me a decided novice in this area of policy studies, but I am convinced that it is an important area that will increasingly command our attention.

Other Thoughts in Brief

Although my main purpose in this chapter has been to sketch out how these phases or elements of study have influenced Canadian policy studies, there are clearly many other strands of the art, craft, and science of Canadian policy studies. I offer brief summary comments on five of these.

First, the study of public administration, understood in this specific instance to be that of broad system-wide political administration – personnel and budgeting systems, modes of departmentalization, accountability regimes, service delivery – remains a vital part of policy studies.[32] Indeed, my sense is that we need more analysis of how such 'systems' affect policy rather than just how bureaucrats as players influence policy. This is all the more true because the core of the recent public service reform agenda has been influenced more by business and economic theory than by traditional public administration concerns.[33]

Second, the impact of the Charter of Rights and Freedoms on policy formation and on policy community strategies and discourse needs more systematic study in different policy fields.[34] Indeed, there are some policy fields where legal cultures and politics and the law are grossly understudied by political scientists (as I am discovering in the field of competition policy).

Third, despite the excellent work of scholars such as Bill Coleman and some business historians,[35] we still lack compelling studies of the power and policy influence of key firms and corporations either in general or in particular policy domains. In the coming decade we need to come up with ways of studying key policy players such as Northern Telecom, or Bombardier, or powerful regional/provincial companies.

Fourth, we still lack systematic comparisons across time of what I will call 'regime-defining' policies or mega policy initiatives. We need to understand better and more conceptually what propels on to the agenda decisions of the scale of the 1980 National Energy Program, the 1986–7 free trade deal, or the 1990 Green Plan, to name three initiatives of this kind of magnitude that need to be compared in this context.

Fifth, there are also powerful public institutions whose policy roles we are still largely ignorant of, in part because they have succeeded in surrounding themselves with an outer band of secrecy and a heavy layer of daunting but largely undeserved mystique. Thus independent books still need to be written on the Bank of Canada, the Department of Finance, and the role of the governing party caucus in policy formation. In general, I have no difficulty in concluding that Canadian (and comparative) policy studies has come along way from my first exposure to it in the mid-1960s. It has far more breadth and depth and a far better empirical base than it had, albeit in a world that is now far less willing to cooperate and that is far more suspicious of social scientists. Work in crafting a PhD degree in public policy at Carleton University's School of Public Administration has further convinced me that policy studies must be a profoundly interdisciplinary enterprise if it is to flourish. Much art, craft, and science continues to be needed for Canadian policy studies to continue to mature, to contribute further to enhancing the quality of Canadian democracy and life, and to contribute to international and comparative scholarly development in policy studies.

Notes

1 My published research has enjoyably encompassed work with political scientist colleagues (Peter Aucoin, Richard Phidd, Vince Wilson, Sharon Sutherland, Michael Prince, Allan Tupper, Glen Toner, Brian Tomlin, and Tom Conway), and economist colleagues (Allan Maslove, Stan Winer, Bill Stanbury, Don McFetridge, Nancy Olewiler, Gilles Paquet, Don Dewees, Michael Trebilcock). It has involved research with: royal commissions from Macdonald to asbestos, to nuclear power; policy think-tanks (C.D. Howe Institute, Economic Council of Canada, Science Council of Canada, Law Reform Commission); and numerous federal, provincial, and international departments and agencies.

2 On the importance of competing ideas in policy analysis, see Simeon, 'Studying Public Policy'; Manzer, 'Social Policy and Political Paradigms'; Doern and Phidd, *Canadian Public Policy.*

3 See, for example, Prince, 'Policy Advisory Groups'; Pal, *Public Policy Analysis.*

4 An early example is Doern and Wilson, eds., *Issues in Canadian Public Policy*; on policy instruments, see Trebilcock et al. *The Choice of Governing Instruments.*

5 Examples of comparative studies include: Blais, ed., *Industrial Policy*;
   Cameron, 'The Growth of Government Spending'; and Hoberg, 'Environmen-
   tal Policy.' On the politics and economics of public policy, see Courchene,
   'Toward the Reintegration of Social and Economic Policy'; Banting, *The
   Welfare State and Canadian Federalism*; Atkinson and Coleman, *The State,
   Business and Industrial Change in Canada.*

6 See Phidd and Doern, *The Politics and Management of Canadian Economic
   Policy*; Doern and Wilson, eds., *Issues in Canadian Public Policy*; Whittington
   and Van Loon, *The Canadian Political System.*

7 V.S. Wilson, *Canadian Public Policy*, ch. 4.

8 See Doern and Aucoin, *Public Policy in Canada*; Prince, 'Policy Advisory';
   Atkinson and Chandler, eds., *The Politics of Public Policy.*

9 Studies by economists include: Hartle, *Public Policy, Decision Making and
   Regulation*; Trebilcock et al., *The Choice of Governing Instruments;* and
   Stanbury, *Business-Government Relations in Canada.* As far as political
   scientists are concerned, see Doern, ed., *The Regulatory Process in Canada*;
   Langford, 'Crown Corporations as Instruments of Policy'; and Schultz,
   'Regulating Conservatively.'

10 Simeon, 'Studying Public Policy'; see also Manzer, 'Social Policy and
   Political Paradigms,' Atkinson and Chandler, eds., *The Politics of Public
   Policy*, and Doern and Phidd, *Canadian Public Policy.*

11 Panitch, ed., *The Canadian State*; Mahon, 'Canadian Public Policy.'

12 See Hartle, *Public Policy, Decision Making and Regulation*; Trebilcock et al.,
   The Choice of Governing Instruments; Stanbury, *Business-Government
   Relations in Canada*; and Acheson and Chant, 'The Bank of Canada.'

13 See Dierkes et al., eds., *Comparative Policy Research*, and Campbell, *Grand
   Illusions.*

14 See Phidd and Doern, *The Politics and Management of Canadian Economic
   Policy*; Doern, ed., *The Politics of Economic Policy.*

15 Dunleavy, *Democracy, Bureaucracy and Public Choice,* and Hodgson,
   Economics and Institutions.

16 See Breton and Wintrobe, *The Logic of Bureaucratic Control*; Hartle, *Public
   Policy, Decision Making and Regulation* and *The Expenditure Budget
   Process*; Sproule-Jones, *Governments at Work.*

17 Skocpol, 'Rediscovering the State.'

18 E.g., Cairns, 'The Embedded State.'

19 See Coleman and Skogstad, eds., *Policy Communities and Public Policy in
   Canada;* Pross, *Group Politics and Public Policy*; and Lindquist, 'Public
   Managers and Policy Communities.'

20 Conway, 'The Marginalization of the Department of the Environment.'
21 Doern and Conway, *The Greening of Canada.*
22 E.g., Brooks, *Public Policy in Canada*; Atkinson, ed., *Governing Canada*; March and Olson, *Rediscovering Institutions.*
23 See Heidenheimer et al., *Comparative Public Policy*; Dierkes et al., eds., *Comparative Policy Research*; Feick, 'Comparative Policy Studies.'
24 E.g., Jones, *Patterns of Social Policy*; Cameron, 'The Growth of Government Spending.'
25 See Hoberg, 'Environmental Policy.'
26 See Simeon, 'Globalization and the Canadian Nation State'; Camilleri and Falk, *The End of Sovereignty?*
27 Doern, *Canadian Competition Policy Institutions in a Global Market*, and 'The Political Economy of Internationalizing Competition Policy.'
28 E.g., Nossal, *The Politics of Canadian Foreign Policy.*
29 See Drache and Gertler, *The New Era of Global Competition*; Doern and Tomlin, *Faith and Fear.*
30 See Doern, *Green Diplomacy.*
31 See Dobson, *Economic Policy Coordination.*
32 E.g., Aucoin, 'Administrative Reform in Public Management'; Kernaghan and Siegel, *Public Administration in Canada*; Sutherland and Doern, *Bureaucracy in Canada.*
33 Various arguments to that effect can be found in Savoie, *The Politics of Public Spending in Canada*; Seidle, ed., *Rethinking Government*; and Albo, Langille, and Panitch, *A Different Kind of State.*
34 For a critique of the effects of judicial review under the Charter, see Mandel, *The Charter of Rights and the Legalization of Politics in Canada.*
35 See Coleman, *Business and Politics.*

3

Public Administration and the Study of Public Policy Making in Canada

RICHARD W. PHIDD

The study of public policy in Canada has been influenced by a variety of disciplinary perspectives. The early Canadian literature was developed by political scientists, but it drew on the work of economists. In the early 1970s G. Bruce Doern and Peter Aucoin published *The Structures of Policy-Making in Canada*. This study of the broad structures of policy making was followed by *Issues in Canadian Public Policy*, which examined selected policy fields; for example, R.W. Phidd examined the evolution of regional development policies in Canada.[1] A later study by Doern and Aucoin added new elements such as organization process and management characteristics and began to utilize the notion of policy or governing.[2]

Doern and Phidd, in *Canadian Public Policy: Ideas, Structure, Process* (1983), developed a comprehensive institutional approach that drew on these earlier works. The Canadian literature on policy making proliferated during the 1980s and in the early 1990s, and this was reflected in the works of Michael Atkinson, Stephen Brooks, William D. Coleman, and Leslie Pal, to name a few. It will be demonstrated below that the most recent focus on institutions in Canadian policy studies is closely related to the organizational behaviour approach to the study of public administration. It is in this context that the chapter attempts to establish linkages between public administration and policy studies.

In this analysis an attempt is made to throw some light on the relationships between public administration and public policy studies in a manner that facilitates understanding of historical as well as contemporary perspectives of this most important field of study. The approach is consistent with analyses such as Ferrel Heady's *Public Administration: A Comparative Perspective* (1979), Colin Campbell's *Governments under Stress* (1983), Charles Levine's *Managing Fiscal Stress: The Crisis in the Public Sector* (1980), and Jeffrey D. Straussman's *Public Administration* (1985). The approach suggests that the study of specific policy issues must be placed in their broader institutional and historical context.

The institutional approach is well emphasized in recent publications such as *Bringing the State Back In* and *Governing Canada*.[3] Theda Skocpol suggests that politics is grounded in society, economy, and culture, as reflected in the organizational arrangements and activities of states. The approach suggests that we conduct research on 'states as actors and as institutional structures with effects in politics.'[4] Two strategies are suggested. On the one hand, states may be viewed as organizations through which official collectivities may pursue distinctive goals realizing them more or less effectively given the available state resources in relation to social settings. On the other hand, states may be viewed more macroscopically as configurations of organization and action that influence meanings and methods of politics for all groups and classes in society. Part I of *Bringing the State Back In* examines states as promoters of economic development and social distribution, and Part II looks at the manner in which states handle transnational relations. The approach leads to a policy focus on organizations and on implementation, which is discussed below.

Neo-Institutionalism and Public Administration

During the 1980s and the 1990s there has been a renewed interest in the study of the state and in the working of institutions. The focus on institutions is inevitably linked to the study of organizations, as depicted by the work of sociologists such as Charles Perrow, Richard Scott, and Richard Hall. March and Olsen, in *Rediscovering Institutions* (1989), emphasized that in many theories of politics developed since World War II, traditional institutions such as the legislature, the legal system, the state, and traditional economic institutions had receded in importance. An emphasis on social organizations characteristic of this era, however, failed to satisfactorily explain public policy making, resulting in increasing attention being refocused on the structures and institutions of government.

The foregoing suggests that public administration and public policy studies should be regarded as existing in a very complex interrelationship. It must be pointed out, therefore, that we may approach the relationship between public administration and public policy studies by identifying at least three perspectives on the subject, which can enhance improved understanding of the nature, scope, and influence of the field of study.

First, there has been a tendency in the area of public administration studies to focus on the *structural aspects* of the study of public sector organizations. The analysts who utilize this approach are sometimes considered to be concerned with the dull or rather dry aspects of public policy making; for example, they may examine the legal setting or the legal framework of governmental policy making. The pathbreaking work of J.E. Hodgetts's *The Canadian Public Service* in the early 1970s, for example, included the examination of the mandate, structure, and even the organization charts of public sector organizations. The early publications by Doern also emphasized the structural dimension of policy studies. These studies may further focus on the implementation of policies already formulated by politicians.

Although dry, the legal foundations of administration and policy must be carefully and critically examined because they point to the core elements of the discipline. The approach helps us to understand issues such as the delegation of authority and responsibility and accountability. More generally, it can be stated that recent studies of organization behaviour in the public sector have combined both classical and contemporary perspectives. This is the case, for example, with William Eddy's *Public Organization Behaviour and Development* (1981). It can be stated in more general terms that the study of comparative public administration and policy has always emphasized this approach, focusing on structural characteristics of administrative agencies and their relation to policy outputs.

Second, there has been a tendency in public policy studies to argue that policy studies are concerned with the *input side* of the operations of the political system. Accordingly, studies concerned with inputs from the environment, including political parties and interest groups, can contribute a great deal to more traditional administrative studies. This approach is significantly aided by the most recent focus on policy communities, which incorporates elements of network analysis.

Within the state agencies, policy making includes within-puts from cabinet ministers and from the governmental bureaucracy. Careful studies of policy making have revealed that the processes of policy formulation and implementation are complex. It should be emphasized that the separate focus on political parties and interest groups characteristic of many policy studies has led to inadequate analyses of the complex interrelationships that exist between political parties, interest groups, and public bureaucracies.[5] The complexities involved suggest that we examine the intricate relationships that may develop between these policy actors.[6] Such an approach involves our examining factors beyond the mere passage of a law by focusing on *implementation* and *feedback mechanisms* in policy and administrative studies.

The policy communities literature has made a significant contribution to bridging this gap between public administration and policy studies.[7] The approach links interest groups to departmental and commercial organizations consistent with earlier works such as Self and Storing's, *The State and the Farmer* (1962). Grace Skogstad's study of Canadian agricultural policies is consistent with their tradition.

A third perspective on public policy making has emerged in recent years and has established some linkages between the two approaches mentioned above. This approach may be conveniently labelled organizational and policy studies. This approach has been aided by the recent focus on policy implementation and evaluation. In many respects the focus on policy implementation has demonstrated that specific policy positions and appropriate tools often cannot be identified in an a priori fashion. Accordingly, the third perspective presented in this framework suggests that policy and administrative studies are inextricably linked and that more serious efforts should be made to integrate the approaches. Failure to do so would simply lead to inadequate assessment of public policy making. A 1983 publication by Richard H. Hall and Robert E. Quinn, *Organizational Theory and Public Policy*, supports this contention. Hall and Quinn suggest that organizations should be perceived in terms of their purposes, their role as instruments of control that serve the interests of corporate elites, and that all large organizations have a public policy role.

The views expressed above were raised earlier by W.I. Jenkins in *Policy Analysis: A Political and Organizational Perspective* (1978). In a section entitled 'Toward an Organizational Perspective' Jenkins suggests that in studying public policy 'we are concerned with political behaviour taking place within and amongst organizational networks.' He suggests that if we move toward 'a political sociology of organizations' one needs to be concerned with the actors and organizations involved in the initiation, formulation, and implementation of policy and, in particular, with a much neglected aspect: administration. Jenkins argues that 'what has up to now passed for an analysis of the political system has either ignored or downgraded the administration.' Accordingly, he concludes:

A focus on the internal structures of political systems draws us towards an organizational perspective on policy and to a realization of the importance of the potential influence of the administrative sphere. Yet in administrative studies the championing of organizational analysis is nothing new. It has been tried before, and, not tested in detail, has rarely been seen as the road to fortune and success.[8]

Jenkins's suggestions are consistent with the more recent emphasis placed on organizational studies by Robert Denhardt and Harold Gortner, among others, who advocate greater study of public sector organizations.[9]

The Canadian state must be viewed as a decision-making and management system continually under change and adaptation. This is consistent with the most recent organization and decision-making theories. Both the political and administrative systems have responded to pressures from the international and domestic environments. We need to conduct more systematic analyses of public sector organizational reforms in order to develop a better appreciation of the origins and the working of institutions and the causes and consequences of their change and adaptation over time.[10]

Doern and Phidd have expanded on these issues and concerns in *Canadian Public Policy: Ideas, Structure, Process* (1992), and in R.W. Phidd's, 'Canadian Public Administration: Challenges, Responses, Adaptation,' which will include when it is completed studies of Foreign Affairs and International Trade Canada, Transport Canada, the Treasury Board Secretariat, Industry Canada, Human Resources Development Canada, and Health Canada. The recent study by James Desveaux, *Designing Bureaucracies: Institutional Capacity and Large Scale Problem Solving* (1995), is consistent with the approach outlined here.

The recent emphasis on globalization and competitiveness and changing international population dynamics have alerted us to the operations of large, complex organizations functioning in a world setting and the continuing need for the studies and findings of scholars working in the public administration and public policy traditions to be integrated. Examining the roles of departments, boards, commissions, regulatory and special operating agencies in policy making helps to bridge the structural, interest group, and organizational perspectives and enhances our comprehension of policy making.

Notes

1 Phidd, 'Regional Development Policy.'
2 Doern and Aucoin, eds., *Public Policy in Canada: Organization and Process.*
3 Evans et al., eds., *Bringing the State Back In*; Atkinson, ed., *Governing Canada.*
4 Skocpol, 'Bringing the State Back In,' 27.
5 An exception is Savoie, *The Politics of Public Spending in Canada.*
6 See Rourke, *Bureaucracy, Politics and Public Policy.*
7 E.g., Coleman and Skogstad, eds., *Policy Communities and Public Policy in Canada.*

8 Jenkins, *Policy Analysis,* 65.
9 See Denhardt, *The Pursuit of Significance*; Gortner, Mahler, and Nicholson, *Organization Theory*; Gray and Jenkins, *Administrative Politics in British Government.*
10 See Dwivedi and Phidd, 'Prime Ministerial Leadership and Public Service Reform.'

4

Canada in the American Arcade: Is Pluralism a Distorting Mirror?

A. PAUL PROSS

Interest groups arouse mixed feelings among Canadians. They have used them since colonial days, but that has not stopped politicians, editorialists, and even group members themselves from decrying their presence in Canadian politics. Between the 1950s and the 1980s interest groups acquired considerable legitimacy and appeared to be accepted as part of the country's evolving political system. In the 1990s, however, a new wave of criticism has engulfed them. They are routinely castigated by politicians, and have lost ground in terms of positional politics and in terms of the resources governments are willing to make available to them.

This debate over the proper place of interest groups in our political system is confused by a tendency to look at pressure group politics through American eyes. This is not surprising. From the founding of the Republic, political institutions and an ideological commitment to individualism encouraged American citizens to exert pressure on government through interest group action, and it was inevitable that their practices and their ideas about pressure groups should have an effect on Canadian thought. In particular, the language, the concepts, and increasingly, the assumptions of pluralism – which is both explanation and justification of American political behaviour – have become a part of Canadian public policy analysis. They have also permeated popular understandings about government and how it should behave.

This discussion is about the influence of American pluralism on Canadian political thought. I shall focus on two critical aspects of pluralism: its confidence in a dynamic, self-correcting political society and its minimalist view of the state. I shall examine Canadian writing in the 'pluralist tradition,' and show that while our literature embraced the first of these two pillars of pluralism, until recently it eschewed the latter. My thesis is that this literature displayed a distinctive Canadian understanding of pluralism, one that reflected the realities of our political economy and that resonated broadly with public opinion. I shall argue that our current tendency to accept indiscriminately the entirety of American pluralist ideology has led us to become confused about the nature of our political society. I conclude that to overcome this confusion we must recognize that Canadian pluralism has distinctive characteristics and we must address ourselves to understanding what they are and how best to use them.

The Early Influence of Pluralism in Canada

Political scientists, like the majority of Canadians, were slow to acknowledge interest group involvement in our political life. J.A. Corry took up the topic in a comparative fashion in the first edition (1946) of *Democratic Government and Politics*, published by University of Toronto Press. R. MacGregor Dawson privately dismissed interest groups as inconsequential,[1] and paid them no attention in *The Government of Canada*, long the preeminent text for students and practitioners of Canadian government. For many years S.D. Clark's study of the Canadian Manufacturers' Association,[2] published in 1939, was the sole scholarly study of organizations, which by 1945 had some 1,700 listings in the *Canadian Almanac and Directory*. In 1953 David C. Corbett presented a paper, 'The Pressure Group and the Public Interest,' to the annual meeting of the Institute of Public Administration of Canada. Several years later another student of public administration, J.E. Hodgetts, devoted a portion of an article on the role of public servants in policy formation to a series of questions that drew attention to the impact of pressure groups on the advice received by governments from their officials.[3] Neither of these pieces was the product of new research into Canadian pressure groups, but in the early 1960s three articles appeared reporting studies of two interest groups – the Consumers' Association of Canada and the Canadian Federation of Agriculture – and of the efforts of affected interests to influence the Diefenbaker government's revisions of the Combines Investigation Act.[4]

A striking feature of these pieces is that they virtually ignore the American literature in the field. Corbett told his audience that part of his paper was 'an exercise in pluralist theory,'[5] and though he cites no specific theorists, he clearly draws on the work of David Truman, whose influential book *The Governmental Process* had been published two years before. Hodgetts notes that Truman's 'study is rich in illuminating hypotheses that deserve to be tested in the context of Canadian administration and politics,'[6] but is much more interested in and influenced by the Anglo-Canadian literature on the role of the public service in the cabinet-parliamentary system. The three case studies are based almost completely on documentary research, the sole reference to the larger literature occurring when Helen Jones Dawson draws on V.O. Key's *Politics, Parties and Pressure Groups* to compare Canadian and American farm organizations.[7]

I conclude from this that, in the 1950s, those Canadian scholars who were aware of the American pluralist literature saw it primarily as a guide to the study of pressure groups. The Americans, after all, by recognizing the role played by interest groups in their political life, had been drawn to develop a literature that was far more extensive than that of any other country. In many respects there was no other literature to turn to. The French student of interest groups, Jean Meynaud, whose work at the University of Montreal made him influential among French-Canadian scholars, complained in 1962 that the Europeans had refused to recognize the significance of interest groups in their national politics. His various studies draw repeatedly on the American literature.[8] J.D. Stewart, in his 1958 study of the influence of British pressure groups on the House of Commons, remarks that 'the pressure group in Britain has not got a substantial literature.'[9] He presents 'a small selection of American works which are useful guides to theories of pressure group methods of research,' which would have served as the foundation for any Canadian scholar's approach to the subject during this period.[10] The most prominent of these are, in fact, cited by J.A. Corry and J.E. Hodgetts in a later edition of *Democratic Government and Politics*.

It is hard to find in these early Canadian studies any recognition of the normative underpinnings of this guiding literature, even though few explanations of political phenomenon are as value-laden as the pluralist accounts of pressure group behaviour in the United States. Perhaps the principal reason for this is that at the beginning, at least, of this formative period pluralism could still be seen as an explanation, rather than a justification, of American political behaviour. As American pluralism evolved certain aspects came to have ideological significance. Its holding that a plural society protects the individual from the state was elaborated by the American Right in such a way that pluralism came to be associated with a commitment to a minimalist state and a rejection of the idea that there is a public interest which it is the responsibility of the leaders of government to discern and maintain.[11] In the 1950s these developments, and the vigorous disputes they generated, were still in the future and it was still possible to treat the work of Truman, Key, Herring, and others as a variant of the liberal democratic philosophy that permeated Canadian political science at the time.[12] Even when the American debate was in full spate, we tended to observe it, in my opinion, with a detached interest. We found in Lowi's typology of distributive, redistributive, and regulatory policies an interesting tool for analysis,[13] but cocooned in the traditions of the cabinet-parliamentary system, we tended to treat his argument in *The End of Liberalism* as part of an essentially American debate.

Another, more subtle, explanation must also be considered. Like Canadians in general, used to making on a daily basis numerous minuscule adjustments to the view of the world that is beamed to us from the United States, academics may have simply adjusted American concepts to 'fit' our own reality. Indeed, the liberal attack on the Right's appropriation of pluralism played into this tendency, because its concern for equity and the public interest resonated with our own brand of liberalism. In Europe, where there is a much sharper contrast between collectivism and individualism, such adjustments could not be assimilated as easily and led to the formulation of the corporatist alternative. Here, as long as we were content to treat the pluralist literature as a guide to research, and to ignore its normative aspects, the approach continued to be received relatively uncritically.

Inevitably a view of political life fashioned to explain and support American institutions could not completely satisfy our own understanding of Canadian realities, however much the two countries have in common and however we may tinker with the American model. Ultimately the concepts of American pluralism jarred with our own understanding of the role and operation of the Canadian state. Several critiques of pluralism emerged in this country. Two were rooted in models developed elsewhere. The Marxist approach treats interest groups as the catspaw of the middle class and therefore incapable of effectively challenging capitalism. Corporatism emphasizes the state's relations with highly structured bodies representing large segments of society, rather than the aspirations of individuals. Both approaches thus challenge the assumption that the pluralist approach accommodates all interests in society and that it is impossible to determine the public interest. Neither approach has won broad support in Canada. Instead, debate over the role of interest groups in public policy formation has been conducted within the framework of a pluralist understanding. However, that understanding has a Canadian twist that has its origins in our traditional view of the state.

Defining Pluralism

A barrier to interpreting the Canadian view of pluralism is the problem of defining the core theory. Aaron Wildavsky once stated that 'the criteria for pluralism are so broad that it is difficult to imagine a community of any size not meeting them.'[14] Definitions are elusive, more likely to be found in lat-ter-day revisions, in theoretical overviews, or in the work of those who, like Phillippe Schmitter, are engaged in building an alternative approach.[15] Those who are credited with actually building pluralism were too concerned with describing and explaining what they thought they saw to clothe themselves in definitional regalia. Moreover, as Grant Jordan has pointed out, what they wrote in the 1950s and 1960s clearly entitles them to dissociate themselves from the body of theory that their critics say they wrote. As far as Jordan is concerned, there is 'no well-elaborated pluralist theory that can be rediscov-ered. Instead there are a multiplicity of ideas about interest groups, loosely tied together by a pluralist tag.'[16]

In other words, where we believed we had a body of thought, we now find a 'multiplicity of ideas,' amorphous and inchoate, yet still considered an approach, even a theory, and a fit subject for debate; one, furthermore, that sparks refinement and rival theories. Even attempts to determine a core of common elements do not help us here because we find that neither friends nor critics of pluralism recognize, much less emphasize, the same core ele-ments. Jordan draws on the high-priests of pluralism – Dahl, Truman, Lindblom, Polsby – to arrive at a set of eight core elements, but they are configured differently from those that appear in Harmon Ziegler's *Plural-ism, Corporatism, and Confucianism.* In the Canadian literature, Leslie Pal's description of pluralism in *State, Class and Bureaucracy* is quite different from the one William Coleman presents in *Business and Politics* and differ-ent again from my description in *Group Politics and Public Policy,* to name but three commentaries.

Rather than bog down in trying to discern what individual scholars thought they saw in what other scholars might have said, I am going to look at the way in which Canadian observers, and to some extent the general public, have approached two positions that are often associated with pluralism. The first derives from the assertion in pluralism that while power is dispersed, fragmented, and unequally distributed, even disadvantaged groups can make their claims heard and have the potential to introduce a necessary dynamism into the polity. The second derives from the belief among some observers that pluralism endorses a minimalist state. Pal, for example, considers plu-ralism to be 'society-centred' and distinguishes the pluralist model of the policy process from 'state-centred' models. Similarly Ziegler sees in plural-ism a rejection of statism, which springs from a conviction that the ultimate value in political life is the protection and promotion of the individual. Indi-vidualism is the outstanding characteristic of pluralism and the force that drives its normative content:

The most frequently derived normative variant of individualism is the doctrine of limited government. If government exists because it serves a purely utilitarian function, its intrusion into personal life must be carefully constrained ...

... If individualists believe that the purpose of government is to shield personal liberty, the pluralist modification furnishes the means for accomplishing this purpose.

... Elite competition, generally expressed by organized interest groups, helps to safeguard individual nonparticipants from governmental abuse, since no set of interests is likely to be ascendant indefinitely.[17]

These two aspects of pluralism – dynamism and state minimalism – have presented Canadians, in the street, the legislature, and the academy, with the classic tension that exists in every polity: the tension between collectivism and individualism. Whether we realize it or not, we are currently joined in that debate at every level of Canadian society.

Dynamic Pluralism and State Centrism

Those who challenge pluralism's insensitivity to the inequitable distribution of power in politics and the limited role it accords the state often characterize it primarily as a description of, and philosophical support for, a competitive, group-dominated politics that treats public policy as merely the residual of rival claims on public goods.[18] Given the stress recent pluralist theorists have placed on superseding the concept of the public interest with pure competition between interests, this criticism is justified. As we shall see, it resonates profoundly in Canada where many, including academics and active members of social movements, look to the state to protect the weak and equate modern pluralism with the rise of the proponents of free-market individualism.

In taking this position, however, present-day critics of pluralism overlook the valuable contribution the approach makes to understanding the dynamic aspects of political life. Pluralism accounts for spontaneity and dynamism in politics far more effectively, for example, than corporatism, whose vision of platoons of hierarchically organized associations marching in lock step seems to exclude the possibility of local, let alone individual, initiative and cannot account for the spontaneous. As a way of describing how change can come about in politics, this aspect of pluralism should have excited more interest among the theoreticians of movements. Their preoccupation with radical change and a fear of co-optation has led them to ignore the lessons that can be learned from incrementalist politics.

As far as political scientists are concerned, their tendency to understate pluralism's treatment of consensus and to undervalue its incrementalist description of change may reflect the discipline's focus on conflict and its interest in high politics, as opposed to the day-to-day accommodations of political life. Even observers of pressure groups prefer to study conflict between major interests within subgovernments rather than coalition politics that draw attentive publics into the policy process. In Canada, at least, one is more likely to find a literature dealing with this type of change within sociology than within political science.[19]

Notwithstanding the approach's unpopularity in academic circles, the language of pluralism is pervasive in our dialogue. It is found in the large – and largely overlooked – literature on public participation in local and urban politics. It is also found in the populism that is commonly associated with the Prairies, but which occurs across the country. Case studies of neighbourhood planning, regional development movements, advocacy groups, and voluntary organizations are also redolent with the conviction of political activists that 'the public' can organize itself and can 'make a difference.' At another level, both participants in and observers of movements invoke concepts of public participation that can be seen as populist interpretations of pluralism. Léon Dion and Micheline de Seve, for example, described the first years of the Quebec independence movement in pluralist terms, finding that 'citizens who had formerly been content to relegate to others the task of defending their interests ... now found themselves awakening to a new kind of active political participation.'[20]

Perhaps this merely indicates that pluralism has successfully used the language of grass-roots politics while in reality promoting a philosophy that organizes the grass-roots out of politics; forcing the mass public to resort to large-scale, revolutionary movements in order to obtain social change. Such an explanation, though, overlooks the fact that thirty years ago pluralism clearly had an appeal for writers working in the liberal democratic tradition who were concerned about equity and equality. Corry and Hodgetts, hailing 'a spontaneous group life without precedent in history,' argue that it is the function of government to mediate or, if necessary, arbitrate between interests in order to secure the public good.[21] Dion maintained that pluralism, after Marxism, was the first systematic refutation of Rousseauian romanticism and the extreme forms of individualism.[22] Its description of a political society that is atomistic, bustling, vibrant, and self-organizing is certainly far broader than both its critics and its latter-day Social Darwinist adherents would have us believe. As Jack Lively has argued, the approach has a concern for consensus, as well as competition, and that aspect of pluralism needs to be rediscovered.[23]

Among Canadian political scientists writing in the liberal democratic tradition, pluralism has lost favour precisely because many of its modern adherents have accentuated its competitive, market-oriented, rather than its consensual aspects. In his 1978 presidential address to the Canadian Political Science Association, Hugh G. Thorburn maintained that the pluralism normally encountered in Canada was 'an American style democracy, emphasizing freedom of association and the pull-haul of interest groups.'[24] He believed that 'the arrival of pluralism of the American variety [had] done much to fan the flames of discontent' in Quebec even as, and because, it sapped the rest of Canada of its independent identity.[25] For Thorburn, pluralism had evolved in Canada as an instrument for 'reconciling political democracy and the control of society by an established elite.'[26] Khayyam Paltiel saw it as a 'private-regarding' ideology, distorting Canadian public life.[27] Even J.A. Corry, who in 1959 had argued from a pluralist perspective that the job of government was to maintain an equilibrium between groups, by 1981 commented with regret that:

governments find it difficult to act resolutely in pursuit of coherent policies if faction, always present in a vigorous, free polity, comes to dominate the field. Faction is rising dangerously near to dominance. This is inevitable in my view, because we now live, in Canada and elsewhere, in what someone has aptly called the Special Interest State.[28]

Practitioners took similar positions. Robert Stanfield, in 1977, became one of the first of many politicians to publicly attack the intrusion of pressure groups into the domain of the political party.[29] Hugh Segal, then in the office of the Ontario premier, attacked 'special interest advocacy, or one-issue political participation' on the grounds that

it fragments the policy development process as well as the political system that is supposed to control that process. And as the process becomes more fragmented, public respect for the way in which public policy is made, and for the forces that have pre-eminence in its development, declines; cynicism and disaffection grow.[30]

Each of these criticisms targets individualistic, competitive, and market-driven pluralism, and thus they are akin to those Lowi, Schattschneider, and others had levelled at American pluralism on its home turf. But this resemblance is superficial. Canadian scholars have long differed fundamentally from their American counterparts in their understanding of pluralism, specifically what it says about the proper role of the state.

Taken at its most abstract much of Canada's pressure group literature is concerned with the nature of the relationship between organized interests and the state. This is in sharp contrast with the United States where a lot of energy has been expended in recent years rediscovering the state and finding that it can at times act autonomously. No student of Canadian politics needs to be reminded that the need for state intervention in virtually every aspect of our lives is a leitmotif of this country's existence.[31] This reality has made Canadians, even today after some years of 'private-regarding' discourse, more receptive than Americans to the concept of an active state and to the belief that a public interest can be discerned.[32]

Accordingly, even the earliest references to pluralism in this country reflect an ambiguity about the American literature's assumption that the role of pluralism is to protect the individual from the state. Corry and Hodgetts applaud the dynamism that pluralism identifies in political life and share the pluralist's confidence in the system's capacity to spontaneously adapt. They find the approach compatible with the liberal democratic ideals that drive their own approach to politics. At the same time, they build into their discussion of pluralism a number of caveats that are distinctly Canadian.[33] The most notable aspect of this is their emphasis on the relationships between interest groups and the bureaucracy.

This emphasis – quixotic when one considers the preoccupation of the American literature with the impact of groups on legislative and regulatory policy making – should not be dismissed as simply reflecting Hodgetts's interest in public administration. The same emphasis occurs in all the early pieces that have been cited here. It was probably no coincidence that the first of them – Corbett's piece – was prepared at the invitation of the Institute of Public Administration of Canada, surely a reflection of the significance some of Canada's leading public servants attached to the relationship. In that piece Corbett commented that 'the relationship between pressure groups and the administrative branch of government bears watching because this is the branch where growth is the most vigorous, and where the strength of democratic control is constantly being tested.'[34] Hodgetts asked whether 'the weakness of our Opposition ... [has] forced the civil service to look elsewhere – notably to organized functional groups – for alternatives to, or criticisms of, the policies they are administering and the choices they are making?'[35] H.G. Thorburn's study of the Diefenbaker government's revision of the Combines Investigation Act showed that the greater part of lobbying for and against specific revisions was directed overwhelmingly at officials and the executive.[36] The view that in Canada interest group influence was more likely to be effective when exercised at the bureaucratic and cabinet level rather than on the legislature, which thus developed with the first modern writings on the subject, was confirmed by Helen Jones Dawson through her studies of the Canadian Federation of Agriculture and the Consumers' Association of Canada and became an important feature of academic studies of Canadian interest group behaviour in the 1970s and early 1980s.[37]

This divergence from the tenor of American pluralism is not trivial. Its significance is suggested in Corry and Hodgetts's justification of government consultation 'with all interests that are strong enough to make their voices heard.' They argue that the purpose of consultation is to achieve an *'arbitration* between interests in the light of all the data that can be discovered from whatever source.'[38] A government that is kept within bounds by the competitive interaction of groups does not arbitrate between them. In other words, the understanding of the role of the state that is implicit in Corry and Hodgetts's discussion is fundamentally different from the understanding that informs American pluralism. As we shall see, that difference is a hallmark of Canadian writing on this subject.

Students of Canadian pressure group politics have articulated this orientation in a variety of ways. It received its clearest statement in the 1970s. David Kwavnick's study of the Canadian Labour Congress presented the influence of government as pervasive.[39] In my own work and that of Helen Jones Dawson, Peter Aucoin, William Stanbury, and R.A. Weir the point recurs.[40] Ronald W. Lang provided a striking description of the dominant role of the bureaucracy in group-agency relations in his study of the government's policy on prescription drug prices during the 1960s. Lang found that the Pharmaceutical Manufacturers' Association of Canada, which represented the major firms, 'rather than enjoying a close, harmonious and mutually dependent status with a particular government department, ... was shunned by all' and therefore failed to obtain the policy concessions it desired.[41]

Today, the Canadian state continues to be a formidable actor in this country's pressure group politics, as I have tried to show in my elaboration of the policy community model.[42] Leslie Pal, in his study of the policies surrounding our unemployment insurance system, concludes that 'state-centred approaches to [understanding] public policy are more promising and fruitful than society-centred theories.'[43] However, the bureaucracy's influence is reduced. The diffusion of power initiated by the reforms of the central policy structures and parliamentary reforms that began in the late 1960s has made it more dependent on the policy communities, including the pressure groups, which essentially guide public policy formation. Pal's most recent study of bilingual, women's, and multicultural programs sponsored by the Secretary of State suggests that once programs are launched, the state's freedom of action is limited by the aspirations and organizational needs of its allies, although its support for those allies is 'indispensable.'[44] In the world of practice, policy analysts are routinely urged to consult with 'stakeholders' as they prepare advice for policy makers. All too often, the 'stakeholders' turn out to be the dominant players in subgovernments, rather than the public at large or even members of the attentive public; the latter being consulted through largely ineffectual exercises in 'public participation.'[45]

The declining influence of the public service can be attributed in part to large-scale political forces. Provincial and federal governments have attacked the scope and power of the public service, ostensibly in the cause of deficit reduction. The introduction of the Charter of Rights and Freedoms has redefined the relationship between the individual and the state, often through the decision of interest groups to test the authority of the state before the courts. Even the academic literature has contributed to the view that the state is less than it used to be. The Canadian corporatist literature, for example, has emphasized the weakness of the Canadian state, and promoted the idea that it is but one of three partners engaged in the management of the economy, even while urging a more coherent and orchestrated approach to economic policy development.[46] Market-oriented pluralism, of course, favours a minimalist state.

How should we assess these developments? Have we descended into a pluralist quagmire of American proportions? Have the forebodings of the late 1970s been realized? Has a private-regarding pluralist philosophy supplanted an earlier state-centred tradition that placed a high value on the public interest?

It is possible that Canada is being consumed by a virulent form of pluralism that is destroying institutions created by a century's painstaking labour in the liberal democratic tradition. But there is a lesson to be learned from our experience with the pluralist literature: rather than exploring the extent to which that literature reflected American political institutions and culture, we adapted it to our own needs. As the literature developed in the United States and internationally, we kept pace, or we thought that we did. As a result, we spoke to the issues raised by pluralism, but we spoke past them as well.

This tendency is best illustrated by the work of Robert Presthus whose application of the pluralist model in Canada is responsible for drawing attention to several aspects of our political life that warranted inquiry: notably that Canadians were much more deferential than Americans – and thus more inclined to accept the diktats of elites – and his equally interesting, yet less noticed, observation of the beginnings of a lively pressure group engagement with Parliament.[47] What the model did not alert him to – possibly because of its emphasis on individualism and its rejection of the concept of the public interest – was the extent to which the state had been able to structure and control its relations with interests. Yet studies of pressure groups based on actual observation of groups in action had since the 1950s emphasized the centrality of the state in Canadian pressure group politics.

For policy analysts there is an important lesson in Presthus's experience. Many of his observations were extremely pertinent, but they missed important dimensions of Canadian politics. They demonstrate that the American pluralist model is a helpful tool, but it does not do the whole job. It exaggerates some aspects of our political experience while suppressing others. The image of ourselves that it presents is recognizable, but distorted.

We do ourselves a disservice, then, if we apply American pluralist concepts indiscriminately to Canadian experience. When historians like Michael Bliss write that Canada has matured from 'an elite-driven, deference-based British colonial system ... into a chaotic, individualistic North American democracy,'[48] we must not assume that our democracy will be identical to that of the United States. Our institutions and our public philosophy interact with individualism to create political behaviour and public policies that are significantly different. Witness our approach to medicare and to gun control. Equally we must not ground observations of Canadian events in too close a reading of the American experience with pluralism. It is true that Canadians are very much influenced by the American media and the American experience in general, but does that mean, for example, that the fragmentation of politics that is so frequently commented upon is entirely a product of those influences? Might not our own experience – province-building, the Charter, parliamentary reform, new practices in policy formation – also contribute to the development of faction? In other words, to what extent are we really confronting pluralist influences? Might our current situation simply be the product of a broader Canadian tradition in which pluralism has an important, but not a defining, part?

Finally we should recognize that Canadian writings in the pluralist tradition do not necessarily adhere to the American tradition of pluralism. Comparativists are wont to assume that the European critique of American pluralism can be applied indiscriminately to the Canadian variant. It is the contention of this paper that this characterization is mischievous. As this discussion has demonstrated, Canadian writers have adapted pluralism to their own understanding of our reality. The comparativist characterization, therefore, not only imputes to these writers a set of assumptions that are attributed – not always correctly – to the American variant, but it overlooks the nuances of what many of us are trying to say about this country. If we are to understand our own country, and contribute meaningfully to its evolution, policy analysts must use international models, like pluralism, with discernment, applying to our situation only those aspects that truly reflect our reality.

Notes

I should like to thank Michael Howlett, Laurent Dobuzinskis, Ted Hodgetts, and two anonymous reviewers for reading earlier versions of this paper and making useful comments. They are not, of course, responsible for any errors that may remain.

1 Helen Jones Dawson in conversation with the writer. His views reflected public attitudes. Despite the longstanding activity of interest groups at national, provincial, and local levels, many Canadians professed a distaste for 'American pressure group tactics.'
2 *The Canadian Manufacturers' Association.*
3 'The Civil Service and Policy Formation,' 475–7.
4 Dawson, 'The Canadian Federation of Agriculture' and 'The Consumers Association of Canada'; Thorburn, 'Pressure Groups in Canadian Politics.'
5 'The Pressure Group and the Public Interest,' 185.
6 'The Civil Service and Policy Formation,' 475, note 19. Hodgetts has since noted that while Truman's work became influential in the 1950s, Corry relied primarily on Stuart Chase's *Democracy Under Pressure* when he wrote *Democratic Government and Politics.* Letter: J.E. Hodgetts to A.P. Pross, 20 Jan. 1995.
7 'The Canadian Federation of Agriculture,' 141, note 33.
8 *Nouvelles études sur les groups de pression en France*, 138–9.
9 *British Pressure Groups*, 245.
10 In addition to Truman's and Key's works, already mentioned, it included Bentley, 'The Process of Government' (1908); Blaisdell, *Economic Power and Political Pressures* (Temporary National Economic Committee, 1941. Monograph No. 26); Stuart Chase, *Democracy and Pressure* (1945); Crawford, *The Pressure Boys* (1939); Dillon, 'Pressure Groups'; and Pendleton Herring, *Group Representation before Congress* (1929).
11 This debate has recently emerged in Canada. See Stanbury, 'A Sceptic's Guide,' and Phillips, 'Of Public Interest Groups and Sceptics.'
12 For an overview of the pluralist literature of this period see Garson, *Group Theories of Politics.*
13 See, for example, Doern, *The Regulatory Process in Canada.*

14 *Speaking Truth to Power*, 276.

15 *Trends Toward Corporatist Intermediation*, 15.

16 'The Pluralism of Pluralism,' 301.

17 *Pluralism, Corporatism, and Confucianism*, 3–4.

18 For example, in Brooks, *Public Policy in Canada*, 2.

19 As, for example, in Cunningham et al., *Social Movements/Social Change*; Clark, Grayson, and Grayson, *Prophecy and Protest*; Harries-Jones, *Making Knowledge Count*. Apart from the writer, Canadian political scientists have shown very little interest in the interaction between attentive publics and subgovernments, and only very recently have Canadian political scientists looked at the dynamics of social movements.

20 'Quebec Interest Groups,' 131. Today it is not unusual for academic observers engaged with feminist, nationalist, and other social movements to describe themselves as 'socialist feminists,' for example, and to claim to set their analyses in Marxist and revolutionary theory, while writing in terms that are distinctly pluralist. See, for example, the discussion of coalition politics in Carolyn Egan et al., 'The Politics of Transformation.'

21 *Democratic Government and Politics*, 299.

22 *Société et politique*, vol. 1, 34.

23 'Pluralism and Consensus.'

24 'Canadian Pluralist Democracy in Crisis,' 723. He defined pluralism as 'an open system which perceives the political process as one of bargaining between organized groups, with the government participating in this process and giving its authority to the accommodation achieved. Like the automatic economy of the classical economists, it produces an automatic society, through continuous group interaction. The government becomes merely "an extension of the political process" (Lowi) – therefore, its legitimacy is undermined, and as a further consequence it fails to pursue rigorous administration. Parliament and cabinet are merely a smallish part of the greater process of group interaction, better called elite accommodation' (724).

25 Ibid., 727.

26 Ibid., 736.

27 'The Changing Environment and Role of Special Interest Groups,' 209.

28 'Sovereign People or Sovereign Governments,' 5. For Corry, the decline of the liberal democratic state was marked by the destructive capacity of special interests to obtain favours at the expense of the rest of society. In 1959 he and Hodgetts had warned:

The job of appeasing interests by giving them privileges that are immediately, if not ultimately, at the expense of others has a divisive rather than a unifying tendency, and it becomes harder to mobilize majorities that will accept all these activities as contributions to the common good or the public interest. Yet whether government activity declines or continues to expand, democratic governments must mediate between interests. (*Democratic Government and Politics*, 306–7)

They conclude that 'mediation will be most successful if it is done in the light of all the available information, including that tendered by the interests themselves' (306–7), and if the majority party has, and holds to, a well-defined perception of the public interest. By 1981, close to the end of his life, Corry had concluded that 'in coping with these complexities and disturbed interrelationships, [governments] have given special concessions and advantages to many groups while denying others or saddling them with special burdens not equally imposed on all'; 'Sovereign People or Sovereign Governments,' 6.

29 'The Fifth George C. Nowlan Lecture,' Acadia University, 7 Feb. 1977 (mimeo). Quoted in Pross, *Group Politics*, 1. In 'The Pressure Group Conundrum,' I discuss more recent attacks by politicians on the activities of Canadian pressure groups. See also Seidle 'Interest Advocacy through Parliamentary Channels.'

30 'A View from the Cabinet Office of Ontario,' 7–8.

31 It is fascinating to find that in Canada, interest groups, the institutions which sit at the very core of the American version of pluralism, commonly owe their creation, and frequently their continued survival, to government intervention. This phenomenon has been noted, explored, and commented upon by most writers in the field (notably Coleman, Paltiel, Pross, Pal, and Stanbury), but its implication for a strictly pluralist interpretation of Canadian pressure group politics has escaped notice. Until recently, at least, Canadians have been prepared to accept a more state-centred pluralism, than their American counterparts. Cf. Berry, *Lobbying for the People*. State sponsorship of groups has been attacked on two fronts in recent years. On the one hand, government financial support has been considerably reduced, partly as a result of the deficit crisis, but also because it has become politically advantageous to attack 'special interests' for their selfish, grasping ways and their 'divisive' behaviour. The Reform Party has been the most outspoken critic of support for groups, but all parties have engaged in it – viz. several incidents at the 1993 Tory leadership convention. Among the academic writers who have looked at the issue, Leslie Pal has recently argued, in *Interests of State*, against state support. This writer noted the propensity for agency manipulation of groups as early as 1983, in a paper that was later published as 'Parliamentary Influence and the Diffusion of Power,' but continues to argue – with

William Stanbury, Kernaghan Webb, and Peter Finkle – that there is a place for such support in Canadian policy making and that it is the way in which support is provided that should be reformed.

32 Thus we find in Corry and Hodgetts a strong defence of the importance of a concept of the public interest and in Paltiel a conviction that the 'private-regarding' ideology of modern pluralism is undermining attempts to create a consensus around a public interest.

33 Perhaps especially Canadian in their blythe failure to draw attention to the variations that they introduce into the American version of pluralism.

34 'The Pressure Group and the Public Interest,' 195.

35 'The Civil Service and Policy Formation,' 477.

36 Thorburn, 'Pressure Groups in Canadian Politics.'

37 I was sufficiently convinced by these findings and by my own research into policy making in Ontario lands and forests administration that I made bureaucratic dominance a key feature of my argument in my own first contributions to the literature ('The Development of Professions in the Public Service' and 'Input versus Withinput'). Today, despite the diffusion of power which I have suggested has diminished bureaucracy's capacity to control its client groups, I continue to treat the bureaucracy as a central, influential and sometimes dominant actor in group-state relations. See *Group Politics*.

38 *Democratic Government and Politics*, 303–4. Emphasis added.

39 *Organized Labour and Pressure Politics*. Kwavnick's study remains one of the best examinations of a Canadian interest group.

40 Dawson, 'National Pressure Groups and the Federal Government,' 39–42; Aucoin, 'Pressure Groups and Recent Changes in the Policy Making Process'; Stanbury, *Business Interests and the Reform of Competition Policy*; Thompson and Stanbury, *The Political Economy of Interest Groups*; and Weir, 'Federalism, Interest Groups and Parliamentary Government.'

41 *The Politics of Drugs*, 296.

42 *Group Politics*, chs. 5 and 6.

43 Pal, *State, Class and Bureaucracy*, 172.

44 *Interests of State*, 272.

45 For example, in the original formulation of the Lobbyists Registration Act and its 1994 revision, the great majority of 'stakeholders' consulted, and certainly the most influential, were lobbying firms. 'LRA Reform Consultations Continue,' *The Lobby Monitor* 5 (29 Nov. 1993), 4.

46 Atkinson and Coleman, *The State, Business and Industrial Change in Canada*.

47 *Elite Accommodation in Canadian Politics*, *Elites in the Policy Process*, and 'Interest Groups and the Canadian Parliament.'

48 *Right Honourable Men*, xv.

5

The Political Economy Tradition and Canadian Policy Studies

STEPHEN MCBRIDE

Political economy has been variously defined as 'the study of power derived from or contingent on a system of property rights; the historical development of power relationships; and the cultural and social embodiments of them';[1] as a focus 'on processes whereby social change is located in the historical interaction of the economic, political, cultural and ideological moments of social life, with the dynamic rooted in socio-economic conflict';[2] and as having as its subject matter 'the production and distribution of societal resources ... [since] ... modern societies depend on two institutions for making such decisions: the state and the market ... the study of both institutions is an integral part of political economy.'[3]

Public policy has attracted the following definitions: 'a course of action or inaction chosen by public authorities to address a given problem or inter-related set of problems';[4] as 'whatever governments choose to do or not to do';[5] and the academic study of public policy becomes an 'attempt to *explain* the evolution of public policy or a particular policy field *over a significant period of time.*'[6]

Juxtaposing these definitions shows considerable complementarity between the two fields of study. Political economy's focus on power leads to a major interest in the state; what the state does or does not do is the focus of public policy studies. In searching for explanation, policy studies can find valuable resources in political economy's concern with the interaction of economic, social, political, cultural, and ideological factors. In particular, focusing on the impact of economic forces poses quite directly the question: Who benefits?[7] Political economy's interest in the interconnection between social, cultural, and economic-political factors is thus helpful in understanding public policy. One seminal article in the mid-1970s suggested that policy analysis incorporates five general approaches to explanation in policy analysis

– the environment of politics, the distribution of power, the prevailing ideas, institutional frameworks, and the process of decision making.[8] Political economy can make a contribution to at least the first four of these approaches. Besides their academic endeavours, political economists often hoped to have some practical impact; much of their work was 'policy-oriented, with a view to changing Canadian priorities and national consciousness.'[9]

In what ways has political economy contributed to our understanding of public policy? How influential has it been in a practical sense? In attempting to answer these questions it will be useful first to provide a brief survey of the variety of concerns and approaches that have informed the Canadian political economy tradition. This discussion will not dwell on one of the liberal variants of political economy, represented in the modern era by public choice theory, partly because it is dealt with elsewhere in this volume, and partly because in Canada, in contrast to some other countries, this brand of political economy has found its home among public policy analysts rather than in the political economy network.

Most observers detect two broad trends in Canadian political economy – one, influenced by the work of Harold Innis and W.A. Mackintosh, focuses on staples theory, and can be regarded, especially in the case of Mackintosh, as a derivative of liberal neoclassical economic theory. The other, influenced by Marxism, has class as its central concept.[10] Both trends have a venerable place in Canadian academe. Both fell out of favour in the 1950s but underwent a revival in the late 1960s. For a decade and a half Canadian political economy represented a growth industry in disciplines such as political science and sociology, and its influence remains substantial.

It is not surprising that Marxist analyses of capitalist society have little influence on the policy makers charged with defending such societies. The practical impact of this variant of political economy is likely, therefore, to be restricted to groups and organizations pushing for fundamental changes to the system. Staples theorists, on the other hand, did enjoy considerable influence on public policy between the late 1930s and 1950s especially where their analyses, as was the case with W.A. Mackintosh, tended also to reflect the rising tide of Keynesianism. Mackintosh became one of the Ottawa 'civil service mandarins' who exercised great influence over the development of policy.[11] Mackintosh authored one of the most influential background studies to the Rowell-Sirois Royal Commission on Dominion-Provincial Relations,[12] the White Paper on Employment and Incomes that promised that postwar Canadian governments would be committed to 'high and stable levels of employment,'[13] and was to have his version of staples theory endorsed by the Gordon Commission in the late 1950s.[14] He had, in short, 'more impact on practical political economy than most academics ever will.'[15] Other political economists of Mackintosh's generation were also concerned with exerting practical influence – frequently the preferred vehicle was the government royal commission. Thus 'hinterland' political economists such as Vernon Fowke took part in investigations of agricultural and transportation policy[16] – one of his most significant contributions was the insistence on the political creation of uneven development through state policy;[17] and others such as George Britnell presented briefs on behalf of their provincial governments.[18] Even Harold Innis, in many ways distrustful of the effects of political involvement on academic scholarship – 'Political economy flourished with political, economic, and religious freedom. It withered with subordination to mathematical abstractions and science, and became the handmaid of centralized power in the modern state'[19] – served on royal commissions.[20] Many political economists journeyed to wartime Ottawa where they enjoyed, if not power, at least influence. Thus the early generation of Canadian political economists were no strangers to the practice of public policy. In this regard, at least, their performance exceeded the aspirations of their successors in the 1970s and beyond.

One central aspect of the Canadian polity, of interest to both political economists and public policy analysts, is a greater degree of state activism when compared to its most common reference point, the United States. Early staples interpretations of Canada's development offered an explanation of Canada's reliance on the state. In a context of scarcity of private capital, and the heavy investment in infrastructure required to transport staple products to foreign markets, the state was the only agency capable of building or financing the necessary canals, railways, and port facilities.[21] Such efforts culminated in a series of 'national policies'[22] which, in combination with later initiatives in the social and cultural areas, characterized Canada as a 'public enterprise culture,'[23] in contrast to the bastion of free and private enterprise to the south.

Staples-based analyses depicted Canada as a disadvantaged actor in an international economy shaped by others. Our disadvantages sprang from geography, history, and technology, and were compounded by the tendency of the indigenous business elite to act as local representatives of international capital.[24] Many of the same concerns were present in the principal stimulus to the revival of political economy – the publication of the Watkins Report[25] in 1968, Kari Levitt's *Silent Surrender*[26] in 1970, an important collection of essays edited by Gary Teeple[27] and the Gray Report,[28] both published in 1972.

Staples theory has been criticized for its 'agentless' character – that is, for viewing history as the product of natural and anonymous forces.[29] The brief account of the inevitability of Canadian statism given above leaves out the obvious political motivations that led state officials to initiate national policies, one of the most powerful of which was the desire to have an existence separate from and independent of the United States. It also ignores the particular balance of forces within and between social classes that was conducive to such initiatives.

Stimulated by the appearance of the Watkins and Gray reports, the revived political economy tradition of the 1970s and 1980s was concerned with understanding Canada's dependent position vis-à-vis the United States – an orientation that led to considerable cross-fertilization between it and neo-Marxian dependency theory. While much of this analysis remained rooted in neo-Innisian pessimism that little could be done about the situation, and therefore had little to say about policy questions, another more optimistic trend was concerned with devising policy responses that might limit dependency.[30] Initially these concerns crystallized around the issue of foreign direct investment (foreign ownership) in Canada. Later, this issue was displaced by a focus on Canada's trading relationship with the United States. Together, these two – foreign investment and free trade[31] – have dominated political economy debates for the last quarter of a century. In analysing them, Canadian political economists have had much to say about the environment of Canadian public policy, the distribution of power, the dominant ideas in society, and the institutional framework in which important policy debates are considered.

While sharing some of the concerns of traditional staples theory, notably attention to resource dependency and the underdevelopment of manufacturing in Canada, many analysts of the 1970s revival assigned greater explanatory power to political factors. A number of these[32] focus on the characteristics of Canada's capitalist class and, while not explicitly Marxist, certainly demonstrate the influence of the renaissance of neo-Marxism. Certainly such analyses concentrate much more on the distribution of power in society than do mainstream staples theorists. Thus Tom Naylor contended that Confederation and subsequent national policies were measures devised by the dominant commercial bourgeoisie to consolidate their dominance of the Canadian economy at the expense of a nascent industrial bourgeoisie. Content to cede manufacturing to foreign investors, the Canadian capitalist class also ceded the commanding heights of the Canadian economy to American multinationals and doomed the Canadian state to dependency and ultimate disappearance: 'A Canadian capitalist state cannot survive because it has neither the material base nor the will to survive.'[33]

If Naylor's depiction of Canadian capitalists resembled the doctrine of 'original sin,' others interpreted Confederation and its aftermath as an attempt by an indigenous capitalist class to engage in a nation-building exercise.[34] If this effort was incompletely successful, this could be attributed to structural determinants – Canada had the misfortune to be situated next door to the dominant capitalist power in its most expansionary phase of development – or to the failure of subordinate classes, in this case farmers, to wrest power from business and to make the nation-building project their own.[35] In the aftermath of the Watkins and Gray reports there was an explosion of national consciousness in Canada, and the prospects for a new national policy to foster greater economic, cultural, and political independence from the United States seemed good. Responding to the new mood the Trudeau Liberals enacted the Foreign Investment Review Agency (FIRA) and created a state-owned oil company, Petro-Canada. Donald Smiley foresaw a new national policy centred on repatriating control of the Canadian economy.[36] Clearly an industrial strategy would form a central component of such a policy; the historical alternative was to embrace free trade and economic integration.[37]

In its 1980–84 term the Trudeau government did adopt an embryonic industrial strategy – its components were the National Energy Program (NEP) and the megaprojects initiatives – in which the federal government was to play a highly interventionist role. The strategy aimed to consolidate Canadian ownership in the energy sector and to use the sector as the cornerstone of an economic development strategy. Thus the new industrial and national policy was 'staples based' and was partly a response to a nationalist agenda created by the revival of political economy in the 1960s.[38] The fact that such policies could be launched seems to indicate either that a nationalist fraction of Canadian capital had come into existence, or that the Canadian state enjoyed considerable autonomy.

Many of the proponents of that agenda, of course, favoured a socialist solution to the problems of dependency. This was not on offer from the Canadian state – though the state was prepared to promote indigenous over foreign-owned capital, its efforts were firmly linked to the interests of private capital accumulation.[39]

Despite its attachment to private enterprise the Liberal attempt at a third national policy encountered major opposition from the United States and from the Canadian business community. The policy had been grounded on assumptions that oil prices would continue to rise. That scenario did not materialize. In this context the Canadian state was all the more vulnerable to pressures from within and without, and the ambitious strategy was abandoned.[40] With the election of the Mulroney government, the state, reflecting the articulated demands of Canadian business,[41] adopted a neoconservative economic strategy.

The new strategy removed constraints on foreign investment, dismantled FIRA and the NEP, and opted for continental free trade.[42] The adoption of this strategy indicated that hopes for a nationalist fraction within Canadian capital had been exaggerated – either indigenous capital had become thoroughly subservient to transnationals, or it had become strong enough, at least in certain sectors, to define its interests in terms of the continental rather than the national economy.[43] This new strategy marked the defeat of the practical influence of the new political economy, which had tended toward nationalist solutions, but provided a range of analytical opportunities. Perhaps some cold comfort was also provided to those political economists who had predicted that the Canadian state would be unwilling or unable to reverse its dependency.

As well as analysing the economic provisions of the Canada–U.S. Free Trade Agreement and, subsequently, the North American Free Trade Agreement, political economists have spelled out the political implications of these quasi-constitutional documents. Indeed, radical political economists were sufficiently far-sighted to identify and warn of these dangers early in the process. Thus Duncan Cameron pointed out in 1986 that free trade represented the main alternative to public sector intervention. It was the basis of a market-driven industrial strategy, if that is not an oxymoron, and concluding a free trade agreement would establish limits on public authority via international agreement. Since international treaties are binding on governments, the trade agreements serve to 'constitutionalize' many of the tenets of neoconservative economics that are included in the agreements. In particular, the ruling assumption is that government interference with market forces is illegitimate. Corporate property rights are generally enhanced by the agreements and those of governments, which have at least the potential to act as expressions of the democratic will of the people, are reduced.[44] The process of shifting to a free trade strategy was much assisted by the conclusions of the Macdonald Report, delivered by a commission whose counsels appear to have been wholly influenced by orthodox free market economists[45] and the representations of the business community.[46] The discontinuity that free trade represented was part of the dissolution of the postwar consensus that occurred in the decade after 1975.

The postwar boom, its subsequent crisis, and the shift to neoconservatism received major attention from political economists. The key issues included efforts to develop a theory of the capitalist state and to apply or illustrate the

theory by investigating particular areas of state activity. Though many political economists resist the label 'policy studies,' their empirical investigation of what the state did fits the classic definition of public policy. Innisian
influences and dependency theory provide an important part of the context
or environment of examinations of the Canadian state and its actions. Even
if these perspectives were not fully integrated into accounts of the state, few
Canadian political economists were insensitive to the constraints and limits
placed upon Canada by its location in the international political economy
and its relation to the United States. To this awareness, neo-Marxian political economy added a focus on the distribution of power in Canadian society,
especially between social classes, and through the incorporation of the
Gramscian concept of hegemony, an interest in the prevailing ideas that influence what the state does. With the shift from Keynesianism to
neoconservatism as the dominant policy paradigm, political economy was
well equipped to analyse this development through the concept of hegemony,
and the later development of regulation theory, briefly discussed below. More
recently, a neo-institutionalist approach to political economy has developed
– an approach that places major emphasis on the institutional, or state-centred, determinants of state activity. Thus recent trends in political economy
encompass the environment, distribution of power, role of ideas and institutions themes identified earlier.

The main departure in the development of 'state studies' was the publication in 1977 of *The Canadian State* edited by Leo Panitch.[47] The collection
included theoretical and historical perspectives on the Canadian state,[48] plus
sections on capitalism and federalism, the connection between class structure and state power, and the state in action – economic and social policy,
ideology, and social control. According to Panitch: 'A fully developed theory
of the state in capitalist society must meet at least three basic requirements.
It must clearly delimit the complex of institutions that go to make up the
state. It must demonstrate concretely, rather than just define abstractly, the
linkages between the state and the system of class inequality in the society,
particularly its ties to the dominant social class. And it must specify as far as
possible the functions of the state under the capitalist mode of production.'[49]

The Canadian State initiated a lively debate, much of which paralleled
similar controversies elsewhere in the Western world. Rival interpretations
– instrumental,[50] structural-functional[51] – had their Canadian adherents.[52]
One issue that soon emerged was the precise relationship between the dominant capitalist class and the state; most participants were at pains to avoid a
crude knee-jerk interpretation that suggested the state was the pliant and
malleable tool of an omnipotent and self-conscious class of capitalists. The

concept that the state acted on behalf of capital but not necessarily at its behest – that the state enjoyed a 'relative autonomy' from capital – was devised and usefully applied in a number of studies.[53] In her study of Canadian textile policy, for example, Rianne Mahon employed a sophisticated blend of class fraction analysis (i.e., conflict between different fractions of the capitalist class) and portraits of intra-bureaucratic competition within the state to explain the failure to prevent deindustrialization in the textile industry. By implication, the analysis applied to the rest of manufacturing, as well as explaining the particular form of industrial strategy emerging in the early 1980s (resource-based megaprojects). Her analysis points to the dominance, within Canadian capital and its state, of a staples-based fraction of capital.

One of the strengths of political economy, and one of its major contributions to policy analysis, has been its focus on the impact of class and, in particular, the power of capital.[54] Whatever its defects, and both the scope and intensity of internal debates within the political economy school indicate there have been many, emphasis on systematic, class-based inequality in society and its political counterpart altered the context in which policy analysis was conducted.[55]

However, the focus on class and the linkage between class and state power came under significant criticism during the 1980s. Class was criticized by feminist theorists for ignoring other forms of inequality, specifically that based on gender. While both feminism and political economy share an understanding of 'power as a fundamental category situated within a historical and materialist context' they differ in that feminist political economists insist that 'all classes are characterized by gender and that gender is fundamental to conflict between classes as well as within them.'[56] While many participants in debates about the relationship between political economy have noted the potential congruence between the two perspectives,[57] few would argue that this has yet been satisfactorily achieved[58] at the theoretical level, though many excellent studies exist that apply some blend of these two perspectives to particular issues.[59]

State theory was attacked primarily for its alleged functionalism,[60] but also for overstating the unity of the capitalist class and, for that matter, the state itself, defects that reduced the theory's usefulness in policy analysis.[61] Functionalism suggests that the state must and always will perform certain functions – typically, accumulation, legitimation, and coercion. Functionalism therefore explains the state's actions in terms of the functional requirements of capital without reference to human agency.

While crude examples of functionalist interpretations were certainly to be found, there were other attempts to integrate a political analysis of class agency into studies that used, at least descriptively,[62] the categorizations of state functions that had been delineated by Panitch and others. In a series of articles, for example, Carl Cuneo[63] used the concept of relative autonomy to explain the state's stance, in the face of class conflict, toward unemployment insurance. And Paul Craven's major study of the state's role in the early industrial relations system in Canada[64] sought to combine a discussion of state functions with an analysis of the ideas and social forces that interacted to form state policy. Used analytically, rather than as explanation, the state function approach had the great merit on focusing attention on the state's outputs and the degree to which they conferred advantage on various social classes.[65] The methodological zealotry displayed by critics of state theory has, however, proved effective, and few works using this approach now appear. The unfortunate effect was that the substantive baby was thrown out along with the 'functionalism-as-explanation' bath water. And class and state analysis declined at the very time that state policy, in Canada and elsewhere, was becoming transparently that favoured by capital and opposed by labour and a variety of social action groups.

The view that state policy increasingly corresponded to capital's articulated self-interest was not shared by all. In a series of works, Atkinson and Coleman, in particular, argued that the capacity of the state, and the degree of unity demonstrated by business, varied considerably depending on what policy area was being investigated.[66] The conclusions emerged from the in-depth examination of interest associations that resulted from the 'discovery' of corporatism in the 1970s. The presence or absence, characteristics, and conditions connected to the emergence of corporatist relations between the state and interest associations spawned a veritable growth industry in the 1970s and 1980s.[67] The concept was generally viewed as having limited application in Canada,[68] but the debate surrounding it led to much valuable work by political economists and others.

In the 1980s many political economists concentrated on analysing and critiquing the new certainties of the right-wing policy agenda. Within comparative political economy it had become commonplace to describe the postwar era in terms of a class compromise which led to a 'postwar consensus,' the substance of which was represented by the formula 'Keynesian welfare state.' The formula thus included a policy commitment to full-employment – explicit in some countries, tacit in others – combined with state provision, or organization through comprehensive insurance schemes, of social security. As a blanket description of the Western capitalist democracies the formula was rather too sweeping and its application to individual cases, including Canada, problematic.[69] Nevertheless the label did capture part of the essence of postwar society and served to distinguish the period from those that preceded and succeeded it. In some versions this Keynesian policy superstructure was said to be founded on a particular phase of the capitalist mode of production – Fordism – the system of mass standardized production and associated patterns of mass consumption. Linking Fordism to Keynesianism, regulation theorists referred to an institutional order that comprised a mode of regulation (Keynesianism), combined with a regime of accumulation (Fordism) and a system of legitimation. During the protracted postwar boom this institutional order exhibited a high degree of stability; from around the mid-1970s it entered a period of crisis manifested by the search for a post-Keynesian or non-Keynesian mode of regulation, a post-Fordist accumulation regime, and a new system of legitimation.[70]

Much of the debate around the decline of Keynesianism has focused on the neoconservative revolution in economic theory and public policy that succeeded it. The renewed focus on ideology could be dubbed 'bringing ideas back in.'[71] The neoconservative assault on the Keynesian consensus[72] has involved at least five major policy departures.[73] These include a redefinition of the goals of economic policy, from full employment to price stability, together with a reduction in the size and role of the state, particularly as it pertains to social and economic policy. Key instruments in achieving this shift include privatization and deregulation, especially the most pervasive form of deregulation – continental free trade; ending and reversing the redistributive role of the state,[74] through changes to the tax system and reduced social services; and reducing the power of trade unions, the organizations of the class that loses as a result of the policy reorientation, and that is most likely to present serious opposition to it. Each of these policy departures has been analysed by political economists. Even if political economy has failed to realize its practical objectives in influencing public policy, it has some claim to have provided the most persuasive account of the sources and consequences of the policy revolution that has transformed Canada in the last decade and a half.

In focusing the goals of macroeconomic policy exclusively on price stability, neoconservatives have advanced a number of rationalizations. One is that there is little governments can do about unemployment,[75] but that governments can have an impact on price stability, primarily through reducing government spending and, in particular, reducing the deficit, said to be caused primarily by excessive spending on social programs. It is clear, however, as a result of investigations by political economists, that the roots of the deficit lie elsewhere. Most of the deficit can be explained by a shortfall in revenues resulting from tax expenditures targeted primarily on the affluent,[76] and from high real interest rates.[77] The main conclusion of political economy policy analysis is that the neoconservative platform is erroneous at best and fraudulent at worst. Contrary to neoconservative claims, governments can do something about unemployment, chronic deficits are not the result of profligate spending on social policies and, indeed, are the product of the neoconservative era, not of the Keynesian one. Not surprisingly, these conclusions have had greater resonance among groups opposed to the government's agenda, rather than in decision-making circles – evidence that the policy studies industry reflects rather than escapes from the ideological tenor of society generally.

Notwithstanding arguments advanced above, retrenchment of social services has been a feature of recent governmental strategy in Canada. There is debate over the extent of retrenchment – erosion is universally conceded;[78] others consider that concentrating on the aggregate level of social spending, which has been sustained or even risen as a result of increased demands on the system, understates the degree of neoconservative restructuring that has actually occurred.[79] Still, there is a perception that progress in dismantling the Keynesian welfare state has been less than neoconservative theorists would have wished. This has been attributed to the federal system itself (that is, to state-centred, institutional factors)[80] and, in the case of specific programs such as unemployment insurance, to a mixture of state- and society-centred factors, 'counter-pressures from affected provinces, regions, unions, employers and social advocacy groups.'[81] Many political economists consider that the free trade agreements will permit the dismantling of social and socio-economic policies such as regional policy to proceed at a faster rate.[82]

Similarly much deregulation and privatization can be linked to the continentalism that led to the free trade agreements. The replacement of the Foreign Investment Review Agency by Investment Canada and the elimination of the National Energy Policy represented a frontal assault on the activist 'new national policy' approach of the Trudeau government.[83] In other areas the Mulroney government sought to portray its deregulatory and privatizing efforts as pragmatically rather than ideologically driven. It seems clear, however, that though the government's practice was cautious, a consistent ideological agenda underlay its moves in these areas.[84]

The rise and fall of the Keynesian era has provided a useful framework for analysing modern industrial relations policy. Certainly the key piece of legislation, federal order-in-council 1003 (1944), coincided with the adoption of a form of Keynesianism by the Canadian state. The federal initiative was widely emulated by provincial governments and thus served as the foundation for a Canadian industrial relations system, notwithstanding provincial jurisdictional primacy over most workers. The intention of state industrial relations policy was 'to enhance collective bargaining with duly certified trade unions. The object here was to avoid the scale of industrial militancy and disruption that had characterized industrial relations during the previous wartime demobilisation (1918–20) and, more recently, in the latter years of the depression and throughout much of the Second World War. The calculation was that trade unions and employers, as responsible representatives of their respective interests, could be brought together through organised collective bargaining.'[85] The calculation seemed to pay off for all the participants for about twenty years. Postwar prosperity, relatively full employment, the flourishing of the Fordist production system, and moderate labour leaders seeking to avoid association with communism or radicalism during the Cold War combined to produce a stable environment for business, and growing wages and security for labour.

The crisis of Fordism and the abandonment of Keynesianism produced a dramatically different environment. Neoconservative industrial relations policy has been characterized as an era of 'permanent exceptionalism' in which 'rights established in the general legislation of the 1940s and 1960s were increasingly removed on an *ad hoc* basis, from particular groups of workers who sought to exercise them and eventually from large segments of the working class altogether for a "temporary period."'[86] One of the chief instruments of permanent exceptionalism has been the regular and increasing use of ad hoc back-to-work legislation. This has been combined with periodic implementation of wage and price controls, and amendment and erosion of the legislative regime governing collective bargaining.[87] These trends have been apparent at both federal and provincial levels.[88] The trends are not unidirectional – it is possible to find legislative expansion of labour's rights as well as restriction. Still, the overwhelming weight of state activity has been toward more coercion and more restriction. This is true even of governments such as Bob Rae's New Democratic government in Ontario, which liberalized the Ontario Labour Relations Act with one hand and engaged in coercion and restraint via its Social Contract legislation with the other. Summing up the trends, Russell argued in 1990: 'What we are presented with is not so much a total restructuring of the industrial relations system as a *de facto* renegotiation, *at the state's behest*, of some of the existing parameters. Once again, union security is exchanged for responsible union conduct *as defined by* existing political priorities. If anything has undergone fundamental revision, it is the nature of the contemporary political agenda and the relative benefits derivable from the trade-off.'[89]

Early in this chapter we posed two questions: In what ways has political economy contributed to our understanding of public policy, and how influential has political economy been in practical terms? Enough has been said above to demonstrate that much of Canadian political economy has had a policy focus and that many excellent policy studies have been produced within the political economy tradition. Clearly much of Canadian political economy has had a left-wing tinge. In the 1930s this was not necessarily an impediment to political influence. The challenge to neoclassical economics by Keynesianism legitimated the building of a welfare state and an active role for government in pursuit of such aims as full employment. However, the past two decades have witnessed the revival and triumph of the political right, and as its academic corollary, the reassertion of a new neoclassical economics. In this context it is unsurprising that political economy's direct influence on policy has been negligible as far as decision making is concerned. Its practical influence has been confined to the social movements and coalitions that have resisted the erosion of the welfare state, continued to advocate full employment, and opposed free trade.

In this period political economy's academic contribution to public policy studies has been significant. Staples and dependency theories have helped delineate the environment in which Canadian public policy making occurs. And while neo-Marxian class theory has never been hegemonic in describing the nature of societal influence on state actors, it has achieved the status of one of several contending theories of power in society that most academic policy analysts find it useful, or at least politic, to consider.

However, it is probably fair to say that mainstream economics provides the hegemonic paradigm for policy studies – in an important sense the policy studies industry replicates the world it is analysing. And, as in the real world, the justifications for neoconservative policies come from the mainstream of the economics profession and the opposition to neoconservative ideas and policies from radical political economy.[90] In sum, political economy has played an important counter hegemonic role in the evolution of policy studies in Canada.

Notes

1 Marchak, 'Canadian Political Economy,' 673.
2 Clement and Williams, eds., *The New Canadian Political Economy*, 7.
3 Howlett and Ramesh, *The Political Economy of Canada: An Introduction*, 9–10.
4 Pal, *Public Policy Analysis: An Introduction*, 2.
5 Dye, *Policy Analysis*, 1.
6 Doern and Phidd, *Canadian Public Policy: Ideas, Structure, Process*, xxi.
7 Atkinson, *Governing Canada: Institutions and Public Policy*, 2.

8 Simeon, 'Studying Public Policy.'
9 Marchak, 'Canadian Political Economy,' 674–5.
10 In their revived versions both trends within political economy exhibit a greater theoretical nature and complexity than this sentence suggests.
11 See Granatstein, *The Ottawa Men: The Civil Service Mandarins, 1935–57*, especially ch. 6; and Owram, *The Government Generation: Canadian Intellectuals and the State*.
12 Mackintosh, *The Economic Background of Dominion Provincial Relations*.
13 Canada, Department of Reconstruction, *White Paper on Employment and Incomes* (Ottawa 1945). This commitment paralleled those being introduced elsewhere. In the Canadian case the commitment had a 'staples theory spin' in that increased staples exports were to be the motor of full-employment policies.
14 Canada, Royal Commission on Canada's Economic Prospects, *Report*.
15 Howlett and Ramesh, *The Political Economy of Canada*, 96.
16 See Phillips, 'The Hinterland Perspective: The Political Economy of Vernon C. Fowke.'
17 On this see Brodie, 'The Political Economy of Regionalism,' 148–50.
18 See Darling, *The Politics of Freight Rates*, 169.
19 Innis, *Political Economy in the Modern State*, 140. See also Berger, *The Writing of Canadian History*, ch. 4.
20 For example on the Turgeon Commission charged with investigating railway freight rates.
21 Innis, *The Fur Trade in Canada: An Introduction to Canadian Economic History*, 400.
22 Fowke, 'The National Policy – Old and New.'
23 Hardin, *A Nation Unaware: The Canadian Economic Culture*.
24 Laxer, 'The Schizophrenic Character of Canadian Political Economy,' *Canadian Review of Sociology and Anthropology* 26, no. 1 (1989), 180–82. The nature and characteristics of Canada's business class provide a linking issue between the revived schools of Canadian political economy.
25 Watkins et al., *Foreign Ownership and the Structure of Canadian Industry*.
26 Levitt, *Silent Surrender: The Multinational Corporation in Canada*.
27 Teeple, ed., *Capitalism and the National Question in Canada*.
28 Gray, *Foreign Direct Investment in Canada*.
29 It nonetheless features in public policy texts as part of the environment shaping Canadian public policy; see, for example, Brooks, *Public Policy in Canada: An Introduction*, ch. 3.
30 For a discussion of the pessimistic version of staples theory associated with Innis, and the more optimistic version associated with W.A. Mackintosh, who

through his participation in government had an important impact on Canadian public policy, see Howlett and Ramesh, *Political Economy in Canada*, ch. 4.

31 In fact the two issues are not as dichotomous as this discussion suggests: 'Aren't today's trade agreements, anyway, just prosaic and misleading names for charters of rights and freedoms for corporations, permitting them to locate their production facilities wherever they please while selling freely everywhere? Some commentators have taken to calling them "free production agreements."' Watkins, 'Foreign Ownership '94 – Buy, Bye Canada,' 30.

32 Notably Naylor, 'The Rise and Fall of the Third Commercial Empire of the St. Lawrence,' and Clement, *The Canadian Corporate Elite*, and *Continental Corporate Power*.

33 Naylor, 'Rise and Fall,' 36.

34 Notably Ryerson *Unequal Union*; see also Laxer, 'Constitutional Crisis and Continentalism,' 202–3, and Resnick, *The Masks of Proteus: Canadian Reflections on the State*, 202–20.

35 Laxer, *Open for Business: The Roots of Foreign Ownership in Canada*, ch. 4.

36 Smiley, 'Canada and the Quest for a National Policy,' *Canadian Journal of Political Science* 8 (1975).

37 See Williams, *Not for Export: Toward a Political Economy of Canada's Arrested Industrialization*, ch. 7.

38 See Clarkson, *Canada and the Reagan Challenge: Crisis and Adjustment, 1981–85*, ch. 4.

39 Pratt, 'Energy: The Roots of National Policy,' *Studies in Political Economy* 7 (1982), 40–41.

40 For a comprehensive analysis of the Trudeau government's retreat from involvement in a 'crisis' with the United States and toward 'adjustment,' see Clarkson, *Canada and the Reagan Challenge*.

41 Langille, 'The Business Council on National Issues and the Canadian State.'

42 For a useful account of the economic policy options see Leslie, *Federal State, National Economy*.

43 See Carroll, *Corporate Power and Canadian Capital*; and Layton, 'Nationalism and the Canadian Bourgeoisie.'

44 See Cameron's introduction to Cameron, ed., *The Free Trade Papers*.

45 See Simeon, 'Inside the Macdonald Commission.'

46 The impact of free trade has received detailed analysis in Cameron and Watkins, eds., *Canada under Free Trade*.

47 Panitch, ed., *The Canadian State: Political Economy and Political Power*.

48 Panitch's own introduction, 'The Role and Nature of the Canadian State,' and Whitaker's 'Images of the State in Canada.'

49 Panitch, 'The Role and Nature of the Canadian State,' 5.

50 For example, Miliband, *The State in Capitalist Society.*

51 For example, Poulantzas, 'The Problem of the Capitalist State,' and *State, Power, Socialism*; O'Connor, *The Fiscal Crisis of the State.*

52 For a useful guide through these debates see Albo and Jenson, 'A Contested Concept.'

53 For example, Mahon's important study of textile policy in *The Politics of Industrial Restructuring.*

54 See, in particular, Langille, 'The Business Council on National Issues and the Canadian State'; Williams, 'Access and Accommodation in the Canadian Welfare State.'

55 Most texts, for example, came to include sections on class-based or Marxian approaches to the study of public policy; see Atkinson and Chandler, eds., *The Politics of Canadian Public Policy*, ch. 1; Doern and Phidd, *Canadian Public Policy: Ideas, Structure, Process*, 2nd ed., ch. 1; and Brooks, *Public Policy in Canada,* 2nd ed., ch. 2.

56 Bakker, 'The Political Economy of Gender,' in Clement and Williams, eds., *The New Canadian Political Economy*, 99–100.

57 See Maroney and Luxton, 'From Feminism and Political Economy to Feminist Political Economy'; and Armstrong and Connelly, 'Feminist Political Economy.'

58 See, for example, Andrew, 'Challenges for a New Political Economy,' in Johnson, McBride, Smith, eds., *Continuities and Discontinuities: The Political Economy of Social Welfare and Labour Market Policy in Canada*, especially 66–8.

59 For example, Armstrong, 'Lessons from Pay Equity,' *Studies in Political Economy* (Summer 1990); and Cohen, *Free Trade and the Future of Women's Work: Manufacturing and Service Industries.* Since the feminist approach to policy studies is represented elsewhere in this volume it will not be dealt with here.

60 See Albo and Jenson, 'A Contested Concept,' in Clement and Williams, eds., *The New Canadian Political Economy*, 209n, who state that functionalism 'impute[s] needs to societies as if they were living bodies; it assumes a teleology without demonstrating the existence of goal-oriented planning mechanisms; and it involves circular reasoning, since any policy adopted is, by definition, functional, unless the system collapses.'

61 Coleman and Skogstad, 'Preface,' in Coleman and Skogstad, eds., *Policy Communities and Public Policy in Canada: A Structural Approach*, ix.

62 Following Gough's famous injunction, 'whilst we must reject any functionalist explanation of the ... state, it is still useful to delineate the functions of the

state, so long as they are used to indicate tendencies at work within the capitalist state,' in *The Political Economy of the Welfare State*, 51.

63 See Cuneo, 'State, Class and Reserve Labour'; 'State Mediation of Class Contradictions in Canadian Unemployment Insurance'; and 'Comment: Restoring Class to State Unemployment Insurance.'

64 Craven, *'An Impartial Umpire': Industrial Relations and the Canadian State, 1900–1911.*

65 The fact that the same policy could contribute to more that one state function was often advanced by critics of the approach. In reality this should only be problematic for those with a unidimensional view of social life.

66 See Atkinson and Coleman, *The State, Business and Industrial Change in Canada*, and 'Strong States and Weak States.'

67 See Panitch, 'Recent Theorizations of Corporatism.'

68 Panitch, 'Corporatism in Canada.'

69 See, for example, Campbell's account of the lukewarm attachment to Keynesianism in Canada in *Grand Illusions: The Politics of the Keynesian Experience in Canada, 1945–75*, and Jenson's account of the peculiar and particular form taken by the Canadian adoption of the new paradigm after the war in '"Different" but not "Exceptional",' and 'Representations in Crisis.'

70 For a stimulating application of these concepts to the Canadian case see Clarkson, 'Disjunctions: Free Trade and the Paradox of Canadian Development.'

71 One of the strengths of regulation theory is, of course, that it forces attention on underlying structural variables as well through its concept of 'regime of accumulation'; see Mahon, 'Post-Fordism: Some Issues for Labour.'

72 For a useful overview see Allen, 'Introduction: The Conservative Revolution in Economic Policy.' A full-length treatment and critique can be found in Gonick, *The Great Economic Debate*, and a shorter, entertaining, yet profound one in Watkins, *Madness and Ruin: Politics and the Economy in the Neoconservative Age.*

73 There have been some efforts to provide holistic accounts of the transformation; for example, see McBride and Shields, *Dismantling a Nation: Canada and the New World Order.*

74 That is, redistributive in the direction of greater equality.

75 For a rebuttal see McBride, *Not Working: State, Unemployment and Neo-Conservatism in Canada*, ch. 2.

76 See Wolfe, 'The Politics of the Deficit'; and McQuaig, *Behind Closed Doors: How the Rich Won Control of Canada's Tax System.*

77 Chorney, *Sound Finance and Other Delusions: Deficit and Debt Management in the Age of Neo-Liberal Economics.*

78 See Banting, *The Welfare State and Canadian Federalism*, 2nd ed.; Mishra, *The Welfare State in Capitalist Societies*; Houle, 'Economic Renewal and Social Policy.'
79 Mullally, 'Social Welfare and the New Right.'
80 Banting, *The Welfare State and Canadian Federalism*, 205–14.
81 Pal, *State, Class and Bureaucracy*, 11.
82 See, for example, the comments of Mishra, *The Welfare State in Capitalist Society*, 99, and Brodie, *The Political Economy of Canadian Regionalism*, 221, 223.
83 For brief accounts of Investment Canada see Hurtig, *The Betrayal of Canada*, ch. 12, and Barlow and Campbell, *Take Back the Nation*, 31–2.
84 Baxter-Moore, 'Ideology or Pragmatism?'
85 Russell 'Assault without Defeat'; for a comprehensive account, from a political economy perspective, of the evolution of Canada's industrial relations system, and the role of labour policy, see Russell's *Back to Work? Labour, State and Industrial Relations in Canada*.
86 Panitch and Swartz, *The Assault on Trade Union Freedoms: From Consent to Coercion Revisited*, 16.
87 For a summary of the legislative assault see Panitch and Swartz, *The Assault on Trade Union Freedoms: From Wage Controls to Social Contract*, Appendix II.
88 For an analysis of an extreme case among the provinces see Shields, 'Building a New Hegemony in British Columbia.'
89 Russell, *Back to Work?*, 273.
90 Some observers attribute the failure of political economy to bring its hegemonic project to fruition to internal divisions and eclecticism within the political economy school itself; see Pal, 'Political Economy as a Hegemonic Project.'

PART TWO

Policy Studies in Practice:
The Rise of Policy Analysis in Canada

6

The Policy Analysis Profession in Canada

STEPHEN BROOKS

I. Introduction

When the government of Canada tabled its first budget in 1867, it was the handiwork of a mere handful of individuals. Not one of them was an economist by training, a not very surprising fact given that economics had not yet emerged as a specialized discipline separate from the traditional study of political economy. The staff of the Department of Finance numbered a slender thirty-eight, most of whom performed clerical and auditing functions. The department's top bureaucrat, William Dickinson, was a relatively obscure person who owed his position to patronage. The budget that he helped produce relied on only the barest information about production, consumption, savings, and investment (the Dominion Bureau of Statistics was not created until 1918). It made no projections about the state of the economy.

Contemporary budget making is a very different affair. Before the Liberal government's 1994 budget was tabled a high-profile exercise in expert consultation was undertaken. Economists, as well as business, labour, and other special interest representatives, were gathered together by Ottawa ostensibly to help chart the course. What ought and ought not to be in the budget, and why, were the subject of numerous analyses by experts in newspapers and magazines and on radio and television. In the end, of course, the budget was formulated by the Department of Finance. But that was about all that was unchanged since 1867. The Department's personnel had increased to about 800, a large percentage of whom were trained economists. The deputy minister, David Dodge, was a nationally renowned economist whose specialty was taxation. In formulating the 1994 budget these officials relied on an enormous amount of routinely collected data, made sense of it by using sophisticated econometrics and a computer model of the Canadian economy.

Projections of the economy's health, and therefore of the government's future revenues and expenditure requirements, were integral parts of the budget process. Expert debate acquired renewed force once the budget was tabled. Economists from academe, private sector think-tanks, banks and other business organizations, and labour unions expressed their views through the mass media as well as more specialized forums. Indeed, budgets are today simply nodal points that help crystallize and publicize an ongoing debate among experts.

Budgets are not, of course, merely the products of expert discourse any more than is true of other public policies. Political considerations are always present and in most circumstances overshadow the advice – usually divided in any case – of policy experts. There is no denying, however, that experts and their specialized knowledge play an infinitely greater role in policy making today than in earlier times. But the difference between 1867 and today is not simply that expert advice has become a routine part of policy making. The role of the expert has acquired social and ideological aspects that were absent in 1867, and only rudimentary before World War II. It is often argued that policy experts were never more influential than during the last world war and the reconstruction that followed. Their dominance was extended under long years of Liberal government, and only shaken a bit by the Diefenbaker interlude of 1957–62. The golden age of the mandarins, which came to an end in the late 1960s, is usually seen as the apogee of bureaucratic-expert influence in Canada. This assessment of the rise and relative decline of the policy expert rests on too narrow an understanding of the expert's role, and a failure to appreciate how the policy-making process has changed in recent decades.

In this chapter I examine the development of the policy analysis profession in Canada. I argue that the *professionalization* of policy analysis should be viewed as a cultural phenomenon that encompasses not only the expert's relationship to the state and to various groups in society, but also the impact of policy experts on the popular consciousness and the general discourse within which more specialized policy discourses are situated. Viewed from this wider angle, the influence of policy analysts and their specialized knowledge have never been greater, not even during the heyday of the mandarinate-on-the-Rideau.

The policy analysis community in Canada has, of course, grown enormously. But the true measure of its significance is not its size but its contribution at all stages of the policy-making process, from shaping the policy agenda, through the formulation and implementation of policies, to policy analysts' impact on the popular reception given to government policies. In tracing the professionalization of policy analysis I am concerned chiefly with how analysts and their craft have become embedded in our culture and governance, in the widest sense.

II. Perspectives on the Policy Analysis Profession

The policy analysis profession may be viewed from three perspectives. We may label these the technical, political, and cultural perspectives. The first draws its inspiration from Max Weber's work on modern bureaucracy and the ascendance of rationally based authority. The second perspective achieved prominence as a result of the Dreyfus Affair in *fin de siècle* France, which triggered the twentieth-century debate on the political role of intellectuals, particularly their relationship to the powerful and their societal obligations. The third perspective can be traced to various sources, among whom Michel Foucault, Pierre Bourdieu, and Neil Postman are probably the best known. It focuses attention on the symbolic meaning of the expert and expertise. It is fair to say that this is the least developed of the three perspectives on the professionalization of policy analysis. I believe, however, that it may be the most important.

From the Weberian perspective, professionalization is a process of acquiring authority based on recognized expert credentials that may include formal training, degrees, certification, and particular types of experience. One's status as a member of a profession depends on the possession of these credentials, and the profession's collective authority rests on the willingness of others to acknowledge the special skills, knowledge, and function of its membership. Economics is an obvious and important example of a field that has undergone professionalization during the twentieth-century. But social workers, criminologists, urban planners, ethicists, pollsters, and a host of other groups have experienced a similar development.

Professionalization in the Weberian sense is inextricably tied to the dynamic of modernization, a dynamic that is characterized by increasing levels of specialization and the displacement of traditional forms of authority by rational ones. Rational authority rests upon the cardinal importance of rules, not persons. Under a rational system of domination, acts are legitimate or not depending on their correspondence to impersonal rules that exist apart from those who administer them. It is a social order under which bureaucrats and experts, elites whose judgments are 'without prejudice or passion,' occupy a dominant place.

The modern state is a rational state. This is true under capitalism *and* communism, and anything in between. It has generated a need for experts whose special knowledge is indispensable to the activities of the state. *The policy analysis profession is, from this perspective, an offshoot of the rationalization and bureaucratization of social relations, and the needs of the administrative state.* It is not, however, exclusively the handmaiden of the state. Policy analysts are found in nongovernmental organizations as well, which is natural enough given that the administrative state and the administrative society are complementary aspects of the same historical process.

The second perspective on the development of the policy analysis profession focuses on its relationship to power. Whose side are they on? Are they wittingly or otherwise defenders of the status quo, and therefore of the powerful, or are they critics, agents of social change, and a tick in the hide of the Establishment? To the extent that the policy analysis profession has developed largely within the state and in response to its needs, one would expect it to play an essentially conservative role in politics. Likewise, where powerful private interests finance the activities of policy analysts and shape the agenda of their research, this will perforce mould the profession, or at least part of it, in a politically conservative direction.

The policy analysis community that exists today is diverse in its ideological tendencies and social affiliations. Nevertheless, a large part of it is directly or indirectly tied to either the state or powerful corporate interests. This segment of the profession exists not merely to meet the needs of state agencies, corporations, and business associations for information and expert analysis, but also to legitimize the interests and actions of their employers/ benefactors in ways ranging from the production and dissemination of studies to interviews with the media.

Social critics such as Noam Chomsky argue that the overwhelming preponderance of what the policy analysis community does buttresses the status quo. He views professionalization as a response to the needs of the corporate elites and the capitalist state. While this view needs to be taken seriously, it understates the significance of non-mainstream elements in the policy analysis community, and the impact of social institutions other than the state and corporations on the development of the profession.

The third perspective on professionalization emphasizes the symbolic and cultural impacts of policy analysts' activities. The policy expert – the university professor commenting on the ethical implications of an assisted suicide law, the think-tank economist interviewed for his views on a government budget, or the criminologist talking about the experience of the victims of crime – has become a routine and even necessary part of popular political discourse. Experts have moved from the shadows (where they have long been influential) into the sunlight of public debate on policy. In doing so, the 'expert' has become an icon in a society whose consciousness and values are powerfully affected by his or her activities. The rise of expert authority does not eliminate the influence of other individuals and groups whose political leverage and social status may rest on the size or attributes of the interests they represent, the position they occupy in the policy-making system, their access to or influence on public opinion, or some other factor that is not associated with technical expertise. However, in the age of the expert most groups and individuals will realize the importance of expressing their views using the word-concepts that are associated with experts and their specialized knowledge, and which have become the lingua franca of policy discourse.

What I am calling the cultural perspective views policy analysis and analysts as having meaning in themselves, apart from whatever ideas and information are associated with them. A researcher commenting on claims about exposure to second-hand smoke and cancer signifies the relevance of scientific expertise to public discourse and policy making. The same is true of the criminologist interviewed on the evening news for his or her views on gun control, or the economist whose assessment of the government's interest rate policy is in the newspaper. Indeed, it cannot have escaped any reflective person's notice that most of the 'sound bites' and printed quotations that experts contribute to the news are either statements of the obvious, things that have been said many times before or, when not mere platitudes, claims or ideas that require supporting arguments and information that is not, however, provided. In these circumstances expertise and the expert are used in magical ways. Far from promoting rational policy debate they act as incantations that cast a spell of scientific authority over the viewpoints they support.

This may sound too cynical, and certainly is not intended to dismiss the relevance of expert knowledge nor diminish the enlightenment that experts can bring to bear on an issue. I merely wish to make the point, a point that has been made more ably by others, that the medium is indeed the message. Just as film footage or photographs of Parliament Hill, the White House, or violence in Jerusalem trigger certain associations in the minds of viewers, 'the expert' also produces associations regardless of the content of his or her remarks. Words like 'study,' 'institute,' 'findings,' 'relationship,' and 'specialist' let us know that we are in the realm of scientific reason. A backdrop of books and the expert's institutional affiliation signify the weightiness and scientific respectability of the person being interviewed. Experts become not merely a medium for the expression of certain thoughts, but a message themselves. The message is that expert knowledge is an indispensable part of policy discourse.

Policy analysis in Canada has undergone professionalization in all three senses in which I have used the term. In the remainder of this chapter I will explore the development of the policy analysis profession, using these three perspectives as my guideposts. I will argue that the influence of policy analysts and their craft rests on their technical skills and expert knowledge in our administrative society (Perspective #1), their relationship to powerful groups in society (Perspective #2), and their role in shaping public consciousness in the age of electronic mass media (Perspective #3). This third basis of their influence is, I would argue, not sufficiently appreciated.

Before proceeding any further I must add a word of caution. Any discussion of the role of intellectuals in Canadian politics really must be two discussions, one of English Canada and the other of French Canada.[1] Although their histories share much in common, they have been shaped by rather different influences and have developed along dissimilar lines. My focus will be mainly on the national level, where policy analysts from both linguistic communities have been important participants.

III. The Formative Period, 1913–1945

It is difficult to pinpoint the moment when the policy analysis profession emerged in Canada, but the early years of this century are probably a fair starting point for several reasons. My choice of 1913 is not entirely arbitrary (though non-political scientists may find it to be shamelessly self-congratulatory). The Canadian Political Science Association (CPSA) was founded in that year, under the leadership of some of the country's leading social scientists, public servants, and reformers. They included people such as Adam Shortt, a Queen's political economist and member of the Civil Service Commission (1908–17), O.D. Skelton, likewise a Queen's political economist who become under-secretary of state for external affairs in 1925, Herbert Ames, a reform-minded businessman whose social scientific credentials were established by his study of working-class Montreal,[2] and Quebec political economist Edouard Montpetit.

The philosophy of the CPSA was summed up in the words of Shortt, its first president, who viewed it as an agent for generating solutions to social problems. Shortt and most of the other leading figures in the fledgling CPSA were solidly in the progressive movement that had emerged in the United States during the late 1800s. This movement was dedicated to closer ties between government and academe, based on the belief that rational inquiry by experts could produce solutions to social and economic problems.[3] Its adherents believed that social service, not the advancement of knowledge for knowledge's sake, ought to be their foremost goal. As was true of the progressive reform movement as a whole, the inspiration for social service was diverse. Some were motivated by religious conviction and a belief that the New Jerusalem was within man's power to achieve.[4] Others were inspired by a more secular faith in reform, in some cases based on socialist principles. These and other differences aside, the original members of the CPSA constituted Canada's first self-conscious coterie of policy analysts, committed to using public policy to remedy the social and economic ills of the country.

The outbreak of World War I brought an early end to the activities of the CPSA. But although it was not reconstituted until 1929, the founding of the organization had signalled the emergence of policy analysis on the Canadian scene. The CPSA crystallized various intellectual tendencies current at the time, giving them an institutional voice.

One of these tendencies was the movement for civil service reform. Not until 1918 were competitive examinations and other requirements of the merit system established parts of federal hiring procedures. Although it applied to only a minority of civil service positions, the merit system represented an important change in the idea and practice of governance, away from amateur administration toward the Weberian ideal of rational bureaucracy. Although few of those appointed under the early merit system could be described as policy analysts, the technical professionalization of the bureaucracy would eventually generate many such positions, beginning most significantly in the Department of Finance.

Positions at the top of the bureaucratic hierarchy continued to be staffed at the prime minister's discretion. But the idea of merit quickly became entrenched at this level too. The 1925 appointment of O.D. Skelton as undersecretary of state for external affairs was certainly not the first case of a formally trained expert being appointed to a top bureaucratic job. Skelton's boss, Prime Minister Mackenzie King, had been appointed deputy minister of the newly created Department of Labour in 1900. King had studied economics at Harvard and Chicago, and was perhaps the Canadian prototype of the expert-turned-administrator. Nonetheless, Skelton's influence on policy during his sixteen years at External Affairs (1925–41) was probably unsurpassed by any previous bureaucrat.

Doug Owram argues that the major turning point in the influence of nonpolitical experts occurred in 1932, when Prime Minister R.B. Bennett was preparing for trade negotiations that took place at the Imperial Economic Conference.[5] Bennett solicited the advice of several professional economists, including Clifford Clark, whom he would appoint as deputy minister of finance within the year. Clark was the first professionally trained economist to hold the position, and built Finance into the unrivalled centre of economic policy analysis within the Canadian state. 'Dr Clark's boys,' as the economists under his direction as came to be known, were among the best and the brightest in Ottawa, and included his eventual successors R.B. Bryce and John Deutsch. What Skelton was to foreign policy, Clark was to domestic policy. Indeed, his personal influence extended far beyond economic matters to include issues of social policy with which the Liberal government was grappling in the 1940s.[6]

The Canadian state was transformed during the 1930s and 1940s, and a key feature of this transformation involved the increasingly influential role of nonpolitical experts within the Ottawa bureaucracy. The 'Ottawa men,' as Jack Granatstein[7] calls them, were both a response to the changing demands on government but also architects of its evolution. They established the policy analysis profession at the heart of the state, a development that most social scientists welcomed as the triumph of reason.

The growing prominence of economists and other social scientists was not merely state-driven. Intellectual developments in Canada had a major impact on the activities and goals of the fledgling policy analysis profession. The social activism that had been advocated by Adam Shortt and the founders of the CPSA gained renewed vigour among intellectuals as Canada slid deeper into the Depression. The League for Social Reconstruction (LSR) was the most obvious sign of this intellectual activism, attracting the energies mainly of left-leaning intellectuals such as Frank Underhill, F.R. Scott, Irene Biss, Eugene Forsey, and Graham Spry. Underhill's vision of the LSR was of a Canadian version of the British Fabian Society, generating ideas that would spur public debate and influence the policies of political parties. The League's ideological affinity to the newly created Co-operative Commonwealth Federation (CCF) prevented it from attracting those intellectuals who did not share its predominantly class-based view of society and who were not willing to write off the traditional parties as agents of reform. Nonetheless, the idea championed by the LSR, namely that the 'intelligent use of the expert to plan the pragmatic intervention of the state to meet social and economic needs,'[8] was one shared by most intellectuals of this generation, and one which provided common ground for individuals as ideologically different as Underhill and Clark.

Faith in technocracy was a distinguishing feature of this first generation of policy analysts. Indeed, technocracy was believed by many to be the solvent of ideological differences. Economist W.A. Mackintosh spoke for most social scientists when he said, 'Our philosophy should always be ready to retreat before science.'[9] Those who went to work for the Canadian state shared a technocratic liberalism – interventionist, confident in the ability of government to manage social and economic problems, but also fundamentally supportive of capitalism and hostile to the idea of a class-based redistribution of wealth. Their credo was the 1945 White Paper on Employment and Income, which laid the basis for the Keynesian welfare state in Canada. Some of those who remained outside the state, and whose intellectual links were with the LSR and/or the CCF, were technocratic socialists – in favour of large-scale economic planning and social entitlements, and mistrustful of capitalism and capitalists. Their credo was embodied in the 1933 *Regina Manifesto*, which set forth the principles and policies of the CCF, and in the LSR's *Social Planning for Canada* (1935).

There were, however, dissenters from the technocratic faith. The most prominent of them was Harold Innis. His contempt for the activist social scientist was expressed on a number of occasions.[10] John Porter goes so far as to blame Innis, whose academic stature was considerable, for what he describes as the depoliticization of higher learning in Canada; that is, its failure to perform the adversarial function that Porter believed to be an essential part of its responsibilities. But Innis was also disdainful of the technocratic liberals who sold their services to the state (despite his own forays into the world of royal commissions on a couple of occasions!). He saw the growing importance of the expert in government as a potential threat to democratic government. Innis's fears echoed those of Lord Hewart's influential broadside against technocratic government, *The New Depotism*.[11] But his criticisms of the statist path that government by experts helped pave ran against the irresistible tide of his times.

In summary, the formative era in the development of the policy analysis profession was characterized by a changing conception of the state and a growing belief in the utility of the analyst's craft for policy making. The positive state required technical expertise, particularly in areas of economic management but increasingly in areas of social and, eventually, cultural policy. To a large degree, therefore, the early professionalization of policy analysis was externally driven, shaped by changes in the state and society. But it was also influenced by internal factors, notably the reformist impulses of many social scientists and the Keynesian philosophy that was rapidly becoming *de rigueur* among economists. Neither those who went to work for the state nor those who sniped at it from the LSR, CCF, and the pages of the *Canadian Forum* believed that the sidelines were the appropriate place for a social scientist. An Innis might fret over this, but the tide of events was against him.

Assessments of this early period in the development of policy analysis generally conclude that the profession constituted what T.S. Eliot called a 'clerisy,' that is, intellectual defenders of the status quo and therefore the servants, wittingly or not, of the powerful.[12] This is not entirely fair, unless we restrict use of the term 'policy analyst' to those who actually worked for the state. If, however, the term is understood more broadly to include politically involved experts wherever they are located – in political parties, the media, academe, or organizations such as the LSR – it is clear that the early profession contained a significant number of critics of the Establishment. That they constituted a minority voice within the profession is, however, undeniable.

IV. Consolidating Its Influence, 1945–1968

The pattern that was set by the end of World War II continued afterward. The machinery of government had become dependent on the technical knowledge of formally trained experts, particularly within key agencies such as the Department of Finance, the Bank of Canada, and the Department of External Affairs. But in other parts of the state and in other policy domains, the growing importance of nonpolitical experts was also evident. Porter's observation that 'the upper levels [of the federal bureaucracy] constitute what is probably the most highly trained group of people to be found anywhere in Canada'[13] was doubtless correct. He found that in 1953, just under 80 per cent of senior officials were university graduates, and close to 90 per cent among deputy ministers. Lest it be thought that their degrees were mainly in law or some traditional area of the humanities, Porter notes that about one-quarter were in science or engineering and about an equal share in the social sciences.[14]

Likewise, the precedent of expert research for royal commissions, established by the Royal Commission on Dominion-Provincial Relations (1937–40), continued during the postwar era. The Royal Commission on National Development in the Arts, Letters, and Sciences (1949–51) commissioned fifty-one special studies in disciplines ranging from chemistry to sociology. The Royal Commission on Canada's Economic Prospects (1955–6) was supported by thirty-three studies, all in economics and many by professional economists. The Royal Commission on Health Services (1961–5) commissioned twenty studies carried out by economists and sociologists. The royal commissions on Banking and Finance (1964) and Taxation (1962–6) produced twelve and twenty-six special studies respectively, most by trained economists. Finally, the 'mother' of royal commissions, the Royal Commission on Bilingualism and Biculturalism (1963–9), commissioned 124 special studies and employed the services of many of the country's most respected historians, political scientists, and sociologists.

The status of the policy analyst had never been greater. At the pinnacle of the profession were the Ottawa 'mandarins,' as they came to be called. These were the key deputy ministers and certain other top-level bureaucrats such as the governor of the Bank of Canada, whose influence on policy during the roughly two decades following World War II was profound. Under twenty-two unbroken years of Liberal government there arose, not surprisingly, doubts about the political impartiality of these experts at the top. But as Reg Whitaker observes, the question of whether the bureaucrats had become Liberals might well be turned around to ask whether the Liberals had become bureaucrats.[15]

The end of Liberal rule in 1957 may indeed have signalled the beginning of the end for the Ottawa mandarinate, as J.L. Granatstein argues. But its decline was not accompanied by a diminished role for expert policy analysis within the state. Despite Diefenbaker's prairie populist rhetoric, no significant restructuring of the machinery of governance took place during his tenure as prime minister. The size of the bureaucracy continued to grow under the Conservatives, although less rapidly than in the early 1950s. More important, the idea of policy making as an enterprise requiring the knowledge and participation of specially trained experts was not seriously challenged. Despite the frostier relationship between the civil service and the Conservatives, and the palpable relief of many top bureaucrats when the Liberals were returned to power in 1962, the administrative state whose roots were put down in the 1930s continued to grow.

Although the policy analysis profession was firmly entrenched in the postwar Keynesian welfare state, its status and influence in society were considerably less secure. For example, very few interest groups employed people whose job could be described as that of a policy analyst and whose training was in the social sciences. Likewise, the mass media rarely called upon social scientists for their analysis of contemporary events. Few journalists had any specialized training in economics, sociology, or international affairs, and the academic community that might have contributed this expertise was, with few exceptions, largely disengaged from day-to-day politics. The university community was still relatively small, and the private sector think-tanks that today are important contributors to policy discourse – the C.D. Howe Institute, the Fraser Institute, the Conference Board of Canada, and the Institute for Research on Public Policy, to mention a few – did not yet exist.

In these respects Canada's policy analysis profession lagged far behind its counterpart in the United States. There, the Ford and Rockefeller Foundations were already major private sources of funding for social scientific research, and the prototypes of the policy think-tanks, such as the Rand Institute and the Brookings Institution, originated in the United States. The explosion in the demand for university education began earlier in the United States, producing both an enormous increase in the number of social science professors and a sharp rise in the share of the population exposed to their ideas, *including the idea of the relevance of the social sciences*. Magazines such as *The Atlantic Monthly*, *Harper's*, and *The New Yorker*, as well as America's newspaper of record, *The New York Times*, regularly featured articles by social scientific experts. But perhaps the single most important development contributing to the consolidation of the policy analysis profession in the United States was the growth of attitudinal surveys and their rapid acceptance by the mass media, public officials, and the general population as scientific and therefore worthy of serious public consideration. By the 1950s, surveys, and those who implemented and interpreted them, already had this stature.

In Canada the turning point in the consolidation of the policy analysis profession occurred in the mid-1960s. No single development was responsible, rather a combination of factors elevated the social profile of the analyst's craft. One was the Royal Commission on Bilingualism and Biculturalism which was assigned the largest research budget and the most ambitious research agenda of any royal commission before or, at least in regard to its scope, since that time. Its 124 special studies sucked into the commission's vortex the energies of most of the country's most prominent social scientists. The impact of their work on the commission's recommendations and on policy provides an instructive lesson in the functions of a mature policy analysis profession.

One of those functions – according to Ira Horowitz the *key* function – is to provide a 'political formula' that justifies the preferences of the powerful.[16] Whereas the legitimizing rhetoric of previous eras drew upon religion, political ideology, and philosophy, that of post-industrial society borrows heavily from the social sciences. No less than previous political formulas, however, the rhetoric of the social sciences is easily enlisted in the service of those who rule.

Gertrude Laing, a B&B commissioner and former head of the Canada Council, agrees. She notes that 'the policy-makers did what people generally do who commission research – they used the B&B report in accordance with their predetermined priorities.'[17] In other words, the chief, if unacknowledged, role of the legions of policy analysts who worked for the commission was to provide a 'political formula' that would justify policies shaped by other forces. This does not imply that there was a consensus among the researchers who worked for the Commission. The 'political formula' they provided consisted of the specialized language of the social sciences and the very fact that social science research was a highly visible part of the policy-making process.

Other factors contributing to the consolidation of the policy analysis profession's stature included the rapid expansion of the university system, the growth in state funding of social science research, the media's increasing use of social science experts, and the 1963 creation of the Economic Council of Canada and the Science Council of Canada in 1966. The era of the mandarin expert was definitely in eclipse, but it was succeeded by that of the institutional expert whose social authority rested largely on his or her affiliation to an organization with a research/analysis role. They were found mainly in universities, think-tanks, and state agencies. On the other hand, the linkages between policy analysts and political parties remained fairly tenuous, except in the case of the New Democratic Party (NDP). Nationalist academics and left-leaning social scientists were important figures in the councils of the NDP. The nationalist Committee for an Independent Canada provided another channel for social and economic criticism by policy experts.

At the same time that the policy analysis profession was becoming more securely embedded in the state and society, it was becoming more specialized and fragmented in its internal structures. After enduring years of an increasingly uneasy relationship, political science and economics formally separated in 1967. Branches within policy-related academic disciplines became increasingly specialized during the 1960s and have since continued to diverge. This specialization has been reflected in both a proliferation of technical journals and a widening gap of incomprehension between what previously were closely allied fields.

Fragmentation advanced on the linguistic front as well. Influenced by the strong currents of nationalism in Quebec during the 1960s, the rift between anglophone and francophone social scientists grew ever larger. In 1964 the Société canadienne de science politique was established as the breakaway francophone, and mainly Québécois, counterpart of the Canadian Political Science Association (in 1979 it would change its name to the Société québécoise de science politique). It was following the lead of the Association canadienne des sociologues, which had split from the Canadian Association of Sociologists and Anthropologists in 1961. The energies of Quebec's francophone social scientists were increasingly channelled through a separate network of organizations, conferences, and journals, the latter of which included *Recherches sociographiques* (1961) and *Sociologie et sociétés* (1961). These would be followed by *Les Cahiers du socialisme* (1978) and *Politique* (1982).

The nationalization of the Quebec-centred francophone social science community was abetted by the actions of the Quebec state. It created several funding agencies and research centres during the 1960s, promoting both the natural and social sciences. By decade's end the Quebec state was the principal source of funding for social scientific research in Quebec, a role held by the Canada Council in the other provinces. The nationalist impetus behind the Quebec government's support for scientific research was reflected in the considerably greater share of Quebec than federal money devoted to the social sciences. Whereas only about 10 to 15 per cent of federal money went to the social sciences, the rest going to the natural and applied sciences, about 40 per cent of Quebec funding was earmarked for the social sciences in the late 1960s and early 1970s.

Despite individual social scientists who straddled the line dividing the two linguistic communities, and occasional efforts at cooperation between organizations representing the two groups, the rupture within the profession was deep and permanent. Many francophone economists and other policy analysts continued to work for the Canadian state, but the centre of gravity for their linguistic wing of the profession had moved decisively to Quebec. Perhaps the most obvious and, for those laypersons who naïvely imagine that professional social scientists of all backgrounds are single-mindedly devoted to discovery of the 'truth,' the most disturbing indication of this rift involves the ongoing battle of the balance sheets between separatists and 'federalists. It pits many Québécois economists (led by former Parti Québécois leader Jacques Parizeau) who maintain that Quebec has been bled economically by its membership in Canada against those members of the profession whose calculations show that Quebec has profited considerably.

In summary, this second era in the development of the policy analysis profession was marked by consolidation of its role within the state and an increase in the profession's social stature in both French-speaking Quebec and in the rest of Canada. The era of the Ottawa mandarins, the first generation of expert bureaucrats, was fading from the scene, only to be replaced by a new generation of specialist administrators whose influence was less personal, more diffuse, and embedded in the very nature of the administrative state that the first generation had helped build. Indeed the post-mandarin generation conformed more closely to Weber's ideal type of the expert administrator. The influence of the first generation had depended too much on the fact that they constituted a personal elite whom circumstances had given the opportunity to exercise an exceptional influence on public affairs. By the time the Diefenbaker Conservatives came to power the influence of the policy specialist-administrator was securely entrenched in the Keynesian welfare state.

Outside the state, the policy analysis profession grew slowly, until the 1960s when it expanded rapidly on the coat-tails of growth in the university system and increased state funding for the social sciences. At the same time the profession became increasingly fragmented, both in terms of the orientation and technical language of the various policy-related disciplines and along linguistic lines. Although a bit of an oversimplification, one may say that the consolidation of the profession in French-speaking Quebec was powerfully influenced by Quebec nationalism and the dense network of ties that arose with the provincial state. In English Canada, however, the period of consolidation took place under the aegis of federal policies and institutions, and this linguistic wing of the profession maintained a much more Canadian outlook than its nationalist Québécois counterpart.

In political terms, the profession continued to play the predominantly conservative role that John Porter attributed to it. A policy analysis community whose growth, prospects, and prestige are tied to state funding, royal commissions, and the universities is unlikely to do otherwise. Pockets of criticism existed within the profession, clustered around the NDP, the Committee for an Independent Canada, and in Quebec the emerging separatist movement. Their influence on the development of the profession and on Canadian politics was, however, marginal. The B&B Commission and the Economic Council of Canada were the defining events for this generation of policy analysts, consolidating the policy-making beachhead that had been won by the earlier generation of reform-minded experts and Keynesian welfare state managers.

V. Policy Analysis in the Age of Scientism, 1968 Onward

The early years of Pierre Trudeau's prime ministership appeared to usher in a new golden era for the policy analysis profession. In place of the bureaucratic mandarins whom Trudeau mistrusted, however, the distinguishing characteristic of this new era would be the policy analysis unit. Trudeau's sometimes gushing enthusiasm for rationality in policy making contributed to the proliferation of such units throughout government. His well-known rhapsody to planning at the Liberals' 1969 Harrison Hot Springs conference was music to many a policy analyst's ear:

We are aware that the many techniques of cybernetics, by transforming the control function and the manipulation of information, will transform our whole society. With this knowledge we are wide awake, alert, capable of action; no longer are we blind, inert pawns of fate.[18]

Trudeau's philosophy of governance helped elevate the status of the policy analysis profession, but the prime minister's contribution was more a nudge toward a destination to which the profession was already heading rather than a decisive push. Other factors were also at work. One of these involved reform of the budgetary process during the 1960s, including the introduction of Planning, Programming, Budgeting (PPB). PPB and its successors require much more information and evaluation than traditional budget making. The decision to separate the Treasury Board from the Department of Finance in 1964 and the growth in Treasury Board Secretariat personnel that followed were signs of the analysis-oriented budgeting approach that was pioneered in the United States and imported into Canada. PPB has come and gone, followed by various incarnations that retain its rational-analytical spirit. Perhaps its most important legacy has been a large bureaucratic apparatus whose central purposes involve preparing information in the forms required by rational budgeting systems and evaluating this information. Hardly any disinterested party would claim that these reforms have produced greater efficiency in government.

The creation of several new bureaucratic agencies and departments was another factor that elevated the status of policy analysts and their craft. They included the Science Council of Canada (1966), the Department of Regional Economic Expansion (1969), the Department of the Environment (1970), the Ministry of State for Urban Affairs (1971), and the Ministry of Science and Technology (1971). Only a few of these organizations have survived the various bureaucratic reorganizations that have occurred over the last two decades, the others having been disbanded or absorbed into other parts of the machinery of state. But the spirit that spawned this cluster of policy-oriented agencies has persisted within departments and agencies throughout government.

Although it is impossible to get a precise fix on the number of bureaucrats whose jobs involve policy analysis, there is no doubt that they number in the thousands. The Department of the Environment is probably typical. It includes more than two dozen units, scattered across its various directorates, whose functions relate exclusively or chiefly to program and policy analysis, planning, and coordination. A sprawling ministry such as Health and Welfare includes hundreds of bureaucrats designated 'policy/program analysts,' 'policy advisers,' 'researchers,' 'consultants,' 'systems analysts,' and 'evaluators.'

Analysis, in its various guises, is very much embedded in the structure of the state and the processes of governance. Its ubiquity should not be confused, however, with influence. Those who have carefully studied policy analysis units and policy analysts agree that their impact is generally small and their numbers far out of proportion to their real influence.[19] Nevertheless, along with royal commissions, task forces, and other special studies that review policy and make recommendations, expert analysis performed within government is assumed to be a necessary part of the policy-making process even if, in the priceless words of one official, it involves 'turning cranks not connected to anything.'[20]

Outside the state, the growth of the policy analysis profession has been even more explosive. The publications and conferences of think-tanks such as the Fraser Institute, the C.D. Howe Institute, the Institute for Research on Public Policy, the Canadian Centre for Policy Alternatives, and the Caledon Institute of Social Policy contribute to the contours of elite discourse on policy issues. Other organizations such as the Canadian Council on Social Development, the Vanier Institute of the Family, the Business Council on National Issues, the National Action Committee on the Status of Women, and the Canadian Labour Congress also draw on the services of social scientists in producing studies, submissions to government bodies, and information intended for the public. Large interest groups and professional lobbying firms provide employment opportunities for policy analysts. The mass media, both print and electronic, have specialized journalists for subjects such as science, the environment, economics, native affairs, defence, health care, and education. These journalists, through their impact on the policy agenda and on the terms of debate surrounding particular issues, are among the most influential of contemporary policy specialists.

The policy analysis community is much less exclusive than once was the case. Before World War II it was entirely reasonable to speak of fewer than 100 persons belonging to the fledging profession – mainly public servants and university professors, but including some journalists and individuals from the private sector.[21] Today it numbers in the thousands. The highly elitist and personal character of the profession has disappeared, replaced by a more institutional quality that would not have surprised Max Weber. Indeed, the transition from an elite whose influence was based largely on personal attributes and group characteristics to a profession whose role and influence depend mainly on characteristics of the state and society is precisely what one expect to happen as a result of modernization in the Weberian sense.

Politically, the question remains whether the policy analysis profession – diverse in terms of the specialized training of its members and their institutional affiliations – can reasonably be summed up using a single label. I would argue that while the profession's political centre of gravity is not fundamentally critical of the social or economic status quo, reformist elements on both the left and right of the ideological spectrum are politically influential. On the right, that part of the policy analysis community whose voice is heard through organizations such as the Fraser Institute, the C.D. Howe Institute, the Business Council on National Issues, the Canadian Taxpayers Federation, and *The Financial Post*, and whose chief standard-bearers are economists, clearly believes that reform of the status quo is necessary. Those on the left, including most policy analysts with ties to the environmental and feminist movements, and to the NDP, believe just as strongly that reforms are needed. Their diagnosis of what is wrong and their prescriptions for change are, of course, very different from those of their right-wing counterparts. Both reform-minded wings of the profession are vocal and successful in capturing media attention for their ideas. In recent years the issues of deficit reduction and social policy reform have emerged as the chief lightning rods attracting their energies and crystallizing their differences.

But what is most significant about this third phase in the development of the policy analysis profession is how analysis and the policy analyst have become integral parts of public life, crucial to the process by which public consciousness is formed. This leads me to *scientism*, the label used by Neil Postman to describe a culture in which social science has assumed the role of touchstone for knowing moral truths. Postman provides a vivid illustration of scientism in action:

I have been in the presence of a group of United States congressmen who were gathered to discuss, over a period of two days, what might be done to make the future of America more survivable and, if possible, more humane. Ten consultants were called upon to offer perspectives and advice. Eight of them were pollsters. They spoke of the 'trends' their polling uncovered; for example, that people were no longer interested in the women's movement, did not regard environmental issues as of paramount importance, did not think the 'drug problem' was getting worse, and so on. It was apparent, at once, that these polling results would become the basis of how the congressmen thought the future should be managed. The ideas the congressmen had (all men, by the way) receded to the background. Their own perceptions, instincts, insights, and experience paled into irrelevance. Confronted by 'social scientists,' they were inclined to do what the 'trends' suggested would satisfy the populace.[22]

There is nothing particularly wrong, of course, and much that is commendable in paying serious attention to public opinion. But what the behaviour of these politicians confronted with the 'data' of pollsters and the interpretations of consultants illustrates is the more general phenomenon of modern society's faith in the techniques and authority of the social sciences. Statements such as, 'recent survey data indicate,' '80 per cent of Canadians believe,' and 'recent polling information demonstrates' are so commonly used in the media that one hardly notices the assumptions regarding knowledge, truth, and the best ways of ascertaining these, that underlie them. Today no one can seriously claim to know the will or mood of the populace without a survey that conforms to the methodological canons of the pollster's trade. This ensures, of course, a central role for the social scientist, both as technician and diviner of public opinion.

But the obsession with polls and measurement is only one of the symptoms of scientism. A more important one, in terms of its social impact, involves what German linguist and philosopher Uwe Poerksen calls *plastic words*.[23] Poerksen uses this term to refer to a special category of words that have originated from everyday experiences but have been appropriated by some branch of the social sciences or some group of knowledge 'experts' and then returned to popular discourse with meanings that are different from their original ones. Moreover, these words are also quite imprecise, despite having a scientific aura. Poerksen argues that 'information,' 'communication,' 'needs,' 'development,' 'planning,' 'sexuality,' and 'identity' are examples of such words. Plastic words like these tend to homogenize experience by imposing a single, albeit rather fuzzy, conceptual grid on the circumstances to which they are applied. Plastic words are, he says, the intellectual equivalent of Lego blocks. Like Lego blocks, they can be combined with one another to build idea structures that people, having grown familiar with these words from their regular use by the media, educators, and government agencies, will find intelligible.[24]

Words like 'development' or 'identities' undergo a process of transformation from social scientific concepts to popularly used terms. They enter the popular lexicon through repeated and routine used by the media, educators, government departments, politicians and political parties, organized interest groups, and public figures. Educated laypersons come to hear and even use words like 'communication' or 'planning' with confidence; not confidence that they understand the precise meaning of the terms (because it is in the nature of plastic words that their meanings are terribly imprecise), but confidence that these terms have meanings that are known to experts.

Once established in the language of popular culture – or re-established, but now wearing the mantle of pseudo-scientific authority – plastic words have a number of consequences:

- **Alienation**. Plastic words drive a wedge between an individual and his or her perception of self. They do so by implying that the realm of experience associated with such terms is better understood by some group of experts whose social authority in these matters is tacitly acknowledged by those who unreflectingly and uncritically use the plastic words. This means that plastic words are, by their very nature, *hierarchical*; they place the layperson who uses them in a sort of clientelistic relationship with those who have special expertise in such matters.
- **Legitimization**. Plastic words legitimize the authority of experts and, simultaneously, 'delegitimize' popular knowledge and the voice of laypersons. This is not to suggest that the advice of experts should be ignored when it comes to public policy, but simply to observe that plastic words have the effect of establishing the expertise of those who, in the course of their professional work as researchers, professors, activists, and intellectuals, construct the social meaning of these terms.
- **Social Respectability**. Plastic words awake in those who hear or read them a sense that something serious is being addressed. As Poerksen says, 'Those words are a little bit electric. There is a suggestion of modernity, of success, or of a positive way of thinking. You give the impression that you live at the cutting edge.' Of course, the same may be said of the latest bit of 'bureau-babble' or business school jargon. The difference is that plastic words enjoy wider currency and are more firmly established in popular language than are these jargon-of-the-month terms.
- **Moral Imperative**. They do not simply describe phenomena; they seem to suggest a need to act. This is obvious in the case of terms like 'violence' and 'deprivation.' Not only do plastic words connote a problem, they also imply that an undesirable state of affairs needs to be changed. They suggest transformation: individuals, institutions, and societies becoming, evolving, moving. Although the vocabulary of the expert may seem to be free of moral judgments – and certainly is defended as such by the experts themselves – moral implications lurk just below the surface.
- **Expansion of the Public Realm**. In the process of their transformation from the vernacular into scientific terms that then re-enter popular discourse, plastic words acquire a universal character. They define human experience in universal and very public ways and so justify implicitly

the expansion of state authority. Ways of thinking about the human condition and *how to improve it* – because the expert is not an expert but
merely an old-fashioned intellectual if his or her knowledge cannot be
used to solve problems – acquire a certain uniformity. Although this
universalizing tendency claims to be democratic, and is widely believed
to be so, it actually undermines the historical and regional uniqueness
of human experience and seriously diminishes the privateness of that
experience.

Through the influence of plastic words, social scientists have achieved a
level of collective influence far beyond what is generally attributed to them.
Policy discourse is replete with word-concepts that proclaim their special
knowledge and establish their social authority. The political influence of
social scientists is diffuse and indirect, operating through a language that
they have pioneered and that colonizes popular discourse and consciousness
through the media, the educational system, and state agencies. The particular data or specific studies that social scientists contribute to policy debates
are usually less important than the word-concepts that form a bridge between the world of expert knowledge and that of everyday experience. Viewed
through the lens of plastic words, this everyday experience is something that
can be transformed and, if the experts are to validate their status and have
any social relevance, is in need of transformation. The fundamental bias of
plastic words is, therefore, in the direction of expert-driven change. The destination of change is less important than transformation itself.

VI. Conclusion

The policy analysis profession has undergone enormous changes since its
inception early in this century. From a small, reform-minded elite it achieved
a secure status within the postwar Keynesian welfare state, and more recently has assumed an influential role in society through its impact on public consciousness and the terms of policy debate. The highly personal influence of the fledgling profession's leading members – individuals such as
Adam Shortt, W.A. Mackintosh, and Clifford Clark – has been replaced by a
more collective influence that is based on the popular authority of social
scientific knowledge in the modern age. Every age requires its priests, sha-
mans, or elders; some group whose role it is to make sense of life and explain its truths to others. Our's turns to policy experts, social scientists, and
pollsters, giving the policy analysis profession a profound influence in the
age of scientism.

Notes

1 See Brooks and Gagnon, *Social Scientists and Politics in Canada.*
2 Ames, *The City below the Hill.*
3 For a discussion of the ideas underlying the progressive movement, see Hawkins, 'The Ideal of Objectivity among American Social Scientists in the Era of Professionalization, 1876–1916.'
4 Allen, *The Social Passion: Religion and Social Reform in Canada, 1914– 1928.*
5 Owram, *The Government Generation.*
6 Porter, *The Vertical Mosaic,* 425–8.
7 Granatstein, *The Ottawa Men: The Civil Service Mandarins, 1935–1957.*
8 Owram, *The Government Generation,* 177.
9 Mackintosh, 'An Economist Looks at Economics,' 316.
10 See Innis, 'The Role of Intelligence,' 286.
11 Hewart, *The New Despotism.*
12 This is certainly John Porter's assessment, as expressed in *The Vertical Mosaic.*
13 Ibid., 433.
14 Ibid., 434.
15 Whitaker, *The Government Party,* 167.
16 Horowitz, 'Social Science Mandarins.'
17 Laing, 'The Contributions of Social Scientists to Policy Making – The B&B Experience,' 171.
18 Quoted in Doern, 'The Development of Policy Organization in the Executive Arena,' 65.
19 See the discussion in Savoie, *The Politics of Public Spending in Canada,* 213–16.
20 Ibid., 214.
21 A good sense of the compactness and similar backgrounds of this elite is provided by Owram, *The Government Generation,* ch. 6.
22 Postman, *Technopoly: The Surrender of Culture to Technology,* 133.
23 Poerksen, *Plastic Words.*
24 I have discussed plastic words and their consequences in 'How Ottawa Bends.'

7

Trends and Fashions in the Marketplace of Ideas

LAURENT DOBUZINSKIS

The 1980s will be remembered as a decade of ideological realignment. Momentous events, such as the collapse of the Soviet system or the wave of privatization initiatives, which began in the United Kingdom under Prime Minister Margaret Thatcher and then rippled throughout the Western world, illustrate the import of that transformation. Democracy – liberal democracy, in fact – and the market economy have emerged as the dominant paradigms in the final days of the twentieth century. These powerful ideas have influenced the practice of policy analysis, and ultimately policy making, although it could be argued that actual programs and the structures of governance in most countries, including Canada, change at a more glacial pace than the content of policy discourse. In turn, current ideological changes have been prompted, at least in some limited measure, by policy research. The popularity of market-based approaches in the United States, for example, has something to do with the sustained attacks that a new generation of policy research institutes or 'think-tanks' launched on 'big government' since the early 1970s. In Canada, the role of think-tanks has been less obvious, but it has not been negligible; other elements of the policy analysis industry have also played an important part (e.g., the Macdonald Commission). Though often labouring in different corners, advocates of participatory approaches to public policy making have also been very active.

Admittedly, the rhetorical flourish of the 1980s has been toned down somewhat in the 1990s. The spectacular downfall of the Mulroney government, the very serious problems faced by the British Conservatives, and the return of the Democrats to the White House, however, do not signal a redefinition of priorities or fundamental assumptions. Today, the middle-ground has moved somewhat to the 'right.' And yet, while dissatisfaction with the interventionist administrative state stands out as the dominant motif, one can

also discern a contrapuntal theme. A call for the democratization of our social and political institution runs through the political discourse of the 'new
social movements' and, albeit on a slightly different key, of the new populism.
Such a call could issue in the practice of a more participatory style of politics, and could force a re-examination of the conventions defining liberal
democracy in the years to come.

The purpose of this chapter is to assess the extent to which prescriptive
policy studies reflect the emerging consensus that the administrative state
has ceased to be a privileged instrument of social and economic reform.[1]
More specifically, my intent is to trace the diffusion of the idea of 'government failure,' on the one hand, and of somewhat more nebulous demands for
a more participatory, less technocratic, style of policy making, on the other.
The materials surveyed are drawn primarily from studies produced by private policy institutes, reports from advisory councils, royal commissions,
and task forces. The extent to which these studies are *in fact* truly influential
is debatable.[2] But, at the very least, they exemplify current thinking among
professional policy analysts and throw some light on the dominant ideas in a
number of important policy communities.

To put it in different terms, I deal mostly with studies that treat policies as
the independent variable: their purpose is to analyse the impacts of selected
policies on the economy or society, often with a view to making specific
policy recommendations. 'Academic research,' especially when conducted
by political scientists, more often than not treats policy decisions as the dependent variable, that is, the political phenomena that need to be explained,
regardless of their real or potential impacts.[3] Of course, this is a valid research agenda; indeed, such studies form the subject matter of most of the
contributions to the present volume. But if one wants to identify the dominant ideas among professional policy analysts, process-oriented studies are
comparatively less significant than result-oriented studies.[4]

In the first section, I offer an overview of the recent development of a
'market for policy ideas' in both the United States and Canada. Then, in the
next three sections, I critically examine the dominant themes underlying the
ideas exchanged in that market. I cannot, within the narrow limits here, do
more than identify a few exemplary cases, but these have been carefully
chosen in order to highlight important trends. I also raise a few questions on
the nature of the theoretical and methodological arguments given in support
of policy recommendations. These can be merely ideological – grounded in
unexamined belief systems – or they can be more innovative, reaching into
the domain of creative theorizing. I would argue that one should demand
from policy analysts that they do more than ritualistically invoke hackneyed

phrases such as 'economic efficiency' or, at the opposite end of the ideological spectrum, 'social justice.' If one is to take the term 'analysis' seriously, it is imperative to probe the depth of that 'analysis' – in fact, doubts
have already been raised in the literature about the capacity of think-tanks to
look beyond parochial interests.[5] The proverbial 'cutting edge' of research
has moved far ahead in a number of fields; significant theoretical advances
have been achieved in new areas, including chaos and complexity theory,
evolutionary approaches to economic modelling, the theory of non-coopera-
tive games, and so on.[6] Important developments also have taken place as a
result of the mobilization of new social movements, for example, the feminist critique of social institutions, or the articulation of various approaches
to environmental ethics. Thus when I have an opportunity to take a critical
stance, I shall ask: Are these advances reflected in the policy studies circulating in the new market for policy ideas?

The Market for Policy Ideas

Harold Lasswell, a pioneer of scientifically based policy analysis, or what
he called 'the policy sciences,' repeatedly stressed the importance of a
contextuating approach. The context within which the current flood of information on policy issues must be situated is the appearance of a market for
policy ideas:[7] a place where the results of policy research are exchanged,
advertised, and debated. This market is more crowded and competitive in
the United States than in Canada, but the difference is one of degree rather
than of kind.

In a sense, the image of a marketplace of ideas is ironic. It evokes a kind
of pluralism, perhaps even an unavoidable relativism, which stands in sharp
contrast with the objectivity and 'one-best-way' approach typically advocated by policy analysts.[8] The fragmentation of knowledge, however, can be
observed even in the natural sciences. Social and economic issues are bound
to generate a diversity of points of view, for not only do they overlap the
boundaries separating intellectual disciplines, but they also are situated at
the crossroads of conflicting political forces. Several mutually reinforcing
factors account for the multiplication and gradual differentiation of the
sources of information and policy advice. These include:

1.   the increasing complexity of policy issues (e.g., the blurring of the dis-
     tinction between domestic and international issues) and the consequent
     need for specialized advice, not only from within the bureaucracy but also,
     and increasingly so, from outside the traditional structures of government;

2. the accelerating fragmentation of the policy process into more or less autonomous policy communities, often competing for scarce resources;

3. the need for policy research organizations, which have sprung up to meet the demand for information and new ideas, to establish their legitimacy by appearing to be continually involved in the discussion of high-profile issues;

4. the negative reaction of the public to the secrecy that until recently surrounded the policy-making process, the arrival in the public arena of articulate policy advocates and public interest groups, and the need for governments to be seen listening to these myriad voices;

5. finally, the move toward an information society in which the production and dissemination of knowledge becomes an end in itself, an 'output' of, rather than an 'input' in, the political system.[9]

At the crucible of these societal trends, the social science community has reacted by adopting more professional and specialized structures (see the previous chapter). One could also add the fact that there is now more uncertainty about the core values guiding the formulation and implementation of economic and social policies. Consequently, there are more opportunities for trying to influence policy making and to reshape societal institutions through the formulation of concrete policy proposals, but also through the articulation of broader analytical frameworks – some would say 'myths.'[10]

As could be expected in Canada, the political economy of policy ideas involves both public and private actors. Not only have new government departments and agencies been created over the last thirty years, often for the specific purpose of generating new policy ideas, but most departments have established their own policy research units, for example, the National Health Research and Development Program at Health Canada.[11] This trend, however, has reversed itself in recent years as budgetary constraints have begun to 'bite' deeper, leading to more streamlined administrative structures. Yet these sources of internal advice have proven to be inadequate because they are generally too preoccupied with short-term issues and lack autonomy – hence the more frequent recourse to external sources of advice. Still in the public sector, there are considerably more independent sources of policy advice, such as parliamentary committees,[12] royal commissions, task forces, and advisory councils 'at arm's length' from government.

Royal commissions are temporary organizations created by order-in-council under the Inquiries Act to investigate a matter of concern to the government of the day. They have been used extensively – indeed more than 400 of them have been created since 1867.[13] However, royal commissions were used to investigate specific incidents such as judicial malpractice, not policy issues, until the creation of the Royal Commission on Dominion-Provincial Relations (Rowell-Sirois Commission) in 1939. Since then several commissions have been concerned with significant policy problems. In at least two cases, one can almost speak of a mobilization of the academic community around the problems identified by the commission: the Royal Commission on Bilingualism and Biculturalism (1963–9) released 124 studies, and the Royal Commission on the Economic Union and Canada's Development Prospects (Macdonald Commission, 1982–5) produced seventy-two studies. Other important commissions include: the Royal Commission on the Status of Women (1967–70), the Royal Commission on Financial Management and Accountability (Lambert Commission, 1977–9), the Royal Commission on Electoral Reform and Party Financing (Lortie Commission, 1989–92), and the Royal Commission on Reproductive Technology (Baird Commission, 1989–93). What has characterized the latest commissions has been the extraordinary emphasis placed on consultation with a wide variety of groups and individuals.

Similar in many ways to royal commissions, but more flexible and informal in their operation, are task forces. Prime Minister Trudeau created several task forces and often assigned important mandates to them, for example, the Task Force on National Unity (Pépin-Robarts, 1979). In more recent years a series of task forces collectively known as Public Service 2000 made a number of far-reaching recommendations for moving the federal public service toward more managerial and service-oriented values and practices.[14]

Federal or provincial advisory councils are established and financed by government but composed of individuals who, for the most part, owe little or no allegiance to the party in power. They serve two functions. The first is to provide an instrument for the expression of a diversity of interests and movements. For example, the Canadian Advisory Council on the Status of Women, until it was abolished in 1994, used to advise the federal government on women's issues. This kind of institutionalized consultation is particularly important for groups that lack financial or other resources, which is usually the case with public interest groups (e.g., women's groups, multicultural societies, etc.). The second and related function consists in the generation of policy research to assist council members in their deliberations and in the preparation of official statements on current issues and/or annual policy reviews. Such research is carried out either internally by the council's staff, or by external researchers who retain full responsibility for their findings and recommendations. The importance given to these two functions varies from council to council, as well as over time for some of them;

for example, the consultation process and consensus-building between business and labour were more central to the activities of the Economic Council of Canada in its early years of existence (i.e., throughout the 1960s and early 1970s) than in later years.[15] Advisory councils will continue to play a valuable role in Ottawa and in several provincial capitals. Experience has proven, however, that their arm's-length relationship with government does not always offer sufficient protection; the dismemberment, first, of the Ontario Economic Council in the mid-1980s, and in 1992 of more than twenty federal councils and similar research units, including the prestigious Economic Council of Canada and the Science Council of Canada,[16] are cases in point. The principal reason given by Finance Minister Don Mazankowski for the winding down of these organizations was that competent and timely policy advice is available from the private sector. Is this truly the case?

Private sector players comprise foundations, nonprofit research institutes ('think-tanks'), interest groups, and consultants. It is precisely the growing influence of these organizations, and of the think-tanks in particular (e.g., the C.D. Howe Institute), that warrants the use of the phrase 'market for policy ideas.' The influence of any single participant in that market is often more indirect than direct; policy makers rarely formulate policy options on the basis of research findings,[17] and they generally seek advice from a variety of sources. Given the very uncertain relationship between the advocacy of an idea and its actual implementation through legislation and administrative measures, image-building becomes an end in itself for many policy research organizations. Think-tanks are in the business of selling their research findings, not only literally as a source of funding, but also metaphorically in their attempt to advertise and promote themselves. They communicate with different publics through many channels: members of their staffs appear before parliamentary committees, grant interviews on radio or television, write columns for newspapers, and so on, in addition to their more traditional activities centred on the publication of research monographs or the planning of conferences and workshops. Public research organizations, which have more limited ways of advertising their products, are in this respect at a disadvantage vis-à-vis their private competitors; this could have been a factor in the winding down of the Economic Council and other similar organizations by the Mulroney government in 1992.[18]

Nonprofit research institutes obtain their funding from private sector sources such as individual donors, corporations, foundations, and interest groups; another important source of revenues for most of these institutes are government research contracts. These institutes are a rather new phenomenon on the Canadian political scene. Even in the United States, where institutes such as the Brookings Institution or the Hoover Institution can trace their roots back to the first decades of this century, think-tanks only began to play a noticeable role in the 1960s; and only since the 1980s have they been recognized as major players in Washington (or, incidentally, to serve as a model for some of their Canadian counterparts).[19] There are now more than a hundred of them in the American capital, including prestigious and well-financed organizations such as Brookings, the American Enterprise Institute, and the Center for Strategic and International Studies, relatively smaller but influential ones such as the (libertarian) Cato Institute or the (left-leaning liberal) Institute for Policy Studies, and many more specialized, and often quite small, less well known organizations; dozens of others can be found far away from the Potomac River, especially on the West Coast (e.g., the Institute for Contemporary Studies). In fact, there are so many of these American institutes that it is rather difficult to classify them or to arrive at general propositions that would apply to all of them. One can distinguish between for-contract research organizations (e.g., the RAND corporation) and what Kent Weaver has called 'universities without students,'[20] that is, institutes doing scholarly research, the results of which are published and widely distributed; but these two categories overlap to a considerable extent. The situation in Canada is somewhat less complicated: there are far fewer institutes. Less than a dozen deserve to be mentioned as significant players; they are: the C.D. Howe Institute, the Canada West Foundation, the Canadian Centre for Policy Alternatives (CCPA), the Canadian Council on Social Development (CCSD), the Conference Board of Canada, the Fraser Institute, and the Institute for Research on Public Policy (IRPP).[21] (The list would be significantly longer if I had included university-based research centres, but I cannot do so within the narrow limits of this chapter.) Canadian institutes are also more focused on domestic issues than their American counterparts: geopolitical and strategic issues, in particular, are less relevant to Canadian policy makers or to the Canadian public.[22] The Canadian institutes are also much smaller, both in terms of the size of their operating budgets and of their staffs. In that respect alone, the disappearance of the Economic Council is significant, since it had a budget almost five times as large as that of all but one of its private sector competitors, and a staff of 118 as compared to ten to twenty for several other well-known organizations.[23] But the ways in which they are funded, set their agendas, conduct research, and distribute the results are not very different from what can be observed south of the border. What differs is the institutional context within which they operate. The Canadian parliamentary system presents fewer opportunities for influencing the policy-making process than the more fragmented and decentralized American congressional system, although the new role assumed by parliamentary committees should remind us that this difference is not as sharp as it used to be.

Policy institutes are active in two ways. They produce and distribute studies on the topics they consider important.[24] These studies can be prepared specifically for the benefit of individual clients, as is often the case with work done by the Conference Board of Canada, or they can be written as contributions to a public policy debate; I am interested only in the latter. A further distinction can be made between publications that state an institute's position more or less officially, on the one hand, and studies that do not coincide with the thinking of the institute's management. This creates a difficulty when trying to determine the overall research orientation of a given institute. But this difficulty is not insurmountable. As a rule, policy research organizations seek to avoid appearing to promote widely divergent policy ideas.[25] Moreover, constraints such as the general preferences of the individuals or groups contributing funds and other resources to their operations create vague yet very real limits.

Think-tanks also set up various types of forums (from international conferences to small workshops and luncheon series) where salient issues are debated by invited politicians, academics, journalists, business leaders, and representatives from nongovernmental organizations. While most institutes manage to achieve some sort of balance between these two principal activities, some devote most of their resources to either one of them; for example, the Ottawa-based Public Policy Forum operates primarily as a vehicle for convening meetings.

Think-tanks loudly proclaim their independence and their commitment to objectivity, but these declarations cannot entirely be taken at face value. The values and preferences of the senior staff members and the overall policy preferences of their sponsors set limits to the range of policy ideas that any given policy research organization can advocate. For example, the very strong commitment to libertarian ideals professed by Walter Block, who for many years played a key role in the Fraser Institute, or the equally strong dedication to social democratic principles evidenced by Duncan Cameron, at the head of the Canadian Centre for Policy Alternatives, have been clearly reflected in the content of the policy recommendations advocated by these two organizations. These are, admittedly, extreme examples. Other think-tanks are more subtle in their choices of research priorities and more prone to advocate a broader range of policy options. But ideological predispositions cannot be ignored altogether. And while it would be simplistic to pretend that donors dictate their preferences, or even consistently agree with the policy ideas defended by the organizations they support, it is only common sense to suggest that they exercise some degree of influence; for example, corporate sponsors would not want to fund an organization whose main research priorities would be to explore ways of achieving greater worker control in the workplace and in the management of the economy. Thus we find that there is a significant difference in the origin of the funds collected by the Conference Board of Canada, the C.D. Howe Institute, and the Fraser Institute, on the one hand, and the Canadian Council for Social Development or the Canadian Centre for Policy Alternatives, on the other hand: the former receive support from the corporate sector, while the latter are funded by community groups and by trade unions (in the case of the CCPA). This contrast is rendered more extreme by the relative weakness of foundations in Canada, for these organizations could afford to play a more neutral role.[26] Consequently, policy analysts respond to a variety of incentives and move in different directions. As the next section shows, these alignments and realignments change over time.

From Market Failure to Government Failure

'There are no "market failures"; on the contrary, government failure is ubiquitous.'[27] While this statement by a former senior member of the Fraser Institute's staff goes further than what most policy analysts sympathetic to a market-oriented perspective think on this subject, it underlines the extent to which ideas about the role of the state have changed (and the fact that it appeared in the pages of *Canadian Public Administration*, of all places, adds an anecdotic confirmation of this remark). Of course, economists have always been more reluctant than other specialists to advocate interventionist policies, but the limits of what is acceptable to most of them have shifted over the years. Up until the late 1970s economists used to pay considerable attention to the question of why markets occasionally fail to produce outcomes that are efficient from a macroeconomic standpoint. Today, however, they appear to be more preoccupied with inefficiencies resulting from government intervention (e.g., rising budgetary deficits; irrational investments in technologically sophisticated but economically unsustainable projects for reasons of national prestige; burdensome regulations that result in unexpected inefficiencies or perverse outcomes; inequities caused by subsidies or restrictive marketing practices that serve the interests of influential pressure groups, and so on).

To look for the roots of the notion of market failure, a brief detour through 'Welfare Economics' is required. This school of thought had its origin in the marginalist revolution brought about at the end of the nineteenth century by Alfred Marshall and William Jevons (although another branch of Welfare Economics was derived by Vilfredo Pareto from Léon Walras's work on general equilibrium). Welfare economists attempted to work out the macroeconomic and social policy implications of the notion of economic equilibrium. But this also led some economists to undertake an analysis of the imperfections that might prevent the realization of such an equilibrium (e.g., monopolies). It is in the context of these preoccupations (particularly among British economists) that one must place the emergence of another theoretical revolution, namely, Keynesian economics – not that Keynes merely built upon earlier neoclassical theories, but rather in the sense that he used these, and A.C. Pigou's writings in particular, as a foil in the development of his own ideas. Keynes's most important idea was that although a market economy is effectively self-regulating, there is no assurance that the particular outcome of these self-regulating processes will be optimal; and to the classical argument that these self-regulating mechanisms produce such outcomes only over the long run, Keynes's famous reply was: 'In the long run, we're all dead!' In particular, he wanted to prove that there is no reason to expect that full employment will always result from spontaneous adjustments in the labour market. Therefore, he advocated balancing the budget over the duration of an economic cycle instead of on a yearly basis, thus making it possible for the government to stimulate aggregate demand during a slow-down of the economy by increasing its spending and possibly incurring a deficit. While the impact of Keynesian economics on Canadian policy makers in the postwar years should not be exaggerated, it remains that mainstream economics in the English-speaking world drifted away from some of the axioms of neoclassical economics. (Germany and Japan did not experience the same conversion.) Consequently, the notion that markets can fail became very familiar to economists. Both Keynesian economics and the more classical analyses of market failures from the standpoint of welfare economics helped to create a climate of opinion according to which government intervention was inescapable. As Robert H. Haveman explains:

By the end of the 1950s, Francis Bator could write with authority on the 'failures of the market.' Moreover, a large literature had been developed, and through it, analytical consensus was attained. In this literature, the characteristics of free market operations were examined, those structural conditions which cause social costs and gains were clarified, the characteristics of public goods were defined, and the reasons why markets fail to produce them were identified ... By 1960, 'market failure' possessed significance which it did not previously have.[28]

Many examples of the application of Keynesian macroeconomic principles to economic policy issues, as well as analyses of a variety of market failures in supplying public goods, can be found in the research program of the Brooking Institution throughout the 1960s and early 1970s.[29] This is not irrelevant to the Canadian scene since Brookings was considered to be a model worth emulating; for example, one of the recommendations made by Ronald S. Ritchie in his 1969 report to the Privy Council Office was that a policy institute modelled on the Brookings Institution be established in Canada.[30] (Eventually, this led to the creation of the Institute for Research on Public Policy in 1972.) But more direct evidence of the prevalence of the market failure model is provided by much of the early work of the Economic Council, and especially of the Science Council.[31]

However, the climate began to change as the 1980s drew closer. A telling example of this evolution is the discernible shift in the orientation of the research program of the C.D. Howe Institute between the early 1970s and the mid-1980s. Then as now, the C.D. Howe Institute has defended a relatively pragmatic attitude. This is not to say, however, and despite the institute's protestations to the contrary, that it is entirely 'objective'; its positions on policy issues are informed to some extent by the concerns of identifiable interests (i.e., corporate interests) and, even more so, by the views of some professional groups (e.g., mainstream economists). Although it would be simplistic to describe the C.D. Howe Institute as merely the (moderate) voice of business, it clearly speaks in a language that business interests understand. But the important point, from my perspective here, is that it does not shoot from the fringes of the mainstream. Contrary to, say, the Fraser Institute, it refrains from expressing extreme views on issues. It occupies a position somewhere in the middle of the policy establishment. Thus as the C.D. Howe Institute's image of the world changes, so does the image held by analysts who can confidently speak (their) truth to power.

The limits set by institute publications to the scope of government intervention in the economy and in social affairs have been redrawn. Never a firm believer in nationalist industrial policy initiatives nor in far-reaching social regulations,[32] the institute nonetheless subscribed to the idea of market failure in the 1970s. To wit, the authors of the institute's 1974 Policy Review and Outlook wrote: 'We recognize that existing market forces may not be sufficiently competitive, [and] that these forces may produce results that are inconsistent with specific national goals,' (but they added prudently that 'we believe that [government] intervention should supplement rather than supplant market forces').[33] Also the C.D. Howe Institute was slow to respond critically to the imposition of the wage and price control program of the mid-1970s.

Furthermore, the institute recognized that governments have a role to play in stimulating employment and in easing the impact of competitive pressures on the well-being of Canadians. In the 1974 Policy Review and Outlook, we read that the Canadian political community has the obligation to provide Canadians with 'an adequate income from unemployment insurance, manpower training allowance, or the welfare system.'[34] And the 1975 review offers a defence of the Unemployment Insurance Act; responding to strong criticisms voiced by the Fraser Institute, Judith Maxwell took pains to explain that 'it could be argued that the Act has been successful in giving Canadians better opportunities to find satisfying employment,' and she concluded that 'it is wrong to blame [it] for basic imbalances which have boosted unemployment to such high levels.'[35]

While a subtle shift toward a more strictly monetarist approach to economic policy was noticeable already under the leadership of Carl Beigie in the late 1970s, an even clearer realignment took place in the 1980s under the direction of Wendy Dobson and then Maureen Farrow. Two themes came to dominate the research program: the urgent and imperative need to eliminate budgetary deficits (especially at the federal level) and the necessity of entering into a trade agreement with the United States. Time and time again, the institute's staff and commissioned authors revisited these issues. On free trade, the institute benefited from the active involvement of Richard Lipsey who wrote extensively on the subject. The idea of government failure as such did not enter the vocabulary of the institute in a striking manner,[36] but its meaning underpins the institute's research program throughout the 1980s. The underlying theme of that program was that opportunities for redressing market failures are limited by fiscal exigencies, which themselves, in a sense, represent a colossal failure on the part of the state to manage its affairs responsibly. As for long-term industrial strategies, the institute has tried to show that they make little sense in the context of globalization. From that perspective, competitiveness will be better achieved through measures that do away with rigidities caused by regulations and other interventionist policies.

In the 1990s the institute has embarked on a more comprehensive and ambitious program under the direction of Thomas E. Kierans. The latest outcome of this redeployment is a project entitled 'The Social Policy Challenge.' Fourteen volumes seek answers to the question of how to 'modernize' the welfare state in the face of two pressing constraints: first, the continually worsening debt burden; and second, the dysfunctional effects of what could be described as relatively generous programs that seem to foster a culture of 'dependency' for entire regions (e.g, the Atlantic provinces) as well as for individuals. The overall rationale for the project is not that the welfare state as a whole has failed, however. The two co-editors of the series, John Richards and William Watson, both affirm that Canada's social programs are one of the country's most valued accomplishments and are justified in principle either because markets occasionally fail or because of obvious equity considerations.[37] However, in practice, these programs often create serious problems of their own. Most volumes in the 'Social Policy Challenge' series offer remarkable examples of nonmarket failures. Examples in the area of housing policy[38] include: rent controls in Ontario or subsidized co-op housing in Vancouver that benefit only a fraction of the households in the target population but make it more difficult for others to find affordable accommodations; the preference given to the construction of social housing as compared to the arguably more flexible and more efficient transfer of money directly to households needing assistance; and the perverse effects of municipal zoning laws that result in higher housing costs. Admittedly more controversial but even more striking examples can be cited with respect to the design and implementation of income maintenance programs. Between the mid-1970s and the mid-1990s, the number of Canadians relying on social assistance has doubled; there are, of course, many causes at work here, but one of them has to be that as welfare payments have remained constant or increased somewhat while real market earnings have declined in that period, 'the relative reward from work has declined [and] the relative reward from "nonwork" has increased.'[39]

What Richards and Watson suggest is that the welfare state must be completely rethought and redesigned. What really matters is to achieve the essential goals of the welfare state in a manner compatible with the preservation of a viable market economy. In other words, the welfare state is not synonymous with the perpetuation of existing programs. It is difficult to determine exactly what the proper balance between the private and public sectors ought to be – indeed, this is precisely what this rather considerable research effort is attempting to establish with some degree of accuracy. But Richards suggests, on the basis on multinational comparisons, that the public sector should account for somewhere between 40 and 50 per cent of the GDP; below the lower range, the welfare state risks being ineffective, while above the 50 per cent mark its costs become overbearing and economic dislocations become noticeable. (In 1992, Canada's general government budget outlays stood at 51.5 per cent of GDP.)[40]

The C.D. Howe Institute speaks for a large segment of the policy analysis community in Canada, but despite its significance, it remains a relatively small organization. To substantiate my thesis I must cite a few other cases.

The Macdonald Commission offers another window on the mid-1980s. Not only did it address practically all the issues that continue to dominate the contemporary policy agenda, from the reform of social programs to free trade and sustainable development, but it set the tone for many subsequent developments. I have alluded already to its very broad and far-reaching mandate. In fact, the commission acknowledged the daunting complexity of its task;[41] in and by itself, this broad mandate and the awareness of the depth of its implications exemplifies a turning point, a realization that the postwar era has come to an end and that a different set of values and assumptions must be worked out. Despite the massive research effort that went into the preparation of background studies and of the final report itself, the commission did not succeed in articulating a comprehensive and compelling set of responses to all the complex problems it had been asked to investigate. Indeed, the report contains its fair share of vacuous rhetoric about the challenges facing Canada. As for the more than 100 research papers and monographs that served as background studies, they were prepared by too many authors coming from too many different disciplines to really coalesce around a single vision. Nevertheless, dominant themes and emphases are discernible, more obviously so in the final report, but also in a more inchoate way throughout most of the background papers.

The role of the 'state' – a term explicitly used in the commission's report even though it is far more common to the vocabulary of academic social scientists and/or social critics than to official prose[42] – is clearly perceived as a problem. Of course, the state is often described as a crucial player in economic and social life.[43] But what is significant is that it is not assumed that the state always can, or even should, play a remedial role, coming to the rescue of failing markets. On the contrary, the report states that

in some important areas we Canadians must significantly increase our reliance on market forces. Our proposals to increase our openness to the international economy and, specifically, to enter into a free-trade agreement with the United States reflect our general preference for market forces over state intervention ... Domestically, we have identified a number of market-distorting, growth-suppressing policies ... We recommend that ... the interventionist policies of the state should facilitate adjustments to those market processes which are growth creating.[44]

In line with this perspective, the commission recommended that Canada enter into a free trade agreement with the United States; it argued against a 'targeted approach' to industrial policy; and it proposed a fundamental overhaul of Canada's social programs.

The contribution of the Economic Council to this debate is difficult to estimate. The sheer volume of reports and studies produced by the council until its dissolution is such that whatever trend one may discern can only be an approximation suffering several exceptions. This being granted, one can tentatively outline three stages in the history of the council. The first phase, from the council's creation until the mid-1970s, was characterized by a perhaps lukewarm but realistic acceptance of the market failure paradigm. The second phase, into which the council eased gradually, evidenced a shift away from this model and the quiet conversion to what was becoming the orthodox view among professional economists about the limits of fiscal instruments and the costs associated with protectionism. This did not amount to a radical turnaround but merely a modest refocusing – after all, at no time was the council staffed by radical critics of the market economy. During that period there was an emphasis on econometric sophistication, and the council came under attack for producing work that did not appear to be relevant to the practical concerns of policy makers.[45] The final stage reflects the priorities set by the council's last chair, Judith Maxwell. They did not result in a substantial evolution of the council's basic philosophy – thus the council's research continued to be guided by current thinking in mainstream economics. But the research goals and the style in which they were communicated changed markedly. In addition to traditional macroeconomic topics such as economic growth, labour markets, and international trade, the council undertook ambitious projects in social policy fields such as education, poverty, or the role of women in the economy, and also explored issues related to governance (e.g., the relation between the design of political institutions and the performance of government functions, on the one hand, and competitiveness, on the other). In other words, the council was attempting in its final years to articulate a synthesis of economic and social policy that could have moved us closer to a resolution of the dilemma posed by the confrontation of the market failure and government failure paradigms. The direction in which these projects was heading parallels in some ways the work done at the C.D. Howe Institute. The goal was to explore ways of rebuilding the welfare state, not from the blueprint of the minimal state, but on the basis of a more modest and efficient public sector. A wide array of social services would still be provided but within stricter constraints than those under which previous governments have lived. And in terms of style, the Economic Council in its last years sought to communicate its message more effectively by attempting to eliminate unnecessary jargon.

If the transition from the idea of market failure to that of government failure often remains implicit in the research done by the organizations mentioned so far, the Fraser Institute's message is more straightforward. Its statement of purpose reads as follows:

[The Fraser Institute] has as its objective the redirection of public attention to the role of competitive markets in providing for the well-being of Canadians. Where markets work, the institute's interest lies in trying to discover prospects for improvement. Where markets do not work, the interest lies in finding the reasons. Where competitive markets have been replaced by government control, the interest of the institute lies in documenting objectively the nature of the improvement or deterioration resulting from government intervention.

But in every instance where Fraser Institute publications deal with market imperfections, the cause of these imperfections turns out to be the rigidities introduced by government intervention. As for examples of 'improvement resulting from government intervention,' the institute has yet to report a single one. Thus the institute is at its best in dealing with cases of more or less evident regulatory failures (e.g., provincial trade barriers)[46] and in pursuing innovative ideas that challenge the tenets of the technocratic faith in the capacity of existing governing instruments to achieve efficient results. (Perhaps one of the best examples of this innovative approach is the institute's contribution to the discussion of environmental policy.)[47] However, its publications are arguably less convincing and may strike readers as being unnecessarily dogmatic when dealing with complex and multidimensional issues. To take just one example, poverty[48] is an issue which evokes a diversity of policy responses that cannot always be translated into either 'pro-' or 'anti-market' positions.

This is not to say that we have now reached a consensus about the respective roles of government and markets. There are noticeable expressions of dissent. Yet even the dissenters have sometimes wavered, and these expressions of dissent are often muted. Or when they are not, they tend to be marginalized by the relative lack of visibility of the sources of dissenting opinions.

Beginning in the 1970s and continuing through the early 1980s, the Science Council of Canada took a very firm position on industrial policy. It did so both explicitly in reports that expressed the council's official views by issuing recommendations urging government to take a more interventionist stance, and implicitly by publishing independent studies that went in the same general direction.[49]

Industrial policy was not the only issue in relation to which the council tried to steer the federal government toward more activist policies. For example, the solutions proposed to environmental questions were formulated in terms of the need for more government investment in research and a strengthening of the regulatory powers of public authorities.[50] In fact, the very creation of the Science Council had been premised on the idea that government must constantly be prodded to develop better policy instruments for encouraging Research and Development (R&D); that is, R&D would presumably stay below what it should be in the absence of government intervention. So much so that the council became the *bête noire* of the Fraser Institute.[51] And, although such a hypothesis would be hard to substantiate empirically, there are good reasons to believe that the council's dirigiste reputation accounts in large measure for the severe budget cut it experienced when the Tories came to power. Under such circumstances, it is worth noting that in 1988 the council issued a statement entitled *Gearing Up for Global Markets*, which made the point that 'while ... the efforts of companies will continue to need some reinforcement by governments, ... a crucial factor in Canada's future international competitiveness will be industry's capacity for self-help.'[52] Indeed, from then on, concepts such as 'partnership,' 'consensus,' or 'cooperation' became buzz words in council publications. While the notion of government failure never entered the Science Council's vocabulary, the stress originally placed on the idea of market failure gave way to a more agnostic attitude. Consequently, the council turned its attention to indirect, context-oriented policies such as the rethinking of priorities in education and university-industry education instead of more direct means such as regulation and subsidies.

One can also glean from the catalogue of the IRPP a few titles that depart more or less radically from the trend toward laissez-faire. To wit, in *Getting Ready for 1999* Tom Kent pleads for major reforms in taxation and company law in order to reverse the concentration in corporate power and individual wealth, and argues in favour of a full employment policy through such means as a new mix of fiscal, monetary, and income adjustment policies together with improvements in social policies. And in *The Privatization Putsch*, Herschel Hardin comes to the defence of public enterprise, and pokes holes into the arguments of the advocates of privatization. But the IRPP has always had a rather eclectic research program; in fact, at the time when these studies were published, the IRPP's program was perhaps more diversified (scattered would not be much of an exaggeration) than ever before or since. On the whole, though, it published more studies that were consistent with, if not wholly supportive of, the general tendency toward market solutions, especially in the international trade policy area. Thus the release of a few atypical studies may not amount to much more than a tolerance for dissent at the margin.

In the early 1980s the Toronto-based Canadian Institute for Economic Policy – an institute that had been founded by a prominent member of the Liberal Party, Walter Gordon – published thirty-one monographs that remained firmly anchored in the market failure paradigm. Indeed, many of these studies articulated a neo-Keynesian approach to economic management. While recognizing that the environment was changing, CIEP authors (e.g., John C.P. McCallum, Abraham Rotstein) argued with remarkable consistency that laissez-faire is a simplistic response to these new challenges. They recommended the adoption of a 'new National Policy' to achieve full employment and to regain control over the resource and manufacturing sectors.[53] (The phrase 'National Policy' refers, of course, to a series of separate economic and political measures adopted, first, and rather unsuccessfully, by Sir John A. Macdonald and continued with better results under the Laurier government.) But the CIEP closed its doors in 1984. This was a planned move; nevertheless this decision was, arguably, ill-timed since it took effect precisely at the moment when the government failure paradigm was beginning to gain a greater measure of acceptance, as evidenced by the work of the Macdonald Commission discussed above.

I turn now to the most dedicated opponents of the new paradigm: the Canadian Centre for Policy Alternatives and the Canadian Council on Social Development. Apart from their continued adherence to the market failure paradigm, these two organizations pursue somewhat different strategies. The CCPA is more, albeit not exclusively, concerned with macroeconomic policy, while the CCSD has examined a wide range of issues related to social policy. In terms of style, the latter usually adopts a more subdued and less partisan tone than the former.[54]

Many of the publications of these two organizations illustrate the dilemma facing the advocates of the social democratic option. While they would like to act as agents of social and political change, they are forced by changing circumstance to fall back to a defensive position. They become so preoccupied with the defence of Keynesian economics and of the values underlying social programs (e.g., universality) that they are unable to propose new policies. To wit, in maintaining that the public debt and budgetary deficits are simply a consequence of economic slowdowns and, therefore, are no more of a problem today than they were in other times, CCPA authors such as Harold Chorney or Mario Seccareccia are in effect saying that Keynesian economics continues to provide all the answers to the challenges of the 1990s.[55] Similarly, on trade issues, the argument implicit in the attacks against the free trade agreement with the United States seems to be that the status quo ex ante was satisfactory. (On NAFTA, however, the CCPA has sought to introduce a new element in the discussion, namely, the democratic quality of the new regime, or rather lack thereof.) Social policy issues, and the various recommendations put forward by these two think-tanks, are more heterogeneous and complex; therefore, it is more difficult to sketch a fair description of their overall thrust. But, on the whole, they express attitudes ranging from moderate and sceptical to very hostile reactions to the idea that social programs might create obstacles to economic growth and competitiveness.

Toward a New Democracy?

To say that the 1980s was the decade of disenchantment with the welfare state, while the 1990s is the decade of democratic renewal, is only a figure of speech, but one that somehow rings true.[56] By that I do not mean to say that the disenchantment with the welfare state has been displaced with concerns over democratic renewal, but rather that the latter is the newest response to the former. Policy analysts have zeroed in on that trend in several ways. In some instances, there is an attempt to present the logic of democratization as providing an alternative to the market-oriented agenda outlined above. However, it would be simplistic to pretend that the current interest in democratic renewal always stems from a deliberate effort to articulate a dialectical analysis of this sort. Indeed, there are even some participants in this debate who maintain that economic and political freedoms are mutually reinforcing values.

A policy research organization that has taken the lead in exploring the subject of institutional reform is the IRPP. Throughout most its existence, the IRPP has been active in the general area of 'governance,' that is, the institutional and cultural problems associated with the conduct of public affairs. This concern has become more central for the institute in recent years; one notices a sharper focus on the democratic principles that give meaning to governance issues in Canada. This is indeed deliberate. The IRPP's 1993 *Annual Report* explicitly states that one of the assumptions guiding its governance program is precisely that 'Canadians have become less deferent to elites and more "rights conscious," and ... they expect to be more fully involved in the formation of public policy.' Native land claims and native self-government, public sector management, including questions of ethics, the implications of the Charter of Rights and Freedoms, and the problem of equitable representation, as well as the impact of new technologies on democratic governance, are some of the issues that have retained the attention of the institute's staff and commissioned authors.[57]

Renewed thinking about democracy in Canada is also evident in a number of other settings. The CCSD, for example, has always paid attention to the role of voluntary organizations in the social policy process. But it now sees in the climate resulting from the adoption of the Charter, the way in which the Meech Lake Accord was debated, and other social transformations (e.g., long-term unemployment) a new set of opportunities and challenges for the voluntary sector. Thus it recommends the development of community-based social and health services; and it has published interesting studies on the theory and practice of community economic development.[58] It also raised the question of the need to democratize the nongovernmental organizations themselves.[59]

Proposals for reforms of our democratic institutions are also apparent in the recommendations of several royal commissions. Moreover, the mandates and/or consultation processes of these commissions demonstrate a heightened concern for democratic values. For example, the Macdonald Commission research program included not only projects about federalism and constitutional reform, but also projects about topics such as citizenship, gender, ethnicity, and public opinion.[60] More recently created commissions have been concerned entirely with issues central to democracy. Perhaps the best example is the Royal Commission on Electoral Reform and Party Financing.[61] One could also mention the Royal Commission on Aboriginal People. The Royal Commission on New Reproductive Technologies is also worth noting because soon after its appointment it was embroiled in conflict. Some members opposed the chair of the commission with regard to the research priorities and conduct of the inquiry, revealing a deep division on the question of the relative weights to be placed on scientific expertise in comparison with ethical and political values.

Publications from the sources mentioned above raise controversial questions, but for the most part they demonstrate a certain degree of objective neutrality. This is not to say, however, that they probe very deep below the surface. They underline some key sociological or legal facts relevant to the issue at stake without pursuing the analysis much further,[62] largely ignoring theoretical foundations built by democratic theory and political philosophy. Contributions from the CCPA, by contrast, do not show the same restraint. Indeed, democratic ideals become rhetorical weapons to be used in battles against the neoconservative camp.[63] Democratization is incompatible with the push for market-based policies, as far as the CCPA is concerned. Besides, the CCPA shows a more 'hands on' attitude, by which I mean that it is not only concerned with making policy recommendations, but also with the mobilization of social activists centred on more or less radical democratic practices.[64] In particular, the CCPA is the only policy organization advocating economic democracy, that is, the extension of the principles guiding political life to the economic sphere.

At the other end of the ideological spectrum, the Fraser Institute has directed its attention to the link between economic freedom and political freedom.[65] For Milton Friedman, whose ideas the Fraser Institute has done much to proselytize in Canada, this link is a very tight one. But the institute's liberty project has attempted to examine that relationship in more detail. The publications that came out of that project introduced a crucial third component complementing the simplistic dichotomy between economic and political freedom, namely, civil liberties; with the result that one can speak of countries enjoying economic and civil freedoms but only limited political freedoms (e.g., Hong Kong). And the project tried to produce quantitative measures and rankings of these variables for most countries of the world; the results are interesting but rest on many debatable assumptions, thus their ultimate value is uncertain.

Variations on a Theme

Of course, the entire range of policy ideas that have been proposed and debated in recent decades cannot all be neatly fitted into the categories analysed above. Many specialized studies deal only remotely, or not at all, with either the notion of government failure or with the shift toward more democratic forms of governance. For example, some of the more technical aspects of international trade deserve to be addressed in their own terms. But several new policy debates, as well as recurring controversies, bring us back more or less indirectly to the central themes identified above.

Environmental policy hinges on a comparison of the relative merits of market-oriented measures and regulatory schemes. But the sustainability of our economic structures also opens up a series of questions about the way in which conflicts over fundamental values can be resolved in a democratic society. Although the efficiency of market versus nonmarket solutions has perhaps received more attention than the difficult political and philosophical issues attendant to clashes over values, both aspects have been given ample consideration.[66]

Canadian federalism and constitutional reform have been approached in recent years from a variety of standpoints that transcend the narrow technical and legalistic dimensions within which these issues used to be discussed. This is due, of course, to events and circumstances far more complex than the role played by think-tanks in constitutional matters. (The profound changes in the Canadian political culture that were brought about by the enactment of the Charter of Rights and Freedoms counts as one of the most important among these events.) Nevertheless, some of these think-tanks were instrumental in the development of a new set of constitutional priorities. The Canada West Foundation, for example, has tirelessly hammered away at the issue of Senate reform, presenting arguments in favour of an elected assembly and examining different formulas for accomplishing that goal.[67] The C.D. Howe Institute, for its part, has done much to shift the debate toward the economic costs of some aspects of the constitutional status quo, and to evaluate the economic implications of proposed changes.[68] The IRPP and other institutes have also waded into the debate.[69] The need to redefine the role of the state in ways that take into account new economic constraints and the urgency of democratic reforms emerge once again as the dominant themes.

Five think-tanks[70] also had a more indirect involvement in constitutional reform. They were invited by the federal government to organize a series of conferences, which brought together elected politicians, experts from various fields, interest group representatives, and a cross-section of 'ordinary Canadians' in an attempt to generate some measure of consensus with respect to the essential aspects of the package of reforms proposed by the Mulroney government in September 1991.

'The Vision Thing'

Even when written by academics, policy studies typically do not devote much space to theoretical reflections. This does not mean that they show no connection to theoretical developments in a variety of disciplines. But when there is a noticeable gap between applied research and new ideas, one is entitled to ask whether such studies deserve to be treated differently from any other sources of information. Does policy research really compel us to rethink policy problems in creative ways, or does it merely add a veneer of pseudo-scientific legitimacy to the claims and counterclaims of competing interests?

Questions of pure economic theory or methodology are actually not absent from the literature surveyed here. The Economic Council, in particular, has published numerous papers on technical aspects of its long-term economic models. But these are of interest to only a small audience, and they add little to our understanding of the broader issues. Other organizations have occasionally addressed issues of principles; for example, the Fraser Institute has often acted as a conduit for the ideas of Milton Friedman on the superior advantages of unrestrained capitalism not only from an economic but also from a moral and political standpoint.[71] On the whole, however, think-tanks are far more concerned with applying whatever theoretical idea is deemed appropriate to the study of a particular issue than with the development of new and original analytical frameworks. This is not in itself a poor choice of strategy. One can hardly imagine how policy analysts could significantly influence the policy-making process if they limited themselves to the discussion of abstract concepts and principles.

The relevant question is not whether policy analysts are good theorists, but whether they can rephrase policy issues in ways that facilitate the discovery of novel solutions, and whether they can do more than merely dress up preconceived ideas in the language of experts. Are think-tanks more than clubs of like-minded policy actors seeking convincing justifications of their interests and value preferences, as Evert Linquist suggests might be the case?

The notions of government failure and of democratic reform are not, in themselves, original contributions. To some extent, they could be viewed as rhetorical tricks lacking substance. They do, however, evoke some powerful ideas and paradigms. The theme of government failure is clearly consistent with the general direction of economic theory in recent decades. Neoclassical economics, which is today synonymous with mainstream economics, offers some support for it, but mostly in terms of a not particularly illuminating comparison between the presumed inefficiency of nonmarket allocative processes and the more efficient operations of firms in a competitive environment. The so-called 'Austrian' school offers a more original, as well as a more radical, critique. Austrian economics refers somewhat loosely to a paradigm developed by Carl Menger, and then by Ludwig von Mises, and F.A. Hayek; a younger generation of critics of neoclassical dogmas keep this tradition alive today. It pays more attention than traditional neoclassical economics to the subjective character of economic decisions and to the uncertainty surrounding market interactions. The hypothetical move toward long-term economic equilibrium in the absence of government intervention is regarded by 'Austrian' economists as far less significant than the capacity of markets to respond spontaneously to dynamic and unexpected changes. From that angle, government failure, due in large measure to a lack of knowledge about immensely complex and detailed interactions among countless economic actors, could cause far more damage than a mere reduction in economic efficiency – hence the uncompromising advocacy of laissez-faire exemplified by Walter Block's comment cited earlier. But while Block arrives at his admittedly radical conclusion through an analysis of the consequences of the knowledge problem, as I have just defined it, this is not an argument commonly used by mainstream policy analysts in Canada.

Economists who adhere to the 'Austrian' paradigm share a concern with dynamic transformations, but it is at the margins of the Austrian school, that is, in the work of Joseph Schumpeter, that this problem is presented as central to economic analysis. Rather than treating technological innovation as an exogenous variable, which is a common assumption, Schumpeter attempted to integrate it into his explanation of economic processes. The Schumpeterian theme of creative destruction – that is, of seeing market economies as being periodically regenerated by technological advances – has been revisited and amplified by a new generation of economists; the outcome of this renewal of interest takes the form of new evolutionary models of economic growth. Viewed from that angle, the idea of government failure is not a final verdict on the role of public institutions in economic life; it opens up new perspectives on institutional reform and cultural change. Although it might prove to be a more arduous task, applying the idea of creative destruction to the public sector and/or to the relationship between governments and their clients could lead to the design of innovative policy-making structures, somewhere between the two extreme poles of complete laissez-faire and hierarchical bureaucratic controls. Have these opportunities been exploited?

The answer is not entirely negative. The underlying theme of the C.D. Howe Institute's 'Social Policy Challenge' project seems to be that the present crisis presents an opportunity for 'reinventing' the welfare state. This theme was also faintly apparent in the institute's studies on international trade published in the mid- to late-1980s; Richard Lipsey, in particular, urged the adoption of a 'macro-climate' approach to industrial policy, which would enable Canada to move to the forefront of technological innovation.[72] The IRPP's strategy of repositioning itself by identifying a manageable set of research priorities, including a sharp focus on institutional reform, is another encouraging sign. And while the gap left by the elimination of the Economic Council has yet to be filled, the search for ways of achieving a more adequate balance between economic and social policies, which had characterized its research program during its final years, has been continued through the (temporary) institutional vehicle of the Queen's University/University of Ottawa Economic Projects. The Government and Competitiveness Project, in particular, provides many examples of government failures that must be addressed urgently (e.g., budget deficits).[73] But the goal of the project, which was 'to explore how the delivery of government services can be reshaped to enhance the incomes of Canadians over the long term,' provided the scope for innovative suggestions in a number of areas, from education to natural resources management to environmental regulation.[74]

This is not to say, however, that policy research has suddenly become much more perceptive and original in recent years. One still finds many 'run-of-the-mill' discussions of fiscal, monetary, and trade issues that do little to enhance the reputation of mainstream economists for creative thinking. As we have seen, critics of these conventional ideas often propose equally stereotypical Keynesian or protectionist responses. Besides, the examples I gave of what appears to be a quasi-Schumpeterian vision of public sector reform are based more on implicit than on explicit theorizing; there is room for more fine-tuning of this emergent vision.

As for the emphasis on democratic reform, it also has been of uneven quality. Many observers of the Canadian political scene would no doubt agree that democratic reforms are needed. The Canadian public is demanding that such reforms be implemented in a variety of areas. But the question is, again, whether think-tanks have pointed the way toward innovative responses. There are, of course, quite a few interesting ideas that can be derived from a careful reading of the many studies I alluded to or of others that could not be mentioned here. Inevitably, an element of subjectivity enters into an evaluation of the quality of that material; thus what some may find enlightening, others may dismiss as trite or unconvincing. Two observations can be made, however, which suggest that policy analysts have not yet given sufficient thought to the manifold implications of the trend toward the democratization of Canadian politics. The first is that while there are many examples of studies dealing with specific democratic issues, to date there has never been a concerted effort to integrate these concerns into a single, coherent, and well-funded research project. (The Lortie Commission comes to mind, but despite the importance of its mandate, it was nevertheless a limited one.) The theoretical literature on democratic theory is rich and continues to expand in promising directions, but its application to practical matters would be best served by the formulation of a comprehensive and well thought out research framework. This is still not the case. Second, as Douglas Torgerson argues in his contribution to this volume, there exists now a path-breaking school of thought in policy analysis that has shown how to integrate a concern for democratic governance *into* the very methodology of policy analysis. The impact of this post-positivist approach in Canada, however, is still fairly limited. Professor Torgerson aptly refers to the Berger Inquiry into the construction of a pipeline in the Mackenzie Valley as a remarkable example – and indeed it was. But this pioneering inquiry took place in the mid-1970s; since then, there has been relatively little movement toward a radical departure from technocratic modes of inquiry by think-tanks, royal commissions, or task forces – except perhaps in the environmental field.[75]

Finally, there remains a more insidious weakness. The policy analysis community as a whole suffers from myopia about its own role within the policy process, and about the logic of that process. As has been suggested already, political scientists are arguably too narrowly concerned with process issues; the staff of the policy research organizations discussed in this chapter, being trained, for the most part, in disciplines other than political science, are arguably too concerned with outcomes. They rarely evidence an awareness of the political context within which the recommendations they propose will be discussed; or when they do, they summarily dismiss political variables as reflecting irrational considerations. The political science literature has in recent years portrayed in considerable detail the policy-making process as a dynamic interaction of policy communities and networks; but that perspective has had very little impact on policy studies concerned with the evaluation of policy decisions and their outcomes. These realities, however, are ignored only at great risk to the credibility of policy analysts. For one thing, policy institutes should recognize that they are rather far removed from the centres of decision making. Their recommendations cannot be implemented without being reinterpreted, redesigned, and repositioned in ways that they could actually explore, but generally do not. Social and political systems have more inertia than is sometimes recognized by reformers. For example, it is one thing to push for deregulation, as most market-oriented think-tanks in the United States have done very successfully insofar as their impact on the rhetoric of two Republican presidents shows; but it is another thing to turn around the political and bureaucratic machines and the interest groups with which they interact, as these same presidents and their cabinets have discovered. With more limited resources, Canadian think-tanks are not in a position to promote policy goals in a vacuum. As Evert Lindquist suggests, the 'authors [of the studies published by policy research institutes] should be encouraged to address the organizational, management and implementation dimensions of [an] issue in detail.' The transition from market failure to government failure, and proposals for a redesign of the policy-making system, can lead to valuable reforms only if sufficient attention is paid to the detailed re-engineering of many bureaucratic agencies.

To conclude, professional policy analysts have facilitated the reception of new ideas and articulated a few of their own. But they must constantly be on guard against intellectual fashions whose complex social, political, and economic implications it should be their job to critically explore. Unfortunately, there are few incentives at work in the policy research community to reward critical thinking – as distinct, that is, from facile criticisms of the truisms of yesterday.

Notes

1 Castles has argued that the questioning of the role of the state has been more sustained and far-reaching in English-speaking democracies (among which he includes Canada) than in other Western democracies; but that is perhaps a moot point: certainly, Prime Minister Thatcher and President Reagan took the lead in that regard. But although very real, the change of direction has been somewhat less radical in Canada, while recent announcements of massive privatization programs in France and Italy suggest that this dichotomy between the English-speaking and other democracies reflects a temporal discrepancy more than anything else. See Castles, 'Changing Course in Economic Policy: The English-Speaking Nations in the 1980s.'

2 Evert Linquist suggests that the actual influence of nonprofit policy institutes is rather limited. 'Think Tanks or Clubs?' 575.

3 While as a rule political scientists pay more attention to process issues than to the impact of policy decisions, Leslie Pal argues in this volume that a new trend toward the comprehensive examination of the societal effects of policies – including the symbolic dimensions of such effects – is emerging. This point is well taken; so far the published results of this new emphasis, however, are still relatively meager. Academic research in economics, on the other hand, is often result-oriented rather than process-oriented, but it suffers from a fascination with quantitative techniques as an end in themselves. Readers who are not thoroughly trained in econometrics cannot make much use of these materials.

4 Like all dichotomies, this is a rather crude distinction, and my comments sometimes bear on sources that fall somewhere in between these a priori categories.

5 See Lindquist, 'Think Tanks or Clubs?'

6 The literature on these topics is too vast to be cited here; for a discussion of the implications of some of these new developments on policy analysis, see Dobuzinskis, 'Modernist and Postmodernist Metaphors of the Policy Process'; see also Kiel, 'Lessons from the Nonlinear Paradigm'; the seminal work on evolutionary approaches to economics is Dosi et al., eds., *Technical Change and Economic Theory*.

7 This metaphor has been used already by two students of American think-tanks; see Smith, *The Idea Brokers*, ch. 9, and Ricci, *The Transformation of American Politics*, 15. I should add that, from my perspective, the metaphor of the market is meant to convey both the idea of a (real or virtual) meeting place and an economic structure where, as Ricci points out, marketing techniques set the norms.

8 I am indebted here to David Ricci for his perceptive analysis of the ironic interplay of the Platonic ideal of a single approach to truth, which is inherent in the technocratic style of most professional policy analysts, on the one hand, and the practical reality of the politics of ideas, on the other hand. See Ricci, *The Transformation of American Politics*, 12–16.

9 One should not forget, however, that 'the policy formulation process is characterized by both an active trade in information and knowledge and by strategies for strenuously withholding information and knowledge' (Doern and Phidd, *Canadian Public Policy*, 2nd ed., 214).

10 I am deliberately using the term 'myth' in both its acceptations, i.e., the trivial sense of error or illusion, and its original sense of the commonly shared understanding of complex phenomena. The subtle game played by think-tanks and other organizations consists in convincing their publics that some policy options are a myth in the first sense, while trying to transform other ideas into myths of the second kind.

11 See Prince, 'Policy Advisory Groups in Government Departments.'

12 The Special Joint Committee of the House of Commons and Senate (Beaudoin-Dobbie Committee), which conducted hearings throughout Canada on the federal government's 1992 constitutional proposals, is a good example.

13 Kernaghan and Siegel, *Public Administration in Canada*, 256. See also Pross, et al., eds., *Commissions of Inquiry*.

14 Canada, *Public Service 2000*, and Tellier, *A Report on Progress*.

15 In fact, the official representatives from the labour movement left the council in 1976 to protest against the imposition of the wage and price control program; union officials never returned to the council, although over the years a number of retired union leaders acted as the unofficial voices of the movement.

16 Although not an advisory council but strictly a research organization, the Law Reform Commission must also be mentioned in this respect.

17 There exists a burgeoning literature on the utilization of social science research in policy making. One of the themes that emerges from this literature is that policy makers very rarely have first-hand knowledge of policy research. Indeed, the social sciences have been criticized for being irrelevant to the practical concerns of government officials who prefer instant and timely advice on the issues of the day. Policy analysis is communicated to them through indirect means (e.g., the media); this leaves much room for misapprehension of research results and other communication failures. Eventually, however, new ideas find their way into the public discourse. For a comparative perspective on these issues see Bulmer, ed., *Social Science Research and Government*; Coleman, 'Policy Research – Who Needs It?'; Dunn, 'Assessing

the Impact of Policy Analysis'; Webber, 'The Distribution and Use of Policy Knowledge in the Policy Process'; Weiss, 'Knowledge Creep and Decision Accretion.' Not much has been written specifically on the Canadian case, but see Lindquist, 'Think Tanks or Clubs?'

18 Judith Maxwell reports that when she took office as chair of the ECC, she was instructed by a high-level official to give the council 'more impact' (personal interview, 21 March 1994). Ironically, it is precisely because she succeeded in so doing with the publication of some controversial reports that, in the opinion of many observers, the council was disbanded. (The most controversial report was the 28th Annual Review, *A Joint Venture: The Economics of Confederation* [1991], which tended to minimize the economic impact that Quebec's secession would have on the rest of Canada and Quebec itself.)

19 See Ricci, *The Transformation of American Politics*, and Smith, *The Idea Brokers*.

20 Weaver, 'The Changing World of Think Tanks.'

21 This is not an exhaustive list, of course. One or two other names could be mentioned (e.g., the Canadian Tax Foundation). Nor have I included organizations that are concerned primarily with local issues (e.g., the Laurier Institute in Vancouver).

22 These issues are not ignored, however; they are of primary concern to, for example, the Canadian Centre for Arms Control and Disarmament or, until its dissolution in 1992, the Canadian Institute for International Peace and Security. On the other hand, while it goes without saying that Canadian think-tanks are much more focused on Canadian issues and institutions than American institutes, the latter (for example, the Brookings Institution or the Twentieth Century Fund) have occasionally produced interesting studies on topics such as Canadian unity or U.S.-Canada trade issues.

23 The only comparably sized private sector organization is the Conference Board of Canada. For more detail on these matters, see Lindquist, 'Think Tanks or Clubs?' 559.

24 These studies are written either by the institute's staff or are commissioned from renowned experts; in rarer cases, unsolicited manuscripts are accepted for publication. Canadian institutes, being typically small, usually publish more commissioned studies than staff-prepared studies, but the situation varies from one organization to another. Most of the studies produced by the Conference Board of Canada are produced internally, while the contrary is true with the Fraser Institute.

25 One possible exception to that rule was the eclectic research and publications program of the IRPP throughout most of the 1970s and 1980s; but this did

cause problems for the IRPP, and the present executive of the institute has adopted a more focused approach; in particular, the IRPP no longer accepts unsolicited manuscripts. (This remark is based on interviews I conducted with members of the institute over the course of several years.)

26 On the role of foundations or, rather, lack thereof, see Lindquist, 'Confronting Globalization and Governance Challenges,' 210–11 and 'Think Tanks or Clubs?' 578.

27 Block, 'Public Finance Texts Cannot Justify Government Taxation,' 229.

28 Haveman, 'Public Expenditures and Policy Analysis: An Overview,' 4–5.

29 One of the most positive evaluations of the responsibilities of the welfare state can be found in Steiner, *Public Expenditure Budgeting*; but other titles in the Brookings Institution series 'Studies in Government Finance' were inspired by a similar paradigm.

30 The report was released to the public in 1971 under the title *An Institute for Research on Public Policy*.

31 On the history of the Economic Council, see Smith, 'The Economic Council of Canada.' The very purpose of the council, namely, to assist the government in its long-term planning efforts toward goal-like full employment, indicates that the dominant thinking at the time of its creation in 1963 was that economic potential cannot be fully realized without direct government intervention.

32 In fact, the C.D. Howe Institute has often acted as critic of the interventionist policies of the Trudeau governments.

33 Maxwell and Beigie, *The Disappearance of the Status Quo*, xx.

34 Ibid., 43.

35 Maxwell, *Restructuring the Incentives System*, 85 and 157; Ernst, 'From Liberal Continentalism to Neoconservatism,' 123.

36 But in a recent contribution to a C.D. Howe Institute publication, Richards offers a very useful and comprehensive treatment of the two concepts of market failure and 'failures of government intervention'; see Richards, 'The Social Policy Round,' 60–8.

37 Richards genuinely believes in the goals that Canada's social programs are trying to accomplish while Watson takes note of the fact that Canadians value these goals without seemingly subscribing to them personally; see Richards, 'The Social Policy Round,' and Watson, 'The View from the Right.'

38 See Fallis et al., *Home Remedies*.

39 Richards, 'The Study in Brief,' in Richards et al., *Helping the Poor*, xii.

40 OECD, cited in Richards, 'Living within Our Means,' 41.

41 Royal Commission on the Economic Union and Development Prospects for Canada, *Report*, vol. 1, 5.

42 Commenting on this aspect of the commission's report, Resnick ('State and Civil Society,' 384) wrote:

> To suggest ... that Canada has crossed the boundary that separates 'government' from 'state' is potentially to suggest a degree of concentrated power and autonomous political authority that one might associate with the political philosophies of ... Hobbes or Hegel. Is it to evoke the majesty of sovereignty, the symbolism of Leviathan ...? Is all this to better prepare the terrain for an ideological counter-offensive against an all-pervasive state ... to point to a world where civil society, and more especially the market place, plays the ascendant role? This seems to me an important part of the Commissioners' intention in deploying the term 'state' so effusively.

43 In several of the monographs and collected essays written by political scientists one finds positive evaluations of past contributions by governments at all levels to the construction of a Canadian political community and of specific institutions that have served Canadians well or are destined to play a progressive role (e.g., the Canadian Charter of Rights and Freedoms); some of these commentators (e.g., André Blais) caution the commission against the risks inherent in the dismantlement of policies and programs designed to alleviate the socially disruptive effects of structural changes. Even some of the studies prepared by economists show that the public sector is not necessarily and inherently less efficient that the private sector; see Borins and Boothman, 'Crown Corporations and Economic Efficiency.'

44 *Report,* 65.

45 For an elaboration of this argument, see my 'Policy Orienteering.'

46 On trade barriers, see Palda, ed., *Provincial Trade Wars.* The institute has also published numerous studies on topics such as rent controls, the restrictive practices of professionals (physicians, lawyers, etc.), and marketing boards.

47 See Block, ed., *Economics and the Environment.*

48 E.g., Sarlo, *Poverty in Canada.* One of the criticisms that the proponents of a more activist social policy agenda could make of this work is that it is premised on what Kerans calls a 'thin' definition of needs, which only considers the objective harm a person whose minimal needs are not met may suffer, in contrast with a 'thick' definition of needs that takes the sociocultural context into account, leading to a concern with relative deprivation. See Kerans, 'Need and Welfare.' For contrary definitions and analyses of poverty in Canada, see Lockhead et al., *The Canadian Fact Book on Poverty – 1994*; National Council of Welfare, *Poverty Profile, 1980–1990*; and Economic Council of Canada, *The New Face of Poverty.*

49 For example, Science Council of Canada, *Forging the Links*, and *Hard Times, Hard Choices*; Britton and Gilmour, *The Weakest Link*; and Jenkin, *The Challenge of Diversity.*

50 See Science Council of Canada, *Canada as a Conserver Society; Policies and Poisons*; Schrecker, *The Conserver Society Revisited.*

51 Critiques of the Science Council's recommendations can be found in, for example, Palda, *Industrial Innovation*, and Chant et al., 'The Economics of a Conserver Society.'

52 Science Council of Canada, *Annual Report, 1988–89*, 12; the same report also notes that this recommendation was well received by the Business Council on National Issues.

53 These points were succinctly presented in a 1979 paper prepared by the institute's executive, *Out of Joint with the Times: An Overview of the Canadian Economic Dilemma;* but they underlie practically all the institute's subsequent publications. For a more recent discussion of whether a new National Policy is needed or is actually an idea whose time has not come, see Eden and Molot, 'Canada's National Policies: Reflections on 125 Years,' and the comments by Tupper and McFetridge.

54 The CCPA has often adopted provocative titles for its monographs, as in *Tory Wreckord, 1984–1993: Thirty-Six Ways the Tories Have Hurt Canadians.*

55 These remarks refer, in particular, to the following works: Chorney, *The Deficit and Debt Management*; Chorney et al., *The Deficit Made Me Do It!*; and Bienefeld et al., *'Bleeding the Patient': The Debt/Deficit Hoax Exposed.*

56 In her 'A More Democratic Canada?' Phillips repeatedly comes back to the theme of the 1990s being the decade when the question of how to enhance democratic governance has moved to the top of the political agenda in Canada.

57 The list of relevant publications includes more than half a dozen titles, which makes it too long to cite here. See also numerous recent articles in the IRPP's magazine *Policy Options*, including Seidle, 'The Angry Citizenry' (Mr Seidle heads the IRPP's governance project).

58 E.g., Ross and Usher, *From the Roots Up*, and Robichaud and Quiviger, *Active Communities.*

59 Canadian Council on Social Development, *Social Policy in the 1990s: The Challenge.*

60 Cairns and Williams, eds., *Constitutionalism, Citizenship and Society in Canada*; *The Politics of Gender, Ethnicity and Language in Canada*; and Johnston, *Public Opinion and Public Policy in Canada: Question of Confidence.*

61 In addition to the four-volume report, the commission produced twenty-three
    research volumes, including several on what could be described as new
    dimensions of democratic theory; for example, the representation of women,
    access by visible minorities to the political system, electoral reform, and
    Canada's aboriginal population.
62 There are exceptions, of course; for example, Taylor, 'Alternative Futures,'
    and Kymlicka, 'Group Representation in Canadian Politics.'
63 The following title gives an idea of the rhetorical fervour characteristic of
    many CCPA reports: Robinson, *North American Trade As If Democracy
    Mattered.*
64 E.g., Leah, *Taking a Stand: Strategy and Tactics of Organizing the Popular
    Movement in Canada.*
65 See Walker, ed., *Freedom, Democracy and Economic Welfare*; Block, ed.,
    Economic Freedom: Toward a Theory of Measurement; and Easton and
    Walker, eds., *Rating Global Economic Freedom.*
66 E.g., Anderson, ed., *NAFTA and the Environment;* Block, ed., *Economics and
    the Environment;* Doern, ed., *The Environmental Imperative*; Royal Commis-
    sion on the Economic Union and Development Prospects for Canada, *Report,*
    Part IV; Davidson and Dence, eds., *The Brundtland Challenge and the Cost of
    Inaction.*
67 See McCormick, et al., *Regional Representation: The Canadian Partnership.*
    The Canada West Foundation publishes numerous short position papers and
    brief statements, which cannot be cited here.
68 Indeed, the C.D. Howe Institute has revisited these issues on several occa-
    sions, and each time in great detail. At the beginning of the 1990s the
    institute launched *The Canada Round* series of monographs and has since
    published a number of occasional papers; e.g., Monahan, 'Cooler Heads Shall
    Prevail: Assessing the Costs and Consequences of Quebec Separation.'
69 The IRPP has recently revived the controversial notion of asymmetrical
    federalism; see Seidle, ed., *Seeking a New Partnership.*
70 Namely, the Atlantic Provinces Economic Council, the Canada West Founda-
    tion, the C.D. Howe Institute, the Institute for Research on Public Policy, and
    the Niagara Institute.
71 In the 1980s the Fraser Institute also had a unique interest in the moral,
    philosophical and economic issues that emerge when religious beliefs are
    confronted with economic realities. The proceedings of two conferences on
    these topics were published.
72 Lipsey and Smith, *Taking the Initiative,* 29. Continuing in this line Lipsey has
    in recent years overseen a major research project on economic growth,

technological innovation, and the structural adaptations of advanced economies for the Canadian Institute for Advanced Research.

73 See Hartle, *The Federal Deficit.*

74 For a sample of representative papers, see West, *Education and Competitiveness,* and *Higher Education and Competitiveness*; Anderson, *Natural Resources and Economic Performance*; Bernard, *Hydroelectricity, Royalties and
Industrial Competitiveness*; Dewees, *Reducing the Burden of Environmental
Regulation.*

75 The British Columbia Commission on Resources and the Environment
(CORE) is a relevant example; it completed its work in 1994 after conducting
an extensive process of consultations out of which a consensus was supposed
to emerge, with the active help of the commissioner (Stephen Owen) acting as
a sort of facilitator and final rapporteur. The end result, however, fell short of
these expectations.

8

Public Administration: A Profession Looking For a Home

DONALD J. SAVOIE

A good number of observers have suggested lately that the public service – in particular, the federal public service – has lost its way. Even its most ardent supporters, including its own recent leaders, believe that the institution needs an overhaul. Gérard Veilleux, former secretary to the Treasury Board, reports that public servants generally 'are losing [their] sense of pride in what [they], as an institution, do.'[1] This, despite numerous attempts in recent years to modernize the Canadian public service.[2] Looking back, it seems that those reform measures that met with some success have scarcely left a trace, while those that are seen to have failed are judged to have produced serious negative side effects.[3] Little wonder then that surveys invariably point to a serious morale problem in the federal public service.[4]

If the Canadian public service has lost the way, one should also ask if the public administration academic community can be far behind. Many practitioners and students of government argue that there ought to be closer ties between the two bodies, although organizations such as the Institute of Public Administration of Canada have successfully promoted such close cooperation for years. As well, many students of government routinely serve on various government advisory groups or as consultants. The point is that the public administration academic community has many opportunities to remain in close contact with the federal public service and to be familiar with its challenges.

Both practitioners and students are aware that the powerful forces now at play shaping the role and work of government are also redefining the role and responsibilities of the federal public service. For the academic, the challenge is to understand the nature and cause of these new forces and to prepare students to become the public servants of tomorrow. Practitioners, meanwhile, are faced with never-ending calls to 'reinvent government' or to 'get government right.' This suggests their past efforts were not up to par and that a new world needs to take shape. Thus they are searching for new ideas and experimenting with various new approaches to overhaul or 'fix' their institution.

The purpose of this chapter is to examine the forces challenging the federal public service and to consider the response of practitioners and the public administration community on university campuses to them. It also looks at some of the events that have shaped current developments, reviews the state of the public administration discipline, and identifies issues and ideas requiring further research.

Catching the Wave

As every student of government knows, the Keynesian revolution captured the Canadian Department of Finance and the federal Treasury, as it did elsewhere. Canadians emerged from the war determined never to permit another depression of the kind witnessed in the 1930s. By war's end, the public's belief in the ability of government to intervene and to manage the economy was high.[5] Large latent demand and rapid population increase, combined with the realization that Ottawa's management of the war effort had been successful, gave governments *carte blanche* to expand. Canadians had learned during the war that governments were able, in moments of crisis, and when moved by an all-consuming goal, to lead the country to high levels of economic activity and employment.[6] Not only did the Allies win the war, but the government had run the war economy well. Unemployment had fallen to zero, and yet prices had been held down. Growth of productivity and real GNP was accelerated, inequalities among social groups diminished, civilian consumption actually increased, there were no balance of payment crises, and foreign exchange rates remained stable. Governments (in particular, the federal government) were now convinced that they possessed a new arsenal of economic policy to achieve high employment and generally to manage the economy.[7]

From the 1950s to the 1980s the federal government did not hesitate to intervene to attenuate the lows in economic cycles and to soften the sting of economic misfortune. During those years, it expanded on all cylinders, and there were very few naysayers. In any event, those few were dismissed in public policy debates as 'reactionaries,' and their influence was hardly felt in government.

The same was also true in many other Western countries. Indeed, in the United States, President Roosevelt declared war on the depression, made the

'New Deal' his battle cry, and embarked on a flurry of activities in his first few hundred days in office. Within two years, Roosevelt had established some sixty new agencies and added 100,000 positions to the public service.[8]

In Britain, William Beveridge produced a report for Churchill's wartime coalition cabinet. *Full Employment in a Free Society* made the case that public policy should have full employment as one of its overriding objectives.[9] Working with a very small staff, Beveridge produced 'one of the greatest and most revolutionary documents in our social history.'[10] The report was 'seized on' in Parliament and Beveridge became a 'national figure, in some way the harbinger of the kind of postwar world people hoped to see. Public opinion, if nothing else, forced the adoption of his report by Parliament.'[11] Earlier, the Royal Commission on the Distribution of Industry and Population (the Barlow Commission) had argued in its final report tabled in 1940 that 'national action' was needed to deal with unemployment and the location of industrial activities.[12] Though the problem of unemployment was at least temporarily resolved through rearmament, the Beveridge and the Barlow reports provided the design for the postwar British welfare state. Archbishop William Temple promoted with considerable success the concept of the 'welfare state,' in contrast to Hitler's 'warfare state.' Being a direct participant in the Keynesian revolution was every bit as exciting for young university graduates as had been being part of the war effort. Later, during the Thatcher years, when the British civil service went through a deep period of self-doubt, its most senior officials would contrast the malaise with the 'self-confidence of those golden postwar years.'[13]

Canada also produced its own landmark reports detailing a new and far more interventionist role for government. The Canadian government presented a major policy paper to Parliament toward the end of World War II that was clearly Keynesian in outlook. It stated: 'The Government will be prepared, in periods where unemployment threatens, to incur deficits and increases in the national debt resulting from its employment and income policy.'[14]

The faith in the ability of government to intervene, and to deliver on promises did not wane in the 1960s. One needs only to think back to Pierre Trudeau's 'Just Society' and John F. Kennedy's 'New Frontier,' both of which captured the minds and imagination of a new generation of university graduates. If the goal was to put a man on the moon, then government was asked to do the job. If the goal was to create economic opportunities where none existed, then government would design ways to create them. If past slights toward groups of people or regions had to be rectified, then government was the institution called upon to fix the problem. It was a time when a government could declare war on poverty and most of its citizens believed that it could actually win the war. As a result, the positive state grew and grew. If we discovered that problems were not being solved, we came back with new, more expensive solutions. The mindset was: if all the king's horses and all the king's men could not put Humpty Dumpty together, then bring in more horses and more men.

Leaving aside the war years, university graduates joined the federal public service in record numbers in the 1960s and early 1970s. In Canada, they came to build the Just Society and confidently joined newly established departments such as the Department of Regional Economic Expansion (DREE) or the expanded Secretary of State. The Government Organization Act of 1969, while including provisions for merging some departments, also established a number of new departments and councils. These included the creation of the departments of Fisheries and Forestry, Communications, Regional Economic Expansion, Industry, Trade and Commerce, Supply and Services, and the establishment of the National Council of Welfare.[15]

University graduates were eager to join an institution with a proud history, strong traditions, and a willingness to embrace and stick by basic principles. They learned by watching how the 'elders' went about their work. Leaders such as Arnold Heeney, Bob Bryce, and Gordon Robertson, among a handful of others, were their role models.[16] They were discreet, shunned the limelight, avoided public controversy, handled delicate issues with dexterity and loyalty, and learned how to work well with their political masters. They could appear before standing committees of Parliament and know when to draw the line between what they could say and what they could not. They knew intuitively what were matters of 'policy' and what were matters of 'administration.' Though the Liberals held power before World War II, during the war years, and for twelve years after the war, the great mandarins also knew how to keep their distance from partisan politics. When the Progressive Conservative Party came to power under John Diefenbaker, they showed that they could transport their loyalty to different political leaders. When the time came to open their ranks to different groups, they responded much better than did the private sector. French Canadians, and later women, were invited to join the senior ranks of the public service sooner and in far greater numbers than they were by even the largest private firms in Canada.

New employees soon learned, if they did not know already, that there were a number of things specific to the public service as an institution. These could be traced back to the writings of Max Weber, the German sociologist, who sought to define in specific terms how the bureaucratic organization should function. The career of a public servant should be regarded more as a vocation than a job. Employment was secure and remuneration was in the form of a fixed salary with a right to a pension. Only under extraordinary circumstances could the employer terminate the appointment. In return, public servants would see their work entirely separated from ownership of the means of administration. Their position was treated as the sole, or at least the primary, occupation of the incumbent. Their work was subject to systematic discipline and control. Promotion was based on seniority, achievement, or both, and would depend on the judgment of superiors. Finally, each office had a clearly defined sphere of competence and they were organized in a clearly defined hierarchy of offices.[17]

The academic community, meanwhile, had long taken an interest in public administration and in the evolution of the Canadian public service. As already noted, the Institute of Public Administration of Canada played – and continues to play – an important role in promoting relations between practitioners and academics and undertakes research in public administration. It publishes the journal *Canadian Public Administration*, in which the great majority of articles are written by academics, and it sponsors a case study program.[18] The institute also publishes a monograph series and a book series, which is also entitled *Canadian Public Administration*.

Much as in the United States, it was the departments of politics or political science at Canadian universities that first defined public administration as a field of study and research.[19] Queen's, Dalhousie, and Carleton universities all went on to develop a school or a graduate program, or both, in public administration. Other universities, including Victoria, the University of Ottawa, and l'Université de Moncton, have also put in place important graduate programs in public administration. In Quebec, the provincial government earmarked special resources to develop the *École nationale d'administration publique*. The school offers a graduate program in public administration and caters to junior and middle level public servants from Quebec and elsewhere wishing to upgrade their skills and gain new knowledge in the theories and practice of public administration. All in all, there are an estimated thirty-six schools and programs in public administration in Canada.

These programs, at least initially, built on the work of a handful of senior scholars. Some of them looked at the legal framework for the operation of government while others recorded the institutional memories of important public sector organizations. Scholars such as R. MacGregor Dawson, J.A. Corry, and Ted Hodgetts come to mind. Professor Hodgetts, for example, wrote a number of influential books and articles on public administration, some of which traced the evolution of key public service institutions in Canada.[20]

Political scientists also dominated the early years of the public administration discipline in Canada as new programs and schools were born. In the late 1960s, Kenneth Kernaghan concluded that the field required 'new approaches to the study and teaching of public administration and the need for contributions from fields other than political science.'[21] In time, Kernaghan would get his wish, or at least half of it. Though thirty years ago public administration was a subfield of political science with some interdisciplinary overtones, it is now an independent field that draws not just on political science but also on economics and law, among other disciplines.

The public administration field caught the wave generated by the growth of the positive state. Governments turned to public administration programs to recruit young university graduates. On campus, interdisciplinary programs became the fashion, in part because university presidents, perched as they are on top of competing and independent programs fighting for a greater share of the pie, readily see the value of cooperation. In addition, the marketplace – in this case governments – was sending out strong messages that they wanted well-rounded university graduates with a number of skills enabling them to work in administration in a post-Glassco world and in various policy fields.[22] This encouraged the universities to place greater emphasis on interdisciplinary programs. All in all, 'university presidents, funding agencies and leading government officials extol interdisciplinarity,' and few other areas offered more promise in this direction than public administration.[23]

Have Process, Will Travel

In Ottawa's post-Glassco world, a great deal of effort was expended on tearing down administrative shackles in order to let the 'manager manage.' Established ways of doing things were no longer appropriate if only because they prevented administrators from being innovative and from actually getting their jobs done. The existence of far too many centrally prescribed rules and regulations was considered cumbersome.

In future, public sector administrators, much like private sector managers, would enjoy greater freedom to plan, to spend, and to manage. For example, there would no longer be a Treasury official looking over their shoulders to decide if they could purchase an electric typewriter or go on a trip. Accordingly, it became not only a great deal easier for managers to get things done but also to get what they wanted in terms of administrative support. Glassco and other reformers in the 1960s did not see this as a possible risk, arguing that officials would now be held accountable for their actions because their programs and their own performance would be evaluated.

In many ways, however, the administration side of government lost its lustre, if not before, then certainly in the post-Glassco era. Administration, finance, and personnel functions were turned over to people who were seen by the mandarins as not being able to make it to the top levels.[24] The road to the top of the federal public service was far easier for the policy specialist. John Meisel explains: 'They are less specialists in the substance of any one area than experts in the general art of policy analysis and in the folkways of bureaucracy. They are ever ready to exclaim – Have tools! Will travel. [They] have become less oriented to certain policy areas and more concerned with their own advancement in the invitingly open and evermore rewarding hierarchy of the government priesthood.'[25] In getting to the top, the policy specialists rarely stayed in one position for longer than two years. By and large, the ambitious public servant was eager to come up with proposed solutions and initiatives, not least because this is what brought greater career rewards. However, there was considerably less visibility, less prestige, and consequently, fewer opportunities for advancement for those left behind to implement the initiatives.[26]

In time, the university programs and schools in public administration would also focus more on policy than on administration. Even the Glassco findings did not encourage the programs to focus on administration or management or to strike new alliances with business and management schools.

There are a number of reasons for this. As already noted, the public administration discipline was created by slicing off sympathetic parts of established disciplines – initially political science and later economics – and then gluing the slices together. Business or management programs meanwhile were rarely invited to participate in shaping the new discipline. David M. Cameron points out that 'explanations of the isolation of the two [i.e., public and business administration or management] are not difficult to find. Business administration achieved institutional maturity before its public cousin, and efforts to organize programs in public administration were frequently opposed by faculties of business who either saw the field as theirs or in competition with theirs. The opposition and the resentment it engendered, still lingers. One should also recognize that our business and management schools sought important financial support from the private sector and it might have been more strategically wise to adopt an anti-government posture than be seen pursuing public sector management issues.'[27]

In any event, the issue in the public administration programs is not – nor has it ever been – to strike a proper balance between public administration and business management. Rather, the issue is one of striking a proper balance between research and study in public policy and public administration.

I argue that insufficient attention is being paid in the various programs to political and administrative accountability, to ethics and values in government relations between permanent officials and Parliament, to the relations between public servants and citizens, and to issues of efficiency and effectiveness in government organizations. There are, of course, some exceptions that serve to prove the rule. Professors Peter Aucoin, Sharon L. Sutherland, Paul Thomas, and Kenneth Kernaghan have continued to produce important studies in the public administration field.[28]

When political scientists and economists came together to develop public administration programs, the only common ground linking the two groups was public policy. Economists, for example, could hardly be expected to become interested in studying the finer points of accountability in a parliamentary system. They could, however, easily become interested in a specific policy field. At the risk of overgeneralization, schools and programs in public administration both emphasized policy studies, with economists doing essentially econometrics within specific policy areas and political scientists doing basically descriptive policy studies.

Governments also sent out signals that policy was more important than administration and, indeed, sponsored the establishment of new policy institutes, including the Institute for Research on Public Policy (IRPP) and a variety of policy research centres on university campuses. In addition, government departments were always on the lookout, with contracts in hand, for reputable academics in return for research, advice, or a detached perspective on specific policy issues. If 'have process, will travel' was the way ahead for officials, then 'have policy advice or policy research' proved very profitable for academics.

Administration thus became policy's poor cousin, relegated to less gifted bureaucrats. Policy and advice to ministers, together with the never-ending need to manage actual or potential political crises, ruled the day. In any case, few inside government believed that outsiders, including scholars in public administration, could ever provide timely advice on administrative issues, such as accountability, relations between politicians and permanent officials and between officials and the Canadian public. They were convinced that first-hand experience of the workings of government was necessary before one could offer prescriptions.

The lure of policy work has had an impact on both academics and practitioners. Slowly but surely a number of the schools and programs in public administration were transformed into schools and programs in public policy. Queen's University, for example, recently turned its master program in public administration into a graduate degree in public policy. Carleton's School of Public Administration launched a PhD program in public policy, not in public administration. The school also lost two of its leading scholars of public administration to the political science department. One observer explains that the school has for some years 'experienced interdisciplinary and ideological difficulties.'[29] The future of Dalhousie University's on-again, off-again public administration program remains uncertain.

Practitioners, meanwhile, saw public confidence in their institution begin to wane in the 1970s. By the 1980s 'bureaucrat bashing' had become one of Canada's favourite sports, as in many other countries.[30] Governments, it seemed, could never get it right anymore. Politicians, the very people public servants were being asked to serve and advise, were some of the first to voice their criticism: Prime Minister Mulroney declared his intention to give 'pink slips and running shoes to public servants'; President Reagan said that he had come to Washington to 'drain the swamp'; and Prime Minister Thatcher let it be known that she disliked senior British officials as a 'breed.'[31]

Many politicians and a good number of observers began to argue that it was administration or management that now needed fixing, not policy. Policy was simple enough, they insisted, because politicians knew exactly what was required on virtually every policy front – less government intervention.[32]

Disillusionment Sets In

Government and budgetary reforms introduced in the 1960s and 1970s were designed to modernize government policy and decision making, to accommodate new demands for public service, and to administer an ever-growing number of programs. In short, the reforms were never designed to attack big government at its roots but rather to equip big government with the necessary tools to meet expectations.

A key component of the reform was a shift to performance-based budgetary systems. In Canada, a new Planning, Programming, Budgeting System (PPBS) took government at both levels by storm.[33] The new system, as is well known, concentrated on objectives to be achieved rather than on the means of achieving them. It purported to promote the benefits of alternative programs, provide a capacity to ascertain the costs in future programs and spending proposals, and evaluate the effectiveness of ongoing programs. Politicians would no longer be asked to make decisions on administrative details but could concentrate on key policy and program issues. There is no doubt that supporters of the positive state felt that they had discovered an extremely powerful tool to assist them in managing an increasing role for government in society. Some even believed that the new system was so powerful that it would actually remove politics from the budgetary process – it would provide such clear and rational answers that ministers would be compelled to embrace them. Al Johnson, then secretary of the Treasury Board, felt the need to reassure politicians that politics would still weigh heavily in the decision-making process. He wrote, for example, that 'PPBS must not seek to substitute science for politics in the decision-making process.'[34]

By the mid-1970s, however, PPBS was pronounced dead in both Canada and the United States. Aaron Wildavsky admitted that he had 'not been able to find a single example of successful implementation of PPBS ... PPBS deserved to die because it is an irrational mode of analysis that leads to suppression rather than correction of error.'[35] In Canada two students of government concluded that 'if anyone did a cost-benefit analysis on the introduction of PPBS, he would be forced to conclude that it was not worth the effort.'[36]

The federal government has since introduced yet more expenditure management systems and decision-making processes, but with very limited success. New cabinet committees have been established, abolished, and established again. A new Policy and Expenditure Management System (PEMS) was tried, but like PPBS it too died, and by all accounts it also deserved to die.[37]

While the government was still trying to implement Glassco and PPBS, the auditor general shocked the nation when he wrote: 'Parliament – and indeed the government – has lost or is close to losing effective control of the public purse.'[38] Quite a few critics blamed Glassco, insisting that the commission tried to import private sector management techniques to government where, given the various constraints, they had no chance to take root and have a positive impact.[39]

The federal public service has been scrambling ever since, trying this and that to fix their institution. Reform measures have been introduced one after another in recent years, ranging from the Increased Ministerial Authority and Accountability (circa 1986), Make or Buy policy (circa 1987), Special Operating Agencies (circa 1989), Public Service 2000 (circa 1990), Shared Management Agenda (circa 1991), Restructuring of Government Operations (circa 1994), and Program Review (circa 1995). However, as noted earlier, those reform measures that have met with some success have hardly left a trace, while those that are seen to have failed are judged to have produced serious negative side effects.

To make matters worse, the federal public service has had to come to terms with the fact that it now has few very friends outside its own ranks. A royal commission on Canada's economic future warned in 1985 that 'the reach of the state has in many ways outrun both our administrative and technical capacities, and our capacity to ensure democratic accountability.'[40] It is interesting to note that the commission identified problems relating to administrative, technical, and accountability issues but not to the government's 'policy process.' Canadians generally also turned sour, telling public opinion surveys throughout the 1980s that 'they had less confidence in the public service than in any other institution, save for the trade union movement, politicians, and more recently the tobacco industry.'[41]

Worse still, traditional allies of the public service began to attack the institution. In Canada, left of centre politicians Flora MacDonald and Lloyd Axworthy went public with their criticism and wrote about their disenchantment with the quality of the public service, both arguing that it was no longer responsive to the wishes of its elected masters.[42] John Kenneth Galbraith, himself a leading proponent of a greater role for government in society, observed that bureaucracy had given government a bad reputation.[43]

In less than fifty years, then, the public service world was turned upside down. An institution that once enjoyed widespread support, that was regarded as capable of achieving ambitious public goals, lost the confidence of the politicians it advised and, if public opinion surveys are to be believed, the people it served. If at the end of World War II the public service was viewed as part of the solution in building a modern Canada, fifty years later it became part of the problem. Calls for change, for new approaches, were being heard everywhere. Bureaucracy itself was now regarded as an important barrier against, rather than a vehicle for, progressive change. Those few who argued against tampering with the machinery of government were this time dismissed by both the political left and right as reactionaries.

Management Consultants: Modern-Day Witch-Doctors

It is hardly possible to overstate the kind of pressure coming from all sides to 'fix' the public service. We have already listed above the various reform measures recently introduced, and there is no need to discuss them in detail. In any event, this has already been done elsewhere.[44]

There appears to be widespread agreement in the Anglo-American democracies that the way ahead for government operations is to turn to the business management model for inspiration and guidance. At the risk of overgeneralization, the underlying theme is: What can be privatized or contracted out should be, and what is left should be run much like a private business. The new public management vocabulary has a number of telling words and phrases, including 'empowerment,' 'service to clients,' 'debureaucratize,' and 'individual motivation.' The new public management also encourages, whenever possible, the establishment of external and internal markets. Again, the call has gone out to 'let the manager manage.' That the very same call was made in the 1960s by Glassco appears to have been lost on the reformers.

Some students of government argue that the new public management reform movement has strong ideological overtones. Christopher Pollitt, for example, states that 'managerialism needs to be understood as an ideology.'[45] The movement also has a more mundane side – it recognizes the need to deal with the serious fiscal problems that have confronted most governments since the early 1980s. Indeed, privatization and the selling of government assets have had as much to do with the need to raise cash as with ideology. Selling government assets also gained in importance when it became clear that, notwithstanding their rhetoric, right of centre politicians, including Mulroney and most of his senior ministers, proved reluctant to cut programs or the level of services.

Fiscal problems also gave a sense of urgency to the need to 'fix' government operations. Who better to provide a quick 'fix' than management consultants? 'Have contract, will travel' to peddle the latest management fashion and fad to government. T.J. Peters and R.H. Waterman's book *In Search of Excellence* was 'highly influential' in government circles in the mid-1980s. They argued that the old command and control structures (read Weberian organizations) were no longer appropriate and that they should be replaced by a flatter and more entrepreneurial management regime. Hardly an original call – see the Hoover Commission in the United States, Glassco in Canada, and Fulton in Britain. It also did not seem to matter a great deal that the book was based mainly on the experience of private firms or that it was criticized for selective use of anecdotal evidence, exaggeration, and simplification.[46]

By the late 1980s, however, the book fell out of fashion. It was not long before another co-authored book became the new flavour of the month, providing plenty of fodder for management consultants out to fix government. In their book *Reinventing Government*, David Osborne and Ted Gaebler argued that what was needed were new government structures that are 'mission rather than rule-driven,' 'decentralized,' and 'entrepreneurial.'[47] Again, it did not seem to matter that the Osborne and Gaebler prescriptions were not new or that they virtually ignored the requirements of democratic accountability in government operations. Every government department and agency in Ottawa set out to define a vision and to look at their customers as 'clients.' The rush to put customers first ignores a number of thorny issues all too familiar to students of public administration. Clients are, of course, more demanding than citizens, less deferential. Clients also tend to take the view that financial resources go from individuals to the state, or in some instances, from the state to individuals, and back to the state: that goods are consumed in a competitive environment with the competition being between the public and private sectors. In short, while citizens can have common purposes, clients are sovereign.

Many practitioners meanwhile are left wondering just who their 'real' clients are, confused about their mission and even their legitimacy. Prison officers can only wonder if 'their' clients are the prisoners or Canadians outside the prison walls; immigration officials are uncertain if 'their' clients are people in Asia or elsewhere trying to gain entry into the country or existing Canadian citizens; and central agency officials are never certain if 'their' clients are line departments, the cabinet, cabinet committees, or other central agencies. The list goes on.

The great majority of students of public administration have dismissed the Osborne and Gaebler prescriptions, arguing that, like Peters and Waterman, they too would soon be out of favour and fully discredited. Rather than dealing with fundamental issues, the book simply employs a value-laden lexicon: the concepts of reinventing, re-engineering, and empowering are used to 'maximize the emotive content of what otherwise has largely been a nonemotive subject matter.'[48] In short, Osborne and Gaebler rely on 'old time religion to sell their message.' However, 'as with other types of evangelical messages the authors expect readers to take a leap of faith and act out the vision they describe.'[49]

Therein lies the rub for the public administration discipline, which is now on the outside looking in as management consultants, one by one, come in to sell their snake oil. Thirty years ago, when the field was still a subdiscipline of political science, the study and practice were 'nearly identical.' James Q. Wilson writes that 'scholars studied government agencies in order to understand and improve them; public executives turned to scholars to get advice and help. A reformist impulse based on shared assumptions about the value of public service animated scholar and practitioner alike ... Today, study and practice have increasingly gone their separate ways.'[50] Little wonder then that not one distinguished academic was involved in drafting the high-profile report in the United States entitled 'Creating a Government That Works Better and Costs Less: Report of the National Performance Review.' Some management consultants and a number of practitioners worked on it. And David Osborne wrote much of the summary report. In Canada, the federal government launched in 1989 an ambitious public service reform exercise, which it labelled PS 2000. The work was carried out by practitioners and some management consultants. To my knowledge not one distinguished academic was involved in drafting the various PS 2000 reports.[51]

Schools and programs of public policy have shown very limited interest in machinery of government issues. Academics with a keen interest in public administration have largely been critical of the recent reform measures. Nevertheless, the fact is that: 'Once, the architects of these changes were drawn from political science; today the architects come from outside political science and the critics from inside it.'[52]

Much of the public administration community has been puzzled at the popularity of the new public management movement and literature. Many wonder why political leaders and even senior government officials would have embraced the literature and turned to ill-informed people for advice on rejigging the public service. Nothing could be more bizarre, since business and management consultants very rarely understand the workings of political-administrative institutions, the scaffolding of political and administrative order. In short, such people are regarded by the public administrative discipline as modern-day witch-doctors completely lost in a world of tradition, values, political accountability, collectivism, and so on.

In his recent article on the 'State of Public Administration,' R.A.W. Rhodes begins by quoting D. Waldo's phrase 'public administration suffers from so many crises of identity that normal adolescence seems idyllic.'[53] He adds that this 'intellectual crisis' is not limited to Britain: the discipline everywhere is attempting to deal with the challenge posed by the new public management. The public administration discipline has long been dominated by an institutionalist tradition concerned with accountability, relationships, political and moral responsibilities, and public service values. While practitioners appear to have shifted their interest to accommodate as best they can the new public management agenda and respond to the wishes of elected politicians, many students of public administration are not prepared to give up that easily. Jonathan Boston summed up the problems with the new public management movement in 1991 when he wrote: 'It has been challenged on the grounds that it enjoys neither a secure philosophical base nor a solid empirical foundation. It has been criticized for its constitutional illiteracy, its lack of attention to the need for probity and due process within government, its insensitivity to varying organizational cultures and its potential for reducing the capacity of governments to deal with catastrophes.'[54]

What is so wrong with the Weberian model that we are now told to cast it aside after it has served governments so well for so long? Aaron Wildavsky put forward a number of such questions when he asked: 'Can we denigrate hierarchy from which bureaucracy derives while still honouring public service? Can there be an effective bureaucracy without respect for authority? What is left for administration if its hierarchical form of organization and its search for efficiency are rejected? Why does one hear so little now about the virtues (as well as the vices) of hierarchy – stability, continuity, predictability – with enthusiasm and pride?'[55]

Others are asking why the focus for change falls so heavily on the public service and not on political institutions. If we ignore issues of accountability, which are central to the effective operation of government, they are bound to come back to haunt us. This has already started with Executive Agencies in Britain and Special Operating Agencies in Canada. How can anyone talk seriously about empowering managers and front-line government employees without putting in place measures to disempower ministers, Parliament, and even the media?

While the public administration community is on the outside looking in, government officials seek as best they can to modernize their operations. Told time and again by the private sector, the media, management consultants, and many politicians that their institution is rule bound, lethargic, expensive, and oblivious to bottom-line concerns in an era of large government deficits, they have gone about reforming their institution, while paying scant attention to university-based schools and programs in public administration.

This trend was perhaps never more obvious than when the federal government decided in the late 1980s to establish a new Management Development Centre to 'turn out top flight public sector managers and to undertake research in public sector management.'[56] The Treasury Board Secretariat looked at the possibility of turning over responsibility for both to the universities. It concluded that university-based research was both less expensive and more substantial than research carried out elsewhere. It also concluded, however, that it would not avail itself of scholarly expertise and instead chose to establish an in-house centre. The report explained that 'every school of public administration in Canada has developed expertise and specialists in virtually every field except public sector management.'[57] It also urged the government to move quickly in setting up the centre, because the public service urgently needed means to strengthen itself and to instill a strong 'corporate culture' among its members. It quoted the Public Service Commission's annual report, which had just declared that 'the sense of pride in service that was the glory of the Public Service not all that long ago is being eroded.'[58]

What the above suggests is that senior practitioners in Ottawa realized that the old order was giving way to a new world whose shape was not at all clear. What was clear was that the institution was being challenged like never before, and the Weberian model, with all its appeal, was breaking down to the point that the public service could no longer be its home. Similarly, the public administration community on university campuses essentially stayed on the sideline, with an occasional foray into the debates to denounce the new public management movement and all its shortcomings. The criticism, however, has had a very limited impact.

Looking Ahead

James Q. Wilson recently observed that 'the study of public administration, along with its practice, will have to be reinvented.'[59] While I accept that a redefinition is needed, I would not suggest that students of public administration drop their preoccupations with questions of accountability, relations between politicians and permanent officials, and public service values. But we need to go beyond rediscovering our roots or returning to the work of Corry and Hodgetts. We must now explore new territory and revisit issues that have never been fully examined. We need to ask fundamental questions about the performance of government departments and agencies and answer why some perform better than others and why some behave one way, while others behave in another.

We also need to define the attributes of a competent senior public servant and then determine how one decides if he or she is performing well. How can the competence of senior government officials be judged? Until now, it appears that the perception of success is what has counted. We have yet to design anything on which we can truly assess performance or even competence. If there is one thing that has struck me above everything else while in Ottawa observing the work of the public service, it is the inability of the system to determine with any degree of reliability and consistency who is competent and who is not. For every ten people who will approve the work of any deputy minister at any one time, I can easily find ten others who will claim that the same person ought never to have been promoted to that level. Unlike in business, sports, law, entertainment, and academe, there are no hard criteria to judge the success of the work of senior public servants. Much more often than not, the key factor behind one's joining the ranks of the deputy ministers is the kind of relationship an individual has with the clerk of the Privy Council on whose advice the prime minister relies when appointing deputy ministers. Deputy ministers may well have always been appointed in this fashion in the past, but it is no longer appropriate in an age of transparency, strong media scrutiny of government operations, and modern means of communications.

We also need to answer the question: What can government do well? The pendulum swing away from government intervention in society is about to fly past the point it should, and in the not too distant future we may well be trying to establish a new equilibrium. There *are* things government can do very well, but the rhetoric of the new right and the need to deal with serious fiscal problems are making it difficult for anyone to identify them. Is James Q. Wilson right in arguing that 'you can have big government, or you can have government that is easy to deal with ... I doubt that you can have both'?[60] We should find out.

We should also take a long hard look at our political and administrative institutions to understand how the Westminster model has evolved in recent years and how this has affected the public service. Parliamentary committees have been or are currently being considerably strengthened, and they have been of late taking certain liberties in their dealings with permanent officials. Yet it is hardly possible to overstate the fact that public administration begins and ends with political institutions, notably Parliament and cabinet.

A related issue is 'empowerment.' We know that ministers want to be fully 'empowered' on policy issues, that everyone wants to 'empower' line departments and front-line employees, that clients should be 'empowered' in shaping the delivery and quality of public service and that parliamentary committees should also be 'empowered' in shaping public policy and programs. This begs the question: Can everyone be empowered? Who is losing influence in the new order? What is happening to the long-established tradition of nonpartisan politically sensitive public servants who offer their political masters neutral advice?

We need a fundamental review of the merits of advising on policy from a sectoral or departmental perspective. The current machinery of government tends to compartmentalize such advice. It was no doubt appropriate at the turn of the century to establish vertical sectoral lines and deal with problems, say, in agriculture, transportation, and industry in relative isolation. Issues and challenges confronting nation-states, however, now increasingly cross departmental lines. If key policy issues are more and more horizontal, then the bureaucratic policy formulation and advisory structures must become horizontal as well. Public servants will have to bring a far broader and more informed perspective to bear on their work, since issues are now much more complicated and interrelated.

The new public management movement is ignoring these new challenges. Indeed, it may well be making matters worse, given its call for a decentralized and empowered machinery of government. Empowerment and hiving off of activities into new executive or special operating agencies will make it more difficult to promote coherence in government policy and action. It will also make it more difficult for the political leadership to secure the necessary information to focus on the broad picture. With the loss of 'sameness' in government departments and operations, one is left with the question: What kind of information will be necessary to gain a cross-cutting look at policy? How will one secure information in a consistent fashion, given that government bureaus are now being asked to look to clients for guidance and are being told that client satisfaction is the measure of their success?

The new public management is sending the public service, as we have known it, in retreat. The public service came to life because people respected professionalism, and disliked organized crime, corrupt politics, and monopoly capitalism.[61] The Weberian model provided the organizational structure and the capacity to insulate public servants from the general labour market. In addition, centralized rules and control were put in place to limit the discretionary power of public servants.

An important milestone in the development of the public service in Anglo-American democracies was the publication of the Northcott-Trevelyan report in 1856. The report, it will be recalled, proposed four key reforms: '1) entry into civil service should be through open competition and examination; 2) promotion should be on merit, based on proper assessments prepared by superiors; 3) a distinction should be established between intellectual and mechanical labour; and 4) measures should be put in place to unify the civil service, including a common basis of recruiting.'[62] The report urged a 'professional' and 'unified' public service because its authors had witnessed first hand what the 'barons of Whitehall,' 'patronage,' and 'incompetence' had done to the war effort in the Crimea. The public service, Northcott-Trevelyan argued, was for 'the unambitious, the indolent or incapable.'[63]

The new public management movement may not be trying to turn back the clock to the era of the unambitious, the indolent, or incapable, but it does argue for a public service that is less insulated from the private sector and for greater managerial discretion in directing staff and resources.[64] It is attacking the notion of a unified public service through the establishment of Special Operating Agencies and by empowering line departments and managers.

The basic premise that a unified civil service is not desirable and that private sector management practices are superior to those found in government suggests that the public service has no intrinsic value. It also belittles the noble side of the profession. Lest we need to be reminded, public servants became public servants because they wanted to serve their country. If they had wanted to be private sector executives, they would have joined private firms or started their own businesses. Recent developments have severely tested the loyalty of public servants to their institution.

All of the above is to say that both students of government and practitioners must begin articulating with a sense of urgency what the public service, as an institution, could look like in ten years. Urgency is needed because the public service must find its way, or a new way. The day will come when citizens will begin to see the value of a strong public service. It may well be, however, that when we look at what is left to build with, we could be in for a surprise. The institution could again have become a home for the 'unambitious, the indolent or incapable.'

We should encourage the studying of public administration from a comparative perspective. Thus far, such studies are thin on the ground. Yet, we can learn a great deal more about the impact of change – even to a specific public service – by comparing the experiences of different countries rather than focusing exclusively on one. Christopher Hood argues that 'if we are to learn how to prevent the ill-effects of over prescribing and catch-all prescriptions, we need to know more about how public administration ideas are diffused internationally.'[65]

In calling for research on new public administration issues, I again recognize the risk of overloading a discipline that already has a tendency to go off in many directions. Indeed, some may well argue that the discipline remains sufficiently burdened that it does not need yet another call to achieve immediacy and relevance to current affairs and problems.[66] That said, I argue that there is probably no task more urgent and more important for both academics and practitioners than to articulate what it is governments do well, what a national public service should look like, and how to improve the operations of government.

Notes

1 Veilleux, 'Notes for an Address to the APEX Symposium,' 5.
2 These reform measures in Ottawa include the 'Increased Ministerial Authority and Accountability (IMAA),' Shared Management Agenda, Make or Buy, Special Operation Agencies (SOAs), and Public Service 2000.
3 Peters made a similar observation in his 'Government Reorganization: A Theoretical Analysis,' 1.
4 Zussman and Jabes, *The Vertical Solitude: Managing in the Public Sector.*
5 Savoie, *The Politics of Public Spending in Canada*, 14.

6 Johnson, *Social Policy in Canada: The Past As It Conditions the Present*, 1.

7 Ibid.

8 See Gormley, *Taming the Bureaucracy: Muscles, Prayers and Other Strategies*, 9.

9 Beveridge, *Full Employment in a Free Society*.

10 Wilson, *Memoirs, 1916–1964: The Making of a Prime Minister*, 64.

11 Ibid.

12 See Parsons, *The Political Economy of British Regional Policy*.

13 Sir Ian Bancroft, quoted in Hennessy, *Whitehall*, 150.

14 Canada, Department of Reconstruction and Supply, *Employment and Income with Special Reference to the Initial Period of Reconstruction*, 21.

15 See Osbaldeston, *Organizing to Govern*, vol. 1, 26.

16 See Granatstein, *The Ottawa Men: The Civil Service Mandarins, 1935–1957*.

17 See Savoie, *Thatcher, Reagan, Mulroney: In Search of a New Bureaucracy*, 24–5.

18 See, for example, Kernaghan, 'Canadian Public Administration Programs and Prospects,' 445.

19 See Savoie, 'Studying Public Administration.'

20 Professor Hodgetts's major works include *The Pioneer Public Service* and *The Canadian Public Service: A Physiology of Government*.

21 Kernaghan, 'An Overview of Public Administration in Canada Today,' *Canadian Public Administration*, 308.

22 The findings of the Glassco Commission, which began to report in the early 1960s, are well known. The commission was strongly critical of personnel and financial management practices in the federal government. It argued 'that various administrative controls were far too cumbersome and that there was a wide variety of checks, counterchecks and duplication and blind adherence to regulations.' See Canada, *The Royal Commission on Government Organization*, vol. 1, 91.

23 Pross, 'Assessing Public Administration Education in Canada,' 622.

24 See Savoie, *Thatcher, Reagan, Mulroney*, ch. 7.

25 Meisel, 'The Reforms and the Bureaucrat,' 12.

26 Savoie, *The Politics of Public Spending in Canada*, 224.

27 Cameron, 'The Discipline and the Profession of Public Administration in an Academic's Perspective,' 502.

28 See, among others, Aucoin, 'Administrative Reform in Public Management,' and Sutherland, 'Responsible Government and Ministerial Responsibility,' 100.

29 Pross, 'Assessing Public Administration Education in Canada,' 620.

30 Savoie, *Thatcher, Reagan, Mulroney*, ch. 1.

31 Ibid.

32 Ibid., ch. 11.

33 See, for example, Adie and Thomas, *Canadian Public Administration: Problematical Perspectives*.

34 Johnson, 'PPB and Decision-Making in the Government of Canada,' *Cost and Management*, 16.

35 Wildavsky, *The Politics of the Budgetary Process*, 184.

36 Adie and Thomas, *Canadian Public Administration*, 141.

37 Savoie, *The Politics of Public Spending in Canada*.

38 Canada, *Report of the Auditor General to the House of Commons for Fiscal Year Ended 31 March 1976*, 10.

39 Mallory, in 'The Lambert Report: Central Roles and Responsibilities,' 517, wrote that 'Glassco failed to address itself to the operation of Cabinet and Parliament.'

40 Canada, Royal Commission on the Economic Union and Development Prospects for Canada, *Report*, 3: 148.

41 Quoted in Sheldon Ehrenworth, 'A Better Public Service Needs Freedom to Manage Its People,' *The Globe and Mail* (Toronto), 15 April 1989, B21.

42 See, for example, MacDonald, 'The Minister and the Mandarins,' 30.

43 John K. Galbraith quoted in *Dimension* (Winter 1986), 13.

44 See, among others, Savoie, *Thatcher, Reagan, Mulroney*.

45 Ibid.

46 See Gray and Jenkins, 'From Public Administration to Public Management,' 85.

47 Osborne and Gaebler, *Reinventing Government*.

48 Moe, 'The Reinventing Government Exercise,' 114.

49 Paul Thomas, 'Book Review,' *Public Sector Management* 3, no. 2 (1993), 27.

50 Wilson, 'Reinventing Public Administration,' 66.

51 See, among others, Kernaghan, 'Career Public Service 2000,' 551–72.

52 Ibid.

53 Rhodes et al., 'The State of Public Administration,' 14.

54 Boston, 'The Theoretical Underpinnings of Public Sector Restructuring in New Zealand,' 20.

55 Wildavsky, 'Introduction,' XIV.

56 Canada, The Canadian Centre for Management Studies, Treasury Board Secretariat, May 1988, 8.

57 Ibid., 6.

58 Ibid., 2.

59 Wilson, 'Reinventing Public Administration,' 67.

60 Ibid.

61 Hood, 'Emerging Issues in Public Administration,' 167.
62 See Savoie, *Thatcher, Reagan, Mulroney*, 45.
63 Quoted in ibid., 44–5.
64 Hood, 'Emerging Issues in Public Administration,' 168.
65 Ibid., 169.
66 I make these same points in 'Studying Public Administration,' 410.

PART THREE

Contemporary Approaches to
Canadian Policy Studies

9

Institutions and Constitutions: Public Choice in Canada

MARK SPROULE-JONES

I. Introduction

Philosophers of science disagree about the growth of scientific knowledge. They dispute the idea that scientific knowledge is cumulative and even that knowledge may be progressive. This paper enters these debates by reassessing the contributions and methodologies of the social science field of public choice. It discovers that the field is fracturing along the lines of two major epistemologies that have been associated with the field since it blossomed in the late 1960s. One part of the field has an epistemology that appears to contain a self-correcting logic, which in turn allows it to adapt and readapt to newer social concerns. The other part has an epistemology that is confined to the issues and concerns of the scholars in the field and, without random shocks, may prosper or whither only to the degree it meets scholastic approval. Perhaps the time will come when a clean break rather than a fracture will characterize the two approaches to public choice.

This paper is thus, in part, a contribution to the philosophy of social science. It is also, in part, a review of the major elements in the public choice contributions to policy studies especially in Canada. These two strands of reasoning represent an effort in the mid-1990s to update the conclusions reached in a comparable paper that was published in 1982.[1]

The paper will rely, as its starting point, on the seminal work of Lakatos[2] on the characteristics of a research program or paradigm. It will attempt to marry together the Popperian argument[3] that knowledge progresses by the logical process of refuting theoretical conjectures, with the views of more recent scholarship that knowledge is contingent on the concerns of a community, scholastic or more broadly defined.[4] It acknowledges that knowledge can as easily be regressive as well as progressive as research approaches compete for legitimacy.[5]

In its review of the basic elements of public choice theory, the paper will select major research topics in the field to illustrate its argument and conclusions. More extensive and detailed reviews can be found in a second generation of texts[6] that followed a first generation written mainly in the 1970s.[7] A wider range of literature can now be found in journals such as *Constitutional Political Economy*, *Rationality and Society* and *The Journal of Theoretical Politics*, to supplement the 'flagship' journal of *Public Choice*.

In its review of the public choice approach to policy studies in Canada, the paper will address studies that vary in the scale of their analyses, but address common issues associated with policy fields. Ten years ago it would not have been possible to include sufficient studies to warrant a separate section for a review paper. The approach is proving increasingly popular in the social sciences in Canada.

The next section of the paper reviews what Lakatos calls the 'hard core' of a research program, its basic concepts that form a network of core theoretical propositions that are not subject to dispute. The third section provides an overview of policy applications in Canada and the major methodological questions raised by these studies. The fourth section argues that the hard core of the theory, as it existed in the early 1980s, differs in the early 1990s in that one of its concepts is missing from much public choice scholarship. The fifth section develops the argument that rival epistemologies account for these two differing approaches to the hard core of the theory. In turn, in the sixth section, I argue that the epistemologies account for differing strategies toward the cumulation of knowledge. It is, I argue, a perspectivist epistemology that seems better adapted to the growth of knowledge. This is because it is driven both by the impetus of its theory for logical consistency and by the concerns of its theory to address policy situations in wider society. Much of public choice has a narrower focus on its own scholastic concerns. The final section of the paper is the conclusion and review of the arguments along with some inferences for the future agenda of policy studies in Canada.

II. The Hard Core

One useful way to synthesize public choice and to understand its research tradition is to examine its basic concepts. We call these concepts, following Lakatos,[8] the 'hard core' of the research program. The hard core comprises the basic assumptions and auxiliary hypotheses that are taken for granted by theorists and not made subject to falsification by empirical testing. Outside the hard core are the guidelines, suggestions and supplementary hypotheses that develop the empirical and analytical range of the research program. These propositions are subject to empirical testing.

It became possible, during the 1980s, to describe the hard-core concepts as consisting of (a) rules; (b) individualism; and (c) the nature of the good.[9] As we shall see in a later section, concept (c), the nature of the good, disappeared from the hard core of many public choice analyses.

Rules

Rules are, in a fundamental sense, norms of behaviour that people follow.[10] They include the constitutional and statutory laws of governments. They may consist of regulations, parliamentary conventions, or even the standard operating procedures of the modern public organization. They may also consist of 'court-made' rules, such as the common law, derived from the resolution of conflicts between persons over contractual and damage claims. And they may include the enforced agreements made with and between families, kin, social networks, and other kinds of collective groupings.

Public choice tends to focus on rules about governments, although recent scholarship on social norms and conventions has broadened its focus. For example, the persistence of cooperative strategies among communities in the face of incentives for individuals to pursue their own narrow self-interest runs contrary to early theory on citizen participation[11] and electoral behaviour.[12] Analytical theory,[13] small group experiments,[14] and field research[15] all suggest that enforced social norms can make cooperation a dominant strategy. The critical question is how to specify precisely which rules can be developed to harmonize 'micro motives and macro behaviour.'[16]

One fruitful approach to this issue is to array rules in an hierarchical or 'stacked' configuration, corresponding to the distinctions posed by the seminal work on constitutional theory, *The Calculus of Consent*.[17] Thus rules about the conduct of community affairs are termed 'operational rules,' and these are subject to change by 'institutional rules' that specify what members of the community have authority to make decisions in particular situations. 'Constitutional rules' are the 'rules about rules' in that they specify the terms and conditions for amendment or change in the institutional rules. Constitutional considerations, in this view, are central to an understanding of consensual agreements.[18] For example, economic transactions take place within rule configurations that include rules abut contracts, torts, the security of property, and other kinds of regulations.[19] Institutional rules, such as dispute settlement mechanisms, can be established by traders or by governments to enforce and revise these operational rules.[20] Recourse to constitutional rules may be available as another level of decision making.[21] Thus a 'stack' of rules that become more and more inclusive as the configuration is revealed is a basic framework for analysing public policy. Policy studies may or may not reveal all these rules; it depends on the exact focus of each study. We shall examine this feature in the third section of this paper.

Analyses of governmental rules themselves centre around two enduring questions of democratic theory. First, how can citizens' preferences be both revealed and aggregated by rules, such as voting rules, without bias or distortion? Second, how can legislatures, bureaucracies, courts, and other institutions remain accountable as agents to citizens as principals? The former question tended to dominate the first full decade of public choice analysis. Studies, largely theoretical, were made of (1) voting paradoxes and their solutions such as spatial voting, (2) majority voting rules and their consequences such as median voter strategies, and (3) the logic of exit, voice, loyalty, and revolution.[22] The second question emerged with greater force in the second full decade. A major effort was placed on understanding the logic of governmental regulations with its consequences for both rent seeking and the macroeconomic performance of nations. Building on the early work of Niskanan,[23] analyses also focused on the malperformance of governmental bureaucracies and the rules, such as legislative scrutiny, that might induce nonefficient equilibria.[24]

These studies illustrate, in part, how the hard-core concept of rules is developed in conjunction with other concepts and assumptions and leads to the research program. Rules are viewed as multiple, complex, and configurative in form and open to the strategies of individual and group actions. They thus mesh with a second hard-core concept, that of individualism.

Individualism

Public choice adopts the concept of methodological individualism in both its metaphysical and substantive meanings.[25] At the metaphysical level, individuals are taken as the ultimate constituents of the social world, whether they act independently or in concert with others. It may be methodologically wise, at times, to use group concepts such as political parties, fisheries cooperatives, or the state in analysis, but these group concepts can be disaggregated into relationships between and among individuals.

Substantively, methodological individualism simply implies that individuals have a variety of motives and act more or less consistently in the light of these motives. Of particular importance in structuring motivations and behaviours are rules. Rules create incentives for particular motives to dominate others, and for information to be revealed about the consequences of different strategies. For example, in simple repetitive situations, where the good is technically simple and easily measured and where the rules permit comparisons between goods, such as in competitive market situations, individuals are motivated by their narrow self-interest to maximize their economic gains.[26] Most decision situations are not, however, of this kind. They tend to permit a variety of behaviours, motives, and adaptations over time, and a variety of social norms may emerge to stabilize these customs. Most theory has now moved well beyond an application of the concept of individualism as homo economicus to a concept of individuals as complex, adaptive, and learning persons interacting within a variety of decision situations.[27] The utilitarian ethic has not completely disappeared, however. It remains vibrant in the law and economics literature and in what the current editor of *Public Choice* calls the 'Chicago School' of writers, which he even more curiously still associates with public choice.[28]

The Nature of the Good

Goods, services, and public policies tend to be used interchangeably in public choice analysis. They refer to assets transformed by human ingenuity from physical and human resources. They are not simple pronouncements or statements of intent from a legislature, bureaucracy, or other public organization. Each good will differ in some technical ways from other goods.

Theory about the technical attributes of goods was developed, particularly in the 1960s and 1970s, by economists from the public finance tradition. Thus Buchanan, Margolis, Olson, Tullock, and others were instrumental in helping to develop and elaborate on the attributes of public goods and externalities.

Two attributes or dimensions of goods have proved to be particularly fruitful. These are the dimensions of, first, divisibility or availability (the terms 'subtractability,' 'rivalness,' and 'joint consumability' are also sometimes used in referring to this dimension). Some goods, like a loaf of bread, are highly divisible; if one person takes an extra slice, another gets one less. Other goods, like clean air, are indivisible, for people living within an airshed; if one person takes one breath more, no other person takes one breath less.

Second, some goods possess the characteristic of excludability. It is technically easy to exclude some people from consuming a loaf of bread or cashing an old age pension cheque, whereas it is technically difficult (or costly) to exclude some people from listening to radio frequencies.

Goods that possess both characteristics perfectly are pure public goods. Common pools are the goods where exclusion is difficult and there is a great deal of divisibility. Both types attract public choice analysis because they induce, under many rule arrangements, strategic behaviour in which individual rationality deviates from collective rationality. Indeed, some analysts find the origins of the state in attempts to deal collectively with 'free riding' and 'tragedy of the commons' situations (Hardin, 1982; Mueller, 1989). Toll goods (high exclusivity and low divisibility) and private goods (high exclusivity and low divisibility) receive less theoretical attention.

Studies on externalities frequently use the Coase theorem (Coase 1960) as a point of departure. This theorem states that, under certain assumptions, bargaining between interdependent generators and recipients of technical externalities can produce a (nongovernmental) equilibrium solution. Coase assumes zero transaction costs for bargainers, and subsequent studies tend to remove this assumption for purposes of analysing strategies and outcomes in different-sized groups (e.g. Sproule-Jones and Richards, 1984).

The basic concepts of rules, individualism, and goods form the core of policy analysis. Their particular application will be now explored.

III. Applications in Canada

The exact elaboration and combination of the hard-core concepts depends on the focus of any application. Some studies deal with applications that are national or international in scale; others deal with applications that are more local or regional in character. We illustrate the applications to the Canadian political economy by focusing on the studies that deal, in turn, with the operational level of policy analysis, the collective choice or institutional level, and (thirdly) the constitutional level of analysis.

Operational Level Studies

At the operational level of analysis, studies have been at pains to emphasize how the nature of the good is a critical factor in determining the set of 'delivery' rules for the provision, production, and regulation of public policies. Thus the rules for the delivery of a 'simple' policy, such as solid waste collection in a city, will differ from the rules developed for a 'complex' policy, such as water quality management in a river basin. As a consequence, policy studies at the operational level often *seem* as if they are independent case studies, but they are theoretically linked through generalizations about their institutional (or higher level) rules. In Canada, operational level 'cases' now exist for fisheries,[29] forestry,[30] water quality management,[31] pleasure boating,[32] commercial shipping,[33] solid waste collection,[34] and fire services.[35]

Three continuing theoretical and methodological issues dominate studies at the operational level. First, many of the policies that are chosen have public good (e.g., water quality), common pool (e.g., fisheries), or externality (e.g., forestry) characteristics, and thus measurement of their outputs or value to their users is difficult to determine. Continued effort to develop valid and reliable indicators in both field settings and experimental laboratory situations is being pursued by the local public administration group at the University of Victoria and by the McMaster University Eco-Research Program.

Second, many of the policies appear to have situational differences, in that their character varies by time and by place. Consequently, some policies do not have a spatial form that is perfectly correlated with Canada, a province, or a local government. The policies may differ, in other words, in some respects for some parts of Canada to the rest. The technical attributes of water quality management for the Fraser River estuary will thus differ from the attributes of a fresh water harbour like that of Hamilton.[36] One needs a 'bottom-up' methodology of discovering the rules for each situational manifestation of the policy rather than a 'top downward' specification of the rules from a particular level and type of government. For example, the federal Fisheries Act is a major pollution control law for coastal British Columbia, but it is not used by the federal government in Ontario, having been delegated to the Province in 1884.

Third, a continuing dilemma exists about the operational status of many of the delivery rules of government. Many rules are simply rules-in-form that are not enforced or invoked in 'the real world.' Those that count may be called rules-in-use. For example, many fishers develop their own community-based regulations for apportioning fishing efforts that acquire over time the status of property rights. These regulations may well be enforced by the community, unlike regulations of the Canadian government enforced inconsistently by professional fisheries officers.[37] A challenge confronts all scholars to discover the rules-in-use, rather than the 'paper' rules or rules-in-form that can dominate legislative and administrative proceedings.

Institutional Level Studies

Studies at the institutional level tend to be dominated by the 'choice of instrument' form of analysis, which evaluates different institutional arrangements from an efficiency perspective.[38] We thus have policy studies dealing with contracting out of services,[39] privatization,[40] crown corporations,[41] special boards,[42] and user fees.[43] These studies complement much of the public administration literature.[44]

Broader studies that embrace both provision or 'demand side' considerations and production or 'supply side' considerations include studies of co-management of fisheries,[45] of Indian bands,[46] of British Columbia local government,[47] and of federal and provincial decision making.[48] The studies of Réjean Landry at Laval are detailed in a subsequent chapter. Some theoretical models[49] still await empirical testing.

There are two methodological issues in institutional level studies in Canada. The first concerns the status of co-management of common law rights and of Indian bands. Co-management of resources by government and by local communities can be understood as a partnership or as a discretionary procedure of government that is embedded in a higher-level constitutional rule for the state. Co-management can be treated as both an institutional level problem or a constitutional level problem. The same can be said of Indian or aboriginal people's decision situations. Occasionally, common law rights can take on the same character, as when the Supreme Court uses a common law principle to determine management rights held concurrently by federal and provincial governments. Thus the common law of 'navigable servitude' is used to grant priority to shipping in navigable waters over other water uses falling under federal and provincial jurisdictions.[50]

Second, a major issue concerns the importance of institutional rules in determining policy outcomes. While the rules can determine the basic logic of public policy, other considerations can also be considered important. The methodological issue concerns the relative importance that one should place on these other considerations. Should one treat conventions, for example, in the same way one treats rules-in-use, or do they have a different conceptualization associated with the temporal contingencies of group solidarity? This methodological question is shared by much political science.[51]

Constitutional Choice

Constitutional level studies based on the hard core of public choice concepts parallel and contribute to the plethora of Canadian analyses generated since the Victoria Constitutional Conference of 1971. Four theoretical models may be distinguished in the literature. First, Breton's model of competitive federalism attempts to explain and justify the rivalry of two levels of government competing in the same jurisdiction.[52] Second, Sproule-Jones's model of exclusive groups (or clubs) attempts to explain the basic logic of (parliamentary) executive federalism that simultaneously exhibits characteristics of competition and collusion.[53] Third, Sabetti contributed to the literature on federalism as a covenant by developing the basis of the Anglo-French compact in Canada.[54] Finally, Sharman argues, in a comparative context, that constitutional rules in Canada are muddled and frequently in conflict.[55] Beyond these few models, public choice leans extensively on political science research in Canada and abroad.

Two major methodological issues persist. First, partly in response to the limited government movement of the 1980s in many Western countries, public choice theorists attempted to gauge the size of the Canadian public sector.[56] This exercise proved to be fraught with difficulties, not least because of the extent of co-production and co-management of services by communities with government agencies as well as by the persistence of systems of community self-help.

Second, the development of an understanding of community-based co-management for natural resources plus the empirical studies of large-scale phenomena that transcend national boundaries[57] suggested that multiple and rival constitutions could coexist in any nation-state such as Canada. In turn, this phenomenon raises issues about the primacy of state law that some historians felt was settled after the Reformation.[58]

These applications in the Canadian context are designed to illustrate the range and ubiquity of the public choice approach to policy studies. However, the approach as a whole began to undergo some fundamental changes in the 1980s. To these we now turn.

IV. Changes to the Hard Core

By 1982 it was possible to write that the hard core consisted of three concepts, all of which were elaborated upon and combined to form sets of analytically connected propositions. Public choice fitted the research program model advanced by Lakatos. By the end of the 1980s, composition of the hard core was subject to dispute.

Buchanan, for example, summarizes his position in a 1990 essay as follows:

Constitutional political economy is a research program that directs inquiry to the working properties of rules and institutions within which individuals interact, and the processes through which these rules and institutions are chosen or come into being. The emphasis on the choice of constraints distinguishes this research program from conventional economics, while the emphasis on cooperative rather than conflictual interaction distinguishes the program from much of conventional political science. Methodological individualism and rational choice may be identified as elements in the hard core of the research program.[59]

In other words, what we call individualism is part of what Buchanan sees as the hard core along with the rules of the games. He is silent on the status of the nature of the good. Lane, as a second example, in a recent text on public policy and management, similarly characterizes the public choice hard core as consisting of individualism and the application of economic reasoning to the public sector.[60] He also disassociates public choice from policy analysis.

As a second kind of example of the proposition that the nature of the good is no longer considered to be a hard-core concept in public choice, consider the recently published set of six volumes assembled by Charles Rowley, editor of *Public Choice*. His selection of the leading 158 articles in the field[61] includes only ten that offer some empirical work based on policy concerns.[62]

There are two consequences of the elimination of the nature of the good from the hard core. First, there is an implication that the rules that fit the empirical world for one good are transferable to the empirical world for any other good. Second, there is an implication that the manifestation of a good at a particular time and in a particular place does not alter the character of goods. Each will be discussed.

The implication of the generality of rules across policy fields belies the character of goods as consisting, at least in part, of nonhuman resources. Take, for instance, the previously mentioned Coase theorem,[63] which states that, under certain assumptions, bargaining between recipient and generator of an externality can lead to an optimal equilibrium (where the value of the marginal damages of an externality to the recipient equals the value of its marginal benefits to the generators). The theorem includes, under its scope, the cases where the damages (or benefits) of an externality can be estimated and also where the damages (or benefits) form a continuous function. The policy case of water pollution illustrates the difficulty of generalizing the theorem. For example, a class of pollutants that create a biological oxygen demand can in most ambient water conditions fit the requirements of (relatively easy) estimation and continuous damage functions. Other pollutants do not fit. Persistent organics that may have toxic effects on biological organisms have different kinds of damages for different species (including humans through food chain mechanisms) and seem to have noncontinuous sublethal and lethal effects. The result is that the rules specified in the Coase theorem have limited applicability across pollution types. In other words, there are policy cases where rules will fit and others where they will not fit. In any river basin or estuary or harbour, for example, different rules embodied in common, statutory, and constitutional laws are fashioned to deal with different kinds of policy externalities.[64]

Once goods or policies are introduced into public choice propositions, then the possible variation in these goods by time and/or place must be potentially considered. Public choice analyses that delete goods from their hardcore theory are thus also likely to overlook these 'situational variables.' To the extent to which cultures develop in response to policy problems that occur in particular times and places, they are assumed away in much of public choice. The theory of common property resources (CPR) is an apt example. Scholars, who ignore policy and its time and place variations, work through CPR theory from a concern with the relative absence of rules to exclude uses from overexploitation of the resource. The inference is then made that collective action through the state is necessary to formulate and enforce exclusionary rules so that the resource is sustained over time.[65] Elinor Ostrom in contrast, in her now classic work *Governing the Commons*,[66] began with a concern to explain what are policy anomalies in conventional theory, namely a range of CPR cases managed successfully by users without state rules. This led her to explore rules developed through institutions of self-government and fashion a general theory that admitted for time and place variations in countries as diverse as Japan, Switzerland, the Philippines, the United States, Canada, and Turkey.

Public choice seems to be fragmenting into two schools, with one school including the nature of the good in its hard core, and the other school placing the nature of the good outside the core to be used only occasionally in empirical work. The latter school seems to be dominated by scholars based in or educated at Rochester, Chicago (economics), and Virginia (later George Mason University). The former school draws especially on institutions such as Indiana, Berkeley, and Chicago (sociology).[67] These institutional nodes of activity oversimplify. We must explore the intellectual origins of the fragmentation.

V. Rival Epistemologies

Epistemologies consist of theories of knowledge that can act, *inter alia*, as strategies of investigation, both analytical and empirical. By the early 1980s a number of collective epistemologies had been explicitly invoked by public choice theorists as strategies of investigation. One such epistemology was that of empiricism, which, in Davis's summary, played two roles:[68]

If the first role of empiricism is the testing of theory, the second is the attempt to bridge the gap between refined theoretical structures and the real world via the method of having the empiricists insist upon asking how concepts may be measured and theories tested.

The epistemology could be used to disconfirm or corroborate propositions in the body of the theory, and it could also be used to explain away any apparent disconfirmatory evidence. This latter was possible because the theory could develop higher-level propositions or axioms as a logically consistent effort to rationalize potentially contradictory evidence. Thus the theory of constitutional choice spawned by *The Calculus of Consent*[69] was originally designed to account for the collective rationality of majority tyranny implicit in the voting paradox literature. It could explain away such analytical phenomena as well as theoretically support empirical investigations of, for example, the frequency of cyclical majorities.[70]

Another kind of epistemology associated with public choice may be characterized as 'perspectivist.' The fullest form of this kind of epistemology as applied to public choice is found in the writings of Vincent Ostrom. In this view, rules are human artifacts that influence the perceptions of individuals, including individuals as investigators of public choice. Of particular importance among rules are language rules that make behaviour meaningful, intelligible, and potentially productive for human communities.[71]

One methodological implication of this view is that challenges to the theoretical propositions of public choice can be reinterpreted as challenges from the perspective of the investigator, who may be trapped within the rules of his or her particular language games. Again, this kind of epistemology insulates the theory from rivals.[72]

Ironically, the two epistemologies have become rival strategies of investigation, leading – it may be argued – to the fracturing of the enterprise. The rival epistemologies overlap in their concern with the status of rules. Hence the character of rules in the two epistemologies illustrates (and perhaps tests) their methodological differences. For the empiricists, rules are collective arrangements to coordinate individual behaviours. They can operate in configurative form or independently. They can also be stated in ways previously described. They possess a range of consequences that may be specified analytically and verified empirically. They possess, and this is the key difference with the perspectivist epistemology, purely an instrumental status. Their relevance is limited to what can be deduced analytically or inferred from empirical evidence.

In contrast, rules for the perspectivist bind the investigator and the subjects of analysis together. Rules will have one set of meanings for the investigator and possibly another set of meanings for individuals whose incentives are structured by these rules. The task of the investigator is, in part, to describe and explain the meanings of the rules that they have for these other individuals. Rules may or may not, therefore, have a simple instrumental character. They may have intrinsic worth that cannot be revealed without explaining their value to the individuals affected by them.

Some examples will illustrate this fundamental difference. Compare Riker's methodology in his now famous treatise on federalism with the methodology of Ostrom or Elazer.[73] Riker's method of assessing federalism is to examine nation-states that have federal and nonfederal structures to see whether there are counter examples to the thesis that federalism promotes freedom. Ostrom and Elazer, in contrast, examine the intellectual origins of constitutional experience in the United States (in particular) to see if the original design principles embodied particular meanings for the designers. These design principles are found in covental theology of the Puritans and can be used to assess current constitutional experience. The fullest explication of this latter approach is to be found in Akenson's exceptional book on South Africa (pre-1994), Israel, and Ulster.[74]

A second example may be drawn from the rent-seeking literature.[75] Rules that limit competition in the supply of goods may indeed be instrumental in generating excess income or rent. Thus farmers may benefit from commodity quotas, tenants from rent control legislation, or university professors from academic tenure. However, the rules in question may have other values, many of which are intrinsic rather than instrumental. Agriculture quotas may have value as an attempt to maintain a rural way of life. Rent controls may have value as a signal of a collective agreement to provide some affordable shelter. Academic tenure may reflect a desire to constrain threats to the circulation of ideas. The approach of a perspectivist epistemology to these phenomena is to supplement, not replace, a calculation of the value of economic rents and the loss to society from rent seeking. The supplement would come in the form of understanding custom, habits, and norms and how these may evolve, following Hayek,[76] into social institutions with efficiency implications.[77] Douglas North has provided us with an impressive macro theory of the evolution of institutional change that places the rules for rent seeking in a broader historical context.[78]

Given the difference in approach between the rival epistemologies as exemplified in the meaning they accord to rules, the question now remains as to why one approach would include the nature of the good in its hard core and the other approach would not include this concept. In order to answer the question, we must return to the topic of the growth of knowledge.

VI. Rival Epistemologies and the Growth of Knowledge

One reason why public choice in general has prospered in the last three decades is that it has contained in its epistemologies a methodological impetus for the growth of knowledge. The impetus is the criterion of logical consistency. Logical consistency refers to the way in which the propositions of the theory are interrelated. They are interrelated such that no conclusion drawn from one set of propositions in the analysis contradicts another conclusion drawn from a different set. The propositions conform to the rules of logic, where logic refers to purely formal relations and does not connote anything existential.[79]

The criterion of logical consistency facilitates the growth of knowledge in two ways. First, it enables any covering law to be developed as an explanation or rationalization of a proposition. In this way, deductive-nomological explanations are formed that can account for a range of empirical circumstances. For example, the theory of rent seeking was first developed to explain the scope of interest group activity in Third World countries.[80] Second, logical consistency allows one or more covering laws in a theory to be used to account for different phenomena than originally considered. Thus Olson was able to use the theory of rent seeking to account for the limited economic growth of many advanced industrial societies, for example.[81] In these two regards, public choice theory grows as would any other theory that develops around a deductive-nomological conception of theory development. Moreover, contradictory explanations can be explained away by developing even more generic nomological arguments. Thus the regulations or rules in societies that permit rent seeking may reflect broader macro conditions about institutional development in rich and poor societies[82] and explain away contradictory propositions such as could be postulated in a different theory. The criterion of logical consistency thus allows the theory both to grow and to be buffered from alternative theoretical challenges.

The rival epistemologies of empiricism and perspectivism both share this characteristic of logical consistency that accounts for the growth of the theory. However, the perspectivist approach also grows in a different direction than does the empiricist approach. The reasons are as follows.

All theory and epistemology is embedded within a particular community. One such community is the academic paradigm or followers of a research program.[83] Through a process of peer review, approval is collectively amassed on the various directions that theory may have developed (by using a criterion such as logical consistency). There may be other communities, however. These might include the intelligentsia of a nation or world region,[84] the 'technical-cognitive interests' in any society,[85] or a society of sovereign equals.[86] The linkages of the relevant community with an empiricist epistemology differ, however, from the linkages with the perspectivist epistemology.

In the empiricist epistemology, or more correctly its standard logical-empiricist form, the linkages are ones of conjecture, refutation (or corroboration), extensions of theory by logical consistency (or other criteria such as anomaly solving), and the further conjecture. By conjecture, I mean the generation of a testable hypothesis from an extant body of theory, and by refutation the use of the canons of empirical validity and reliability to assess the degree of proof. These linkages form a self-contained methodological system. They are self-contained within the community of intellectual adherents that can pose the conjectures, assess the refutations, extend the theory, and make further conjectures. It has a kind of 'inner rationality' of its own, and need not reach beyond its community to consider issues that affect wider communities than scholars. This is the reason why much of public choice theory now has no incentive to include the nature of the good as its hard core. The nature of the good, by definition, characterizes policies without scholastic communities at different times and places. It takes public choice beyond the systemic basis of its methodology. Policies or goods may therefore be included in public choice analysis, but they are not a necessary part of the hard core. They are simply part of the positive heuristic developing the range of the research program.[87]

A perspectivist epistemology implies more. Its methodology requires linkages beyond those formed with a community of scholars, because it must try and grasp the meanings of its theoretical propositions to nonscholastics in communities in particular times and places. One way of establishing these kinds of linkages is through systematically including the nature of the good or the manifestations of a public policy in its hard core of theoretical propositions.[88] The perspectivist tradition within public choice does not have a self-contained methodological system, therefore. It grows through logical consistency, but its premises are rooted, through the medium of policy analysis, in a very different kind of community.

An apt example that contrasts the two forms of growth may be the subfield of constitutional political economy. The empiricist tradition is exemplified in the innovative journal *Constitutional Political Economy*. Articles focus on key theoretical conjectures, the occasional empirical refutation or confirmatory evidence for these conjectures, the extension of the theoretical conjectures by logical consistency and then further conjecture. The agenda is set by the conjectural puzzles associated with rule utilitarianism, constitutional contracting, evolutionary bases of constitutional and common laws, constitutional change through judiciaries, secession and referendums, and allocational and distributive impacts of constitutional formulas. Many of these agenda items have been set by classical political theorists and subsequently amended by modern theorists such as Buchanan, Hayek, Nozick, and Rawls.

In contrast, the *Res Publica* tradition associated with the Indiana University Workshop in Political Theory and Policy Analysis focuses on policy concerns in large and small communities and how these translate into different rule configurations. The goods studied include water supply systems, irrigation systems, policing, fisheries, shipping, and environment, and these are conducted in regimes as diverse as Nepal, Nigeria, Poland, and Canada. Studies progress both within the theoretical program by using the criterion of logical consistency (such as extending the theory of common property rights) and also by reference to policy concerns within nonscholastic communities (such as law and order in impoverished Indian bands).[89]

In sum, epistemologies can provide their own logic for the growth of knowledge. The epistemologies associated with public choice are no exception. They push the accumulation of knowledge through applying the concept of logical consistency to theoretical conjectures associated with their hard core of basic concepts. For much of public choice, this is sufficient. This is because its epistemology derived from an empiricist tradition is self-contained, involving only academic communities in advancing theory and accepting conjectures and refutations. For another part of public choice, this strategy is supplemented by a concern with the nature of the good as a hard-core concept. The strategy extends the theory outward to policy communities as well as inward to theoretical communities. The separate enterprises are leading, it may be suggested, to the fracturing of the public choice enterprise.

VII. Conclusion

In the last thirty years, there has been a concerted effort to understand and explain the growth of scientific knowledge. One especially fruitful approach – in that it has applicability across a variety of disciplines – comes from the work of Kuhn on academic paradigms[90] and later modifications of the approach by Lakatos[91] (1974). In these views, the central elements of a theory, such as hard-core concepts and primitive terms and assumptions, are adopted by scholars in different fields. Knowledge grows from these central elements to solve anomalies in extant theory, which may overturn current knowledge (Kuhn) or lead to its gradual disappearance (Lakatos).

This paper argues that knowledge in the public choice field has grown through the methodology of logical consistency rather than anomaly solving. Knowledge is expanded through deductive logic or through application of logic to new issues. However, two differing epistemologies that are associated with public choice differ in the degree to which they go further than the logical consistency criterion in establishing new agendas for study. One epistemology that includes the nature of the good in its hard core, and which has a perspectivist form, adds to the logical consistency criterion an additional concern to explain policy situations where rules, goods, and individualism conflux. This is because it argues that the necessary meanings that individuals bestow on rules can only be adequately described when policy questions are addressed. This epistemology reaches outward beyond its internal logic to understand extrascholastic concerns as manifested in policy situations. This outward thrust complements its 'inner rationality' of following the impetus of logical consistency.

The other epistemology is driven by the logical consistency criterion. It is associated with an empiricist epistemology, particularly a logical-empiricist one. Over time, the agendas set by this epistemology differ from the perspectivist one. It is a 'closed loop' epistemology that contains no method to 'correct' its logic by reference to the nonscholastic world of policy analysis. Policies are treated as an interesting but not a necessary part of the theoretical endeavour.

The two epistemologies are gradually, and perhaps inexorably, fracturing the field of public choice. In broader terms, it seems as if the growth of knowledge can take place in a cumulative fashion only if a common epistemology emerges for a field. It also seems as if knowledge can be expanded through 'inner' methodologies such as that of logical consistency or extrascholastic concerns such as policy analysis. The former methodology, on its own, can lead to arid and narrow scholasticism and perhaps gradual disappearance of the field. The latter can lead to adjustment and readjustment to nonscholastic concerns over time. It takes, perhaps, a particular kind of epistemology rather than just any epistemology to yield enduring and cumulative progress in any scholastic endeavour.

If this analysis is correct, there are a number of implications that follow for the analysis of policies in Canada. First, there is likely to be a continued deviation between policy analysis using the perspectivist epistemology and scholarship that remains attached to the logical-empiricist epistemology. The perspectivist policy studies may increasingly resemble other policy analyses in the discipline more than they resemble the public choice empiricist studies. This is already the case with studies at the constitutional level of analysis. Second, as policy studies increase, there will be a concomitant need to document and review the field in order to build theory through logical consistency. Policy studies can become merely eclectic without theoretical integration on a regular basis. Third, it may mean that a new name might be necessary to distinguish the policy studies in public choice from the (now) established version of public choice. The public may then be able to choose, as it were, between the two forms of scholarship.

Notes

A shorter version of this paper was presented at the 'Workshop on the Workshop,' a Conference on the occasion of the 20th Anniversary Celebration of the Workshop in Political Theory and Policy Analysis, Indiana University, Bloomington, 15–20 June 1994. I am grateful to Peter Bogason, Barbara Carroll, and Vincent Ostrom for comments.

1   Sproule-Jones, 'Public Choice and Natural Resources.'
2   I. Lakatos, *Criticism and the Growth of Knowledge.*
3   K. Popper, *The Logic of Scientific Discovery; Conjectures and Refutations.*
4   E.g., Kekes, *A Justification of Rationality*; Laudan, *Progress and Its Problems*; Habermas, *Theory of Communicative Action.*
5   Alexander and Colomy, 'Traditions and Competition.'
6   E.g., Mueller, *Public Choice II*; Johnson, *Public Choice*; Dunleavy, *Democracy, Bureaucracy and Public Choice*; Ordeshook, *A Political Theory Primer.*
7   E.g., Bish, *The Public Economy of Metropolitan Areas*, 1971; Riker and Ordeshock, *An Introduction to Positive Political Theory*; Mueller, *Public Choice*; Abrams, *Foundations of Political Analysis*; Hardin, *Collective Action.*
8   Lakatos, *Criticism and the Growth of Knowledge.*
9   Sproule-Jones, 'Public Choice and Natural Resources'; Ostrom, *Rules, Laws and Common Pool Resources.*
10   Sproule-Jones, *Governments at Work.*
11   E.g., Olson, *The Logic of Collective Action.*
12   E.g., Downs, *An Economic Theory of Democracy.*
13   E.g., Axelrod, *The Evolution of Cooperation.*
14   E.g., Orbell et al., 'Covenants Without the Sword'; Ostrom et al., 'Covenants With and Without a Sword.'

15 E.g., Ostrom et al., *Rules, Laws and Common Pool Resources.*
16 Schelling, *Micromotives and Macrobehavior.*
17 Buchanan and Tullock, *The Calculus of Consent.*
18 Buchanan, *The Economics and the Ethics of Constitutional Order.*
19 Commons, *Legal Foundations of Capitalism.*
20 Benson, *The Enterprise of Law.*
21 Ostrom, *The Meaning of American Federalism.*
22 See, for example, the contents of Mueller's first edition text *Public Choice,* published in 1979.
23 Niskanen, *Bureaucracy and Representative Government.*
24 See Mueller's second edition, *Public Choice II,* for contrasts with edition one.
25 Sproule-Jones, 'Methodological Individualism.'
26 Kiser and Ostrom, Workshop in Political Theory and Policy Analysis Working Paper, 1987.
27 Mansbridge, *Beyond Self Interest*; Wildavsky, 'Why Self-Interest Means Less outside a Social Context.'
28 Rowley, *Public Choice Theory.*
29 Davis, *Atlantic Fisheries and Coastal Communities,* 1984; Pinkerton et al., *Cooperative Management of Local Fisheries*; Matthews, *Controlling Common Property.*
30 Pinkerton, 'Co-Management Efforts as Social Movements.'
31 Sproule-Jones, *The Real World of Pollution Control,* 1981; *Governments at Work.*
32 Sproule-Jones, *Governments at Work.*
33 Ibid.
34 McDavid, 'The Canadian Experience With Privatizing Solid Waste Services'; McDavid and Schick, 'Privatization versus Union-Management Cooperation.'
35 McDavid, 'Part-Time Firefighters in Canadian Municipalities.'
36 Sproule-Jones, *Governments at Work.*
37 Matthews, *Controlling Common Property.*
38 Trebilcock et al., *The Choice of Governing Instrument*; Kitchen, *Efficient Delivery of Local Government Services.*
39 Bish, 'Improving Productivity in the Government Sector'; McDavid and Schick, 'Privatization versus Union-Management Cooperation.'
40 Harrison and Stanbury, *Canadian Public Administration,* 1990; Stanbury, *Provincial Public Finances,* 1991
41 Vining and Boardman, 'Ownership vs. Competition.'
42 Sproule-Jones, *Agencies, Boards and Commissions.*
43 Sproule-Jones, 'User Fees.'

44 Reese, 'Decision Rules in Local Economic Development'; Kernaghan, 'Partnership and Public Administration.'

45 Pinkerton et al., *Cooperative Management of Local Fisheries.*

46 Cassidy and Bish, *Indian Government: Its Meaning in Practice.*

47 Bish, *Local Government in British Columbia.*

48 Sproule-Jones, *Governments at Work.*

49 Breton and Wintrobe, 'Bureaucracy and State Intervention'; *The Logic of Bureaucratic Conduct.*

50 Sproule-Jones, *Governments at Work.*

51 Atkinson, *Governing Canada.*

52 Breton, *Report of the Royal Commission on the Economic Union and Development Prospects for Canada*; and Breton and Scott, *The Economic Constitution of Federal States.*

53 Sproule-Jones, *Public Choice and Federalism in Australia and Canada*; 'The Enduring Colony'; *Governments at Work.*

54 Sabetti, Workshop on Covenant and Politics, Center for the Study of Federalism.

55 Sharman, 'Parliamentary Federations and United Government.'

56 Lermer, *Probing Leviathan*; Auld and Kitchen, *The Supply of Government Services.*

57 Sproule-Jones, 'Multiple Rules and the Nesting of Public Policies.'

58 Berman, *Law and Revolution.*

59 Buchanan, 'The Domain of Constitutional Economics'; see also Buchanan, 'The Public Choice Perspective,' and 'The Constitution of Economic Policy.'

60 Lane, *The Public Sector*, 154–60.

61 Rowley, ed., *Public Choice Theory.*

62 The criteria for selection of 'empirical work based on policy concerns' was that the article had, at a minimum, to use a policy case as an example and that this case should be at least one paragraph long. The criterion allowed for cases based on 'casual empiricism' as well as primary and secondary source empirical investigations.

63 Coase, 'The Problem of Social Cost.'

64 Sproule-Jones, *Governments at Work.*

65 See Lane, *The Public Sector*, 1993, 12–46; or Johnson, *Public Choice*, 1991, 324–6, for example.

66 *Governing the Commons.*

67 For other classifications along institutional lines, see Mitchell, *Public Choice*, 1988, and Rowley, *Public Choice Theory.*

68 Davis, *Mathematical Applications in Political Science*, 1969, 36.

69 Buchanan and Tullock, *The Calculus of Consent.*

70 Tullock, 'Why So Much Stability?'
71 Ostrom, 'Artisanship and Artifact,' and *The Meaning of American Federalism.*
72 In my 'Public Choice and Natural Resources' I denoted a third epistemology, that of rationality. However, it may also be considered to be a subset of the logical-empirist view. Also the perspectivist approach, as noted, includes a variety of subapproaches, only the major of which is detailed here.
73 Riker, *Federalism*; Ostrom, 'Can Federalism Make a Difference?'; Elazar and Kincaid, 'Government, Politics, and Constitutionalism.'
74 Akenson, *God's Peoples.*
75 E.g. Buchanan et al., *Toward a Theory of the Rent Seeking Society.*
76 Hayek, *The Sensory Order.*
77 Koford and Miller, *Social Norms and Economic Institutions*, 1991.
78 North, *Structure and Change in Economic History*; *Institutions, Institutional Change and Economic Performance.*
79 Sproule-Jones, 'Public Choice and Natural Resources.'
80 Krueger, 'The Political Economy of the Rent Seeking Society.'
81 Olson, *The Rise and Decline of Nations.*
82 North, *Institutions, Institutional Change and Economic Performance.*
83 Kuhn, *The Structure of Scientific Revolutions.*
84 MacKenzie, *The Study of Political Science Today.*
85 Habermas, *Theory of Communicative Action.*
86 Tocqueville, *Democracy in America.*
87 Lakatos, *Criticism and the Growth of Knowledge.*
88 I do not assert it is the only way.
89 There is no good single review study available. Many of the appropriate references can be found in Ostrom, *The Meaning of American Federalism*, Sproule-Jones, *Governments at Work*, or Ostrom et al., *Rules, Laws and Common Pool Resources.*
90 Kuhn, *The Structure of Scientific Revolutions.*
91 Lakatos, *Criticism and the Growth of Knowledge.*

10

Rational Choice and Canadian Policy Studies

Applications of rational choice models to policy analysis attempt to base
policy analysis on microlevel explanations of aggregate decisions. These
models start with assumptions about individuals and the context of decision
making, and then draw logical policy implications from these assumptions.
The rational choice literature can be differentiated according to the assumptions that are made regarding the motivations of individuals and the nature
of the decision-making context. Therefore, I begin with an examination of
the main assumptions of the rational choice approach; then I evaluate the
strengths and weaknesses of policy studies based on rational choice models.
Finally, I consider the merit and demerits of methodological options for structuring theoretical and empirical policy studies, with a view to propose future
directions of research.

The Rational Choice Approach

In order to understand the implications of different conceptions of rational
choice models and to compare their strengths and weaknesses, a description
of the most important components of each type of model is needed. With
respect to policy studies, it is useful to differentiate three types of rational
choice models: the rational actor theory, the interdependent rational actor
model, and institutional rational choice modelling. Before considering each
alternative, it is necessary to define the three components upon which the
generic model of rationality is based. Faced with two or more alternatives,
an *actor* makes a decision that generates certain *outcomes*; these outcomes,
in turn, produce *consequences* for the actor.

A debatable but generally accepted assumption states that the actor does not directly evaluate his or her actions but only their consequences. Therefore, evaluation works from consequences to actions.

Rational Actor Model

The simplest form of rational choice model is based on the assumption of certainty. In this form, it is assumed that actions fully determine outcomes and, likewise, that outcomes fully determine consequences. It is assumed that the actor associates each alternative action with specific outcomes and then selects the action that produces the outcomes he or she prefers. This simple model implies that rational choice theory includes normative and positive analytical dimensions. Rational choice models embody a normative view in pointing out what action an actor *should* select in order to obtain a given consequence, but they also provide a positive standpoint for describing, explaining, and predicting the choice of actions. Rational choice models help to describe the conditions surrounding individual choices of actions as well as to explain and predict individual choices in terms of a few simple assumptions about how individuals determine their preferences. This simple model assumes that individual choices of actions are consistent (i.e., transitive). That is, if an individual prefers A_1 to A_2 and A_2 to A_3, then he or she also prefers A_1 to A_3.

Although it has implicitly served as a benchmark model, this simplest model has been criticized and its unrealistic assumptions rejected in early Canadian policies studies.[1] Still considered to be a plausible theoretical approach,[2] this type of deductive model is nevertheless criticized as providing theoretical insights that induce policy analysts to read public policies in terms of rational choices, instead of facilitating the derivation of hypotheses that can be tested through systematic empirical observation.[3] The discrepancies between the assumptions of the rational actor model and the actual process of decision making have been forcefully pointed out by Braybrooke and Lindblom.[4] The rational actor model is not a satisfactory research tool for policy analysis because its assumptions do not match reality. First, it assumes that actors possess the computational abilities required to associate actions to outcomes and outcomes to consequences. Second, it assumes that actors have consistent and stable preference orderings of consequences. It is easy to agree that these assumptions are unrealistic. However, it is even more important to point out that this elementary rational choice model is not useful because it rests on unsatisfactory assumptions about the institutional context of policy making. It implicitly postulates a world inhabited by isolated individuals where institutions do not matter. These shortcomings are taken into consideration by game theory and institutional rational choice models.

Interdependent Rational Actor Model

The rational actor model described above assumes that individuals maximize their personal interests in complete isolation. The *interdependent* rational actor model assumes that individual decisions are made in a context of interdependence and, therefore, pay more attention to the institutional arrangements appropriate to induce social interactions that generate mutually compatible individual decisions. This model is based on two assumptions: (1) a rational individual seeks to maximize his or her utility; and (2) in a decision-making context of voluntary action, the basic form of social interaction that generates compatible individual decisions is the market.

In a context of interdependence, rational choice is based on expectations about what others might do. Game theory has been developed to investigate decision-making situations involving two or more actors in which the outcome is contingent upon the combined actions of the actors.[5] From the standpoint of game theory, the crucial assumptions concern the suppositions that each actor makes about the strategy used by the others players. These suppositions can be clarified once one has specified seven items: (1) the list of actors; (2) the policy objectives of these actors; (3) the actions available to each actor; (4) a list of potential outcomes; (5) the relationship between actions and outcomes; (6) the relationship between outcomes and policy objectives; (7) the perception developed by each actor on items 1 to 6, and their respective perceptions about the perceptions of others (this last condition is usually referred to as a situation where 'common knowledge' prevails).

In the area of policy studies, game theory has been used to investigate the problems that arise when individuals have 'opportunities to get something for nothing.'[6] Such opportunities exist either whenever one can freely extract resources from a common pool,[7] or whenever one can freely decide whether or not to contribute to a common fund of resources.[8] Extracting water from a groundwater basin or fishing in the ocean correspond to the first type of opportunity,[9] whereas contributing time and money to a group promoting improvement of water quality or contributing to the production of a good requiring a team effort[10] are examples of the second type.

Decision-making situations that induce individuals to get something for nothing create collective action problems often referred to as social dilemmas.[11] The most famous social dilemma is the prisoner's dilemma.[12] Let us describe briefly the conditions creating such a dilemma. There are two actors who both face the alternatives of either contributing or not contributing to the preservation of a common pool of resources. In the configuration of strategic interaction depicted in Table 1, each player has a dominant strategy: not to contribute. In game theory, it is assumed that a strategy dominates another strategy if, and only if, it gives to the one player who adopts it an outcome at least as good as any other, whatever the strategy chosen by the other player. A rational player, that is, one who tries to achieve the best possible outcome, always selects a dominant strategy. In a situation like that depicted in Table 1, neither player has an incentive to depart from the dominant strategy. If one player decides to abandon his or her dominant strategy in order to contribute to the common pool of resources, while the other sticks to his or her dominant strategy, the contributor gets a payoff of 1 whereas the other obtains 4. Therefore, each player sticks to his or her dominant strategy even though each player would obtain a better payoff if both were to simultaneously adopt the strategy of contributing (the payoff for each would increase from 2 to 3). This paradox is attributable to four conditions: the players have the right to freely choose their strategy; both players would benefit from a joint strategy of contribution; however, the existence of a strongly stable, albeit deficient, equilibrium means that each player lacks an incentive to contribute if the other does not; and, indeed, each player is motivated to stick to his or her dominant strategy even if it is expected that the other will contribute.

The logic has led many students of collective action to conclude that institutional arrangements based on voluntary contribution to the production of public goods and public policies are likely to generate suboptimal outcomes, especially when there are good reasons for free riding.[13] In the field of policy studies, this conclusion has been used as justification for government intervention.[14] Indeed, if rational actors make decisions in a context of market institutional arrangements based on voluntary action, and also if the outcomes of aggregated individual actions generate public goods (which are goods available to everyone without the possibility of excluding anyone, once they are provided), then rational individuals are likely to prefer not to contribute. Therefore, many authors have concluded that the production of public goods requires the coercive instruments of government intervention. Appealing as it may seem, this rationale does not provide sufficient information on the relationship between specific public goods problems and specific policy instruments.

TABLE 1
The Prisoner's Dilemma Game

| | | Player B | |
		Do not contribute	Contribute
Player A	Do not contribute to the common pool of resources	2,2	4,1
	Contribute	1,4	3,3
		Outcomes: 4=best; 1=worst	

In Canada, the federal, provincial, and municipal governments have all attempted to compensate for this type of market failure by developing financial and regulatory policy instruments. Governments have tried to influence decisions in the fisheries by providing subsidies, imposing quotas on captures, and providing incentives stimulating the creation of institutions of self-governance.[15] McDavid has conducted numerous empirical studies on the incentives created by government interventions in the area of service delivery.[16] However, empirical investigations of the involvement of individuals in interest groups – a problem that can be compared to contributing voluntarily to a common fund of resources – have not been based on the model of the interdependent rational actors. In Canada, recent empirical studies on the interactions between participation in interest groups and public policy have shown a tendency to be based on the policy community framework.[17]

However, game theory has been a tool of predilection chosen by many students of constitutional politics, especially in their various attempts to model interdependence between Quebec and the rest of Canada.[18] Although rich in interpretations, these applications tend to suffer from several methodological limitations. In order to test empirically a rational choice theory, one needs to identify clearly in advance what is predicted. In the case of game theory, one needs: (1) to identify a configuration of strategic interactions; (2) to determine the equilibrium solution or equilibria solutions of the game; and (3) to have access to empirical observations concerning the actual decisions made by the participants in the game. Let us consider each of these points. The identification of a configuration of strategic interaction is not as easy as it might seem at first sight. Let us recall that there are seventy-eight different configurations of strategic interactions for 2x2 ordinal games (games where two players have two strategies at their disposal).[19] Given that the preferences, decision rules, alternative strategies, and equilibria solutions are difficult to observe, the proportion of unobservable terms is so high that it is almost impossible to establish whether or not a situation corresponds to a specific configuration (out of the seventy-eight), as well as to confirm or invalidate the theoretical predictions regarding the equilibria solutions observed in real decision-making situations. Finally, the fits between the predicted solutions and the empirical tests are difficult to evaluate because the researchers tend to collect instances and illustrations concerning only the most memorable moments and the most visible strategies in constitutional debates. In short, this literature does not offer systematic empirical tests, and it is based on many unobservable terms.

In view of these practical difficulties, one has to agree with Brian Martin that 'game theory may not be very good in arriving at precise strategies in complex situations, but it is useful in helping one to think about the situation in an ordered way.'[20] Steven Brams proposed major changes to render game theory truly dynamic by assuming that most games have a history.[21] He assumes that players are in a particular state and that they can attempt to improve their situation by switching their strategies. Brams also suggests that players think ahead about the consequences of countermoves to their moves, counter-countermoves, and so on, hence contributing to extend the strategic analysis into a distant future. Very interesting from a theoretical standpoint, the changes proposed by Brams do not resolve the difficulties encountered in previous attempts to test game theory empirically. As for James Morrow's excellent review of recent theoretical developments in game theory, it too fails to provide the tools required for empirical testing.[22]

The interdependent rational actor model opens up interesting perspectives on the kind of complex strategic interactions that occur in most policy issues. To that extent, it offers a better tool than the individual rational actor model. However, both types of models embody unsatisfactory assumptions regarding the institutional context of policy making. Rational choice models like game theory consider the institutional context of decision-making situations in a highly abstract manner that does not reflect a sufficient dose of realism to serve as a problem-solving tool for policy analysts and policy makers. In the game theory perspective, the institutional arrangements defining the decision-making situations are considered as exogenous factors, that is, they are given and stable. The purpose of institutional rational choice models is to tackle this problem of underspecification by incorporating contributions from transaction cost theory and contract theory.

Institutional Rational Choice Models

Interdependent rational actor models are predicated on the idea that the same individuals will make different decisions in different decision-making situations. The institutional rational choice models add the further assumption that institutional arrangements play a determining role in defining these decision-making situations. With respect to policy studies, institutional rational choice models deal with two related questions: How do different institutional arrangements affect policy outcomes? And how are institutional arrangements affected by individual preferences and individual strategies? Contrary to game theory, where institutional arrangements are viewed as exogenous factors, institutional rational choice models attempt to endogenize institutional arrangements.

The claim that institutional arrangements matter is not new. It goes back to Aristotle who, in addition to assimilating political science to the study of institutions, attempted to see how different constitutional arrangements affect what we today call policy outcomes. What is new are the numerous attempts to integrate institutional and behavioural variables in the same theoretical models.[23]

Institutional rational choice models assume that the actions of rational actors are coordinated through contractual arrangements. Contracts are agreements among individuals stipulating what specific actions each party has to accomplish at some point in the future, and what rewards or penalties are associated with compliance or noncompliance with agreed-upon commitments. In this micro-perspective, institutions are generated from aggregations of networks of contracts (or 'nexus of treaties').[24] Therefore, the incentives created by institutions are determined by differences in the nature of the contractual terms that individuals develop to solve specific problems. In micro-institutional rational choice models, the analysts do not place the emphasis on the institutional structure or on the policy, but on the transaction itself.[25]

With respect to policy analysis, the transaction costs associated with contracts are the resources expended in planning, adopting, implementing, and evaluating public policies. The operationalization of this approach involves five conceptual stages: (1) stating the behavioural assumptions affecting contracts; (2) dimensionalizing transactions in terms of cost consequences; (3) developing a grammar of generic contractual arrangements; (4) developing a theory of incomplete contracts; and (5) developing criteria for evaluating the policy outcomes. Let us examine these points in turn.

Behavioural Assumptions

Micro-institutional rational choice models rest on two critical behavioural assumptions, namely, bounded rationality and opportunism. The scope of the assumption of rationality has been enlarged by Herbert Simon[26] so as to refer to behaviour that is 'intendedly rational, but only limitedly so.' The idea of intended rationality means that individual behaviour is oriented toward the attainment of goals. Riker and Odershook[27] have developed a convincing argument stating that if individual decisions were not goal-oriented, it would be impossible to explain regularities that occur in the domain of human behaviour. But the cognitive competence of individuals is limited. From this point, one has deduced that individuals do not seek to maximize but simply to 'satisfice' their interests, in other words, they seek to obtain no more than a satisfactory level of benefits. In a context of limited rationality, institutional arrangements influence the decisions made by individuals. Furthermore, individuals are induced to invest in the creation and maintenance of institutional arrangements because such arrangements generate routine-like decisions that do not require computation of optimal solutions. In this approach, institutions do matter.

However, institutional arrangements are never comprehensive in the sense that they never exhaust all the possibilities of interactions occurring among individuals. Although they facilitate decision making because they define the limits of behaviour, institutional arrangements always include some grey zones of ambiguity. In the words of contract theory, it is impossible to design comprehensive *ex ante* contracts. The point here is that incomplete contracts – or incomplete institutional arrangements – create room for opportunism, that is, an incentive to satisfy individual self-interest. If the terms of a contract are ambiguous, one of the co-contracting individuals is likely to exploit this fact for his or her own advantage. It is not necessary to assume that all individuals involved in a decision-making situation behave in an exploitative manner; it suffices to assume that it is probable.

These two behavioural assumptions have important implications for the development of institutional arrangements. In a decision-making context where contracts are unavoidly incomplete due to bounded rationality, and where incomplete contracts create incentives for opportunism, individuals are induced to invest in the creation and maintenance of institutional contractual arrangements that organize transactions so as to minimize simultaneously the recourse to cognitive competence and the occurrence of opportunism.[28] These theoretical implications are especially relevant for policy analysts.

Dimensionalizing Transactions

Interdependent interactions among individuals are governed by contracts. The specific terms of actual contracts are devised so as to deal with specific problems occurring in actual transactions, that is, the resources that are transferred from one individual to another.

The transactions that fall in the domain of policy analysis are those transactions that must be governed by state interventions because they affect third parties. The role of the government is to intervene whenever voluntary private transactions fail. However, one has to identify the critical dimensions of transactions in order to understand why transaction failures occur and how government interventions can alleviate these failures. According to O.E. Williamson,[29] transactions differ in three crucial ways: asset specificity, uncertainty, and frequency. Bryson and Smith, Ring,[30] and Brousseau[31] add a fourth critical dimension: measurability.

Transactions may depend on prior investments made in physical assets, human assets, site assets, or dedicated assets. The specificity of these prior investments is conditioned by the degree to which the use of these assets for alternative purposes, and by alternatives users, is costly. In short, high prior investments in asset specificity create incentives for acting opportunistically, and opportunism is likely to lead to transaction failures.

Uncertainty and frequency of transactions directly affect the costs of transacting and the contractual terms governing the relations among the parties. All other things being equal, the higher the uncertainty imposed on decision makers, the greater the likelihood of transaction failures. On the other hand, transaction failures are less likely whenever the level of uncertainty is low, and whenever the frequency of transactions has no influence because the transactions do not involve high prior investment in asset specificity. However, transactions that require high prior investment in asset specificity are influenced by the frequency of transactions. Therefore, the less frequently a set of assets can be used in similar transactions, the more difficult it is to capture the costs of transacting on the market, and as a consequence, the greater is the likelihood of transaction failures due to opportunistic behaviour.

A transaction involves the transfer of resources among co-contracting parties. Assets brought in the transactions can be easily measurable if they possess two intrinsic characteristics: a unit of measurement and a quantity of units. In all other cases, assets are not easily measurable. A measurable asset is easily observable whereas a contribution based on assets difficult to measure is difficult to assess and is likely to generate problems of moral hazard and problems of adverse selections.

TABLE 2
Generic Characteristics of Transactions

Generic Variations on Characteristics				
Type of Characteristics	Variation #1	Variation #2	Variation #3	Variation #4
Asset specificity	high and symmetric	high and asymmetric	low and symmetric	low and asymmetric
Uncertainty	high	low	N/A	N/A
Frequency	high	low	N/A	N/A
Degree of measurement	easy for each influx of assets	difficult for at least one influx of assets	N/A	N/A

These analytical dimensions generate a table describing the generic characteristics of transactions. Each type of transaction generates specific problems of interactions (coordination) among co-contracting parties, and as consequence, each type of transaction is likely to generate specific contractual arrangements (Table 2).

These critical dimensions determine the terms defining the institutional arrangements of contracts and the institutional structures made up by networks of contracts.

A Grammar of Generic Contractual Arrangements

The basic question posed by the literature on transaction cost economics is: Which institutional arrangements and which institutional structures can best minimize transaction costs? The traditional answer has been to provide a choice between the market or the hierarchy.[32] Brousseau[33] has proposed to go beyond this simplistic dichotomy in a very interesting way. He assumes that a contract seeks (1) to ensure coordination among individuals so as to capture a quasi-rent, that is, the difference between the payoff associated with the initial terms of a contract and the payoff resulting from the implementation of alternative contractual terms (this difference is a quasi-rent entirely attributable to the selection of specific contractual terms); (2) to redistribute the payoffs (quasi-rent) resulting from cooperation; and (3) to ensure compliance to prior commitments.

According to Brousseau,[34] all contracts include four categories of mechanisms:

1.   **routine:** a mechanism appropriate to base one's decisions on the know-how accumulated by others instead of investing resources to recreate existing public know-how;
2.   **authority:** a mechanism appropriate to redefine the allocation of assets and behaviour of the co-contracting parties whenever unanticipated circumstances occur;
3.   **monitoring:** a mechanism appropriate to assess the contributions made by the parties so as to improve efficiency and to resolve potential conflicts regarding the distribution of the quasi-rent among the co-contracting parties;
4.   **incentives:** mechanisms to meet problems of moral hazards by providing rewards or imposing sanctions on the co-contracting parties.

These mechanisms are complementary: the first mechanism is devised to save on investments in information; the second aims to ensure some flexibility; whereas the last two mechanisms are developed to attenuate opportunistic behaviour.

Contracts are sets of clauses devised to reach the three objectives mentioned above based upon the four mechanisms just defined. According to Brousseau,[35] all contracts can be captured through basic clauses concerning (1) technical coordination; (2) execution of the commitments; (3) partition of the payoff; and (4) duration of the contracts.

Problems of technical coordination among co-contracting parties can be solved by devising clauses based on different combinations of authority and routines. Technical coordination requires that the co-contracting parties agree upon: (1) the choice of a goal (final output); (2) the choice of the assets brought by the different parties; and (3) the temporal and spatial uses of the assets.

The choice of a goal refers to problems of strategic coordination. This clause, let us call it A, can vary in three different ways: (1) *routines*: the contract defines in a comprehensive manner the objective of the co-contracting parties. One has therefore a complete contract; in cases of disagreement, the co-contracting parties are left with no option but exit;[36] (2) *centralized authority*: in this case, one of the co-contracting parties has the discretionary right to modify the objective of the contract. This type of contract is incomplete; (3) *decentralized authority*: the objective of the contract is renegotiable. Again, the contract is incomplete.

Organizational coordination refers to the assets brought to the transaction by the co-contracting parties so as to achieve the objective of the contract. Let us refer to this clause as clause B. Again, it can take three different forms: (1) *routines*: the co-contracting parties stick to bringing the assets defined *ex ante* in the contract and any discrepancy between agreed-upon and actual contribution generates a contract annulment, that is exit; (2) *centralized authority*: one of the co-contracting parties has the right to modify the contribution expected from the contracting parties; and (3) *decentralized authority*: the co-contracting parties can renegotiate the nature of their contributions in the transaction.

Finally, operational coordination refers to temporal and spatial coordination concerning how the assets brought into the transaction are to be used. Clause C can vary along three different patterns: (1) *routines*: production delays and sites of delivery are entirely defined *ex ante* (no renegotiation is allowed); (2) *centralized authority*: one of the co-contracting parties has the discretionary right to modify the production delays and the sites of delivery; and (3) *decentralized authority*: the co-contracting parties can renegotiate on a continuous basis the production delays and the sites of delivery.

Execution of commitments is based on two types of mechanisms: warranties and monitoring clauses concerning guaranties designed to create some protection for a party harmed by the defection of another party by increasing the exit cost. Clause D embodies three generic solutions: (1) *no warranty*: the exit costs and opportunistic behaviour are entirely determined by the specificity of the assets brought by the co-contraction parties; (2) *unilateral implementation*: one of the co-contracting parties provides a guarantee to the other and this guarantee can be appropriated by the latter in cases of noncompliance with the commitments agreed upon; and (3) *bilateral implementation*: a relation of interdependence is created in cases whereby each co-contracting party provides a guarantee to the others.

Monitoring refers to clause E, and it deals with mechanisms devised to verify whether or not each party has observed its commitments. Brousseau[37] distinguishes four alternatives: (1) *self-governance*: verification is made by each co-contracting party (a contract is cancelled whenever a party does not stick to its commitments); (2) *public external arbitrator*: the execution of the commitments is placed under the control of public judiciary institutions; (3) *supervisor*: one of the co-contracting parties has the right to control the execution of the commitments and has the power to punish defection; and

(4) *private agent*: a third party is hired to make investigations and collect information regarding the execution of the commitments.

The distribution of the payoffs among the co-contracting parties refers to clause F. It deals with the rules defining how the quasi-rent is shared among the participants. It is useful to distinguish at least two generic patterns: (1) *payoff based on individual contributions*: the payoff obtained by the co-contracting parties is based on the effective contribution made by each party; (2) *payoff based on collective output*: the payoff is divided according to *ex ante* negotiation without reference to effective contribution.

Finally, Brousseau[38] claims that duration (clause G) is a crucial factor affecting transaction efficiency. Three pure cases may be distinguished: (1) fugitive contracts are valid for only one transaction; (2) *short term*: the co-contracting parties cannot modify the assets that they brought in the transactions; however, the contract is valid for a series of transactions; and (3) *long term*: assets brought in the transactions can be renegotiated.

According to Brousseau,[39] all these analytical distinctions may be used to generate a grammar of contracts that goes far beyond the usual dichotomy opposing markets and hierarchies (Table 3). In the perspective of this grammar, a transaction occurring in the market is defined as $A_1 B_1 C_1 D_1 E_2 F_1 G_1$, whereas a transaction taking place within a hierarchical structure may be described as $A_2 B_2 C_2 D_2 E_3 F_3 G_3$. If one considers political parties and interest groups as coalitions, the contractual terms governing the transactions among their members may be described as $A_1 B_3 C_3 D_3 E_1 F_2 G_3$. Finally, institutional arrangements of self-governance may be described as transactions governed by contractual agreements $A_3 B_3 C_3 D_1 E_1 F_2 G_3$. As one can see, a grammar of contracts provides a set of generic contractual terms that facilitate comparison among contracts.

Toward a Theory of Incomplete Contracts

Different types of transactions generate different types of contractual arrangements. Rational individuals attempt to negotiate contracts that incorporate the best alternative for each category of clauses (A, B, C ... G). In this context, one may assume that individual choices about contractual clauses depend upon the assets owned by the co-contracting parties as well as upon the efficiency of the alternative contractual clauses considered by the co-contracting parties. Attempts to explain and predict individual decisions fit in a positive approach, whereas attempts to assess the efficiency of different contractual arrangements fit in a normative approach. Let us consider each approach in turn.

TABLE 3
Grammar of Contracts

Generic Variations of Clauses				
Type of Clauses	Variation #1	Variation #2	Variation #3	Variation #4
A Strategic Coordination	Routine	Centralized Authority	Decentralized Authority	N/A
B Organizational Coordination	Routine	Centralized Authority	Decentralized Authority	N/A
C Operational Coordination	Routine	Centralized Authority	Decentralized Authority	N/A
D Warranty System	No Warranty	Unilateral Implementation	Bilateral Implementation	N/A
E Monitoring Mechanism	Self-governance	Public External Arbitrator	Supervisor	Private Agent
F Division of Payoff Among Parties	Marginal Productivity	Equal Share	Fixed Sum	N/A
G Duration of Contracts	Fugitive	Short Term	Long Term	N/A

Adapted from Brousseau, 1993, p. 126.

A Positive Approach to Contractual Arrangements

In the Williamson tradition, one usually assumes that individual decisions can be explained and predicted from incentives to devise contractual arrangements that minimize transaction costs. However, Jacquemin[40] and Brousseau[41] suggest that individual decisions regarding the choices of contractual clauses are more likely to depend upon incentives to maximize individual gains resulting from transactions than upon incentives to minimize the costs of transacting. In the same vein, students of public policy[42] assume that policy makers are induced to compensate the transaction costs incurred by private parties for the production of public goods because the costs of excluding nonpayers from consuming such goods discourage their production through private contracts.

Rational individuals are incited to jointly use their assets to generate quasi-rents. The assets brought to the transactions by the different participants usually differ in their degree of specificity. In turn, this asymmetry in asset specificity affects the incentives to cooperate. Thus, following Brousseau, one may assume that:

the party controlling the least specific assets (A_i) can be more easily replaced by another contracting party (A_j). Therefore, B is induced to attempt to increase its share of the quasi-rent.

However, the party controlling the least specific assets (A_i) is protected against the opportunistic behavior of B because its lower degree of asset specificity can be used jointly with many other potential contracting parties $(A_j, A_k,$ etc.).[43]

Whenever the degree of asset specificity is asymmetrically distributed among participants, one has an agency problem where the participant controlling the assets having the highest degree of specificity (the principal) is induced to support contractual arrangements that increase its share of the quasi-rent while protecting its assets against the opportunistic behaviours of the agent. On the other hand, when asset specificity is symmetrically distributed among participants, they are induced to minimize the costs of transacting if their assets have a low degree of specificity because they have to compete with other participants having similar assets. However, the participants are not induced to minimize the costs of transacting when their assets are highly specific because they are less likely to be sensitive to the competitive pressures originating from the nonparticipants in the contract. Table 4 depicts these four analytical cases.

TABLE 4
Incentives Created by Different Degrees of Asset Specificity

		B's Degrees of Asset Specificity	
		low	high
A's Degrees of Asset Specificity	low	Incentives to minimize transaction costs	A = rent-seeking principal B = agent
	high	A = agent B = rent-seeking principal	No incentives to minimize transaction costs

Charlotte Twight[44] has rightly pointed out that a party involved in the negotiations of contractual arrangements can be induced to augment transaction costs facing the other parties. Following her interpretation, 'the predicted extent of transaction-cost-augmenting behavior is shaped by the direct costs and benefits expected by, and the degree of competition faced by, decision-makers contemplating such measures.'[45] She has attempted to identify the key determinants of government manipulation of transaction costs as well as to develop a taxonomy of governmental transaction costs augmentation. The conceptual distinctions introduced above suggest that the incentives to manipulate the transaction costs depend upon two generic characteristics of transactions: the degree of uncertainty and the degree of measurement. Let us first consider the issue concerning the degree of measurement.

The more easily the assets brought into a transaction by a party can be assessed (high degree of measurement), the more difficult it is to attempt to manipulate the perceptions concerning their actual value, and conversely. One may assume that the parties controlling the assets that are the most difficult to measure have incentives to attempt to negotiate contractual arrangements that increase their share of the quasi-rent generated by the contract. The parties controlling assets easily measurable can easily be replaced. Again, one has another case of a principal-agent problem.

TABLE 5
Incentives Created by the Degree of Measurement of the Assets Brought into the Transactions

		B's Degree of Measurement of Assets	
		low	high
A's Degree of Measurement of Assets	low	A = high incentives B = high incentives to manipulation	A = high incentives B = low incentives to manipulation
	high	A = low incentives B = high incentives to manipulation	A = low incentives B = low incentives to manipulation

The assets brought into transactions are jointly invested to produce something that could not be produced independently. However, this joint investment generates payoffs that have a low or a high degree of uncertainty depending upon the transactions. The more uncertain the occurrence of a payoff resulting from a joint investment of assets, the higher are the incentives to attempt to alter the perceptions concerning the cost-benefit appraisal of the other parties involved in a contract. In more concrete terms, it means that whenever incentives to manipulation are high, one is induced to artificially augment the costs perceived by one's opponents while artificially reducing the costs perceived by one's supporters. The debates surrounding the cost of the separation of Quebec from the rest of Canada provide a good illustration of the behaviour generated by incentives to transaction cost manipulation.

TABLE 6
Incentives Created by Different Levels of Uncertainty Concerning the Payoffs Produced by Joint Investments of Assets

		B's Degree of Uncertainty of Payoffs	
		low	high
A's Degree of Uncertainty of Payoffs	low	A = low incentives to manipulation B = low incentives	A = low incentives to manipulation B = high incentives
	high	A = high incentives to manipulation B = low incentives	A = high incentives to manipulation B = high incentives

A Normative Approach to Contractual Arrangements

A normative approach to contractual arrangements attempts to assess efficiency and distributional equity associated with different types of contractual arrangements. Co-contracting parties are induced to select contractual arrangements that are efficient. Efficiency can be assessed in terms of production costs, coordination costs, and incentive costs. Production costs refer to resources invested in the assets used jointly to produce a good or a service; coordination costs refer, as indicated earlier, to the costs incurred to assume technical coordination; finally, incentive costs are generated by the resources that each party is induced to spend in order to deter opportunism. A contract will be considered efficient whenever it minimizes these three types of costs per unit of goods produced.

The criterion of distributional equity is a normative criterion used to assess the degree of acceptability concerning the distributional impact of the payoffs resulting from the contractual arrangements.[46] The distribution of the payoffs among the co-contracting parties may be considered as more or less politically acceptable. Unsatisfied interest groups and unsatisfied politicians are therefore induced to use this normative criterion in order to justify governmental interventions that seek to redistribute differently the payoffs resulting from (private) contractual arrangements.[47] It is important to point out that the policy sciences still lack 'efficient' normative criteria of evaluation, especially regarding the distributional impacts of the payoffs or outcomes of public policies.

Empirical applications based on micro-institutional analysis are not numerous, and they tend to suffer from difficult methodological problems. The empirical studies made by Williamson,[48] North,[49] Trebilcock,[50] Migué and Marceau,[51] and Ostrom, Schroeder, and Wynne[52] demonstrate that it is very difficult to evaluate, even to approximate, the resources involved in the transaction costs. This empirical problem is due to the fact that contracts are unavoidably incomplete and that contract theory is not a theoretical tool that has been formalized sufficiently to generate explanations and predictions based on deductive reasoning or mathematical analytical solutions.

A significant fraction of the Canadian literature on policy instruments is based – at least implicitly – on a contractual approach. Contractual clauses relating governments to other parties have been studied in the literature on public enterprises,[53] regulation,[54] taxation,[55] and service delivery.[56] The Canadian literature on policy instruments has developed many taxonomies of policy instruments that could be considered as grammars of policy instruments. These studies focus attention on the institutional arrangements of policy making and policy delivery. The policy instruments are the tools employed by governments to produce and deliver their interventions. The most significant contributions to this literature have been reviewed and analysed by Howlett.[57] Categorizations of policy instruments tend to be constructed according to notions concerning governing resources, or continuous models are used that rank instruments from the least to the most coercive.[58] Most of these taxonomies are based on highly abstract concepts, and although their proponents[59] have derived hypotheses from them, they are usually not considered as elements of more general institutional theories of policy choice.

With respect to normative evaluation, Landry and Blouin[60] have attempted to determine to what extent governmental assistance provided to manufacturing firms aims at compensating for market failures in order to improve economic efficiency or, alternatively, seeks to compensate politically unacceptable outcomes in order to improve distributional impacts. They have found that the ten provinces do in fact base their policy interventions on the simultaneous use of both criteria.

In spite of the theoretical and methodological difficulties discussed above, micro-institutional rational choice models based on transaction-costs theory constitute a research program that is promising but that still has to demonstrate its potential for the advancement of knowledge in the area of policy studies.

Conclusion on Future Directions

Rational choice models can be differentiated according to their assumptions regarding the attributes of individuals and the nature of the decision-making context. The rational actor model does not provide a satisfactory policy research tool because, in addition to many unrealistic assumptions concerning the attributes of the individuals, it implicitly postulates that interdependence among individuals does not matter and that the institutional arrangements determining the policy-making context do not matter. The interdependent rational actor model developed by the theory of games provides a good theoretical tool in helping to think about complex strategic interactions that occur in most policy issues. However, the theory of games considers the institutional context of the policy-making situations as exogenous factors modelled in a highly abstract manner.

Institutional rational choice models are more convincing because they endogenize the relevant micro-institutional arrangements by using various conceptual tools from the economic theory of transaction costs, the economic theory of contracts, as well as the principal agent theory. Although these models provide more appropriate tools for capturing the institutional complexities of policy-making situations, they have lost some of the predictive ability that characterizes the theory of games. To that extent, the micro-institutional rational choice models face the same challenge that contributed to discredit traditional political science dedicated to the study of (macro)-institutional structures: the ability to provide appropriate descriptions but no ability to go from description to explanation and prediction based on deductive models. In spite of this mitigated diagnosis of the current state of the micro-institutional rational choice models, they will inform future directions of research. Their contribution to the advancement of knowledge in political science and in policy studies will be significant insofar as they will yield formal descriptions of the linkages that exist between the attributes of individual actors and the attributes of the micro-institutional arrangements defining the decision-making situations. This evolution from description to explanation and prediction is likely to require systematic empirical studies such as those conducted by Elinor Ostrom and her colleagues at Indiana University and Mark Sproule-Jones at McMaster University, as well as systematic experimental studies such as those conducted by Norman Frohlich from the University of Manitoba and his colleague Joe Oppenheimer from the University of Maryland.

Notes

1 Doern and Aucoin, *Public Policy in Canada*; Landry, ed., *Introduction à l'analyse des politiques*.
2 Pal, *Public Policy Analysis: An Introduction*, 30–2.
3 Howlett and Ramesh, *Studying Public Policy: Policy Cycles and Policy Subsystems*, ch. 2.
4 Braybrooke and Lindblom, *A Strategy of Decision: Policy Evaluation as a Social Process*.
5 Ordershook, *A Political Theory Primer*; Ordershook, *Game Theory and Political Theory*; Axelrod, 1984; Brams, 1985; Zagare, *Game Theory: Concepts and Applications*.
6 Green and Shapiro, *Pathologies of Rational Choice Theory: A Critique of Applications in Political Science*.
7 Ostrom, *Governing the Commons: The Evolution of Institutions for Collective Action*; Ostrom, Roy, and Walker, *Rules Games and Common-Pool Resources*.
8 Olson, *The Logic of Collective Action* (Cambridge: Harvard University Press, 1965).

9 Bromley, ed., *Making the Commons Work: Theory, Practice and Policy*; Ostrom, *Crafting Institutions for Self-Governing Irrigation Systems*.
10 Miller, *Managerial Dilemmas: The Political Economy of Hierarchy*.
11 Brams, *Paradoxes in Politics: An Introduction to the Nonobvious in Political Science*; Dawes, *Rational Choice in an Uncertain World*; Greenberg, *The Theory of Social Situations: An Alternative Game Theoretic Approach*.
12 Rapoport and Chammak, *Prisoner's Dilemma*.
13 Olson, *The Logic of Collective Action*, Cambridge; Frohlich, Oppenheimer, and Young, *Political Leadership and Collective Goods*; Harding, *Collective Action*; Taylor and Ward, 1982; Hampton, 1987.
14 Hanuch, *Anatomy of Government Deficiencies*; Wolf, *Markets or Governments: Choosing between Imperfect Alternatives*; Brander, *Government Policy toward Business*, ch. 1; Strick, *The Economics of Government Regulation: Theory and the Canadian Practice*, Part 1.
15 Anai, 'Policy and Practice in the Atlantic Fisheries'; Pinkerton, ed., *Cooperative Management of Local Fisheries*; Davis, 'Property Rights and Access Management in the Small Boat Fisheries.'
16 McDavid, *Service Delivery in Canadian Public Economics*; McDavid, 'The Canadian Experience with Privatizing Residential Solid Waste Collection Services,' 602–8.
17 Pross, *Group Politics and Public Policy*; Coleman and Skogstad, eds., *Policy Communities and Public Policy in Canada: A Structural Approach*.
18 Imbeau, 'Procedural Constraints and Conflictual Preferences in Collective Decision-Making'; Imbeau, 'Voting Games and Constitutional Decisions'; James, 'Rational Choice? Crisis Bargaining over the Meech Lake Accord'; Landry, 'Interest Groups and the Political Economy of the Constitutional Debates in Canada'; Young, 'The Political Economy of Secession,' *Constitutional Political Economy*.
19 Rapoport and Guyer, 'A Taxonomy of 2x2 Games'; Rapoport, Guyer, and Gordon, *The 2x2 Game*; Brams, *Theory of Moves*.
20 Martin, 'The Selective Usefulness of Game Theory,' *Social Studies of Sciences*.
21 Brams, *Theory of Moves*.
22 Morrow, *Game Theory for Political Scientists*.
23 Landry, 'La nouvelle analyse institutionnelle'; Shepsle, 'Studying Institutions'; Sproule-Jones, 'Public Choice and Natural Resources'; Sproule-Jones, 'Institutions, Constitutions and Public Policies'; Ostrom, *Governing the Commons*.

24 Williamson, 'The Firm as a Nexus of Treaties'; Brousseau, *L'économie des contrats*; Brousseau, 'L'approche néo-institutionnelle de l'économie des coûts de transaction.'
25 Bryson and Smith Ring, 'A Transaction-Based Approach to Policy Intervention.'
26 Simon, *Administrative Behavior*.
27 Riker and Ordeshook, *An Introduction to Positive Political Theory*.
28 Williamson, *The Economic Institutions of Capitalism*; Williamson, *Markets and Hierarchies, Analysis and Antitrust Implications*.
29 Williamson, *The Economic Institutions of Capitalism*.
30 Bryson and Smith Ring, 'A Transaction-Based Approach to Policy Intervention,' 211.
31 Milgram and Roberts, *Economics, Organization and Management*, 33.
32 Williamson, *Markets and Hierarchies*.
33 Brousseau, *L'économie des contrats*.
34 Ibid.
35 Ibid.
36 Hirschman, *Exit, Voice, and Loyalty: Responses to Decline in Firms, Organizations and States*.
37 Brousseau, *L'économie des contrats*.
38 Ibid., 124.
39 Ibid.
40 Jacquemin, *Pouvoir et sélection dans la nouvelle économie industrielle*.
41 Brousseau, *L'économie des contrats*, 148.
42 Wolf, *Markets or Governments: Choosing between Imperfect Alternatives*; Brander, *Government Policy toward Business*; Strick, *The Economics of Government Regulation: Theory and Canadian Practice*.
43 Brousseau, *L'économie des contrats*, 151.
44 Twight, 'Political Transaction-Cost Manipulation'; Twight, 'Constitutional Renegotiation'; Twight, 'Government Manipulation of Constitutional-Level Transaction Costs.'
45 Twight, 'Political Transaction-Cost Manipulation,' 200.
46 Wolf, *Markets or Governments*.
47 Landry and Blouin, 'Comparaison des stratégies d'aide manufacturières aux entreprises.'
48 Williamson, *The Economic Institutions of Capitalism*.
49 North, *Institutions, Institutional Change and Economic Performance*; North, *Structure and Change in Economic History*.
50 Trebilcock, *The Limits of Freedom of Contract*.

51 Migué and Marceau, *Le monopole public de l'Éducation.*

52 Ostrom, Schroeder, and Wynne, *Institutional Incentives and Sustainable Development: Infrastructure Policies in Perspective.*

53 Brook, *Who Is in Charge? The Mixed Ownership Corporation in Canada*; Stanbury and Kierans, *Papers on Privatization*; Stanbury, 'Privatization by Federal and Provincial Governments in Canada: An Empirical Study'; Tupper and Doern, eds., *Privatization, Public Policy and Public Corporations in Canada*; Bernier, 'Privatization in Québec.'

54 Schultz, 'Deregulation Canadian-Style' in Bernier and Gow, eds., *A Down-Sized State?*; Schultz and Alexandroff, *Economic Regulation and the Federal System*; Block and Georgermer, eds., *Breaking the Shackles: Deregulating Canadian Industry.*

55 Maslove, ed., *Taxes as Instruments of Public Policy.*

56 Veit, 'Purchase of Service Contracting in the Social Services in Canada'; McDavid, 'The Canadian Experience with Privatizing Residential Solid Waste Collection Services'; McDavid, 'Privatization of Residential Solid Waste in Richmond, British Columbia'; McDavid, 'Part-time Fire Fighters in Canadian Municipalities,' *Canadian Public Administration* 29, no. 3 (1986); McDavid and Schick, 'Privatization versus Union-Management Cooperation: The Effects of Competition on Service Efficiency in Municipalities,' *Canadian Public Administration* 30, no. 3 (1987); McDavid, 'Factors Predicting Police Costs in Canadian Municipalities,' *Canadian Police College Journal* 16, no. 2 (1992).

57 Howlett, 'Policy Instruments, Policy Styles, and Policy Implementation: National Approaches to Theories of Instrument Choice'; Howlett and Ramesh, *Studying Public Policy: Policy Cycles and Policy Subsystems.*

58 Linder and Peters, 'Instruments of Government: Perceptions and Contexts,' 9; C. Hood, *The Tools of Government* (Chatham House Publishers 1986); Doern and Phidd, *Canadian Public Policy: Ideas, Structure, Process* (Toronto: Methuen 1983).

59 Trebilcock, Hartle, Prichard, and Dewees, *The Choice of Governing Instrument*; Woodside, 'Policy Instruments and the Study of Public Policy'; Landry and Pesant, *Politicians, Incentives and Policy Instruments: Theory and Evidence.*

60 Landry and Blouin, 'Comparaison des stratégies d'aide manufacturières aux entreprises.'

11

Policy Networks, Policy Communities, and the Problems of Governance

MICHAEL M. ATKINSON
AND WILLIAM D. COLEMAN

The past decade has witnessed two important and related changes in the academic study of public policy. First, society-driven models of the policy process have given way to models in which the institutions of the state are understood to have considerable autonomy. The idea that policy emanates from interests that are organized in society has not, by any means, been entirely eclipsed, but there has been a general recognition that original images of responsive politicians and compliant bureaucrats need to be amended. Students of comparative state theory have led this revival of interest in the autonomous role of state institutions, but rational choice theorists have assisted by emphasizing the self-interested behaviour of state officials. Although researchers in these traditions have little in common methodologically (or ideologically for that matter), they share the belief that the state is not an inert entity shaped by historical struggles and liable to capture by society's strongest interests. Rather, the state is an active agent, moulding society and serving the interests of office-holders sometimes as much as, or more than, the interests of citizens.

Second, traditional pluralist conceptions of the organization of societal interests have been expanded and, to some degree at least, amended. Models of the policy process in which a host of groups compete with one another to organize and represent a rich variety of interests shared by overlapping segments of society are now seen to be relevant only in selected instances. Whatever its genealogy, pluralist imagery has given way to a variety of alternative models that stress the difficulties of organizing and maintaining interests, the uneven character of organization, and the privileged status of business.

To some extent, these changes in conceptual apparatus are linked to changes in the real world. It is cliché to note that governments have grown in size and complexity. Some areas of governance, in particular the management of macroeconomic policy instruments, began only with World War II. Other areas, including the expansion of social welfare systems, were responses to the Great Depression. Part of the Keynesian legacy is that political authorities in advanced capitalist societies are now held responsible for ensuring that their citizens enjoy a minimum standard of social well-being. Where it was once assumed that the decisions of firms and individuals alone created economic dislocation, governments are now obliged to share a large measure of responsibility.

Public sector managers have discovered that in shouldering this responsibility, they cannot rely exclusively on traditional organizational forms styled on the Weberian model of bureaucracy. Accordingly, state managers have searched for new means to accomplish unfamiliar, and often unwelcome, tasks. Independent regulatory agencies were among the first organizational innovations. They have been followed in recent years by mixed corporations, joint ventures, and most recently, service-oriented public bureaucracies. For modern states, the problem has become one of maintaining ultimate control yet sharing the exercise of public authority. Public officials want to escape blame, but also to claim credit. They want to husband political power, but they must mobilize social forces to obtain it in the first place. As a result, the range of state forms has expanded considerably, encouraging a reconsideration of established policy models.

Of course, changes in policy-making models are also a function of intellectual dynamics. Postwar pluralist imagery was a direct reaction against the idea that constitutional formulas – for example, ministerial responsibility or the separation of powers – were the sole or primary key to understanding governance. Pluralist descriptions of the policy process directed attention away from the structure of the state and toward the more fluid, less predictable world of group politics. The subsequent return to institutions and the structure of government – captured conveniently in the phrase 'bringing the state back in' – has been an almost predictable reaction to the reaction. Although pluralist models were originally defended as realistic, rather than idealistic, these versions of the policy process are no longer seen as entirely authentic themselves. Somehow, room had to be made for the state's capacity to define legitimate interests, shape political organization, and incorporate societal actors into policy making. Those who never doubted the importance of legislatures, executives, and bureaucracies are now invited to propose their own versions of state-society relationships.

'Policy network' and the related notion of 'policy community' constitute two of the most important conceptual innovations to emerge from this more catholic approach to the policy process. Although these terms have different meanings in different hands, they suggest a renewed attempt to be both encompassing and discriminating in describing the policy process: encompassing because they refer to actors and relationships in the policy process that take us beyond political-bureaucratic relationships; discriminating because they suggest the presence of many communities and different types of networks. They allow that the world of state-society relations is richly varied and deny that there is any advantage in positing a single model.

In this article we evaluate recent attempts to define and use the policy community/policy network concepts, then turn our attention to three sets of problems that beset these conceptual formulas. First, we speculate on whether these notions are nothing more than minor variations on the dominant pluralist theme. The weakness of pluralist versions of the state is reflected in the problems that network and community concepts encounter in incorporating the influence of macropolitical institutions. Second, given that these concepts have been developed primarily for study at national and subnational levels, it is not clear how they can accommodate the internationalization of many policy domains. Finally, while it is evident that networks and communities change, very little theorizing has been done on the subject of diachronic dynamics.

Networks and Communities

Most students of the policy process want to generalize. They may be experts in one or another policy area, but they typically aspire to say something about policy making in general, ideally something that applies to a number of different political systems. Hence the search for a 'magic bullet,' a concept or image that travels across policy domains and political systems yet retains some measure of relevance and distinctiveness. Such a concept would encourage comparisons, suggest hypotheses, and help draw together knowledge of an increasingly fragmented policy process.

Such fragmentation has become a particularly significant obstacle to the generation of a coherent body of knowledge. Study after study has shown us that, within the same political system, things work differently in agriculture, transportation, monetary policy, and so on. We have been forced to accept that, in advanced capitalist economies, the policy process differs considerably across policy domains. Some domains are dominated by a few actors representing a limited set of interests; in others the organizational ecology is complex and the interests are widely varied. Many policy domains remain the preserve of conventional trade associations, but many others also contain single-issue groups, professional lobbyists, and think-tanks under varied sponsorship. Nor do sectors provide a way out: studies of the same policy sector across different states yield diverse findings as well.

In an increasing number of policy areas, possessing technical capacity and detailed information has become crucial to effective participation. For those who have such expertise, the exchange of information between state and private actors can create privileged relationships to which the uninitiated are excluded. In some of these policy arenas the technical requirements are so demanding that societal actors have been delegated the authority to implement policy. In others the state has resources at least as impressive as those possessed by the most powerful forces in society. Here state actors jealously guard their prerogatives and resist collaboration or even information sharing.

So, generalizations do not come easily. Researchers now recognize that in all countries the pattern of governance will vary (sometimes significantly) across policy subsystems. The dominant pattern in agriculture may be fundamentally different from the one that prevails in, say, energy. Any images or models of the policy process have to be sufficiently elastic to stretch across a variety of policy sectors.

'Policy network' and 'policy community' are one set of concepts that appear to possess the required elasticity. For many years sociologists employed the concept of a network in studies of social communication in small groups and in large organizations. More recently, the concept has been used in the study of communication patterns that favour product innovation in congeries of small firms.[1] Political scientists have used the term 'policy network' more loosely to refer to dependency relationships that emerge between both organizations and individuals who are in frequent contact with one another in particular policy areas.[2] The term 'policy community' has a more anthropological flavour. Heclo and Wildavsky, for example, used this term to denote the 'shared framework' within which the Treasury decision making takes place.[3] Although the term has been employed in a number of ways since, it still suggests 'a commonly understood belief system, code of conduct, and established pattern of behaviour.'[4]

The metaphoric character of these terms in political science has invited definitional disputes. For example, there are those who propose that 'network' should be the master concept, and that policy community is best understood as a type of network. Thus Rhodes defines policy community as a network characterized by stable relationships, restrictive membership, vertical interdependence, and insulation from other networks and institutions.[5] Networks that are less stable, less restrictive, and so on, are given different names. Wilks and Wright employ an alternative approach.[6] For them, the policy community refers to all actors or potential actors who share either an interest in a policy area or a common 'policy focus' and who, over time, succeed in shaping policy. They reserve the term 'policy network' for describing the nature of the 'linking process' that occurs within this community. Coleman and Skogstad adopt essentially the same distinction. For them, a policy network refers to 'the properties that characterize the relationships among the particular set of actors that forms around an issue of importance to the policy community.'[7] Thus the 'community' refers to the actors; the 'network' refers to the relationships among actors, particularly in the subgovernment.

Although some have suggested that this dispute be settled by definitional fiat,[8] it seems unlikely that forced closure will end the terminological debate that has emerged. Part of the reason that researchers use identical terms to refer to rather different phenomena is that the phenomena themselves – relationships among societal actors, politicians, and bureaucrats – are rather more complex than first imagined. All researchers seek roughly the same objective: a way of describing complex relationships in particular policy areas that will assist in understanding policy outcomes. However, as concepts, neither network nor community can convey very much of this complexity. They are broad, inclusive terms that have so far retained their essentially metaphorical qualities. Lending more precision to these concepts requires further conceptual refinement, and it is this endeavour that leads to terminological disagreements.

Of course, the reason these concepts are attracting any interest at all is their evident relevance for two key questions of policy analysis, namely who participates and who wields power. On the first of these questions, who participates, both 'network' and 'community' convey the impression of order in the midst of chaos. Those who have studied policy making in advanced capitalist systems know that interpersonal and interorganizational relations have become extraordinarily complex. For researchers the initial task is to trace interactions, first at the level of individuals, then groups and finally communities. Sociologists are past masters at this enterprise. By breaking down social exchanges into their component parts and then reassembling them into networks, they have worked toward theories that explain how particular patterns are sustained.[9]

Hugh Heclo's concept of 'issue network' echoes this sociological approach. He uses the term to suggest a policy making process that is fragmented and populated by a wide and unpredictable number of participants.[10] Heclo focuses his discussion at the micro level, that is, on the relationships that prevail among individuals. The backgrounds of these individuals and their career profiles are the key to the emerging system he finds, a system that borders on chaos. Kriesi's study of networks in Switzerland, which borrows even more directly from sociological network analysis, reveals, in contrast, a highly structured and ordered political system.[11]

Not everyone shares this preference for anchoring networks and communities in exchanges among individuals. Others have employed the term 'network' exclusively at the meso level, the level of groups and organizations.[12] Rather than build their networks from the bottom up, beginning with individuals in contact with one another, they have begun with public and private organizations in a system.

But whatever the level of analysis, communities or networks have conceptual appeal because they convey, simultaneously, the impression of inclusiveness and exclusiveness. Networks have shape and identity, but they are also open systems that do not have clear boundaries. Communities suggest a more organic connection among participants, but they too are relatively open. The question then becomes: How open? And with that question comes several others: What is the price of admission and how integrated is the network or community?

As Jordan points out, early formulations of the network concept by American political scientists used expressions such as 'whirlpools of activity' and 'web of relationships in the subsystem' to convey the image of fluid relationships that involved participants from a variety of institutional sites in decentralized systems of mutual dependence.[13] Subsequent research uncovered considerable variation in the integration of networks. Perhaps the most integrated network is the so-called 'iron triangle,' a concept developed in the 1960s in the United States to describe a mutually supportive relationship between relevant congressional committees, interest associations, and government bureaus. Iron triangles suggest a closed system in which cooperation is based on the support that each party gives the others and the political and economic surpluses generated are privately appropriated.

Although this image still enjoys some currency in the United States, its applicability beyond the American congressional system has always been suspect. Some of these triangular and, in parliamentary systems, bipartite structures have proven remarkably resistant to outside intrusion, as Wilson's study of 'wilderness politics' in Canada illustrates.[14] But the pattern is one of increasing complexity. Even in the United States, the iron triangle concept applies only to a limited and perhaps shrinking number of policy areas.[15] If anything has characterized the policy process in recent years it is the entry of a proliferation of voluntary associations and public interest groups that were previously thought to be unorganized and virtually unorganizable.[16]

These groups, and other institutional actors such as local governments, corporations, and universities,[17] have interrupted cosy relationships and given legislators and others the tools to break up even iron triangles.

So while iron triangles may exist, they sit on a continuum as exemplars of one of the most integrated of a wide range of policy networks. This variation in networks has been illustrated well by Laumann and Knoke whose study of the energy and health sectors in the United States has set the standard among sociologists who aim at the careful dissection of policy networks. Calling health and energy 'policy domains,' these authors develop exchange models of organizational interaction in which 'resources' are the medium of exchange and 'events' the conditions under which organizational exchange takes place.[18] Among other things, their analysis indicates that the health domain is characterized by far more integrated networks than those found in energy and that different organizations dominate in each domain: professional organizations in health; business organizations in energy. But each domain possesses an underlying stability: in each there is an array of identifiable associational actors.

This is a first step in the use of the network and community concepts, but it does not take us far enough. For one thing, Laumann and Knoke's research confirms what casual observers already recognize, namely that specific decision-making events draw on only a limited number of those who might potentially be involved. The fact that policy networks are relatively open-ended means that it is not possible to predict with any confidence just who will participate in which event. Thus the authors conclude that the energy and health domains are highly differentiated and that policy outcomes 'are the product of decentralized contention among a plurality of organizations.'[19] This conclusion is a sound and cautious one, but it is not very encouraging. Networks can be identified, but that information alone will be of very little use in predicting policy outcomes.

Part of the problem is methodological. The network and community concepts, to their credit, have refocused attention on political actors in interaction. By their nature, communities suggest people in communication with one another; networks suggest contact. These concepts return individual actors to centre stage and invite researchers to map their relations with one another. The difficulty is that sophisticated attempts to map interactions and create complex network typologies too often pay inadequate attention to the content of relationships. We are told that networks consist of exchange relationships, but what is the structural context in which these exchanges take place? Are there relationships of power and dependency that transcend and colour individual transactions?

If the answer to this last question is 'yes,' then we will have to reach beyond transactional analysis to posit the structural conditions under which interaction occurs. That is, networks will have to be distinguished from one another by more than their level of integration, their degree of openness, or even by the coalitions that have formed around certain policy options. As Scharpf points out, even when the substance of policy choices is factored into the analysis of networks, the connection between the networks on the one hand, and process and outcome variables on the other, is often underdeveloped.[20] To bridge that gap it will be necessary to focus on institutional variables, such as the levels of centralization and professionalism that characterize organizations in a network, and on ideological variables, such as the intellectual foundations of dominant world views in particular policy areas.[21]

This kind of network analysis has already begun. The structural properties of state agencies and organized interests have been used to generate a typology of policy networks based on distinctive patterns of power and dependency. Policy networks have been described as corporatist, state-directed, collaborative, or pluralist not simply on the basis of who participates, but also on the basis of the distribution of organizational resources within the network.[22] This structural interpretation of policy networks does not include an ideological dimension, but there is no reason why networks cannot also be distinguished in terms of ideological resources. The point is that research premised on an appreciation of the content and structure of networks will have to press well beyond the question of how integrated or open they are. The latter properties are probably best understood as features of the policy community. Networks, on the other hand, should be distinguished by the properties that characterize the relationships inside these communities.

Ambiguities surrounding the use of these terms should not be allowed to overshadow the fact that the concepts of network and community have assisted public policy studies. They have shifted attention from policy making in national institutions to policy making in subsystems and sectors. In the process, institutionally imposed boundaries to research have been broken down and replaced by a more fluid and less restricted view of the policy process. The original idea that groups are exclusively policy advocates has given way to the view that some groups, particularly those with appropriate organizational qualities, are capable of sharing in the exercise of political power. Moreover, societal participation in the policy process is by no means restricted to interest groups. The network and community concepts leave open to empirical research the question of which societal actors, possessed of which institutional properties, participate in a given policy domain. Any actors holding technical knowledge – whether these be expert committees of trade associations, large corporations, universities, private research institutes, or even trade unions – can become potentially crucial participants in the policy process of any advanced capitalist economy.

Just as the network and community concepts have broadened and deepened the analysis of societal actors, they also have forced a reconsideration of the role of formal bureaucratic institutions in the policy process. From this perspective, it is no longer clear that technical and policy knowledge can always be marshalled and managed in hierarchies. In many instances rigid bureaucratic structures are giving way to self-organizing networks as means of coping with the complexity created by conditions of reciprocal interdependence.[23] Similarly, networks are also ways of compensating for the deficiencies of market coordination, since price signals cannot be relied upon to produce mutually beneficial exchanges or optimal levels of cooperation.

In short, networks and communities are natural conceptual responses both to the limits of markets and hierarchical arrangements, to the enormous expansion in the types of societal actors involved in policy making, and to the dispersion of specialized policy resources.[24] As Pross has noted, there is little point in continuing to work with concepts designed for a period when 'lobbying and government were much less complicated.'[25] Unfortunately, it is not possible to conclude with a complete endorsement of the theorizing that has been done or the research that has been conducted under this conceptual umbrella. Apart from the conceptual issues already touched upon, those who would use the network/community concepts must cope with three challenges: theorizing the connection between networks, communities, and broader political institutions, integrating international levels of decision making into studies that have been confined to the nation-state only, and conceptualizing patterns of change in networks.

Reaggregating the State: The Problem of Pluralism

By breaking the policy process into sectoral and subsectoral components, the policy community and policy network concepts have countered the tendency to generalize haphazardly about macropolitical processes. For example, this research has offered a critique of the strong state/weak state distinction and has argued for a more nuanced appreciation of strength and weakness based on the characteristics of sectoral policy networks.[26] Nevertheless, some room must be left for the reintegration of macropolitical structures into the analysis of policy outcomes. Having disaggregated the state, researchers in this tradition are faced with the problem of reaggregating it. They must consider how sectoral networks and communities affect the pattern of policy outcomes at the macro level and how national political institutions condition policy networks and policy communities.

So far, this question has not dominated theorizing. On the contrary, the study of policy networks has tended to reinforce an image of the state traditionally found in pluralist theory. In this version, state authority is seriously fragmented, agencies and bureaus are in open competition, a rich variety of interest groups compete for the attention of policy makers, and disjointed incrementalism is the dominant policy style. Moreover, research under the network and community banner has uncovered patterns of interaction that reinforce the pluralist message. In their search for a centre or core within the complicated system of policy networks in the United States, John Heinz and his colleagues turned up very little.[27] Using reputational techniques and the analysis of interactions, they identified a set of Washington lobbyists ('notables' in their words) whose contacts with one another form the basis for elite networks in four policy domains: health, energy, labour, and agriculture. Remarkably, they found very few generalists, that is, people who are active across these areas: 'Even though our list of notables includes Washington representatives of great prominence, accomplishment, and reputed influence, we find no identifiable "core" actors.'[28] What Heinz et al. did find was a well-developed division of labour in which the structure of networks is dictated by the substantive specialization of the representative.

Little wonder then that those whose work has been primarily at the micro and meso levels have concluded that 'the modern industrial polity is a complex of formal organizations in conflict with one another over the collective allocation of scarce resources'[29] and that the best way to describe the overall structure of policy domains is 'elite interest group pluralism.'[30] Some students of policy communities prefer to treat the state as a separate entity, rather than one that shares authority with groups,[31] but the conceptual apparatus and methodological tools of network analysis militate against this presumption. Self-organizing networks are not limited by institutional boundaries, and there is no 'stopping rule' that prevents them from expanding to include state officials or public bureaucracies.[32] Thus Laumann and Knoke probably capture the implications best when they describe the state as 'a complex system of government and nongovernmental organizations that struggle for power and legitimacy in the making of public policies affecting domain participants.'[33] The distinction between state and society virtually disappears in this formulation and 'the appropriate unit of analysis for studies of policy formation is not the state understood in the institutional sense, but the state as a collection of policy arenas incorporating both governmental and private actors.'[34]

The blending of a pluralist view of the state and network analysis emphasizes the idea of variation in power relationships at the sectoral and subsectoral levels, but discourages comparison at the level of nation-states. If the state is nothing more than 'a collection of policy arenas,' then it is to these arenas that we should presumably repair. Comparisons of policy arenas in different states make sense, but efforts to compare the policies of whole nations are probably misguided. Network analysis gives within-system variation pride of place, and discourages those who believe that different national practices and traditions have a potential impact on policy outcomes. The fact that many students of networks and communities seem to be satisfied with a rather anaemic view of the state is perfectly understandable under these circumstances. If the state can be successfully disaggregated and if policy networks hold the key to understanding policy outcomes, then there is little incentive to reconstitute the state or conceive of it as anything other than an assembly of organizational actors. Logically, then, comparative public policy will take the form of comparisons within sectors but across nations.

It is not quite so easy, however, to dismiss macropolitical structures. Researchers have found it difficult to explain cross-national differences in policy by referring to sectoral variables alone. This problem emerged clearly in the research on corporatism and corporatist policy networks. At the outset, the concept was used to characterize governance arrangements at the macropolitical level that involve negotiations between the state and 'social partners,' usually over economic policy. More recently, the concept has come to be used to denote a model of policy making in which the state bargains with interest associations who monopolize representation in particular sectors of the economy and assume various responsibilities for implementing policy.[35] In closed forums, societal and state actors develop consensual arrangements for both generating and distributing resources. The key to corporatism is the organization of societal interests. Both political order and policy solutions are made possible by the organization of political interests into hierarchies of groups that bargain with the state over critical policy issues. In its most complete form, these hierarchies incorporate all organized interests into peak organizations capable of entering into the negotiation of investment and production decisions. Thus we have a combination of hierarchy and network.

The corporatist model has been widely adapted for study at the sectoral level,[36] but it has not been possible to shake off the impact of macropolitical structures. The political organization of the dairy sector, probably the policy domain most consistently organized along corporatist lines, illustrates the profound impact of these variables. There are, it is true, broad similarities among the dairy industries in Western democracies: protectionism is common, lobbying is highly developed, and interest associations participate in both policy formulation and implementation. Yet there are important differences as well: bargaining takes place within comprehensive peak associations in Austria and Sweden, but not in other countries; the delegation of authority to interest associations is more extensive in Austria, Sweden, Switzerland, and Germany than it is in Britain, the United States, and Canada.[37] These kinds of differences are not readily explained by cross-country variations in industry structure or in bureaucratic expertise related to dairying. To account for differences in the networks that have emerged, researchers have been obliged to resort to broader, macropolitical factors.

Research inspired by the corporatist agenda has taken us beyond the (by now) uncontroversial view that the policy process is likely to be different from one domain or sector to another, to the point at which we must acknowledge that at least some of these differences are differences in kind, not degree. It is not merely a matter of how many actors are involved, or how frequent their contacts are with one another; corporatist research has shown that relationships differ in their fundamental assumptions. These fundamental assumptions are often derived from macropolitical arrangements. For example, the competitive-adversarial character of American politics has been invoked to account for the resistance to corporatist forms in the United States. Corporatist and collaborative networks are simply less likely to develop in institutional environments that nurture pressure pluralism. Conversely, Dyson's identification of the German polity as one with a developed public law state and a highly associative society suggests an environment more nurturing of collaborative networks.[38] Pluralist forms are not equally encouraged in all systems, so no one should be surprised that more restrictive and hierarchical networks will emerge where the virtues of pluralism have a weaker hold over the political imagination.

In short, notwithstanding the growing popularity of network studies and the continued vitality of pluralist models of policy making, thoughts of jettisoning macro-level variables seem rather premature. Even among those who urge the use of the network and community concepts, there is an acknowledgment that system-level norms set the context in which networks are formed. For example, Maurice Wright, after reviewing the institutional norms of parliamentary government in Britain – the rule of law, natural justice, and parliamentary privilege – suggests that 'these and other systemic norms provide the general contours of policy and behaviour, the details of which are filled in at the level of different policy areas and, within them, sectors and sub-sectors.'[39] Jack Hayward makes a similar observation in discussing industrial policy in France: 'A country's peculiar policy style, the institutional and cultural legacies that constitute the normative framework by reference to which policy is defined and that changes relatively slowly, must not be equated with the day-to-day behaviour of members of the policy community.'[40] The distinction gives rise to what Hayward calls the 'dual policy style,' which in turn accounts for the apparent inconsistencies in the French policy process, namely the image of a strong bureaucratic state capable of anticipatory policy, and the reality of short-term reactive policy making in fragmented policy communities.

There is certainly no shortage of system-level variables that could conceivably influence the structure of policy networks. Different styles of regulation, different modes of representation, and different levels of institutional autonomy are all potentially important macro-level variables.[41] However, the integration of these variables with the concepts of network and community has not proceeded very far. In fact, these latter variables seem to do little more than provide 'the general contours' (Wright) and constitute 'the normative framework' (Hayward). Their relationship to meso and micro level variables is not specified.

If these variables are to be drawn together more systematically, it is most likely that research will begin by suggesting how macro-level variables influence the formation and operation of policy networks. But these macro-level variables cannot be invoked haphazardly; they must be consciously connected to the development of policy networks. Coleman has shown, for example, how national policy styles – the 'dual polity' in France, the 'accommodative, liberal corporatist polity' in Germany, and the 'adversary polity' in Britain, the United States, and Canada – affect the level of integration and cooperation within the business associations of these countries.[42] Adversary politics at the national level generally retards business mobilization.

Within some policy domains, such as environmental regulation and occupational health and safety, however, there may be significant differences within adversary systems. In these domains, Britain, for example, has developed a relatively informal and flexible system of regulation that places minimal demands on business; in the United States, responsible agencies rely heavily on their rule-making authority and often display an inflexible attitude toward their 'clients.'[43] The point is that a properly specified model of policy outcomes will have to define macro-level variables accurately and appreciate that their effects may differ from one policy domain to another within the same system.

Model specification is made more difficult by the fact that the relationship between network and community variables, on the one hand, and macro-level variables on the other, is a reciprocal one. The operation of networks, for example, will eventually change national policy styles, albeit very slowly. If the emergence of particular types of networks changes the manner in which policy is made in advanced industrial economies, then presumably these networks cannot but gradually influence the evolution of the state.

Progress toward a multilevel model of the policy process, in which networks and communities play a critical role, will be hampered by a slavish devotion to pluralist images of the state. Although the modern state may be a highly fragmented and divided entity, it is not reducible to its parts nor can it be dissolved into a collection of policy networks. In constitutional democracies, no policy making institution is an entirely independent entity. The state consists of a set of executive, administrative, deliberative, and adjudicative institutions whose peculiar character and relationship to one another will influence the integration of policy communities, the structure of policy networks, and the values nurtured in both. The concept of the state recognizes that these institutions are drawn together in the practice both of normal politics, that is, the authoritative allocation of values, as well as of crisis politics, those more dramatic occasions on which the state uses its coercive tools to enforce compliance. The state's capacity to structure and restructure, organize and reorganize, will differ from system to system, but proceeding to analyse the policy process as if broad state institutions are irrelevant is a misuse of the concepts of network and community.

The Internationalization of Policy Domains

The concept of a policy network has been developed primarily to assess national policy making from a domestic point of view. When two or more countries are compared, the study normally involves the analysis of respective domestic networks. Thus, whether the studies are comparative or limited to one country, the stress is on the identification of constellations of national or subnational state agencies, politicians, interest groups, and political parties. In short, with the important exception of policy analysis within federal regimes, policy networks have tended to be studied at a single level of a political system.

Yet the need to incorporate both national and international levels into policy analysis has become increasingly pressing over the past two decades. The list of policy areas affected by international negotiations, whether at a regional or a global level, has lengthened considerably to include telecommunications, banking, securities trading, and environmental regulation to name but a few.[44] This growing interdependence of national and international arenas should provide some direction for future developments in the policy networks approach.

In the first place, specialists in international relations have encountered the same interdependence and, in response, have drawn heavily on the same sets of variables that are crucial to students of policy networks. Second, international relations theorists have employed game theory to model policy processes that take place at two levels. In short, the conceptual challenges posed by the internationalization of policy networks can be met, in part at least, by capitalizing on the work of international relations theorists.

Specialists in international relations have begun to distinguish what might be called traditional foreign policy from new, emerging areas of international policy making.[45] In contrast to traditional foreign policy, these new policy arenas tend to be more rule-oriented than power-oriented and to depend less on classic diplomacy but more on managing technical expertise and issues. Accordingly, Winham notes, the cultural and nationalist dimensions of foreign policy give way to demands imposed by bureaucratic procedures, information handling, and issue management. In addition, these more technical and rule-oriented international negotiations have an increasingly pronounced impact on national policy making and on the day-to-day lives of individual citizens.

Not surprisingly, then, some of the policy analysis emerging from international relations resembles the study of domestic policy networks. Winham's study of the Tokyo Round of GATT negotiations admirably illustrates the convergence. In assessing the factors that determine success at the negotiating table, he stresses the importance of control over domestic politics.[46] 'Control' in this context refers to the ability of national representatives to deal with three sorts of pressures: domestic economic interest groups, the constellation of concerned bureaucratic agencies, and 'internal' governments (national governments in the EEC, states or provinces in the United States and Canada). Variations in the intensity of these pressures across nation-states (interest groups were strong in the United States, provinces important in Canada, the bureaucracy in Japan) are then used to explain developments at the negotiating table. In effect, Winham is arguing that in order to account for the twists and turns of international trade negotiations, one has to understand the structure of domestic policy networks.

Peter Cowhey reaches similar conclusions in his consideration of the 'international regimes' literature. Drawing upon a study of telecommunications, he argues that traditional approaches to international regimes have slighted the role of domestic politics. He writes: 'National politicians have been unlikely to accept any global regime that fails to reinforce the preferred domestic regime. Global regime change, therefore, has been most likely to occur when new coalitions successfully challenge domestic regulatory bargains in countries with significant impact on the world market.'[47] 'Coalition' is the key word in this statement: it requires an examination of the structure of domestic policy networks, their internal divisions, and the interests of their members. In fact, Cowhey describes domestic politics as 'the primary source of regime change.'[48]

From the field of comparative public policy, scholars interested in policy convergence have found themselves dealing simultaneously with domestic and international variables. In his careful review of the literature, Bennett argues for distinguishing among convergence in policy goals, policy content, policy instruments, policy outcomes, and policy styles.[49] The latter concept embraces factors that come under our discussion of policy networks and communities.[50] He invokes phenomena such as emulation, diffusion, harmonization, and penetration to explain convergence. In doing so, Bennett and other students of convergence combine domestic network analysis with international institutional processses.

Not only is there some convergence in policy analysis between international relations approaches and policy network/policy community approaches, but international relations research has also yielded some theoretical progress for studying multilevel policy networks. Robert Putnam's work on 'two-level games' represents one sophisticated attempt to treat these international-domestic linkages. He begins with an assertion that echoes Winham and Cowhey: 'A more adequate account of the domestic determinants of foreign policy and international relations must stress politics: parties, social classes, interest groups (both economic and non-economic), legislators, and even public opinion and elections, not simply executive officials and institutional arrangements.'[51] In this formulation, the emphasis on domestic political coalitions is crucial for understanding the size of the 'win sets' – the set of all possible agreements for which a national negotiator could gain majority support from domestic constituents. Examples of factors deemed crucial to determining the size of a national win set include: the distribution of power, preferences, and conditions among national constituents; the relative autonomy of central decision makers from these constituents; and the strength of the state.[52]

Putnam characterizes 'two-level games' in the following way:

At the national level, domestic groups pursue their interests by pressuring the government to adopt favorable policies, and politicians seek power by constructing coalitions among those groups. At the international level, national governments seek to maximize their own ability to satisfy domestic pressures, while minimizing the adverse consequences of foreign developments. Neither of the two games can be ignored by central decision-makers, so long as their countries remain interdependent, yet sovereign.[53]

He adds that national political leaders sit at both game boards. Moves that may be rational at one board, may be irrational at the other.

Several ideas are introduced to link the two games conceptually. Putnam decomposes the negotiation process into two stages: the first leading to a tentative agreement among negotiators at Level I (international) and the second involving ratification of the tentative agreement at Level II (national). He then suggests the idea of a 'win set' noted above: the set of possible Level I agreements that will satisfy a Level II constituency. This notion of a win set provides the real link between the two games. The larger the win set, the higher the probability an agreement will be reached.

The question then becomes: What determines the size of a given win set? Putnam replies, as noted above, that domestic factors (the relative power and preferences of the members of the policy community and the properties of domestic political institutions), plus the strategies of Level I negotiators, are the critical variables. Negotiators will face a number of questions: Do they try to expand the size of the win set to maximize the chances for agreement? Do they keep the win set relatively small in order to maintain a strong bargaining situation? The more complete our understanding of policy networks, the better our appreciation of the strategies of politicians, including their attempts to improve bargaining positions by making side payments to influence the size of win sets.

Putnam's model of two-level games will be particularly useful in policy arenas where national-level actors are the key players, both domestically and internationally. The model assumes that domestic pressures are channelled through a national negotiator who alone plays at both game boards. Although it is widely applicable, this assumption does not hold in several key policy scenarios. For example, it will be less useful in the presence of what Nye and Keohane have termed 'transnational relations': 'contacts, coalitions, and interactions across state boundaries that are not controlled by the central policy organs of governments.'[54] Where transnational relations proliferate, the model breaks down. To illustrate, there are many interest associations that not only lobby their own national governments, but also join together into international organizations that exercise pressure at an international level. Similarly, multinational firms are able to act simultaneously through a number of national interest associations, fostering a kind of indirect cooperation on the international level. These are not insuperable problems for Putnam's model as long as national negotiators retain 'control,' to use Winham's term. But when this control lapses and transnational relations are plentiful, the model does not readily apply and others need to be constructed.

Putnam's model also does not work well when Level I games include an international organization with its own bureaucratic apparatus. The presence of such an international organization will encourage the development of parallel interest organizations leading to a more complex set of negotiations. Consider, for example, the European Union and its policy-initiating institution, the European Commission. Endowed with a separate legal status and important powers, including a monopoly on the proposing of new directives, the Commission is truly a supranational organization and not merely the sum of the contributions of the twelve member countries. Thus the initiative for proposing new policies or directives in the first place comes not from the European Council, but from the Commission. The very existence of the Commission has spawned an intensive development of interest representation at the European level. Furthermore, since the Commission has its hand on the pen when it comes to proposing legislation, national interest associations and bureaucratic agencies seek linkages with it, either directly or through their permanent representatives in Brussels. According to some national associations, these ties to the European Commission are almost as important as those with national government representatives.

In the European Union, two-level games, the extensive interchanges that occur between national and international levels, are no longer funnelled through a single national negotiator sitting at both game boards as Putnam's model assumes. In fact, national negotiators exercise rather little control over many of the interlevel interactions taking place. In brief, other models must be sought when the games become so complex that national interest groups, international interest groups, and international governmental organizations join national negotiators in playing at both game boards.

Once again, a multilevel model of the policy process is needed. The attraction of network analysis is that it promises to bridge national and international levels. The danger, as before, is that researchers will proceed as if traditional distinctions – this time between national and international relations – have dissolved. Networks are governed by sets of rules that determine how decisions are made and who participates in policy making.[55] These rules are bound to be different in the national as opposed to the international sphere. Any effective multilevel model in which policy networks play a central role must take account of these differences.

Policy Networks and Political Change

The analysis of policy communities and policy networks tends to be dynamic only in the sense that one learns about patterns of interaction among various actors, the content of those interactions, and the structures that channel communication. In this respect, network studies have provided useful snapshots of the policy process at a particular point in time, but they have devoted less attention to the changes in processes and outcomes. If policy network approaches are to make a lasting contribution to comparative public policy, they must first explain how policy networks change, and then determine the relationship between network change and policy change. The conceptual tools needed for addressing such questions exist already, albeit implicitly, in policy network analysis. What is required is a conscious effort to specify the key elements in a dynamic model. Three sets of variables recommend themselves as crucial to a fuller understanding of network change.

The first set of variables bears on the issue of boundary shifts. We have already suggested that policy communities are open systems. Inevitably, some members will be closer to the core of the system than others. Their interactions will be stable and continuous compared to the relatively spasmodic involvement of those on the margins. If 'policy community' is used simply to identify those who shape policy outcomes in the long run, the community itself can then be divided and subdivided into those who are relatively close to, or far from, key decisions. For example, Coleman and Skogstad, following Pross, divide the policy community into two segments: a 'subgovernment,' which makes policy in a given field, and an 'attentive public,' which follows and attempts to influence policy making but does not participate directly in it.[56]   *ex: media + polls*

The distinction between those included in the making of policy and those excluded has become a key variable in policy studies. For example, Alan Cawson and his colleagues refine the Weberian concept of 'social closure' and give it a central role in their analysis of policy in the European electronics industry.[57] As they observe, a considerable amount of the energy of firms is devoted simply to the task of keeping others out of the community or at least on the margin. Just who is excluded is revealing about the character of the network that emerges. As Hancher and Moran argue, distinguishing between the included and the excluded 'encourages us not only to examine relations between those who enjoy inclusion, but also to examine the characteristics of the excluded. That the structure of power is shaped by modes of exclusion from any political process is an elementary truth.'[58]

The next step is to study inclusion and exclusion over time. Do some actors move from the attentive public into the subgovernment? Are others forced out? Are new actors gathering on the margins of the subgovernment pressing to be included? What are the consequences for policy making of these kinds of changes? What are the conditions that explain changes in patterns of inclusion and exclusion? Determining the answers to these questions will facilitate the understanding of policy innovation and change.

Recent research suggests that change in the membership of policy communities becomes particularly crucial when new entrants are also carriers of new ideas and theories about policy. As Goldstein and Keohane note, 'actions taken by human beings depend on the substantive quality of available ideas, since such ideas help to clarify principles and conceptions of causal relationships, and to coordinate individual behavior. Once institutionalized, furthermore, ideas continue to guide action in the absence of costly innovation.'[59] Hence, policy network approaches need to incorporate more sophisticated analysis of ideas if they are to account for policy change.

Recognition of the importance of political ideas has shaped several recent studies of public policy that share much in common with the policy network approach. In a study of pesticide regulation in the United States, George Hoberg elaborates the concept of a 'regulatory regime.'[60] In addition to the institutional characteristics of state and societal actors, and the notions of boundary and decision-making rules normally found in network studies, he adds three other components: the dominant values guiding public policy, the knowledge base available to policy makers, and the norms that legitimize various approaches to policy. Hoberg then documents the transformation in regulatory regimes through a careful analysis of the interaction between these structural and ideational factors.

Like Hoberg, Paul Sabatier elaborates a concept, 'policy subsystem,' that includes a mix of structures and of ideational factors.[61] But he also adds two considerations to the analysis. First, he suggests that most policy subsystems will contain more than one 'advocacy coalition,' each with its own belief system and preferred policies. Under 'normal' conditions, one of these coalitions will be dominant and will be in control of relevant state agencies and societal actors. Second, even under 'normal' politics, Sabatier notes that some 'policy learning' will take place. Such learning may improve the understanding of how the variables in a policy maker's belief system are logically and causally related. Resulting refinements in policy makers' belief

systems represent an important force for policy change within a policy subsystem or policy network.

Specialists in international political economy also tend to highlight the
interaction between structures and ideas. Particularly important here is the
concept of an epistemic community. As described by Haas, an epistemic community is a 'network of professionals with recognized expertise and competence in a particular domain or issue area.'[62] As experts committed to a particular ideational road map and a related set of normative beliefs, members
of an epistemic community can play a crucial role in times of crisis when
politicians are looking for new approaches. In his analysis of the international telecommunications regime, Cowhey develops this approach showing
the competition between those believing telecommunications to be a natural
monopoly and those who hold that such services would benefit from normal
market pressures.[63] Kapstein follows a similar approach in analysing the
progress toward a risk-based measure of capital for international banks.[64]

These first two sets of factors – boundary rules and policy ideas – must be
tied to a third set of more external changes if the evolution of networks is to
be linked to policy innovation and change. Changes in one policy network
might have consequences for another. For example, reorganizing a network
dealing with assistance to the poor in order to promote neoliberal principles
may have spillover effects to a network organized around the delivery of
child-care policy. More broadly, Sabatier hypothesizes that the core of a
government's approach to policy is unlikely to be revised significantly without a change in government that leads to a redistribution of the balance of
power among advocacy coalitions within a policy community. He adds that
crucial changes in the social and economic environment might also create
stress in a dominant advocacy coalition.

Certainly these hypotheses are consistent with Hoberg's findings: changes
in environmental regulatory regimes are triggered first by disturbances in
society and the economy in the late 1960s and second by the election of
Ronald Reagan in 1980. Cowhey's analysis of telecommunications shows the
importance of neoliberal governments to regime change in telecommunications. Such governments have been highly unwilling to supply institutional
protection for rather exclusionary networks. Finally, Moran, in his analysis
of financial regulation, cites both the internationalization of financial markets and changes in U.S. government perspectives on financial markets in
explaining changes in policy in Britain and Japan.[65]

Of course, there is nothing innovative about pointing to broad social or
economic changes or to ideological shifts in government when seeking to
explain policy innovation and program changes. But at the moment the study

214 Contemporary Approaches

of policy networks includes very little reflection on the impact of these variables. Network and community analysis tends to be rooted in the realm of normal politics. Yet studies of major policy changes show that environmental disturbances are quite capable of crushing networks and dispersing communities. Of course, this need not happen. Broad shifts in the political and socio-economic environment external to policy communities are filtered through sophisticated and rather complex arrangements before policy changes occur. Networks may delay and even channel the direction of policy change, but just how much they contribute to the process, or even benefit by it, has been a neglected topic. What we do know is that significant macro-level changes often do not translate into actual public policies and programs. Which networks survive environmental shocks and which ones collapse is a topic that must find its way onto the agenda of those who intend to use the network and community concepts.

The methodological implications of these arguments for network/community studies are clear: in addition to determining the relative capacity and resources of various community members, and to assessing the degree of dependency and autonomy that prevail among actors in policy networks, analysts must seek to ascertain the more general principles and norms underlying interpretations of the policy field. They must observe these principles and norms over time, and they should be alert to the possibility of competing beliefs within the given policy community. Examples of how such information can be obtained and assessed are already available in the many excellent studies of belief systems of politicians and bureaucrats.[66] The challenge is to obtain such information from a broad and diffuse policy community that includes political parties, interest associations, trade unions, large enterprises, as well as public officials, and politicians. Kaplan's study of the Canadian trucking industry and Grant, Paterson, and Whitson's work, comparing the German and British chemical industries, provide useful models in this regard.[67]

In summary, policy network approaches need to be recast conceptually if they are to be used in the study of policy innovation and change. Crucial to the analysis of the change is an inclusive conception of the policy community that enables researchers to identify participants in the policy-making process as well as those who are excluded but attentive. Studies should be carried out over time in order to assess the durability of various types of policy networks, their openness to outside influences, and the shifts that occur between the included and the excluded. Greater attention must be paid to the cognitive frameworks of all members of the policy community, to the relative strength of coalitions of community members supporting alternative sets of ideas, and to the potential for policy learning.

Conclusion

This review of policy network/policy community approaches, and the assessment of their problems, leaves grounds for optimism. These approaches appear to serve as a kind of conceptual crossroads for ongoing theoretical and empirical research. As we have indicated, they provide a useful junction for the converging fields of international political economy and comparative public policy. They also invite discussions between those studying executive and legislative structures of government, those focusing on interest intermediation, and those analysing party politics and party government. More broadly, insights from important branches of sociology – network analysis and the sociology of ideas – and from economics – industrial organization, the structure of the firm, and institutional transactions – can be, and in some cases have been, incorporated into the analysis of networks and communities. Cawson et al. note the importance of selecting a methodology that transcends rather than reproduces the boundaries set by academic disciplines.[68] Certainly, the bridging of disciplinary boundaries always proves to be inspiring and useful in the social sciences.

Yet the convergence of various streams of research on the network/community concepts presents dangers as well. In particular, it may foster an endless series of conceptual disputes and counter-disputes. Theoretical progress may stall and empirical research may retreat behind more comfortable, and more familiar, disciplinary boundaries. Averting these dangers requires that empirical research and conceptual development continue to proceed hand-in-hand. The limitations of particular definitions and the utility of insights from diverse subdisciplines will only emerge as scholars actually study the complex policy-making systems of today's governments. We are hopeful that the network/community approaches may advance the study of these systems and, in the process, assist in the development of more broadly based theories of state-society relations.

Notes

This chapter is a revised version of an article that originally appeared in *Governance: An International Journal of Policy and Administration* 5 (April 1992).

1 See Powell, 'Neither Market Nor Hierarchy,' in Staw and Cummings, eds., *Research in Organizational Behavior.*
2 See Benson, 'A Framework for Policy Analysis,' in Rogers et al., eds., *Interorganizational Coordination*, 148.

3 Heclo and Wildavsky, *The Private Government of Public Money.*
4 Pross, *Group Politics and Public Policy*, 98.
5 Rhodes, *Beyond Westminster and Whitehall.*
6 Wilks and Wright, 'Conclusion: Comparing Government-Industry Relations,' in Wilks and Wright, *Comparative Government-Industry Relations.*
7 Coleman and Skogstad, 'Policy Communities and Policy Networks,' in Coleman and Skogstad, eds., *Policy Communities and Public Policy in Canada*, 26.
8 Jordan, 'Subgovernments, Policy Communities and Networks.'
9 For example, see Willer and Anderson, eds., *Networks, Exchange and Coercion.*
10 Heclo, 'Issue Networks and the Executive Establishment,' in King, ed., *The American Political System.*
11 Kriesi, 'The Structure of the Swiss Political System,' in Lehmbruch and Schmitter, eds., *Patterns of Corporatist Policy-Making.*
12 Rhodes, 'Policy Networks'; van Waarden, 'Dimensions and Types of Policy Networks.'
13 Jordan, 'Subgovernments, Policy Communities and Networks.'
14 Wilson, 'Wilderness Politics in B.C.,' in Coleman and Skogstad, eds., *Policy Communities and Public Policy in Canada.*
15 Jordan, 'Iron Triangles, Woolly Corporatism and Elastic Nets,' 99.
16 See Walker, 'The Origin and Maintenance of Interest Groups in America'; Olson, *The Logic of Collective Action.*
17 Salisbury, 'Interest Representation.'
18 Laumann and Knoke, *The Organizational State.*
19 Ibid., 378–80.
20 Scharpf, 'Games Real Actors Could Play.'
21 Goldstein and Keohane, 'Ideas and Foreign Policy,' in Goldstein and Keohane, *Ideas and Foreign Policy: Beliefs, Institutions, and Political Change.*
22 Coleman and Skogstad, 'Policy Communities and Policy Networks'; Atkinson and Coleman, 'Strong States and Weak States'; Cawson, Holmes, and Stevens, 'The Interaction between Firms and the State in France,' in Wilks and Wright, *Comparative Government-Industry Relations.*
23 Scharpf, 'Games Real Actors Could Play.'
24 Kenis and Schneider, 'Policy Networks and Policy Analysis,' in Marin and Mayntz, eds., *Policy Networks: Empirical Evidence and Theoretical Considerations.*
25 Pross, *Group Politics*, 132.
26 Atkinson and Coleman, 'Strong States and Weak States.'

27 Heinz et al., 'Inner Circles or Hollow Core?' in Heinz et al., *The Hollow Core: Private Interests in National Policy Making*.
28 Ibid., 380–1.
29 Laumann and Knoke, *The Organizational State*, 377.
30 Rhodes and Marsh, 'New Directions in the Study of Policy Networks.'
31 Pross, *Group Politics*, 12.
32 Scharpf, 'Games Real Actors Could Play,' 44.
33 Laumann and Knoke, *The Organizational State*, 382.
34 Ibid., 9.
35 See Schmitter, 'Reflections on Where the Theory of Neo-Corporatism Has Gone,' in Lehmbruch and Schmitter, eds., *Patterns of Corporatist Policy-Making*; Cawson, *Corporatism and Political Theory*.
36 Although not without criticism, see Cox, 'The Old and New Testaments of Corporatism.'
37 There are a number of sources that discuss the dairy sector in comparative perspective. See van Waarden, 'Bureaucracy around the State,' in Streeck and Schmitter, eds., *Private Interest Government*, and the studies in Grant, ed., *Business Interests, Organizational Development and Private Interest Government: A Study of the Food Processing Industry*. Additional material comparing Canada, the United States, and Britain is in Grant, *Government and Industry: A Comparative Analysis of the US, Canada, and the UK*. The U.S. industry is studied further in Hollingsworth, Lindberg, and Young, 'The Governance of the American Dairy Industry: From Regional Dominance to Regional Cleavage,' in Coleman and Jacek, eds., *Regionalism, Business Interests and Public Policy*, and in Young, 'Does the American Dairy Industry Fit a Meso-Corporatism Model?'
38 Dyson, *The State Tradition in Western Europe*, ch. 2.
39 Wright, 'Policy Community, Policy Network and Comparative Industrial Policies,' 600.
40 Hayward, *The State and the Market Economy*, 19.
41 van Waarden, 'The Historical Institutionalisation of Typical National Patterns in Policy Networks between State and Industry.'
42 Coleman, 'State Traditions and Comprehensive Business Associations.'
43 Vogel, *National Styles of Regulation*.
44 See Cowhey, 'The International Telecommunications Regime'; Kapstein, 'Resolving the Regulator's Dilemma: International Coordination of Banking Regulations'; Moran, *The Politics of the Financial Services Revolution: The USA, UK, and Japan*, and 'Regulating Britain, Regulating America'; Chuppe, Haworth, and Watkins, 'Global Finance: Causes, Consequences and Prospects

for the Future'; Grant, Paterson, and Whitson, *Government and the Chemical Industry: A Comparative Study of Britain and West Germany.*

45 Winham, *International Trade and the Tokyo Round Negotiation*, 363–7.

46 Ibid., 343.

47 Cowhey, 'The International Telecommunications Regime,' 171.

48 Ibid., 373.

49 Bennett, 'Review Article,' 218.

50 For an application, see Coleman, 'Policy Convergence in Banking.'

51 Putnam, 'Diplomacy and Domestic Politics,' 432.

52 Ibid., 442–50.

53 Ibid., 434.

54 Nye and Keohane, 'Transnational Relations and World Politics,' in Nye and Keohane, eds., *Transnational Relations and World Politics*, xi.

55 Scharpf, 'The Joint-Decision Trap,' and 'Decision Rules, Decision Styles and Policy Choices.'

56 Coleman and Skogstad, 'Policy Communities and Policy Networks.'

57 Cawson et al., *Hostile Brothers: Competition and Closure in the European Electronics Industry.*

58 Hancher and Moran, 'Organizing Regulatory Space,' in Hancher and Moran, eds., *Capitalism, Culture and Economic Regulation*, 277.

59 Goldstein and Keohane, 'Ideas and Foreign Policy,' 5.

60 Hoberg, 'Reaganism, Pluralism, and the Politics of Pesticide Regulation.'

61 Sabatier, 'Knowledge, Policy-Oriented Learning, and Policy Change.'

62 Haas, 'Introduction: Epistemic Communities and International Policy Coordination,' 3.

63 Cowhey, 'The International Telecommunications Regime.'

64 Kapstein, 'Resolving the Regulator's Dilemma.'

65 Moran, *The Politics of the Financial Services Revolution: The USA, UK, and Japan.*

66 Putnam, *The Beliefs of Politicians*; Aberbach, Putnam, and Rockman, *Bureaucrats and Politicians in Western Democracies*; Campbell and Szablowski, *The Superbureaucrats*; Campbell, *Governments under Stress.*

67 Kaplan, *Policy and Rationality: The Regulation of Canadian Trucking*; Grant, Paterson, and Whitson, *Government and the Chemical Industry: A Comparative Study of Britain and West Germany.*

68 Cawson et al., *Hostile Brothers*, 11.

12

New Agendas for Research on Policy Communities: Policy Analysis, Administration, and Governance

EVERT A. LINDQUIST

The concept of policy community has rapidly gained currency in both the Canadian and the comparative political science and public policy literature. The approach, which aims to analyse the constellation of actors in a particular policy domain or sector, as well as the nature, basis, and extent of their interrelationships, has proven to be a compelling way to address the complexities of contemporary political and policy-making realities while, at the same time, embracing previous approaches to understanding politics and the policy process.

Despite the rapid progress of this perspective, there is a palpable sense of unease about its future in recent reviews of the literature.[1] I share the unease about the trajectory of the literature for several reasons. First, there is a risk that community analysis could become a modern form of systems theory, encompassing all actors or variables, but without a compelling theoretical edge. Another problem is the proliferation of concepts attempting to capture different kinds of communities, networks, and associations that often intersect, overlap, or operate at different levels of analysis – each formulation has been developed for a specific analytic purposes, but little attempt is made to relate them to each other. Such conceptual problems, of course, reflect the complexities of modern politics and governance they seek to capture, but they also raise the prospect of debate over terminology, which promises to yield little in the way of additional explanatory power or conceptual integration.

My final concern is more directly linked to the purpose of this volume and derives from a sense that policy community concepts are not conceived as policy tools that rival those of other disciplines and that we are missing opportunities to influence policy debates. This view is motivated by a more general concern about the ambitions of political scientists in the design of public policy and governing processes. Should we simply attempt to comprehend policy and political developments, and be content with *ex post* analysis, the typical posture of policy studies? Or are we trying to develop new tools for governments, organized interests, academics, and citizens alike that will help them better comprehend and tackle their policy, administrative, and professional problems? Are we confidently trying to advance distinctive analytic and synthetic perspectives that will complement or compete with the policy advice of economists, lawyers, and natural scientists?

Though policy community concepts are not the only analytic tools available to political scientists, they do constitute distinctive means for contributing to contemporary policy debates and are consistent with the importance political scientists attach to institutions and values. This chapter attempts to apply policy community concepts and logic to the real worlds of policy analysis and public management, and suggests some promising areas for empirical research. I suggest that the approach should be of use to policy analysts, administrators, and those who seek to manipulate policy networks – and those who seek to study them. If this sort of application is promising, more effort is required to delineate the essential elements of community analysis, to demonstrate the salience and power of the approach as a political science tool for comprehending and addressing policy and administrative issues, and to fill gaps in our empirical knowledge. An implication is that relatively less energy should be directed to generating new concepts or searching for an integrating theoretical umbrella.

This chapter begins by exploring how policy community concepts help to better understand the changing world of the policy analyst, but suggests that our empirical knowledge of policy analysis practice is tenuous. The second part returns to the roots of the British literature, and considers the potential of the approach for understanding the interior dynamics of a public service, in particular, the interactions among central agencies and operating departments. The third part takes up the task of modelling how policy actors inside and outside the state attempt to manipulate policy communities.

Policy Analysts in Policy Communities: What Do We Know?

The literature on policy communities and networks emerged during the 1980s in order to better account for new dynamics in policy making. Contributors sought to acknowledge, first, that more actors were contributing to debates over public policy and were involved in policy development and implementation, and second, that interrelationships among these actors vary across policy domains or sectors. What is striking, however, is the extent to which the focus has been on organizations as the unit of analysis, ignoring or downplaying the changing role of individual actors. Indeed, one reason why Hugh Heclo's seminal contribution on 'issue networks' has tended to fit uneasily with the Canadian literature on policy communities – in addition to the fact that congressional politics served as the backdrop for his analysis – is because it emphasizes individuals as much as institutions. From the standpoint of this volume, this is particularly unfortunate because arguably it was the proliferation of policy analysts in institutions throughout policy communities during the 1960s and the 1970s that alerted observers to the fact that a wider circle of actors in the policy process had analytic competencies and influence.[2]

Traditional understandings of the policy process presumed that experts or analysts spent either all or the better part of their careers with one institution, and that there was a limited range of organizations with influence where they could work. Hence the common phrase 'policy analysts in the bureaucracy,' which suggested that experts and analysts were coterminous with certain institutions. For Heclo, the concept of issue networks captured the less stable career patterns of policy experts, a more fluid labour market, the emergence of more complex and interrelated policy issues with increasingly blurred boundaries, and increased fragmentation of authority in traditional institutions. These trends were conducive to greater mobility for analysts and made it less likely that they would spend entire careers in one organization; experts now have a greater number of organizations to work for or associate with, often simultaneously. Analysts are more like free agents in professional sports; they are decoupled from the institutions that were once the key repositories of policy knowledge. In turn, managing policy analysis can now be more like directing a holding company than a bureau.[3] These developments have been amplified by the revolution in communications technology.

These trends, however, should not be interpreted as signalling the demise of institutions in the policy process. Indeed, policy community concepts are intended to show that the number of institutions involved in policy making has expanded and to make more transparent the fact that, in some sectors, many nongovernmental actors are influential. Despite the mobility of analysts, institutions remain focal points for policy analysis because they have the capability to mobilize resources to sponsor such work, whether it be a single study or a team project. In this connection, a policy community offers many 'sites' for the conduct of policy analysis, each with different attributes including degree of access to policy makers, type of inquiry that is sponsored, the terms and conditions of employment (remuneration, full or part-time association, etc.), and the extent to which value congruence is expected between the analysts and the larger institution.[4]

While the undeniable trend is that state actors generally rely on, or are influenced more by, societal actors, it remains that the authorities, power, and resources needed to sponsor policy analysis continue to accrue with certain actors in policy communities. Pross argues that the institutions comprising the subgovernment – dominant state and societal actors – seek to maintain the status quo, although the precise distribution varies in subgovernments and networks that address different issues. Indeed, in some networks, key societal interests or associations may have expertise that rivals that of state actors, or is organized more effectively. It follows that the energies of analysts working for these institutions, unless affected by external shocks or presented with other compelling reasons, should be directed toward managing or defending their interests and existing policy regimes. Conversely, Paul Pross suggests that more critical and creative insights are more likely to emerge from *outside* the subgovernment in the attentive public, which – depending on the policy network and issues at hand – may consist of advisory groups and government councils, parliamentary committees, nonprofit policy institutes, new social movements, nongovernmental organizations, and academics.[5]

This formulation now raises few eyebrows but constitutes an interesting reversal of earlier conventional wisdom. Since the 1950s it was presumed that creative policy analysis was most likely to emerge from policy units located *in* the bureaucracy, comprised of a group of analysts with sufficient resources and properly organized to accomplish those feats. The corollary was that, beyond articulating interests and preferences – often in a critical manner – actors in the attentive public did not have sufficient capacity to analyse complex problems and thus had little influence on the design of policies and the implementation of programs. But circumstances have changed, and not just because more actors in policy communities have better access to policy expertise. During the late 1980s governments began to rely more heavily on the expertise residing in consulting firms, interests groups, think-tanks, and universities. This shift in demand was partly attributable to political leaders who did not fully trust the advice of public servants, but it was also a response to the fact that many senior officials and even subgovernment actors as managers of existing policy and administrative regimes were in a coping mode – they had less internal capacity to commit to innovative policy analysis because they were consumed with managing the transactions required during a time of significant expenditure restraint and delayering of senior management in the public service. Moreover, ministers and senior officials are increasingly comfortable with soliciting the advice of outsiders because there are more *former* officials available to consult who left the public service as promotion opportunities became increasingly scarce.

Whether subgovernment analysts are less creative than counterparts in the attentive public and whether the relative gap in capacity to design policy and implement programs has indeed closed are certainly debatable issues, and the answers are bound to be highly contextual. The reality, however, is that global competition and debt problems are forcing governments at all levels and even the most vested interest groups to consider how to dramatically restructure policy regimes. The intriguing and critical issue is how to *link* creativity with analytic capacity throughout policy communities and networks. In this connection, Paul Sabatier's concept of 'advocacy coalitions' – the constellations of individual and institutional actors from inside and outside the state in a particular policy community who share similar beliefs and worldviews, but who may or may not be tightly organized – is useful. The concept highlights why actors inside the state are inclined to exchange information and insights with actors outside the state, and who they might act in concert with to move more proposals higher on the political agenda. Thus, depending on the issue and the government in power, certain experts and institutions in the attentive public will have greater currency than others – beliefs and ideology will often provide an important basis for dialogue and learning, and for increasing the chances that creative or solid ideas will be connected with sound assessments of their feasibility.[6]

This formulation raises the prospect of conflict across advocacy coalitions by institutions and analysts alike, which has prompted observers to explore how the dynamic works. John Kingdon sees this process as competitive, where policy entrepreneurs advocate, debate, and vet new ideas and assessments of existing policies and programs before a more limited set of credible alternatives are injected into public debates. In his model, this is but one stream feeding into the policy process, providing alternatives to be weighed by policy makers and the public when a policy window opens. Sabatier depicts this as an ideologically driven process involving protracted conflict, but suggests that analysts and professions may serve as moderating influences by providing standards for evaluating ideological claims and by providing relatively neutral sites for debating issues. A similar role may be played by actors *within* advocacy coalitions who encourage colleagues to test old ideas and to embrace new views. Reflecting a concern about the distance between policy makers and academic policy research, Duncan MacRae argues that the salience and feasibility of academic research should be tested by specialists in state agencies and other organizations involved in policy making.[7] In an era of declining resources and of restructuring, the need to vet findings across traditional boundaries and to develop research networks across institutions to properly address issues are matters of increasing importance.

•

The above remarks should indicate the great potential of a community perspective for understanding the diversity in career paths, roles, and location of analysts in the policy process. Never have we had a richer array of concepts and models for capturing the organizational environments in which analysts work and the many, often subtle, different interrelationships of which they are a part. We reviewed concepts such as issue networks, policy communities and networks, subgovernments, the attentive public, and advocacy coalitions. But this barely scratches the surface. To the list we could add transnational or global networks, epistemic communities, technical communities, associational networks, professional and quasi-professional associations, and new social movements. Moreover, there has emerged a variety of more theoretical conceptualizations of policy analysis in the form of post-positivist and post-modern interpretations.[8]

Collectively and separately, these formulations capture how the external environment in which policy analysts work is changing, and they demonstrate the many role-sets of analysts. Moreover, the view of a more complicated, more diffuse world for policy analysts has been echoed in recent assessments. In a thought-provoking lecture, Richard French argued that policy analysis in the form of the policy sciences fuelling rational government has lost its credibility, and that the result has been a shift 'from analysis to process, from policy to positioning, from modern to postmodern government.' Similar charges have been levelled in an even more provocative manner by Johh Ralston Saul in *Voltaire's Bastards*.[9] While many officials in the federal public service would not agree with the view that policy analysis has been either impotent or pernicious, they would agree that the policy capacity of departments waned during the 1980s. The federal government's Canadian Centre for Management Development has responded to this widespread concern by launching a new set of courses and lectures for senior managers.

However, I would like to argue that recent theoretical insights and critiques from all quarters are hollow. Their common attribute is the lack of any plausible rendering of how contemporary policy analysis is *actually* conducted, let alone any attempt to depict how such practice might vary in different organizational contexts. While mainstream textbooks dutifully acknowledge the proliferation of econometric firms, policy consulting groups, and think-tanks of all kinds in policy communities, they continue to insinuate that policy analysis still proceeds according to the rational model. Recent contributions have done an excellent job of conveying the *possibilities* for where policy analysis might be conducted in public bureaucracies or who it might be contracted to, but these articles, unfortunately, tell us little about the state of analytic practice.[10]

Academic portrayals of policy analysis practice in Canada are based on data that are increasingly out of date. We have precious little empirical data, either in qualitative or quantitative from, that impart a better sense of what policy analysts currently do, what instruments they employ, what career patterns they have, or even where they are located (i.e., do most analysts work in bureaucratic policy units?). There has been a proliferation of texts on public policy and analysis in Canada, but they provide superficial accounts of the state of analytic practice, relying heavily on a secondary literature that is sometimes decades out of date. It is sobering to realize that contributions such as those of Arnold Meltsner and Aaron Wildavsky, whose writings inspired many Canadian academics and provided insight into the problems and realities of policy analysis as an emergent profession, were written over fifteen years ago. While it is tempting to point to David Good's study of the tax policy branch of the Department of Finance, his research interviews were conducted during the mid-1970s. The recent turn toward interpretive and post-positive models and critiques of policy analysis does not mitigate this more fundamental problem. Indeed, some of the critics and new perspectives may only be catching up with where professional practice has been for some time.[11]

Before we invest more energy toward theoretical development, it is essential that Canadian academics show they understand how policy analysts actually do their work. This points to the need for more empirical research, which undoubtedly will serve to stimulate additional theoretical insights and questions. The gap is so large that empirical contributions of many kinds – qualitative, quantitative, and prescriptive – stand to make important contributions.

Qualitative Studies. An excellent place to begin would be with a study that replicates or updates Good's *Politics of Anticipation.* While tax analysis is only one form of policy analysis, the advantage would be that the researcher could control for the type of analysis and readily determine deviations from past practice. Other studies might investigate how policy analysis is conducted and organized in federal, provincial, and municipal agencies, perhaps comparing findings with those of Good or perhaps a study like that of

Martha Feldman on the conduct of policy analysis in the U.S. Department of Energy. Another approach would be to track a single policy issue over a period of time and then analyse the work of policy analysts and policy units located throughout a policy network; the idea would be to compare work done on the same issue in different organizational contexts, to explore the impact of different ideological suppositions, the amount of resources and expertise that were available, and the data that were generated or drawn upon.[12]

Quantitative Studies. A complementary approach would be to conduct baseline studies to document the number and the size of bureaus responsible for policy analysis in a federal, provincial, or municipal government, and then determine whether they have grown or decreased in size over the years. A related study might track the career paths of entry-level analysts over, say, a ten-year period; or, conversely, review the career paths of several senior analysts in a public service. Given the hypotheses of French and other observers, it would be useful to have a study that compares the status and evolution of policy analysis units with the fortunes of bureaus responsible for program evaluation and for communications. Finally, another much needed study would undertake a census of nonprofit institutes, academic centres, individual academics, and consulting firms at work in different policy sectors.

Venturing Designs. We need studies that address the issue of how to create or to overhaul policy capacity, and to redress the gaps in skill levels and approaches, in order to meet contemporary policy challenges that have emerged in every sector. One recent study examines how three federal departments created 'adhocracies' to design policy innovations, but only scratches the surface of an increasingly important topic. We know contemporary policy development now involves much more than assembling a critical mass of analysts to grapple with the technical aspects of a complex policy challenge and must also embrace the difficult tasks of consultation, consensus-building, contracting-out, and communications. We also know that the mix of technical expertise, consultation, and management considerations will vary from context to context. The issue of design extends beyond improving the policy capacity of government agencies to considering how analytic resources dispersed across policy communities can be better mobilized. One example of this approach is the Centre for Studies in Higher Education, a network of educational policy research centres funded by the Office of Educational Improvement in the U.S. Department of Education.[13] A similar approach has recently been advocated by Judith Maxwell, who has called for the creation of a Policy Research Network to replace and surpass the analytic capacity of the former Economic Council of Canada by drawing on more diverse expertise in a more flexible manner without a large, costly bureaucracy.

Central Agencies and Administrative Policy Networks

In this section the object of analysis shifts from policy analysts to officials who function more as managers or administrators, moving squarely into the realm of administrative policies intended to ensure accountability and the efficient operation of government programs and the public service as a system. This may seem an odd application, but it is worth recalling that a precursor to the British literature on policy networks, Heclo and Wildavsky's *Private Government of Public Money*, focused on the norms and culture of senior officials in central agencies and operating departments. As British scholars began to examine substantive policies, the concept of community was reserved to describe a stable network of actors with *shared* interests and norms who shaped a policy regime (what Canadian scholars refer to as subgovernments), while network was employed to capture the wider set of actors outside the state with interests in policies, or what Canadians have referred to as policy communities.[14]

These recent investigations by scholars on both sides of the Atlantic have greatly contributed to our understanding of policy making, but it has come at some cost. Much of the energy of political scientists has been recently devoted to identifying entire policy networks, and less attention has been focused specifically on state organization or public administration. However, I would like to argue that, for scholars interested in traditional topics of public administration, the interest in policy communities has produced conceptual advances that can be usefully *reapplied* to study how central agencies and departments relate to each other, and to better comprehend the dynamics of communities and networks in a bureaucratic or administrative context.

In a recent article I attempted to show how policy community concepts could be of use to government officials in operating departments since many must comprehend their external environments in order to monitor, develop, and implement public policies. Depending on the department, and the position of an official, he or she might have to deal with several policy networks. Moreover, when taking up new positions inside or across departments, officials must assess and adjust to substantially different external environments.[15] Since the article was published, several officials have told me they found the analysis helpful, but one such compliment was intriguing because it did *not* come from an official working in an operating department; nor did he primarily interact with provincial governments, interest groups, think-tanks, or citizens. Rather, the official worked in a federal central agency, the Treasury Board Secretariat, and more specifically, in the area of information management, then under the aegis of the Administrative Policy Branch. Initially, I was incredulous that such concepts could illuminate how central bureaus went about their work, but on reflection, his insight pointed to a promising research agenda, one that should show how central agencies exercise influence within public services, and how they are responding to larger pressures to restructure public services.

Let me first assert that, as with the writing on policy analysis, there are huge gaps in our understanding of central agencies. By central agencies, I am referring to the constellation of agencies, which may vary across governments, that have responsibility for managing and regulating a public service, and may include cabinet offices, finance or treasury departments, public or civil service commissions, and management or treasury boards – although it is usually the latter that have the most responsibilities in this regard. Many observers discuss the counterproductive or ineffectual management initiatives of governments and central agencies, the competition and overlap among central agencies, or focus on their pernicious influence on policy development and on the management of departments.[16] However, such studies tend to focus on one element of central agency operations such as the revenue or expenditure budget process, review their range of responsibilities at a high level of abstraction, and do not provide detailed assessments of how they function as organizations nor how they interact with departments. One way to remedy this gap is to encourage more studies that focus on the tasks, culture, challenges, and evolution of central agencies and constituent bureaus. Such contributions would be significant, but if based on standard approaches employed to study public organizations, they might not come to grips with issues and adjustments relating to the rapidly changing nature of governance, which affect central agencies and operating departments alike.

Governments have become more open and permeable, and old conceptual frames may no longer capture all that is important or changing. To focus only on the outputs of central agencies, or of particular bureaus, may miss where most of the decisions and innovations are actually made within government, and therefore fail to provide an accurate account of their role and influence. Officials, of course, owe their primary allegiance to departments and their deputy ministers, whether they work for central agencies or departments, but often they identify more with colleagues *elsewhere* in the public service who worry about similar problems, and who may serve as their most important networks for professional learning. An alternative way to envision a public service, then, is in terms of specific professional functions and tasks (personnel, legal work, finance, evaluation, contracts, budgets, regulation, employment equity, etc.), and the cadre of officials throughout a public service responsible for elements of those functions. Given the inclination to decentralize responsibilities based on managerialist or new public management principles, as well as budgetary pressures that also impact on the centre, many central agencies are no longer the dominant and controlling entities they once were; they have actively sought to relinquish many tools for overtly shaping the design and implementation of programs. To the extent that central agencies exert influence, it must increasingly be achieved in more subtle ways.

With these larger developments in mind, one can see why the policy community approach could be useful for exploring the role and organization of central agencies. The approach emerged as political scientists realized that, in order to account for policy outcomes, it was necessary to understand how organized interests, whether business or labour organizations, exerted influence on policy development and implementation by governments and their agencies. Indeed, it was acknowledged that often experts associated with such groups – and with universities, think-tanks, consulting firms, and social movement organizations – possessed information and knowledge rivalling or even surpassing that of officials on some issues, but such conclusions were highly contingent on the policy network under review. What permits application of community concepts to central agencies is the fact that, like state organizations, they are buffeted by trends similar to the diffusion of power observed within domestic policy networks as well as their permeability to outside influences.

How can the community analysis be applied to studying central agencies? First, the structuralist approach suggests we disaggregate the community – in this case, the constellation of organizations comprising the public service – and identify different realms of administrative responsibilities and the associated networks of officials situated in central agencies and operating departments. The general domains of responsibility, as well as more specific issues in each, include the following: *budget making* (expenditure analysis, estimates production, reserve management); *management innovation* (budgetary flexibilities, alternative delivery mechanisms, departmental assessments, service quality); *human resource management* (collective bargaining, benefits administration, classification, redeployment, training); *administrative policy* (purchasing, freedom of information and privacy, information technology, real property); *affirmative action* (women, minorities, disabled, aboriginals, and sometimes official languages); and *financial management* (audit, evaluation, financial control systems). This list is not exhaustive, but it does indicate the extent and diversity of responsibilities.

Casual observation suggests that identifying the network of actors throughout a public service involved in developing, implementing, and then evaluating administrative policies in each domain is promising. Some of these networks have thrived for some time; others have emerged only recently. For example, a seminal study of the federal public service noted the existence and emergence of councils during the 1960s associated with personnel management, records management, materials management, electronic data processing, and financial management.[17] Many of those councils still exist, although some have different labels or have divided or been consolidated as the challenges evolved and the expertise required to address them shifted. On the other hand, new networks have been recently created at the federal level in order to implement a service standards initiative, to facilitate exchange of information across special operating agencies, and to further communication and explore possibilities for savings among departments located in particular regions.

Identification and description of such networks will be an important contribution, but observers must also probe for how the representatives of central bureaus and departments relate, and how these interactions differ across networks. Since each revolves around unique administrative challenges, the character or culture of the network should change accordingly; each bureau will have different tasks and authorities, and a unique basis for interacting with departments. For example, central agencies typically have authority over the complex of human resource policies (staffing and training), but usually delegate most responsibility for administration to operating departments, and therefore adopt more of a monitoring posture. On the other hand, the tasks of central agency units responsible for negotiating collective agreements with public sector unions are considerably different; they may have far more in common with the 'opponents' who sit across the bargaining table than with colleagues in central bureaus or in departments. Estimates divisions consist largely of analysts responsible for monitoring and serving as a liaison to particular departments. However, they tend to interact with departments on a bilateral basis, book numbers, and are less involved in facilitating the exchange of ideas and practices across programs and departments; such associations take on the character of intelligence or diplomatic networks.

Conclusions about the general standing of a central bureau in an administrative network may not tell the whole story – the relative capacity of a bureau with respect to departments may vary within a single network. Some departments may have greater competency in certain functional areas and therefore be better positioned to negotiate with or outflank the centre. This capability may be due to the fact that some departments are so large that central agency staff cannot challenge its functional expertise or because some pressing items on the administrative agenda 'crowd out' detailed monitoring of and debate over other items. Some departments may be so innovative or be moving so quickly that a central bureau may not be able to thoroughly assess some initiatives; on the other hand, some departments may be considerably weaker in the same areas and may actively require central agency assistance.

One weakness of the structural approach is that it tends toward a static analysis of the structure and power differentials within policy communities and is less amenable to dealing with how institutional environments evolve.[18] This also presents difficulties when studying administrative policy regimes, particularly given the general shift from the central agency dominance to the decentralization associated with managerialism. One remedy is to take several snapshots of an administrative policy community at different times; another is to rely on models that directly address change. Sabatier's *advocacy coalition* framework, which emphasizes the importance of modelling competing systems of values and beliefs within policy networks, is a useful supplement to the structuralist perspective. However, a direct application would produce limited results, since conflict over administrative concerns is not likely to be motivated by the same ideological views as clashes over policy and political issues. The basis for conflict is more likely to involve the clash of different *professional* worldviews. When examining administrative policies such as real property management – purchasing, leasing, and disposing of property – an observer should try to identify two or three competing schools of thought on appropriate administrative regimes and degrees of centralization. The extent to which central agency control is extended or reduced, or certain management innovations initiated or diffused, may depend on which ministers or deputy ministers occupy key positions in a network, their views, and whether they take an active interest in such issues.

The last point underscores the fact that, as with policy networks, outside forces can profoundly influence not only the distribution of power within administrative policy networks and the regimes that guide them, but also the viability and fortunes of entire networks. These forces include the change of governments, broad economic and social trends, and perhaps developments in other policy communities – administrative policies should be affected by evolving government priorities, pressures on the public service due to the growth of programs, and how governments choose to react to criticism or crises. For example, the creation of the federal Office of the Comptroller General in 1978 was a response to criticism of the government's record of financial management during the 1970s, and widespread concern about overregulation led to the creation of a regulatory reform bureau in the Treasury Board Secretariat during the early 1980s.

However, despite evolving environmental influences, many central bureaus remain stable over the years and maintain their status, whether high or low. How can this stability be explained? Drawing on organization theory, one approach is to ask whether bureaus operate in domains with weak or strong institutional environments, and with weak or strong technical environments. Certain bureaus, such as estimates and staff relations divisions, have task environments where the imperatives, regardless of either the policy or administrative disposition of governments or particular ministers, are clear: budgets must be produced, collective agreements must be negotiated, and new policies must be costed. Many officials at the centre bemoan the fact that 'transactions' crowd out other activities; but this is simply another way of saying that some activities undertaken by certain bureaus are valued more highly by the system than others. Other bureaus may persist because governments and sometimes the public service must respond to demands and expectations emanating from their institutional environment (think of the creation of bureaus devoted to employment equity and financial management); some theorists argue that such entities often function as buffers to appear responsive and deflect criticism but may not be connected to the technical core or critical tasks of a central agency – however, they remain intact due to their symbolic importance.

As certain central bureaus become less critical in meeting either the technical or symbolic needs of the government or of the public service, the values they represent become increasingly precarious; they have less claim to resources, and they are more susceptible to reorganization and marginalization.[19] With fewer resources and moral backing, such bureaus must attempt to achieve their administrative objectives through persuasion and levering the resources of departments; if an administrative network does not exist, it may make sense to create one.

•

Identifying administrative policy communities and networks is a worthy enterprise, but the approach outlined above effectively serves to deconstruct central agencies because it calls for a focus on specific bureaus and how they relate to departments. With respect to the analysis of substantive policy networks, Atkinson and Coleman have observed that having 'disaggregated the state, researchers in this tradition are faced with the problem of reaggregating it. They must consider how sectoral networks and communities affect the pattern of policy outcomes at the macro level and how national political institutions condition policy networks and policy communities.' If we replace 'national political institutions' with 'the government and central agencies,' and replace 'policy networks and policy communities' with 'administrative policy networks,' the problem becomes quite clear: we should attempt to comprehend central agencies in their entirety, as complete organizations. We have, in the terminology of Lawrence and Lorsch, focused more on 'differentiation' than 'integration.'[20]

It cannot be emphasized enough that the issue of integration in central agencies is not a theoretical invention; it is a critical issue for ministers and deputy ministers who lead central agencies. They must respond to government priorities and the need to appear 'in control' to such critics as the media and auditor generals, while worrying about the cumulative impact of scores of administrative policies emanating from myriad central bureaus or program managers in departments. However, an unexpected theoretical by-product of a focus on administrative policy communities is that it may provide insights for scholars interested in substantive policy networks and who are frustrated about how to connect meso analysis with macro or systemic developments. Central agencies, particularly at the national level, are – along with the cabinet and its committees – the crucibles for decision making, for responding to such forces, and making difficult choices that shape the fortunes of policy communities.

How and to what extent do central agencies attempt to integrate? How can such a process be modelled and analysed? Since central agencies and their bureaus regulate and monitor the same departments, how do they organize and coordinate their dealings with these clients? One approach is to assess the how bureaus impact on their respective subenvironments (the reporting and operations of departments) and surmise the extent of interaction effects of responding to administrative policies across subenvironments.[21] If the interaction effects are high, this suggests a need for coordinating or integrating mechanisms inside central agencies. However, many officials in departments feel such mechanisms, if they exist, are rarely effective. For example, despite efforts by central agencies to increase flexibilities for department managers at the federal level – such as the removal of person-year controls and the move to more flexible budget regimes – many senior department managers claim that centrally negotiated collective agreements, workforce adjustment regimes, and repetitive budgeting negate much of this latitude. Different kinds of interaction problems, of course, suggest that the centre should respond at different levels and with different means. Should central agencies provide 'one window' service to departments or do they rely on informal or ad hoc processes to facilitate adjustments in response to policies working at cross-purposes? Another approach for understanding how integration is, or is not, achieved is to review key decision-making processes and to determine the extent to which various central bureaus contribute. The most obvious candidates are estimates and budget processes, routine submissions to management or treasury boards, collective bargaining, assessments of departmental performance, and responses to oversight agencies such as auditor generals and privacy commissions.

This leads to a third line of investigation. Central agency leaders increasingly worry about the cumulative impact of the many demands emanating from their bureaus on operating departments. The tolerance for 'unintegrated' regulation and management initiatives by central agencies is now very low for two reasons. First, the increasing size of ministerial portfolios, the delayering of senior management teams in departments, as well as resource reductions have dramatically exposed the transaction costs of dealing with the centre. Second, to the extent that public services will be subjected to fundamental restructuring due to deficit reduction agendas, it will be increasingly difficult for central agencies to escape pressures to downsize and to restructure their policy regimes. The upshot is that governments and central agencies must delineate new integrative processes, structures, and administrative policy regimes. This will raise issues about accountability and the essential roles of central agencies. These changes will have profound implications for the quality of governance; and they deserve considerably more debate among academics who, in addition to monitoring these developments, should venture new designs, a theme central to the section below.

Community Analysis as Instrument: Reshaping Networks

The two previous sections concluded that policy makers and observers will be confronted with the challenge of reshaping policy and administrative networks. The issue and challenge of design underscores the fact that policy communities and networks of all kinds can be manipulated or at the very least influenced by individuals and institutions; they are not necessarily condemned to their status or degree of influence. While the literature has addressed the dynamics of policy communities, most attention has been directed to comprehending the external forces that impact on policy communities.[22] But change may also be induced by actors *within* policy communities. We need to analyse more carefully by what means the agendas, structure, and relative power of communities can be influenced.

It is in this connection that we must ask whether or not community analysis has developed in such a way as to provide a new set of design tools for political scientists, policy analysts, and public managers. Can scholars who study policy communities move beyond producing 'knowledge of' the policy process to actively considering in what ways they can provide 'knowledge in' the process?[23] Can community analysis be employed as a diagnostic and prescriptive tool? Whether social science concepts provide tools and insights for those who seek to effect change is a useful test of their relevance. Here is a preliminary list of ways that community concepts might assist political leaders, officials, academics, and other observers.

Environmental Scanning. First, community concepts can be employed by policy practitioners and observers alike to go beyond simple issues analysis in order to identify changes in institutional environments. This entails monitoring the capacity of actors in policy communities, whether they be rivals or colleagues, and to determine whether they are gaining or losing their comparative analytic advantage, coordinating capacity, or constituency support. An exemplar of another form of scanning is found in Atkinson and Coleman's *The State, Business and Industrial Change*, which explored the evolution of industrial policy networks. In my view, the literature has fixated on the structural templates they delineated and downplayed a key element of their seminal contribution. In their case studies, Atkinson and Coleman first attempted to determine the trajectory of the policy sector (i.e., Is a sector in decline, in ascendancy, or relatively stable?) and then undertook a diagnosis of the structural characteristics and capacity of a policy network – this permitted them to establish whether or not there was a mismatch between policy-making challenges and institutional arrangements. As a result, they were in a position to venture prescriptions about how these arrangements could be modified.

Instruments for Manipulation. If scanning and diagnosis suggests that a policy or administrative network needs to be altered one way or another, what are the means by which political or bureaucratic leaders can reshape or move a network in new directions? Here it is useful to draw on the ideas of Robert Young and of Kenneth Benson. Young provides us with a useful perspective as a by-product of his effort to supplement the conventional public choice model of interest groups and state actors involved in an episodic game to maximize votes at elections. Young develops an alternative model, where groups attempt to sell votes and information in exchange for greater influence on policy makers, and in doing so draws attention to the notion of 'tectonic policies.' Such policies seek to alter the resources of actors playing in an ongoing political game and to reshape the playing field and its rules. These policies include: *beneficial* policies, which serve to generally advantage one set of actors over another; *contextual* policies, which entail adjusting regulatory or statutory frameworks to guide the interactions of actors in a given network; *generative* policies, which provide subsidies and other benefits to groups; and *positional* policies, which grant access to state actors by means of advisory committees or consultation opportunities. Benson would group Young's tectonic policies in the larger category of 'authoritative' strategies, and would observe that they involve micromanaging the network, which involves altering the flow or the point of entry of resources into an entire network. These strategies, which he terms 'manipulative,' rely on the self-organizing capacity of the network to effect the ultimate changes.[24] Together, these insights portray all public policies as potential means, whether used selectively or in combination, for reshaping policy communities, although the effects could be lasting or temporary in nature. The terminology employed by both authors is awkward, but the insights are valuable and should be applied systematically to case studies on policy and administrative networks.

Encouraging Stewardship. Young acknowledges that his approach constitutes a rather cynical account of politics – or, as applied in this chapter, the dynamics of policy and administrative networks – which emphasizes the acquisition and retention of power. However, there is a less cynical approach that seeks to reshape policy networks for other purposes. This approach is more concerned with increasing the responsiveness of policy networks and their ability to learn in order to address emerging policy challenges.[25] Members of advocacy coalitions may 'learn' in response to threats from, or to gain advantage over, competitors, but policy communities can also be viewed as organic entities that have certain capacities to learn and adapt, raising the issue of how entire networks can be moved to new planes of debate and problem solving. This perspective should lead observers to analyse policy communities from the standpoint of stewardship, and to determine whether or not there is one or more individuals or institutions committed to how well the network or community functions as a whole, even if comprised of many autonomous institutions and individuals.

Nurturing Expertise, Forums, and Networks. This subject area is simply an extension of the point made above, and brings the chapter back full circle to the issue of how academics and policy analysts can play a more effective and perhaps socially more useful role in the policy process. In order to do so, there must be an assessment of whether or not relying on the available expertise and forums will lead to productive debates that will adequately address new policy challenges. If they are deemed inadequate, this augers poorly for leaders identifying and nurturing the emergence of new professional and quasi-professional areas of expertise, and the design of new forums for the exchange of information. Another possibility is simply to commission new studies or to create new databases. Relatedly, and as noted at the end of the agenda for future research on policy analysis, some actors might consider how to reconfigure or better link expertise spread throughout a policy community in order to be more productive. This might be achieved either by installing better communications infrastructure or by establishing a network that addresses new subjects in a more concerted manner.

It is important to realize that many can play the governance game. The desire to manipulate policy networks is not limited to ministers and key officials, and also includes the leaders of business groups, labour unions, nonprofit organizations, new social movements, and even foundations; in the case of administrative networks, the parallel is that senior officials, auditor generals, and other outside actors may also seek to alter the organization and content of administrative policy regimes. Kenneth Benson has suggested that, for actors with neither the authority nor resources to pursue manipulative or authoritative strategies for altering entire networks, they must settle instead for more limited cooperative or disruptive strategies that focus on one or perhaps a few other actors in the network. One recent case study shows how the Canadian government and several foundations helped build a vital policy community to deal with Asia-Pacific issues by creating advisory bodies, by sponsoring research and training programs, and by encouraging bilateral associations and exchanges between Canada and other countries.[26] To enjoin debate on several issues, Canadian nationalists have created several organizations such as the Action Canada Network, the Council of Canadians, and the Canadian Centre for Policy Alternatives. Although their resources are quite limited and their leaderships overlap considerably, the number of entities gives the movement greater prominence in policy debates.

Thus, in addition to government efforts to influence the institutional fabric of policy communities, these examples should suggest that many groups do not limit their energies to influencing policy outcomes, which may result only in short-term gains. Indeed, increased focus on the management, evolution, and manipulation of policy and administrative communities will have more than practical implications; it should make the politics inside policy and administrative networks more transparent and easier for observers to comprehend.

Conclusion

This paper has set out agendas for research that could take the policy community literature in new directions, calling for more attention to be directed to the role of policy analysts in policy communities, to the organization of central administrative processes, and to the problems of institutional design and manipulation of policy and administrative networks. The agendas, of course, constitute an application of concepts that have been developed to date and reflects the research interests and policy training of the author, and of the emphasis of this volume, and therefore should not be interpreted as constituting the only directions in which future research on policy communities should proceed. The traditional concerns of the literature are still salient – we need more studies of policy networks in uncharted policy domains, and closer analysis of how these networks evolve over time.

Some readers will no doubt worry that employing policy community concepts to understand the role of policy analysts and how central agencies perform their tasks will stretch the approach too far. Indeed, Atkinson and Coleman have already flagged the problem of researchers moving too blithely from one level of analysis to another without paying sufficient attention to the different rules and norms governing interactions in a different context. Nevertheless, they ultimately viewed the moving of concepts across regional or national boundaries in a positive light, noting they served to provide 'a useful junction for the converging fields of international political economy and comparative public policy.'[27] It is hoped these forays into the domains of policy analysis and central agencies will be viewed in a similar light. Indeed, I have suggested that the study of administrative policy communities may provide one possible avenue for supplementing the traditional mode of community analysis that, in its current guise, seems committed to the project of disaggregating the state, since it is central agencies that assist governments in their attempts to impose coherence over a range of policy concerns.

Finally, the fact that political scientists now have a conceptual apparatus that can be applied to different levels of analysis should be interpreted as a promising development. Whenever a complex organizational system can be identified – and no matter whether political scientists and public administration theorists happen to be looking up, down, or sideways from their usual stomping grounds – they are now likely to discern policy networks and communities, very much in the manner of fractal and chaos theorizing.[28] Political scientists have discovered a useful set of analytic tools that will allow them to enjoin debates on the design of public policy and of institutions based on a solid method, one rooted squarely in the institutional traditions of the discipline and of public administration. This is a timely development because we live in a time of significant institutional and social change. We should contribute to these debates on policy and governance with more than historical analysis and critical commentary; we should also actively evaluate proposals for their institutional implications and underlying values, and then propose our own solutions, even if we are not likely to be as certain as colleagues working in more prescriptive traditions.

Notes

1 See Jordan, 'Sub-Governments, Policy Communities and Networks'; Rhodes, 'Policy Networks'; Atkinson and Coleman; 'Policy Networks, Policy Communities and the Problems of Governance'; and Howlett and Ramesh, *Studying Public Policy*, ch. 6.
2 See Laumann and Knocke, *The Organizational State: Social Choice in National Policy Domains*; and Heclo, 'Issue Networks and the Executive Establishment.' On the rise of policy analysis as a profession, see Meltsner, *Policy Analysts in the Bureaucracy*; and Wildavsky, *Speaking Truth to Power: The Art and Craft of Policy Analysis*.
3 See Boston, 'Purchasing Policy Advice.'
4 On the different attributes of different organizational sites where policy analysis and research might be conducted, see Lindquist, 'The Third Community, Policy Inquiry, and Social Scientists.'
5 On different policy networks, see Atkinson and Coleman, *The State, Business, and Industrial Change*; and Coleman and Skogstad, *Policy Communities and Public Policy in Canada*. For the argument that subgovernments prefer to maintain the status quo, see Pross's *Group Politics and Public Policy*. The discussion in the text leaves aside the issue of whether expertise, particularly inside the state, can be reconfigured to undertake policy innovation, and under what circumstances subgovernments might be driven to innovate. For more detail, see Desveaux, Lindquist, and Toner, 'Organizing for Policy Innovation in Public Bureaucracy.'
6 See Sabatier, 'Knowledge, Policy-Oriented Learning, and Policy Change.'
7 On these points, see Kingdon, *Agendas, Alternatives and Public Policy*; Sabatier, 'Knowledge, Policy-Oriented Learning, and Policy Change';

Lindquist, 'Public Managers and Policy Communities'; and MacRae, 'Building Policy-Related Technical Communities.'

8 For examples of different networks in which experts participate, see the chapters that comprise Brooks and Gagnon, eds., *The Political Influence of Ideas: Policy Communities and the Social Sciences*. See also 'Epistemic Communities as Enemies of Habit-Driven Institutions,' 4–46, in Haas, *When Knowledge Is Power*. For examples of post-positive and post-modern approaches, see Fischer and Forester, eds., *The Argumentative Turn in Policy Analysis and Planning*; and Togerson, 'Interpretative Policy Inquiry,' and 'Between Knowledge and Politics.'

9 See French, 'Postmodern Government,' 43; and Saul, *Voltaire's Bastards: The Dictatorship of Reason in the West*. For explication of the concept of role-sets, see Merton, 'On Sociological Theories of the Middle Range.'

10 See Boston, 'Purchasing Policy Advice'; and Hollander and Prince, 'Analytic Units in Federal and Provincial Governments.'

11 On this point, see Lindquist, 'Postmodern Politics and Policy Sciences.'

12 See Feldman, *Order without Design: Information Production and Policy Making*. One such attempt can be found in Lindquist, 'Behind the Myth of Think Tanks,' which reviews the contributions of government agencies and task forces, interest groups and associations, government councils, nonprofit institutes, and academics on energy policy, pension reform, and tax policy process reform during the 1970s and early 1980s.

13 See Fuhrman, 'The Centre for Policy Research on Education.' On adhocracies and policy innovation, see Desveaux, Lindquist, and Toner, 'Organizing for Policy Innovation in Public Bureaucracy.'

14 See Heclo and Wildavsky, *The Private Government of Public Money: Community and Policy Inside British Politics*. For reviews the British literature, see Jordan, 'Sub-Governments, Policy Communities and Networks'; and Rhodes, 'Policy Networks.'

15 Lindquist, 'Public Managers and Policy Communities.

16 For an overview of central agencies, see Thomas, 'Central Agencies.' For more detail, see Donald Savoie's masterful study of the expenditure budget process, *The Politics of Public Spending*; Douglas Hartle's *The Expenditure Budget Process of the Government of Canada*; and Colin Campbell's *Governments under Stress*, and *The Superbureaucrats*, the latter co-authored with George Szablowski.

17 See Hodgetts, *The Canadian Public Service: A Physiology of Government*.

18 On this point, see Lindquist, 'Public Managers and Policy Communities.'

19 See Myer and Rowan, 'Institutionalized Organizations'; Meyer, Scott, and Deal, 'Institutional and Technical Sources of Organization Structure'; and Clark, 'Organization Adaptation and Precarious Values.'

20 See Atkinson and Coleman, 'Policy Networks, Policy Communities and the Problems of Governance,' 163; and Lawrence and Lorsch, *Organization and Environment: Managing Differentiation and Integration.*

21 On the notion of the subenvironments of units within organizations, see Lawrence and Lorsch, *Organization and Environment.*

22 The Canadian literature on policy communities does acknowledge that external forces impinging on a given policy sector constitute the largest potential for significant change, but does not model these forces systematically. Sabatier and Jenkins-Smith explicitly model the forces that impact on policy communities in their *Policy Change and Learning: An Advocacy Coalition Approach,* including changes in government and the resulting political and bureaucratic appointments to positions of authority, developments in other policy domains, and secular domestic and international trends.

23 For this well-known distinction, see Lasswell, *A Pre-View of Policy Sciences.*

24 See Young, 'Tectonic Policies and Political Competition'; and Benson, 'The Interorganizational Network as a Political Economy.' Benson identifies two other strategies to be discussed below.

25 On learning and stewardship in policy communities, see Sabatier, 'Knowledge, Policy-Oriented Learning, and Policy Change'; Lindquist, 'Public Managers and Policy Communities'; and Howlett and Ramesh, *Studying Public Policy,* ch. 9.

26 See Benson, 'The Interorganizational Network as a Political Economy'; and Lindquist, 'Balancing Relevance and Integrity.'

27 See Atkinson and Coleman, 'Policy Networks, Policy Communities and the Problems of Governance,' 176.

28 See Gleick, *Chaos: Making a New Science.*

13

Discourse, Identity, and Voice: Feminist Contributions to Policy Studies

SUSAN D. PHILLIPS

Feminism is a rich and diverse analytic perspective that at its core involves a transformative politics committed to removing gender-based injustices and empowering women in their communities, workplaces, and families, as well as through public policies. Although feminism has influenced a generation of scholars who have tried to reorient their disciplines by expunging androcentric bias, the impact of feminism on policy studies is a more recent development. In many respects, feminist policy analysis is still struggling to gain credibility in a field historically dominated by the model of rational economic man. Thus it remains poorly understood and relatively invisible. Indeed, feminism is often wrongly assumed to be applicable to policy studies only on matters that deal directly with 'women's issues,' such as child care and social policy, but to have little relevance for so-called 'hard' economic policy issues. The reach and potential utility of feminism for policy studies, however, is much broader than often presumed for several reasons.

At the very minimum, feminism adds gender to policy analysis, regardless of the issue at hand. One of the basic insights of feminism is to differentiate gender from sex. While sex describes biological difference, gender connotes 'socially constructed and historically variable relationships, cultural meanings, and identities through which biological sex differences become socially significant.'[1] Gender, therefore, is not a fixed characteristic, but refers to the constructed, subjective identities through which we see and experience the world. It is not only a component of individual identity, but is also an aspect of political and social structures. The world is pervasively shaped by gendered relations, which can be institutionalized in the state, in organizations, culture, and public policies, although the nature of these relations may change over time.

A feminist approach to policy studies does not stop at adding gender. It also necessitates a fundamental conceptualization of how we formulate and use knowledge, and this has significant epistemological and methodological implications. The starting point of feminist research is a critique of positivism and, in particular, the attempt by social science to adopt positivist premises of a static, perspectiveless 'truth' and objective, 'neutral' concepts of knowledge. Positivist science is seen as erroneously separating the knower from knowledge, knowledge from its sociohistorical context, and facts from values and as positing the superiority of experts above people. It also inappropriately regards language and discursive systems as simply passive containers of ideas. As an alternative, feminism has generated analysis that views knowledge claims as forms of discourse. Thus theory becomes relational, knowledge grounded, and the analyst part of the analysis. As Torgerson outlines in the following chapter, other post-positivist perspectives, such as hermeneutics and deconstruction, are also concerned with language and discourse. While post-modernism is often viewed as a natural ally for feminism, what separates feminism from most forms of post-modernism is that it is rooted in and necessarily linked to an emancipatory politics. Feminism thus focuses on discourse in action – discourse as social interaction and political struggle – that considers how both socio-economic structures and individual agency create systems of meaning and how they influence policy outcomes. From a feminist vantage point, policy problems cannot be taken as given or absolute, but are perspective dependent; policy design must be examined for its differential effects based on gender, class, race, age, community, and other dimensions, and these effects need to be evaluated and understood from the lived experiences of those groups or communities affected.

As an analytical perspective linked to a political movement, over the past decade feminism has grappled seriously with the concept of 'difference,' both differences between women and men and differences among women. From these debates over difference emerges a second major contribution to policy studies: a concern with identity and identity politics. Feminism has always been attentive to representation and has evolved a stance that cautions against blanket categorization that imposes identities, experiences, and names on individuals that they would not choose for themselves. One way of avoiding stereotyping or presuming a coherence among members of a category that may not exist is to focus on identities – representations of self formulated with reference to collectivities that are socially constructed and self-named.[2] The prescriptive side of the concern with difference and the equitable representation of people in policy making has produced its third contribution to policy studies: an emphasis on 'voice.' Identities often find a voice through a 'politics of difference' in which representation is not only expanded to include a diversity of groups and communities, especially formerly silenced ones, but participation in policy making takes place directly by individuals and their chosen community representatives, rather than by societal elites. Ultimately, feminism would take policy making in the direction of dramatically altered democratic practices that would provide greater representation and participation for all citizens.

This chapter provides an overview of a feminist perspective on policy studies and, in particular, its development of the notions of discourse, identity, and voice. It begins with the basic step of treating gender as a category of analysis, although as we will see, the definition and treatment of gender is itself problematic. Second, it explores different ways in which feminist policy studies have responded to the misplaced objectivity of positivist models, and finally, it considers the implications for the politics of policy. Throughout the chapter, my focus is on the converging aspects of feminism as they inform the study and practice of policy analysis. In stressing these elements of convergence within feminism, however, I am not suggesting that feminism is a unified theoretical approach. Indeed, the alternative explanations of injustice and oppression offered by different strands of feminism – socialist, radical, liberal, or post-modern feminism – are often highly discordant. Explication of these differences, however, is also beyond the scope of this chapter.

Bringing Gender In

Feminist analysis begins with the claim that all social and political life is gendered and that gender as a social construction is not a fixed biological characteristic, but is relational, temporal, and context specific. If, as feminist scholars point out, gender is institutionalized in state structures and public policy in often relatively obvious and sometimes glaringly discriminatory ways, why has it taken so long for investigation of these gendered relations to take place and why are policy analysts still often reluctant to examine them? The answer is not that policy analysts have been predominantly male or overtly sexist or just plain stupid; rather, the reasons can be traced to liberalism as a political philosophy and its influence on contemporary notions of citizenship. Liberalism is seen by many feminists to degender policy analysis in at least two ways. First, the concept of citizen embedded in liberalism posits a universality, abstracted from social and economic contingencies: the citizen is portrayed as an individual without gender, class, race, or community. Many feminists argue that the consequence of the universal citizen is that women have been required to deny aspects of themselves and conform to the unitary norms of citizenship.[3] Pateman, one of the strongest feminist critics of liberalism, goes even further to argue that this norm of citizenship, in fact, has never been gender neutral.[4] Rather, she asserts that citizenship has been made in the male image so that when women were considered in classical liberal theory, they have been either subordinated to men or subsumed under the male model of citizen. For Anne Phillips, the challenge for feminism is not to deny sexual difference and any possibility of abstraction, but to bring both genders in:

Sexual differentiation is already writ large in political theory, in a manner that has so far served men. The solution is not to eliminate all such references, but to recast the story with both sexes on stage. Human identity is sexually differentiated, and exists in a bodily form. Those who seek to deny the body, who deal only in the abstraction of 'the individual' or 'the citizen,' who think it should make no difference whether these individuals are women or men, will be writing in one sex alone as their standard. Women can be encompassed on an equality with men only if sexual difference is first of all acknowledged.[5]

The second way in which liberalism has encouraged analysts to ignore gender is by presenting a false dichotomy of the public and private spheres. Public refers to the sphere (in symbolic and institutional terms, as well as geographic space) that is open and accessible and that not only permits contests over values and relationships – that is, politics – but anticipates and promotes such contests. In contrast, because relationships and values – and therefore, injustices as well – in the private are occluded from public view, they have not been open to debate or been the subject of politics. Feminism's questioning of this dichotomization highlights the ways that some activities and values, especially those of caring and care giving, are presumed to be the responsibility of private individuals (mainly women) rather than society as a whole. This has depoliticized and devalued caring as an activity.[6] The public/private dichotomy also obscures many aspects of women's lives. It perpetuates a gendered division of labour in the domestic domain, discounts a great deal of work done by women, excludes from political attention many issues affecting the equality of women, and restricts women's opportunities to participate in public life. One of the successes of the women's movement (along with other contemporary social movements) has been to make the private and personal political: to question and debate the nature of the structures, relations, and values in the traditionally private sphere. Yet, as Young notes, to say the personal is political does not deny a distinction between public and private. Rather, it implies and advances two fundamental political principles: '(a) no persons, actions, or aspects of a person's life should be forced into privacy; and (b) no social institutions or practices should be excluded a priori from being a proper subject for public discussion and expression.'[7] It is important to note, however, that while many feminists are highly critical of the legacy of classical liberalism, not all feminists would argue that the solution is to abandon liberalism. On the contrary, many liberal feminists, such as Okin, argue persuasively that the liberal principles of justice can be used to reformulate both the public and private spheres.[8]

Feminist scholars – whether working from a liberal or neo-Marxist theory of the state – have attempted to correct for the gender blindness of traditional policy studies by bringing gender in as an independent category of analysis. Two main avenues of exploration have been followed in feminist policy studies: one path has been to consider how the effects of public policy may have differential impacts according to gender, and the related route has been to examine how gender relations are structured and represented by the state generally or within the bureaucracy specifically. Since its emergence in the 1970s, the trend in feminist policy analysis has been to move away from more deterministic and functionalist models (in which patriarchy, discrimination, and oppression were often assumed and women portrayed as relatively powerless in the face of these structures) to more nuanced and textured analyses in which comparative study, specific historical struggles, and the mechanisms of women's agency are central concerns.

Inclusion of gender as a means of investigating both the gendering effects of policy and the ways in which gender relations are structured by state institutions and practices has covered a wide array of policy fields.[9] For instance, Cohen has examined the negative and unanticipated effects of the Canada–U.S. Free Trade Agreement on women, and Maloney provides a thorough and thoughtful analysis of the impact of the Canadian tax system on women.[10] MacDonald and Connelly successfully integrate gender relations with a class analysis to explain how the political and economic changes in the fishing industry in Nova Scotia have differentially affected women and men.[11] Feminist analysis of the use of environments and services within Canadian cities and women's responses to economic restructuring have emerged as an important new direction in urban policy studies.[12]

Notwithstanding the range of policy fields investigated from a feminist perspective, the most developed area of research has focused on the welfare state and social policy. This is not surprising given women's special relationship with the welfare state both as clients (recipients of social assistance) and as employees (social programs tend to be delivered predominantly by women as social workers and care givers). The growing number of women as single parents and the strong likelihood that they and their children will live in poverty means that research on the ways in which gender relations are embedded in the institutions and policies that provide social services is of critical importance.

Early work in this area by McIntosh and other socialist feminists presented a theory of 'dual systems' – capitalism and patriarchy – as explanations of women's oppression.[13] McIntosh theorizes that capitalism and the state reproduce gender oppression because both support a specific type of family (based on a male wage-earner and dependent female who performs domestic service). This ensures that women do the unpaid domestic labour and are available to the labour force as a 'reserve army of labour' – available to move in and out of paid work as required, but generally at lower pay and often in part-time work.

More recent work by a number of Scandinavian scholars has also studied women's relationship with the welfare system by focusing on their multiple roles as clients, employees, and citizens. These multiple relationships, argues Hernes, have not empowered or enhanced the autonomy of women, but instead have created greater dependencies on the part of most women who come into contact with the welfare state, in part because women, as citizens, do not have powerful organizations to defend their interests.[14] Siim observes that the effects of the Scandinavian welfare states on women's lives have been somewhat more contradictory because, on one hand, the state has aided in reproducing the sexual division of labour while, on the other hand, it has also created greater equality, especially in the labour market and education systems.[15] There is a consensus among these writers, however, on what is required to reduce dependencies: greater participation by women in the determination of their social needs and empowerment as mothers, workers, *and* citizens.

Other feminist research has concentrated on more detailed empirical analysis of the differential gender effects of particular policies. An interesting study by Nelson, for example, examines the original administrative design and practices of the two early American social programs – 'Workmen's' Compensation and Mothers' Aid – which respectively established the criteria for subsequent social insurance programs and welfare programs.[16] The administrative origins and paternalistic assumptions embedded in these programs created a legacy of a two-channel welfare system in which one channel has been designed for (white) industrial workers and the other for poor mothers with young children. From the beginning, the administrative style and practices of Workmen's Compensation were relatively unobtrusive because they were based on standardized forms and eligibility rules determined by 'scientific' formulas (related to the extent and duration of a worker's disability) and involved little monitoring of how recipients spent their benefits. The Mothers' Aid program, in sharp contrast, was committed to establishing a woman's capacity to care, and its administrative style was highly moralistic and discretionary with considerable authority vested in caseworkers to apply eligibility standards, determine needs, and assess the behaviour of recipients. One closely monitored requirement, for example, was that mothers be 'morally fit,' a term that included sexual behaviour, use of alcohol and tobacco, presence of boarders, and housekeeping skills.[17] Little's work reveals that precisely the same moral tone has historically dominated and continues to characterize the delivery of social assistance to single mothers in Ontario. Not only must they prove their worthiness as both recipients and as mothers, but the scrutiny imposed by the state has helped to 'reinforce dominant race, class and gender interests in society at large.'[18]

It is not surprising that feminists have been among some of the strongest critics of the neoliberal and neoconservative governments of Reagan, Thatcher, and Mulroney.[19] Their criticism has been aimed at the underlying ideology of neoliberalism, which could be interpreted as a kind of social Darwinian survival of the fittest consumer, that is, an assumption that all citizens have more or less equal resources and capacities to access or create opportunities, thereby justifying market mechanisms as solutions to social problems. They have also been critical of neoconservatism's emphasis on 'family values,' which many fear simply masks a commitment to encourage women to return to the home.[20] In a comparative study of proposals for national child-care policies in Canada and the United States in the late 1980s, Teghtsoonian demonstrates that the underlying anti-statist and pro-market ideology of the neoconservative governments and leading interest group opponents was expressed in slightly different ways in the two countries.[21] Neoconservatives' 'pro-family' stance (expressed as the desire to prevent the erosion of parental prerogatives by state authority), however, transcended the border. Together these neoconservative values converged and were instrumental in defeating the child-care proposals.

Other feminist scholars have turned from the macro to the meso level of analysis: from broad state structures and policy regimes to the bureaucracy itself to explain gendered relations in public policy. Stivers makes the case that, despite its supposed neutrality, public administration has systemic masculine characteristics.[22] In particular, the images of expertise, leadership, and virtue in public administration – the mainstays of administrative power – have masculine features that not only bestow political and economic privilege, but do so at the expense of women (the specific ways in which this occurs are documented in considerable detail by Stivers). She is not particularly optimistic. While important for addressing justice issues, employment equity and other strategies for promoting women within the bureaucracy are unlikely to change the tenor and value of public administration. The only route to real change, Stivers suggests, is through 'exploring public administration's gender dilemmas, instead of denying their existence' and thereby recasting our thinking about the entire nature of administration.[23]

As Orloff explains in her excellent review of the literature on gender and the welfare state, the most significant recent developments in feminist policy studies are more extensive comparative research and greater emphasis on the vehicles through which women and their organizations have agency and influence in the policy process.[24] Three brief examples illustrate just how far feminism has moved over the past two decades from theorizing patriarchy and assuming inequality, as the dual systems theorists did, to providing sophisticated comparative analyses of specific ways in which gender relations are expressed through public policies. First, Jenson has focused attention on the agents and discourses that have shaped policies through her detailed comparisons of the social policy regimes in France with those of other countries. In one study, Jenson explains why, at a critical moment of industrialization at the turn of the century, France developed extensive policies protecting women and their children while the United States was very resistant to such legislation.[25] Her analysis explains that in France the prevailing gender identity for women was one of 'citizen-producer,' an identity that validated labour force participation by both single and married women, whereas in the United States working women were relatively invisible. The concern of the French state at the time was to avoid depopulation by reducing infant mortality caused by a hasty return to work by new mothers. The nationalist interests of the state were supported by business, labour, the Catholic Church, and feminists alike.[26] In contrast, the combined strength of liberalism and federalism in the United States put the courts in a superior policy-making position, and American legal doctrine gave primacy to the protection of freedom of contract at individual workplaces. Within the polity, there were few demands for protective legislation because trade unions feared the effects of female employment on men's wages and the feminist movement was focused on women's 'nurturing' qualities.

Second, Balbo offers a compelling analysis of the evolution in the relationship between state and family, beginning with the creation of the modern state in France in the eighteenth and nineteenth centuries through the establishment of the modern welfare state in Britain in the 1940s to 1960s and ending with the contemporary 'post-welfare' state.[27] Balbo's work adds to the study of social policy regimes by demonstrating why it is necessary to take into account women's unpaid labour as an essential supplement to state-provided services and as a strategic link among service-delivery institutions. Her thesis is that women have actually been gaining strength over the course of the evolution of the welfare state due to their increasingly strategic position. She argues that 'because of services provided by women either free or at low cost, an enormous number of needs, although recognized as legitimate demands in a welfare state or service society, do not compete for scarce resources. Therefore, they do not become a political demand capable of generating pressures, strains, and conflict.'[28] Such demands are not reflected as part of state policy, but are part of the overall social policy delivery system – precisely because of the unpaid, often unacknowledged work of women.

Finally, Skocpol's book on the origins of the American welfare state provides an excellent illustration of how much richer – and, indeed, more accurate – analysis can become by incorporating gender.[29] Skocpol acknowledges that she began her investigation into why the United States did not develop a modern European-style welfare state (in spite of the fact that by 1900 the American government provided generous benefits for civil war soldiers) by using a state-centred framework that emphasizes formal policy and government officials. Yet, as she progressed with the research, it became evident that women's voluntary organizations (in a period when women had not yet won the right to vote) had been more influential than state officials in getting legislation providing social spending for mothers.[30] The exclusion of women from electoral politics, Skocpol argues, encouraged them to develop a solidarity around gender, form autonomous organizations, and forge alliances with other reformist groups. Women used these organizations and alliances to create a maternalist political conscience at a time when industrial workers were not very class-conscious and to pressure all levels of government to establish social policies to help mothers and their families.[31] The inclusion of gender became more than 'background information' to the story that Skocpol initially had set out to tell: 'Gender relations and identities were not just a footnote to my overall story; they were centrally intertwined with the structural and cultural patterns of American politics ... My state-centered theoretical frame of reference had evolved into a fully "polity-centered approach."'[32]

This overview leads us to an important question: What can we see as policy analysts by using gender as a lens or category of analysis that we would not have seen without it? First, the inclusion of gender makes analysis more complete by making visible the activities and political processes that have been rendered invisible in traditional policy studies. We can, for example, more fully understand the significant role of unpaid labour in the domestic sphere and appreciate the importance of alternative political spaces, such as voluntary organizations and social movements, as mechanisms for political representation. Second, analysis that takes gender into account challenges popular – but often faulty – assumptions, corrects stylized facts, and removes systemic bias that arises from the supposition that (elite) men's experience represents all human experience.[33] As discussed in more detail below, it also forces us to look at ourselves as analysts and to question our own assumptions and methodologies that we bring to the research endeavour. Third, new questions are often raised and existing categories and theories are sometimes reconfigured. Feminist scholarship on the welfare state, for instance, has given rise to a plethora of new questions about its origins, practices, and effects. Finally, gendered analysis leads us to ask about the possibilities for change. In what ways might public policies be designed to alter gender relations in progressive ways?

Problematizing Gender: Identity and Voice

It would be misleading to leave the impression that feminist scholars accept gender as a consistent and coherent category that differentiates women from men but that admits few significant differences within the category. On the contrary, one of the most debated points among feminists in recent years has been the extent to which women share an 'essence' as women, or at least share sufficiently similar experiences, to be treated as a category of analysis at all. Although feminists have always regarded gender as a social and political construct, rather than as merely a descriptive label, the legitimacy of the concept has come under attack recently from two main sources: postmodernism, which is sceptical of any universal and generalizing claim, and from women of colour, aboriginal, and other minority women who see that the focus on women as a category has been advanced from a voice of privilege by white, middle-class, heterosexual women.[34] The anti-essentialist position is that gender cannot be isolated from race, class, nationality, sexual orientation, and other identities. As Spelman, one of the most influential anti-essentialist scholars, cautions, 'though all women are women, no woman is only a woman. [We] must give up the hunt for the generic woman – the one who is all and only woman, who by some miracle of abstraction has no particular identity in terms of race, class, ethnicity, sexual orientation, language, religion, nationality.'[35] The experiences of culture and identity as well as the realities of sexism and oppression, the anti-essentialist position argues, are both qualitatively and quantitatively different for minority women.

This fragmentation of the category presents a problem for feminist analysis, albeit a very different one than that presented by early feminist assumptions that ignored difference. If all women have distinctive identities as a result of being situated in multiple communities, who is left in the category simply called 'woman'? A number of feminists have attempted to reconcile the charge that feminism has not been sufficiently sensitive to difference with the aims of creating an inclusive political movement. The dilemma is that feminist politics would evaporate without a critical mass of women who share a collective identity as women sufficient to mobilize as a political force. Young argues that treating individuals as individuals would simply exile feminism into the folds of liberalism and, in fact, would extend the potential for oppression rather than celebrate diversity.[36] One strategy for dealing with this dilemma, argued perhaps most articulately by Okin, is that analysis must be attuned to difference. She concludes that 'gender itself is an extremely important category of analysis and that we ought not to be paralyzed by the fact that there are differences among women. So long as we are careful and develop our judgments in light of empirical evidence, it is possible to generalize about many aspects of inequality between the sexes.'[37]

Another solution is to concentrate on identity politics that are based on a conception of the subject as positional or relative. Identity is a political point of departure and a motivation for action, rather than a set of objective needs; it builds on the commonalities as a political movement, yet permits sufficient flexibility to remain sensitive and attentive to women in a wide range of situations. As Jenson notes, 'these ideas about who we are ... are never fixed in time, nor do they fall from the sky. They are created out of the political actions of groups and individuals who work to make themselves heard, their positions respected, and their demands met.'[38] Using the notion of identity, the position and concept of women is not defined according to innate characteristics – the approach that has been attacked as essentialist – but in relation to external and constantly shifting contexts that include a network of other players and structural factors, such as economic conditions, cultural dimensions, and political institutions.[39] It is from this relative position that values are interpreted, alliances constructed, and injustices experienced. Thus identity is conceived to be sufficiently fluid and relative that it avoids the static bonds and homogenizing tendencies of essentialism.

Feminism's conceptualization and problematization of gender as a category has had two direct implications for the content of policy and the politics of representation. The first issue is whether policies aimed at removing gender-based inequality and injustice should be premised on treating women and men in the same way (because sex is seen to be irrelevant) or if equality can be better achieved by treating women and men differently (in recognition of their sexual and social differences). A good example of how this sameness/difference debate has been played out relates to workplace protective legislation. Should women, especially women of childbearing age, be restricted from doing certain kinds of work that involve toxic chemicals or other hazards that may harm their reproductive systems? A similar argument pertains to whether women should be allowed to participate fully in military combat units. Increasingly, feminists are arguing that sameness (undifferentiated treatment) is not a requirement for equality, and in many cases more equitable and appropriate treatment might be achieved by recognizing difference and making policy sufficiently flexible to accommodate and address differences. Indeed, in an excellent review of a wide range of historical and contemporary policy debates in which the sameness/difference dimension has been prominent (e.g., affirmative action, divorce and child custody, and maternity benefits), Bacchi argues that equating equality with sameness and setting up equal treatment as being in opposition to differential treatment is a conceptual and semantic conceit.[40] It serves only to mystify the underlying political issues and conditions that force women into a choice between them in the first place. As Scott states, 'it denies the way in which difference has long figured in political notions of equality and it suggests that sameness is the only ground in which equality can be claimed.'[41] In this light, the Canadian Charter of Rights and Freedoms could be seen as an instrument that attempts to promote equity both through protection of straightforward equality before and under the law *and* through the differential treatment afforded by affirmative action programs.

The second implication for the policy process also relates to difference, but to differences among women, as discussed above. While feminism has always been concerned with enhancing representation, not only of women but of all marginalized groups, the problematizing of gender has given rise to a 'politics of difference' that, while an issue for other social movements, has had the greatest impact on the women's movement. A politics of difference is based on a vision of 'a heterogeneous public that accepts and affirms group differences'[42] and is centred on the metaphor of voice – participation that includes some measure of power. The mode of representation under a politics of difference shifts from representation by elites, whether elected, state, or interest group elites, to direct representation and participation by people who personally share in the experiences of the social and cultural groups for whom they claim to speak.[43] Difference politics is necessarily a politics of identity, one that 'involves competing accounts of the grounds of identity not just of the group or collectivity concerned but of the individual self.'[44] Through such politics, emphasis is being shifted from *what* is being claimed to *how* and by *whom* claims are made.

An illustration by Findlay shows how new attempts to enhance representation by the state through consultation and employment equity may be more of a problem than a solution to concerns raised by marginalized communities because, while such measures appear to include a variety of people, they still have embedded within them hierarchies of privilege.[45] In the name of employment equity and public consultation, the city of Toronto began in the 1980s to employ more people from 'designated groups' (women, racial minorities, aboriginal people, and people with disabilities) and to create citizen advisory committees that would address issues of particular concern to these groups. Instead of empowering minority communities, however, Findlay contends that the city's practices actually diminished their voice because representation by designated groups within the administration, who tend to be in relatively powerless positions, replaced direct representation by community activists. Because the equity initiatives artificially separated race and disability from gender, visible minority women, aboriginal women, and women with disabilities fell through the cracks; this ultimately further privileged white women at the expense of minorities. In addition, the relationship of the city with the citizen committees tended to be mediated by city advocates who organized consultations and provided their own expertise and advice to politicians and bureaucrats. The point of this example is that just as feminism has been challenged by women of colour and other less privileged women to grapple with the concept and the politics of difference, feminism is pushing governments to re-examine their own practices of representation and consultation to assess who is really being represented and who decides which are the legitimate claims and appropriate claimants to be heard.

Feminist Epistemologies: Context and Discourse

When women become feminists the crucial thing that has occurred is not that they have learned any new facts about the world but that they come to view those facts from a different position, from their own position as subjects.[46]

Feminism has not only grappled with gender as a subject of analysis, but it has also challenged established conceptions of knowledge. The attempts to construct alternative epistemologies are based on a critique of positivist social science and specifically that: (1) positivism separates the knowers (scientists or policy analysts) from knowledge (the subject matter) through its commitment to objectivity and its claims that facts are independent of the values of scientists; (2) by searching for the development of generalized laws, it tends to decontextualize the subject and knowledge; (3) language is assigned to a passive role in representing individuals' mental processing; and (4) it presumes a superiority of the scientists with little responsibility to the participants in knowledge construction or to larger publics.[47]

With what alternative epistemologies and research methodologies would feminism replace these premises of positivism that it finds so wanting? In contrast to more radical interpretations, my view is that feminist epistemology does not dismiss or preclude all systematic inquiry and quantitative methodologies; rather, its aim is to contextualize and situate inquiry in certain specific ways. First, feminism's response to positivism's insistence on objectivity – the claim that proper scientific analysis can be produced only by dispassionate and value-free methods of inquiry in which the researcher is distinctly separate from the object of investigation and has no particular point of view toward it – is that science, especially social science, is never value free, but relies on interpretation by the researcher. The misplaced concern with objectivity, argues Hawkesworth, is the fear that the idiosyncratic experiences, biases, and perceptual quirks of the observer will impair understanding of the phenomenon under investigation.[48] This masks the real concern, however, which is the role of social values: 'rather than being perceived as potential sources of error, social values such as racism and sexism that filter perception, mediate arguments, and structure research investigations escape critical reflection.'[49] By recognizing that the researcher is an integral part rather than a distant relative of the research endeavour, feminist scholars argue that they have, in fact, enhanced sensitivity to social values that traditional conceptions of objectivity inappropriately obscure. Because no positivist method is sufficiently powerful to eliminate all social bias, the challenge is to deal directly and upfront with the point of view of the investigator. The case for 'feminist standpoint theory' advanced by Harding uses women's lives and experiences – their standpoints (which as socially mediated and experientially based viewpoints are quite different from preconceived theoretical or ideological positions) – and it recognizes that all human beliefs are socially situated.[50] This approach, Harding argues, will result in stronger objectivity because it exposes the historical, sociological, and cultural relativism of the theorist and encourages us to ask the question: Whose values and whose standpoints does this research represent?[51]

The second point in the construction of a feminist epistemology is recognition of the significance of context. All knowledge is situated, not only relative to the investigator, but in a specific historical, social, economic, and political context. Understanding of the subtleties of people's experiences cannot be garnered through generalized and universal theories that present the context as presumed by the researcher. Rather, the methods of investigation must be subject salient and context sensitive so as to reflect accurately these experiences from the perspective of the subject. The focus on the importance of context is naturally coupled with an insistence that language is not a neutral or passive container of ideas, but an active force in knowledge production. Language is seen to be constitutive, not merely expressive of concepts, and serves as the means through which people represent themselves as individuals and as part of collectivities. One implication of the politics of language is that all concepts potentially become 'essentially contestable concepts,' in Connolly's terms, which means that understanding of the political life of a community necessarily involves knowledge of the conceptual and discursive systems within which that life moves.[52] The significance of both language and context suggests, as Yeatman does, that 'subjects are understood to be discursively positioned within the conjunctural historical moment of contested narratives of who they are and where they are going.'[53]

The primary vehicle for exploring these contested concepts and narratives in policy studies has been discourse analysis. Discourse is not simply a language or text, but 'a historically, socially, and institutionally specific structure of statements, term categories and beliefs.'[54] Of course, discourse analysis is not unique to feminism, and even within feminism there are several distinct approaches to the study of discourse, notably post-modern and poststructural feminism.[55] For policy studies, however, it is important that discourse as meaning be linked with a subject as the supplier of that meaning and that language and text be understood in relation to the actions of these subjects.

One of the leading scholars using a discourse analysis that includes subjects as both active agents and subjects of structure is Jane Jenson. In her autobiographical exploration of how feminism influenced her elaboration of 'permeable fordism,' Jenson rejects the disempowering formulations and politics of post-structuralism and other discourse analysis in favour of a discourse considered as historical agency:

One of the crucial legacies of those feminist analyses which take seriously the notion that gender relations are social constructions and that social constructions result from both structures and agency – that is, that people make their own history but not under conditions of their own choosing – is a move towards analyses which examine the dialectic between the abstractions of structures and the specificity of historical circumstances.[56]

The emphasis on both structure and agency has led Jenson to the development of the notion of the 'universe of political discourse,' which is defined as the universe of socially constructed meaning resulting from political struggle.[57] In the course of contest over meaning, actors seek to name themselves and construct collective identities, represent themselves to themselves and to others, and give legitimacy to their causes. The political struggle that occurs within the universe of political discourse sets the boundaries of what are considered to be legitimate claims and relevant actors, determines the possibilities for alliances and advocacy strategies, and limits what are deemed by policy makers to be feasible policy options. Jenson's concept is by no means a free-for-all pluralist struggle in which all collectivities can be mobilized and heard; on the contrary, she is unequivocal that the power relations within such a universe are seldom equal. In particular, state institutions have considerable power to determine who will be represented by structuring how representation occurs, by inviting certain people to consult and being more accommodating to some collective identities than others.[58] Clearly, not all possible actors and positions will achieve representation on this terrain of struggle because the universe filters and delineates claims and in fact determines what is 'political' in the first place.

Jenson's research strategy for analysis of discourse starts with the policy in a specific historical context, rather than with given sets of actors. By tracing the policy, analysis can describe the actors, their positions and discourses, and their ultimate success (or failure). One example of Jenson's application of the universe of political discourse, the struggle for protective legislation, is discussed above. Another illustration is drawn from her investigation of how women came to acquire political rights in France.[59] It is an intriguing question as to why the country that invented universal (manhood) suffrage in 1789 took until 1944 to grant equivalent political rights to women. We cannot understand the reasons that women got the vote in France, however, by imposing 1990s discourses of individual rights and gender equality; rather, the prevailing and competing discourses, as carried by particular actors, have to be explored in their historical setting. Jenson's analysis of the alignment of social movements, political parties, the Catholic Church, and the state reveals that suffrage was primarily advocated as votes for 'mothers' rather than women and that even the feminist movement at times promoted a 'family' vote (in which husbands' and wives' ballots are linked) and frequently debated suffrage exclusively within the framework of French society as republican or Catholic. She concludes that it was not until a realignment occurred in the universe of political discourse that political rights for women were finally attained. In the end, 'the decision was rationalized as a reward for service in the Resistance, not in terms of a fundamental right of women to full equality and citizenship.'[60]

Other Canadian scholars have made extensive use of discourse analysis to explain more contemporary public policy issues. In separate analyses, Maroney and Hamilton focus on the alternative discourses of nationalism, feminism, and demography that have shaped Quebec's pro-natal policies in this century.[61] Walker shows how the fundamental and in many respects most difficult stage of the struggle by the women's movement to get the issue of 'wife battering' on the political agenda was one of conceptual definition.[62] This struggle involved getting the issue understood – and named – in terms of a feminist discourse of 'violence against women' (which entails solutions involving systemic change), rather than in the language of a professional discourse of 'family violence' (which would give primacy to attempts by social workers to treat 'troubled families') or as a sociolegal discourse of 'violence' (in which law-and-order solutions on the part of the police and the justice system to enforce sanctions against 'assault' would predominate).

Analysis of discourse in this genre begins with context and positional subjects, rather than with generalized assumptions about the types of policy arguments usually associated with these particular subjects and issues. Unequal structures, inadequate opportunities to be heard, and the gendering effects of the discourses are not theorized or assumed, but investigated through empirical analysis. Through examination of concrete cases, comparisons across discourses, historical moments, and countries of the ways in which gender is institutionalized and reproduced in government policies becomes possible.

The final point in the creation of alternative feminist epistemologies is the rejection of the notion of superiority of the scientist over the subject. Instead, feminism stresses that science does not end with the phase of inquiry and discovery, but also includes a stage of justification and persuasion in which the results of research are allowed to be challenged, refuted, and defended.[63] Moreover, the products of inquiry seldom remain in the possession of the researcher, but get injected into culture and politics. Because it remains embedded in a politics of empowering women, feminism affirms a social responsibility on the part of the researcher and on the part of the policy process itself. For the researcher, this responsibility involves a commitment to communicate research in terms and through channels accessible to those outside academe or the scientific community because access to analysis and the opportunities to offer critical scrutiny of it are an important step toward empowerment. Researchers also need to recognize that they may not be asking the same questions – let alone coming up with the same answers – as people touched by the analysis. In fact, as Sprague and Zimmerman suggest, 'if we who are in relatively privileged social positions take the standpoints of those who are at the bottoms of social hierarchies, it is unlikely that our questions will be the same as theirs ... If we want to claim to be doing feminist research, however, we should be able to see how addressing our questions will facilitate their answers.'[64]

The responsibility of the policy maker is to ensure that research on a particular policy issue facilitates understanding of the full range of standpoints and perspectives, and in particular that the politically marginalized groups of society have the opportunity to give voice to their alternative constructions and interpretations of research. This returns us to be point of understanding the collective identities in society and allowing them to have their voices heard.

Conclusion

Feminist policy research is often erroneously equated with the examination of 'women's issues' or with simply adding women to the analysis. But feminism's contributions to policy analysis go much deeper than this. As both theory and politics, feminism over the past decade has grappled seriously with concepts of difference. Thinking about a politics of difference has enormous potential to inform policy making processes because one of the major concerns for democracy in the 1990s centres on the nature of representation and, in particular, on extending representation to usually silent constituencies and to groups as well as individuals and on shifting to forms of more direct rather than elite representation.[65] Feminism – although not feminism alone (see the following chapter) – has also produced new approaches to the construction and use of knowledge in policy analysis.

This chapter has argued that from these two basic discussions within feminism – related to difference and to epistemology – there have emerged three important contributions to policy studies. First, the focus on discourse illustrates that subjects are situated in discursive contexts and that commonly used notions are often contestable concepts. Policy debates thus can best be understood through investigating the specific contexts, discourses, and experiences of actors in these contested narratives. Second, policy analysis should not impose categories upon people and experience, but must examine the collective identities that people construct and name for themselves. The third contribution, the notion of voice, points to the fact that such identities are usually created through political struggle and, once formed, continue to struggle to create political spaces for their discourses and to participate in policy making. Feminism's concern with inequality and injustice in representation serves to remind us that democratic states have a responsibility to ensure that some voices are not consistently silenced, while others are regularly privileged. The challenge for feminism over the next decade will be to remain relevant to policy studies through providing extensive empirical and comparative analyses and to ensure that the debates over difference serve as the means for making politics inclusive, rather than allowing them to become the fissures that tear feminism apart.

Notes

My appreciation is expressed to Laurent Dobuzinskis, Jane Jenson, Brian Little, Rianne Mahon, and Leslie Pal for their thoughtful and constructive comments on the first draft of this chapter. Undoubtedly, my assessment, which focuses on feminism's positive contributions to policy studies, rather than its limitations, will be seen as unduly restrictive by many readers. My objective is not to preclude criticism of feminism as an analytical approach. Rather, my premise is that the themes and convergence within feminism must be explicated and understood before its shortcomings can be critically addressed.

1 Laslett and Brenner, 'Gender and Social Reproduction,' 382. Peterson also provides an excellent discussion of the insights gained for policy analysis, specifically in the context of international relations, by distinguishing gender from sex. Peterson, 'Introduction,' 9–10.
2 On the naming of collective identities, see Jenson, 'Understanding Politics,' 61–2.
3 Anne Phillips, *Democracy and Difference*, 56.
4 Pateman, *The Disorder of Women*, 14.
5 Phillips, *Democracy and Difference*, 57.
6 Tronto, *Moral Boundaries*, especially ch. 6.
7 Young, *Justice and the Politics of Difference*, 120.
8 Okin, *Justice, Gender, and the Family*. In their book, which offers advice to the women's movement regarding political strategy, Gelb and Palley also assert that a feminist agenda can be advanced and meaningful change achieved within a liberal state, as long as the movement's tactics are conso-

nant with a pluralist polity and, in particular, if primarily incremental change is pursued and confrontational politics avoided. Gelb and Palley, *Women and Public Policies.*

9 For an excellent overview of feminist contributions to policy studies with a particular focus on the United States, see Hawkesworth, 'Policy Studies with a Feminist Frame,' which is a special issue of *Policy Sciences* dedicated to feminist perspectives. A good review of recent books on feminism and public policy is provided by Ackelsberg, 'Feminist Analysis of Public Policy.'

10 Cohen, *Free Trade and the Future of Women's Work*; Maloney, 'What Is the Appropriate Tax Unit for the 1990s and Beyond?' See also Cassin, 'Equitable and Fair,' 104–34. Maloney's analysis reveals how the disincentives created by the current tax system have a far greater impact on women's decisions to enter the paid labour force than on men's decisions and shows how these disincentives have been the product of faulty assumptions about why women work outside the home. In particular, it generally has been assumed that women are the secondary wage-earners in the household and that they chose to work outside the home for personal enjoyment once their children are older or to purchase discretionary 'luxuries' for the household. Therefore, it has been argued that women are willing to accept lower-paying jobs or part-time work in order to give priority to their child rearing responsibilities. In demonstrating the fallacy of these assumptions, Maloney provides statistics that indicate that for a vast majority of women in the paid labour force, a job is an economic necessity rather than a luxury. Although the proportion of women employed in part-time jobs (32.6 per cent) greatly exceeds that of men (12.8 per cent), a 1985 Labour Force Survey indicates that the primary reason is not that women prefer part-time work. On the contrary, 28 per cent of women in part-time work said that it was all they could find. Finally, it is noteworthy that women suffer a higher unemployment rate than men.

A related concern for feminists who study tax policy is the degree to which and how income is shared within the family. On this point, see Woolley and Marshall, 'Measuring Inequality within the Household,' and Okin, *Justice, Gender, and the Family,* who explores broader questions of justice in families.

11 MacDonald and Connelly, 'Class and Gender in Fishing Communities,' 61–85.

12 On feminist analysis of urban environments and policy, see Mackenzie, 'Women's Responses to Economic Restructuring,' 81–100; Andrew, 'The Feminist City,' 109–22, and the collection edited by Andrew and Milroy, *Life Spaces.*

13 McIntosh, 'The State and the Oppression of Women'; Wilson, *Women and the Welfare State*. Jenson is highly critical of McIntosh's dual systems approach because it generalizes about reproduction and capitalism from a particular period and a particular state in which an ideology of familialism and the family wage contributed to the oppression of women. See Jenson, 'Gender and Reproduction: Or, Babies and the State,' 9–14.

14 Hernes, 'The Welfare State Citizenship of Scandinavian Women,' 139–59.

15 Siim, 'The Scandinavian Welfare States,' 255–70; see also Borchorst and Siim, 'Women and the Advanced Welfare State,' 128–57.

16 Nelson, 'The Origins of the Two-Channel Welfare State,' 123–51.

17 Ibid., 144. An examination of contemporary American social policy as conducted by Sapiro demonstrates that it is still far from gender neutral. In the case of social policies that have been aimed specifically at women, notably Aid to Families with Dependent Children (AFDC), Sapiro's assessment is that they still serve to force women into greater, not less, dependency. 'Its [AFDC's] intention has been to enable them to *care* for their families and not, by and large, to *provide* for them in the sense that is expected of a breadwinner.'

18 Little, '"Manhunts and Bingo Blabs,"' 245. For an overview of the major issues and developments in social policy in Canada from a feminist perspective, see Cohen, 'Social Policy and Social Services,' 264–84.

19 For critiques of the gendering effects of neoliberalism/neoconservatism, see Eisenstein, 'Liberalism, Feminism and the Reagan State'; Waylen, 'Women and Neo-liberalism'; and Wilson, 'Thatcherism and Women.' Bashevkin, 'Confronting Neo-Conservatism,' provides a very interesting analysis of the impact of neoconservatism in the United States, the United Kingdom and Canada on the women's movement.

20 In her assessment of the impact of Thatcherism on women, Wilson observes that Thatcherism did not secure the subordination of women by forcing a return to the home, as had been feared by many critics, but it nevertheless made most women's lives harder, poorer, and more dangerous as they increasingly have been exploited in the worst paid and least protected jobs. Wilson, 'Thatcherism and Women,' 299.

21 Teghtsoonian, 'Neo-Conservative Ideology and Opposition to Federal Regulation,' 97–121.

22 Stivers, *Gender Images in Public Administration*. See also Ferguson, *The Feminist Case Against Bureaucracy*. A related genre of research that originated in Australia has focused on the extent to which individual feminists working in state bureaucracies – who are often labelled 'femocrats' – have had an influence on public policy to the advantage of women. For a sampling

of the femocrat literature, see Eisenstein, 'The Australian Femocratic Experiment,' 69–83, Sawer, *Sisters in Suits*, and Yeatman, *Bureaucrats, Technocrats, Femocrats*, chs. 4 and 5, and, in the Canadian context, see Findlay, 'Facing the State,' 31–50.

23 Stivers, *Gender Images in Public Administration*, 123.
24 Orloff, 'Gender and the Social Rights of Citizenship,' 305.
25 Jenson, 'Paradigms and Political Discourse,' 220–58.
26 Ibid., 241–2.
27 Balbo, 'Family, Women and the State,' 201–19.
28 Ibid., 211.
29 Skocpol, *Protecting Soldiers and Mothers*.
30 In a similar but earlier interpretation of the same turn-of-the-century reform period in Canada, Andrew argues that women's groups were crucial to the development of social welfare policies. A wide range of issues, including child care, mothers' pensions, education, temperance, and reforms aimed at juvenile delinquents, were taken up as women's issues: 'They were women's issues because women were seen as particularly affected by the problem but also because women had been involved in the solutions.' Andrew, 'Women and the Welfare State,' 11. See also Bacchi, *Liberation Deferred?*
31 Skocpol, *Protecting Soldiers and Mothers,* 57. As these voluntary organizations weakened from the 1920s onward, however, the sustained pressure for the creation of a full-fledged maternalist welfare state also diminished
32 Ibid., x.
33 Peterson, 'Introduction,' 6. See also Woolley, 'The Feminist Challenge to Neoclassical Economics,' 485–500.
34 Okin, 'Gender Inequality and Cultural Differences,' 6. For discussions of some of these concerns in the Canadian context, see Ng, 'The Social Construction of Immigrant Women in Canada,' 269–86; Pierson, 'The Mainstream Women's Movement and the Politics of Difference,' 186–214; Simms, 'Beyond the White Veil,' 175–81; and many of the chapters in Carty, ed., *And Still We Rise*. A distinctive feature of feminist politics in Canada has been that women in Quebec have evolved different organizations, been involved in somewhat different debates than women in English Canada, and have commanded a distinct voice in national, especially constitutional, politics. For a small sampling of the English literature on women in Quebec see Clio Collective, *Quebec Women: A History*, and Dumont, 'Women of Quebec.'
35 Spelman, *Inessential Woman*, 187.
36 Young, 'Gender as Seriality,' 718.
37 Okin, 'Gender Inequality and Cultural Differences,' 20.
38 Jenson, 'Understanding Politics,' 55.

39 Alcoff, 'Cultural Feminism versus Post-Structuralism,' 433.
40 Bacchi, *Same Difference*, 264–5.
41 Scott, 'Deconstructing Equality-versus-Difference,' 46.
42 Young, *Justice and the Politics of Difference*, 10.
43 A good example of the politics of difference in action was the debate surrounding the Canadian Panel on Violence against Women. The major national women's groups that initially supported the panel withdrew their support because it appeared that the panel sought only token representation from visible minority and disabled women. For a discussion of the implications of this case for representation, see Phillips, 'Who's Listening? Who's Speaking?'
44 Yeatman, 'Gender as Seriality,' 83; see also Jenson, 'Understanding Politics.'
45 Findlay, 'Problematizing Privilege,' 207–24.
46 Alcoff, 'Cultural Feminism versus Post-Structuralism,' 434.
47 This critique is drawn primarily from Code, *What Can She Know?* 27–70; Kenneth Gergen, 'Feminist Critique of Science and the Challenge of Social Epistemology,' 27–48; Mary Gergen, 'Toward a Feminist Metatheory and Methodology in the Social Sciences,' 87–104; Grosz, 'The In(ter)vention of Feminist Knowledges,' 92–104; Hawkesworth, *Beyond Oppression*, 130–48; Sprague and Zimmerman, 'Overcoming Dualisms,' 255–80; and Yeatman, *Postmodern Revisionings of the Political,* 13–41. For pioneering work on feminist methodologies, see Smith, *The Everyday World as Problematic.*
48 Hawkesworth, *Beyond Oppression*, 140, and 'Policy Studies within a Feminist Frame.'
49 Hawkesworth, 'Policy Studies within a Feminist Frame,' 21.
50 Harding, 'Feminism, Science, and the Anti-Enlightenment Critique,' 83–106, and *Whose Science, Whose Knowledge?* For an excellent application of feminist standpoint theory to policy analysis, see Rixecker, 'Expanding the Discursive Context of Policy Design.'
51 A critique commonly levelled against feminist epistemology is that it borders on and, in some cases, becomes relativism. If each individual's experiences are as relevant as anyone else's, it is impossible to develop any conceptualization of knowledge or any degree of generalization beyond one's self. The response by Harding, 'Feminism, Science, and the Anti-Enlightenment Critique,' and most other feminist scholars is that feminist standpoint theory is relational, not relativist: it does occupy a position (that of the gendered subject), rather than having no fixed position at all. On this point, see Gorsz, 'The In(ter)vention of Feminist Knowledges,' 100; Rixecker, 'Expanding the Discursive Context of Policy Design'; and Yeatman, *Postmodern Revisioning of the Political*, 20.

52 Connolly, *The Terms of Political Discourse*, 39.

53 Yeatman, *Postmodern Revisionings of the Political*, 120.

54 Scott, 'Deconstructing Equality-versus-Difference,' 35.

55 For a good discussion of post-structuralism, see MacDonald, 'The Trouble with Subjects,' and on post-modern feminism see Riley, *'Am I That Name?'* and the collection edited by Nicholson, *Feminism/Postmodernism*.

56 Jenson, 'Different but Not Exceptional,' 66.

57 Jenson, 'Gender and Reproduction,' 26.

58 Jenson, 'Understanding Politics,' 59.

59 Jenson, 'Changing Discourse, Changing Agendas,' 68–75. Jenson provides many other interesting examples; see 'Gender and Reproduction,' 14–46, and 'The Limits of "and the" Discourse,' 155–72.

60 Jenson, 'Changing Discourse, Changing Agendas,' 68–9.

61 Maroney, '"Who Has the Baby?"' 237–65; Hamilton, 'Pronatalism, Feminism and Nationalism.'

62 Walker, 'The Conceptual Politics of Struggle,' 317–42. Other Canadian examples of the application of discourse analysis include Brodie, Gavigan, and Jenson, *The Politics of Abortion*; McKeen, 'The Wages for Housework Campaign'; and Whitworth, 'Planned Parenthood and the New Right.'

63 The concern that policy analysts have a responsibility for both discovery ('the art') and justification ('the craft') is a point made by other post-positivists, but is put most eloquently by Wildavsky, *Speaking Truth to Power*, especially 389.

64 Sprague and Zimmerman, 'Overcoming Dualisms,' 273.

65 On group representation, see Kymlicka, 'Group Representation in Canadian Politics,' 61–90, and Young, *Justice and the Politics of Difference*, 185–91.

14

Power and Insight in Policy Discourse: Post-Positivism and Problem Definition

DOUGLAS TORGERSON

With the decline of positivism, methodological departures in the social sciences and humanities have drawn attention to language as a medium enveloping both the conduct and subject matter of inquiry. The effort to get to the simple facts – to grasp directly the brute, hard data constituting an unproblematically objective world – is displaced, if not wholly abandoned, by a focus on language, texts or text analogues, discursive practices. In the policy literature, this broad linguistic twist in methodological deliberations has allowed for the emergence of a post-positivist genre that, including hermeneutic, critical, and deconstructive elements, focuses attention on policy discourse.[1]

Post-positivism in policy analysis encourages attention to policy discourse generally in terms of *meaning*, but particularly in terms of an interplay between *power* and *insight*. Policy discourse is treated in three distinct ways. For hermeneutics, meaning is an achievement of participants who overcome differences, working through misunderstandings in order to attain a mutuality of communication. Critique challenges the supposed mutuality of prevailing communication and maintains that meaning is enforced by dominant interests in a manner that obscures and distorts actual relationships, thereby blocking the path to genuine understanding. Deconstruction questions the very possibility of stable, coherent, genuine communication; meaning, whether hermeneutically or critically understood, is treated by deconstruction as an arbitrary closure that excludes other possibilities and depends upon potent, though contingent and unstable, frames of reference.[2]

Questions of meaning arise clearly in relation to the task of defining policy problems. As David Dery has indicated, the very idea of 'problem definition' is suggestive of a 'constructivist' as opposed to an 'objectivist' posture: 'problems ... are not objective entities' that somehow simply 'exist "out there" ... in their own right,' but are identified and defined through the imposition of 'certain frames of reference.'[3] Thus understood, problem definition appears as an element of policy analysis that cannot escape at least implicit recourse to post-positivist concepts. Explicit attention to the post-positivist genre, moreover, suggests that problem definition occurs in discursive contexts where contests over meaning exhibit the ambivalent potential of either inhibiting or eliciting insight. This ambivalence can be seen in policy discourse as typically practised in administrative organizations; and the dynamic can also be found in open contexts of democratic politics, particularly where social movements intervene to challenge prevailing conventions.[4]

In examining the post-positivist genre of policy studies, this essay seeks to elucidate both the general character of post-positivism and the significance of differences among hermeneutic, critical, and deconstructive approaches. While proceeding generally from a post-positivist orientation, the essay itself makes no attempt to resolve these differences in a definitive manner. Post-positivism can well be understood not as a single, coherent approach, but as an unresolved – perhaps unresolvable – contention among different approaches to perplexities of meaning. Post-positivism, nonetheless, does possess a certain coherence and identity by virtue of its contrast with positivist and technocratic conventions of objectivism. As we shall see, the post-positivist genre tends to unsettle policy discourse in prevailing technocratic and administrative forms while reinforcing policy discourse as a form of commentary in broader social and political contexts.

I. Policy Discourse and Political Language: A Tale of Three Rhetorics

Attention to policy discourse reveals, as one might expect, that it is not univocal, but includes different practices – indeed, different rhetorics. Inquiry has often been thought to exclude rhetoric in principle, to be required to adhere to a pure, somehow neutral language of its own. Positivism proved particularly effective in reinforcing this view; and with its crisp, quiet style, policy analysis has typically appeared consistent with this requirement.[5]

Yet policy analysis cannot avoid contact with a language of politics characterized, at different times, by diversity and ambiguity, deception and revelation, charm and bombast. Whether the goal is merely to comprehend the policy process, or is somehow to shape it, policy analysis cannot escape some sort of involvement with a wider world of political language that is openly and obviously rhetorical. Yet contemporary policy analysis tends not to display its rhetorical character: its rhetoric is a quiet one, typically em-

ploying the measured precision of a technocratic idiom or confining itself to
a realm of cloistered consultations.

A view generally common to post-positivist perspectives is that rhetoric
is to be found in the most surprising places; for no text, no genre, no linguistic world can stand altogether apart from others, insulated and secure in its
own purity and neutrality.[6] J.A. Throgmorton has made a significant contribution to the post-positivist genre by developing this point in the context of
policy analysis. Indeed, he moves beyond the simple recognition of a rhetorical dimension in policy analysis to discriminate more finely among different rhetorics, distinct modes of discourse. Drawing upon Throgmorton's
approach, it is possible to identify three rhetorics of policy analysis – science, advice, and commentary – each with a distinct style and idiom, and
each addressed to a particular audience.[7] As science, policy analysis is, in
principle, directed to a scientific community; as advice, policy analysis is
intended for the ears of clients in narrow political and organizational contexts; as commentary, policy analysis informs a broader public. The three
rhetorics come into play on different occasions, variously creating problems
or opportunities for different actors in the policy process.

This tripartite scheme of science, advice, and commentary cannot capture
all the complexities and nuances of policy discourse as it is practised today
in diverse arenas with participants of varying interests and perspectives. If
viewed historically, though, the scheme does possess significant coherence
and comprehensiveness. Its elements correspond to three particular types of
political language that have developed with the advent of the modern state:
in the contemporary context of the administrative state, these types of political language have come together in a distinctive, composite form, as policy
discourse.

Broadly speaking, the subtlety, irony, and discretion of a deliberately rhetorical craft of advice in Renaissance counsel gradually gives way to an anti-
rhetorical rhetoric which, under the banner of science, employs a tightly
constricted idiom, fostering the impression of being measured, precise, entirely rational. With the Enlightenment, this shift is sustained by scientific
developments, but is also accompanied by the emergence of a public that –
while generally restricted to educated, propertied men – is disposed to engage in open deliberations, in the give and take of continuous commentary
on public affairs.

In the Renaissance, discretion and irony are key elements of a discourse
which, oriented to the practice of counsel in princely circles, is attuned to
the complexities and vicissitudes of power.[8] Evident, for example, in
Machiavelli, the style and concerns of the period are especially remarkable

in Thomas More. While disdaining 'the busy trifles of princes,'[9] the author of *Utopia* enters skilfully – albeit reluctantly – into the flatteries and deceptions of court life.[10] Keenly aware that 'novel ideas' cannot effectively be 'thrust on people' who are opposed to them, More pronounces 'academic philosophy' out of place 'in the councils of kings,' for there 'great matters are debated with great authority.' Yet he identifies 'another philosophy' which, suited to context, is 'more practical for statesmen' – one 'which knows its stage, adapts itself to the play in hand, and performs its role neatly and appropriately.' Make no attempt, he advises, to 'force upon people new and strange ideas which you realize will carry no weight'; try instead 'to handle matters tactfully' through an 'indirect approach.'[11] The counsellor to the prince is thus an adviser within a cloistered domain, discreetly proposing options in accord with prudence and, perhaps, virtue.

The effort to found a modern science of politics begins in the seventeenth century with an explicit rejection of rhetoric in favour of an uncompromisingly rationalistic philosophy. Indeed, the technocratic idiom of the administrative state is already anticipated in Hobbes; reacting against the Renaissance effort to join eloquence and wisdom, he rigorously disassociates the two, emphasizing how eloquence, as an appeal to the passions, could be readily joined with a lack of judgment in engendering social discord.[12] He seeks instead a precise, literal language of emotional neutrality, a language of mechanism in accord with the emerging mechanistic worldview. Hobbes rejects the 'ornaments and graces,' 'the paint and false colours of language': for 'the first grounds of all science are ... poor, arid, and, in appearance, deformed.'[13] While himself speaking openly and directly of the passions, Hobbes thus offers what has been characterized as a 'passage' from the rhetoric of the Renaissance to the 'tight-lipped style' that characterizes later political science: through his 'magnificent logic machine' he reduces human passions to units of a mechanism and teaches a method of restraint and calculation.[14] Using 'Metaphors, Tropes, and other Rhetorical figures, instead of words proper,' he insists, is a cause of absurdity and hence 'not to be admitted' in the search for truth.[15] Despite his vigorous rejection of rhetoric, Hobbes the rhetorician stands forth. Systematically formulated and punctuated by potent imagery, his teaching is meant not only to inform the sovereign, but also – under the spectre of social chaos – to tame the populace. Hobbes's *Leviathan* opens with a metaphor that remains, perhaps, the most striking image in the history of political thought. Through this image, paradoxically, he presses his view that political order and authority require a restrained, careful language devoid of such imagery.[16] Today, the prevailing idiom of policy discourse tacitly defers to rather similar images of order and authority, though typically without making the openly rhetorical gestures evident in Hobbes. In the context of his time, Hobbes seems not yet prepared for the technocratic consistency of an invisible rhetoric.

Public opinion, as it emerges with the Enlightenment, is not 'mere' opinion; it arises from an educated public actively involved in discussion.[17] However constrained by idiom, ideology, and exclusivity, this public world of commentary unavoidably entertains troublesome issues. In this context, established power is drawn into question and cannot maintain its legitimacy solely by an appeal to traditional symbols: power and authority are openly contested.

This questioning, however, tends to turn upon itself, as is especially evident during the nineteenth and twentieth centuries. In the context of a mass, industrial society, democratic movements tend to intrude upon the privileged civility of public life, drawing into question the basic terms of discussion and demanding that authority be democratically responsible. Yet, just as the public expands democratically, serious discussions guiding public policy increasingly retreat behind the closed doors of the administrative state. Public discourse tends to be displaced by propaganda – by a systematic circulation of images geared to channelling mass behaviour, to shaping an objectified 'public opinion,' rather than enhancing discussion. It is indeed at this juncture in the development of the modern state that policy analysis begins to enter the scene as a distinctive activity.[18]

In the contemporary context of policy analysis, the rhetoric of science displays a crucial ambivalence: in principle addressed to a broad scientific community, it has a decidedly technocratic accent and speaks particularly to experts in the echelons of administrative organizations. Here, however, listless technocratic exchanges are typically enlivened by the practice of advice: the invisible rhetoric of technocracy is insufficient and must be supplemented by more openly rhetorical gestures, by a give and take of opinion, and by active attention to context.[19] While the rhetoric of advice is thus clearly heard along the corridors of the administrative state, these routine departures from the technocratic idiom are no more deliberately made public than the discreet advice of a Renaissance counsellor to a prince. Now as then, advice is given behind closed doors; out in the open – in a mass, industrial society – technocratic style and imagery typically pervade the official pronouncement.

The rhetoric of advice thus remains muffled in a cloistered domain. At the same time, the rhetoric of science no longer is able to inform the active kind of public life that developed with the Enlightenment, but is instead pressed into the service of legitimation. In contrast, commentary influences analysis from the outside and appears, at first glance, to be alien, perhaps opposed, to the very idea of policy analysis. In an 'age of organization,' a key theme of commentary portrays technocracy as a source of distortion and confusion that undermines the potential for democratic public life.[20] Inasmuch as it openly speaks only a language of science – or only a language of discreet advice – conventional policy analysis can, at most, marshall only a thin and superficial response to this challenge.[21] The voice of science does project soothing and impressive technocratic imagery, but this very imagery is now often vulnerable to questioning, even ridicule, portrayed as part of a ritual of smoke and mirrors that obscures the exercise of power. With a curious twist, indeed, the concerns of commentary begin to infiltrate policy analysis itself: there is discussion of the potential for a type of policy analysis that could itself challenge technocracy while seriously promoting a more democratic form of public life.[22]

The concerns of commentary, linked to complementary methodological developments, encourage the advent of a post-positivist genre tending to press policy analysis beyond neat professional, disciplinary, or organizational boundaries to promote an arena of policy discourse open not only to experts, but also to a broader public. This is not to argue, of course, that there has been any fundamental realignment of policy discourse in the administrative states of the industrially advanced societies, but that alternative modes of policy discourse have made a significant appearance in the professional literature. The significance of these modes of discourse is somewhat enhanced, moreover, because they tend to resonate sympathetically with the perspectives and concerns of social movements posing challenges and alternatives to prevailing practices. Yet, forsaking familiar and accepted language, post-positivist moves appear to open onto a strange, threatening, and confusing world. This is forbidding territory. Consistent claims to the rationality of policy discourse cannot, however, avoid the risk of venturing into it.

II. Analysis in Wonderland: The Advent of Post-Positivism

Even though policy analysis once seemed secure in its technocratic convictions, some of the intellectual terrain has shifted. This change did not begin in prevailing institutions or the mainstream professional literature, but in the context of methodological dispute. Although the foundations of positivist social science previously seemed invulnerable, they came under sustained criticism in the 1970s and were undermined by a variety of intellectual currents seeking a post-positivist reorientation of inquiry. The stable, self-sufficient world of objectivism was unsettled, along with the supposedly neutral language designed to codify and control it.[23]

Anti-technocratic social movements questioning the administrative state and other features of advanced industrial society at times disrupted objectivist presuppositions by contesting forms of problem definition typical of conventional policy deliberations. This tendency was reinforced in the 1980s as the broad methodological unrest came to enter the professional policy literature in the form of explicit initiatives promoting a post-positivist reorientation of the field.[24] The Berger Inquiry in Canada loomed large in this context and helped to suggest what such a reorientation might practically mean.[25]

The methodological turmoil threw technocratic discourse into question and at least carried the threat of profound dislocation. Certainly, established disciplinary and institutionalized power offered ways to ignore and resist, even perhaps to overwhelm, such a challenge. Yet the advent of significant resistance to technocratic discourse was no mere accident; it was, at least in part, a reflection of technocratic limitations in addressing problems – methodological limitations, that is, rooted in the inadequacies of objectivism in grappling with complexities of meaning.

Since such complexities of meaning cannot – despite technocratic appearances – be avoided even in the texts of extremely narrow, technical forms of policy research, the post-positivist wonderland looms as a necessary adventure for the most reluctant of analysts.[26] Looked at through the wrong end of the telescope, all the features of this wonderland seem to merge into an undifferentiated blur. However, the approaches examined here – hermeneutic, critical, and deconstructive – exhibit important differences in their methodological and practical implications for policy discourse. These differences are more readily recognized than resolved, however, so that the post-positivist genre and its significance for policy discourse are bound to remain matters of contention.

Hermeneutics

Hermeneutic inquiry is concerned with how human beings understand themselves and one another through a shared scheme of categories that renders meaningful a world of interpersonal relationships and social institutions. Through the conventions of a 'life-world' or 'form of life,' language allows for meaningful communication in a shared symbolic world. Human conduct indeed becomes incomprehensible apart from the meaning it has for those engaged in it. The positivist fixation on objective observation thus appears as a delusion; for inquiry cannot proceed unless one becomes 'clued in' to the meanings that sustain this world.[27]

Hermeneutics tries to come to grips with materials that are initially problematic – strange, confusing, incomplete – in order to render them familiar, clear, and whole. A subtle process of understanding and interpretation thus becomes the mode of access to valid evidence, and the ground of inquiry thereby shifts from objective facts to shared meaning. The inquirer comes to share in a meaningful context, proceeding with interpretive skills that develop as interpretation advances.

If positivism took the objective detachment of the analyst as necessary to its method of inquiry, hermeneutics views this detachment as an obstacle to overcome. For interpretation is reflexive, rooted in self-understanding; even as it aims at understanding others and other ways of life, it seeks a kind of knowledge that develops, refines, and reforms the self-awareness of the inquirer. Indeed, the interpretive orientation appears not only as a method of investigation, but also as a way in which the inquirer might share more fully in understanding the human condition, overcoming ruptures in the understanding of self and others.

The identity of the inquirer as a competent participant in the sphere of meaningful human interaction emerges, in any event, not as a peripheral feature of the individual researcher to be replaced by a posture of detached observation, but as an indispensable condition for the very possibility of social research. The identity of the investigator thus becomes a central issue. By acknowledging social and political life as a realm open to interpretation, one makes the very possibility of inquiry dependent upon an inquirer capable of penetrating this realm and understanding it as a participant. The strictly objective observer would have no avenue of access.

Charles Taylor, in particular, has argued that social inquiry is inescapably hermeneutic since it can be pursued only by inquirers who are 'in on' the shared meaning of a social world.[28] Taylor explicates the significance of this point by following Paul Ricoeur's view of social life on the 'model of the text.'[29] Just as in literary interpretation, so in social life generally, one confronts a text (or text analogue) and offers a reading of it. This reading is dependent, however, upon a reading of the context. Meaning is discerned, then, not through rigid attention to text or context, but through an interplay between the two in which a pattern is recognized. How does one validate an interpretation? There appears to be no way out other than an appeal to consistency with other interpretations, and we thus enter the well-known problem of the 'hermeneutic circle.' Interpretation hinges upon other interpretations such that we appear locked within a circle of interpretations without any firm foundation upon which to ground ourselves. For Taylor, however, to seek such a foundation is to be misled by an absurdly high demand for certainty.[30] The implication of his position, as others have formulated it, is that 'insight and judgment are an essential part of any inquiry.'[31]

This general position in the philosophy of the social sciences supports proposals for policy analysis to follow in a post-positivist direction by adopting a hermeneutic orientation.[32] Closely associated with traditional concepts of 'prudence' dating back through the Renaissance to antiquity, hermeneutics has been portrayed as especially significant to the practice of counsel.[33] Policy analysis, it is argued, must 'capture the meaning of action' through sensitive 'contextualizing descriptions' that do not merely enumerate facts or catalogue information. Interpretive explications must 'construct narrative sequences linking conventional meaning, intention, and action'; they must 'make situations come alive once more in the medium of the social scientist's language.'[34]

There is, moreover, a moral posture implicit in a hermeneutic orientation since it abandons a focus on control over objectified processes in favour of participation in a human community. Indeed, as one conceives the policy process 'interpretively,' it has been argued, one can understand that it 'is, accordingly, inherently democratic or communitarian in intent.' 'Likewise, interpretive policy inquiry is inherently normative in its intent to foster human development through improved self-understanding rather than through strategic manipulation.'[35]

From a hermeneutic perspective, no policy analyst – however apparently removed from the human world – can really stand apart. Efforts to do so do not bring 'objectivity,' only an objectivist delusion. Objectivity is gained, if at all, only through the reflexive self-monitoring by inquirers of their own research practice. Objectivism deflects sustained reflection, renders the self opaque, and thus closes off effective interpretation of both oneself and others. Continuing interpretation means maintaining communication, together with the openness it demands.

Critique

Critique acknowledges the hermeneutic interplay between text and context as a central feature of inquiry, but claims that hermeneutics remains too much within its own circle. The alleged consequence is that the hermeneutic orientation, seeking always for the restoration of meaning, is altogether too trusting and fails to inquire into modes of domination which obscure themselves even as they shape the context of inquiry. By introducing a note of suspicion, critique suspends the hermeneutic quest for meaning with a move that objectifies the subject matter, asking after cause rather than simply meaning. Just as, in the case of psychopathology, the analyst questions not only what the patient is saying, but also why, so critique focuses attention on a socio-economic context as a source of delusion. This is a context that, while constituted through meaningful social interaction, typically escapes notice in terms of conventional categories. To draw this context to attention is to alter its significance, to render it potentially subject to change through deliberation and decision.[36]

Being at odds with positivist and technocratic presuppositions, the hermeneutic focus in policy inquiry seems to have a certain critical aura. Yet it is important to note that this actually arises from the rejection of a critical posture. While crucially significant to post-positivism, hermeneutics hearkens back to a mode of inquiry that is pre-positivist, indeed pre-Enlightenment. By deliberately avoiding an objectifying moment in its examination of context, hermeneutics remains within a circle; any critical aura is produced merely by a rejection of Enlightenment-inspired efforts to break out of the circle. This methodological stance translates, in political terms, into a predisposition to accept rather than challenge traditional practices and institutions.[37]

In promoting rationality, critique follows in the spirit of the Enlightenment, but presses this spirit to the point of turning rationality against itself. That is to say, critique points to the limitations of the prevailing form of rationality in advanced industrial society, but does so in the name of a larger reason which an objective context of delusion blocks from realization. Since this larger rationality remains unrealized, critique has faced a perplexing problem in conceptualizing and portraying the rational standard that is to guide its own conduct of inquiry. Jürgen Habermas's effort to address this problem has taken the step of reformulating the concept of rationality in terms of communication,[38] and it is Habermas's conception that has had the most decisive impact on attempts to bring critique to policy discourse.[39]

Grounded upon a appeal to reason, conventional policy discourse and the administrative state are particularly vulnerable to critique in terms of Habermas's communicative rationality. If rationality presupposes communication and if communication presupposes openness, then the monological and cloistered character of technocratic decision making is a recipe for distorted communication and cannot sustain its claim to legitimacy on the basis of rationality. Discourse in a context free from domination becomes the precondition for rationally grounded inquiry and decision.[40]

Critique is thus not only opposed to technocratic discourse, but also tends to be at odds with the practice of counsel in established institutions.[41] Instead, critique is interested in how prevailing discourses and institutions distort communication and thus inhibit a rational form of public life. In this way, critical discussion is oriented to commentary that both exposes how modes of domination constrain communication and anticipates the possibility of a communicative rationality freed from domination. The logic of policy critique does not stop at revealing the delusive character of discourses and institutions, but moves on to affirm alternative approaches to policy deliberation.

Proposals for 'discursive designs' in policy deliberation emerge directly from a critical focus on communication.[42] The point of departure is that the prevailing form of policy reason is constricted by an instrumental orientation that deflects attention from the communicative context. Critique is thus oriented to rationality not merely as analysis or calculation, but as a form of life supported by norms that allow for free inquiry, reflection, and discussion. That is to say, critique indicates that allegiance to rationality ultimately issues in a call for institutional forms marked by an openness that is unachieved in prevailing policy arenas.

The idea that a constricted policy reason might be replaced by a broader kind of policy reason has issued in a specific protocol to guide the consideration of policy initiatives.[43] Questions to be raised address concerns not only about instrumental effectiveness, but also about the appropriateness of proposals to specific settings and to a range of normative criteria. As a challenge to conventional policy discourse, this protocol is designed to focus attention on typically neglected issues. The intent, moreover, is to broaden participation in policy deliberation to include not only technical experts, but segments of the populace that are typically excluded. The thrust of the proposal is to construct a form of policy deliberation that promotes and prizes 'participatory expertise.'[44] Yet, designed to promote a rational form of policy deliberation, this proposal must insist upon orderly procedure and cannot permit inclusion and participation on just any terms. Carried to this point, the logic of policy critique follows the call of a larger reason, but confronts a difficulty that has troubled critical inquiry whenever it has affirmed concrete proposals. What ensures that this new rationality will not institute a new form of domination?[45]

Deconstruction

For deconstruction, the meaning of any text depends upon the construction of a stable reference point, a key to interpretation, that is arbitrary. The very discrimination between text and context, for example, provides the boundary necessary to give the text a coherent, meaningful identity. Accordingly, deconstruction focuses upon the apparent margins of a text to show both how the marginal may be construed as central and how textual boundaries are bound up with other textual patterns: the determinate opposition between text and context is displaced by the interplay of an indeterminate textual network. Thus, in Jacques Derrida's famous formulation, 'there is nothing outside the text.'[46]

The quest for meaning – whether in a hermeneutic or critical form – gives way to a quest for additional meanings, to a proliferation of interpretive possibilities that belies claims to the singular identity and meaning of any text, as well as to the authority of any key to interpretation. Whatever portrays itself as ultimate becomes portrayed as arbitrary, and its privilege is thereby thrown into question.[47]

Deconstruction, while introducing instability into the interpretive enterprise, remains dependent upon meaningful constructions that are never, strictly speaking, refuted: instability arises as the constructions are shown to be partial, insufficient in themselves. A deconstructive move thereby depends upon a reconstructive move, an interpretive moment that (re)constitutes the meaningful orientation of inquiry. While at least implicitly repeated in each deconstructive exercise, such an interpretive moment informs the historical advent of deconstruction as a method and movement disrupting the smooth stream of Western rationalism. Deconstruction throws into question rationality claims, indeed the very propensity to put reason at the centre of things – what Derrida calls 'logocentrism.' Deconstruction thus emerges historically as dependent upon a particular reception of the Western tradition. The point for deconstruction, again, is not to refute this tradition, but to show that – despite its own pretentions – the tradition is partial, necessarily incomplete, unavoidably open to other possibilities.[48]

As a response to a tradition that it constructs as logocentric, however, deconstruction is unavoidably informed by images of a context: while subject to deconstructive moves showing it to be arbitrary, this context nonetheless is typically portrayed as possessing a stubborn power. Indeed, particularly as sketched in the work of Michel Foucault, the context appears as a formation of discursive practices, of 'power/knowledge,' which constructs and maintains social identities. While he stresses that these discursive practices emerged as responses to specific, local problems of social control, Foucault nonetheless portrays an ensemble of administrative practices as constituting the characteristically 'disciplinary' form of modern society, state, and economy.[49]

However secure it may seem, the power/knowledge of disciplinary society has its vulnerabilities. Indeed, the formulation power/knowledge deconstructs the logocentric idealization of knowledge as pure, neutral cognition essentially independent of its object and instead presents knowledge as inescapably implicated in not only the control but also the very construction of its object. Discursive practices dependent upon the notion of a pristine knowledge thus become questionable, and this questioning extends particularly to the rationality claims of the conventional policy literature. The discursive practices characteristic of the policy field can thus be portrayed as stabilizing the privileged and marginalized identities of disciplinary society in the name of a questionable rationality.[50]

The deconstruction of stigmatized identities in social policy provides a particularly apt illustration. The stigmatization of the impoverished through social policy practices is an old story.[51] Current discourse on welfare has, however, been portrayed as a 'readable text' through an explicitly deconstructive treatment. Deconstruction serves to highlight the gendered way in which the discourse constructs and perpetuates stigmatized identities through 'invidious distinctions' such as 'self-sufficiency/dependency, deserving/undeserving, responsible/promiscuous': 'On this reading, welfare policy operates to reproduce two-parent families by stigmatizing and denigrating mother-only families for being the cause of their own problems.' The troubles of poor women with children are thus perpetuated by a discursive practice that helps to 'construct female-headed, single-parent families as a marginal "other" suited for inferior benefits and punitive therapeutic practices.' Attention is thereby deflected not only from important difficulties arising from contemporary economic developments, but also from the questionable privileges intrinsic to the prevailing alignment of social power. The entire focus of the discourse thus conveniently allows for the neglect of an obvious point: 'the problems that beset poor, female-headed families' are rooted significantly in 'poverty itself.'[52]

Deconstruction unsettles the apparently fixed opposition between a privileged centre and neglected margins. The positions and identities of marginalized groups and types of individuals, as constructed by the power/ knowledge of disciplinary society, are thus opened to change. In particular, the prospect emerges that the marginalized may develop discursive practices to define and redefine their identities in relation to prevailing forms of social privilege. Policy discourse incorporating such a deconstructive move tends to promote a repositioning of the policy field and becomes particularly significant to the rhetoric of commentary.[53] However, commentary cannot here be conceived in terms of an essentially universal and homogeneous public sphere, but pertains to discursive practices in particularized spheres.

Through its concern with marginalized identities, deconstruction appears to verge on critique, to involve a recognition of domination and a critical judgment of it. Methodologically, however, deconstruction not only stops short of critique, but actually poses critique as itself something to deconstruct.[54] Deconstruction denies itself the self-centred stability necessary to support any standard of critical judgment. To maintain a standpoint of critique, for example, Habermas relies upon an ideal of genuine communication that provides a model for the institutionalization of discourse in a revitalized public sphere. Such an ideal, the deconstructionist replies, is a mere fiction, a unifying image that obscures and denies the diversity, tension, and indeterminacy of communication; itself a product of a rationalist bias, this image reinforces patterns of social discipline that accord a privileged position to the purveyors of rational technique while, in effect, channelling potential resistance into support for the established order.[55] Against proposals for a larger rationality to guide policy considerations, deconstruction would pose a destabilization of all rationality claims and, indeed, any standard by which to maintain the legitimacy of public deliberations and decisions. By stressing the arbitrary features of any stable point of reference, deconstruction would introduce a question mark into any coherent approach to policy.[56]

Movement in a post-positivist direction certainly presses policy discourse beyond the technocratic domain that prizes the idiom of science: hermeneutics, critique, and deconstruction all tend to disrupt this realm. However, these three forms of post-positivism retain their differences. Hermeneutics is at home in a world of counsel, but contains no principle to restrict itself there: the approach thus unavoidably gestures also to a common public world of commentary. Critique gestures even more insistently to this world as a goal to be achieved; but in denying the legitimacy of the prevailing public world, critique introduces troubling elements of distance and suspicion. Deconstruction intervenes into the public world of commentary, but harbours no illusions of ultimately restoring or achieving a comfortably legitimate realm of common understandings: the accent of deconstruction is on difference and contention. Any attempt to arbitrate among these varieties of post-positivism is beyond the scope of this chapter, but the potential political significance of these methodological disputes is clear enough: the tendency is to broaden the focus of attention in policy discourse in a manner that has particular implications for problem definition.

III. Beyond Technocracy: Canadian Policy Discourse at the Turning Point?

Disillusionment with conventional policy discourse and the advent of alternative initiatives did not simply wait upon the emergence of the post-positivist genre in the professional literature, but informed and helped to shape it. This has particularly been the case in Canada. Here, in retrospect, post-positivist concepts allow us to recognize both disillusionment and new initiatives in policy events that, in pointing beyond technocratic discourse, were – at least in a conceptual sense – of pivotal significance.

The apotheosis of technocracy in Canadian policy discourse was reached in the early Trudeau era, a period of 'technocratic hubris'[57] when earlier proposals to promote governmental efficiency culminated in systematic and intensive efforts to apply techniques drawn from management science, microeconomics, and cybernetics. Despite the prevalence of technocratic imagery and style, policy discourse in the period was marked by ambivalence between developments taking two principal forms – one arising from the formal and informal hierarchies of the administrative apparatus, the other responding to the rise of democratic social movements.

By appealing to reason and neglecting power, technocratic discourse not only projects a neutral image of itself, but simultaneously ignores and obscures its own context. Conceived as a rational system, technocracy is at odds with traditional hierarchies and privileges: for analysis to be unbiased and for relevant information to move appropriately through the channels of the system, all elements must be responsive, must submit themselves to the demands of a larger logic. Consequently, when, in the early Trudeau era, 'responsiveness'[58] emerged as a watchword of government, the technocratic mystique could make analysts believe that a policy system would emerge in accord with their designs. At the same time, the newly responsive system could be democratic. Curiously combined with the technocratic discourse was the imagery of participatory democracy, echoing the dramatic emergence of democratic social movements in the 1960s and early 1970s.

Happy images of reason and democracy could thus coalesce in a vision, particularly favoured by the prime minister, of a cybernetic system, a grand pattern of information flows, in which political leaders, expert officials, and an active citizenry would all have appropriate input.[59] Nonetheless, another meaning of responsiveness proved more significant than what was suggested by either technocratic or democratic images: the new system was to reinforce responsiveness to the traditional top of the administrative apparatus, particularly the cabinet and the prime minister.[60]

Technocratic discourse displays a preference for automation through a fixation on the goal of reducing decisions to programmed decisions.[61] The central image involves precisely specified steps of administrative procedure, conceptualized in terms of the transmission and processing of information through a complex network of multiple feedback loops. The project requires a comprehensively and consistently applied terminology, a common linguistic framework. The technocratic discourse of the time remained fragmented, however, along fairly conventional administrative and disciplinary lines. Finance, for example, guarded its macroeconomic framework and traditional privileges. Cabinet and its immediate sphere exhibited disciplinary eclecticism and retained prerogatives of discretion and judgment. The main effort to develop and promote a comprehensive and consistent framework tended to remain isolated at a subordinate level, particularly in the Planning Branch of the Treasury Board Secretariat, under Deputy Director Douglas Hartle.[62]

In this position during the early 1970s, Hartle was a major advocate of 'technocratic solutions,' as he later came to call and criticize them.[63] One of Hartle's main problems was his inability to get necessary information in the appropriate form, especially policy directives from cabinet that would clearly specify goals and objectives. Vagueness or ambiguity in such matters is both incongruous with technocratic expectations and perplexingly incomprehensible. The attempt to understand the meaning of policy directives thus led a one-time champion of technocracy to disillusionment and an insight into power.

The sleek technocratic veil obscured something unsightly, something even reminiscent of what Hobbes wished to avoid. Hartle described attempts to change 'administrative techniques and processes' as part of 'a continuous battle of the "war of all against all"':

Those who advocate changes in techniques and processes are for the most part, consciously or unconsciously, guns for hire: they seek changes in the existing power structure. They are responding, sometimes without awareness, to the incentive systems that apply to themselves and the groups they serve.[64]

Inhibiting this unwelcome insight, technocratic discourse is guided by linguistic conventions that presuppose the image of an abstract and anonymous decision maker somehow rising above politics: the 'advocates of these new technocratic solutions talk and write as if they were trying to persuade an all-powerful, all-wise, all-loving dictator. Politics, human nature and institutional structures are essentially ignored.'[65] Those who advocate technocratic solutions, Hartle concludes, are 'naïve,'[66] and he does not exclude himself:

My mistake ... was to think that if only the game-playing would stop and serious analysis begin, 'better' policies would emerge. In truth the strategic behaviour embodied in the process was the substance and the analysis only the form of negotiation in many and perhaps most instances.[67]

Admitting that he 'foolishly' failed to 'take into account the fundamental incentive system,' Hartle finds the strategic use of information to be central to the policy process.[68] Especially in program evaluation, adequate analysis demands a knowledge of 'the "real" purposes' of a program, yet this is precisely the kind of knowledge that is regularly denied the analyst: 'More often than not these real purposes are not admitted, at least officially.'[69] In characterizing the overall process, Hartle portrays a system quite at odds with the technocratic ideal, for certain interests have distinctly greater access to informed participation than do others. The system can be characterized as an '*unconscious* conspiracy to suppress information' which, if revealed, could work a 'profound' change in power relationships.[70]

To understand the meaning of his technocratic frustrations, Hartle could not strictly remain within the positivist framework that allowed technocratic expectations to be raised in the first place. While he at least tacitly had to enter into interpretation – into the domain of hermeneutics, indeed of critique – Hartle has not explicitly ventured far from his earlier framework, but has retained the postulate of the rational economic actor and has proposed a contextually enriched game-theoretic model.[71] Commenting on 'the two Douglas Hartles' – the 'proponent of rational planning' and the 'critic of technocratic management'[72] – Richard D. French has argued for even greater 'distance' from conventional 'assumptions and practices' regarding knowledge and power; Hartle's disillusionment, he suggests, points to a post-positivist turn.[73]

Disillusionment with technocracy was played out during the time not only at the level of an occasional practitioner's recognition of analytic limitations or at the level of general methodological questioning. For technocratic discourse did not simply carry with it explicit commitment to a form of analysis, but also implicitly reinforced governance in accord with conventional ideas celebrating universal human progress toward an advanced technological civilization. Technocratic commitment thus introduced a particular bias to policy deliberations in that, as Giandomenico Majone has put it, 'technological expertise' tends to be inadequate to assess its own consequences: 'The initial assumption is that the innovation will achieve what the innovator claims for it and that it will have no negative consequences that could reduce the attractiveness of its practical implementation.'[74] Even if this bias could often go unnoticed in technocratic circles, it was causing alarm in a broader social context where conventional ideas of progress were being sharply criticized by rising social movements – e.g., environmentalist, feminist, aboriginal – that were to exert significant impacts on both the study and conduct of public policy.

In this context, the advent of social and environmental impact assessment signalled both a continuity with technocratic discourse and a dramatic departure from it, for presuppositions of progress were drawn into question. Indeed, when in 1974 Thomas Berger set about to fulfil the federal mandate of the Mackenzie Valley Pipeline Inquiry to assess the impact of a major pipeline proposal for the Canadian North, he displayed the potential of nontechnocratic policy deliberation.[75]

A fundamental difference of opinion emerged during the inquiry, along the lines of what Berger called two conflicting 'philosophies.'[76] Committed to the project of modernizing the North, one position supported the pipeline proposal – and industrial projects in general – primarily by appealing to the prospect of expanded job opportunities. This argument, however, entered upon a political scene in which aboriginal groups had, over a number of previous years, been mounting concerted resistance to government initiatives seeking an assimilation of aboriginal peoples into Canadian society. At the same time, these groups had also been opposed to emerging technocratic features of the administrative state.[77] Supported by scholars who challenged the project of modernization, the main aboriginal groups advanced an alternative oriented to the prospect of socio-economic self-determination. Without entirely excluding industrial initiatives, wage employment, and private business, this position placed an accent upon community development, cooperative enterprise, and the strengthening of the renewable resource sector.

Berger's conclusion in favour of self-determination was supported by a process of inquiry which, by encouraging different modes of discourse, provided a relatively open forum contrasting sharply with technocratic procedures. Research led to debate, with one impact study challenging another. Yet scholarship was but one dimension of the process. Both nationally and regionally, members of the public were deliberately drawn into the debate, encouraged by ready access to information, the availability of funding, and a form of inquiry that created space for both experts and citizens – and allowed all to speak in their own language.[78] This encouragement was met by an extraordinary response, especially from aboriginal people. Indeed, for Berger, their views, as expressed in community hearings, appeared decisive:

No academic treatise or discussion, formal presentation of the claims of native people by the native organizations and their leaders, could offer as compelling and vivid a picture of the goals and aspirations of native people as their own testimony. In no other way could we have discovered the depth of feeling regarding past wrongs and future hopes, and the determination of native people to assert their collective identity today and in the years to come.[79]

While endorsing self-determination, Berger also concluded that the conventional project of modernizing the North was ethnocentric and superficial, particularly with regard to the notion that the expansion of employment opportunities was an unmixed blessing. Supported by native testimony and anthropological research portraying the complex impact of wage employment in the context of aboriginal communities, Berger stressed that the people involved were 'not simply poor people' who happened to need jobs: 'They are people whose values and patterns of social organization are in ways quite different from those that underlie the modern industrial world.'[80] To assess the pipeline proposal adequately, Berger maintained, one must overcome any 'lingering reluctance to take the views of native people seriously when they conflict with our own notions of what is in their best interests.'[81]

The Berger Inquiry provoked considerable controversy, not only over its conclusions but also concerning its analytic adequacy. A key strategy of refutation was to repeat conventional standards of research in positivist and technocratic terms and then to find Berger's report 'inadequate' according to this standard. In these terms, for example, Berger did not adequately weigh benefits and costs in light of 'all relevant information.'[82] Although writing before the explicit emergence of a post-positivist genre in policy research, Berger nonetheless proceeded with a view of inquiry that was quite at odds with that of his conventional critics. Stressing tendencies to overestimate the benefits of 'a large-scale industrial project,' to be misled by 'the comforting illusion that you are dealing with hard data,' and to think 'that all problems can be foreseen and resolved,'[83] he went on to argue that a complex issue cannot be handled through technocratic procedures, but only through 'the exercise of human judgment.'[84] While his critics sought to advance authoritative accounts of the correct form and appropriate role of analysis in public policy deliberations, Berger identified a pervasive bias tending to obscure 'the nature of human affairs.'[85]

With Berger, the conventional policy discourse supporting established power alignments was challenged by another mode of discourse, and the challenge produced a dramatically new problem definition concerning social impact. The social impact research of pipeline proponents followed the usual assumption that the expanded economic activity brought by the project would offer increased employment opportunities to an underdeveloped region, thereby allowing the people of the area to join in the benefits of industrialization. Opponents, however, not only raised questions about the type and duration of employment, or about the impact of the pipeline on the resource base of traditional economic activities, but also about the assumption that employment was necessarily beneficial in the context of aboriginal communities. Wage employment was portrayed not as a solution to the social pathologies of an underdeveloped region, but as an intrusion that disrupted traditional patterns of community production and sharing, thereby constituting a source of those pathologies. With employment thus seen not so much as part of the solution as part of the problem, the conventional definition of the problem was turned upside down. The legitimacy of corporate and state plans for the region was thus significantly weakened because this legitimacy was largely dependent upon the conventional problem definition.

The inquiry proved significant for the aboriginal peoples of the region, not so much for the influence of the inquiry on the pipeline decision as for the experience gained in the course of the inquiry process. Although, as Berger would portray them, aboriginal peoples had long been in acquiescent subordination to powerful forces of Canadian society, these peoples had begun to assert themselves; and the inquiry reinforced this tendency by providing a forum for the development and presentation of a coherent position demanding self-determination. This position, crafted both by aboriginal community participants and by allied academic consultants, countered a conventional ethnocentrism oriented, either implicitly or explicitly, to the eventual assimilation of aboriginal peoples into the mainstream of Canadian society.

The Berger Inquiry has been described as a catalyst to a political transformation in the region that saw important institutional innovations combined with the emergence of the aboriginal peoples as a significant force in shaping patterns of development.[86] While the inquiry has been sharply criticized on conventional grounds – particularly for failing to match the expectations of a sound cost-benefit analysis – the process served to focus attention on the ethnocentric limitations of conventional analytic assumptions. More broadly, not only did the inquiry challenge prevailing positivist and technocratic notions, but it can be seen in retrospect as having implicitly ventured into a post-positivist domain of hermeneutics, critique, and deconstruction.

Questioning the role of wage employment requires hermeneutic insight into the meaning of economic activities in aboriginal communities. Critique is apparent in the images of domination advanced through the inquiry process, and a clear standard of critique appears evident in the demand for self-determination. No sooner is the demand constructed, however, than its meaning becomes a matter of contention. In a deconstructive manner, the identity of aboriginal peoples collectively and autonomously seeking a common goal is destabilized and thrown into question. Calling wage employment the problem rather than the solution ignores the complexities of crafting concrete alternatives; there are, indeed, many potential meanings of self-determination and no unquestionable criteria by which to choose among them.

The insights arising in the 1970s from Hartle's disillusionment and Berger's breakthrough meant that Canadian policy discourse had, at least in conceptual terms, reached a turning point: the promise of a decisive move beyond technocracy, involving a transformation of theory and practice. It is hardly surprising that the turn was not taken in any clear and decisive fashion. The image of the 'kaleidoscope in grey'[87] captures well the idea that, despite interminable rituals of policy review and reorganization, change in the administrative state – in Canada and elsewhere – is caught within generally fixed patterns of discursive practice. Even though the rhetoric of advice is typically practised at decisive moments in the policy process, a positivist and technocratic rhetoric of science remains central, routinely invoked to secure a legitimating aura of rationality. Participatory exercises oriented to a rhetoric of commentary can, as in Berger, partly counter the hold of the positivist and technocratic form by appealing to traditional notions of judgment and by invoking democratic images. Yet to challenge prevailing policy discourse directly on post-positivist methodological grounds is to confront an imposing apparatus of institutionalized language and power.

IV. Power and Insight in Problem Definition

Positivism in policy discourse not only involved a form of methodological commitment, but typically also featured a technocratic commitment to the orderly governance and progress of advanced industrial society. With these twin commitments, the positivist orientation possessed characteristic biases in problem definition that have become increasingly visible. This visibility has come not with post-positivist methodological developments alone, but also with the emergence of movements that have, in different ways, questioned, challenged, or even opposed what they have perceived as the prevailing order of society and pattern of development. Here policy discourse centred in the domain of commentary acts back upon the more restricted contexts of science and counsel.

The dual advent of post-positivism and oppositional social movements has introduced into policy discourse unconventional perspectives that provoke insights into typical practices of problem definition, revealing their biases and promising alternative ways of framing problems. The occasion for such insight is, of course, constrained by institutionalized power, as is evident in a broad social context. Yet a useful perspective on the interplay between power and insight can be gained in the context of administrative organizations where, in both theory and practice, determined efforts are made to find the 'optimal' balance[88] of encouraging insight while discouraging the disruptions that insight might provoke.

Since it cannot be reduced to the calculative ideal of a formal model, the task of problem definition has been troubling to the self-image of the administrative organization. Taking pride in its rationality, such an organization typically encounters a paradox that organization theorists have puzzled over ever since Max Weber's account of rationalization and bureaucratization became a central point of reference – i.e., a paradox of organizational rationality arising from the opposition of requirements for both creativity and disciplined behaviour.[89]

Organization theory has increasingly addressed this difficulty by stressing the importance of creativity. This has particularly been the case with the advent of a post-positivist tendency to focus on the images and metaphors of organizational life.[90] Explicit attention to organizational discourse – probing its 'deep images' and 'assumptions' – has thus been suggested as a key to handling organizational problems, particularly to the task of crafting 'imaginative' and 'creative' strategies.[91] Similarly, there has been a call for a 'technology of foolishness':[92] 'the operation of normal rationality' in organizations so threatens the emergence of novel ideas that new notions require 'mechanisms' not only to 'shield them,' but also to protect the foolishness and playfulness required to develop them.[93]

Yet by encouraging playfulness and novelty, activities not clearly consistent with an established order, the technology of foolishness poses the risk of breaking explicit and implicit rules, of violating boundaries, of transgressing the normal patterns and well-worn pathways of organizational discourse. Consequently, to remain consistent with established organizational power, the technology of foolishness needs to encourage a 'serious' and 'appropriate' playfulness.[94] The promise of foolishness as a source of insight into organizational problems is implicitly withdrawn as soon as the foolishness threatens to render visible – and hence disturb – organizational power.

The dynamic of power and insight is replicated more broadly on the larger social stage. Here, however, power contests tend to be more overt, and the potential for mobilizing resistance thereby tends to be enhanced. Policy discourse is thus kept within conventional boundaries only with difficulty, and the potential for disruption is ever-present. Yet the broader social context is not left untouched by the world of administrative organizations. Indeed, when he assessed the significance of the bureaucratic form for modern society, Weber was unequivocal: 'The whole pattern of everyday life,' he said, 'is cut to fit this framework.'[95] For Weber, bureaucratization was part of the advent of a rationalized 'cosmos' which left nothing untouched and against which resistance would be futile.[96] Today the limits of this cosmos are partly registered in the significant social movements that have arisen to challenge it. Limits, however, are also evident in dysfunctions of this rationalized cosmos, and the effort to promote a responsible foolishness can be counted as one recognition, among many, of a problem.

What is the problem? With its technocratic fixation, conventional policy discourse is unable to say: for, to exaggerate only slightly, the problem is this very fixation. The advent of post-positivism in policy discourse may, in contrast, be viewed as part of a wider intellectual tendency which, by explicitly identifying a problem in the epistemological focus and institutional development of advanced industrial society, creates openings for the consideration of alternatives that would otherwise be neglected. In a policy context, the post-positivist concern with meaning reinforces patterns of problem definition that draw upon unconventional insights. Indeed, in relation to recent social movements, post-positivist policy discourse engages with entire forms of oppositional knowledge – e.g., environmentalism and feminism – which are being developed from such insights.[97]

V. Conclusion

The post-positivist genre intersects with developing social movements in a manner that disrupts prevailing patterns of policy discourse and anticipates realignments of power.[98] Neither homogeneous nor univocal, post-positivism promises no clearcut pattern of development, but continuingly contentious relations among its hermeneutic, critical, and deconstructive elements. Nonetheless, by being at odds with technocratic discourse while generally resonating sympathetically with oppositional social movements, post-positivism does reinforce the possibility of previously unimaginable forms of policy discourse. The prospect of moving beyond a technocratic orientation did not, of course, await the advent of post-positivism, but anticipated and influenced it.

Against the backdrop of the kaleidoscope in grey, the dynamic of power and insight – and its unpredictability – is evident in the promotion of discursive designs for policy deliberations.[99] Before the Berger Inquiry was even completed, for example, it was described as an anomalous and transitory exercise: nothing like it would ever again be permitted by the powers that be. Nonetheless, the Berger Inquiry has exerted an impact that remains evident some two decades later in the context of anti-technocratic efforts. In the wake of Berger, there were various initiatives to modify the technocratic focus of policy discourse, particularly by locating discourse both in broad public inquiries and in similar forums on a more modest scale.[100] Such initiatives continue today – e.g., with the advent of round tables on sustainable development – and the Berger Inquiry still looms large: it furnishes an exemplary model for citizens who challenge experts in public hearings, and it still influences the design and operations of large-scale public inquiries such as the Royal Commission on Aboriginal Peoples.[101] With the once unchallenged supremacy of technocratic discourse thrown into doubt – as in the case of Hartle's disillusionment – there was scope for the Berger Inquiry to exert a continuing influence on the shape of Canadian policy discourse.

Even in the central arenas of the administrative state, the limits of technocratic discourse are often apparent, particularly in the tension between the rhetoric of science and the rhetoric of counsel. Yet, while the counsellor may adopt the role of jester and employ a technology of foolishness,[102] the weight of institutional power in cloistered settings is such that it typically constrains insight within narrow patterns of discourse, even if these constraints prove inimical to the very interests of the institution in question.[103] Here insight appears starkly contradictory, both necessary and impossible – or, at least, as containing an ambivalent potential of both promise and threat.

The insights arising from the post-positivist policy genre and oppositional social movements would seem, then, not to be entirely incompatible with the prevailing order of advanced industrial society. These insights, typically first circulating in the rhetorical context of commentary, may also enter the contexts of science and counsel in ways that significantly mark both problem definition and policy development. But the insights are, again, typically ambivalent, apparently needed by that order while often antagonistic to it. Insight promises flexibility, innovation, and adaptability. But insight is also unpredictable, hence possibly uncontrollable – potentially threatening to prevailing power formations and the types of policy discourse that have served to sustain them.

Notes

I would like to thank Laurent Dobuzinskis, John Dryzek, Frank Fischer, Mary Hawkesworth, Jeanette Hofman, Les Pal, Sandy Schram, and Dvora Yanow for helpful comments and encouragement. I am especially grateful to an anonymous reviewer for an excellent suggestion on organizing the material. An earlier version of this essay was presented at the Annual Meetings of the American Political Science Association, New York, 2 September 1994.

1 See, e.g., Fischer, *Politics, Values, and Public Policy: The Problem of Methodology*; Dryzek 'Policy Analysis as a Hermeneutic Activity'; Paris and Reynolds, *The Logic of Policy Inquiry*; Jennings 'Interpretation and the Practice of Policy Analysis'; Ascher, 'Policy Sciences and the Economic Approach in a "Post-Positivist" Era'; Hawkesworth, *Theoretical Issues in Policy Analysis*; Stone, *Policy Paradox and Political Reason*. The term 'post-positivist' may have its problems, but it should be regarded not only in relation to the cautious methodological strictures of twentieth-century neopositivism, but also in relation to the confident linking of expertise and industrialism in the earlier positivism of the nineteenth century (on this distinction, see Torgerson, 'Between Knowledge and Politics'). The advent of the post-positivist policy genre can perhaps be gauged by a difference in emphasis of two review articles appearing five years apart: the first, Amy's 'Toward a Post Positivist Policy Analysis' (1984) tentatively suggests a movement in the direction of post-positivism while the second, Fischer's 'Beyond the Rationality Project' (1989), speaks more confidently of a 'post-positivist challenge' to prevailing conventions. Moreover, when the first edition of Pal's introductory text, *Public Policy Analysis*, appeared in 1987, it reflected only some early post-positivist developments, but the second edition in 1992 notes the clear emergence of 'a strong current' of post-positivism, at xi. Tribe's studies 'Policy Science' and 'Technology Assessment and the Fourth Discontinuity' (appearing in the early 1970s) criticized the prevailing positivism of policy discourse as it had emerged in the postwar era, yet already noted counter-tendencies within the field. Such counter-tendencies point not only to exigencies of practice that could not be contained by a positivist framework (see Torgerson, 'Reuniting Theory and Practice') but also to a still significant, though declining, influence of pragmatism in the social sciences. That post-positivism could find a certain resonance in the policy literature (see, e.g., Forester's 'The Policy Analysis-Critical Theory Affairs') is largely due to this influence. Of particular significance, moreover, was the work of Harold D. Lasswell, who not only advanced his conception of the 'policy sciences' as a deliberate adaptation of Deweyan pragmatism, but also anticipated key features of post-positivism by drawing extensively on figures such as Freud and Marx (see Torgerson, 'Contextual Orientation in Policy Analysis'). For further discussion, see Torgerson, 'Priest and Jester in

the Policy Sciences,' and 'Policy Analysis and Public Life: The Restoration of *Phronesis*?'

2 This characterization of types of post-positivism is no doubt contestable. The point is to focus attention on methodological differences within post-positivism. In particular, 'deconstruction' is used as a methodological point of reference in preference to the more diffuse anti-foundationalist sensibility often suggested by the term 'post-modernism' (cf. Schram, 'Postmodern Policy Analysis: Discourse and Identity in Welfare Policy'; Rosenau, 'Anticipating a Post-Modern Policy Current?'; Dryzek and Torgerson, 'Democracy and the Policy Sciences'; White, *Political Theory and Postmodernism*). While the post-positivist policy literature does not, of course, always follow the sharp distinctions developed in this essay, these distinctions do delineate salient contours of the discourse and indicate the agenda for an important discussion.

3 Dery, *Problem Definition in Policy Analysis*, xi, 4.

4 This point is developed along somewhat different lines in Torgerson, 'Oppositional Knowledge: Policy Sciences and Transformative Politics.' Cf. Carroll, ed., *Organizing Dissent*.

5 See Tribe, 'Policy Science'; Fischer, *Technocracy and the Politics of Expertise*; Winner, 'Cybernetics and Political Language.' Also see Nelson, Megill, and McCloskey, 'Rhetoric of Inquiry.'

6 Despite family resemblances among genres, Habermas wishes to maintain distinctions according to the predominance of different linguistic functions (see his *The Philosophical Discourse of Modernity*, 183–210). Doing so would appear crucial to his version of critical theory.

7 This typology draws loosely on Throgmorton, 'Rhetorics of Policy Analysis.' The category of 'commentary' is influenced by Wolin's 'Political Theory and Political Commentary.'

8 On the centrality of rhetoric in the Renaissance, see Kristeller, *Renaissance Thought*, ch. 1.

9 More to Erasmus, quoted in Chambers, *Thomas More*, 145.

10 Chambers, *Thomas More*, 150–1, 163–4; cf. 113. Cf. Machiavelli's discussion of counsel in *The Prince*, chs. 22–3; on discretion, in particular, see the comments of his Florentine contemporary, Francesco Guicciardini, *Maxims and Reflections (Ricordi)*, Series C, esp. 2, 7, 186. For a relevant discussion of Machiavelli, see Torgerson, 'Interpretive Policy Inquiry.'

11 More, *Utopia*, 48–50. Despite his reluctance to become involved, More here also suggests a sense of duty: 'If you cannot pluck up wrongheaded opinions by the root, if you cannot cure according to your heart's desire vices of long standing, yet you must not on that account desert the commonwealth.'

12 Hobbes, *De Corpore*, 2.

13 Hobbes, *De Corpore Politico*, 209–12.

14 Jacobson, *Pride and Solace: The Scope and Function of Political Theory*, 63. Also see Farr, 'Political Science and the Enlightenment of Enthusiasm'; Hirschman, *The Passions and the Interests*. Francis Bacon (e.g., 'Of Counsel') both continues the Renaissance tradition of counsel and anticipates modernity (see Faulkner, 'Visions and Powers: Bacon's Two-fold Politics of Progress'). Hobbes's relationship with Bacon would appear significant in this regard (see Peters, *Hobbes*, 17–18).

15 Hobbes, *Leviathan*, 114–15.

16 See Ryan, *Marxism and Deconstruction*, 2–5.

17 This account largely follows Habermas's *The Structural Transformation of the Public Sphere*; cf. Calhoun, ed., *Habermas and the Public Sphere*.

18 Harold D. Lasswell, the chief proponent of a policy orientation in the social sciences, began his career as a student of propaganda. Already in the mid-1920s, as he was working on propaganda, Lasswell had conceptualized a project wherein the social sciences would serve as a prime source of intellectual leadership for modern society. In this, he was influenced by progressivism, particularly as advanced by his mentor, Charles E. Merriam. For details, see Torgerson, 'Origins of the Policy Orientation,' and 'Policy Analysis and Public Life.'

19 Cf. Bari, 'L'expert comme conseiller du prince.'

20 Wolin, *Politics and Vision*, ch. 10; also see Habermas, *Toward a Rational Society*.

21 See, e.g., McAdams, 'The Anti-Policy Analysts.'

22 See, e.g., Forester, 'The Policy Analysis-Critical Theory Affair'; Torgerson, 'Between Knowledge and Politics'; Dryzek, 'Policy Sciences of Democracy'; Fischer, *Technocracy and the Politics of Expertise*.

23 See, e.g., Bernstein, *The Restructuring of Social and Political Theory*.

24 See n. 1 above.

25 See the discussion of Berger in section III below. Also see, for example, Dryzek, 'Policy Analysis as a Hermeneutic Activity'; Torgerson, 'Between Knowledge and Politics.'

26 The allusion to Lewis Carroll is indebted to Archibald's 'The Pitfalls of Language, or Analysis through the Looking Glass,' an apt linguistic analysis showing how supposedly technical inquiries enter, even if unaware, into a hermeneutic wonderland.

27 For a survey of hermeneutics, see Palmer, *Hermeneutics*; the leading theoretical exposition is Gadamer's *Truth and Method*. The term 'life-world' was drawn by Schutz (e.g., *The Phenomenology of the Social World*) from the late

phenomenology of Husserl and developed in the context of social inquiry (also see Berger and Luckmann's *The Social Construction of Reality*); in his *The Idea of a Social Science*, Winch did something similar for the idea of 'form of life,' drawn from Wittgenstein's late linguistic analysis. Whether such different schools of interpretation are appropriately discussed under the heading of hermeneutics is a reasonable question. Habermas's *On the Logic of the Social Sciences* suggests points of convergence as well as differences among them; also see Bernstein's *Restructuring*. Gadamer's 'On the Scope and Function of Hermeneutical Reflection,' of course, makes an even more sweeping claim for the scope of hermeneutics.

28 Taylor, 'Interpretation and the Sciences of Man,' 13.
29 Ricoeur, 'The Model of the Text.'
30 Cf. Hirsch, *Validity in Interpretation*.
31 Rabinow and Sullivan, 'The Interpretive Turn,' 7.
32 Understandably, given this sharp break with a technocratic posture, a recurring feature in discussions of interpretive policy analysis is a tendency to view interpretation as the foundation for a particular 'genre' or 'model' of inquiry (e.g., Jennings, 'Interpretive Social Science and Policy Analysis'; Dryzek, 'Policy Analysis as a Hermeneutic Activity'). While the present discussion largely reinforces this tendency, it is important to recognize the hermeneutic premise that is thereby obscured: *viz.*, that interpretation is no side-show but an inescapable dimension of all inquiry into human social life. This is due to the reflexive character of human conduct and institutions: human beings, individually and collectively, are persistently self-interpretive; they seek to make sense of themselves and their world, and such effort becomes incorporated into the life-world categories and conventions which sustain a form of life – i.e., into common sense (see Taylor, 'Interpretation'). This point provides for the recognition that positivist modes of analysis have ignored rather than escaped interpretation. To take a prominent example, the model of the rational economic individual, which looms large in much of the policy literature, generally involves the notion of a set of fixed and coherent preferences responding, according to complete information, to the impersonal conditions of market exchange. The individual is regarded as a calculator of costs and benefits according to a given set of preferences and options. Although inadequate to the diversity of human experience, this concept is not just some arbitrary notion. Developed in a culture of 'possessive individualism' (see Macpherson, *The Political Theory of Possessive Individualism*), the concept portrays a highly anonymous and abstract type of activity and may thus be viewed as an implicit interpretation and analytic accentuation of tendencies toward anonymous and abstract action types (see Schutz, *The*

Phenomenology of the Social World) already present in social life, particularly in the domain of market activities. The real question is not whether the task of interpretation is to be undertaken, but how deliberately and how well it is to be done.

33   See Jennings, 'Interpretation and the Practice of Policy Analysis'; Bari, 'L'expert comme conseiller du prince.' Cf. Torgerson, 'Policy Analysis and Public Life.'

34   Jennings, 'Interpretive Social Science and Policy Analysis,' 21. On narrative see, e.g., Kaplan, 'Reading Policy Narratives.'

35   Healy, 'Interpretive Policy Inquiry,' 387; cf. Torgerson, 'Interpretive Policy Inquiry.'

36   See Habermas, *On the Logic of the Social Sciences*; Radnitzky, *Contemporary Schools of Metascience*, vol. 2. On Habermas, see McCarthy, *The Critical Theory of Jürgen Habermas*. On critical theory generally, see Held, *Introduction to Critical Theory: Horkheimer to Habermas*. On suspicion in interpretation, see Ricoeur, 'Psychoanalysis and the Movement of Contemporary Culture.' In this context, it is thus possible to speak of a critical hermeneutics in which a distancing from the subject matter through deliberate objectification and suspicion is an indispensable moment of inquiry.

37   For further discussion, see Torgerson, 'Interpretive Policy Inquiry,' and 'Priest and Jester in the Policy Sciences.' Also see Ricoeur, 'Ethics and Culture: Habermas and Gadamer in Dialogue,' and Gadamer's discussion of Habermas in 'On the Scope and Function of Hermeneutical Reflection.'

38   Habermas, *The Theory of Communicative Action*, 2 vols., and 'Toward a Theory of Communicative Competence.' Also see Benhabib, *Critique, Norm, and Utopia*.

39   This influence, already explicit in Tribe's early contribution, 'Technology Assessment and the Fourth Discontinuity,' is evident later in, for example, Fischer, *Politics, Values and Public Policy*, and 'Critical Evaluation of Public Policy'; Forester, 'The Policy Analysis-Critical Theory Affair'; Dryzek, 'Policy Analysis as a Hermeneutic Activity,' and 'Discursive Designs'; and Torgerson, 'Interpretive Policy Inquiry.'

40   See Forester, 'The Policy Analysis-Critical Theory Affair'; Torgerson, 'Interpretive Policy Inquiry.'

41   See Fischer, *Technocracy and the Politics of Expertise*, and 'Participatory Expertise.'

42   See Dryzek 'Discursive Designs,' and 'Designs for Environmental Discourse.' Berger's innovations (see section III below) provided a key illustration for Dryzek and others.

43 See Fischer, *Politics, Values, and Public Policy*, 'Critical Evaluation of Public Policy,' *Technocracy and the Politics of Expertise.*

44 See Fischer, *Technocracy and the Politics of Expertise*, and 'Participatory Expertise.'

45 See the exchange between Torgerson, 'Reuniting Theory and Practice,' and Fischer, 'Reconstructing Policy Analysis.' Also see Torgerson, 'Policy Analysis and Public Life.'

46 Derrida, *Of Grammatology*, 158. Also see Leitch, *Deconstructive Criticism*, ch. 6.

47 See Leitch, *Deconstructive Criticism*, ch. 5.

48 Cf. Lyotard, *The Postmodern Condition.*

49 See Foucault, *Power/Knowledge*, and *Discipline and Punish.* Also see Dreyfus and Rabinow, *Michel Foucault: Beyond Structuralism and Hermeneutics*, 153–67; Leitch, *Deconstructive Criticism*, 143–59.

50 See Pal, 'Knowledge, Power, and Policy.'

51 See Pinker, *Social Theory and Social Policy*, ch. 2.

52 Schram, 'Postmodern Policy Analysis,' 257, 261.

53 See Schram, 'Postmodern Policy Analysis'; Schneider and Ingram, 'Social Construction of Target Populations'; Throgmorton, 'Rhetorics of Policy Analysis'; Dobuzinskis, 'Modernist and Postmodernist Metaphors of the Policy Process'; Rosenau, 'Anticipating a Post-Modern Policy Current?'

54 Derrida maintains that 'deconstruction is not a critical operation, the critical is its object; deconstruction always bears, at one moment or another, on the confidence given the critical, critico-theoretical, that is to say, deciding authority.' Quoted in Leitch, *Deconstructive Criticism*, 261.

55 See, e.g., Lyotard, *The Postmodern Condition*; Rorty, 'Habermas and Lyotard on Postmodernity'; Nagele 'Freud, Habermas and the Dialectic of Enlightenment.'

56 See McCarthy, 'The Politics of the Ineffable'; Fraser, 'The French Derridians'; Dryzek and Torgerson, 'Democracy and the Policy Sciences'; White, *Political Theory and Postmodernism.* Derrida's apparent equation of deconstruction and justice ('Deconstruction,' he states, 'is justice'), 'Force of Law,' 15, is in this regard neither entirely clear nor unequivocal, but does open the possibility for another interpretation.

57 See French, *How Ottawa Decides*, 20; also see Dobuzinskis, 'Rational Policy-Making'; Szablowski, 'The Optimal Policy-Making System.'

58 Langford, *Transport in Transition*, 7ff.

59 See Doern, 'The Policy-Making Philosophy of Prime Minister Trudeau and His Advisers.'

60 See Langford, *Transport in Transition*, 214–15.
61 See Lasswell, 'Current Studies of the Decision Process'; cf. Simon, *The New Science of Management Decision*, esp. 31.
62 French, *How Ottawa Decides*, ch. 2.
63 Hartle, *The Expenditure Budget Process in the Government of Canada*, 95; cf. Hartle, 'Operational Performance Measurement in the Government of Canada,' and 'A Proposed System of Program and Policy Evaluation.'
64 Hartle, 'Techniques and Processes of Administration,' 24.
65 Hartle, *The Expenditure Budget Process in the Government of Canada*, 95.
66 Ibid., 57.
67 Hartle, 'An Open Letter to Richard Van Loon (with a Copy to Richard French),' 97.
68 Hartle, Comment, 20.
69 Hartle, 'An Open Letter,' 91.
70 Hartle, *The Expenditure Budget Process in the Government of Canada*, 112 (emphasis in original).
71 See Hartle, *A Theory of the Expenditure Budget Process*, and *The Expenditure Budget Process in the Government of Canada*.
72 French, *How Ottawa Decides*, 34.
73 See French, 'Did Ottawa Plan? Reflections on My Critics,' 104; also see French, *How Ottawa Decides*, 20, 157.
74 Majone, *Evidence, Argument, and Persuasion in the Policy Process*, 5–6.
75 This account of the Berger Inquiry draws upon Torgerson, *Industrialization and Assessment*, and 'Between Knowledge and Politics.'
76 Berger, *Northern Frontier, Northern Homeland: The Report of the Mackenzie Valley Pipeline Inquiry*, vol. 2, 3–6; cf. vol. 1, 148ff.
77 See Doerr, 'Indian Policy,' and Doern, 'The Budgetary Process and the Policy Role of the Federal Bureaucracy,' 105.
78 See Gambel, 'The Berger Inquiry.'
79 Berger, *Northern Frontier, Northern Homeland*, vol. 2, 228.
80 Ibid., vol. 1, 148.
81 Ibid., vol. 2, 228.
82 Stabler, 'The Report of the Mackenzie Valley Pipeline Inquiry, Volume 1: A Socio-Economic Critique,' 57–8.
83 Berger, *Northern Frontier, Northern Homeland*, vol. 1, 143, 160–1.
84 Ibid., vol. 2, 229.
85 Ibid., vol. 1, 161.
86 Abele, 'The Berger Inquiry and the Politics of Transformation in the Mackenzie Valley,' 79, ch. 6, and 'Canadian Contradictions.'
87 Van Loon, 'Kaleidoscope in Grey.'

88 March, 'Footnotes to Organizational Change,' 181.
89 See, e.g., March, 'The Technology of Foolishness.' This point is developed in
    Torgerson, 'The Paradox of Organizational Rationality: Uncertainty Absorp-
    tion and the Technology of Foolishness.'
90 See, e.g., Morgan, 'More on Metaphor,' and *Images of Organization.*
91 Smircich and Stubbart, 'Strategic Management in an Enacted World,' 730–1.
92 March, 'The Technology of Foolishness.'
93 Ibid., 179.
94 Ibid., 181.
95 Weber, *Economy and Society*, vol. 1, 223.
96 Weber, *The Protestant Ethic and the Spirit of Capitalism*, 181, and 'Science
    as a Vocation,' 139.
97 See Ackelsberg, 'Feminist Analyses of Public Policy'; Hawkesworth, 'Policy
    Studies within a Feminist Frame'; Torgerson, 'Limits of the Administrative
    Mind: The Problem of Defining Environmental Problems,' 'Oppositional
    Knowledge,' 'The Uncertain Quest for Sustainability: Public Discourse and
    the Politics of Environmentalism'; Paehlke and Torgerson, 'Toxic Waste as
    Public Business.' Problem definition may thus be considered in relation to the
    more explicitly contentious context of agenda setting. See Pal, *Public Policy
    Analysis*, 2nd ed., ch. 6; also see Kingdon, *Agendas, Alternatives, and Public
    Policy*; Cobb and Elder, 'The Politics of Agenda Building.'
98 Pal, *Public Policy Analysis*, 2nd ed., 234, argues that 'modern democracies
    are increasingly irritated by closed policy processes, and levels of contested
    debate seem to be rising, not diminishing. The prospects for vigorous, non-
    technocratic, if often difficult and vexatious, democracy have never seemed
    better.'
99 See Dryzek, 'Discursive Designs,' 'Designs for Environmental Discourse.'
100 The early assessment of Berger was provided by Dosman, *The National
    Interest: The Politics of Northern Development, 1968–77*, 217. On subsequent
    public inquiries, see Salter and Salco, *Public Inquiries in Canada*; Torgerson,
    Industrialization and Assessment, ch. 7. More generally, see Kathlene and
    Martin, 'Enchancing Citizen Participation: Panel Designs, Perspectives and
    Policy Formation.'
101 On round tables, see Bruton and Howlett, 'Differences of Opinion.' For
    references to Berger in the context of a remarkable case study of a recent
    public hearing, see Richardson et al., *Winning Back the Words: Confronting
    Experts in an Environmental Public Hearing*, 41–2. A focus of attention in
    the Royal Commission on Aboriginal Peoples is the promotion of 'aboriginal
    voice,' a concern reflected, for example, in the commission's 'Ethical
    Guidelines for Research.' George Erasmus, a co-chair of the commission, is

from the Northwest Territories and played a significant role as an aboriginal leader (Chief, Assembly of First Nations) during the course of the Berger Inquiry. See Erasmus and Dussault, 'Opening Statement by the Co-Chairs,' for a discussion which, without mentioning Berger, is clearly marked by the influence of his inquiry. I am indebted to Les Pal and Frances Abele (Deputy Director, The North) for background information on the commission.

102 See Torgerson, 'Priest and Jester in the Policy Sciences.'

103 The literature on participation in policy analysis may, in this regard, be read as often offering testimony to missed opportunities. See, e.g., Aronson, 'Giving Consumers a Say in Policy Development: Influencing Policy or Just Being Heard?'; Fischer, 'Citizen Participation and the Democratization of Policy Expertise: From Theoretical Inquiry to Practical Cases'; Durning, 'Participatory Analysis in a Social Service Agency'; Richardson et al., Winning Back the Words. Identifying the interests of an institution is, of course, a complex matter of interpretation and contention.

15

Comparative Policy Studies in Canada: What State? What Art?

COLIN BENNETT

The modern tradition of comparative public policy studies originated in the early 1970s. It was mainly promoted by the community of Europeanists working within (or trained in) American political science departments. In one of the pioneering works in the field, Arnold Heidenheimer and his colleagues define comparative policy analysis as the 'the study of how, why and to what effect different governments pursue particular courses of action or inaction.'[1] The subfield thus embraces descriptive, explanatory and evaluative questions.

The rise of comparative policy analysis within American political science can be understood in the light of wider trends and problems in the discipline as a whole. The 1960s had seen a dichotomy between the building of abstract general theories (such as systems theory) and, by contrast, the analysis of the impact of psychological, sociological, and economic variables on political choice. By the late 1960s, the subfield of comparative politics had reached a crisis point, split between the study of 'macropolitics' and 'microphenomena.'[2] In its attempt to move away from the more static and ethnocentric study of institutions, 'the political baby had been thrown out with the institutional bathwater.'[3]

Coinciding with this tension within comparative politics, American political science was undergoing a search for 'relevance,' inspired in part by David Easton's 1969 presidential address to the American Political Science Association.[4] The behavioural revolution had pushed the discipline above the everyday world of politics and the urgent public issues of the day. Easton identified a 'pervasive intellectual tendency' to rethink the nature of the discipline and make it relevant to 'specific social issues.' The rise in public policy analysis (and its comparative offshoot) was a product of this rethinking, and of a renewed faith in the ability of political scientists to make a contribution to the resolution of social problems. Comparative policy analysis thus arose in the early 1970s from the policy analyst's quest for relevance and from the comparativist's search for middle-range theory about the processes and structures of government.

The potential rewards from comparative policy analysis are descriptive, theoretical, and evaluative. First, and most simply, the addition of a policy dimension to behavioural and institutional analysis provides a more complete and balanced description of the performance of different political systems.[5] Explicit comparison of policy also helps avoid culture-bound generalizations. The policy studies literature has been predominantly American in origin and focus. The conceptual and theoretical developments have been derived chiefly from case studies of American social programs, at state and federal levels. Comparative analysis can provide a basic corrective to the American dominance of policy studies specifically, and political science generally.

Second, comparative policy analysis should be able to tell us a great deal about the dynamics of different political systems. The underlying assumption is that by comparing policy *output* in different national settings, we might better understand the range of social, economic, cultural, and institutional variables that account for any variation. The policy is the starting-point. By asking the 'why here, not there' or the 'why like that here, and like that there' questions, we may gain theoretical insights about the wider capabilities and features of different political systems.[6]

This potential is especially notable when *new* policy problems hit the agendas of different states at the same time. These provide a kind of naturally occurring experiment, subjecting different polities to a common and simultaneous challenge. Thus transnational forces that might (according to a deterministic logic) promote a convergence of policy responses, confront a distinctive set of national attitudes and institutions that may cause interesting divergences. In particular, the comparison of policy responses to new technologies provides a potentially valuable way of assessing how different states have responded to the same challenge.

Third, and from a more evaluative standpoint, comparison can potentially make a significant contribution to the solution of major policy problems. Ad hoc comparisons are continually made in political rhetoric, in everyday conversation, and in journalism. There is an understandable tendency to invoke evidence from abroad to support political arguments. The political scientist can offer a more systematic analysis of such questions. An understanding of the different circumstances under which public policy has emerged and been implemented allows a careful analysis of policy options and of the conditions under which they might be transplanted from one political system to another.[7]

The comparative policy analyst can thus engage in a form of quasi-experimental research. In this interpretation, the function of comparative policy analysis is 'to extend the process of policy search, policy formulation, and evaluation across jurisdictional frontiers of a single policy, and thus to enrich the problem-solving capabilities of any society.'[8] Different societies arguably have distinct 'policy equipment' or a repertoire of 'policy tools.'[9] The concomitant effort is to attempt to understand why instruments appear in the repertoire of some systems and not others. And once the relevant inhibitions to the diffusion of specific policy techniques are established, it is possible to state the conditions necessary for the transfer of a particular tool to a given polity. The normative implications are, therefore, unavoidable: 'Comparative policy analysis is condemned to be part of the argument over desirable policy.'[10]

The comparative analysis of public policy seemingly holds potential for richer case studies, for wider theoretical knowledge about the determinants of public policy, as well as for practical application. Many scholars have realized these values with the result that a substantial, and growing, body of comparative literature now supplements research in most policy sectors – economic, environmental, educational, social, and so on.

This article attempts to assess the extent to which the analysis of *Canadian* public policy has been influenced by these wider traditions. Comparative policy research is, however, sharply dichotomized in terms of methodological approach and preference. The first is the comparative case study of a limited number of countries. The contrasting approach applies statistical techniques to a larger cross-section of countries to seek correlations between a range of institutional, socio-economic, and cultural variables and some aspect of public policy.

I will demonstrate that, while there are a sprinkling of works that integrate the Canadian case into both case study and cross-sectional research, the comparative policy tradition has never been seriously embraced by Canadian policy analysts. Moreover, overseas scholars have also been reluctant to come to Canada, study public policy here, and take the lessons learned back to their respective jurisdictions. There are some theoretical, conceptual, and disciplinary reasons for this failure. I will conclude, however, by arguing that there is a great potential for comparative policy analysis in several areas of Canadian public policy.

I. Comparative Case Analysis of Canadian Public Policy

The first, and most common, strategy for comparative policy research remains the comparative case study of a limited number of countries. The emphasis is upon the reasons for, and consequences of, policy actions in context. Under this methodology, public policy is conceived as an inherently complex, multidimensional, and dynamic phenomenon that cannot adequately be operationalized by surrogate indicators pulled from context in order to search for statistical measures of association. The case study approach is based on the examination of more complex interactions between clusters of causal relationships rather than the singular causal links common to behavioural analysis. The proponents argue that the rich, contextual case study provides a more satisfying understanding of the causes, operation, and impact of public policy.

Case studies should not just attempt to explain the idiosyncratic features of one case or scientific observation. As Sidney Verba noted: 'The unique historical event ... must be considered as one of a class of such events even if it happened only once.'[11] This advice is particularly salient for the policy analyst. Idiosyncratic policy studies are often 'who did what' accounts, and are based on the 'implicit premise, or hope that once a certain critical mass of descriptive studies had been reached theory would almost automatically break through.'[12] On the contrary, the case study in the strict sense of the term should be a 'scientific observation ... intended to monitor or explicate some larger phenomenon and thus is to be planned under the impetus of theory rather than the excrescent accumulation of whatever data happen to turn up.'[13]

With a determination to compare cases within a theoretical framework derived from existing literature and using the same analytical constructs, we can potentially: (1) more easily identify the universe from which the cases are drawn; (2) select comparable cases and thus maintain a low variance in the control variables in relation to that of the operative variables; and (3) test hypotheses openly drawn from prior knowledge about likely patterns and trends. Accordingly, Lijphart defined the 'comparable cases strategy' as:

the method of testing hypothesized empirical relationships among variables on the basis of the same logic that guides the statistical method, but in which the cases are selected in such a way as to maximize the variance of the independent variables and to minimize the variance of the control variables.[14]

A cursory analysis of the major Canadian political science, public policy, and public administration journals reveals a paucity of comparative case analysis of Canadian public policy in this genre. Most article-length pieces in Canadian journals in which some aspect of Canadian public policy is treated in comparative perspective tend to have an explicitly evaluative purpose, where the aim is to describe an overseas approach to a policy problem and to attempt to draw positive or negative lessons. Most examples of these are found in *Canadian Public Administration* and are conducted by policy analysts located in institutions other than academic political science departments. Michael J. Daly, for instance, investigates the Swedish approach to public pension fund investment, and asks whether there are some positive lessons for Canada.[15] Sanford Borins asks the same question with respect to public sector management in Japan.[16] Conversely, Frances Fisken suggests the negative lessons that should be drawn from urban policy analysis in the United States.[17] Only one article in another journal, Paul Lanoie's analysis of government intervention in occupational safety policy (published in *Canadian Public Policy*), was found within this genre.[18]

Lesson-drawing is not only of practical advantage, it also provides a possible explanation as to why some options were chosen over others in policy debate. This is my argument with respect to the development of both a Canadian privacy policy, as well as one relating to access to government information.[19] A careful investigation of the way that evidence about American and British law in these areas was utilized in Canadian policy debate offers some key insights into the selection of specific statutory language and policy instruments. That evidence may enter policy debate as a way to push an issue to an institutional agenda, as a way to mollify pressure, in order to emulate the actions of an exemplar, in order to optimize the search for the best policy, as well as to legitimate conclusions already reached.[20]

Comparative policy analysis can also help explicate patterns of cross-national convergence and divergence. The deterministic logic of the 'convergence thesis' (popular in the 1960s and 1970s) has given way to a more realistic understanding of the complex and subtle ways that similar countries might differ in their responses to similar problems. This is one of George Hoberg's main messages in his studies of chemical regulation in Canada and the United States.[21] The conventional wisdom that paints Canadian regulatory policy dependent on and convergent with American actions is simply untrue. First, there are several interesting divergences between Canadian and American responses in this area. Second, when convergence is apparent, it is not simply attributable to externalities associated with American action that force Canada to harmonize its policy. Hoberg demonstrates that for some issues at least, Canadian policy makers may emulate American standards simply because they provide the best approach.

Michael Howlett tests the thesis about the convergence of public policy styles between the United States and Canada through a case study of judicial decisions on the environment.[22] He concludes that there is (as yet) no pattern of convergence in terms of an increased legalization or judicialization of Canadian environmental policy making. Both Hoberg and Howlett demonstrate that when the detailed twists and turns of public policy are examined, and set within a clear comparative framework, the explanations for policy adoption are far more complex (and interesting) than when the policy analysis adheres more rigidly to an approach derived from some more recently fashionable theoretical school in the field.

In a similar vein, Katherine Teghtsoonian studies the failure of both Canada and the United States to regulate child-care services, a neglected corner of the subdiscipline. Teghtsoonian roots this failure in converging strands of neoconservative ideology, that do, however, exhibit a different tone on both sides of the border. The research is justified because the two countries 'offer roughly comparable contexts within which to explore policy debates on the subject.'[23]

Beyond these articles cited, one would be hard-pressed to find further comparative policy analysis within major Canadian journals. We therefore need to look to book-length treatments in which the details of different national policies can be more thoroughly described and explained. Here we find a few noteworthy research projects.

A relatively early attempt at comparative policy research was completed by Christopher Leman. His study of welfare reform in Canada and the United States is founded on the assumption that:

despite ostensible similarities in the collapse of welfare reform in Canada and the United States, welfare politics actually differ dramatically. This difference is particularly intriguing because the two countries have so much in common, a fact that makes it possible to isolate the reasons for the difference in welfare politics.[24]

Other book-length comparisons tend to be collaborative efforts. The most notable example is the first publication from the Canada–U.S. Project in the School of Policy Studies at Queen's University. This draws together scholars from both countries in around forty different comparative projects, most of which have a policy focus. The central aim of the project is 'to explore and compare the ways in which society, economy, policy and institutions in the two countries have been affected by – and responded to – a number of recent challenges. On the one hand are the challenges arising from the changing global environment ... On the other hand is the need to adapt and respond to changing domestic societies.'[25] Within this broad framework, the coordinators have asked their researchers on both sides of the border to consider questions about adaptation, constraint, and convergence and divergence. At writing, however, the overall results of this project have not been published.

It is indicative that most of the studies cited so far have attempted to compare Canada with the United States. This emphasis does, of course, complement the more longstanding tradition of analysing Canada–U.S. relations (discussed by Mildred Schwartz in her contribution to this volume), and the wider debate within the Canadian foreign policy literature about bilateral versus multilateral agendas. It also, at least implicitly, connects with the literature on the differences between American and Canadian political cultures. In some analyses of North American culture, more explicit hypotheses are investigated about the possible policy implications of the more 'individualistic' American political culture versus the more 'communitarian' culture in Canada.[26]

Comparisons with the United States make some sense from a practical point of view (ease of access to policy makers, data availability, proximity, and so on). From a strictly methodological viewpoint, however, comparisons with other parliamentary systems might be more revealing for some policy analyses. Both policy makers and political scientists in Canada have a natural tendency to look south of the border first for policy comparisons and lessons, even though other countries might provide greater institutional, cultural, and legal compatibilities.[27]

But we have to search high and low for comparative case studies that integrate countries other than the United States into the framework. Lou Pauly's analysis of banking regulation in the Pacific Rim is one example.[28] He writes detailed case studies on the United States, Canada, Japan, and Australia before assessing the wider question about policy convergence. He assesses the roles played by four sets of actors in opening up financial markets: domestic banks, domestic governments, foreign banks, and foreign governments. In each case, the actions of a different set of actors provided the critical catalyst for policy change.

The broader the comparison (both in terms of countries and sectors), the less detail can be observed by the author(s) in question. Wyn Grant (a British political scientist) makes this trade-off in his comparison of industrial policy in the United Kingdom, Canada, and the United States.[29] Six different industries are analysed: dairying, forestry, chemicals, steel, electricity, and long-distance railways. The advantages are that we gain a broad under-standing of these different states' regulatory styles. The disadvantage is that within the general sweep of the analysis much detail is lost, detail that may be critically important in any one regulatory context.

The comparative method does not necessarily imply an explicit multicase strategy selected by one researcher. Comparative policy analysis can proceed within and between many single-country volumes and over several years. This is the approach taken within the series of books edited for Temple University Press by Douglas Ashford, Peter Katzenstein, and T.J. Pempel. Carolyn Tuohy, in her Canadian contribution to the series, argues that 'what appears distinctive about Canadian institutions is their extraordinary capacity to embody conflicting principles within structures ambiguous enough to allow for ad hoc accommodations over time – what I have called Canada's "institutionalized ambivalence."'[30]

This depiction of a distinctive policy 'style' emerges from an analysis of different cases of policy making within Canada and a careful comparison of the capacity of the Canadian state to respond to the same challenges as its counterparts overseas. But comparative evidence is utilized selectively in order to point out the distinctive features of Canadian institutions and society and of how they interact to produce public policy.

A collection of case studies driven by a similar conceptual scheme or theoretical framework, and using similar types of data to measure equivalent and clearly defined concepts, is logically no different from the comparative method. The paucity of such literature suggests, however, that the problems of achieving a level of consistency are enormous. In practice, the link between single-case analyses, other studies conducted by different authors, and existing theory is often tenuous. On the other hand, the multicase approach pursued by one author offers a greater potential for theoretical and conceptual consistency, but also a broader range of methodological and practical difficulties for the researcher.

II. Canadian Public Policy in Cross-Sectional Studies

The largest number of cases that one author can conceivably integrate into one comparative policy design using a case study approach is probably around four. Even with this number, the investment required in developing sufficient expertise in the range of historical, cultural, and institutional factors that might possibly influence policy choice is enormous. Authors that attempt such comparisons typically narrow the scope of policy to be compared, thus limiting the potential range of actors and institutions to be considered. But even at this level, the number of cases is typically too low to permit generalizations beyond the countries studied.

In seeking wider generalizations and possibly cumulative theoretical development, the contrasting approach applies statistical techniques to a larger cross-section of countries. An effort is then made to define a systematic variation in some aspect of public policy output or outcome, and then to pull from context selected political, cultural, socio-economic, and institutional variables in order to find statistical measures of association. Inquiry is thus normally limited to explaining variation in dependent variables definable in terms amenable to interval-level measurement. Thus research in this tradition tends to focus on economic variables, such as the determinants of unemployment or inflation rates, the size of the public economy, the extent of income distribution, and so on.

There is an enormous volume of literature in this genre dating back to the mid-1960s. Much relies on OECD statistics, supplemented by other indices that have been created by political scientists to measure variables such as the ideological orientation of the government, the strength of labour unions, the presence of corporatist modes of intermediation, and so on. Two big questions have dominated this literature: how to explain variation in some aspect of the size of government (such as the public economy, or welfare effort); and whether (and to what extent) policy outcomes are shaped by the parties in power, as opposed to being the almost automatic by-product of economic or technological development.

Most of these studies will include Canada as one of many cases. Few, however, have been conducted by Canadian political scientists. And few have attempted to use cross-sectional data on advanced industrial states to say anything specifically about Canadian public policy, as opposed to testing more general hypotheses about patterns and trends.

An exception would be some of the studies completed for the Royal Commission on the Economic Union and Development Prospects for Canada (the Macdonald Commission): David Cameron's analysis of the growth of government spending in the Western world reaches some specific conclusions about the determinants of growth in Canada: 'Both the cross-national analysis of the expansion of government spending in 20 nations over the past two decades and the longitudinal analysis of the growth in federal and total government spending in Canada over the past five decades demonstrate that political factors have exerted an independent effect on the growth of government spending.' He points specifically to the 'organizational attributes of labour movements, the frequency of control of government by leftist parties and the openness of the Canadian economy.'[31]

Julia O'Connor is more interested in spending, more specifically on welfare programs. The Canadian welfare state occupies a peculiar position within the comparative perspective. It presents a 'mixed picture' across four dimensions of welfare effort – decommodification, solidarity, redistribution, and full employment. Expenditures on education and health are the best aspects of its welfare effort; those on employment and social transfers are relatively low by OECD standards.[32] This kind of work, however, is not generally undertaken by Canadian political scientists. Rarely is Canada singled out for comment in this way from the broad sweep of cross-sectional analysis.

The difficulty of conceptualizing and operationalizing the dependent policy variable, of identifying possible variation in independent variables, and of reducing these concepts to an operational level with relevant, accurate, complete, and equivalent data across a large enough number of countries is formidable, often insuperable. Moreover, as Anthony King argues, cross-sectional studies 'in some ways resemble photographs taken from a high-flying aircraft; the main features stand out, but much detail is lost – and the lost detail may be important.'[33]

III. Comparative Public Policy in Canada: The Constraints

The above review does not claim to be exhaustive. We have seen that there are a number of largely descriptive studies that attempt to outline the contours of Canadian policy in some kind of comparative perspective. There are also incentives for those in Canada to draw lessons from policy experiences elsewhere, and for a few outside to look to Canadian policy as exemplary. There are few political scientists, however, who have explicitly used comparative policy analysis in order to learn something more broadly about the Canadian state and society.

In no way, therefore, can comparative policy analysis be said to be a 'tradition' in Canada (in the same way that political economy is a tradition, for example). There are some reasons for this. Some are inherent in the very difficult enterprise of comparative policy analysis. Others are more peculiar to Canadian political science. The constraints can be categorized as theoretical, conceptual, and professional.

Theoretical Dilemmas

The determinants of public policy are multiple and various. Along with other areas of comparative politics, comparative public policy is fraught with the 'too many variables, small "N"' problem.[34] Attempts to integrate and categorize potential variables to provide guidance for empirical research have not been successful; often the drive for exhaustiveness limits a framework's value as a device to direct our attention to salient and sharply defined explanatory factors.[35]

On the other hand, efforts to construct more parsimonious frameworks may suffer from the normative bias of the author. For those operating from Marxist or Gramscian assumptions, public policy is the expression of the economic interests of the dominant class. For the pluralist, policy is the result of group competition and political bargaining. For the elite theorist, the critical factor is the natural tendency for large organizations to be dominated by a small number of committed and knowledgeable officials. For the public choice theorist, the focus of attention is the promotion and protection of self-regarding interests. But each approach is, to some extent, a 'self-validating standpoint,' suggesting what to look for, and what not to look for, but providing no empirically valid explanation for systemic variation.[36]

The attempt to explicate policy differences and similarities across different systems is fraught with a central dilemma. The bewildering array of potential independent variables, operating at different levels of analysis that might shape public policy, can rarely, if ever, be tested and compared within the same causal model. Hence the comparativist needs to be selective, running the risk of allowing arbitrary or value-laden considerations to influence the choice of cases and the construction of the comparative framework.

As one of the few federal and parliamentary states in the world, Canada poses a particular problem for the comparativist. The inclusion of the Canadian case within any comparative study will complicate the range of institutional variables that might account for policy variation. In other words, it is difficult to think of many comparisons that could be made with Canada that would approximate what Przeworski and Teune call a 'most similar systems design.'[37] With the exception of comparisons with Australia (certainly becoming more popular among Canadian and Australian institutional experts), it is difficult to conceive of a choice of cases that fits the standard prescription for comparative methodology, as defined by Lijphart, that 'maximizes the variance of the independent variables and minimizes the variance of the control variables.'[38]

A second theoretical dilemma, which is perhaps more pronounced when Canada is included for comparison, finds expression as 'Galton's problem.' Are similar outcomes and events in different countries explained by contextual variables, where policy responses are hypothesized to be the by-product of common socio-economic or technological development, or are they best explained through diffusion? The former approach assumes an independence of cases and that empirical relationships found between system-level variables in a significant number of countries are indeed true causal links. The latter, cognizant of 'Galton's problem,' presupposes linkages and influences across state boundaries that blur the independence of individual observations. This may be regarded as a serious methodological problem that reduces (maybe to one) the independent events that may logically be analysed.

Again this poses a particularly severe dilemma for the Canadian case, given the close economic and political ties with the United States. Thus analysts of Canadian public policy must always be cognizant of the international sources of domestic public policy.[39] In particular, they must consider the externalities imposed by American policies or actions that affect some aspect of Canadian welfare. Perhaps the most notable examples are in the environmental sphere, in which the United States has literally exported its pollution to Canada.[40]

The Conceptualization of Public Policy

The more familiar conceptualization sees public policy as an 'output' of the structures and processes of the political system. Policy is a dependent variable. Its emergence, production, and character are shaped by that system and the interests that support it. Donald Hancock suggests that the majority of comparativists 'interpret policy outcomes as the product of antecedent economic, social or political factors.'[41]

However, there is another school of thought, which has followed the lead of Lowi in conceptualizing policy as an *independent* variable. Political conflict arenas are determined by the expectations of policy makers, 'so that for every type of policy there is likely to be a distinctive type of political relationship.'[42] This assumption underpins the work of Douglas Ashford who, most prominently among comparative policy analysts, has insisted that policy is a 'structural factor in the organizational, distributional and historical regularities of states achieving their goals.'[43] But this view, taken to its logical extreme, would suggest that the nature of the problem faced is the most important feature in determining the politics surrounding its resolution, and that different states would then tend to converge in their approaches to solving similar problems.[44]

Others question whether 'policy' is a variable at all. Hugh Heclo has argued that 'policy does not seem to be a self-defining phenomenon; it is an analytic construct, the contents of which are identified by the analyst rather than by the policy maker of pieces of legislation or administration.'[45] Moreover, in some languages (including French) the words 'policy' and 'politics' are indistinguishable, creating a further barrier to the development of equivalent constructs.

Public policy is also a multidimensional phenomenon.[46] It has at least five different aspects: policy *goals* (the explicit or implicit intentions behind the policy); policy *content* (defined as the more formal manifestations of government policy); policy *instruments* (the institutional tools chosen to administer or regulate the policy); policy *outcomes* (the negative or positive consequences of implementation; and policy *styles* (the typical processes through which different policies are formulated).

Similarity and variation can occur across each of these dimensions.[47] Indeed, it is not uncommon to find a cross-national convergence across one aspect of a public policy, and yet a striking divergence across another. Hoberg's review of four comparative environmental works, for instance, reaches the conclusion that: 'The four studies under review are remarkable for their overwhelming consensus that, while regulatory *outcomes* are highly similar across countries, the political *processes* by which these outcomes are reached display persistent differences.'[48]

The Disciplinary Constraints

The reasons outlined above are in some respects inherent within the entire subfield. To be sure, Canada poses some peculiar methodological difficulties of equivalence for any scholar wanting to integrate a Canadian case into a wider comparative study. But all societies to some extent pose their own unique difficulties. To understand why there are *so* few comparative studies of Canadian public policy we have to look to certain disciplinary reasons that have more to do with the behaviour and motivations of researchers in Canada and outside.

There would certainly be more comparative research of Canadian public policy if Canadian politics were of greater interest to American political scientists. Kent Weaver has tried to explain why the incentives for American political scientists to study Canada are so low. Using rational choice arguments, it is clear to Weaver that there are strong incentives for American political scientists to avoid investing time and resources into studying a country that is not within the dominant scholarly concerns of American political science. A paucity of mentors, training opportunities, funding sources, research materials, and potential journal outlets all militate against aspiring American political scientists doing dissertation research on Canadian politics or policy.[49]

Moreover, from the point of view of the American perspective, Canada is a 'one-country region,' whereas most American-trained comparativists (and the academic positions they compete for) are defined in regional terms – Western European, East Asian, South Asian, Latin American, African, and so on. Few departments can afford to devote slots explicitly to the study of any one overseas country. The logical regional comparison for Canada, the United States, tends also to be studied from a noncomparative perspective. Americanists are expected to have more precise institutional or behavioural expertise (Congress, the presidency, public law, mass behaviour, and so on). For reasons that have to do with the definition of 'subfields' in American political science, Canada tends to 'fall through the cracks.'

There are similarly persuasive professional reasons why political scientists within Canada do not embrace comparative methodology. To some extent this is a reflection of the wider lack of attention to comparative studies generally, and in particular to the absence of a Canadian journal specifically devoted to comparative research. Comparativists in the United States have natural outlets in journals such as *Comparative Politics*, *Comparative Political Studies*, and *Governance*. European journals such as the *Journal of Public Policy* and the *European Journal for Political Research* provide additional outlets, especially for those interested in transatlantic comparisons. There are no real equivalents for the Canadian 'comparativist.'

If Canadian politics is rarely studied elsewhere, there has been a natural tendency to ensure that it is thoroughly covered within Canadian departments. This is related to a wider disciplinary incentive to promote a version of the discipline that can be defined as 'Canadian' and distinguished in both intellectual terms and with regard to research focus from what some see as the universalizing tendencies of American political science. 'Comparison' is not seen by some in Canada as an inevitable and general perspective, but as a quite precise methodology, imbued with the positivist overtones of American behaviouralism. 'Comparative politics/policy' thus means more than a cross-national perspective, it means the 'comparative *science* of politics,' which is of course anathema to many Canadian students of politics who proceed from post- or anti-positivist assumptions.

It is also worth pointing out, in passing, that some research *within* Canada is comparative in perspective and methodology. The regional heterogeneity of the country means that any cross-provincial study has to be cognizant of the range of comparative methodological issues that raise their head in cross-national research. *Small Worlds*, for instance, is a study of comparative politics. Elkins and Simeon had to consider issues of concept definition (e.g., political culture), equivalence of concepts, levels of analysis, data availability, and so on.[50]

For a number of equally compelling reasons, however, I will argue in conclusion that this lack of attention to comparative policy work is undesirable. Moreover, for a variety of reasons that have to do with the inconvenient progress of international political and economic affairs, it will be inevitable that more and more Canadians will look outside for comparative reference points, and more and more outsiders will look to Canada as an exemplar.

IV. Comparative Public Policy in Canada: The Promise

Comparative public policy is not one 'art.' It embraces a range of different empirical and normative questions and may lead to a number of different quantitative and qualitative methodologies. Whatever the definition of this 'art,' however, one finds few examples within Canadian political science. The issue is the extent to which these first examples of comparative policy research will be emulated and whether the technique will permeate the consciousness and research techniques of policy analysts within Canada. In this regard, I would point to four very fruitful areas for further research.

First, there is enormous scope for comparative studies of regulatory policy. The comparative analysis of how states respond (or not) to similar challenges potentially provides insights into the capacity of the Canadian state to manage change: whether its style of policy making is reactive or anticipatory, consensual or conflictual; whether the policy responses are forced to converge with actions overseas; whether distinctive Canadian policy instruments are selected; and whether the policy responses are relatively successful by comparison. When new problems are raised to the institutional agendas of different states, especially those posed by the development of new technologies, they provide a kind of naturally occurring experiment that reduces many of the problems of equivalence that are attached to policies with longer histories and entrenched institutional interests.

A second area relates to the literature on policy communities and networks. Policy analysts within different countries, as well as international relations scholars, have recently converged on quite similar conceptualizations of policy communities, epistemic communities, advocacy coalitions, and so on, to characterize the loose amalgam of experts that surround many issues and that often have a decisive influence on public policy.[51] The market integration within North America through NAFTA will only increase these cross-national linkages within different policy sectors.

A third area of future research lies in the dynamic of policy learning or lesson-drawing.[52] Richard Rose has argued that comparative political scientists can say a lot more about the conditions under which the actions of other states are emulated.[53] We now have some quite precise hypotheses about the conditions for lesson-drawing that can fruitfully be examined within comparisons of public policy in Canada and elsewhere. We need a lot more research on the way that evidence about overseas policy enters and is utilized in Canadian policy debates.

Finally, the recent publicity over the Canadian health-care system in the United States would suggest a potential for more American policy analysts to look to the Canadian approach in a number of related areas. U.S. policy making is notoriously parochial, as many comparative studies have shown. The willingness to explore foreign approaches to health care, and the extraordinary way in which lessons about the Canadian case have been bandied about in recent political debate, might signal a greater openness to the exploration of overseas approaches in other policy sectors. That would mean a concomitant need for more comparative policy analysis in the United States.

Despite all the compelling theoretical, conceptual, methodological, and practical reasons for *not* conducting comparative policy research, the familiar maxim (originally attributed to Rudyard Kipling speaking about England) will remain true: 'What know they of Canada, who only Canada know?' 'There is no nation, without other nations,' Dogan and Pelassy assert.[54] By the same token, there is no national public policy, without other nations' public policy. At a basic intuitive level, our knowledge of Canadian public policy will inevitably be understood with reference to policy events elsewhere.

Notes

I am grateful to Manon Moreau and Darren Osadchuk for the research assistance on which this paper is based.

1 Heidenheimer et al., *Comparative Public Policy,* 2–3.
2 LaPalombara, 'Macro-Theories and Micro-Applications in Comparative Politics.'
3 Rustow, 'Modernization and Comparative Politics.'
4 Easton, 'The New Revolution in Political Science.'
5 Leichter, 'Comparative Public Policy.'
6 An argument made in more detail in Bennett, *Regulating Privacy*, 1–2.
7 Rose, *Lesson-Drawing in Public Policy.*
8 Anderson, 'Comparative Policy Analysis,' 122.
9 See Hood, *The Tools of Government.*

10 Anderson, 'The Logic of Public Problems,' 41.
11 Verba, 'Some Dilemmas in Comparative Research,' 114.
12 Heclo, 'Review Article: Policy Analysis,' 89.
13 Ibid., 88.
14 Lijphart, 'The Comparable-Cases Strategy in Comparative Research,' 164.
15 Daly, 'The Swedish Approach to Investing Public Pension Funds.'
16 Borins, 'Management of the Public Sector in Japan.'
17 Frisken, 'Canadian Cities and the American Example.'
18 Lanoie, 'Government Intervention in Occupational Safety.'
19 .Bennett, 'The Formation of a Canadian Privacy Policy'; and 'How States Utilize Foreign Evidence.'
20 Bennett, 'How States Utilize Foreign Evidence,' 33.
21 Hoberg, 'Risk, Science and Politics'; Hoberg, 'Sleeping with an Elephant'; Harrison and Hoberg, 'Setting the Environmental Agenda in Canada and the United States.'
22 Howlett, 'The Judicialization of Canadian Environmental Policy.'
23 Teghtsoonian, 'Neo-Conservative Ideology and Opposition to Federal Regulation of Child Care Services.'
24 Leman, *The Collapse of Welfare Reform*, xiii.
25 Banting et al., *Policy Choices*, 2.
26 Lipset, *Continental Divide;* Finbow, 'Ideology and Institutions in North America.'
27 Bennett, 'How States Utilize Foreign Evidence,' 51.
28 Pauly, *Opening Financial Markets.*
29 Grant, *Government and Industry.*
30 Tuohy, *Policy and Politics in Canada*, xvii. Other books in the series include: Heclo and Madsen, *Policy and Politics in Sweden;* Katzenstein, *Politics and Policy in West Germany*; Pempel, *Policy and Politics in Japan*; Ashford, *Politics and Policy in France*; Ashford, *Politics and Policy in Britain.*
31 Cameron, 'The Growth of Government Spending,' 46.
32 O'Connor, 'Welfare Expenditure and Policy Orientation,' 143.
33 King, 'What Do Elections Decide?' 316.
34 Lijphart, 'Comparative Politics and the Comparative Method.'
35 Lockhart, 'Explaining Social Policy Differences Among Advanced Industrial Societies,' 336.
36 Lowi, 'American Business, Public Policy, Case Studies and Political Theory.'
37 Przeworski and Teune, *The Logic of Comparative Social Inquiry.*
38 Lijphart, 'The Comparable-Cases Strategy Comparative Research.'
39 See Gourevitch, 'The Second-Image Reversed'; Almond, 'Review Article: The International-National Connection.'

40 Hoberg, 'Sleeping with an Elephant.'

41 Hancock, 'Comparative Public Policy,' 288.

42 Lowi, 'American Business, Public Policy, Case Studies and Political Theory,' 688.

43 Ashford, 'The Structural Analysis of Policy or Institutions Really Do Matter,' 92.

44 Bennett, 'Review Article: What Is Policy Convergence and What Causes It?' 217.

45 Heclo, 'Review Article,' 85.

46 See Greenberg et al., 'Developing Public Policy Theory.'

47 Bennett, 'Review Article,' 218.

48 Hoberg, 'Technology, Political Structure and Social Regulation,' 359.

49 Weaver, 'Through the One-Way Mirror.' Weaver draws upon his own experience of studying railway policy in North America: Weaver, *The Politics of Industrial Change: Railway Policy in North America* (Washington, D.C.: Brookings Institution 1985).

50 Elkins and Simeon, *Small Worlds.*

51 See Haas, 'Introduction'; Sabatier, 'An Advocacy Coalition Framework of Policy Change and the Role of Policy-Oriented Learning Therein'; Atkinson and Coleman, 'Policy Networks, Policy Communities and the Problems of Governance.'

52 Bennett and Howlett, 'The Lessons of Learning.'

53 Rose, *Lesson-Drawing in Public Policy.*

54 Dogan and Pelassy, *How to Compare Nations*, 5.

16

National Policy Studies in Comparative Perspective: An Organizing Framework Applied to the Canadian Case

CAROLYN HUGHES TUOHY

Students of public policy face a fundamental trade-off. How broadly comparative should be their scope, or how finely textured their analysis of a particular case? The wider the comparative sweep across time and nations, the more likely it is that broad patterns of activity will be revealed, and that an explanation can be developed, based on the observation of consistent relationships between variables. The closer the focus on a particular case, the greater the number of variables that can be taken into account, and the more likely the investigator is to develop the close familiarity that allows for an interpretation of behaviour and events. The judgments that individual scholars make about the trade-off between comparative scope and textured focus have yielded a wide range of approaches within the field of public policy – from studies based on the analysis of aggregate data drawn from a dozen or more countries, through studies more closely targeted at three or four countries, to studies focused on one country against a comparative background, to 'idiographic' country-specific studies with little if any comparative context.

The study of Canadian public policy, almost by definition, falls closer to the country-specific than to the multinational end of this spectrum. For the most part, those who have addressed issues of Canadian public policy in the past have concerned themselves almost exclusively with Canada.[1] Canada is often included among the 'data points' in quantitative analyses of large databases; but relatively little of this work is done by Canadian scholars, or scholars with a particular interest in Canada.[2] There are, however, a few recent examples of the inclusion of Canada in three- or four-country studies of particular policy arenas. Increasingly, moreover, students of Canadian public policy are being careful to locate Canada in a comparative context in setting up their research questions.

In this chapter, I shall be concerned with the work of those scholars who study Canada in a comparative context, whether in the context of a comparative study of a small set of nations, or as a single point of focus within a broader comparative field. And I shall argue that the generation and exploration of research questions, for students of Canadian public policy and of comparative public policy more generally, is enhanced by this closely focused comparative work. This is true for two reasons. First, a close focus allows for the exploration of explanatory factors and dimensions of policy that are not amenable to measurement in the quantitative terms that are necessary in working with large samples of cases. Second, a close focus allows for an investigation of the *dynamics of the joint effects* of multiple variables.

This is not to argue against the quantitative analysis of multination datasets as an appropriate methodology in comparative public policy. Indeed, the more closely focused studies that I shall discuss in this chapter benefit from the development and testing of hypotheses in this broader comparative work. My argument is rather that the comparative study of public policy embraces a range of approaches that yield different kinds of knowledge. Within that range, the close and textured study of a limited number of cases holds an important place.

This chapter presents an organizing framework within which various approaches to the comparative study of public policy can be considered. This framework is then used to locate a number of studies of Canadian public policy in comparative perspective. Finally a more extensive discussion of my own work focusing on the Canadian case against a comparative field is provided.

When attempting to explain policy decisions, students of public policy usually differentiate between two categories of data: independent and dependent variables. The former are causally related to the latter. In other words, the dependent variables, or outputs, are more or less strictly determined by the independent variables.

Independent Variables

Economic and Technological Factors

In this category are factors such as the level of economic development, the size and organization of the national economy or the economic sector under review, and the interrelationship between sectoral, regional, national, and international economies. In the 1970s considerable debate was waged around the issue of the relative weight of economic factors in explaining policy outcomes. Neo-Marxist analysis assigned a privileged role to this category of explanatory variables, arguing that public policies derive from the functional imperatives of capitalist economies – imperatives that are fundamentally contradictory.[3] Other analysts, without accepting the theoretical framework of neo-Marxism, developed and tested empirical models to show that, over a broad range of nations, the level of economic development is strongly associated with gross measures of public policy such as the level of public expenditure relative to the size of the economy, and hypothesized that over time public policies would converge among states with similar levels of economic development.[4]

Yet other scholars, however, pointed to the continuing differentiation in the policies of advanced industrial nations when compared to each other and not to a global set of nations. Within the smaller set of advanced industrial nations, the level of economic development was less important than other factors, such as institutional structure and partisan control of government, in explaining policy differences.[5] Furthermore, an influential line of analysis was opened up with the exploration of the effect on policy of the degree of openness (to international trade) of a nation's economy, as opposed to its level of economic development.[6]

In the wake of these debates, most students of comparative public policy accept the importance of multifactorial explanations of policy differences, and include economic factors within the set of factors to be included.

Ideas

Most scholars recognize the need to take into account the impact of ideas upon public policy; but much more work is needed to understand the mechanisms by which ideas are generated and brought to bear on policy decisions. In a classic study, Anthony King identified differences across nations and over time in the ideas that drive policy.[7] The best Canadian example of this approach is Ronald Manzer's eloquent and insightful tracing of the evolution of Canadian public policies to uncover the underlying 'public philosophy.'[8]

For those who seek causal explanations of public policies, the investigation of the impact of ideas presents particular problems. It is difficult to identify 'ideas' independently of the policies that they inform. Work such as Manzer's melds explanation and interpretation in an attempt to identify broad developments in the 'public philosophy' and then to show how that philosophy is manifest in particular policy arenas. A related but distinct approach is one that attempts through various sociological techniques to identify the 'political culture' of a nation (or subnational unit) – a common set of assumptions about political life. This culture is generated in a social crucible in which economic forces, historical and demographic factors, and institutional structures all form part of the mix.

Some scholars attempted to relate differences in political culture systematically to differences in policy outputs.[9] In a classic critique of the concept of political culture as an explanatory variable, and particularly its relevance to the study of public policy, Elkins and Simeon argued that political culture shapes public policy by 'setting the agenda,' by establishing the range of alternatives considered. And they argued that culture has this effect through its interaction or 'joint effects' with other factors.[10]

Picking up and developing this theme, a number of students of public policy have sought to understand the mechanism through which ideas are brought to bear on policy by focusing on the intersection between ideas, interests, and institutions.[11] In the Canadian context, this theme has recently been developed by Keith Banting and Michael Atkinson, among others.[12] This raises the third and fourth categories of independent variables in the model.

Interests

The two dominant modes of public policy analysis in political science in the latter part of the twentieth century – pluralism and class analysis – each take interests as their starting point. Perhaps more attention has thus been paid to the role of interests in shaping public policy than to any other set of factors. Class analysis (including but not limited to neo-Marxist analysis) essentially holds that interests, and the power of interests (although it does not generally use that term), are defined by the structure of capitalist society and hence are fundamentally grounded in economic relations. Pluralists, on the other hand, view the points of genesis of interests and the bases of their power to be multiple and competing, and include not only economic relations but also belief systems, demographic characteristics such as ethnicity, gender, and age, positions within organizations, including state institutions, and so on. Hence for pluralists the influence of interests on policy is seen as a function of their degree of mobilization, their access to resources, and their strategic behaviour.

Essentially, then, these two approaches have differed in the degree of structure or fluidity that they attribute to the organization of interests in society, and in the range of bases of interest that they recognize.[13] Increasingly, however, the distinction between these two modes of analysis is eroding. Pluralists recognize that the structure of capitalist society establishes constraints on policy, and privileges certain interests, notably business interests. Class analysts, for their part, recognize that capitalist social formations comprise complex structures of class fractions, and that there are a variety of models for the expression of the policy imperatives of capitalist society. Both modes of analysis, moreover, have increasingly paid attention to the role of the state. In particular, there has been great interest in the effects of 'corporatist' modes of organization and interaction with the state.

Institutions

Much has been written about the renaissance of interest in the role of institutions in the policy process, often referred to as the 'new institutionalism.' This label covers a wide variety of approaches, from public-choice-based formal analysis of incentives and decision rules in organizations to finely detailed historical descriptions of changes in policy-making structures and the impact of those changes on policy outcomes. Even the definition of the term 'institution' is not consistent. Some scholars use the term in its classic sociological sense to mean an organization whose structures and processes become imbued with value in themselves and acquire a 'character' that persists over time.[14] Others treat institutions as structured relationships in both state and society – in Peter Hall's words, 'the formal rules, the compliance structures, and standard operating practices that structure the relationship between individuals in various units of the polity and economy.'[15]

Defining institutions as patterned or structured relationships, however, does not distinguish the concept of institution from others such as 'policy style' – a concept to be discussed below. It is preferable, rather, to restrict the use of the term to *state* structures: that is, structures through which *authority* is exercised, and that is the sense in which I use it here. Focusing on institutions as authority structures highlights the essence of their role in conflict resolution.

For some 'new institutionalists,' state institutions assume a privileged role in the explanation of policy outputs. They represent a 'crystallization' of the effects of economic factors, ideas, and interests;[16] and they constitute the primary vehicle through which these factors are brought to bear on policy. But they also generate ideas and interests through a process of institutional evolution over time.[17] This 'new institutionalist' position is close to what I want to argue in this chapter. The framework presented here, however, supposes that the policy process is conceptually distinct from its institutional milieu. The policy process, that is, is shaped largely but not entirely by the way in which various factors have been crystallized in institutions. It is also shaped by the continuing flux of economic forces, ideas and interests. Before turning to the policy process itself, however, let us consider the nature of the outputs of that process.

Policy Dimensions

I identify three dimensions of policy outputs. A dimension that I will call 'distributional' relates to the allotment of tangible benefits and costs across various interests in society. A second dimension, which relates to issues of identity, status, and belief, is the 'symbolic' dimension of policy. The third dimension is 'structural' – it relates to the allocation of positions of influence in the making and implementation of policy.[18] These dimensions are not mutually exclusive – a given policy may well have distributional, symbolic, and structural implications. But policies differ in the level of their distributional, symbolic, and structural content.

Distributional Policies

Much of the literature on comparative public policy, it is fair to say, concerns distributional policies, and more particularly the fiscal policies of governments. What is the level of public expenditure for particular purposes, either in absolute terms or as a proportion of Gross National Product? What is the level of taxation and the structure of the tax system? Fiscal policies are not the only policies with high distributional content. Regulatory policies involve the exercise of the authority of the state to establish constraints upon private activity, with significant distributional implications.

Symbolic Policies

Measures of government expenditure do even less to capture the symbolic dimension of policy. Using the authority of the state to influence or control a given type of behaviour sends a powerful set of signals. It signals that such behaviour warrants the attention of the state – that it needs to be sanctioned, in either the positive or the negative sense, through the authoritative apparatus of the state. The corollary signal is that such behaviour cannot be left entirely to be determined through 'private' or nonauthoritative mechanisms such as the market or the family. The symbolic dimensions of policies, then, have the capacity to engage even those for whom the policies are likely to have little tangible effect. They signal something about the nature of the collectivity in which individuals hold membership, and about the status of those individuals and/or their beliefs within that collectivity. The mobilization of groups around issues of abortion policy and family law are testimony to the power of such symbols.

The distributional and symbolic dimensions of a given policy may be mutually reinforcing; but they may also cut in somewhat different directions. The banning of extra-billing in Canada and the related compensatory changes for the medical profession, for example, represented on balance a set of tangible gains for the profession, but a symbolic loss.[19] As another example, social policy reforms in Canada, the United States, and Europe in the 1980s and early 1990s had distributional and symbolic implications that were in some tension. They tended to enhance benefits while signalling an intention to make eligibility for these benefits increasingly contingent on participation in market-oriented activities. There are important symbolic implications in structuring social benefits as outright entitlements on the basis of membership in the political community on the one hand, or as contingent upon contributions, demonstration of need, or participation in training or public works programs on the other. The balance between entitlement and contingency in the design of social programs sends important signals about the legitimacy of the state and the market respectively.

Structural Policies

Finally, public policies can have important structural implications – that is, implications for the positions of authority of various actors in the policy process – for the degree and nature of their access to the sanctions of the state in enforcing their preferences. Constitutional policy – establishing the basic law that determines the distribution of authority among state institutions, and representation within those institutions – is the primary example of a policy type with a very large structural dimension. Other kinds of policy, such as those relating to industrial relations or professional regulation, also rank very high on this dimension. In yet other cases, policies undertaken, at least ostensibly, for primarily distributional purposes may also have important structural implications.

For example, reforms in the health-care arena in a number of nations, notably Britain, the Netherlands, and New Zealand, in the late 1980s and early 1990s, have attempted to enhance the role of market forces within a publicly funded system by distinguishing more sharply between the roles of 'providers' and 'purchasers' of health care within the system and by encouraging competition between providers. The reforms are aimed (at least ostensibly) at increasing the efficiency of the system. They also have the important symbolic effect of signalling a preference for exchange- (or market-) based over authority- (or state-) based mechanisms. Perhaps even more important, they have profound implications for the positions of influence of various types of health-care providers and administrators over the allocation and distribution of publicly financed benefits.

Comparative studies of the structural dimensions of public policy are relatively few. Institutional factors, as noted above, are more commonly treated as 'independent' variables. Studying the structural dimensions of policy, however, treats institutions as 'dependent' variables, shaped by policy outputs. But there is a reciprocal relationship, or cycle of causality, between institutions and policy outputs; and there is much to be learned from investigating each direction of causality. For example, there is a substantial body of work on the effects of 'corporatism,' as noted above, on a variety of policy outputs and outcomes. There is less comparative work on the structural effect of policies directed at creating corporatist arrangements, although there has been particular interest among Canadian scholars in this regard.[20]

The Policy Process: Keys to the Black Box

The policy process often appears as a 'black box' into which a range of conceptually distinct factors flow, and from which a set of policy outputs emanate. Significant numbers of studies, especially those based on quantitative analysis of aggregate data, essentially ignore this mechanism of mediation. If we are to unlock this black box, we need a way of conceiving the interrelationships that occur in the policy process. In particular, we need a way of conceptualizing the relationship between *interests* and *institutions*. Why the focus on these two categories of variables? Because it is in their intersection that we discover the *agency*, the source of action, that brings about policy change. It is through their positions in the structure of mobilized interests and in the institutions of the state, in other words, that *political actors* become involved in policy making. One critical aspect of this intersection, though by no means the only one, is the role of political parties.

Policy Networks

One way of conceptualizing the interrelationships within the policy process, and one that has gained considerable currency in the study of public policy in Canada and elsewhere, is the concept of the 'policy community' or the 'policy network.' This approach essentially maps out the relations between interests and institutions, and attempts to show how the pattern of influence represented by these maps yields particular policy outcomes. This is a case-based approach whose methodology is to build up an inventory of cases so that the relationship between certain types of policy networks and certain types of policy outcomes can be established.

Much of the work following this approach in the Canadian context has been concerned with the different effects of 'pluralist' and 'corporatist' networks. Coleman and Skogstad, for example, have developed a sixfold typology of networks based on differences in the cohesiveness of the organization and the autonomy of the state.[21] So far, no consistent set of hypotheses has been built up using the 'policy network' approach, although certain hypotheses – such as whether certain types of networks are more stable than others, or are more capable of responding to certain types of policy challenges – suggest themselves as possible topics for investigation as an inventory of cases builds up.

Policy Styles

A second, more encompassing but less well developed concept for unlocking the black box of the policy process is the notion of 'policy style.' This concept has gained some currency as scholars have sought a way of drawing their insights about the particular characteristics of the policy process in given nations into a broader comparative context.[22] Richardson and his colleagues, using concepts derived from institutional analysis, saw policy style as the 'standard operating procedures' for making and implementing policies in a given society, and the related set of 'legitimising norms for policy activity' (at p. 2). Their working hypothesis was that nations develop distinctive policy styles that are common across policy sectors.

In theory, the concept of policy style could embrace a number of variables – and indeed Richardson and his colleagues experimented with quite exhaustively defined matrices of six or more variables and five or six policy styles.[23] For comparative purposes, however, they judged such a model to be unmanageable; and they reduced the model to two variables yielding four possible types of policy style. One variable concerned the degree to which the approach to problem solving was anticipatory or reactive; the other concerned the degree to which the relationship between the state and other actors was one of consensus or imposition.

The concept of 'policy style' bears some similarity to the concept of 'political culture,' and it has been plagued by somewhat similar problems. The very breadth and flexibility that made it attractive as a bridge from the 'idiographic' to the comparative also made it almost infinitely malleable. To gain a comparative edge, scholars such as Richardson and his colleagues turned to the development of parsimonious typologies. The problem has been that policy processes, like social belief systems, defy 'type-casting.' As different scholars have tried to fit particular policy processes to 'types' and vice versa, the definition of types has continued to shift. Even the group of scholars who contributed to the Richardson volume had mixed success in applying a consistent typology of policy styles. (A similar problem, it should be noted, bedevils attempts to develop typologies of 'policy networks.' Contributors to the Coleman and Skogstad volume cited above, for example, are not consistent in their use of the typology set out in the introductory chapter.)

National Distinctiveness in Comparative Context

One set of scholars has attempted an approach somewhat similar to the 'policy style' approach, but has sought to gain comparative power through the consistent use of a common conceptual framework in which to make an argument. Each of the authors of the series of books on *Policy and Politics in Industrial States,* of which I am one, sought to identify the distinctive characteristics of the policy process of a particular nation by looking at the ways in which economic and technical factors, ideas, and especially interests and institutions intersected in that policy process *in comparison to other nations* treated in the series. More or less explicitly, the conceptual framework set out above in terms of independent and dependent variables was applied to each nation, while drawing comparisons and contrasts to other nations.

Like those who attempt to identify typologies of 'policy styles,' those who look for the distinctive characteristics of national policy processes adopt the working hypothesis that those characteristics are common within a given nation across policy arenas. The distinctive national process may, however, be more or less successful in resolving conflict and responding to policy challenges in different policy arenas. Each author investigated a number of different policy arenas, differing in the extent to which they entailed distributional, symbolic, and structural policy outputs. I shall return to the application of this framework to the Canadian case below.

Methodological Implications

The methodology for investigating relationships suggested by the framework presented here depends upon which types of relationships are under investigation. Broad patterns of relationship between economic factors, certain types of interest configuration, and certain institutional characteristics, on the one hand, and the distributional dimension of policy on the other, lend themselves to investigation across a wide range of nations using quantitative techniques. Economic variables, relating as they do to aggregations of discrete units of exchange, lend themselves to quantitative measurement. There have also been a number of attempts to express the structure of interest organization – and particularly the structure of business and labour – in quantitative terms for purposes of comparison. David Cameron and others, for example, have developed measures of labour unity and power.[24] Working at the intersection of interests and state institutions, various scholars have developed scales of 'corporatism' to express the degree of cohesion of business and labour interests and their integration into the policy-making process.[25] There are various ways of expressing gross institutional characteristics in quantitative terms for purposes of comparative analysis. The degree of centralization/decentralization, for example, can be measured in terms of the proportion of all government revenues accruing to the central level. Institutional characteristics such as federalism or parliamentary government can be expressed as dummy variables. As for the distributional aspects of policy, measures of public expenditure in various categories are fairly readily accessible through national accounts, and in many cases are standardized through the OECD.

To the extent that investigators are interested in capturing more finely nuanced characteristics of economic organization, ideas, interests, and institutions, or the symbolic or structural dimensions of policy outputs, or especially the joint effects of a variety of factors as they intersect in the policy process, they will be drawn to methods that allow for the development of close familiarity with particular systems. The measurement of ideational variables, in particular, for the purposes of comparative analysis is much more problematic than is the case for economic variables. The electoral strength of parties of varying ideological stripes is sometimes taken as a proxy for the strength of various ideas; but as I have argued, parties are best considered as vehicles of intersection between ideas, interests, and institutions within the policy process itself. Understanding the role of ideas requires a qualitative and interpretive methodology and a close familiarity with the subject – requirements that militate against a broad cross-national sweep. Much the same is true of an appreciation of the symbolic dimensions of policy. Similarly, those concerned with institutional structures and structural policy dimensions generally wish to capture a level of detail that requires the analysis to be limited to a small set of nations.

Students of Canadian public policy are beginning to be represented among those who undertake such closely focused comparative work. The following section reviews several such contributions; the next deals at some length with my own analysis of Canadian public policy within the framework presented here.

Applictions to the Canadian Case

Canada as One of a Small Set of Nations to be Compared

Closely focused studies of Canadian public policy in comparative context fall into two categories: those in which Canada is included in a small set of cases to be compared; and those that focus on the Canadian case against a comparative background. In the first category are studies by Leman (1977), Thomas (1988), Bruce (1989), Pierson and Weaver (1993), Banting (1992), Perl (1993), and Teghtsoonian (1993), among others.

Several examples of the inclusion of Canada in comparative studies of a small set of nations have been generated by the contemporaneous occurrence of conservative governments in Canada, the United States, and the United Kingdom in the 1980s.[26] Pierson and Weaver, for example, have found that the extent to which the Mulroney and Thatcher governments and the Reagan administration were successful in achieving their respective objectives for reform in public pensions was mediated by institutional differences. The parliamentary systems of Canada and Britain provided the concentrated authority necessary for governments to realize their objectives, in contrast to the congressional system in the United States. But institutional differences alone were not sufficient to explain cross-national differences in outcomes. Parliamentary systems concentrate not only authority but accountability; and the willingness of the Thatcher and Mulroney governments to impose losses upon various groups under those circumstances differed markedly. Understanding this difference in turn takes us into the ideological bases of the respective governments.

Other examples of the inclusion of Canada in comparative studies with one or more other nations derive from the fortuitous (from a research perspective) 'natural experiments' that have occurred as Canadian and American public policies diverged from a common base in arenas such as health care and labour relations, over the period from the 1960s through the 1990s. In the 1960s the configuration of interests in the health-care arena was very similar in Canada and the United States. Nonetheless, comprehensive national health insurance was introduced in Canada, and a much more circum-scribed version limited to the elderly and the poor was introduced in the United States. As a result, the two policy arenas subsequently evolved in quite different ways. From the perspective of the comparative study of pub-lic policy, these developments have two important implications. In the first place, the developments of the 1960s mean that we have to look primarily outside the health-care arena itself to the broader policy processes of the two nations if we are to understand the differences in policy outputs.[27] Sec-ond, the differences in the subsequent evolution of the two policy arenas draws our attention to the feedback of policy on economic factors, ideas, interests, and institutions.

National health insurance in Canada increased the role of state institu-tions in the health-care arena while reinforcing existing structures of health-care delivery with their associated economic relationships and configura-tions of interest, and became a defining element of the Canadian public mythology. In the United States, in the absence of national health insurance, market forces have led to the domination of the health-care arena by large corporate interests without parallel in Canada. In turn, these evolving differ-ences in the Canadian and American arenas have meant that the repertoire of feasible policy instruments has come to differ as well.[28]

In the labour relations arena, we also observe a pattern of divergence be-tween Canada and the United States from a roughly similar base in the 1960s. At that time, unionization rates and the structure and mix of labour organi-zations were similar in the two countries – as was the model of labour legis-lation, which in Canada had been influenced strongly by postwar develop-ments in the United States. Subsequently, however, labour was able to con-solidate and in some cases extend its legislative gains in Canada, while in the United States these gains were progressively eroded. Again, an under-standing of these developments takes us to differences in the broader policy processes of the two nations, and particularly the role of social democratic parties in Canada.[29] Furthermore, these developments also demonstrate the feedback of policy outputs on economic factors, ideas, interests, and institu-tions. Within the reinforced legislative framework in Canada, organized la-bour was able to maintain its economic and political power to an extent much greater than that in the United States, where unionization rates precipitously declined from the 1960s to the 1990s. This survival positioned organized labour in Canada to play a role in the evolution of tripartite and bipartite institutions that was not possible for its counterpart in the United States.[30]

Canada against a Comparative Field

The above examples illustrate the gains to be made in the understanding of public policy in Canada and more generally by pursuing research questions that arise in a comparison of Canada with one or more nations in a way that allows for the tracing out of intersecting variables and feedback loops. A second approach to the study of Canadian public policy in comparative perspective, as noted, is to retain a primary focus on Canada while ensuring that research questions are framed in a broader comparative context. This is essentially the way in which Keith Banting approaches the study of Canadian income maintenance policy, and Atkinson and Coleman approach the study of Canadian industrial policy.[31] The work of these scholars can be interpreted within the organizing framework presented in this chapter. They begin by asking how Canadian public policy outputs have resembled or differed from those in other industrialized nations, in response to roughly similar challenges of advanced capitalism. They trace their explanations back to the way in which relevant economic factors, ideas, the organization of interests and institutions, and the intersection of those interests in the policy process compare between Canada and other nations.

Atkinson and Coleman, for example, locate Canada among a group of nations whose industrial policies tend to be 'reactive' rather than 'anticipatory.' They find the explanation for the particular Canadian version of reactive industrial policy in the intersection between a 'firm-centred' industrial culture derived from an economic history linking Canada to Britain and the United States, a fragmented structure of business and labour interests derived from a branch-plant and regionally based economy, and a 'weak state' ideological tradition reinforced by the institutions of federalism. Each of these factors can be fully understood only in relief, against comparisons with nations having more sectorally or nationally oriented industrial cultures, more cohesively organized business and labour interests, and with 'strong state' traditions, as in Europe and Japan.

In my own work, in a book in the series on 'Policy and Politics in Industrial States' cited above, I have extended this approach to develop an argument about the distinctive features of the Canadian public policy process across policy arenas.[32] The next section of this chapter outlines that argument.

The Distinctiveness of the Canadian Policy Process

To understand the Canadian policy process, it is necessary to understand that a fundamental ambivalence about the role of the state versus the role of the market, about the level of primary identification with the political community (national versus regional), and about the rights and responsibilities of the individual versus those of the collectivity has been incorporated into the institutions of the Canadian state. In comparative context, the degree and nature of this ambivalence is thrown into relief:

Canada is not, of course, the only industrial nation whose policy processes are characterized by ambivalence ... But in different ways in each of these cases, as in Britain, France, the United States, Australia, and other nations with which Canada might be compared, the questions of the boundaries of the state, its relative degree of centralization or decentralization, and its role in the protection and advancement of individual or collective rights are matters either of consensus or of fairly consistent polarization. In Canada these questions are addressed virtually *de novo* with new policy issues ... More importantly, Canadian ambivalence is *institutionalized:* It is 'built in' to the structures of the state.[33]

What we see in Canada, then, is 'institutionalized ambivalence.' The institutional system legitimizes competing principles. It combines a written and an unwritten constitution, and the principle of parliamentary supremacy with a constitutional charter of rights. Its federal system is one of the most fiscally decentralized among industrialized nations, in terms of the proportion of tax revenue accruing to the federal government; but it embodies a court-sanctioned federal 'spending power' that allows the federal government to spend, and to attach conditions to its spending, in areas of exclusive provincial jurisdiction. Institutional relationships, particularly those between national and provincial governments, but also those between legislatures and courts, are defined sufficiently ambiguously that ad hoc accommodations can be reached among competing interests as issues arise, without an agreement ever being reached on underlying principles.

This is an argument that privileges the explanatory role of institutional factors. But it sees institutions as responding over time to fundamental tensions arising from the interplay of ideas, economic relations, and interests in a process of historical evolution. The roots of ambivalence that Canadian institutions embody are threefold: the relationship with the United States, the relations between francophones and anglophones, and the relationship between regions of the country.

From the perspective of comparative public policy, the relationship with the United States must be seen as the defining feature of the Canadian economy. Canadians, then, find themselves both bound to and threatened by an international superpower, the largest Western industrial economy and the primary exemplar of an ideology of individualism, limited government, and reliance on the market. This relationship underlies Canadian ambivalence about the appropriate roles of the public and private sectors, and about 'individualist' and 'collectivist' ideological strains. This ambivalence about the role of the state is, moreover, compounded by ambivalence about the political community itself – an ambivalence that has its historical roots in the relations between anglophones and francophones and in the regionalized nature of the Canadian economy and society.

The legacy of the British 'Conquest' of New France in the mid-eighteenth century is one of deep ambivalence for Canadians, francophone and anglophone, inside and outside Quebec. On the one hand, the Conquest and subsequent British policies of tolerance and cooperation with French-Canadian elites shaped Quebec's distinctiveness within Canada, and Canada's distinctiveness vis-à-vis the United States. On the other hand, the search for a mutually agreeable way to accommodate the 'French fact' within Canada is an ongoing source of tension and conflict. Christian Dufour has summarized French-Canadian ambivalence as follows: 'English is a deeply ambivalent and perturbing element of the Quebec identity: at the same time both friend and foe, a part of ourselves that makes us stronger and the conqueror that wants our blood.'[34] Charles Taylor describes the anglophone counterpart to this ambivalence: 'The French component of the Canadian identity is both cornerstone and potentially loose foundation, a source of fission and rupture.'[35]

This ambivalence distinguishes Canada from more polarized, ethnically divided nations such as Belgium or more accommodative ones such as Switzerland. And it underlies the tension between individualist and collectivist, and regional and national orientations that characterize Canadian attitudes to conceptions of right and views of the political community. Collectivist and regional orientations are stronger in Quebec than elsewhere in Canada, but tensions exist across the country. The increasingly multicultural and multiracial nature of Canadian society further fuels these tensions.

The legacy of anglophone-francophone relations is related to a third source of ambivalence: the regionalized nature of the Canadian economy and society. Canadian regionalism arises from superimposed economic, linguistic, cultural, and governmental cleavages within defined geographic areas. The structure of regional economies varies markedly; and regional economic disparity, measured in terms of inequalities in the distribution of average personal after-tax income across regions, is substantial relative to most other Western industrial nations.[36] The concentration of francophones in Quebec and differential patterns of immigration in other parts of the country have,

together with economic differences, given rise to regional identities and loy-
alties that compete with attachments to the nation as a whole. As is the case
in most industrialized states, these regional differences are reflected in voting patterns. But to a greater extent than is the case in other federal systems,
Canadian voters are likely to 'split their votes,' to support different parties
at federal and provincial levels of government.[37]

An understanding of this institutionalized ambivalence, deriving from
fundamental economic and social tensions with long historical roots, is an
important key to understanding Canadian public policy. But it is not a description of the policy process itself. To understand that process, we need to
look to the intersection of Canada's ambivalent institutions with the structure of interests in given policy arenas. Historically, the policy process has
been one of accommodation among elites, in which mediating interests have
played a critical role:

Traditionally, the Canadian political system has dealt with divergent principles
and interests by institutionalizing them – particularly in its federal system, but
also in the relationship between the legislatures and the courts. It has provided
contending elites with institutional footholds, within a structure ambiguous
enough to allow them room to manoeuvre in reaching mutual accommodations.
The ability of such a system to resolve conflict and to facilitate coherent policy
development depends, however, on the structure of the interests represented by
elites. More specifically, it requires that there be some form of *mediating* interest.
What we must look for in attempting to understand the Canadian policy process
are the *opportunities for mediation that are provided by institutional ambiguity
and the candidates for the mediator's role.*
The elite groups most likely to play mediating roles are those whose own
internal ambivalence renders them open to compromise. That ambivalence may in
turn derive from the group's particularly cross-pressured position within the field
of interests, or from the fact that it aggregates a number of divergent interests. The
possibility of agreement is also enhanced where the range of interests that must be
comprehended is relatively narrow. Different policy arenas, then, vary considerably in their capacity to produce mediators, and in the magnitude of the mediator's
task.[38]

For those who have attempted to identify the distinctive characteristics of
policy processes in comparative terms, an important question is whether it is
possible to identify a process that is common across policy arenas within a
given nation, or whether the process varies with each policy arena. The Ca-

nadian case occupies a middle ground in this respect. The general rule – look for institutional ambiguity and mediating interests – is common across policy arenas in Canada. But the structure of interests and the potential for conflict resolution differs dramatically across arenas. This places the Canadian case intermediate between the case of some European nations and Japan on the one hand and the United States on the other. In the former group, some scholars have found it possible to identify a form of intersection between institutions and interests that is fairly common across policy arenas.[39] In the United States, on the other hand, an exceptional degree of fragmentation in the institutions of the state and in the organization of societal interests allows for the emergence of different types of politics within different policy arenas.[40]

In *Policy and Politics in Canada: Institutionalized Ambivalence,* I have traced out the policy process in a number of policy arenas, with regard to policies involving different degrees of distributional, symbolic and structural implications. Three examples will serve to illustrate the argument: health care, economic adjustment and labour market policy, and constitutional policy.

Health-Care Policy

Despite periodic media reports of crisis, Canadian health-care policy is generally viewed in comparative perspective as a success story. In distributional terms, it provides universal, comprehensive first-dollar coverage of medical and hospital services. Although the proportion of total health-care spending in Canada that comes from public sources (about three-quarters) lies close to the OECD average, the structure of the Canadian health-care financing system is unusual in that the public and private sectors are segmented from, not parallel to, each other. In other words, the vast bulk of medical and hospital services are financed entirely out of public funds – there are no private alternatives. The private sector comprises expenditures on drugs outside hospitals, dental services, eyeglasses and other prostheses, and amenities such as private rooms in hospital. For almost all medical and hospital services, then, Canadians in all income categories face no out-of-pocket costs. In terms of total health-care expenditures (public and private), Canada ranks with a group of European nations (including Germany, Austria, Sweden, and France) in which health spending accounts for between about 8 and 10 per cent of GDP. This contrasts on the one hand with the case in Britain, in which total health care expenditures amount to just over 7 per cent of GDP, and on the other hand with the United States, whose largely private health-

care system is also very expensive, with total health-care spending account-
ing for almost 14 per cent of GDP.

In symbolic terms, Canadian medicare has become, as noted above, virtually a defining element of Canadian public mythology. Polls have consistently demonstrated that medicare is by far the most popular public program
in Canada, and cross-national polls reveal that Canadians are more satisfied
with their health-care system than are citizens of other nations.[41] This level
of public support exists not only because of the tangible benefits that medicare yields, though that is clearly an important factor; it exists also because
medicare is a central part of Canadian public mythology. It has become an
important element by which Canadians distinguish themselves from other
nations, and particularly from the United States. During the heated and
wrenching public debate over the free trade agreement with the United States
in 1988, politicians opposing the agreement (including the then leader of the
federal Liberal Party) repeatedly invoked medicare as one of the things that
distinguished Canada from the United States, and alleged that it was threatened by the agreement. Public opinion polls showed that this allegation was
the most effective way of galvanizing opposition to the FTA.[42]

Structurally, Canadian medicare has maintained the medical profession's
position of influence to a greater extent than has been the case in either the
United States or Britain, the two nations to which Canadian physicians most
commonly look for comparison. The introduction of Canadian medicare essentially froze in place the system of health-care delivery that existed in the
1960s and underwrote its costs. In Britain, in contrast, the introduction of
the National Health Service in the 1940s was accompanied by wholesale
reorganization. And in the United States, the absence of national health insurance has led to a vicious cycle of regulation and corporate strategic behaviour.

Medical groups in Canada are aware of the different trade-offs that underlie these different systems. Even in briefs critical of government policy,
they typically present the Canadian system as one of the best in the world,
while expressing some concerns about its future.[43] The twin spectres of the
U.S. system (intrusive regulation, corporate dominance, inadequate coverage) and the British system (inadequate resources, excessive rationing) are
frequently evoked. Attitude surveys of physicians find large majorities on
balance satisfied with their conditions of practice and positively oriented
toward medicare – although sizeable pockets of discontent remain.[44] A comparative survey of physicians in Canada, the United States, and western
Germany in 1991 found that although a majority of physicians in each country believed that some fundamental changes in their health systems were

necessary, satisfaction with the health system was higher among Canadian and German physicians than among American physicians. When respondents were asked to identify the most serious problems with their system, the sharpest differences arose between Canadian and American physicians, whose judgments of their respective systems appeared virtually as mirror images of each other. Canadian physicians were more likely to complain of limitations on the supply of well-equipped medical facilities. American physicians, on the other hand, were more likely to identify delays or disputes in processing insurance forms and in receiving payment, the inability of patients to afford some aspect of necessary medical care, external review of clinical decisions for the purpose of controlling health costs, and limitations on the length of hospital stays as serious problems with their system.[45]

In these medical attitudes lies one of the keys to understanding the policy process in the Canadian health policy arena. They underlie the accommodations between the medical profession and the state in various provinces that are at the heart of Canadian medicare. Torn between the threats to clinical autonomy posed by the state and the market, medical associations have both explicitly and implicitly mediated conflicts within the health-care arena, including conflicts within their own memberships, between those who advocate market-based and state-based approaches. Within the resulting system of 'private practice/public payment,'[46] the economic discretion of physicians is limited while their clinical autonomy is preserved within broad resource constraints.

This pattern of provincial-level accommodation was possible in health care for essentially two reasons – one relating to the institutional structure and the other to the structure of interests. Health care is a matter of exclusive provincial jurisdiction. Notwithstanding the federal government's use of its spending power in the arena to establish the broad parameters of medicare, the provinces retained the authority to develop programs within those parameters. Furthermore, interregional spillovers in the health-care arena are relatively small, compared to a number of other policy arenas: health-care providers and consumers in one province were not likely to be greatly helped or harmed by what was done for providers and consumers in another.

Economic Adjustment Policy

The health-care arena has been spared the degree of interregional conflict that has debilitated the Canadian policy process in some other arenas. Where interregional conflicts must be resolved, cross-provincial mechanisms are required. Lines of cleavage are more complex, the role of the mediator is more difficult, and the candidates for the mediator's role are fewer. The arena of economic adjustment policy provides a case in point. In that arena, the chasm between business's concern to protect the autonomy of the individual firm and labour's insistence on full-employment strategies has been cross-cut by regional fissures and governmental jurisdictional rivalries. Neither business nor labour has the degree of cohesive national organization required to mediate these conflicts. As a result, policy has been determined largely through intra- and intergovernmental contests, marked not only by turf battles for jurisdiction but by disputes about the appropriate role of the state itself. The distributional dimension of economic adjustment policy, that is, has often been overtaken by structural and symbolic concerns.

Federal political parties have attempted to negotiate this rocky terrain as mediators, but they found only the narrowest of common ground: a focus on the protection of those most disadvantaged by economic forces – the poorest regions and failing or marginally competitive firms. This focus has satisfied no one and has been the subject of ongoing criticism from business, labour, and governments themselves. There have been limited experiments with structural changes drawing business and labour into tripartite or bipartite boards and agencies, particularly with regard to labour market policy, but these bodies remain embryonic and very vulnerable to shifts in business, labour, or government agendas.[47] In general, despite periodic reorganizations of institutions and programs, and despite the rhetoric of increasing competitiveness and flexibility, there has been little fundamental change in policy.

The one major policy initiative in the arena of economic adjustment in the 1980s – the signing of the free trade agreement with the United States – was decided outside the regular channels of elite accommodation, through an extraordinary appeal to the mass public in the 'referendum' of the 1988 federal election. Even so, this appeal yielded a 'resounding maybe,'[48] as the electorate returned the party supporting free trade, the Conservatives, with a majority of seats in the House of Commons but cast the majority of votes for the two parties opposing the agreement, the Liberals and the NDP.

In comparative perspective, Canada can be seen not to be alone in lacking consensus on the appropriate balance of state and market forces in the economic adjustment arena. In Britain, for example, this balance has been highly contested.[49] Nor is it alone in the significance of regional considerations in this arena in both federal and unitary states.[50] What is most striking about the Canadian case in comparative perspective is rather a unique *conjunction* of factors: a fundamental lack of consensus regarding the role of the state, regional disparities and sensitivities, strong regional (provincial) governments, and the lack of a mechanism to mediate interregional disputes.

Perhaps the most instructive comparison is with Germany, where the intersection of institutions and interests has yielded a process more capable of conflict resolution. As in the Canadian case, regional concerns have played a significant role in German economic adjustment policy. In the former West Germany, the regionally concentrated industries of coalmining and steel presented significant challenges of economic adjustment in the 1960s, 1970s, and 1980s.[51] Land governments, though less powerfully endowed with policy instruments than Canadian provincial governments, participated actively in the development and implementation of industrial strategies of response. But there the parallels with Canada cease.

As Katzenstein has argued, the operation of Germany's 'decentralized state' is facilitated by its 'centralized society' – its complex networks of organized industrial, financial, and labour interests – and by institutional features of the state-society relationship.[52] Notable among these features are a centripetal party politics, flexible federal arrangements, and a range of parapublic institutions bringing major interests (particularly business and labour) together in administrative arms of the state. Canada shares only one of these characteristics – constitutional flexibility. In contrast to Germany's multilayered institutional linkages, moreover, the exploitation of Canada's constitutional flexibility depends heavily upon relations among political executives. Nor in Canada does partisanship provide a strong basis upon which interregional alliances can be struck. In contrast with Germany's more integrated and centralized system, the Canadian party system is sharply divided between federal and provincial levels.

Constitutional Policy

The conflict-resolution potential of the Canadian policy process, with its reliance upon institutional ambiguity, elite accommodation, and mediating interests, then, varies across policy arenas. It is, moreover, a process that has been under unprecedented strain in the 1980s and 1990s. In part, this strain has been the result of the massive policy challenges presented by economic globalization and shifts in domestic demography, with attendant changes in the configuration of interests. In part, however, it has also been the result of a decline in the legitimacy of the process itself. In turn, that decline in legitimacy can be attributed in part to the mixed success of the policy process in responding to the policy challenges of the 1980s and 1990s. But it has also, in a sense, been self-inflicted – inflicted, that is, by the political executives who have been such key actors in the process of elite accommodation. By embracing the project of constitutional reform on a number of occasions over the period from the 1960s to the 1990s, these elites have threatened the 'institutionalized ambivalence' that has enabled the process to function in the face of a lack of agreement on underlying principles.

The arena of constitutional politics in Canada is more fraught with interregional conflicts than any other. And the stakes are high: the significant structural content of constitutional policy means that gains made in this regard will place the winners in positions to influence subsequent policies. Furthermore, as the basic law of the land the constitution is high in symbolic value, and constitutional policy hence generates a highly charged and volatile form of politics.

For most of its history, Canada lived with a constitutional system that was the quintessence of institutionalized ambivalence, with its unwritten and written components, its capacity to be interpreted to yield concepts such as the federal 'spending power,' and the lack of a specified domestic process for agreeing upon amendments, leaving the formal power to amend with the British Parliament. However unsatisfactory in terms of legal sovereignty, the constitution did prove itself admirably flexible. Nonetheless, the quest for 'patriation' of the constitution periodically gained momentum. During the 1960s, in the wake of the 'Quiet Revolution' and the attendant 'constitutional radicalization' of Quebec,[53] that momentum accelerated. Patriation had to involve an amending formula; and it thereby 'opened up' the constitution for other reforms. Accordingly, it attracted a number of agendas, dominant among which were those of contending federalist and nationalist elites in Quebec. And in this process it was the federalist Quebec elite, and particularly those of its members who sought political careers in Ottawa, that held the potential to play the key mediating role.

The policy process through which constitutional reform was pursued was, in fact, typically Canadian in its reliance on elite accommodation: it was conducted almost exclusively through negotiations between federal and provincial political executives – through the structures of 'executive federalism.' It also sought to maintain the Canadian hallmark: the incorporation of competing principles through provisions that would need to be interpreted in specific circumstances over time. It resulted, in 1982, in the patriation of the constitution through the adoption of an amending formula, and in the entrenchment of a constitutional Charter of Rights and Freedoms. The Charter itself, however, balanced constitutional entrenchment of rights against the unwritten principle of parliamentary supremacy that Canada had inherited from Britain.[54] In its first section the Charter provides that the rights and freedoms therein shall be subject to 'such reasonable limits prescribed by law as shall be demonstrably justified in a free and democratic society.'

The 1982 constitution was, however, adopted over the objections of the Parti Québécois government of Quebec. Attempts to secure passage of a set of reforms acceptable to the successor Liberal governments in Quebec came to naught. Any such reforms had to address explicitly the place of Quebec within Canadian federalism – whether it was to be a province like the others or whether it was to have special status; whether, in other words, Canadian federalism was to be symmetrical or asymmetrical. The written constitution and its interpretation, as well as practice in federal-provincial programs over the years, contain elements of each of these principles.[55] Attempting to make these provisions more explicit in constitutional form could only exacerbate the conflicts that institutional ambiguity had muted.

The first attempt after 1982 to 'bring Quebec in' to the constitution, the Meech Lake Accord, was squarely in the tradition of the Canadian policy process: it was drawn up through a closed process of negotiation between federal and provincial executives; and its phrasing, in particular its recognition of Quebec as a 'distinct society' within Canada, was a masterpiece of artful ambiguity. It nonetheless fell victim, under the constitutional amendment process adopted in 1982, to a fatal delay in which the initial fragile elite consensus unravelled and public opposition built. In the process, the pattern of elite accommodation that had led to the accord was itself increasingly called into question. In 1992, two years after the expiry of the Meech Lake attempt, the federal and provincial heads of government reached another agreement, the Charlottetown Agreement. This time, however, in recognition of the declining legitimacy of closed executive processes, they sought legitimacy for the agreement by submitting it to a national referendum.

The referendum proved to be a strategic error. The Charlottetown Agreement was not endorsed. It had attracted a wider range of agendas than had the Meech Lake Accord (including the agendas of groups who believed that they had been excluded from the process and substance of Meech Lake). If, therefore, the Charlottetown Agreement contained 'something for everyone,' it also contained something for everyone to oppose. A broad national referendum debate, conducted in an atmosphere charged with high symbolic import, was not the forum in which to seek endorsement of the careful trade-offs and ambiguities of the Charlottetown Agreement. It is not, indeed, contemplated in the amendment process set out in the 1982 constitution, which places ratification in the hands of legislatures. The decision to go to a referendum was a political judgment, and a telling marker of the extent to which political executives believed that the classic Canadian policy process of elite accommodation had lost its legitimacy, at least in the arena of constitutional policy.

Challenge and Change

Is the Canadian policy process indeed undergoing a metamorphosis? In the early 1990s the strengthening – especially in the form of the rise of the Reform Party – of the populist strain that is never far beneath the surface of Canadian politics gave further credence to the view that the legitimacy of processes of elite accommodation was in question. So far, however, the challenge to the legitimacy of processes of elite accommodation has been strongest in the arena of constitutional politics. The extent to which it will spill over into other arenas is not clear. A comparative perspective on the durability of policy processes may help to address this question.

Much more comparative work needs to be done in understanding the dynamics of change in national policy processes over time. As it is, there are a few cases in which there has been a frontal challenge to the essential features of a national policy-making process. The case of Britain in the Thatcher era stands out. Margaret Thatcher brought to government an ideological and exclusionary style that contrasted sharply with the established process of adversarial negotiation.[56] The Thatcher challenge was given strength by the perceived dysfunctionality of the established process. Studies of the British policy process in the 1970s attributed Britain's economic status as the 'sick man of Europe' to the fact that the negotiation process had bogged down. 'Institutional sclerosis'[57] and 'pluralistic stagnation'[58] were terms used to describe the British disease. The degree to which the Thatcher era brought about a permanent change in the policy process remains as yet unclear, however. At the beginning of the Thatcher era, Jordan and Richardson argued that the policy process was proving resistant to change, in part because of its very pragmatism. By the mid-1980s, Anthony King saw a more marked shift, without judging whether it would be permanent. And by the end of the Thatcher era, Marsh and Rhodes distinguished between the policy-making and implementation phases of the policy process, and argued that the impact of Thatcherism had been much greater on the former than on the latter – that the process of negotiation and the influence of various interests was simply shifted to a different point in the policy process.[59] This may bear out Jordan and Richardson's point that the 'logic of negotiation [in the British context] is difficult to escape.'[60]

A similar point might apply in the Canadian case. There is a 'logic,' in a nation in which agreement on fundamental principles cannot be reached, to a policy process in which political actors have room to manoeuvre, to reach accommodations as issues arise within an ambiguously defined framework. It is a process that depends upon the development of relationships over time, and on myriad interrelated trade-offs. It is a process, then, that depends heavily upon the relationship among political executives and the leadership of affected interests, who must be granted considerable latitude by their supporters. It is, in that sense, an 'elite' process. Current challenges may open the Canadian policy process to a wider range of 'elite' groups. They will also make informal accommodations among elites more difficult to achieve and to maintain. But the policy process has evolved in response to enduring facts of Canadian political life, and it continues to be replicated across a range of policy arenas, from health care to labour market policy. The logic of Canadian-style elite accommodation may also prove 'difficult to escape.'

Summary

Political scientists make *arguments* to enhance the understanding of political phenomena. We make interdependent choices about the kinds of phenomena we want to explain, the kinds of argument we want to make, and the kinds of data we can compile. Some kinds of argument imply a reliance on quantitative analysis of large samples for support. Other kinds of argument depend on tracing out the logic that underlies phenomena observed through closer examination of a limited number of cases.

This chapter has presented a case for closely focused work in comparative public policy. Within an organizing framework that identifies key categories of variables and emphasizes the intersections among them, it has used the case of Canada to demonstrate the potential of a country-specific focus within a comparative field. It has argued that distinctive characteristics of the Canadian policy process – a process of ad hoc accommodation among elites within an ambiguous institutional framework, which relies heavily upon the role of mediating interests – can be identified and understood using this approach. It has also identified part of the agenda for future work – in particular with regard to the conditions under which the distinctive characteristics of national policy processes may undergo a fundamental change.

Such an approach must sacrifice scientific rigour in the interest of deeper exploration of the national case: it does not allow for the testing of hypotheses through the consistent measurement and control of variables across a wide range of cases. But it should not sacrifice *discipline*. The framework presented in this chapter is a general one, but it reflects a growing consistency in the types of variables and intersections of variables that are considered in the comparative study of public policy. To the extent that arguments about the effects of variables in specific countries give attention to these variables, and are developed always with an eye to relevant cross-national comparisons, the literature of comparative public policy and the understanding of specific cases will be enriched.

Notes

1 This 'idiographic' approach to studies of Canadian public policy developed despite the existence of landmark comparative studies of government in Canadian political science, notably Corry and Hodgett's *Democratic Government and Politics*. These comparative studies of government did not, however, extend to the policy process or its outcomes.
2 One notable exception is the work of Julia O'Connor. See, for example, 'Convergence or Divergence.'
3 See O'Connor, *The Fiscal Crisis of the State.*
4 See Wilensky, *The Welfare State and Equality*; Dye, 'Politics vs. Economics.'
5 See Castles and McKinlay, 'Does Politics Matter.'
6 Cameron, 'The Expansion of the Public Economy.'
7 King, 'Ideas, Institutions and the Policies of Governments.'
8 Manzer, *Public Policies and Political Development in Canada.*
9 See Peters et al., 'Types of Democratic Systems.'
10 Elkins and Simeon, 'A Cause in Search of its Effects, or What Does Political Culture Explain?'
11 Hall, *The Political Power of Economic Ideas.*
12 See Banting, *The Welfare State and Canadian Federalism*, and Atkinson, 'Introduction: Governing Canada.'
13 Les Pal has pointed out that feminist analysis shares with neo-Marxism an emphasis on the extent to which interests are structured around a single base of power – in this case patriarchy (Pal, *Public Policy Analysis: An Introduction*, 29).
14 See March and Olsen, 'The New Institutionalism.'
15 Hall, *Governing the Economy*, 18; see also Thelen and Steinmo.
16 See Hall, *Governing the Economy.*
17 See Weaver and Rockman, eds., *Do Institutions Matter? Government Capabilities in the United States and Abroad*, and Steinmo et al., *Structuring Politics: Historical Institutionalism in Comparative Perspective.*
18 Various scholars have wrestled with the appropriate terminology for this third dimension of policy – the terms 'constitutional' (Day and Klein, 'Constitutional and Distributional Conflict'), 'constituent' (Lowi, 'The State in Politics'), and 'positional' (Aucoin, 'Theory and Research') have variously been used.
19 See Tuohy, 'Medicine and the State in Canada.'

20 See Banting, *The State and Economic Interests*, and Tuohy, 'Interests and Institutions in the Occupational Health Arena.'
21 'Introduction' to *Policy Communities and Public Policy in Canada.*
22 See Premfors, 'National Policy Styles and Higher Education in France, Sweden and the United Kingdom'; Richardson, ed., *Policy Styles in Western Europe*; Freeman, 'National Styles and Policy Sectors'; and Hoberg, 'Environmental Policy.'
23 Richardson, *Policy Styles in Western Europe*, 11; see also Olsen et al., 'Norway.'
24 Cameron, 'Social Democracy, Labour Quiescence, and the Representation of Economic Interests in Advanced Capitalist Society.'
25 See Lehmbruch, 'Concertation and the Structure of Corporatist Networks'; and Schmidt, 'The Welfare State and the Economy in Periods of Economic Crisis.'
26 See Thomas, 'Public Policy and the Resurgence of Conservatism in Three Anglo-American Democracies'; Pierson and Weaver, 'Imposing Losses in Pension Policy'; and Teghtsoonian, 'Neo-Conservative Ideology and Opposition to Federal Regulation of Child Care Services in the United States and Canada.'
27 See Tuohy, 'The Clinton Proposal.'
28 See Tuohy, 'Health Policy and Fiscal Federalism.'
29 See Bruce, 'Political Parties.'
30 See Tuohy, *Policy and Politics in Canada: Institutionalized Ambivalence*, 159–210.
31 Banting, *The Welfare State and Canadian Federalism*; and Atkinson and Coleman, *The State, Business and Industrial Change in Canada.*
32 Tuohy, *Policy and Politics in Canada: Institutionalized Ambivalence.*
33 Ibid., 4–5.
34 Dufour, *A Canadian Challenge*, 97.
35 Taylor, 'A Free Independent Quebec in a Strong, United Canada,' 48.
36 See Jenkin, *The Challenge of Diversity.*
37 LeDuc, 'Partisan Change and Dealignment in Canada, Great Britain and the United States.'
38 Tuohy, *Policy and Politics in Canada*, 347–8.
39 See Richardson, *Policy Styles in Western Europe*; Pempel, *Policy and Politics in Japan*; Heclo and Madsen, *Policy and Politics in Sweden*; Katzenstein, *Policy and Politics in West Germany*; Muramatsu and Kraus, 'The Conservative Policy Line and the Development of Patterned Pluralism.'
40 See Heclo, 'Issue Networks and the Executive Establishment.'
41 Blendon, 'Three Systems.'

42 Johnston and Blais, 'A Resounding Maybe.'
43 Tuohy, *Policy and Politics in Canada*, 144–5.
44 Stevenson, Vayda, and Williams, 'Medical Politics after the Canada Health Act.'
45 Blendon et al., 'Physicians' Perspectives on Caring for Patients in the United States, Canada and West Germany,' 1015.
46 Naylor, *Private Practice, Public Payment.*
47 See Fournier, 'Consensus Building in Canada,' and Tuohy, 'Interests and Institutions in the Occupational Health Arena.'
48 Johnston and Blais, 'A Resounding Maybe.'
49 Grant and Wilks, 'British Industrial Policy.'
50 Blais, 'Industrial Policy in Advanced Capitalist Economies,' 28–31.
51 See Esser, Fach, and Dyson, '"Social Market" and Modernization Policy,' and Katzenstein, *Policy and Politics in West Germany*, 101–2.
52 Katzenstein, *Policy and Politics in West Germany: The Growth of a Semisovereign State.*
53 Russell, 'The Politics of Frustration,' 14–15.
54 This principle is 'written' in the sense that the Constitution Act, 1967, provides in its preamble for a 'constitution similar in principle to that of the United Kingdom.'
55 See Mallory, 'Confederation,' and Tuohy, *Policy and Politics in Canada*, 59–62.
56 See Jordan and Richardson, 'The British Policy Style or the Logic of Negotiation?' and King, 'Margaret Thatcher.'
57 Olson, *The Rise and Decline of Nations.*
58 Beer, 'British Pressure Groups Revisited.'
59 Marsh and Rhodes, *Implementing Thatcherite Policies: Audit of an Era.*
60 Jordan and Richardson, 'The British Policy Style or the Logic of Negotiation,' 108.

17

Comparing Canada and the United States: Why Comparisons?

MILDRED A. SCHWARTZ

Similarities between Canada and the United States in conditions arising from shared geography, a British heritage, democratic practices, and a multi-ethnic population often give rise to similar problems. This makes the two countries an attractive setting for comparing public policies because we can begin with an expectation that both face the same problems. When they respond, we have a basis for asking why particular policies were selected.[1] Each country gives a fixed point of comparison for the other, much like one sibling allows us to judge the growth and achievements of a second.[2] Just the proximity of Canada and the United States attracts comparison because of sheer visibility as well as the dominance of the United States.[3] Proximity creates relations between the two in areas of environment, security, and trade, which are then the subject of policies. The results of these features make Canada–U.S. policy comparisons a rich field of research.

Comparing Canada and the United States in preference to focusing on each country independently expands the possibilities for explanation. Even a sample of only two cases permits more convincing generalizations than are possible with a single case. Conversely, restricting comparison to two similar cases rather than attempting to work with larger samples of countries controls the amount of variation that will be found. Working with manageable numbers of both similarities and differences, Canada–U.S. comparisons allow the researcher to hone in on the particular factors that distinguish between them.

For all of these reasons, the field of Canada–U.S. comparative research continues to grow and to merit comment. In an earlier review of the field, I classified works according to their contributions to three lines of explanation, whether directed to differences in policies, to changing relations between the two countries, or to policy effects.[4] In this paper my focus once again is on major arguments or explanations for similarities and differences in policy choices and outcomes. Here I make an effort to fit these writings into a more inclusive theoretical context, with illustrations mainly from works published in the past ten years.

Structures and Institutions

The simplest argument that could be made in comparing Canadian and U.S. public policy is that similar conditions give rise to similar kinds of policies with similar kinds of outcomes. It is not, however, an argument easily found in the literature. I suspect that the reason is not because there are, in fact, no such existing commonalities, but that they are not sufficiently interesting to researchers.

The most common perspective begins with different policies or with differences in policy results and attributes them to differences in political structures, organizations, or institutions.[5] Existing structures constrain what and when new policy choices can be made, which alternatives are selected, and how they will be implemented. Organizations and institutions have histories that give them the power to limit policy alternatives. Those histories also shape the ways in which they themselves are able to change. In general, writers are in strong agreement that the one area that continues to set the two countries apart from each other is their political institutions. Their arguments can be summarized to say that differences in structures and institutions are sufficient to explain national differences in the content and impact of the policies themselves.

Institutionalist explanations are used, for example, to account for why different avenues were taken to constitutionally protect equal rights for women, with subsequent failure in the United States but success in Canada.[6] Among the factors enumerated are the procedures for constitutional amendment in the United States, the Canadian practice of governmental assistance in organizing interest groups, the ability to focus on the national level in Canada in relation to a small political elite, and the diffuseness of local forums of influence in the United States. Structural factors are also used to explain why policy making on acid rain has been easier in Canada than in the United States. Canada's advantages include responsible government, jurisdictional overlap, government control over key polluting industries, and the committee structure in the House of Commons. Related institutions in the United States all operate in ways that make agreement on policies more difficult.[7]

Each country's institutions are a continuing barrier against outside influences on policy by ensuring that past history and practices will influence the present. Once structures and institutions are in place, they acquire a taken-for-granted nature in the sense that their effects are not easily linked to the intentions of individual political actors. This is illustrated by the greater decline in mortality rates among native peoples in the United States compared to Canada.[8] The explanation turns out to be a temporally remote one, tied to 'the legacy of the greater impact of nineteenth-century urban reform on American than Canadian Indian policy,'[9] which resulted in setting up a system of health care on reservations whose consequences are still felt. The unanticipated effects from existing institutions may be surmised from how the United States and Canada approach issues of immigration and refugees. Although there are numerous structural factors that differentiate the ways in which immigration policy is made in the two countries, their larger geopolitical role probably explains more of the content of those policies. Canada's skills-based immigration policy is the result of greater scope for economic interests, reinforced by the role played by provinces and the discretionary power enjoyed by the minister responsible and his or her ministry. Actors can play their roles without regard to the same kind of foreign policy concerns that colour the behaviour of Congress and the president.[10]

But not everyone working within an institutional framework agrees that comparison results in finding differences. Attention can be drawn instead to the ways institutions, although initially different, adapt to changing circumstances in ways that makes them alike. In the organizational literature, this is conceptualized as institutional isomorphism.[11] Although this theoretical language is not used explicitly in comparing the two countries, it can be read into a variety of arguments about existing or impending similarities.

One illustration of how institutional isomorphism may be associated with change is implied in observations by William Alpert et al. about growing similarity in Canadian and U.S. tax harmonization policies.[12] In then asking whether the adoption of similar policies is the result of change in the larger country, leading to a parallel response in the smaller, they suggest a kind of coercive isomorphism, in which change in one organization (or larger entity) is the result of pressures from others on which it depends or from cultural expectations about the most appropriate way for organizations of that type to behave.[13] Alternatively, Alpert and associates ask whether change has its roots in 'common intellectual influences,' a possibility they are more inclined to accept. This too is a form of isomorphism, resulting from normative pressure to adopt uniform standards, like those needed to promote professional autonomy. The likelihood of such normative change is enhanced through specialized educational standards and network ties among practitioners.[14]

These two forms of isomorphic change are completed by a third – mimetic isomorphism resulting from imitation instigated by uncertainty. That is, in circumstances when information is confusing or where the outcome of particular choices is difficult to ascertain, there is a tendency to adopt prevailing practices.[15] There is considerable overlap among all three forms, including the likelihood that similar changes may either be produced deliberately or may arise from unconscious imitation. Despite this imprecision, or perhaps because of it, institutional isomorphism suggests rationales for finding that different institutions and different policies may still produce similar outcomes. For example, despite the different ways language policies are set in the two countries, similar tensions have still evolved between the central governments, as the protectors of minority rights, and provincial or state governments, as sources of restriction on those rights.[16]

Whatever the attractiveness of isomorphic arguments, these have not been particularly well received, however. Take the thesis that the new emphasis on constitutionally guaranteed rights in the 1982 Charter of Rights and Freedoms will lead to an Americanization of Canadian politics by the attention that the courts will now be forced to give to U.S. precedents used in interpreting the Bill of Rights. That thesis is rejected by Russell,[17] who sees the courts continuing to rely on English precedents in support of parliamentary supremacy. Even the new activism of the courts, prompted by the Charter, is unlikely to produce changes in the direction of the U.S. judicial model because of the unusual importance of federalism in Canada. Russell's argument appears to be buttressed by a recent collection of essays, which concludes that the political institutions and constitutional histories of the two countries are so different that they have little positive impact on each other.[18] Similarly, Howlett rejects the possibility of convergence on how the courts treat environmental policy on the grounds that constitutional and other institutional forms are too persistently different.[19]

In general, the new institutionalism downplays the role of agency in producing given outcomes. According to this perspective, not only do organizations and institutions continue because of their historical rootedness and taken-for-granted character, but even the processes through which they are maintained tend to be unquestioned. In the most extreme form of this argument, it is virtually impossible for actors to take deliberate actions that would more than marginally affect adaptation because the environments in which states and organizations operate are so complex and ever-changing. Although we do not find this latter argument among those who offer institutional ex-

350 Contemporary Approaches

planations for either similarities or differences in Canada–U.S. policies, it might just as well be there, given the low level of attention to the processes by which choices are made or policies implemented. Yet consideration of such processes, now recognized as necessary to flesh out gaps in institutional analysis in general,[20] is needed to incorporate the political nature of the policy world. The current tendency to explain Canadian and U.S. policies and their outcomes by structures and institutions may account for differences and similarities, but it does so with broad brush strokes and underevaluates the potential for change.

An approach to the role of agency consistent with expanded institutional explanations is one that focuses on issues of power and answers questions of how and by whom policy agendas are set, and how strategic choices are selected from among alternatives. For example, Hoberg's reconstruction of why the pesticide alachlor was banned in Canada but kept on the market in the United States considers how the same scientific information was differently evaluated.[21] In Canada, both within the larger environment and the bureaucratic one, there were contending interests with different stakes in the outcome, which the responsible minister had to weigh as competing costs and benefits to himself and his ministry. While the outcome could be described as an example of institutional constraints, the more detailed picture shows how those constraints unfold in a manner not entirely predictable from formal structures or institutional practices.

Most new policies begin with expectations that they will be clear instruments of change. In contrast, most institutionalists begin with expectations that change is slow and incremental, the result of adapting to environmental pressures. There is, then, a kind of paradox involved in institutional explanations of policy change that may be resolved through attention to processes and agencies of power. Some sense of the need for this approach is implied, though not spelled out, when dealing with health care, where there is currently a great deal of interest in whether the United States could adopt a Canadian-style program. At the same time as he advocates the single-payer (Canadian) approach, Bodenheimer points to the actions of specific interest groups in the United States that are using their resources to resist any policy change they perceive as costly to them.[22] Their ability to take these actions are one kind of institutional constraint on change. Will they be, however, the most important? Marmor, who has been among the strongest advocates of a single-payer policy, argues that political actors have the ability to make strategic choices that could adapt Canadian policy to the U.S. institutional milieu.[23]

Culture

Structural and institutional explanations of U.S. and Canadian policies have one rival to their pre-eminence in cultural explanations. Probably the strongest exponent of the cultural basis for differences between the United States and Canada is S.M. Lipset. By culture he means a set of fundamental value-orientations whose origins lie in the foundings of the two societies.

One was Whig and classically liberal and libertarian – doctrines that emphasize distrust of the state, egalitarianism, and populism – reinforced by a voluntaristic and congregational religious tradition. The other was Tory and conservative in the British and European sense – accepting of the need for a strong state, for respect for authority, for deference – and endorsed by hierarchically organized religions that supported and were supported by the state.[24]

These values became the basis of new institutions and organizations and were sustained through the socialization of new members, including immigrants from countries with quite different values. Even major social changes affecting the two countries have not obliterated the essential cultural differences between them.

Researchers in this cultural mode deal with the emergence of new issues in the context of prevailing cultural standards. For example, Haussman explains the inclusion of protection for women's rights in Canada's Charter to an underlying collectivist orientation, although her willingness to link the failure of the Equal Rights Amendment in the United States to a form of classical liberalism that 'traditionally has denied women the right to participate in the public sphere'[25] stretches the credibility of her argument. Cultural premises about collective rights are also raised in the case of why native peoples in the United States have a harder time implementing claims to autonomy despite the fact that they already possess formally guaranteed claims. Fleras and Elliott attribute the blockage to the American public's unwillingness to accept a concept of group rights.[26] In quite a different kind of example dealing with energy policy, Uslaner concludes that policy differences are essentially cultural in origin.[27] That is, conflict between federal and provincial governments over energy regulation reflects more deeply rooted and still unresolved struggles over the federal state and the weaker sense of Canadian national identity associated with it.

Cultural explanations are normally used to account for differences between the two countries' policies, and cultural sources of divergence are generally described as longstanding and stable. One exception to this trend is found in the work of Nevitte et al., who look at convergences in values in the direction of what has been called 'post-materialist.'[28] Value change is expressed in preferences for personal freedom and autonomy and a sense of belonging rather than material rewards. These changes are linked to policy with respect to support for free trade.

One appeal of the cultural perspective is that it can be used to give starting points to policies that reach beyond any particular set of structures or circumstances. For example, in the case of differences in labour laws, it is argued that their current content arises because 'laws do not fall from the sky; they reflect the prevailing norms and mores of the wider society.'[29] But there is something intrinsically unsatisfying about this approach; it sounds tautological, implying that something is because it is. It points out the dangers of seeking theoretical justification in an outmoded anthropology, where a uniform and consensual culture is tied to a homogeneous society, in which present-day cultural forms and practices, linked together in a compatible whole, are attributed to some immutable and unchanging past.

There is a place for cultural explanations of policy, but to become more useful they first need to be linked to a more explicit definition of culture appropriate to complex societies. That includes acknowledging the existence of cultural diversity and competition and of incompatibilities among cultural systems. It should be able to account not only for the persistence of cultural patterns and the ways these constrain policy innovations, but also for the avenues through which cultures change. One step in enlarging the utility of cultural analyses is to give primacy to issues of power in ways similar to what I suggested for institutional analyses. Orloff, in her basically structural analysis of pension policies in Canada and the United States (and Britain), does this by distinguishing ideologies around which groups can mobilize and from which elites can plan strategies and form coalitions.[30] Or, as I wrote in my earlier review of comparative policy, 'arguments based on the importance of ideas or ideology for directing policy choices need more explicit evidence of the ties between beliefs and the actions of policy elites.'[31]

Conclusions

To sum up this brief overview of Canada–U.S. policy comparisons, I see the major trends in explaining policy content or impact to have either a structural/institutional or a cultural focus. In either case, the emphasis is mainly on differences between the two countries. My reaction to both approaches is to advocate greater attention to agency in order to reintroduce power into the policy realm.

If my review of cultural explanations appears truncated by my effort to classify most studies within the structural or institutional framework, this is not accidental. I even gloss over the fact that a number of the studies included in the institutional camp also use cultural explanations. I do this because I do not see the sharp dichotomy between social structure and culture that is implied by some writers.[32] Cultures create organizations and institutions, just as organizations and institutions create cultures. Culture provides frameworks of meaning for social organizations, and institutions are sources of meaning for social actors. All are by definition highly stable, yet they all change, often slowly, but also at times with revolutionary speed.[33]

For the student of policy, it is important to recognize 'that most types of organizations confront multiple sources and types of symbolic or cultural systems and they exercise some choice in selecting the systems with which to connect.'[34] To take this admonition seriously, those who compare Canada with the United States will need to do more than describe the content or outcome of policies and then attribute a causal source in either structure or culture. They need to work within a more explicitly theoretical framework that lets them empirically test connections. That theory (or theories) will require a more complex conception of structures, institutions, and culture that differentiates among elements, depending on whether they are relatively fixed or undergoing change. For the purposes of policy analysis, those concepts need to be politicized in the sense of capturing the identity of those with the power to bring about or impede change and the situations when power is most usable.

Over the past thirty years, comparative studies of U.S. and Canadian public policy have continued to increase. They provide a vigorous milieu for research because they tell us so much about ourselves, whether those selves are Canadians or not. The opportunities ahead in the next thirty years should be even greater, and they deserve to be grasped with even more theoretical venturesomeness.

Notes

1 Card and Freeman, 'Introduction,' 2, describe this potential for comparison as a 'natural experiment.'
2 Lipset, *Continental Divide,* xiii, argues that the best way to 'gain insight' into each country is through study of the other.
3 Thomas, 'Introduction,' 9–10, recognizes that proximity stimulates an 'availability error,' in which comparisons are made from what immediately

comes to mind through recent observation and experience. Systematic comparisons then are a way of overcoming that kind of error.

4 See Schwartz, 'Comparing U.S. and Canadian Public Policy.'
5 These concepts are often used interchangeably in the political science literature, but I will make distinctions among them when appropriate. For current views of institutionalism, see March and Olsen, *Rediscovering Institutions*, and DiMaggio and Powell, 'The Iron Cage Revisited.'
6 See Black, 'Ripples in the Second Wave.'
7 See Wilcher, *The Politics of Acid Rain Policy in Canada, Great Britain and the United States.*
8 Kunitz, 'Public Policy and Mortality among Indigenous Populations of Northern America and Australasia,' 650–1.
9 Kunitz, ibid., 653.
10 See Reimers and Troper, 'Canadian and American Immigration since 1945.'
11 See DiMaggio and Powell, 'The Iron Cage Revisited.'
12 See Alpert et al., 'Introduction.'
13 DiMaggio and Powell, 'The Iron Cage Revisited,' 67–9.
14 DiMaggio and Powell, ibid., 70–4.
15 DiMaggio and Powell, ibid., 69–70.
16 See Vaillancourt, 'An Economic Perspective on Language and Public Policy in the United States and Canada.'
17 See Russell, 'The Diffusion of Judicial Review.'
18 See McKenna, *The Canadian and American Constitutions in Comparative Perspective.*
19 See Howlett, 'The Judicialization of Canadian Environmental Policy.'
20 See DiMaggio and Powell, 'Introduction.'
21 See Hoberg, 'Risk Science and Politics.'
22 See Bodenheimer, 'Universal Health Insurance "Canadian Style."'
23 See Marmor, 'Health Care Reform in the United States.'
24 Lipset, *Continental Divide: The Values and Institutions of the United States and Canada*, 2.
25 Haussman, 'The Personal is Constitutional,' 112.
26 See Fleras and Elliott, *Aboriginal-State Relations in Canada, the United States, and New Zealand.*
27 See Uslaner, 'Energy Policy and Federalism in the United States and Canada.'
28 See Nevitte et al., 'Directions of Value Change in North America.'
29 Calvert, 'The Divergent Paths of the Canadian and American Labour Movements,' 383.
30 Orloff, *The Politics of Pensions: A Comparative Analysis of Britain, Canada, and the United States*, 58–9.

31 Schwartz, 'Comparing U.S. and Canadian Public Policy,' 568.
32 E.g., Finbow, 'Ideology and Institutions in North America.'
33 See DiMaggio and Powell, 'Introduction'; March and Olsen, *Rediscovering Institutions: The Organizational Basis of Politics.*
34 Scott, 'Unpacking Institutional Arrangements,' 181.

PART FOUR

Prospects for the Near Future

18

Missed Opportunities or Comparative Advantage? Canadian Contributions to the Study of Public Policy

LESLIE A. PAL

Taking the measure of a large subfield such as policy studies – even in only one country – is no easy task. At the very least it demands a solid description of previous work and some review of current approaches. Fortunately, the preceding essays in this volume have provided detailed reviews of the evolution of policy studies in Canada as well as of some key analytical frameworks. This chapter will therefore indulge in a rare luxury – it will evaluate the state of the art of Canadian policy studies in terms of an unabashedly idiosyncratic set of benchmarks. The assessment is based on what I judge to be five major developments in the field over the past decade. These developments are not peculiar to Canada – they represent fresh orientations or approaches that have swept the field as a whole. The argument is that in some respects Canadian scholarship should have a comparative advantage in these areas, given our own institutional arrangements or biases within the research community.

The argument may have a carping quality to it, but the Canadian research community is small and scattered, and the few dozen scholars who define public policy as their prime focus simply cannot do everything. Nonetheless, wish lists can serve a purpose if they remind us of things that we might like to tackle should the time and resources ever become available. The larger point behind the exercise is to encourage work in which Canadian scholarship should have some competitive edge, as well as work that is geared more precisely to our domestic circumstances. A quick review of the Social Sciences Citation Index of individuals from the Canadian Political Science Association's Directory who list 'public policy' as their first area of scholarly interest shows the 'index' of foreign citations of Canadian work is low to zero.[1] As a group, our international impact is minimal. Thinking about our comparative advantages and fresh opportunities may help change that.

Contemporary Areas of Inquiry in Policy Studies

It is difficult to discern trends in anything and biases inevitably structure what one considers to be important. Moreover, policy research tends to shade off into sociology, economics, history, and political science, so that what one sees as a trend depends very much on how one draws the boundaries of the field in the first place. Policy-relevant research is conducted in a variety of disciplines, and so we need to have a generic set of features to define the field.

A policy focus has at least three characteristics. First, the analyst is principally concerned with the outputs and outcomes of the policy process. Political scientists interested in public policy are usually adept at some specific feature of the process or the system, from political parties to the Charter, yet insofar as they work with a policy focus they harness their empirical research to understanding why outputs (laws, regulations, and policy) and outcomes or effects are what they are.

Second, a policy focus draws upon approaches and theories specifically designed to deal with outputs and outcomes. Given that it is impossible to completely sever the policy process from the larger political process, or indeed from sociological and economic forces, policy research inevitably uses the full array of theoretical work in the social sciences. But policy research is in part distinguished by its resonance with the corpus of policy-relevant literature and debates. Early examples would include Harold Lasswell's work,[2] and the robust debate over whether 'politics matters' in explaining policy outcomes.[3] More recent examples are the attempts to theorize the ways in which ideas affect policy making, either through institutions[4] or through particular types of 'advocacy coalitions.'[5]

Finally, a policy focus usually (though not always) has a visibly pragmatic and even ameliorative edge. Policy researchers are often very close to being policy analysts, and in turn trench on being policy advocates. A concentration on outputs and outcomes begets an interest in improving things. Some of this comes directly from the founding disciplines that underpin policy research. Economics operates with explicit concepts about efficiency and optimality. Sociology has been powerfully affected by notions of social inequality. Political scientists are, by and large, cautious liberal democrats, and the pragmatic orientation in the management sciences is virtually axiomatic. While the temptation to apply one's expertise in order to improve the world is universal, policy research tends to magnify it since the object of analysis is government actions and their effects.

This definition should help clarify this chapter's purpose. Understanding the 'state of the art' in Canada must mean measuring what we do against the larger body of policy-relevant and policy-specific theory. However, the 'state of the art' should have the additional purpose of saying something useful about the public policy process as our fellow citizens perceive (suffer?) it. This second objective is trickier than it seems, and so this chapter's proxy for usefulness is whether we are leaving some promising avenues of policy research unexplored. This is perhaps a typically academic way of defining usefulness, but it is a beginning.

The chapter will explore five fresh orientations or themes that have arisen in policy studies in the last decade. They are deliberately eclectic and broad, and deal with how we think about policy, how we explain it, and how we frame its driving forces and the effects that it has. They are: (1) the rise of post-modern/post-positivist approaches to policy analysis; (2) the increasing attention to the noninstrumental dimensions of public policy; (3) the renewed attention to institutions as key factors in explaining the policy process; (4) the internationalization of domestic policy processes; and (5) the question of public policy and the political community.[6] These approaches and themes have affected both the policy literature and the real policy world. Thinking about them theoretically forces us to grapple with the practical issues entangled with them. Moreover, the Canadian policy research community has some comparative advantages in each of them.

Post-Modern/Post-Positivist Approaches to Policy Analysis

The traditional, empirical, and positivist approach to policy analysis has yielded ground recently to what Hawkesworth dubs the 'post-positivist' approach,[7] or what Fischer calls 'critical policy analysis.'[8] Informed by Habermas, Foucault, deconstructionists, critical legal theory, the regulation school in Marxism, and feminist theory, this is an eclectic kitbag of conceptual tools and approaches. Indeed, it almost resists systematization, since that would be a form of reification and hierarchy. Nevertheless, there are some recognizable features to the approach.[9] Its central axiom is that social and political reality is constructed rather than simply 'there' as something to be empirically discovered. By the 1990s this seems a fairly tepid sort of claim, but it echoes long and sometimes bitter debates over the nature of reality and science. Put crudely, the positivist approach separated facts from values, assuming that it was possible to determine facts through empirical investigation. The facts so discovered were the basis of true knowledge and would form the consensual basis for policy making. True knowledge of this type could be discovered only through rigorous technique and sophisticated methodology. There was thus a strong role for expertise in the policy process, a role that was not entirely subordinate to the citizenry. Experts could claim the keys to the kingdom since their prescriptions were grounded in fact and in rational methods. The exemplar of this vision of policy analysis is the evaluation movement, particularly in the 1960s and 1970s.

Various streams have nurtured the post-modern/post-positivist reaction, but they all start by disagreeing with the facticity of the world and the division between facts and values. If reality is never unfiltered, and if the potential number of filters or perspectives is infinite, then how is social reality structured as an intersubjectively valid universe of discourse? How, in short, is it possible for people who wear different lenses to see the same thing? One answer is social power, and both Marxist and feminist theory have contributed to arguments that public policy is strongly shaped by class and patriarchy. Another related approach is to look at the social construction of reality itself through language. Edelman was a pioneer of this approach, looking at the ways in which symbols and words are used politically,[10] and more recent variants have stressed the role of argument and persuasion in policy analysis[11] and the organizing power of conceptual frameworks on policy definition.[12] This has been supplemented by analyses of specific policy discourses in order to understand the linguistic and conceptual manoeuvres that help some problem definitions succeed and others to fail.[13]

The post-modern/post-positivist thrust in the contemporary policy sciences also has implications for the understanding of policy expertise and democracy. Since all 'reality' is constructed, the reality of the policy expert is just as much a product of artifice as any other reality. Experts consequently retain very little pre-eminence over competing perspectives. This in turn reconfigures the balance between expertise and democracy, since without experts the policy process is up for grabs. A premium therefore is placed on communicative competence, the ability to forge valid arguments to make a policy point. Given the impossibility of deciding whose reality is right, this perspective emphasizes participation, trying to ensure the widest possible consultation. This reflects both democratic values and a conviction that the 'best' policy is not defined in technical terms but in large part by support and consensus.

Canadians should have a comparative advantage here because in many ways this country is a post-positivist or post-modern political community. First, its own political institutions are marked by what Tuohy has called ambivalence and ambiguity.[14] This ambivalence is matched by a political community of contestation, where every social movement from women, ethnic groups, language minorities, and gays and lesbians champions its cause through and with the Charter of Rights and Freedoms against perceived social injustice and discrimination. Every polity has its social movements, but only in Canada have they enjoyed substantial financial and moral support from governments.[15] The culture of minoritarianism has gone further here than it has in most other liberal democratic states.[16] This is extraordinarily fertile ground for the study of social movements themselves, but more importantly for the understanding of the key themes at the heart of post-positivist policy analysis. Canadian interest groups – think only of the National Action Committee on the Status of Women or EGALE (Equality for Gays and Lesbians Everywhere) – are practised in the art of policy contestation in post-positivist terms. They critique policies not in cost-benefit terms, but in terms of rights, participation, democracy, and equality.[17] The Canadian left is also more prominent than its American counterpart, both in the form of organized political parties, incumbent governments, and in academe. Post-positivist analyses have a leftish flavour, and given the weight of the left in this country's political and intellectual elites, we should be leading the field.[18]

In fact, while the work coming out of fields such as Canadian political economy and women's studies is quite voluminous, it is driven by methodological considerations that have little connection to the policy literature. It occupies a different theoretical terrain, one informed primarily by contemporary Marxist and feminist theory. The consequence, however, is that several of the key epistemological and procedural issues that are central to the work of writers such as Frank Fischer, Helen Ingram, Mary Hawkesworth, or Deborah Stone[19] are either unaddressed or muted. There is some scattered work on social movements,[20] but very little of it examines them from the perspective of the policy process. And while it is easy to cite examples of work that does address the post-modern aspects of political discourse arising from such movements and what Charles Taylor has called the 'malaise of modernity,'[21] very little of it is in dialogue with a policy literature that has been wrestling with similar problems for over a decade.

Ironically, what at first blush might appear as a comparative advantage may also be an intellectual liability. This country's political culture and a good deal of its public policy resonates with post-modern themes, and for that very reason may inhibit dispassionate analysis of the construction of social problems. Most Canadian academics who could be classified as working within a post-positivist paradigm are openly *parti pris* and ready to express their solidarity with the disadvantaged and oppressed, as those groups are conventionally defined. The same analytical tools can shed light on how unconventional social movements and policy actors work to construct their situations as policy problems requiring immediate attention, but the results would likely have a politically incorrect flavour. Prime examples include the analysis of the human rights movement as an 'industry' that manufactures minorities,[22] or the pro-Charter movement as a 'court party.'[23] In 1993 the federal government released a survey of women's experiences of sexual harassment. Widely touted as ground-breaking, it concluded that half of all Canadian women had experienced 'violence' at some point in their lives since the age of sixteen.[24] Like any survey, this one had to be constructed, and at a deeper level it contributed to the ongoing construction of the 'reality' of gender relations. Yet had Ontario's 'framework' document on zero-tolerance been adopted by the province's universities and colleges, raising such a point, even with the textual camouflage of a Paglia,[25] might have led to an investigation.[26]

Policy and the Noninstrumental Dimension

One of the most interesting questions in the policy literature is the independent effect of policies and state practices on society. This is a bigger question than whether policies work, or whether they hit the intended target. Impact in this sense is broader and pertains to effects on, for example, political support, the structure and nature of political discourse, social practices, political cohesion, and legitimacy. It is the difference between asking whether unemployment insurance provides an adequate income, and what effect unemployment insurance has on work incentives or a sector of the economy such as the fishery. It is the difference between asking whether Joanny can read as a result of educational policy, and whether Joanny carries around sexual or racial stereotypes as a result of educational policies. What is the effect of destreaming on social equity as opposed to educational attainment? Does funding advocacy groups make a difference to the tone and temper of political discourse? These are 'regime' questions that assume there is more than an instrumental connection between public policies and their outcomes. Policies are organically connected to both the body social and the body politic. Another term for this might be 'macro-evaluation.'

Thinking about policy in these terms is as familiar as the feedback loops in systems theory and hardly constitutes anything new at the level of theory. Most empirical research on public policy takes into account at some point the effect of policy legacies, acknowledging the broad causal impact of previous policies on present behaviour. At another level, however, this does represent a fresh focus. Reflecting the points made earlier about mainstream public policy analysis, the traditional approach was marked by both instrumentalism and utilitarianism. The first encouraged analysis of public policy primarily as problem-solving tools. Policy is an instrument designed to tackle some specific circumstance and presumably improve upon it. This perspective is faithful to an important aspect of policy as it is made and discussed in the real world: we want transportation policy to make transportation better, social policy to alleviate poverty, and so o n. But policies also have a symbolic or referential dimension of meaning. Chopping rail lines to remote regions does have an instrumental, transportation policy dimension, but inevitably drags in issues associated with what the railway 'means' to Canadians. Social policy is not a matter merely of income replacement ratios – it is read as a barometer of society's obligations as well as of its 'standards.'

The utilitarianism underlying traditional approaches to public policy is linked to this point. The conventional approaches, especially those inspired by rational choice theory, have taken values as exogenous. Public policy therefore is basically about setting incentive systems for a given set of preferences. But preferences or utility functions are grounded in values, and these values 'emerge from lessons taught by family, friends, and community.'[27] Values can change, and moreover, people's responses to public policy are grounded in these values. Ultimately, therefore, this forces attention to the effects of public policy on value formation and value change, on the bedrock of policy preferences. This line of inquiry has opened a broad discussion on the nature of democratic practice as itself producing citizenship and what Mansbridge calls 'public spiritedness.'[28] If people respond to public policy in terms of fundamental value orientations, then perhaps the most important value orientation of all is the willingness to act as a citizen, to seriously consider the balance of private as against the public interest. It implies a willingness to believe in such a thing as the public interest in the first place, and actualize it through participation.[29]

Canada should be an international leader in this sort of reflection on public policy for two reasons. The first is the peculiar embeddedness of identity politics in Canada. Whether as a result of the Charter,[30] longer-term policies on citizenship undertaken since 1968,[31] or post-materialist influences,[32] Canadian political discourse places a premium on claims made in terms of identity,[33] a premium that has been reinforced by globalization and the dissolution of the traditional state.[34] Identity claims are saturated in noninstrumental reasoning because, as a yardstick to measure policy, identity always asks, 'What does this *mean* in relation to *who I am or wish to be*?' The second reason is the wide acceptance by Canadian governments and policy actors of the fundamental injustice of many key Canadian institutions. If Canada has a passion for identity, it also has an apparent passion for equity. Its bundle of equity, human rights, anti-discrimination, and multicultural policies is among the most advanced in the world. Together, they stand as testaments to at least the rhetorical acceptance that Canadian society is beset by deep strains of racism, sexism, homophobia, and so on. In this environment, policy discourse constantly echoes concerns about both the 'messages sent' by policies and their implications for the larger structure of domination. Destreaming as an educational strategy, for example, probably has more to do with attacking the class structure than it does with educational achievement. Integration of the disabled in the classroom seeks the amelioration of discrimination more than it does some narrowly educational goal. Employment equity and pay equity are economic policies seeking social justice.

In practice therefore, Canadian public policy shows strong streaks of noninstrumentalism. The academic community has not seized upon this advantage, however. In part, this would require the analysis of instrumental policies in terms of their dimensions of meaning, as well as of policies explicitly intended to alter values and meaning systems (e.g., exhortative policies). Two fine examples of the first are Franks's *The Myths and Symbols of the Constitutional Debate in Canada* and Shkilnik's *Poison Stronger than Love*.[35] The 1993 Ontario debate over same-sex families provides a wonderful example of the second. But the sustained work in these comparatively rich fields is quite meager. Again, it may be that the Canadian academic policy community is too wrapped up in championing these policies to take a dispassionate perspective on their internal logic and consequences. For example, why has no one done an analysis of the expanding logic of equity claims? Equality seekers hate hierarchy, but what could be more hierarchical than saying, for the purposes of equity employment, that there should only be four target groups (women, the disabled, visible minorities, and aboriginals)? The 1992 pay equity hearings in Ontario, for example, saw just this sort of dynamic with at least three new types of groups (gays and lesbians, francophone minorities, and the 'double discriminated') demanding to be included with the traditional groupings.

Institutions

Institutional analysis, *pace* March and Olsen[36] and Weaver and Rockman,[37] is the logical successor to 'state-centric' theories of politics and policy making. The focus here, in terms of explanatory modes of analysis rather than practical or pragmatic policy making, is to think about the ways in which institutions channel political action, constitute political possibilities, and constrain behaviour.[38] There are different approaches within this broad area, of course, from sociological 'rule systems' theory[39] to public choice and voting theory. All share the central insight, however, that formal institutions and their underlying principles shape political outcomes.

Canadians should have a comparative advantage here, and in this case the opportunity has not been missed as much as in the others. Indeed, it is probably the one area of policy studies where Canadians have made their mark internationally, though less at the broad theoretical level than through the study of one institutional reality, federalism. Federalism (and constitution making) has been the grand obsession of Canadian politics for the last quarter-century,[40] and if there is one institutional variable that has attracted sustained Canadian scholarly inquiry in terms of its impact on policy, then this is it. Within political science the leading students of federalism and the constitution (e.g., Donald Smiley, Richard Simeon, Keith Banting, Peter Russell, Alan Cairns) are the best known among the international scholarly community. The very preponderance of federalism and constitutional issues in our practical politics has encouraged Canadian students of public policy to focus on institutions almost naturally. The Charter of Rights and Freedoms has also stimulated work on the institutional structure of the courts and the judicial rules of the game as they affect policy making.[41]

Nonetheless, there are still some missed opportunities here. A critical one is exploiting the comparative dimension of institutional analysis. Taking institutions seriously at minimum means taking rule systems and their logic seriously. At a general level, this should encourage an interest in the way that policy issues get processed in different institutional arenas. As issues move from the courts to the legislature, for example, the logic of the arenas will compel different strategies and patterns of behaviour. In this sense, institutional analysis is almost always comparative, but it could be more explicitly so. For example, 'issue tracking' through institutional arenas could yield a better understanding of how the policy process works. Another approach might be to compare policy formulation and development at different levels of the political system: How do municipalities, provinces, and the national government handle similar policy questions? Work could also be more comparative in the more traditional sense of the term in studying Canadian patterns and contrasting them with other countries. This has perhaps gone furthest in the study of elections and of federalism, though comparative judicial studies is a burgeoning subfield. An outstanding opportunity for comparative institutional analysis is the European Union. Canadians, given their recent constitutional history, have a comparative advantage in observing the techniques of constitutional and political circumlocution in disaggregated political systems (e.g., opting out, cost-sharing equalization). These could profitably be applied to the comparative study of emerging forms of European federalism.

Another potentially fruitful area of institutional inquiry is in what Elster has called forms of 'local justice,'[42] ways in which nongovernmental institutions (e.g., corporations, voluntary agencies, etc.) organize and address issues that inevitably have a political aspect. This is important, because too much institutional analysis is anchored in traditional political institutions. This restricts the study of the full range of practical solutions and rule systems that people generate to deal with generic problems of distribution and resource allocation. In thinking about something such as consultation, for example, it is tempting to examine forms that governments have adopted and modified in their latest passion to 'empower citizens.' However, the nongovernmental sector is likely experimenting with a wider variety of consultative forms that could shed light on the inner logic of communicative action. Another example is forms of self-government among aboriginal peoples. Comparative and microscopic analysis of actual arrangements reveals a richer variety of institutional patterns than might be generated through a more logical and deductive approach to the issue.

Internationalization of Domestic Public Policy

There has been a traditional division of labour between international relations and domestic politics. Indeed, the notion of 'international public policy' is itself of relatively recent vintage, since international bodies are often at best the site of politics, not of policy. This is obviously changing with the end of the Cold War, the increase in U.N. actions, and the emergence of supranational blocs such as the European Union and NAFTA. With these developments has come a double-sided movement that is readjusting the nature of both international and domestic policy making. First, international politics, standards, and institutions are increasingly salient for domestic issues. Human rights and environmental standards are the best examples, where domestic policy making can no longer take place outside of a framework informed by international developments and actors.

The second is the projection of domestic issues onto the international stage.[43] This may simply be a matter of degree, but conceivably could also involve a qualitative change in the type and nature of appeals and actions taken internationally to further domestic policy issues. The 1993 opinion of the U.N. Human Rights Committee on Bill 178 and the report of the Committee on Economic, Social, and Cultural Rights on Canadian social policy are cases in point where domestic policies are challenged through a loop that includes some international forums.[44] Canadian aboriginals have essentially done the same thing with the Great Whale project, and B.C. forest policy has faced similar challenges outside national borders from the Sierra Club and international eco-lobbyists. In May 1994 a complaint was lodged with the U.N. Human Rights Committee in Geneva by two Ontario francophones, arguing that the province's policies amounted to 'genocide' of the francophone population.[45]

Canada's comparative advantage here is clear. The country's colonial history and proximity to the United States (not necessarily different things) should give us an edge in thinking about the international context of domestic issues. NAFTA is a perfect laboratory for the examination of the constraints and opportunities posed by harmonization. Canada's overseas development budgets have been delivered to a much greater extent by NGOs than is true of other countries, and our social activists are involved in numerous international networks. Canada has even been a rhetorical leader in the emerging areas of international diplomacy such as human rights and the environment. Despite these and other characteristics, Canadian students of public policy have not been noticeably on the forefront of thinking through the consequences of the internationalization of public policy. The traditional scholarly division of labour holds here as much as it does elsewhere, and so while Canada has many distinguished students of international relations, very few of them have turned their attention to domestic policy making. Students of domestic policy have only rarely thought through the consequence of internationalization, and insofar as they have concentrated on the Canada–U.S. Free Trade Agreement and NAFTA, they have taken a dim view of the process.

The research possibilities are nonetheless quite exciting. Policy communities, for example, are increasingly permeable to international connections and networks. Indeed, in thinking about the ways in which international groups connect to domestic ones, we may need to rethink the dynamics of policy communities in ways that highlight their fluidity and flexibility. Another subject is the ways in which policy discourse changes to incorporate arguments about international forces. If policy making is about making arguments, then the internationalization of policy should be reflected in the ways in which policy issues are defined and debated. This is perhaps one of the most intriguing aspects of internationalization, since it taps the ways in which 'internationalization' becomes an operative code for policy actors within their policy fields. Yet another avenue of inquiry is the concrete ways in which international standards and agreements come to be projected into the national and subnational arena. International declarations are often dismissed, for example, as being unimportant because they are nothing more than expressions of sentiment. What we sometimes forget is that domestic policy actors take their cues from these declarations and act in a myriad of ways to actualize them within their spheres of competence. U.N. declarations and statements about human rights, for example, have an empty and ritualistic quality to them, until one realizes that there are dozens of interest groups and agencies operating at the community level who work diligently to promote and popularize those principles. Their work on hearts and minds may induce important value shifts.

Nation-State and Political Community

The phenomenon of internationalization has posed fundamental questions about the nation-state, sovereignty, and political community. Globalization of the international economy, telecommunications, ease of travel and information exchanges, and the demise of east-west tensions have created the possibility of a global society or community.[46] Many of the same forces, of course, are pushing not toward the dissolution of the nation-state but to rising demands for ethnically homogeneous states. Mass migrations will put pressure on Western states. These forces pose two fundamental challenges to the traditional configuration of the nation-state and its political community. The first pushes the state's competencies up to international levels, while the second undermines the firmness of its social foundations by corroding the bonds that tie citizens within a state to each other. The state thus faces a powerful tension: its citizens are less and less inclined to see themselves primarily as members of the national political community, but the state itself still is the main conduit for key social and economic programs that citizens demand as part of a developed welfare state.

The reasons why Canada should have a comparative advantage in this area of inquiry are painfully obvious. First, there is the bracing debate over Quebec sovereignty. The 1993 Charlottetown referendum campaign stimulated some interesting proposals for institutional realignment that would have changed the nature of state sovereignty in this country quite substantially. A new round of constitutional negotiations has now begun as a result of the very narrow victory of the 'No' side in the October 1995 referendum on Quebec sovereignty. However, it is still too early to judge what the outcome of these latest efforts will be. While the political debate has not been inspiring, the language of national integration and disintegration comes naturally to Canadians. Second, Canada is already, and has been for some time, a multiethnic, multicultural, and immigrant society. Aside from the Quebec question, then, Canadians have had to address the question of national unity and identity along this axis as well. Finally, the aboriginal question has of late evolved considerably beyond the mere recognition of treaty rights to self-government and even sovereignty. The Charlottetown Accord was prepared to recognize aboriginal self-governments, but no one at the time was able to offer a satisfactory explanation as to how it would work in terms of quasi-states operating within national boundaries.

Again one can easily think of some outstanding examples of work that has probed some of these areas. Certainly Canadian scholarship on aboriginal questions is world-class, as is the work of some political theorists on the nature of liberalism and communitarianism. But descending from these heights, there is relatively little policy work that probes these questions and issues explicitly. How can we design states that engender loyalty in contexts where citizenship is fragmented? What are the possible bases of a social contract in heterogeneous societies? Are there general principles to be drawn from the way that some existing aboriginal self-government arrangements are managed? Might they be applied to other circumstances? The world at large, not just Canada, is in desperate need of models of cohabitation, of constitutional designs that address the functional requirements of states along with the community bonds that ensure that those states survive as viable entities. It may be that this is a realm more suited to philosophy than policy studies, but the need is there nonetheless.

Conclusion

The preceding discussion has doubtless been at too general a level. For some, policy studies consist of work done on specific policy issues or areas, such as housing, social policy, garbage disposal, and so on. The journals show a wide variety of work in these specific policy fields, and most of it is of high quality. This chapter has tried to emphasize another dimension of the community's scholarly work, the one that connects the results of this more focused research to broad theoretic and practical issues in the nature of the state. Canadian public policy research will always be of interest to other Canadians, but it should also speak to larger themes in the literature and to the changing nature of the policy process itself.

The five developments discussed in this chapter are a subset of a host of other interesting questions that researchers could pose to themselves. Nonetheless, they do represent important debates and, moreover, ones for which Canadian conditions and circumstances provide some comparative advantage to our own researchers. The Canadian work that does exist in these areas is often excellent but either concentrates exclusively on Canada or is too thin on the ground to build up a critical mass of scholarship that would attract wider attention. With some effort, however, we should be able to capitalize on these unique circumstances and develop their general applicability. In so doing, Canadian policy research would simultaneously further both its domestic and global relevance.

Notes

1 The Canadian Political Science Association provided the names of fifty-one members who had listed public policy as their first area of research. I devised an index by comparing their citations as a percentage of an average constructed from the citations for three recognized policy scholars (Theodore Lowi, Claus Offe, and Francis Castles).
2 Lasswell, *A Pre-View of the Policy Sciences.*
3 For a contemporary version of this discussion, see Castles and Mitchell, 'Identifying Welfare State Regimes.'
4 Hall, *Governing the Economy.*
5 Sabatier and Jenkins-Smith, eds., *Policy Change and Learning: An Advocacy Coalition Approach.*
6 I have left out rational choice because it is less new than the others and because it seeps into institutional analysis quite strongly. Nonetheless, it is hugely important in contemporary policy analysis. Readers should refer to the section in this book devoted to rational choice for a full discussion.
7 Hawkesworth, *Theoretical Issues in Policy Analysis.*
8 Fischer, 'Participatory Expertise.'
9 See Torgerson in this volume for more detail.
10 Edelman, *Constructing the Political Spectacle.*
11 Majone, *Evidence, Argument and Persuasion in the Policy Process*; deLeon, *Advice and Consent*; and Fischer and Forester, eds., *The Argumentative Turn in Policy Analysis and Planning.*
12 Best, *Images of Issues.*
13 Stark, 'Political-Discourse Analysis and the Debate over Canada's Lobbying Legislation.'
14 Tuohy, *Policy and Politics in Canada: Institutional Ambivalence.* A book that explores this theme in Canadian political institutions is Archer, Gibbins, Knopff, and Pal, *Parameters of Power.*
15 See Pal, *Interests of State.* See also the introduction on 19 May 1994 in Ontario of the first North American legislation that would have treated same-sex couples identically to heterosexual couples.

16 Cairns, 'The Fragmentation of Canadian Citizenship'; Zolf, 'Comparisons of Multicultural Broadcasting in Canada and Four Other Countries'; Helly, 'The Political Regulation of Cultural Plurality.'

17 Razack, *Canadian Feminism and the Law: The Women's Legal Education and Action Fund and the Pursuit of Equality*; Pal, 'Advocacy Organizations and Legislative Politics'; Vickers et al., *Politics As If Women Mattered: A Political Analysis of the National Action Committee on the Status of Women.*

18 Not only on the left: see the French and Lindquist debate in *Optimum*; French, 'Postmodern Government'; Lindquist, 'Postmodern Politics and Policy Sciences'; and French 'Retrieving the Policy Sciences.'

19 Fischer, *Technocracy and the Politics of Expertise*; Ingram and Rathgeb, eds., *Public Policy and Democracy*; Hawkesworth, *Theoretical Issues in Policy Analysis*; Stone, *Policy Paradox and Political Reason.*

20 Carroll, ed., *Organizing Dissent: Contemporary Social Movements in Theory and Practice.*

21 Taylor, *The Malaise of Modernity.* And also see Taylor, *Multiculturalism and 'The Politics of Recognition.'*

22 Knopff and Morton, *Charter Politics*; Knopff, *Human Rights and Social Technology: The New War on Discrimination.*

23 Morton, 'The Charter Revolution and the Court Party.'

24 'The Violence against Women Survey,' *The Daily* (Statistics Canada), 18 November 1993.

25 Paglia, *Sexual Personae: Art and Decadence from Nefertiti to Emily Dickinson.*

26 The Ontario government announced its executive order to universities regarding the framework in October 1993. It would have forbidden 'gestures and remarks' related to race, ancestry, place of origin, colour, ethnic origin, citizenship, creed, sex, sexual orientation, disability, age, marital status, family status, the receipt of public assistance, record of provincial offences or pardoned federal offences that caused offence to anyone or created a 'negative environment.' Provincial universities slowly gathered themselves to resist the framework, at which point the government softened it to a 'guide.'

27 Aaron, Mann, and Taylor, 'Introduction,' 3.

28 Mansbridge, 'Public Spirit in Political Systems.'

29 Dryzek, *Discursive Democracy*; Forester, *Planning in the Face of Power.*

30 Bryden, Davis, and Russell, eds., *Protecting Rights and Freedoms: Essays on the Charter's Place in Canada's Political, Legal, and Intellectual Life*; Seidle, ed., *Equity and Community.*

31 Pal, *Interests of State*; Manfredi, *Judicial Power and the Charter: Canada and the Paradox of Liberal Constitutionalism.*

32 Nevitte, 'New Politics, the Charter and Political Participation.'

33 A leading text in Canadian studies, for example, is aptly entitled *Passion for Identity.*

34 Minogue, 'Identity, Self, and Nation'; Kincaid, 'Peoples, Persons and Places in Flux.'

35 Franks, *The Myths and Symbols of the Constitutional Debate in Canada*; Shkilnyk, *A Poison Stronger than Love.*

36 March and Olsen, *Rediscovering Institutions.*

37 Weaver and Rockman, eds., *Do Institutions Matter?*

38 Atkinson, ed., *Governing Canada: Institutions and Public Policy.*

39 Burns and Flam, *The Shaping of Social Organization.*

40 Russell, *Constitutional Odyssey: Can Canadians become a Sovereign People?*

41 See the special issue of the *Osgoode Hall Law Journal* devoted to this question: *Osgoode Hall Law Journal* 30, no. 3.

42 Elster, *Local Justice.*

43 Ponting, 'Internationalization.'

44 Bill 178 was reviewed in April 1993 by the U.N. Human Rights Committee, and the Economic, Social, and Cultural Rights Committee report was issued in May 1993.

45 'Ontario Killing French Ways, UN Panel, Told,' *The Globe and Mail*, 25 May 1994, A5.

46 Rosenau and Czempiel, eds., *Governance without Government.*

19

Afterword: 'New' Directions in Canadian Policy Studies

RICHARD SIMEON

In this chapter I wish to offer some observations about the recent development of policy studies in Canadian political science, the strengths and weaknesses of some of the approaches that have recently come to the fore, and
the agenda for future research and development. I agree with almost everything Bruce Doern has written (see Chapter 2). Our field is part art, craft,
and science, and his body of work superbly exemplifies all three. I especially like his scepticism about the abuse of the term 'neo-', since I agree
that the Canadian tradition in political science never really departed from
institutionalism, and the state-society link has been fundamental in the great
Canadian works on public policy, such as those of Innis, Mallory, Smiley,
Corry, and others. I recall that Smiley labelled an article I published in 1972
as representing a 'neo-institutional' approach, and Bruce Doern rightly points
out that his early work with Aucoin on the 'inner state' would later have
been labelled neo-institutional. I think one reason the 'bring the state back
in' literature was so positively received in Canada is precisely that it was so
consistent with what we had been doing all along. So there's not much new
under the sun – what we see instead is a shifting of emphasis back and forth.

I generally agree with his characterization of developments in the field. I
would emphasize the enormous contribution neo-Marxism has made to debates about the role and nature of the state. I would also underline (see Chapter
14 by Torgerson) the influence of other paradigms – feminism, post-modernism, deconstructionism – in shaping the policy research agenda and in
reaffirming the importance of ideas in policy analysis. I would also under-
score the extent to which the policy research agenda tracks events: for example, in the shift from analysis of the growth of the welfare state to studies
of fiscal crisis, of economic policy, and so on.

I am sympathetic to what Richard Phidd (see Chapter 3) is trying to do – that is, to reintegrate public policy with more traditional concerns of public administration and organizational theory – and the need to establish linkages between the more macro and micro explanations. There is a lot to be said for his emphasis on a longer time horizon. But my main reactions are, first, that he states the need for such approaches without telling us much about how to go about doing it; and, second, that we are in fact, through volumes such as *Policy Communities and Public Policy* or *Governing Canada: Institutions and Public Policy*, already quite far along in the enterprise he seeks.

Since I wrote the article on 'Studying Public Policy' in 1976, there has been an extraordinary growth and maturation of policy studies in Canada. Courses and publications have proliferated. We now have at least four general texts in public policy and policy analysis (Doern and Phidd; Pal; Brooks; Atkinson) along with some excellent readers. There is a growing tendency to give more general texts a policy focus. In 1976 *Canadian Public Policy* was in its infancy; *Policy Options* had not yet started. The immensely useful *How Ottawa Spends* series had not yet begun. (As a parenthetical plea, let me suggest that every couple of years it be interspersed with a companion *How Provinces Spend*).

The field has become much more comparative (see Chapters 15, 16 and 17), not only in the sense that more explicitly comparative studies are being undertaken, but also in the sense that Canadian research draws very heavily on the comparative literature (as in the influence of neocorporatism, neoinstitutionalism, and the like). Increasing numbers of Canadian scholars (Banting and Coleman, for example) are participating in international collaborative work. There has also been more fruitful cooperation across disciplines, especially with economics.

Impressive case studies now cover a vast array of policy fields. There has been a large, and valuable, convergence among those who have approached policy from different ideological or theoretical approaches – witness Bruce Doern's long list of collaborators. Our scholarship has become much more theoretically self-conscious and explicit. And there have been impressive conceptual contributions: Coleman and Skogstad on policy communities and networks, George Hoberg's work on policy styles, and so on.[1] The field is strong and healthy.

In my 1976 article I argued that the role of policy research was to provide a window to a broader understanding of the political system. It was not, and should not be seen as, directed to influencing and reforming the policy process, or giving policy advice. This purist academic position caused me some grief when shortly after I became director of the Queen's University School of Public Administration, with a mandate to educate public servants and to argue how relevant and helpful our research really is.

It does seem true that, despite the greater richness of the field, our impact on the real world of policy making remains very limited, with a few exceptions such as constitutional policy. Economists, as we often lament, have had enormously more influence on policy that we have. In government organization it is works in public management emanating from business schools that one sees on officials' desks and that get taught in public sector management programs. In other policy areas I think one could make a case that legal researchers have had more impact than we have.

I do not know if we should worry about this: I suspect most of us are ambivalent about the purpose of policy studies, though few of us, I believe, are without some reformist impulses. But we have been very modest about prescription and evaluation. Our focus has been on explanation, finding the determinants of policy. Interestingly, Leslie Pal has a table in which he labels the links between determinants and policy content as 'academic' policy analysis, and the links between content and implementation/evaluation as 'applied' policy analysis. He argues further that these are quite different and distinct enterprises. Maybe, but surely good applied analysis requires a good understanding of determinants; and surely there is much room for more scholarly analysis, both empirical and normative, of outcomes and impacts.

In any case, we *are* modest about prescription. We tend to look backward, why things are as they are, rather than forward to what they might be. When we talk of policy legacies and such, we convey the impression that continuity is more important than change. Our emphasis on constraint, multicausality, and unintended consequences makes us sceptical about the possibilities for reform. Nor do our models – despite, or even because of, their richness – have the powerful, true-believer 'have I got a model for you' message of, say, the economists. In addition, for us policy content is usually secondary. George Hoberg knows about all there is to know about environmental policy; so does Grace Skogstad about agricultural policy, and Bruce Doern on trade policy; but our discipline does not give them a mandate to make recommendations about good policy in these areas. However, if state capacity to manage complex societies is increasingly the issue, then there is indeed room for a contribution on our part to the real world of policy and policy making.

Despite our increased conceptual rigour, the field continues to be characterized by eclecticism in our search for explanations of policy. There can be debates about the relative weight to accord societal factors or institutional factors, and different scholars can make different judgments on that, but everybody agrees that both sets are important; that neither can be ignored in any full account of policy; and that what we are most interested in is precisely the nexus, the interlinking of state and societal factors. One of the major contributions of the policy community/policy network literature is that this is precisely where it locates the research project. It is interesting to note that in a recent book by Atkinson and his colleagues,[2] for every assertion of the centrality of institutional factors there seems to be an equally strongly stated caveat: well, of course they do not explain everything, they are contingent, and so on. So there is a lot more to be done in theorizing the state-society linkage.

We are still faced with a plethora of factors linked to policy outcomes: global and international forces, the domestic social and economic environment, the role of ideas, ideologies, and cultures, macro and micro institutional structures, and so on. Indeed, the list of relevant factors that analysts point to has grown rather than declined, and we are not very good at weighting them against each other. So parsimony is not our strong suit, despite the desire of the public choice theorists to make it so. This does not bother me. I think it is simply a reflection of the complexity of the field, and the resulting need for multicausal, multidimensional analysis if any plausible account of policy is to be given.

I do think, though, that it is worth recalling a simple point in my 1976 article: that how we invest our resources depends very heavily on what we want to explain. Is it big macro questions such as the size of the welfare state, or more micro questions about why this or that change in the unemployment insurance program was adopted? The research tools will be quite different. Explaining similarities across all Western industrial societies points to quite different explanations (more societal, less institutional) than explaining variations among them. Similarly, the tools for explaining the undoubtedly high degree of continuity in public policy are different from those we use to explore change. So I do think we can do a better job of sorting out the interplay of the many factors we explore if we are a bit more self-conscious about what it is about policy we want to explain.

As I have noted, the major recent innovations have built on the neo-institutional or neostatist literature, and on the interaction of state and societal forces in policy communities and networks. I think this is enormously useful and has produced very important insights – for example, in a more nuanced view of state autonomy, and the notion of variations not only across countries but also across policy sectors. The approach provides a very powerful descriptive framework, allowing us to integrate a great many variables. It is, however, perhaps better as a descriptive framework than an explanatory one; and perhaps better at understanding continuity than change.

There is a very large irony here, though. The growth in emphasis on state autonomy, on institutions, and on varied policy networks comes precisely at a time when a whole variety of forces seem to argue for a more macro approach. Why emphasize what goes on within the state when global forces seem, at least in some eyes, to be draining independence, autonomy, and the ability to make choices away from national governments? When the dominant image is of the constrained state; when the policy instruments available to them are increasingly limited; when the levers they do have to pull do not seem to be attached to anything; when capital mobility and the impact of global problems exceed the regulatory grasp of the state; when debts and deficits also constrain state innovation? Or, to use another example, it seems ironic to move way from Marxist approaches at a time when, even as communism as an operative political movement is in collapse, the dynamics of national and international capitalism seem to be of overwhelming importance in shaping the policy agenda.

All of this suggests that the chief questions for policy analysts today are the macro ones: What are the capacities of states to manage their environments; are states now facing the restructuring, both in policy and institutions, that parallels what has gone on in the private sector; how can we reconceptualize the role of the state in the face of changes both in the global environment and in the domestic society, where existing institutions, policy styles, and policy networks are increasingly under challenge? While the work I am referring to is not unaware of these sorts of issues, these are not the questions the analysis of policy networks and communities is primarily designed to answer. So one might suggest that we may be fiddling while Rome burns.

On the other hand, we might argue that the constraints and limits placed on the state by these larger forces are easily exaggerated and that in any case they are not new; that there remains important room for policy choice; that governments do have some degrees of freedom, though these are likely to vary across policy areas. This is indeed a very important area for research. It also suggests the value of Weaver and Rockman's emphasis on state capacities: To what extent do institutional structures, and the organization of state and society in policy networks, vary in their ability to formulate and implement responses to the various challenges they face from the external environment?[3]

This suggests some thoughts about items that might be on the agenda for future policy studies. First, we need much more work on the implications of globalization for public policy. That globalization has a pervasive impact has become conventional wisdom, but its impact on public policy agendas and on the policy-making process has been little studied. To what extent does it shape the policy agenda? To what extent does it change the constellation of domestic cleavages and shift the power relations between them – as in a shift in influence from the less mobile to the mobile? To what extent does it constrain policy instruments and policy goals? To what extent does it promote convergence in policy outcomes across systems with different traditions and institutions? How do these pressures and constraints on policy instruments vary from sector to sector? How does it change policy networks and the organization of interests? Do global pressures necessarily weaken and disorganize interests and the state; or can they, as Coleman and Skogstad suggest, sometimes strengthen them? What are the implications of globalization for democratic politics and policy effectiveness? There is much to build on here in the work of Hall, Katzenstein, and others.[4]

Parallel to this, I think we need more work on policy and process responses to increased social and ideological diversity and to the emergence of new social movements – in terms of the ways they alter the character of policy networks, challenge traditional policy styles, engender new processes of consultation, and so on. Hoberg's pluralism by design and his discussion of the growth of multipartite bargaining and legalism in the Canadian environmental field is the kind of thing I mean.[5]

Third, we need more work on the politics and policy of debts and deficits, both in terms of failure and success in managing them and their implications for policy across other sectors. Fourth, there is much room for more explicitly normative questions. To take one example, in *Governing Canada* Sharon Sutherland situates her chapter on the public service and public policy around the question: 'How can democracy as a form of self-government of citizens by citizens be squared with the reality of a state that is dependent upon professional bureaucrats?' Stated a bit more broadly, how can the requirements of democracy – representativeness, openness, participation, consultation, etc. – be reconciled with concerns for greater policy effectiveness – the ability to take hard decisions, to act decisively, to allocate costs, to orient policy to the longer term, and so on? There are major tensions between two sets of potentially competing reform agendas and a need to think more about what we mean by 'state capacities.' Much of the literature on the United States and Canada sees them as 'weak states' and betrays a hankering for 'strong states' in the European tradition. I am not at all sure that is a very useful distinction, nor that 'strong' states are necessarily more effective than weak ones. Moreover, the terms effectiveness and capacity need to be debated; like 'efficiency' they have meaning only in terms of some prior normative conception: effectiveness, for what?

Finally, even as we continue to try to get a better handle on the dynamics of policy and policy formation in the systems as they exist, I think we too have to engage in a broader enterprise of rethinking the role, purpose, and nature of government and the state in light of massive social and economic changes both globally and nationally. In that sense, while not wanting to denigrate the institutionalists, I do want to stress that it is essential to keep our eye on the context, the environment, the social, economic, and attitudinal settings in which governing structures and policy networks are embedded, and to underline the need to trace the linkages between them.

Notes

1 Coleman and Skogstad, eds., *Policy Communities and Public Policy*; Hoberg, 'Environmental Policy.'
2 Atkinson, ed., *Governing Canada.*
3 Weaver and Rockman, eds., *Do Institutions Matter?*
4 See Hall, *Governing the Economy*; Katzenstein, *Small States in World Markets.*
5 See Hoberg, 'Environmental Policy.'

Bibliography

Aaron, Henry, Thomas E. Mann, and Timothy Taylor. 1994. 'Introduction.' In *Values and Public Policy*. Washington: Brookings Institution, 3–15.

Abele, F. 1983. 'The Berger Inquiry and the Politics of Transformation in the Mackenzie Valley.' PhD Thesis, York University, Toronto.

– 1987. 'Canadian Contradictions: Forty Years of Northern Political Development.' *Arctic* 40, no. 4, 310–20.

Aberbach, Joel D., Robert D. Putnam, and Bert Rockman. 1981. *Bureaucrats and Politicians in Western Democracies*. Cambridge: Harvard University Press.

Abrams, R. 1980. *Foundations of Political Analysis*. New York: Columbia University Press.

Acheson, K. and John Chant. 1971. 'The Bank of Canada: A Study in Bureaucracy.' Unpublished paper, Department of Economics, Queen's University.

Ackelsberg, Martha A. 1992. 'Feminist Analyses of Public Policy.' *Comparative Politics* 24:477–93.

Akenson, D.H. 1991. *God's Peoples*. Montreal and Kingston: McGill–Queen's University Press.

Adie, Robert F. and Paul G. Thomas. 1982. *Canadian Public Administration: Problematical Perspectives*. Scarborough, Ont.: Prentice-Hall.

Albo, Gregory and Jane Jenson. 1989. 'A Contested Concept: The Relative Autonomy of the State.' In W. Clement and G. Williams, eds., *The New Canadian Political Economy*. Montreal: McGill-Queen's University Press.

Albo, Gregory, D. Langille, and Leo Panitch. 1993. *A Different Kind of State*. Toronto: Oxford University Press.

Alcoff, Linda. 1988. 'Cultural Feminism versus Post-Structuralism: The Identity Crisis in Feminist Theory.' *Signs* 13, no. 3, 405–36.

Alexander, J.C. and P. Colomy. 1992. 'Traditions and Competition.' In G. Ritzer, ed., *Metatheorizing*. Newbury Park: Sage Publications, 27–52.

Allen, Richard. 1971. *The Social Passion: Religion and Social Reform in Canada, 1914–1928*. Toronto: University of Toronto Press.

Allen, R.C. 1992. 'Introduction: The Conservative Revolution in Economic Policy.' In R. Allen and G. Rosenbluth, *False Promises: The Failure of Conservative Economics*. Vancouver: New Star Books.

Almond, Gabriel A. 1989. 'Review Article: The International-National Connection.' *British Journal of Political Science* 19:237–59.

Almond, Gabriel and Sidney Verba. 1963. *The Civic Culture*. Princeton: Princeton University Press.

Alpert, William T., John B. Shoven, and John Whalley. 1992. 'Introduction.' In *Canada–U.S. Tax Comparisons*. Chicago: University of Chicago Press, 1–23.

Ames, Herbert. 1897. *The City below the Hill*. Montreal.

Amy, D.J. 1984. 'Toward a Post Positivist Policy Analysis.' *Policy Studies Journal* 13:207–11.

Anderson, Charles W. 1971. 'Comparative Policy Analysis: The Design of Measures.' *Comparative Politics* 4:117–31.

– 1978. 'The Logic of Public Problems: Evaluation in Comparative Policy Research.' In D. Ashford, ed., *Comparing Public Policies*. Beverly Hills: Sage.

Anderson, F.J. 1993. *Natural Resources and Economic Performance*. Discussion Paper 93–03. Government and Competitiveness Project, Queen's University School of Policy Studies.

Anderson, James E. 1984. *Public Policy-Making*, 3rd ed. CBS College Publishing.

Anderson, Terry L., ed. 1993. *NAFTA and the Environment*. Vancouver: The Fraser Institute.

Andrew, Caroline. 1984. 'Women and the Welfare State.' Presidential Address to the Canadian Political Science Association.

– 1992. 'The Feminist City.' In Henri Lustiger-Thaler, ed., *Political Arrangements: Power and the City*. Montreal: Black Rose Books, 109–22.

– 1994. 'Challenge for a New Political Economy.' In A.F. Johnson, S. McBride and P.J. Smith, eds., *Continuities and Discontinuities: The Political Economy of Social Welfare and Labour Market Policy in Canada*. Toronto: University of Toronto Press, 62–75.

Andrew, Caroline and Beth Moore Milroy, eds. 1988. *Life Spaces: Gender, Household, Employment*. Vancouver: UBC Press.

Archer, Keith, Roger Gibbins, Rainer Knopff, and Leslie A. Pal. 1995. *Parameters of Power: An Introduction to Canadian Political Institutions*. Toronto: Nelson.

Archibald, K.A. 1980. 'The Pitfalls of Language, or Analysis through the Looking Glass.' In G. Majone and E.S. Quade, eds., *Pitfalls of Analysis*. Chichester: John Wiley, 1980.

Armstrong, P. and P. Connelly. 1989. 'Feminist Political Economy: An Introduction.' *Studies in Political Economy* 30 (Autumn), 5–12.

Armstrong, P. and H. 1990. 'Lessons from Pay Equity.' *Studies in Political Economy* 32 (Summer), 29–54.

Aronson, J. 1993. 'Giving Consumers a Say in Policy Development: Influencing Policy or Just Being Heard?' *Canadian Public Policy* 19, no. 4, 367–78.

Ascher, W. 1987. 'Policy Sciences and the Economic Approach in a "Post-Positivist" Era.' *Policy Sciences* 20:3–9.

Ashford, Douglas E. 1978. 'The Structural Analysis of Policy, or Institutions Really Do Matter.' In Douglas E. Ashford, ed., *Comparing Public Policies: New Concepts and Methods*. Beverly Hills: Sage.

– 1981. *Policy and Politics in Britain: The Limits of Consensus*. Philadelphia: Temple University Press.

– 1982. *Policy and Politics in France: Living with Uncertainty*. Philadelphia: Temple University Press.

– 1988. 'Ordaining Power: Discovering the State through Policy Studies.' Paper prepared for the Conference on Comparative Policy Studies, University of Pittsburgh, 18–21 May.

Atkinson, Michael M. 1993. 'Introduction: Governing Canada.' In Michael M. Atkinson, ed., *Governing Canada: Institutions and Public Policy*. Toronto: Harcourt Brace Jovanovich, 1–16.

– ed. 1993. *Governing Canada: Institutions and Public Policy*. Toronto: Harcourt Brace Jovanovich.

Atkinson, Michael and M. Chandler, eds. 1983. *The Politics of Canadian Public Policy*. Toronto: University of Toronto Press.

Atkinson, Michael M. and William D. Coleman. 1988. 'Policy Networks, Policy Communities and the Problems of Governance,' *Governance* 5:154–80.

– 1989. *The State, Business and Industrial Change in Canada*. Toronto: University of Toronto Press.

– 1989. 'Strong States and Weak States: Sectoral Policy Networks in Advanced Capitalist Economies.' *British Journal of Political Science* 19:47–67.

Aucoin, Peter. 1971. 'Theory and Research in the Study of Policy-Making.' In G. Bruce Doern and Peter Aucoin, eds., *The Structures of Policy-Making in Canada*. Toronto: Macmillan.

– 1975. 'Pressure Groups and Recent Changes in the Policy Making Process.' In A. Paul Pross, ed., *Pressure Group Behaviour in Canadian Politics*. Toronto: McGraw-Hill.

– 1986. 'Organizational Change in the Machinery of Government: From Rational Management to Brokerage Politics.' *Canadian Journal of Political Science* 19, no. 1, 3–27.

- 1990. 'Administrative Reform in Public Management: Paradigms, Principles, Paradoxes and Pendulums.' *Governance* 3, no. 2, 115–37.
- et al. 1988. *The Centralization-Decentralization Conundrum: Organization and Management in Canadian Government.* Halifax: IRPP.
Auld, D. and H. Kitchen. 1988. *The Supply of Government Services.* Vancouver: The Fraser Institute.
Axelrod, R. 1984. *The Evolution of Cooperation.* New York: Basic Books.
Bacchi, Carol Lee. 1983. *Liberation Deferred? The Ideas of the English-Canadian Suffragists, 1877–1918.* Toronto: University of Toronto Press.
- 1990. *Same Difference: Feminism and Sexual Difference.* Sydney: Allen and Unwin.
Bacon, F. 1985. 'Of Counsel.' In his *The Essays*, edited by J. Pitcher. Harmondsworth: Penguin, 120–4.
Badaracco, Joseph L. Jr. 1985. *Loading the Dice: A Five-Country Study of Vinyl Chloride Regulation.* Cambridge, Mass.: Harvard Business School Press.
Bakker, I. 1989. 'The Political Economy of Gender.' In W. Clement and G. Williams, eds., *The New Canadian Political Economy.* Montreal: McGill-Queen's University Press.
Balbo, Laura. 1987. 'Family, Women, and the State: Notes toward a Typology of Family Roles and Public Intervention.' In Charles S. Maier, ed., *Changing Boundaries of the Political.* Cambridge: Cambridge University Press, 201–19.
Banting, Keith, ed. 1986. *The State and Economic Interests.* Volume 32 of the Research Studies for the Royal Commission on Economic Union and Development Prospects for Canada. Toronto: University of Toronto Press.
- 1987. *The Welfare State and Canadian Federalism*, 2nd ed. Montreal: McGill-Queen's University Press.
- 1992. 'Economic Integration and Social Policy: Canada and the United States.' In Terence M. Hunsley, ed., *Social Policy in the Global Economy.* Kingston: Queen's University School of Social Policy, 21–44.
Banting, Keith, Michael Hawes, Richard Simeon, and Elaine Willis, eds. 1991. *Policy Choices: Political Agendas in Canada and the United States.* Kingston: School of Policy Studies, Queen's University.
Bari, J-P. 1986. 'L'expert comme conseiller du prince: Réflexions sur la pratique du conseil en matière politique.' *Annuaire Suisse de Science Politique* 29:55–80.
Barlow, M. and B. Campbell. 1991. *Take Back the Nation.* Toronto: Key Porter Brooks.
Bashevkin, Sylvia. 1994. 'Confronting Neo-conservatism: Anglo-American Women's Movements under Thatcher, Reagan and Mulroney.' *International Political Science Review* 15, no. 3, 275–96.

Baxter-Moore, N. 1991. 'Ideology or Pragmatism? The Politics and Management of the Mulroney Government's Privatization Program.' Paper presented to the Annual Conference of the British Association for Canadian Studies, University of Nottingham (April).

Beer, Samuel. 1980. 'British Pressure Groups Revisited: Pluralistic Stagnation from the Fifties to the Seventies.' *Public Administration Bulletin* 32:5–16.

Benhabib, S. 1986. *Critique, Norm, and Utopia: A Study of the Foundations of Critical Theory*. New York: Columbia University Press.

Bennett, Colin J. 1990. 'The Formation of a Canadian Privacy Policy: The Art and Craft of Lesson Drawing.' *Canadian Public Administration* 33:551–70.

– 1991. 'How States Utilize Foreign Evidence.' *Journal of Public Policy* 11:31–54.

– 1991. 'Review Article: What Is Policy Convergence and What Causes It?' *British Journal of Political Science* 21:215–33.

– 1992. *Regulating Privacy: Data Protection and Public Policy in Europe and the United States*. Ithaca: Cornell University Press.

Bennett, Colin J. and Michael Howlett. 'The Lessons of Learning: Reconciling Theories of Policy Learning and Policy Change.' *Policy Sciences* 25:275–94.

Benson B.L. 1990. *The Enterprise of Law*. San Francisco: Pacific Research Institute for Public Policy.

Benson, J.K. 1975. 'The Interorganizational Network as a Political Economy.' *Administrative Science Quarterly* 20:229–49.

– 1982. 'A Framework for Policy Analysis.' In D. Rogers et al., eds., *Interorganizational Coordination*. Ames: Iowa State University Press.

Berger, C. 1976. *The Writing of Canadian History*. Toronto: Oxford University Press.

Berger, P.L. and T. Luckmann. 1967. *The Social Construction of Reality: A Treatise in the Sociology of Knowledge*. New York: Anchor Books.

Berger, T. 1977. *Northern Frontier, Northern Homeland: The Report of the Mackenzie Valley Pipeline Inquiry*, 2 vols. Ottawa: Supply and Services Canada.

Berman, H.J. 1984. *Law and Revolution*. Cambridge: Harvard University Press.

Bernard, Jean-Thomas. 1993. *Hydroelectricity, Royalties and Industrial Competitiveness*. Discussion Paper 93–04. Government and Competitiveness Project, Queen's University School of Policy Studies.

Bernstein, R.J. 1976. *The Restructuring of Social and Political Theory*. Philadelphia: University of Pennsylvania Press.

Berry, Jeffrey M. 1977. *Lobbying for the People: The Political Behavior of Public Interest Groups*. Princeton: Princeton University Press.

Best, Joel. 1989. *Images of Issues: Typifying Contemporary Social Problems*. New York: de Gruyter.

Beveridge, William. 1960. *Full Employment in a Free Society*, 2nd ed. London: Allen and Unwin.

Bienefeld, Fred et al. 1993. *'Bleeding the Patient': The Debt/Deficit Hoax Exposed*. Ottawa: Canadian Centre for Policy Alternatives.

Bish, R.L. 1971. *The Public Economy of Metropolitan Areas*. Waco: Markham Press.

– 1986. 'Improving Productivity in the Government Sector.' In D. Laidler, ed., *Responses to Economic Change*. Toronto: University of Toronto Press.

– 1990. *Local Government in British Columbia*, 2nd ed. Richmond: Union of B.C. Municipalities.

Black, Naomi. 1992. 'Ripples in the Second Wave: Comparing the Contemporary Women's Movement in Canada and the United States.' In Constance Backhouse and David H. Flaherty, eds., *Challenging Times: The Women's Movement in Canada and the United States*. Montreal and Kingston: McGill-Queen's University Press, 94–109.

Blais, André. 1985. *Industrial Policy*. Toronto: University of Toronto Press.

– 1986. 'Industrial Policy in Advanced Capitalist Economies.' In André Blais, ed., *Industrial Policy*. Volume 44 of the Research Studies for the Royal Commission on Economic Union and Development Prospects for Canada. Toronto: University of Toronto Press, 1–54.

Blais, André, Donald Blake, and Stéphane Dion. 1993. 'Do Parties Make a Difference? Parties and the Size of Government in Liberal Democracies.' *American Journal of Political Science* 37:40–62.

Blendon, Robert J. 1989. 'Three Systems: A Comparative Survey.' *Health Management Quarterly* 11, no. 1, 2–10.

– et al. 1993. 'Physicians' Perspectives on Caring for Patients in the United States, Canada and West Germany,' *New England Journal of Medicine* 328, no. 14, 1011–16.

Bliss, Michael. 1994. *Right Honourable Men: The Descent of Canadian Politics from Macdonald to Mulroney*. Toronto: Harper Collins.

Block, Walter, ed. 1989. *Economics and the Environment: A Reconciliation*. Vancouver: The Fraser Institute.

– 1991. *Economic Freedom: Toward a Theory of Measurement*. Vancouver: The Fraser Institute.

– 1993. 'Public Finance Texts Cannot Justify Government Taxation: A Critique.' *Canadian Public Administration* 36, no. 2, 225–62.

Bodenheimer, Thomas. 1993. 'Universal Health Insurance "Canadian-Style": Will It Come to the United States?' *American Review of Canadian Studies* 23 (Spring), 37–45.

Borchorst, Anette and Birte Siim. 1987. 'Women and the Advanced Welfare State – A New Kind of Patriarchal Power?' In Anne Showstack Sassoon, ed., *Women and the State*. London: Routledge, 128–57.

Borins, Sanford F. 1986. 'Management of the Public Sector in Japan: Are There Lessons to be Learned?' *Canadian Public Administration* 29:175–96.

Borins, Sanford F. and B.E.C. Boothman. 1985. 'Crown Corporations and Economic Efficiency.' In D.G. McFetridge, ed., *Canadian Industrial Policy in Action*. Toronto: University of Toronto Press.

Boston, J. 1991. 'The Theoretical Underpinnings of Public Sector Restructuring in New Zealand.' In J. Boston et al., eds., *Reshaping the State: New Zealand's Bureaucratic Revolution*. Melbourne: Oxford University Press.

– 1994. 'Purchasing Policy Advice: The Limits to Contracting Out.' *Governance* 7, no. 1, 1–30.

Brams, Steven J. 1976. *Paradoxes in Politics: An Introduction to the Nonobvious in Political Science*. New York: The Free Press.

– 1985. *Rational Politics: Decisions, Games and Strategy*. New York: Academic Press.

– 1994. *Theory of Moves*. Cambridge: Cambridge University Press.

Braybrooke, David and Charles E. Lindblom. 1963. *A Strategy of Decision: Policy Evaluation as a Social Process*. New York: MacMillan.

Breton, A. 1985. 'Supplementary Statement.' In *Report of the Royal Commission on the Economic Union and Development Prospects for Canada*. Ottawa: Ministry of Supply and Services, 485–526.

Breton, A. and A.D. Scott. 1978. *The Economic Constitution of Federal States*. Toronto: University of Toronto Press.

Breton, A. and R. Wintrobe. 1979. 'Bureaucracy and State Intervention.' *Canadian Public Administration* 22:208–26.

– 1982. *The Logic of Bureaucratic Control*. Cambridge: Cambridge University Press.

Brickman, Ronald, Sheila Jasanoff, and Thomas Ilgen. 1985. *Controlling Chemicals: Regulatory Politics in Europe and the United States*. Ithaca, N.Y.: Cornell University Press.

Britton, John N.H. and James M. Gilmour. 1978. *The Weakest Link: A Technological Perspective on Canadian Industry Underdevelopment*. Science Council of Canada, Background Study No. 43. Ottawa: Supply and Services.

Brodie, Janine. 1989. 'The Political Economy of Regionalism.' In W. Clement and G. Williams, eds. *The New Canadian Political Economy*. Kingston: McGill-Queen's University Press.

– 1990. *The Political Economy of Canadian Regionalism*. Toronto: Harcourt Brace Jovanovich.

Brodie, Janine, Shelley A.M. Gavigan, and Jane Jenson. 1992. *The Politics of Abortion*. Toronto: Oxford University Press.

Bromley, Daniel W., ed. 1992. *Making the Commons Work: Theory, Practice and Policy*. San Francisco: The ICS Press.

Brooks, Stephen. 1993. *Public Policy in Canada*, 2nd ed. Toronto: McClelland and Stewart.
– 1994. 'How Ottawa Bends: Plastic Words and the Politics of Social Morality.' In S. Phillips, ed., *How Ottawa Spends 1994–95: Making Change*. Ottawa: Carleton University Press.
Brooks, S. and A.G. Gagnon. 1988. *Social Scientists and Politics in Canada: Between Clerisy and Vanguard*. Kingston and Montreal: McGill-Queen's University Press.
– eds. 1990. *Social Scientists, Policy, and the State*. New York: Praeger.
– eds. 1994. *The Political Influence of Ideas: Policy Communities and the Social Sciences*. New York: Praeger.
Brousseau, Eric. 1989. 'L'approche néo-institutionnelle de l'économie des coûts de transaction.' *Revue française d'économie* 4, no. 4, 123–66.
– 1993. *L'économie des contrats*. Paris: Presses Universitaires de France.
Bruce, Peter G. 1989. 'Political Parties and Labour Legislation in Canada and the U.S.' *Industrial Relations* 28, no. 2, 115–41.
Bruton, J. and M. Howlett. 1992. 'Differences of Opinion: Round Tables, Policy Networks, and the Failure of Canadian Environmental Strategy.' *Alternatives: Perspectives on Society, Technology and Environment* 19, no. 1, 25–8, 31–3.
Bryden, Philip, Steven Davis, and John Russell, eds. 1994. *Protecting Rights and Freedoms: Essays on the Charter's Place in Canada's Political, Legal, and Intellectual Life*. Toronto: University of Toronto Press.
Bryson, John M. and Peter Smith Ring. 1990. 'A Transaction-Based Approach to Policy Intervention.' *Policy Sciences* 23, no. 3, 205–29.
Buchanan, J.M. 1983. 'The Public Choice Perspective.' *Journal of Public Finance and Public Choice* 1:17–25.
– 1987. 'The Constitution of Economic Policy.' *American Economic Review* 77:243–50.
– 1990. 'The Domain of Constitutional Economics.' *Constitutional Political Economy* 1:1–18.
– 1991. 'The Contractarian Logic of Classical Liberalism.' In Buchanan, ed., *The Economics and the Ethics of Constitutional Order*. Ann Arbor: University of Michigan Press, 125–36.
Buchanan, J.M. and G. Tullock. 1962. *The Calculus of Consent*. Ann Arbor: University of Michigan Press.
Buchanan, J.M. et al., eds. 1980. *Toward a Theory of the Rent Seeking Society*. College Station: Texas A&M University Press.
Bulmer, M., ed. 1987. *Social Science Research and Government: Essays on Britain and the United States*. London: George Allen and Unwin.
Burns, Tom and Helena Flam. 1987. *The Shaping of Social Organization: Social Rule System Theory with Applications*. London: Sage.

Cairns, Alan C. 1985. 'The Embedded State: State-Society Relations in Canada.'
In Keith Banting, ed., *State and Society: Canada in Comparative Perspective.*
Toronto: University of Toronto Press, 53–86.
– 1993. 'The Fragmentation of Canadian Citizenship.' In William Kaplan, ed.,
Belonging: The Meaning and Future of Canadian Citizenship. McGill-Queen's
University Press, 181–220.
Cairns, Alan and Cynthia Williams, eds. 1985. *Constitutionalism, Citizenship and
Society in Canada.* Toronto: University of Toronto Press.
– eds. 1985. *Public Opinion and Public Policy in Canada.* Toronto: University of
Toronto Press.
– eds. 1985. *The Politics of Gender, Ethnicity and Language in Canada.* Toronto:
University of Toronto Press.
Calhoun, C., ed. 1992. *Habermas and the Public Sphere.* Cambridge: The M.I.T.
Press.
Calvert, John. 1987. 'The Divergent Paths of the Canadian and American Labour
Movements.' *The Round Table* 303 (July).
Cameron, David M. 1987. 'The Discipline and the Profession of Public Adminis-
tration in an Academic's Perspective.' *Canadian Public Administration* 25, no.
1, 496–50.
Cameron, David. 1978. 'The Expansion of the Public Economy: A Comparative
Analysis.' *American Political Science Review* 72, no. 4, 1243–61.
Cameron, David R. 1984. 'Social Democracy, Corporatism, Labour Quiescence,
and the Representation of Economic Interest in Advanced Capitalist Society.'
In John R. Goldthorpe, ed., *Order and Conflict in Contemporary Capitalism.*
Oxford: Oxford University Press, 143–78.
– 1985. 'The Growth of Government Spending: The Canadian Experience in
Comparative Perspective.' In Keith Banting, ed., *State and Society: Canada in
Comparative Perspective.* Toronto: University of Toronto Press, 21–52.
– ed. 1986. *The Free Trade Papers.* Toronto: James Lorimer.
Cameron, David and M. Watkins, ed. 1993. *Canada under Free Trade.* Toronto:
James Lorimer.
Camilleri, Joseph A. and Jim Falk. 1992. *The End Of Sovereignty?* Aldershot:
Elgar.
Campbell, Colin. 1983. *Governments under Stress: Political Executives and Key
Bureaucrats in Washington, London and Ottawa.* Toronto: University of
Toronto Press.
Campbell, Colin and George Szablowski. 1979. *The Superbureaucrats.* Toronto:
Macmillan.
Campbell, R.M. 1987. *Grand Illusions: The Politics of the Keynesian Experience
in Canada.* Peterborough: Broadview Press.

Canada. 1945. Department of Reconstruction and Supply. *Employment and Income with Special Reference to the Initial Period of Reconstruction.* Ottawa: King's Printer.

– 1962. Royal Commission on Government Organization. *Report.* Ottawa: Queen's Printer.

– 1976. *Report of the Auditor General to the House of Commons for Fiscal Year Ended 31 March 1976.* Ottawa: Supply and Services Canada.

– 1985. Royal Commission on the Economic Union and Development Prospects for Canada. *Report.* Ottawa: Supply and Services Canada.

– 1989. *Public Service 2000: The Renewal of the Public Service of Canada.* Ottawa: Supply and Services Canada.

Canadian Council on Social Development. 1991. *Social Policy in the 1990s: The Challenge.* Ottawa: Canadian Council on Social Development.

Canadian Institute for Economic Policy. 1979. *Out of Joint with the Times: An Overview of the Canadian Economic Dilemma.* Ottawa: Canadian Institute for Economic Policy.

Card, David and Richard B. Freeman. 1993. 'Introduction.' In David Card and Richard B. Freeman, eds., *Small Differences that Matter: Labor Markets and Income Maintenance in Canada and the United States.* Chicago: University of Chicago Press, 1–19.

Caroll, W.K. 1986. *Corporate Power and Canadian Capital.* Vancouver: University of British Columbia Press.

– ed. 1992. *Organizing Dissent: Contemporary Social Movements in Theory and Practice.* Toronto: Garamond Press.

Carty, Linda, ed. 1993. *And Still We Rise.* Toronto: Women's Press.

Cassidy, F. and R.L. Bish. 1989. *Indian Government: Its Meaning in Practice.* Halifax: Institute for Research on Public Policy and Oolichan Books.

Cassin, A. Marguerite. 1993. 'Equitable and Fair: Widening the Circle.' In Allan M. Maslove, ed., *Fairness in Taxation: Exploring Principles.* Toronto: University of Toronto Press, 104–34.

Castles, Francis G. 1993. 'Changing Course in Economic Policy: The English-Speaking Nations in the 1980s.' In F.G. Castles, ed., *Families of Nations: Patterns of Public Policy in Western Democracies.* Aldershot: Dartmouth.

Castles, Francis G. and Deborah Mitchell. 1992. 'Identifying Welfare State Regimes: The Links between Politics, Instruments, and Outcomes.' *Governance* 5 (January), 1–26.

Castles, Frank and Robert D. McKinlay. 1979. 'Does Politics Matter: An Analysis of the Public Welfare Commitment in Advanced Democratic States.' *European Journal of Political Research* 7:169–86.

Cawson, Alan, P. Holmes, and A. Stevens. 1987. 'The Interaction between Firms and the State in France: The Case of Telecommunications and Consumer Electronics.' In Wilks and Wright, eds., *Comparative Government-Industry Relations*. Oxford: Oxford University Press.

Cawson, Alan, Kevin Morgan, Douglas Webber, Peter Holmes, and Anne Stevens. 1991. *Hostile Brothers: Competition and Closure in the European Electronics Industry*. Oxford: Clarendon Press.

Chambers, R.W. 1963. *Thomas More*. Harmondsworth: Penguin.

Chant, John F., Donald McFetridge, and Douglas A. Smith. 1990. 'The Economics of a Conserver Society.' In W.E. Block, ed., *Economics and the Environment: A Reconciliation*. Vancouver: The Fraser Institute.

Chase, Stuart. 1945. *Democracy Under Pressure: Special Interests vs the Public Welfare*. New York: Twentieth Century Fund.

Chorney, Harold. 1988. 'Sound Finance and Other Delusions: Deficit and Debt Management in the Age of Neo-Liberal Economics. Department of Political Science, Working Paper No. 4. Montreal: Concordia University.

– 1989. *The Deficit and Debt Management: An Alternative to Monetarism*. Ottawa: Canadian Centre for Policy Alternatives.

– et al. 1992. *The Deficit Made Me Do It! The Myths about Government Debt*. Ottawa: Canadian Centre for Policy Alternatives.

Chuppe, Terry M., Hugh R. Haworth, and Marvin G. Watkins. 1989. 'Global Finance: Causes, Consequences and Prospects for the Future.' *Global Finance Journal* 1:1–20.

Clark, B.R. 1956. 'Organizational Adaptation and Precarious Values: A Case Study.' *American Sociological Review*, 327–36.

Clark, S.D. 1939. *The Canadian Manufacturers' Association*. Toronto: University of Toronto Press.

Clark, S.D., J. Paul Grayson, and Linda M. Grayson. 1975. *Prophecy and Protest: Social Movements in Twentieth-Century Canada*. Toronto: Gage.

Clarkson, S. 1985. *Canada and the Reagan Challenge: Crisis and Adjustment*. Toronto: James Lorimer.

– 1989. 'Disjunctions: Free Trade and the Paradox of Canadian Development. In D. Drache and M. Gertler, eds., *The New Era of Global Competition*. Montreal: McGill-Queen's University Press.

Clement, Wallace. 1975. *The Canadian Corporate Elite*. Toronto: McClelland and Stewart.

– 1977. *Continental Corporate Power*. Toronto: McClelland and Stewart.

Clement, W. and G. Williams, eds. 1989. *The New Canadian Political Economy*. Kingston: McGill Queen's University Press.

Clio Collective. 1987. *Quebec Women: A History*. Toronto: Women's Press.

Coase, R.H. 1960. 'The Problem of Social Cost.' *Journal of Law and Economics*
3:1–44.

Cobb, R.W. and C.D. Elder. 1971. 'The Politics of Agenda Building: An Alternative Perspective for Modern Democratic Theory.' *Journal of Politics* 33, no. 4,
892–915.

Code, Lorraine. 1991. *What Can She Know? Feminist Theory and the Construction of Knowledge*. Ithaca, N.Y.: Cornell University Press.

Cohen, Marjorie Griffin. 1987. *Free Trade and the Future of Women's Work:
Manufacturing and Services Industries*. Toronto: Garamond Press.

– 1993. 'Social Policy and Social Services.' In Ruth Roach Pierson, Marjorie
Griffin Cohen, Paula Bourne, and Philinda Masters, eds., *Canadian Women's
Issues: Volume I, Strong Voices*. Toronto: James Lorimer, 264–84.

Coleman, David. 1991. 'Policy Research – Who Needs It?' *Governance* 4, no. 4,
420–53.

Coleman, James. 1990. *Foundations of Social Theory*. Cambridge: The Belknap
Press of Harvard University Press.

Coleman, James and Thomas J. Fararo. 1992. *Rational Choice Theory*. Newburry
Park: Sage Publications.

Coleman, William D. 1988. *Business and Politics: A Study of Collective Action*.
Montreal: McGill-Queen's University Press.

– 1990. 'State Traditions and Comprehensive Business Associations: A Comparative Structural Analysis.' *Political Studies* 38:231–52.

– 1994. 'Policy Convergence in Banking: A Comparative Study.' *Political Studies*.

Coleman, William and Grace Skogstad. 1990a. 'Policy Communities and Policy
Networks: A Structural Approach.' In Coleman and Skogstad, eds., *Policy
Communities and Public Policy in Canada*. Toronto: Copp Clark Pitman.

– eds. 1990b. *Policy Communities and Public Policy in Canada*. Toronto: Copp
Clark Pitman.

Commons, J.R. 1932. *Legal Foundations of Capitalism*. Madison: University of
Wisconsin Press.

Connolly, William E. 1983. *The Terms of Political Discourse*, 2nd ed. Princeton:
Princeton University Press

Conway, Thomas. 1993. 'The Marginalization of the Department of the Environment: Environment Policy, 1971–1988.' Unpublished Doctoral Dissertation,
Carleton University, Ottawa.

Corbett, David C. 1953. 'The Pressure Group and the Public Interest.' *Proceedings of the Annual Conference*, Institute of Public Administration of Canada,
185–95.

Corry, J.A. 1981. 'Sovereign People or Sovereign Governments.' In H.V. Kroeker,
ed., *Sovereign People or Sovereign Governments*. Montreal: Institute for
Research on Public Policy, 3–12.

Corry, J.A. and J.E. Hodgetts. 1959. *Democratic Government and Politics.* Toronto: University of Toronto Press.

Courchene, Thomas. 1990. 'Toward the Reintegration of Social and Economic Policy.' In Bruce Doern and Bryne Purchase, eds., *Canada at Risk?* Toronto: C.D. Howe Institute, 125–48.

Cowhey, Peter F. 1990. 'The International Telecommunications Regime: The Political Roots of Regimes of High Technology.' *International Organization* 44:169–200.

Cox, Andrew. 1988. 'The Old and New Testaments of Corporatism: Is It a Political Form or a Method of Policy-Making?' *Political Studies* 36:294–308.

Craven, Paul. 1980. *'An Impartial Umpire': Industrial Relations and the Canadian State, 1900–1911.* Toronto: University of Toronto Press.

Cuneo, C. 1979. 'State, Class and Reserve Labour: The Case of the 1941 Canadian Unemployment Insurance Act.' *Canadian Review of Sociology and Anthropology* 16, no. 2, 147–70.

– 1980. 'State Mediation of Class Contradictions in Canadian Unemployment Insurance.' *Studies in Political Economy* 3:37–65.

– 1986. 'Comment: Restoring Class to State Unemployment Insurance.' *Canadian Journal of Political Science* 19.

Cunningham, Frank, Sue Findlay, Marlene Kadar, Alan Lennon, and Ed Silva. 1988. *Social Movements/Social Change: The Politics and Practices of Organizing.* Toronto: Between the Lines.

Daft, Richard. 1992. *Organization Theory and Design.* New York: West Publishing.

Daly, Michael. J. 1981. 'The Swedish Approach to Investing Public Pension Funds: Some Lessons for Canada?' *Canadian Public Administration* 24:257–71.

Darling, H. 1980. *The Politics of Freight Rates.* Toronto: McClelland and Stewart.

Davidson, Alex and Michael Dence. 1988. *The Brundtland Challenge and the Cost of Inaction.* Montreal: Institute for Research on Public Policy.

Davis, A. 1984. 'Property Rights and Access Management in the Small Boat Fishery.' In C. Lamson and A.J. Hanson, eds., *Atlantic Fisheries and Coastal Communities.* Halifax: Dalhousie Ocean Studies Program.

Davis, O.A. 1969. 'Notes on Strategy and Methodology for a Scientific Political Science.' In J.L. Bernd, ed., *Mathematical Applications in Political Science.* Charlottesville: University Press of Virginia, 22–38.

Dawes, Robyn M. 1988. *Rational Choice in an Uncertain World.* New York: Harcourt Brace Jovanovich.

Dawson, Helen Jones. 1960. 'The Canadian Federation of Agriculture.' *Canadian Public Administration* 3, no. 2, 134–49.

– 1963. 'The Consumers Association of Canada.' *Canadian Public Administration* 6, no. 1, 92–118.

- 1975. 'National Pressure Groups and the Federal Government.' In A. Paul Pross, ed., *Pressure Group Behaviour in Canadian Politics*. Toronto: McGraw-Hill, 27–58.

Dawson, R.M. 1970. *The Government of Canada*, revised by N. Ward. Toronto: University of Toronto Press.

Day, Patricia and Rudolph Klein. 1992. 'Constitutional and Distributional Conflict in British Medical Politics: The Case of General Practice, 1911–1991.' *Political Studies* 40:462–78.

deLeon, Peter. 1988. *Advice and Consent: The Development of the Policy Sciences*. New York: Russell Sage.

Denhardt, Robert B. 1993. *The Pursuit of Significance: Strategies for Managerial Success in Public Organizations*. Belmont, Calif.: Wadsworth Publishing.

Derrida, J. 1976. *Of Grammatology*, trans. by G.C. Spivak. Baltimore: Johns Hopkins University Press.

- 1992. 'Force of Law: The "Mystical Foundation of Authority."' In D. Cornell, M. Rosenfeld, and D. Carlson, eds., *Deconstruction and the Possibility of Justice*. London: Routledge, 3–67.

Dery, D. 1985. *Problem Definition in Policy Analysis*. Lawrence: University of Kansas Press.

Desveaux, James. 1995. *Designing Bureaucracies: Institutional Capacity and Large Scale Problem Solving*. Stanford: Stanford University Press.

Desveaux, J., E.A. Lindquist, and G. Toner. 1994. 'Organizing for Policy Innovation in Public Bureaucracy: AIDS, Energy, and Environmental Policy in Canada.' *Canadian Journal of Political Science* 27, no. 3, 493–538.

Dewees, Don. 1993. *Reducing the Burden of Environmental Regulation*. Discussion Paper 93–07. Government and Competitiveness Project, Queen's University School of Policy Studies.

Dierkes, Meinolf, H. Weiller, and A. Berthoin Antal, eds. 1987. *Comparative Policy Research*. Aldershot: Gower.

DiMaggio, Paul J. and Walter W. Powell. 1991a. 'Introduction.' In Walter W. Powell and Paul J. DiMaggio, eds., *The New Institutionalism in Organizational Analysis*. Chicago: University of Chicago Press, 1–38.

- 1991b. 'The Iron Cage Revisited: Institutional Isomorphism and Collective Rationality in Organizational Fields.' In Walter W. Powell and Paul J. DiMaggio, eds., *The New Institutionalism in Organizational Analysis*. Chicago: University of Chicago Press, 63–82.

Dion, Léon. 1971. *Société et politique: La vie des groupes*. Québec: Les Presses de l'université Laval.

Dion, Léon and Micheline de Seve. 1974. 'Quebec Interest Groups: The Search for an Alternative Political System.' *Annals of the American Academy of Political and Social Science* 413:124–44.

Dobson, Wendy. 1991. *Economic Policy Coordination: Requiem or Prologue?* Washington: Institute for International Economics.

Dobuzinskis, Laurent. 1977. 'Rational Policy-Making: Policy, Politics, and Political Science.' In T.A. Hockin, ed., *Apex of Power: The Prime Minister and Political Leadership in Canada*, 2nd ed. Scarborough: Prentice-Hall, 211–28.

– 1987. 'Policy Orienteering.' *Policy Options* (October), 3–6.

– 1992. 'Modernist and Postmodernist Metaphors of the Policy Process: Control and Stability vs. Chaos and Reflexive Understanding.' *Policy Sciences* 25, no. 2, 355–80.

Doern, G.B. 1971. 'The Development of Policy Organizations in the Executive Arena.' In G.B. Doern and P. Aucoin, eds., *The Structures of Policy-Making in Canada*. Toronto: Macmillan, 39–78.

– 1971. 'The Bugetary Process and the Policy Role of the Federal Bureaucracy,' 79–112.

– 1977. 'The Policy-Making Philosophy of Prime Minister Trudeau and His Advisers.' In T.A. Hockin, ed., *Apex of Power: The Prime Minister and Political Leadership in Canada*, 2nd ed. Scarborough: Prentice-Hall, 189–96.

– ed. 1978. *The Regulatory Process in Canada*. Toronto: Macmillan.

– 1981. *Government Intervention in the Canadian Nuclear Industry*. Montreal: Institute for Research on Public Policy.

– ed. 1985. *The Politics of Economic Policy*. Toronto: University of Toronto Press.

– ed. 1990. *The Environmental Imperative*. Toronto: C.D. Howe Institute.

– ed. 1990. *Getting It Green: Case Studies in Canadian Environmental Regulation*. Toronto: C.D. Howe Institute.

– 1993. *Green Diplomacy*. Toronto: C.D. Howe Institute.

– 1994a. *Canadian Competition Policy Institutions in a Global Market*. Toronto: C.D. Howe Institute.

– 1994b. 'Canadian Competition Policy Institutions: A Macro and Micro Political Analysis.' Paper Prepared for the Conference on National Competition Policy Institutions in a Global Market, School of Public Administration, Carleton University, Ottawa, 26–27 May.

– 1994c. 'The Political Economy of Internationalizing Competition Policy: From Regimes to Institutions?' Paper Prepared for the Conference on National Competition Policy Institutions in a Global Market, School of Public Administration, Carleton University, Ottawa, 26–27 May.

Doern, G. Bruce and Peter Aucoin, eds. 1971. *The Structures of Policy-Making in Canada*. Toronto: Macmillan.

– eds. 1978. *Public Policy in Canada: Organization and Process*. Toronto: Macmillan.

Doern, G. Bruce and Tom Conway. 1994. *The Greening of Canada: Federal Institutions and Decisions*. Toronto: University of Toronto Press.

Doern, G. Bruce, Allan Maslove, and Michael Prince. 1988. *Public Budgeting in Canada: Politics, Economics and Management*. Ottawa: Carleton University Press.

Doern, G. Bruce and Richard W. Phidd. 1983. *Canadian Public Policy: Ideas, Structure, Process*. Toronto: Methuen.

– 1992. *Canadian Public Policy: Ideas, Structure, Process*, 2nd ed. Toronto: Nelson Canada.

Doern, G. Bruce and Bryne Purchase, eds. 1990. *Canada at Risk? Canadian Public Policy in the 1990s*. Toronto: C.D. Howe Institute.

Doern, G. Bruce and Brian Tomlin. 1991. *Faith and Fear: The Canada–U.S. Free Trade Story*. Toronto: Stoddart.

Doern, G. Bruce and Glen Toner. 1985. *The Politics of Energy: The Development and Implementation of the NEP*. Toronto: Methuen.

Doern, G. Bruce and Allan Tupper, eds. 1988. *Privatization, Public Enterprise and Public Policy in Canada*. Halifax: Institute for Research on Public Policy.

Doern, G. Bruce and Vince Wilson, eds. 1974. *Issues in Canadian Public Policy*. Toronto: Macmillan.

Doerr, A.D. 1974. 'Indian Policy.' In G.B. Doern and V.S. Wilson, eds., *Issues in Canadian Public Policy*. Toronto: Macmillan, 36–54.

Dogan, Mattei and Dominique Pelassy. 1984. *How to Compare Nations: Strategies in Comparative Politics*. Chatham, N.J.: Chatham House.

Doron, Gideon. 1992. 'Rational Choice and the Policy Sciences.' *Policy Studies Review* 11, no. 34, 359–69.

Dosi, Giovanni et al., eds. 1988. *Technical Change and Economic Theory*. London: Pinter Publishers.

Dosman, Edgar J. 1975. *The National Interest: The Politics of Northern Development, 1968–75*. Toronto: McClelland and Stewart.

Downs, A. 1957. *An Economic Theory of Democracy*. New York: Harper and Row.

Drache, Daniel and M.S. Gertler, eds. 1991. *The New Era of Global Competition*. Montreal: McGill-Queen's University Press.

Dreyfus, H.L. and P. Rabinow. 1983. *Michel Foucault: Beyond Structuralism and Hermeneutics*, 2nd ed. Chicago: University of Chicago Press.

Dryzek, J.S. 1982. 'Policy Analysis as a Hermeneutic Activity.' *Policy Sciences* 14:309–29.

– 1987. 'Discursive Designs: Critical Theory and Political Institutions.' *American Journal of Political Science* 31:656–79.

– 1989. 'Policy Sciences of Democracy.' *Polity* 22, no. 1, 97–118.

– 1990. 'Designs for Environmental Discourse.' In R. Paehlke and D. Torgerson, eds., *Managing Leviathan: Environmental Politics and the Administrative State*. Peterborough: Broadview Press, 97–111.

– 1990. *Discursive Democracy: Politics, Policy and Political Science*. Cambridge: Cambridge University Press.

Dryzek, J.S. and D. Torgerson. 1993. 'Democracy and the Policy Sciences: A Progress Report.' *Policy Sciences* 26, no. 3, 127–37.

Dufour, Christian. 1990. *A Canadian Challenge/le défi québécois*. Vancouver: Oolichan.

Dumont, Micheline. 1995. 'Women of Quebec and the Contemporary Constitutional Issue.' In François-Pierre Gingras, ed., *Gender and Politics*. Toronto: Oxford University Press.

Dunleavy, Patrick. 1991. *Democracy, Bureaucracy and Public Choice*. London: Harvester Wheatsheaf; New York: Prentice-Hall.

Dunn, William N. 1992. 'Assessing the Impact of Policy Analysis: The Function of Usable Ignorance.' In W.N. Dunn and R.M. Kelly, eds., *Advances in Policy Studies since 1950*. New Brunswick, N.J.: Transaction Books.

Dunn, W.N. and R.M. Kelly, eds. 1992. *Advances in Policy Studies Since 1950*. New Brunswick, N.J.: Transaction Books.

Durning, D. 1993. 'Participatory Policy Analysis in a Social Service Agency: A Case Study.' *Journal of Policy Analysis and Management* 12, no. 2, 297–322.

Dwivedi, O.P., ed. 1982. *The Administrative State in Canada: Essays in Honour of J.E. Hodgetts*. Toronto: University of Toronto Press.

– 1986. 'The Environmental Challenge for Canada: Policy Developments and Administrative Changes.' In L.R. Moise et al., eds., *Organizational Policy and Development*. University of Louisville, 253–81.

Dwivedi, O.P. and R.W. Phidd. 1994. 'Prime Ministerial Leadership and Public Service Reform.' Paper presented at the Canadian Political Science Association Annual Meeting, Calgary, Alberta (June).

Dye, Thomas R. 1976. *Policy Analysis: What Governments Do, Why they Do it and What Difference it Makes*. University: University of Alabama Press.

– 1979. 'Politics vs. Economics: The Development of the Literature of Policy Determination.' *Policy Studies Journal* 7:652–62.

Dyson, Kenneth H.F. 1980. *The State Tradition in Western Europe*. Oxford: Martin Robertson.

Easton, David. 1969. 'The New Revolution in Political Science.' *American Political Science Review* 63:1051–61.

Easton, Stephen and M. Walker, eds. 1992. *Rating Global Economic Freedom*. Vancouver: The Fraser Institute.

Economic Council of Canada. 1991. *A Joint Venture: The Economics of Confederation*. 28th Annual Review. Ottawa: Supply and Services Canada.

- 1992. *The New Face of Poverty: Income Security Needs of Canadian Families.* Ottawa: Supply and Services Canada.

Eddy, William B. 1981. *Public Organization Behaviour and Development.* Cambridge, Mass.: Winthrop Publishing.

Edelman, Murray J. 1988. *Constructing the Political Spectacle.* Chicago: University of Chicago.

Eden, Lorraine and Maureen Molot. 1993. 'Canada's National Policies: Reflections on 125 Years.' *Canadian Public Policy* 19, no. 3, 232–51.

Egan, Carolyn, Linda Lee Gardner, and Judy Vashti Persad. 1988. 'The Politics of Transformation: Struggles with Race, Class, and Sexuality in the March 8th Coalition.' In Frank Cunningham, Sue Findlay, Marlene Kadar, Alan Lennon, and Ed Silva, eds., *Social Movements/Social Change: The Politics and Practices of Organizing.* Toronto: Between the Lines, 20–47.

Eisenstein, Hester. 1995. 'The Australian Femocratic Experiment: A Feminist Case for Bureaucracy.' In Myra Marx Ferree and Patricia Yancey Martin, eds., *Feminist Organizations.* Philadelphia: Temple University Press, 69–83.

Eisenstein, Zillah. 1987. 'Liberalism, Feminism and the Reagan State: The Neoconservative Assault on (Sexual) Equality.' *The Social Register*, 236–62.

Elazar, D.J. and J. Kincaid. 1980. 'Government, Politics and Constitutionalism.' *Publius* 10:3–30.

Elkins, David J. and Richard E.B. Simeon. 1979. 'A Cause in Search of Its Effect, or What Does Political Culture Explain?' *Comparative Politics* (January), 127–45.

- 1980. *Small Worlds: Provinces and Parties in Canadian Political Life.* Toronto: Methuen.

Elster, Jon. 1992. *Local Justice.* New York: Russell Sage Foundation.

Engeman, T.S. 1982. 'Hythloday's Utopia and More's England: An Interpretation of Thomas More's *Utopia.' Journal of Politics* 44:131–49.

Erasmus, G. and R. Dussault. 1992. 'Opening Statement by the Co-Chairs.' In *Opening Statements on the Occasion of the Launch of the Public Hearings of the Royal Commission on Aboriginal Peoples.* Winnipeg, Manitoba, 21 April.

Ernst, Alan. 1992. 'From Liberal Continentalism to Neoconservatism: North American Free Trade and the Politics of the C.D. Howe Institute.' *Studies in Political Economy* 39 (Autumn), 109–40.

Esping-Andersen, Gosta. 1990. *The Three Worlds of Welfare Capitalism.* Princeton, N.J.: Princeton University Press.

Esser, Josef, Wolfgang Fach, and Kenneth Dyson. 1984. '"Social Market" and Modernization Policy.' In Kenneth Dyson and Stephen Wilks, eds., *Industrial Crisis: A Comparative Study of the State and Industry.* New York: St. Martin's Press, 102–27.

Evans, Peter et al. 1988. *Bringing the State Back In*. New York: Cambridge University Press.

Fallis, George et al. 1995. *Home Remedies: Rethinking Canadian Housing Policy*. Toronto: C.D. Howe Institute.

Farr, J. 1988. 'Political Science and the Enlightenment of Enthusiasm.' *American Political Science Review* 82, no. 1, 51–69.

Faulkner, R.K. 1988. 'Visions and Powers: Bacon's Two-fold Politics of Progress.' *Polity* 21:111–36.

Feick, Jurgen. 1992. 'Comparative Policy Studies: A Path Towards Integration.' *Journal of Public Policy* 12, Part 3 (July–Sept.), 257–85.

Feldman, M.S. 1989. *Order without Design: Information Production and Policy Making*. Stanford: Stanford University Press.

Ferguson, Kathy E. 1984. *The Feminist Case against Bureaucracy*. Philadelphia: Temple University Press.

Finbow, Robert. 1993. 'Ideology and Institutions in North America.' *Canadian Journal of Political Science* 26 (December), 671–97.

Findlay, Sue. 1987. 'Facing the State: The Politics of the Women's Movement Reconsidered.' In Heather Jon Maroney and Meg Luxton, eds., *Feminism and Political Economy*. Toronto: Methuen, 31–50.

– 1993. 'Problematizing Privilege: Another Look at Representation.' In Linda Carty, ed., *And Still We Rise: Feminist Political Mobilizing in Contemporary Canada*. Toronto: Women's Press, 207–25.

Finkle, Peter with Kernaghan Webb, W.T. Stanbury, and Paul Pross. 1994. *Federal Government Relations with Interest Groups: A Reconsideration*. Ottawa: Consumer and Corporate Affairs Canada.

Finn, Ed, ed. 1993. *The Tory Wreckord, 1984–1993: Thirty-Six Ways the Tories Have Hurt Canadians*. Ottawa: Canadian Centre for Policy Alternatives.

Fischer, F. 1980. *Politics, Values, and Public Policy: The Problem of Methodology*. Boulder, Colo.: Westview Press.

– 1985. 'Critical Evaluation of Public Policy.' In J. Forester, ed., *Critical Theory and Public Life*. Cambridge: The M.I.T. Press, 231–57.

– 1989. 'Beyond the Rationality Project: Policy Analysis and the Postpositivist Challenge.' *Policy Studies Journal* 17:941–51.

– 1990. *Technocracy and the Politics of Expertise*. Newbury Park: Sage Publications.

– 1992. 'Participatory Expertise: Toward the Democratization of Policy Science.' In W.N. Dunn and R.M. Kelly, eds., *Advances in Policy Studies since 1950*. New Brunswick, N.J.: Transaction Publishers, 351–76.

– 1992. 'Reconstructing Policy Analysis: A Postpositivist Perspective.' *Policy Sciences* 25:333–9.

- 1993. 'Citizen Participation and the Democratization of Policy Expertise: From Theoretical Inquiry to Practical Cases.' *Policy Sciences* 26, no. 3, 165–87.

Fischer, F. and J. Forester, eds. 1993. *The Argumentative Turn in Policy Analysis and Planning*. Durham: Duke University Press.

Fleras, Augie, and Jean Leonard Elliott. 1992. *Aboriginal-State Relations in Canada, the United States, and New Zealand*. Toronto: Oxford University Press.

Forester, J. 1985. 'The Policy Analysis–Critical Theory Affair: Wildavsky and Habermas as Bedfellows?' In J. Forester, ed., *Critical Theory and Public Life*. Cambridge: The M.I.T. Press, 258–80.

Forester, John. 1989. *Planning in the Face of Power*. Berkeley: University of California Press.

Foucault, M. 1979. *Discipline and Punish: The Birth of the Prison*, trans. by A. Sheridan. New York: Vintage.

- 1980. *Power/Knowledge*, edited by C. Gordon. New York: Pantheon.

Fournier, Pierre. 1986. 'Consensus Building in Canada: Case Studies and Prospects.' In Keith Banting, ed., *The State and Economic Interests*, vol. 32 of the Research Studies for the Royal Commission on Economic Union and Development Prospects for Canada. Toronto: University of Toronto Press, 291–336.

Fowke, V.C. 1967. 'The National Policy – Old and New.' In W.T. Easterbrook and M.H. Watkins, eds., *Approach to Canadian Economic History*. Toronto: McClelland and Stewart.

Franks, C.E.S. 1993. *The Myths and Symbols of the Constitutional Debate in Canada*. Kingston: Institute of Intergovernmental Relations.

Fraser, N. 1989. 'The French Derridians: Politicizing Deconstruction or Deconstructing the Political?' In her *Unruly Practices: Power, Discourse and Gender in Contemporary Social Theory*. Minneapolis: University of Minnesota Press, 69–92.

Freeman, G.P. 1985. 'National Styles and Policy Sectors: Explaining Structured Variation.' *Journal of Public Policy* 5:467–96.

French, Richard D. 1980. *How Ottawa Decides: Planning and Industrial Policy-Making, 1969–1980*. Toronto: James Lorimer.

- 1983. 'Did Ottawa Plan? Reflections on My Critics.' *Canadian Public Administration* 26, no. 1, 100–4.

- 1992. 'Postmodern Government.' *Optimum* 23 (Summer), 42–51.

- 1993. 'Retrieving the Policy Sciences.' *Optimum* 24 (Summer), 51–53.

Frisken, Frances. 1986. 'Canadian Cities and the American Example: A Prologue to Urban Policy Analysis.' *Canadian Public Administration* 29:345–76.

Frohlich, Norman, Joe A. Oppenheimer, and Oran R. Young. 1971. *Political Leadership and Collective Goods*. Princeton: Princeton University Press.

Frohlich, Norman and Joe A. Oppenheimer. 1993. *Choosing Justice: An Experimental Approach to Ethics*. Berkeley: University of California Press.

Fuhrman, S.H. 1992. 'The Centre for Policy Research on Education: An Overview.' In C.H. Weiss, ed., *Organizations for Policy Analysis: Helping Government to Think*. Newbury Park: Sage, 81–98.

Gadamer, H-G. 1977. 'On the Scope and Function of Hermeneutical Reflection.' In his *Philosophical Hermeneutics*, trans. by D.E. Linge. Berkeley: University of California Press, 18–43.

– 1989. *Truth and Method*, 2nd ed., trans. by Joel Weinsheimer and Donald G. Marshall. New York: Crossroad.

Gambel, D.J. 1978. 'The Berger Inquiry: An Impact Assessment Process.' *Science* 199/4332:946–52.

Garson, David. 1978. *Group Theories of Politics*. Beverly Hills: Sage.

Geertz, Clifford. 1981. *Negara: The Theatre State in Nineteenth Century Bali*. Princeton, N.J.: Princeton University Press.

Gelb, Joyce and Marian Lief Palley. 1987. *Women and Public Policies*, rev. ed. Princeton: Princeton University Press.

Gergen, Kenneth J. 1988. 'Feminist Critique of Science and the Challenge of Social Epistemology.' In Mary M. Gergen, ed., *Feminist Thought and the Structure of Knowledge*. New York: New York University, 27–48.

Gergen, Mary M. 1988. 'Toward a Feminist Metatheory and Methodology in the Social Sciences.' In Mary M. Gergen, ed., *Feminist Thought and the Structure of Knowledge*. New York: New York University, 87–104.

Gleick, J. 1987. *Chaos: Making a New Science*. New York: Penguin.

Goldstein, Judith and Robert O. Keohane. 1993. 'Ideas and Foreign Policy: An Analytic Framework.' In Goldstein and Keohane, eds. *Ideas and Foreign Policy: Beliefs, Institutions, and Political Change*. Ithaca: Cornell University Press.

Goldthorpe, John, ed. 1984. *Order and Conflict in Contemporary Capitalism*. New York: Oxford University Press.

Good, D.A. 1980. *The Politics of Anticipation: Making Canadian Federal Tax Policy*. Ottawa: School of Public Administration, Carleton University.

Gormley, William T. 1989. *Taming the Bureaucracy: Muscles, Prayers and Other Strategies*. Princeton: Princeton University Press.

Gortner, Harold F.G., Julianne Mahler, and Jeanne Bell Nicholson. 1987. *Organization Theory: A Public Perspective*. Chicago: Dorsey.

Gouh, I. 1979. *The Political Economy of the Welfare State*. London: Macmillan.

Gourevitch, Peter. 1978. 'The Second Image Reversed: The International Sources of Domestic Politics.' *International Organization* 32:881–911.

Granatstein, J.L. 1982. *The Ottawa Men: The Civil Service Mandarins, 1935–1957*. Toronto: Oxford University Press.

Grant, Wyn P., ed. 1987. *Business Interests, Organizational Development and Private Interest Government: A Study of the Food Processing Industry.* Berlin: de Gruyter.
– ed. 1989. *Government and Industry: A Comparative Analysis of the US, Canada, and the UK.* Aldershot: Edward Elgar.
Grant, Wyn P., William Paterson, and Colin Whitson. 1988. *Government and the Chemical Industry: A Comparative Study of Britain and West Germany.* Oxford: Clarendon Press.
Grant, Wyn and Stephen Wilks. 1983. 'British Industrial Policy: Structural Change, Policy Inertia,' *Journal of Public Policy* 3:15–28.
Gray, Andrew and Bill Jenkins. 1995. 'From Public Administration to Public Management: Reassessing a Revolution?' *Public Administration* 73, no. 1, 75–100.
Gray, A. and W.I. Jenkins. 1985. *Administrative Politics in British Government.* Sussex: Wheatesheaf Books.
Green, Donald P. and Ian Shapino. 1994. *Pathologies of Rational Choice Theory: A Critique of Applications in Political Science.* New Haven: Yale University Press.
Greenberg, George D. et al. 1977. 'Developing Public Policy Theory: Perspectives from Empirical Research.' *American Political Science Review* 71:1532–43.
Greenberg, Joseph. 1990. *The Theory of Social Situations: An Alternative Game-Theoretic Approach.* Cambridge: Cambridge University Press.
Grosz, E.A. 1988. 'The In(ter)vention of Feminist Knowledges.' In Barbara Caine, E.A. Grosz, and Marie de Lepervanche, eds., *Crossing Boundaries: Feminisms and the Critique of Knowledges.* Sydney: Allen and Unwin, 92–104.
Guicciardini, F. 1972. *Maxims and Reflections (Ricordi)*, trans. by M. Domandi. Philadelphia: University of Pennsylvania Press.
Gusfield, Joseph R. 1963. *Symbolic Crusade.* Urbana: University of Illinois Press.
Haas, E.B. 1990. *When Knowledge Is Power: Three Models of Change in International Organizations.* Berkeley: University of California Press.
Haas, Peter M. 1992. 'Introduction: Epistemic Communities and International Policy Coordination,' *International Organization* 46:1–35.
Habermas, J. 1970. 'Toward a Theory of Communicative Competence.' *Inquiry* 13:360–75.
– 1971. *Knowledge and Human Interests.* Boston: Beacon Press.
– 1971. *Toward a Rational Society*, trans. by J.J. Shapiro. Boston: Beacon Press.
– 1984. *Theory of Communicative Action.* Boston: Beacon Press.
– 1984/87. *The Theory of Communicative Action*, 2 vols., trans. by T. McCarthy. Boston: Beacon Press.
– 1987. *The Philosophical Discourse of Modernity*, trans by F. Lawrence. Cambridge: The M.I.T. Press.

- 1988. *On the Logic of the Social Sciences*, trans. by S.W. Nicholsen and J.A. Stark. Cambridge: The M.I.T. Press.
- 1989. *The Structural Transformation of the Public Sphere*, trans. by T. Burger. Cambridge: The M.I.T. Press.
Hall, Peter. 1986. *Governing the Economy*. New York: Oxford University Press.
- ed. 1989. *The Political Power of Economic Ideas*. Princeton: Princeton University Press.
Hall, Richard H. *Organizational Structure and Process*. Englewood Cliffs, N.J.: Prentice-Hall.
Hall, Richard H. and Robert E. Quinn. 1983. *Organizational Theory and Public Policy*. Beverly Hills: Sage Publications.
Hamilton, Roberta. 1995. 'Pronatalism, Feminism and Nationalism.' In François-Pierre Gingras, ed., *Gender and Politics*. Toronto: Oxford University Press.
Hancher, Leigh and Michael Moran. 1989. 'Organizing Regulatory Space.' In Hancher and Moran, eds., *Capitalism, Culture and Economic Regulation*. Oxford: Clarendon Press.
Hancock, M. Donald. 1983. 'Comparative Public Policy: An Assessment.' In Ada W. Finifter, ed., *Political Science: The State of the Discipline*. Washington D.C.: American Political Science Association.
Hanusch, Horst, ed. 1983. *Anatomy of Government Deficiencies*. New York: Springer-Verlag.
Hardin, Hershel. 1974. *A Nation Unaware: The Canadian Economic Culture*. Vancouver: J.J. Douglas.
- 1989. *The Privatization Putsch*. Halifax: Institute for Research on Public Policy.
Hardin, R. 1982. *Collective Action*. Baltimore: Johns Hopkins University Press.
Harding, Sandra. 1990. 'Feminism, Science, and the Anti-Enlightenment Critique.' In Linda J. Nicholson, ed., *Feminism/Postmodernism*. New York: Routledge, 83–106.
- 1991. *Whose Science, Whose Knowledge? Thinking from Women's Lives*. Ithaca: Cornell University Press.
Harries-Jones, Peter, ed. 1991. *Making Knowledge Count: Advocacy and Social Science*. Montreal: McGill-Queen's.
Harrison, Kathryn and George Hoberg. 1991. 'Setting the Environmental Agenda in Canada and the United States: The Cases of Dioxin and Radon.' *Canadian Journal of Political Science* 23:3–28.
Harrison, K. and W.T. Stanbury. 1990. 'Privatization in B.C.' *Canadian Public Administration* 33:165–97.
Hartle, D.G. 1972. 'Operational Performance Measurement in the Government of Canada.' *Optimum* 3, no. 4, 5–17.
- 1973. 'A Proposed System of Program and Policy Evaluation.' *Canadian Public Administration* 16, no. 2, 243–66.

- 1976. 'Techniques and Processes of Administration.' *Canadian Public Administration* 19:21–33.
- 1976. *A Theory of the Expenditure Budgetary Process.* Toronto: University of Toronto Press.
- 1976. Comment. In Sandra Gwyn, ed., 'Refugees from Ottawa: Five Public Servants and Why They Left.' *Saturday Night* (March), 20.
- 1978. *The Expenditure Budget Process in the Government of Canada.* Toronto: Canadian Tax Foundation.
- 1979. *Public Policy, Decision Making and Regulation.* Montreal: Institute for Research on Public Policy.
- 1983. 'An Open Letter to Richard Van Loon (with a Copy to Richard French).' *Canadian Public Administration* 26, no. 1, 84–94.
- 1988. *The Expenditure Budget Process of the Government of Canada: A Public Choice–Rent-Seeking Perspective.* Toronto: Canadian Tax Foundation.
- 1993. *The Federal Deficit.* Discussion Paper 93–30. Government and Competitiveness Project, Queen's University School of Policy Studies.
Haussman, Melissa H. 1992. 'The Personal is Constitutional: Feminist Struggles for Equality Rights in the United States and Canada.' In Jill M. Bystdzienski, ed., *Women Transforming Politics: Worldwide Strategies for Empowerment.* Bloomington: Indiana University Press, 108–23.
Haveman, Robert H. 1970. 'Public Expenditures and Policy Analysis: An Overview.' In R.H. Haveman and J. Margolis, eds., *Public Expenditures and Policy Analysis.* Chicago: Markham.
Hawkesworth, M. 1988. *Theoretical Issues in Policy Analysis.* Albany: SUNY Press.
- 1990. *Beyond Oppression: Feminist Theory and Political Strategy.* New York: Continuum.
- 1994. 'Policy Studies within a Feminist Frame.' *Policy Sciences* 27:97–118.
- ed. 1994. *Feminism and Public Policy.* Special issue of *Policy Sciences* 27, no. 2–3.
Hawkins, Hugh. 1976. 'The Ideal of Objectivity among American Social Scientists in the Era of Professionalization, 1876–1916.' In C. Frankel, ed., *Controversies and Decisions.* New York: Russell Sage Foundation, 89–102.
Hayek, F.A. 1953. *The Sensory Order.* Chicago: University of Chicago Press.
Hayward, Jack. 1986. *The State and the Market Economy.* Brighton: Wheatsheaf.
Heady, F. 1979. *Public Administration: A Comparative Perspective, Second Edition Revised and Expanded.* New York: Marcel Dekker.
Healy, P. 1986. 'Interpretive Policy Inquiry: A Response to the Limitations of the Received View.' *Policy Sciences* 19:381–96.
Heclo, Hugh. 1972. 'Review Article: Policy Analysis.' *British Journal of Political Science* 2:83–108.

- 1978. 'Issue Networks and the Executive Establishment.' In Anthony King, ed., *The New American Political System*. Washington, D.C.: American Enterprise Institute for Public Policy Research.
Heclo, Hugh and Henrik Madsen. 1987. *Policy and Politics in Sweden: Principled Pragmatism*. Philadelphia: Temple University Press.
Heclo, H. and A. Wildavsky. 1974. *The Private Government of Public Money: Community and Policy inside British Politics*. London: Macmillan.
Heidenheimer, Arnold J., Hugh Heclo, and Carolyn T. Adams. 1983. *Comparative Public Policy: The Politics of Social Choice in Europe and America*, 2nd ed. New York: St. Martin's Press.
- 1990. *Comparative Public Policy*, 3rd ed. New York: St. Martin's Press.
Heinz, John P., Edward O. Laumann, Robert L. Nelson, and Robert H. Salisbury. 1993. *The Hollow Core: Private Interests in National Policy Making*. Cambridge, Mass.: Harvard University Press.
Heinz, John P., Edward O. Laumann, Robert H. Salisbury, and Robert L. Nelson. 1990. 'Inner Circles or Hollow Core? Elite Networks in National Policy Systems.' *Journal of Politics* 52:356–90.
Held, D. 1980. *Introduction to Critical Theory: Horkheimer to Habermas*. Berkeley: University of California Press.
Helly, Denise. 1993. 'The Political Regulation of Cultural Plurality: Foundations and Principles.' *Canadian Ethnic Studies* 25: 15–35.
Hennessy, Peter. 1989. *Whitehall*. London: Fontana.
Hernes, Helga Maria. 1985. 'The Welfare State Citizenship of Scandinavian Women.' In Kathleen B. Jones and Anna G. Jónasdóttir, eds., *The Political Interests of Gender*. London: Sage Publications, 135–59.
Hewart, Gordon. 1929. *The New Despotism*. London: E. Benn.
Hirsch, J.D., Jr. 1974. *Validity in Interpretation*. New Haven: Yale University Press.
Hirschman, Albert O. 1970. *Exit, Voice, and Loyalty: Responses to Decline in Firms, Organizations and States*. Cambridge: Harvard University Press.
- 1977. *The Passions and the Interests: Political Arguments for Capitalism before Its Triumph*. Princeton: Princeton University Press.
Hobbes, T. 1962. *De Corpore Politico*. In W. Molesworth, ed., *The English Works of Thomas Hobbes*, reprint of the 1840 ed., vol. 4. Scientia Aalen.
- 1962. *De Corpore*. In W. Molesworth, ed., *The English Works of Thomas Hobbes*, reprint of the 1839 ed., vol. 1. Scientia Aalen.
- 1968. *Levitathan*, edited by C.B. Macpherson. Harmondsworth: Penguin.
Hoberg, George. 1986. 'Technology, Political Structure and Social Regulation: A Cross-National Analysis.' *Comparative Politics* 18:357–76.
- 1990. 'Reaganism, Pluralism, and the Politics of Pesticide Regulation.' *Policy Sciences* 23:257–89.

- 1990. 'Risk Science and Politics: Alachlor Regulation in Canada and the United States.' *Canadian Journal of Political Science* 23:257–78.
- 1991. 'Sleeping with an Elephant: The American Influence on Canadian Environmental Regulation.' *Journal of Public Policy* 11:107–32.
- 1993. 'Environmental Policy: Alternative Styles.' In Michael Atkinson, ed., *Governing Canada: Institutions and Public Policy.* Toronto: Harcourt Brace Jovanovich, 307–42.

Hodgetts, J.E. 1955. *Pioneer Public Service: An Administrative History of the United Canadas, 1841–1867.* Toronto: University of Toronto Press.
- 1957. 'The Civil Service and Policy Formation.' *Canadian Journal of Economics and Political Science* 23, no. 4, 467–79.
- 1973. *The Canadian Public Service: A Physiology of Government, 1867–1970.* Toronto: University of Toronto Press.

Hodgson, Geoffrey. 1993. *Economics and Institutions.* Cambridge: Polity Press.

Holland, K., F.L. Morton, and B. Galligan, eds. 1994. *Federalism and the Environment.* Westport: Greenwood Press.

Hollander, M.J. and M.J. Prince. 1993. 'Analytic Units in Federal and Provincial Governments: Origins, Functions and Suggestions for Effectiveness.' *Canadian Public Administration* 36, no. 2 (Summer), 190–224.

Hollingsworth, Roger, Leon Lindberg, and Brigitte Young. 1989. 'The Governance of the American Dairy Industry: From Regional Dominance to Regional Cleavage.' In William Coleman and Henry Jacek, eds., *Regionalism, Business Interests and Public Policy.* London: Sage Publications.

Hood, Christopher C. 1986. *The Tools of Government.* Chatham, N.J.: Chatham House.
- 1995. 'Emerging Issues in Public Administration.' *Public Administration* 73, no. 1, 165–90.

Horowitz, Ira. 1970. 'Social Science Mandarins: Policymaking as a Political Formula.' *Policy Sciences* 1, no. 3, 339–60.

Houle, F. 1990. 'Economic Renewal and Social Policy.' In A.-G. Gagnon and J. Bickerton, eds., *Canadian Politics: An Introduction to the Discipline.* Peterborough, Ont.: Broadview Press.

Howlett, Michael. 1991. 'Policy Instruments, Policy Styles, and Policy Implementation: National Approaches to Theories of Instrument Choice.' *Policy Studies Journal* 19, no. 2, 1–21.
- 1994. 'The Judicialization of Canadian Environmental Policy: A Test of the Canada-United States Convergence Thesis.' *Canadian Journal of Political Science* 27 (March), 99–127.

Howlett, Michael and M. Ramesh. 1992. *The Political Economy of Canada: An Introduction.* Toronto: McClelland and Stewart.

– 1995. *Studying Public Policy: Policy Cycles and Policy Subsystems.* Toronto: Oxford University Press.

Hurtig, M. 1991. *The Betrayal of Canada.* Toronto: Stoddart.

Imbeau, Louis-M. 1990. 'Voting Games and Constitutional Decisions: The 1981 Constitutional Negotiation in Canada.' *Journal of Commonwealth and Comparative Politics* 28, no. 1, 90–105.

– 1992. 'Procedural Constraints and Conflictual Preferences in Collective Decision-Making: An Analysis Based on the Constitutional Decision of November 1981 in Canada.' *International Journal of Conflict Management* 3, no. 3, 181–206.

Ingram, Helen and Steven Rathgeb, eds. 1993. *Public Policy and Democracy.* Washington: Brookings Institution.

Innis, H.A. 1935. 'The Role of Intelligence: Some Further Notes.' *Canadian Journal of Economics and Political Science* 1, no. 2 (May) 280–6.

– 1946. *Political Economy in the Modern State.* Toronto: Ryerson.

– 1956. *Essays in Canadian Economic History.* Toronto: University of Toronto Press.

– 1970. *The Fur Trade in Canada: An Introduction to Canadian Economic History.* Toronto: University of Toronto Press.

Jackson, Peter M. 1992. 'Economic Policy.' In David Marsh and R.A.W. Rhodes, eds., *Implementing Thatcherite Policies: Audit of an Era.* Buckingham: Open University Press, 11–31.

Jacobson, N. 1978. *Pride and Solace: The Scope and Function of Political Theory.* Berkeley: University of California Press.

Jacquemin, A. 1985. *Pouvoir et sélection dans la nouvelle économie industrielle.* Paris: Economica.

James, Patrick. 1992. *'Rational Choice? Crisis Bargaining over the Meech Lake Accord.'* Paper presented at the Annual Meeting of the Canadian Political Science Association, Charlottetown, P.E.I.

Jenkin, Michael. 1983. *The Challenge of Diversity: Industrial Policy in Canadian Federalism.* Background Study No. 50 for the Science Council of Canada. Ottawa: Minister of Supply and Services.

Jenkins, W.I. 1978. *Policy Analysis: A Political and Organizational Perspective.* Suffolk: Martin Robertson.

Jenkins, W.I. and Andrew Gray. 1985. *Administrative Politics in British Government.* Sussex: Wheatsheaf Books.

Jennings, B. 1983. 'Interpretive Social Science and Policy Analysis.' In D. Callahan and B. Jennings, eds., *Ethics, the Social Sciences and Policy Analysis.* New York: Plenum Press, 3–35.

– 1987. 'Interpretation and the Practice of Policy Analysis.' In F. Fischer and J.
  Forester, eds., *Confronting Values in Policy Analysis.* Newbury Park: Sage
  Publications, 128–52.
Jenson, Jane. 1986. 'Gender and Reproduction or Babies and the State.' *Studies in
  Political Economy* 20 (Summer), 9–46.
– 1987. 'Changing Discourse, Changing Agendas: Political Rights and Reproduc-
  tive Policies in France.' In Mary Fainsod Katzenstein and Carol McClurg
  Mueller, eds., *The Women's Movements of the United States and Western
  Europe.* Philadephia: Temple University Press, 64–88.
– 1988. 'The Limits of "and the" Discourse: French Women as Marginal Workers.' In Jane Jenson, Elisabeth Hagen, and Ceallaigh Reddy, eds., *Feminization
  of the Labor Force: Paradoxes and Promises.* New York: Oxford University
  Press, 155–72.
– 1989. 'Paradigms and Political Discourse: Protective Legislation in France and
  the United States before 1914.' *Canadian Journal of Political Science* 22, no.
  2, 235–58.
– 1989. '"Different" but not "Exceptional": Canada's Permeable Fordism.'
  Canadian Review of Sociology and Anthropology 26:69–94.
– 1990. 'Representations in Crisis: The Roots of Canada's Permeable Fordism.'
  Canadian Journal of Political Science 23, no. 4, 653–84.
– 1990. 'Different but Not Exceptional: The Feminism of Permeable Fordism.'
  New Left Review 184 (Nov./Dec.), 58–68.
– 1994. 'Understanding Politics: Contested Concepts of Identity in Political
  Science.' In James P. Bickerton and Alain-G. Gagnon, eds., *Canadian Politics*,
  2nd ed. Peterborough, Ont.: Broadview Press, 54–74.
Johnson, A.W. 1971. 'PPB and Decision Making in the Government of Canada.'
  Cost and Management (March–April), 16–24.
– 1987. *Social Policy in Canada: The Past As It Conditions the Present.* Halifax:
  Institute for Research on Public Policy.
Johnson, D.G. 1991. *Public Choice.* Mountain View, Calif.: Bristelcone Books.
Johnston, Richard. 1985. *Public Opinion and Public Policy in Canada: Questions
  of Confidence.* Toronto: University of Toronto Press.
Johnston, Richard and André Blais. 1988. 'A Resounding Maybe,' *The Globe and
  Mail* (Toronto), 19 December, A7.
Jones, C. 1985. *Patterns of Social Policy.* London: Tavistock.
Jordan, A. Grant. 1981. 'Iron Triangles, Woolly Corporatism and Elastic Nets:
  Images of the Policy Process.' *Journal of Public Policy* 1:95–123.
– 1990. 'Sub-Governments, Policy Communities and Networks: Refilling the Old
  Bottles?' *Journal of Theoretical Politics* 2, no. 3, 319–37.
– 1990. 'The Pluralism of Pluralism: An Anti-Theory?' *Political Studies* 38:286–
  301.

Jordan, Grant and Jeremy Richardson. 1982. 'The British Policy Style or the Logic of Negotiation?' In Jeremy Richardson, ed., *Policy Styles in Western Europe*. London: George Allen and Unwin, 80–110.

Kaplan, Harold. 1989. *Policy and Rationality: The Regulation of Canadian Trucking*. Toronto: University of Toronto Press.

Kaplan, T.J. 1993. 'Reading Policy Narratives: Beginnings, Middles, and Ends.' In F. Fischer and J. Forester, eds., *The Argumentative Turn in Policy Analysis and Planning,*. Durham: Duke University Press, 167–85.

Kapstein, Ethan B. 1989. 'Resolving the Regulator's Dilemma: International Coordination of Banking Regulations.' *International Organization* 43:323–47.

Kathlene, L. and J.A. Martin. 1991. 'Enchancing Citizen Participation: Panel Designs, Perspectives and Policy Formation.' *Journal of Policy Analysis and Management* 10:46–63.

Katzenstein, Peter. 1985. *Small States in World Markets: Industrial Policy in Europe*. Ithaca: Cornell University Press.

– 1987. *Politics and Policy in West Germany: Growth in a Semisovereign State*. Philadelphia: Temple University Press.

Kekes, J. 1976. *A Justification of Rationality*. Albany: State University of New York Press.

Kelman, Steven. 1981. *Regulating America, Regulating Sweden: A Comparatice Study of Occupational Safety and Health*. Cambridge, Mass.: The M.I.T. Press.

Keman, Hans, Heikki Paloheimo, and Paul Whiteley, eds. 1987. *Coping with the Economic Crisis*. Beverly Hills: Sage Publications.

Kenis, Patrick and Volker Schneider. 1991. 'Policy Networks and Policy Analysis: Scrutinizing a New Analytical Toolbox.' In Bernd Marin and Renate Mayntz, eds., *Policy Networks: Empirical Evidence and Theoretical Considerations*. Boulder, Colo.: Westview.

Kent, Tom. 1989. *Getting Ready for 1999: Ideas for Canada's Politics and Government*. Halifax: Institute for Research on Public Policy.

Kerans, Patrick. 1994. 'Need and Welfare: "Thin and "Thick" Approaches.' In Andrew F. Johnson, Stephen McBride, and Patrick J. Smith, eds., *Continuities and Discontinuities: The Political Economy of Social Welfare and Labour Market Policy in Canada*. Toronto: University of Toronto Press.

Kernaghan, Kenneth. 1968. 'An Overview of Public Administration in Canada Today.' *Canadian Public Administration* 11, no. 3, 291–308.

– ed. 1983. *Canadian Public Administration: Discipline and Profession*. Toronto: Butterworths.

– 1991. 'Career Public Service 2000: Road to Renewal or Impractical Vision?' *Canadian Public Administration* 34, no. 4, 551–72.

– 1993. 'Partnership and Public Administration.' *Canadian Public Administration* 36:57–76.

Kernaghan, Kenneth and David Siegel. 1991. *Public Administration in Canada: A Text*, 2nd ed. Scarborough, Ont.: Nelson.

Kettle, Donald F. 1993. *Sharing Power: Public Governance and Private Markets.* Washington, D.C.: Brookings Institution.

Kiel, L. Douglas. 1991. 'Lessons from the Nonlinear Paradigm: Applications of the Theory of Dissipative Structures in the Social Sciences.' *Social Science Quarterly* 72:431–42.

Kincaid, John. 1994. 'Peoples, Persons and Places in Flux: International Integration versus National Fragmentation.' In Guy Laforest and Douglas Brown, eds., *Integration and Fragmentation: The Paradox of the Late Twentieth Century.* Kingston: Institute of Intergovernmental Relations, 53–84.

Kindler, Donald R. and Thomas R. Palfrey. 1993. *Experimental Foundation of Political Science.* Ann Arbor: University of Michigan Press.

King, Anthony. 1973. 'Ideas, Institutions and the Policies of Governments: A Comparative Analysis.' *British Journal of Political Science* 3, 291–314; 4, 409–423.

– 1981. 'What Do Elections Decide?' In David Butler, Howard R. Penniman, and Austin Ranney, eds., *Democracy at the Polls: A Comparative Study of Competitive National Elections.* Washington, D.C.: American Enterprise Institute.

– 1985. 'Margaret Thatcher: The Style of a Prime Minister.' In Anthony King, ed., *The British Prime Minister*, 2nd ed. London: Macmillan, 96–140.

Kingdon, J.W. 1984. *Agendas, Alternatives and Public Policy.* Boston: Little, Brown.

Kiser, L.L. and E. Ostrom. 1982. 'Reflections on Elements of Institutional Analysis.' Workshop in Political Theory and Policy Analysis Working Paper, Indiana University.

Kitchen, H. 1993. 'Efficient Delivery of Local Government Services.' Discussion Paper 93–15. Kingston: Queen's University School of Policy Studies.

Knopff, Rainer. 1989. *Human Rights and Social Technology: The New War on Discrimination.* Ottawa: Carleton University Press.

Knopff, Rainer and F.L. Morton. 1991. *Charter Politics.* Toronto: Nelson.

Knott, J.H. and A.J. Miller. 1987. *Reforming Bureaucracy: The Politics of Institutional Choice.* Englewood Cliffs, N.J.: Prentice-Hall.

Koford, K.J. and J.B. Miller, eds. 1991. *Social Norms and Economic Institutions.* Ann Arbor: University of Michigan Press.

Krasner, Stephen. 1984. 'Approaches to the State: Alternative Conception and Historical Dynamics.' *Comparative Politics* 18:223–46.

Kriesi, Hanspeter. 1982. 'The Structure of the Swiss Political System.' In Gerhard Lehmbruch and Philippe Schmitter, eds., *Patterns of Corporatist Policy-Making.* London: Sage.

Kristeller, P. 1961. *Renaissance Thought.* New York: Harper and Row.

Krueger, A.O. 1974. 'The Political Economy of the Rent Seeking Society.' *American Economic Review* 64:291–303.

Kuhn, T.S. 1970. *The Structure of Scientific Revolutions.* Chicago: University of Chicago Press.

Kunitz, Stephen J. 1990. 'Public Policy and Mortality among Indigenous Populations of Northern America and Australasia.' *Population and Development Review* 16 (December), 647–72.

Kwavnick, David. 1972. *Organized Labour and Pressure Politics.* Montreal: McGill-Queen's University Press.

Kymlicka, Will. 1993. 'Group Representation in Canadian Politics.' In F.L. Seidle, ed., *Equity and Community: The Charter, Interest Advocacy and Representation.* Montreal: Institute for Research on Public Policy.

Laing, Gertrude. 1979. 'The Contributions of Social Scientists to Policy Making – The B&B Experience.' In A.W. Rasporich, ed., *The Social Sciences and Public Policy in Canada.* Calgary: University of Calgary.

Lakatos, I. 1974. 'Falsification and the Methodology of Scientific Research Programmes.' In I. Lakatos and A. Musgrave, eds., *Criticism and the Growth of Knowledge.* Cambridge: Cambridge University Press, 91–196.

Landry, Réjean, ed. 1980. *Introduction à l'analyse des politiques.* Québec: Les Presses de l'Université Laval.

– 1984. 'La nouvelle analyse institutionnelle.' *Revue Québécoise de science politique* 6:5–22.

– 1990. 'Biases in the Supply of Public Policies to Organized Interests: Some Empirical Evidence.' In W.D. Coleman and G. Skogstad, eds., *Policy Communities and Public Policy in Canada: A Structural Approach.* Toronto: Copp Clark Pitman, 291–311.

– 1991. 'Party Competition in Quebec: Direct Confrontation or Selective Emphasis.' In H. Thorburn, ed., *Party Politics in Canada.* Scarborough, Ont: Prentice-Hall, 401–14.

– 1992. 'L'analyse de contenu.' In B. Gauthier, ed., *Recherche sociale: De la problématique à la collecte des données.* Sillery: Les Presses de l'Université du Québec, 337–60.

– 1992. 'The Imperfect Market for a Constitutional Deal.' *Inroads.* (Fall), 46–57.

– 1993. 'Administrative Reform and Political Control in Canada.' *International Political Science Review* 14, no. 4, 334–49.

– 1993. 'Interest Groups and the Political Economy of the Constitutional Debates in Canada.' *Business in the Contemporary World* 5, no. 1, 116–29.

– 1993. 'Les traditions de recherche en science politique.' *Revue Québécoise de science politique* 23:7–20.

Landry, Réjean and Chantal Blouin. 1994. 'Comparaison des stratégies d'aide manufacturières aux entreprises.' In J. Crête and L.M. Imbeau, eds., *Politiques provinciales comparées*. Québec: Presses de l'Université Laval, 297–328.

Landry, Réjean and Marc Pesant. 1994. *Politicians, Incentives and Policy Instruments: Theory and Evidence*. Groupe de recherche sur les interventions gouvernementales, unpublished manuscript, 35 pp.

Landry, Réjean, Marc Pesant, and Paule Duchesneau. 1994. 'Limites du contrôle par les règles comme instrument de gestion: comparaison des centres d'accueil publics et privés d'hébergement pour personnes âgées.' *Canadian Journal of Program Evaluation* 9, no. 1, 69–96.

Lane, J.E . 1994. *The Public Sector*. London: Sage.

Lang, Ronald W. 1974. *The Politics of Drugs: The British and Canadian Pharmaceutical Industries and Governments – A Comparative Study*. Farnborough: Saxon House.

Langford, J.W. 1976. *Transport in Transition: The Reorganization of the Federal Transport Portfolio*. Montreal: McGill-Queen's University Press.

Langford, John. 1979. 'Crown Corporations as Instruments of Policy.' In Bruce Doern and Peter Aucoin, eds., *Public Policy in Canada*. Toronto: Macmillan, 239–74.

Langille, David. 1987. 'The Business Council on National Issues and the Canadian State.' *Studies in Political Economy* 24:41–85.

Lanoie, Paul. 1992. 'Government Intervention in Occupational Safety: Lessons from the American and Canadian Experience.' *Canadian Public Policy* 18:62–75.

LaPalombara, Joseph. 1968. 'Macro-Theories and Micro-Applications in Comparative Politics: A Widening Chasm.' *Comparative Politics* 1:52–78.

Laslett, Barbara and Johanna Brenner. 1989. 'Gender and Social Reproduction: Historical Perspectives.' *Annual Review of Sociology* 15:381–404.

Lasswell, Harold D. 1955. 'Current Studies of the Decision Process: Automation versus Creativity.' *Western Political Quarterly* 8, no. 3, 381–99.

– 1971. *A Pre-View of the Policy Sciences*. New York: Elsevier.

Laudan, L. 1977. *Progress and Its Problems*. Berkeley: University of California Press.

Laumann, E.O. and D. Knocke. 1987. *The Organizational State: Social Choice in National Policy Domains*. Madison: University of Wisconsin Press.

Lawrence, P.R. and J.W. Lorsch. 1967. *Organization and Environment: Managing Differentiation and Integration*. Boston: Graduate School of Business Administration, Harvard University.

Laxer, Gordon. 1989. 'The Schizophrenic Character of Canadian Political Economy.' *Canadian Review of Sociology and Anthropology* 26, no. 1, 178–92.

– 1989. *Open for Business: The Roots of Foreign Ownership in Canada*. Toronto: Oxford University Press.

- 1992. 'Constitutional Crisis and Continentalism: Twin Threats to Canada's Continued Existence.' *Canadian Journal of Sociology* 17, no. 2, 199–247.

Layton, J. 1976. 'Nationalism and the Canadian Bourgeoisie: Contradictions of Dependency.' *Canadian Review of Studies in Nationalism* 3, no. 2, 146–71.

Leah, Ronnie. 1992. *Taking a Stand: Strategy and Tactics of Organizing the Popular Movement in Canada.* Ottawa: Canadian Centre for Policy Alternatives.

LeDuc, Lawrence. 1985. 'Partisan Change and Dealignment in Canada, Great Britain and the United States.' *Comparative Politics* 17:379–98.

Lehmbruch, Gerhard. 1984. 'Concertation and the Structure of Corporatist Networks.' In John Goldthorpe, ed., *Order and Conflict in Contemporary Capitalism.* New York: Oxford University Press, 60–80.

Leichter, H. 1977. 'Comparative Public Policy: Problems and Prospects.' *Policy Studies Journal* 5:583–96.

Leitch, V.B. 1983. *Deconstructive Criticism.* New York: Columbia University Press.

Leman, Christopher. 1977. 'Patterns of Policy Development: Social Security in the United States and Canada.' *Public Policy* 25:261–91.

- 1980. *The Collapse of Welfare Reform: Political Institutions, Policy, and the Poor in Canada and the United States.* Cambridge: The M.I.T. Press.

Lermer, G., ed. 1984. *Probing Leviathan.* Vancouver: The Fraser Institute.

Leslie, Peter. 1987. *Federal State, National Economy.* Toronto: University of Toronto Press.

Levine, Charles. 1980. *Managing Fiscal Stress: The Crisis in the Public Sector.* New Jersey: Chatham House.

Levitt, K. 1970. *Silent Surrender: The Multinational Corporation in Canada.* Toronto: Macmillan.

Lijphart, Arend. 1968. 'Typologies of Democratic Systems.' *Comparative Political Studies* 1: 3–44.

- 1971. 'Comparative Politics and the Comparative Method.' *American Political Science Review* 65:683–93.

- 1975. 'The Comparable-Cases Strategy in Comparative Research.' *Comparative Political Studies* 8:158–77.

Lindblom, C.E. 1977. *Politics and Markets.* New York: Basic Books.

Linder, S.H. and B.G. Peters. 1989. 'Instruments of Government: Perceptions and Contexts.' *Journal of Public Policy* 9, no. 1, 35–8.

Lindquist, E.A. 1989. 'Behind the Myth of Think Tanks: The Organization and Relevance of Canadian Policy Institutes.' Doctoral Dissertation, Graduate School of Public Policy, University of California at Berkeley.

- 1990. 'The Third Community, Policy Inquiry, and Social Scientists.' In S. Brooks and A.G. Gagnon, eds., *Social Scientists, Policy, and the State.* New York: Praeger, 21–51.

- 1991. 'Confronting Globalization and Governance Challenges: Canadian Think Tanks and the Asia Pacific Region.' In *Think Tanks and Governance in the Asia-Pacific Region*. Halifax: Institute for Research on Public Policy.
- 1992. 'Public Managers and Policy Communities: Learning to Meet New Challenges.' *Canadian Public Administration* 35, no. 2, 127–59.
- 1993. 'Postmodern Politics and Policy Sciences.' *Optimum* 24, no. 1 (Summer), 42–50.
- 1993. 'Think Tanks or Clubs? Assessing the Influence and Roles of Canadian Policy Institutes.' *Canadian Public Administration* 36, no. 4, 547–79.
- 1994. 'Balancing Relevance and Integrity: Social Scientists and Canada's Asia-Pacific Policy Community.' In S. Brooks and A.G. Gagnon, eds., *The Political Influence of Ideas: Policy Communities and the Social Sciences*. New York: Praeger, 135–62.

Lipset, Seymour Martin. 1990. *Continental Divide: The Values and Institutions of the United States and Canada*. New York: Routledge.

Lipsey, Richard G. and Murray G. Smith. 1986. *Taking the Initiative: Canada's Trade Options in a Turbulent World*. Toronto: C.D. Howe Institute.

Little, Margaret Hillyard. 1994. '"Manhunts and Bingo Blabs": The Moral Regulation of Ontario Single Mothers.' *Canadian Journal of Sociology* 19, no. 2, 233–47.

Lively, Jack. 1978. 'Pluralism and Consensus.' In P. Birnbaum, J. Lively, and G. Parry, eds., *Democracy, Consensus and Social Contract*. Beverly Hills: Sage, 185–201.

Lockhart, Charles. 1984. 'Explaining Social Policy Differences among Advanced Industrial Societies.' *Comparative Politics* 16:335–50.

Lockhead, Clarence et al. 1994. *The Canadian Fact Book on Poverty – 1994*. Ottawa: Canadian Council on Social Development.

Lowi, Theodore J. 1964. 'American Business, Public Policy, Case Studies and Political Theory.' *World Politics* 16:677–715.
- 1966. 'Distribution, Regulation, Redistribution: The Functions of Government.' In R.B. Ripley, ed., *Public Policies and Their Politics: Techniques of Government Control*. New York: W.W. Norton, 27–40.
- 1969. *The End of Liberalism: Ideology, Policy, and the Crisis of Public Authority*. New York: Norton.
- 1972. 'Four Systems of Policy, Politics and Choice.' *Public Administration Review* 32, no. 4, 298–310.
- 1985. 'The State in Politics.' In Roger Noll, ed., *Regulatory Policy and the Social Sciences*. Berkeley: University of California Press, 67–105.

Lyotard, J-F. 1984. *The Postmodern Condition: A Report on Knowledge*, trans. by G. Bennington and B. Massumi. Minneapolis: University of Minnesota Press.

MacDonald, Eleanor. 1991. 'The Trouble with Subjects: Feminism, Marxism and the Questions of Poststructuralism.' *Studies in Political Economy* 35 (Summer), 43–71.

MacDonald, Martha and M. Patricia Connelly. 1989. 'Class and Gender in Fishing Communities in Nova Scotia.' *Studies in Political Economy* 30 (Autumn), 61–85.

Mackenzie, Suzanne. 1986. 'Women's Responses to Economic Restructuring: Changing Gender, Changing Space.' In Roberta Hamilton and Michèle Barrett, eds., *The Politics of Diversity: Feminism, Marxism and Nationalism*. Montreal: Book Centre, 81–100.

Mackenzie, W.J.M. 1970. *The Study of Political Science Today*. New York: Macmillan.

Mackintosh, W.A. 1937. 'An Economist Looks at Economics.' *Canadian Journal of Economics and Political Science* 3, no. 3 (August), 311–457.

– 1939. *The Economic Background of Dominion-Provincial Relations*. Ottawa: Printer to the King.

Macpherson, C.B. 1964. *The Political Theory of Possessive Individualism: Hobbes to Locke*. Oxford: Oxford University Press.

– 1979. 'By Innis out of Marx: The Revival of Canadian Political Economy.' *Canadian Journal of Political and Social Theory* 3, no. 2, 134–8.

MacRae, D. 1987. 'Building Policy-Related Technical Communities.' *Knowledge* 8, no. 4, 431–62.

Mahon, Rianne. 1977. 'Canadian Public Policy: The Unequal Structure of Representation.' In Leo Panitch, ed., *The Canadian State*. Toronto: University of Toronto Press, 165–98.

– 1984. *The Politics of Industrial Restructuring*. Toronto: University of Toronto Press.

– 1991. 'Post-Fordism: Some Issues for Labour.' In D. Drache and M. Gertler, eds., *The New Era of Global Competition*. Montreal: McGill-Queen's University Press.

Majone, Giadomenico. 1989. *Evidence, Argument, and Persuasion in the Policy Process*. New Haven: Yale University Press.

Mallory, J.R. 1977. 'Confederation: The Ambiguous Bargain.' *Journal of Canadian Studies* 12, no. 3, 18–23.

– 1979. 'The Lambert Report: Central Roles and Responsibilities.' *Canadian Public Administration* 22, no. 4, 517–29.

Maloney, Maureen. 1992. 'What Is the Appropriate Tax Unit for the 1990s and Beyond?' Paper prepared for the Ontario Fair Tax Commission, Toronto.

Mandel, Michael. 1991. *The Charter of Rights and the Legalization of Politics in Canada*. Toronto: Thompson.

Manfredi, Charles P. 1990. 'The Use of United States Decisions by the Supreme Court of Canada under the Charter of Rights and Freedoms.' *Canadian Journal of Political Science* 23 (September), 499–518.

Manfredi, Christopher P. 1992. *Judicial Power and the Charter: Canada and the Paradox of Liberal Constitutionalism.* Toronto: McClelland and Stewart.

Mansbridge, Jane. 1993. 'Public Spirit in Political Systems.' In Henry Aaron, Thomas E. Mann, and Timothy Taylor, eds., *Values and Public Policy.* Washington: Brookings Institution, 146–72.

Mansbridge, T.J. 1990. 'The Rise and Fall of Self Interest in the Explanation of Political Life.' In Mansbridge, ed., *Beyond Self Interest.* Chicago: University Press, 3–24.

Manzer, Ronald. 1981. 'Social Policy and Political Paradigms.' *Canadian Public Administration* 24, no. 4, 641–8.

– 1985. *Public Policies and Political Development in Canada.* Toronto: University of Toronto Press.

March, J.G. 1989. 'Footnotes to Organizational Change.' In his *Decisions and Organizations.* Oxford: Basil Blackwell, 167–86.

– 1989. 'The Technology of Foolishness.' In his *Decisions and Organizations.* Oxford: Basil Blackwell, 253–65.

March, James G. and Johan P. Olsen. 1984. 'The New Institutionalism: Organizational Factors in Political Life.' *American Political Science Review* 78:734–49.

– 1989. *Rediscovering Institutions: The Organizational Basis of Politics.* New York: The Free Press.

Marchak, P. 1985. 'Canadian Political Economy.' *Canadian Review of Sociology and Anthropology* 22, no. 5, 673–709.

Marmor, Theodore E. 1993. 'Health Care Reform in the United States: Patterns of Fact and Fiction in the Use of Canadian Experience.' *American Review of Canadian Studies* 23 (Spring), 47–64.

Maroney, Heather Jon. 1992. '"Who Has the Baby?" Nationalism, Pronatalism and the Construction of a "Demographic Crisis" in Quebec, 1960–1988.' In M. Patricia Connelly and Pat Armstrong, eds., *Feminism in Action: Studies in Political Economy.* Toronto: Canadian Scholars' Press, 237–65.

Maroney, H.J. and M. Luxton. 1987. 'From Feminism and Political Economy to Feminist Political Economy.' In Maroney and Luxton, eds., *Feminism and Political Economy, Women's Work, Women's Struggles.* Toronto: Methuen.

Marsh, David and R.A.W. Rhodes, eds. 1992. *Impementing Thatcherite Policies: Audit of an Era.* Buckingham: Open University Press.

Martin, Brian. 1978. 'The Selective Usefulness of Game Theory.' *Social Studies of Sciences* 8, no. 1, 85–110.

Maslove, Allan. 1989. *Tax Reform in Canada: The Process and Impact.* Ottawa: Institute for Research on Public Policy.

Maslove, Allan, Bruce Doern, and Michael Prince. 1986. *Federal and Provincial Budgeting.* Toronto: University of Toronto Press.

Matthews, D.R. 1993. *Controlling Common Property*. Toronto: University of
   Toronto Press.
Maxwell, Judith. 1975. *Restructuring the Incentives System*. Montreal: C.D. Howe
   Research Institute.
Maxwell, Judith and Carl Beigie. 1974. *The Disappearance of the Status Quo*.
   Montreal: C.D. Howe Research Institute.
McAdams, J. 1984. 'The Anti-Policy Analysts.' *Policy Studies Journal* 13:91–101.
McBride, Stephen. 1992. *Not Working: State, Unemployment and Neo-Conserva-
   tism in Canada*. Toronto: University of Toronto Press.
McBride, S. and J. Shields. 1993. *Dismantling a Nation: Canada and the New
   World Order*. Halifax: Fernwood.
McCarthy, T. 1979. *The Critical Theory of Jürgen Habermas*. Cambridge, Mass.:
   The M.I.T. Press.
– 1991. 'The Politics of the Ineffable: Derrida's Deconstructionism.' In Michael
   Kelley, ed., *Hermeneutics and Critical Theory in Ethics and Politics*. Cam-
   bridge, Mass.: The M.I.T. Press, 146–68.
McCormick, Peter, Ernest C. Manning, and Gordon Gibson. 1981. *Regional
   Representation: The Canadian Partnership*. Calgary: Canada West Foundation.
McDavid, J.C. 1985. 'The Canadian Experience with Privatizing Solid Waste
   Services.' *Public Administration Review* 45:602–8.
– 1986. 'Part-Time Fire Fighters in Canadian Municipalities: Cost and Effective-
   ness Comparisons.' *Canadian Public Administration* 30:472–88.
McDavid, J.C. and G.K. Schick. 1987. 'Privatization versus Union-Management
   Cooperation.' *Canadian Public Administration* 30:472–87.
McIntosh, Mary. 1978. 'The State and the Oppression of Women.' In A. Kuhn and
   A. Wolpe, eds., *Feminism and Materialism*. London: Routledge and Kegan
   Paul, 254–89.
McKeen, Wendy. 1994. 'The Wages for Housework Campaign: Its Contribution to
   Feminist Politics in the Area of Social Welfare in Canada.' *Canadian Review of
   Social Policy* 33 (Spring-Summer), 21–43.
McKenna, Marian C., ed. 1993. *The Canadian and American Constitutions in
   Comparative Perspective*. Calgary: University of Calgary Press.
McQuaig, Linda. 1987. *Behind Closed Doors: How the Rich Won Control of
   Canada's Tax System*. Markham, Ont.: Viking.
Meisel, John. 1983. 'The Reforms and the Bureaucrat: A Remedial Dissonance?'
   Alan B. Placent Memorial Lecture (8 April). Ottawa: Carleton University.
Meltsner, A.J. 1976. *Policy Analysts in the Bureaucracy*. Berkeley: University of
   California Press.
Merton, R.K. 1967. 'On Sociological Theories of the Middle Range.' In *On
   Theoretical Sociology*. New York: The Free Press, 39–72.

Meyer, J.W. and B. Rowan. 1977. 'Institutionalized Organizations: Formal Structure as Myth and Ceremony.' *American Journal of Sociology* 83, no. 2, 340–63. Also reprinted in Powell and DiMaggio (1991).

Meyer, J.W., W.R. Scott, and T.E. Deal. 1981. 'Institutional and Technical Sources of Organization Structure.' In H.D. Stein, ed., *Organization and the Human Services*. Philadelphia: Temple University Press, 151–78.

Meynaud, Jean. 1962. *Nouvelles études sur les groups de pression en France.* Paris: A. Colin.

Migué, Jean-Luc and Richard Marceau. 1989. *Le monopole public de l'Éducation.* Sillery: Les Presses de l'Université du Québec.

Miliband, Ralph. 1969. *The State in Capitalist Society.* London: Weidenfeld and Nicholson.

Miller, Gary M. 1992. *Managerial Dilemmas: The Political Economy of Hierarchy.* Cambridge: Cambridge University Press.

Minogue, Kenneth. 1994. 'Identity, Self, and Nation.' In Guy Laforest and Douglas Brown, eds., *Integration and Fragmentation: The Paradox of the Late Twentieth Century.* Kingston: Institute of Intergovernmental Relations, 85–99.

Mishra, Ramesh. 1990. *The Welfare State in Capitalist Societies: The Politics of Retrenchment and Maintenance in Europe, North America, and Australia.* Toronto University of Toronto Press.

Mitchell, W.C. 1988. 'Virginia, Rochester and Bloomington.' *Public Choice* 56:101–20.

Moe, Ronald C. 1994. 'The Reinventing Government Exercise: Misinterpreting the Problem, Misjudging the Consequences.' *Public Administration Review* 54: 111–22.

Monahan, Patrick. 1995. 'Cooler Heads Shall Prevail: Assessing the Costs and Consequences of Quebec Separation.' C.D. Howe Institute Commentary, no. 65. Ottawa: Renouf.

Monroe, Kristen Renwick, ed. 1991. *The Economic Approach to Politics: A Critical Reassessement of the Theory of Rational Actions.* New York: Harper Collins.

Moran, Michael. 1990. 'Regulating Britain, Regulating America: Corporatism and the Securities Industry.' In Colin Crouch and Ronald Dore, eds., *Corporatism and Accountability: Organized Interests in British Public Life.* Oxford: Clarendon Press.

– 1991. *The Politics of the Financial Services Revolution: The USA, UK, and Japan.* London: Macmillan.

More, Thomas. 1964. *Utopia.* New Haven: Yale University Press.

Morgan, G. 1983. 'More on Metaphor: Why We Cannot Control Tropes in Administrative Science.' *Administrative Science Quarterly* 28:601–7.

– 1986. *Images of Organization*. Beverly Hills: Sage Publications.

Morton, F.L. 1992. 'The Charter Revolution and the Court Party.' *Osgoode Hall Law Journal* 30 (Fall), 627–53.

Mueller, D.C. 1979. *Public Choice*. Cambridge: University Press.

– 1989. *Public Choice II*. Cambridge: University Press.

Mullaly, Robert. 1994. 'Social Welfare and the New Right: A Clan Mobilization Perspective.' In A.F. Johnson, S. McBride and P.J. Smith, eds., *Continuities and Discontinuities: The Political Economy of Social Welfare and Labour Market Policies in Canada*. Toronto: University of Toronto Press, 76–94.

Muramatsu, Michio and Ellis S. Kraus. 1987. 'The Conservative Policy Line and the Development of Patterned Pluralism.' In K. Yamamura and Y. Yasuba, eds., *The Political Economy of Japan: Volume 1, The Domestic Transformation*. Stanford: Stanford University Press, 516–54.

Nagele, R. 1981. 'Freud, Habermas and the Dialectic of Enlightenment: On Real and Ideal Discourses.' *New German Critique* 22:41–62.

National Council of Welfare. 1992. *Poverty Profile, 1980–1990*. Ottawa: Supply and Services.

Naylor, C. David. 1986. *Private Practice, Public Payment: Canadian Medicine and the Politics of Health Insurance, 1911–1966*. Montreal: McGill-Queen's University Press.

Naylor, R.T. 1972. 'The Rise and Fall of the Third Commercial Empire of the St. Lawrence.' In G. Teeple, ed., *Capitalism and the National Question*. Toronto: University of Toronto Press.

Nelson, Barbara J. 1990. 'The Origins of the Two-Channel Welfare State: Workmen's Compensation and Mothers' Aid.' In Linda Gordon, ed., *Women, the State and Welfare*. Madison: University of Wisconsin Press, 123–51.

Nelson, J.S., A. Megill, and D.N. McCloskey. 1987. 'Rhetoric of Inquiry.' In J.S. Nelson, A. Megill, and D.N. McCloskey, eds., *The Rhetoric of the Human Sciences: Language and Argument in Scholarship and Public Affairs*. Madison: University of Wisconsin Press, 3–18.

Nevitte, Neil. 1991. 'New Politics, the Charter and Political Participation.' In Herman Bakvis, ed., *Representation, Integration and Political Parties in Canada*. Toronto: Dundurn Press, 355–417.

Nevitte, Neil, Miguel Basañez, and Ronald Ingelhart. 1992. 'Directions of Value Change in North America.' In Stephen J. Randall, ed., *North America without Borders? Integrating Canada, the United States, and Mexico*. Calgary: University of Calgary Press, 245–59.

Ng, Roxana. 1986. 'The Social Construction of Immigrant Women in Canada.' In Roberta Hamilton and Michèle Barrett, eds., *The Politics of Diversity: Feminism, Marxism and Nationalism*. Montreal: Book Centre, 269–86.

Nicholson, Linda J., ed. *Feminism/Postmodernism*. New York: Routledge.

Niskanen, W.A., Jr. 1971. *Bureaucracy and Representative Government*. Hawthorne: Aldine-Atherton.

North, Douglass C. 1981. *Structure and Change in Economic History*. New York: Norton.

– 1990. *Institutions, Institutional Change and Economic Performance*. Cambridge: Cambridge University Press.

Nossal, Kim. 1989. *The Politics of Canadian Foreign Policy*, 2nd ed. Scarborough: Prentice-Hall.

Nye, Joseph and R.O. Keohane. 1972. 'Transnational Relations and World Politics: An Introduction.' In Nye and Keohane, eds., *Transnational Relations and World Politics*. Cambridge: Harvard University Press.

O'Connor, James. 1973. *The Fiscal Crisis of the State*. New York: St. Martin's Press.

O'Connor, J.S. 1988. 'Convergence or Divergence: Change in Welfare State Effort in OECD Nations, 1960–1980.' *European Journal of Political Research* 16:277–99.

– 1989. 'Welfare Expenditure and Policy Orientation in Canada in Comparative Perspective.' *Canadian Review of Sociology and Anthropology* 26:127–50.

Okin, Susan Moller. 1989. *Justice, Gender and the Family*. New York: Basic Books.

– 1994. 'Gender Inequality and Cultural Differences.' *Political Theory* 22, no. 1, 5–25.

Olsen, Johan, Paul Roness, and Harald Saetren. 1982. 'Norway: Still Peaceful Coexistence and Revolution in Slow Motion?' In Jeremy Richardson, ed., *Policy Styles in Western Europe*. London: George Allen and Unwin, 47–79.

Olson, Mancur. 1965. *The Logic of Collective Action*. Cambridge, Mass.: Harvard University Press.

– 1982. *The Rise and Decline of Nations*. New Haven: Yale University Press.

Orbell, J.M. et al. 1991. 'Covenants without the Sword.' In K.J. Koford and J.B. Miller, eds., *Social Norms and Economic Institutions*. Ann Arbor: University of Michigan Press, 117–34.

Ordershook, Peter C. 1986. *Game Theory and Political Theory*. Cambridge: Cambridge University Press.

– 1992. *A Political Theory Primer*. New York: Routledge.

Orloff, Ann Shola. 1993. 'Gender and the Social Rights of Citizenship: The Comparative Analysis of Gender Relations and Welfare States.' *American Sociological Review* 58 (June), 303–328.

– 1993. *The Politics of Pensions: A Comparative Analysis of Britain, Canada, and the United States, 1880–1940*. Madison: University of Wisconsin Press.

Osbaldeston, G.F. 1989. *Keeping Deputy Ministers Accountable*. Toronto: McGraw-Hill Ryerson.

– 1992. *Organizing to Govern*, 2 vols. Toronto: McGraw-Hill Ryerson.

Osborne, David and Ted Gaebler. 1992. *Reinventing Government*. Reading, Mass.: Addison-Wesley.

Ostrom, Elinor. 1986. 'An Agenda for the Study of Institutions.' *Public Choice* 48:3–25.

– 1990. *Governing the Commons*. Cambridge: University Press.

– 1992. *Crafting Institutions for Self-Governing Irrigation Systems*. San Francisco: ICS Press.

– et al. 1992. 'Covenants with and without a Sword.' *American Political Science Review* 86:404–17.

Ostrom, Elinor, Gardner Roy, and James Walker. 1994. *Rules, Games, and Common-Pool Resources*. Ann Arbor: University of Michigan Press.

Ostrom, Elinor, Larry Schroeder, and Suzan Wynne. 1993. *Institutional Incentives and Sustainable Development: Infrastructure Policies in Perspective*. Boulder: Westview Press.

Ostrom, Vincent. 1973. 'Can Federalism Make a Difference?' *Publius* 3:197–238.

– 1980. 'Artisanship and Artifact.' *Public Administration Review* 40:309–17.

– 1991. *The Meaning of American Federalism*. San Francisco: ICS Press.

Owram, Doug. 1986. *The Government Generation: Canadian Intellectuals and the State, 1900–1945*. Toronto: University of Toronto Press.

Paehlke, R. and D. Torgerson. 1992. 'Toxic Waste as Public Business.' *Canadian Public Administration* 35, no. 3, 339–362.

Paglia, Camille. 1990. *Sexual Personae: Art and Decadence from Nefertiti to Emily Dickinson*. New Haven: Yale University Press.

Pal, Leslie A. 1988. *State, Class and Bureaucracy: Canadian Unemployment Insurance Policy*. Montreal: McGill-Queen's University Press.

– 1989. 'Political Economy as a Hegemonic Project.' *Canadian Journal of Political Science* 22, no. 4, 827–39.

– 1990. 'Knowledge, Power, and Policy: Reflections on Foucault.' In S. Brooks and A.-G. Gagnon, eds., *Social Scientists, Policy, and the State*. New York: Praeger, 139–58.

– 1992. *Public Policy Analysis: An Introduction*, 2nd ed. Scarborough: Nelson.

– 1993. *Interests of State: The Politics of Language, Multiculturalism and Feminism in Canada*. Montreal: McGill-Queen's University Press.

– 1994. 'Advocacy Organizations and Legislative Politics: The Effect of the Charter on Interest Group Lobbying over Federal Legislation, 1989–91.' In F. Leslie Seidle, ed., *Equity and Community: The Charter, Interest Advocacy and Representation*. Montreal: Institute for Research on Public Policy, 119–57.

Palda, Filip, ed. 1994. *Provincial Trade Wars: Why the Blockade Must End*. Vancouver: The Fraser Institute.

Palda, Kristian S. 1985. *Industrial Innovation: Its Place in the Public Policy Agenda*. Vancouver: The Fraser Institute.

Palmer, R. 1969. *Hermeneutics*. Evanston, Ill.: Northwestern University Press.

Paltiel, Khayyam Z. 1982. 'The Changing Environment and Role of Special Interest Groups.' *Canadian Public Administration* 25, no. 2, 198–210.

Panitch, Leo, ed. 1977. *The Canadian State*. Toronto: University of Toronto Press.

– 1979. 'Corporatism in Canada.' *Studies in Political Economy* 1:43–92.

– 1980. 'Recent Theorization of Corporatism: Reflections on a Growth Industry.' *British Journal of Sociology* 31, no. 2, 159–87.

Panitch, L. and D. Swartz. 1988. *The Assault on Trade Union Freedoms: From Consent to Coercion Revisited*. Toronto: Garamond.

– 1993. *The Assault on Trade Union Freedoms: From Wage Controls to Social Contracts*. Toronto: Garamond.

Paris, D.C, and J. F. Reynolds. 1983. *The Logic of Policy Inquiry*. New York: Longman.

Parsons, D.W. 1986. *The Political Economy of British Regional Policy*. London: Croom Helm.

Pateman, Carole. 1989. *The Disorder of Women*. Stanford: Stanford University Press.

Pauly, Louis. 1988. *Opening Financial Markets: Banking Politics on the Pacific Rim*. Ithaca, N.Y.: Cornell University Press.

Pempel, T.J. 1982. *Policy and Politics in Japan: Creative Conservatism*. Philadelphia: Temple University Press.

Perl, Anthony. 1993. *Comparative Transport Finance: The Institutional Logic of Infrastructure Development in Canada, France and the United States*. PhD Dissertation, Department of Political Science, University of Toronto.

Peters, B. Guy. 1991. 'Government Reorganization: A Theoretical Analysis.' Paper presented to the Annual Meeting of the Canadian Political Science Association, Kingston, Ontario (June).

– 1992. 'The Policy Process: An Institutionalist Perspective.' *Canadian Public Administration* 35, no. 2, 160–80.

Peters, B. Guy, John C. Doughtie, and M. Kathleen McCulloch. 1977. 'Types of Democratic Systems and Types of Public Policy.' *Comparative Politics* (April), 327–55.

Peters, R. 1967. *Hobbes*. Harmondsworth: Penguin.

Peterson, V. Spike. 1992. 'Introduction.' In V. Spike Peterson, ed., *Gendered States: Feminist (Re)Visions of International Relations Theory*. Boulder: Lynne Rienner Publishers, 1–29.

Phidd, Richard W. 1974. 'Regional Development Policy.' In G.B. Doern and V.S. Wilson, eds., *Issues in Canadian Public Policy*. Toronto: Macmillan.

Phidd, Richard W. and Bruce Doern. 1978. *The Politics and Management of Canadian Economic Policy*. Toronto: Macmillan.

Phillips, Anne. 1993. *Democracy and Difference*. University Park, Pa.: Pennsylvania State University Press.

Phillips, P. 1978. 'The Hinterland Perspective: The Political Economy of Vernon C. Fowke.' *Canadian Journal of Political and Social Theory* (Spring/Summer), 73–96.

Phillips, Susan. 1993. 'A More Democratic Canada?' In S. Phillips, ed., *How Ottawa Spends, 1993–94: A More Democratic Canada?* Ottawa: Carleton University Press.

– 1993. 'Of Public Interest Groups and Sceptics: A Realist's Reply to Professor Stanbury.' *Canadian Public Administration* 36, no. 4, 606–16.

– forthcoming. 'Who's Listening? Who's Speaking? Political Strategies of the Canadian Women's Movement.' In Radha Jhappan, ed., *Women's Legal Strategies*. Toronto: University of Toronto Press.

Pierson, Paul D. and R. Kent Weaver. 1993. 'Imposing Losses in Pension Policy.' In R. Kent Weaver and Bert A. Rockman, eds., *Do Institutions Matter? Government Capabilities in the United States and Abroad*. Washington, D.C.: Brookings Institution, 110–50.

Pierson, Ruth Roach. 1993. 'The Mainstream Women's Movement and the Politics of Difference.' In Ruth Roach Pierson, Marjorie Griffin Cohen, Paula Bourne, and Philinda Masters, eds., *Canadian Women's Issues: Volume I, Strong Voices*. Toronto: James Lorimer, 186–214.

Pinker, R. 1973. *Social Theory and Social Policy*. London: Heinemann Educational Books.

Pinkerton, E., ed. 1989. *Cooperative Management of Local Fisheries*. Vancouver: UBC Press.

– 1993. 'Co-Management Efforts as Social Movements.' *Alternatives* 19 (November), 33–8.

Plumptre, T.W. 1988. *Beyond the Bottom Line: Management in Government*. Halifax: IRPP.

Poerksen, Uwe. 1995. *Plastic Words: The Tyranny of a Modular Language*. University Park: Pennsylvania State University.

Ponting, J. Rick. 1990. 'Internationalization: Perspectives on an Emerging Direction in Aboriginal Affairs.' *Canadian Ethnic Studies* 22:85–109.

Popper, K.R. 1968. *The Logic of Scientific Discovery*. London: Hutchinson.

– 1969. *Conjectures and Refutations*. London: Routledge and Kegan Paul.

Porter, John. 1965. *The Vertical Mosaic*. Toronto: University of Toronto Press.

Postman, Neil. 1993. *Technopoly: The Surrender of Culture to Technology*. New York: Vintage Books.

Poulantzas, Nicos. 1969. 'The Problem of the Capitalist State.' *New Left Review* 58:67–78.

– 1978. *State, Power, Socialism*. London: NLB.

Powell, Walter. 1989. 'Neither Market Nor Hierarchy: Network Forms of Organization.' In Barry M. Staw and Larry L. Cummings, eds., *Research in Organizational Behavior*. Greenwich, Conn.: JAI Press.

Powell, W.W. and P.J. DiMaggio, eds. 1991. *The New Institutionalism in Organizational Analysis*. Chicago: University of Chicago Press.

Pratt, L. 1982. 'Energy: The Roots of National Policy.' *Studies in Political Economy* 7:27–60.

Premfors, Rune. 1981. 'National Policy Styles and Higher Education in France, Sweden and the United Kingdom.' *European Journal of Education* 16, no. 2, 253–62.

Presthus, Robert. 1971. 'Interest Groups and the Canadian Parliament: Activities, Interaction, Legitimacy, and Influence.' *Canadian Journal of Political Science* 4, no. 4, 444–60.

– 1973. *Elite Accommodation in Canadian Politics*. Toronto: Macmillan.

– 1974. 'Preface,' and 'Interest Groups in International Perspective.' *The Annals of the American Academy of Political and Social Science* 413 (May).

– 1974. *Elites in the Policy Process*. Toronto: Macmillan.

Prince, Michael. 1978. 'Policy Advisory Groups in Government Departments.' In Bruce Doern and Peter Aucoin, eds., *Public Policy in Canada*. Toronto: Macmillan.

Pross, A. Paul. 1967. 'The Development of Professions in the Public Service: The Foresters in Ontario.' *Canadian Public Administration* 10, no. 3, 376–404.

– 1975. 'Input versus Withinput: Pressure Group Demands and Administrative Survival.' In A. Paul Pross, ed., *Pressure Group Behaviour in Canadian Politics*. Toronto: McGraw-Hill, 148–72.

– 1985. 'Parliamentary Influence and the Diffusion of Power.' *Canadian Journal of Political Science* 18, no. 2, 235–66.

– 1986. *Group Politics and Public Policy*. Toronto: Oxford University Press.

– 1990. 'Assessing Public Administration Education in Canada,' *Canadian Public Administration* 33, no. 4, 618–32.

– 1992. *Group Politics and Public Policy*, 2nd ed. Toronto: Oxford University Press.

– 1994. 'The Pressure Group Conundrum.' In James Bickerton and Alain-G. Gagnon, eds., *Canadian Politics*. Toronto: Broadview.

Pross, A. Paul, Christie Innis, and John A. Yogis. 1990. *Commission of Inquiry*. Toronto: Carswell.

Przeworski, Adam and Henry Teune. 1970. *The Logic of Comparative Social Inquiry*. New York: Wiley.

Putnam, Robert A. 1973. *The Beliefs of Politicians*. New Haven: Yale University Press.

– 1988. 'Diplomacy and Domestic Politics: The Logic of Two-Level Games.' *International Organization* 42:427–460.

Rabinow, P. and W.M. Sullivan. 1979. 'The Interpretive Turn: Emergence of an Approach.' In P. Rabinow and W.M. Sullivan, eds., *Interpretive Social Science*. Berkeley: University of California Press.

Radnitzky, G. 1968. *Contemporary Schools of Metascience*, Vol. 2, *Continental Schools of Metascience*. Goteborg, Sweden: Scandinavian University Press.

Rapoport, Anatol and Albert M. Chammak. 1970. *Prisoner's Dilemma*. Ann Arbor: University of Michigan Press.

Rapoport, A. and M. Guyer. 1966. 'A Taxonomy of 2x2 Games.' *General Systems* 11:203–14.

– 1976. *The 2x2 Game*. Ann Arbor: University of Michigan Press.

Razack, Sherene. 1991. *Canadian Feminism and the Law: The Women's Legal Education and Action Fund and the Pursuit of Equality*. Toronto: Second Story.

Reese, L.A. 1993. 'Decision Rules in Local Economic Development.' *Urban Affairs Quarterly* 28:501–13.

Reimers, David M. and Harold Troper. 1992. 'Canadian and American Immigration Policy since 1945.' In Barry R. Chiswick, ed., *Immigration, Language, and Ethnicity: Canada and the United States*. Washington, D.C.: AEI Press, 15–54.

Resnick, Philip. 1987. 'State and Civil Society: The Limits of a Royal Commission.' *Canadian Journal of Political Science* 20, no. 2, 379–401.

– 1990. *The Masks of Proteus: Canadian Reflections on the State*. Montreal: McGill-Queen's University Press.

Rhodes, R.A.W. 1986a. '"Power-Dependence" Theories of Central-Local Relations: A Critical Assessment.' In M. Goldsmith, ed., *New Research in Central-Local Relations*. Aldershot: Gower.

– 1986b. *Beyond Westminster and Whitehall*. London: Unwin Hyman.

– 1990. 'Policy Networks: A British Perspective.' *Journal of Theoretical Politics* 2, no. 3, 293–317.

Rhodes, R.A.W. and David Marsh. 1992. 'New Directions in the Study of Policy Networks.' *European Journal of Political Research* 21:181–93.

Rhodes, R.A.W., C. Dargie, and B. Tutt. 1995. 'The State of Public Administration: A Professional History, 1970–1995.' *Public Administration* 73, no. 1, 1–16.

Ricci, David M. 1993. *The Transformation of American Politics: The New Washington and the Rise of Think Tanks*. New Haven: Yale University Press.

Richards, John. 1994. 'Living within Our Means.' In W.G. Watson, J. Richards, and D.M. Brown, eds., *The Case for Change: Reinventing the Welfare State*. Toronto: C.D. Howe Institute.

– 1994. 'The Social Policy Round.' In W.G. Watson, J. Richards, and D.M. Brown, eds., *The Case for Change: Reinventing the Welfare State*. Toronto: C.D. Howe Institute.

– et al. 1995. *Helping the Poor: A Qualified Case for 'Workfare.'* Toronto: C.D. Howe Institute.

Richardson, Jeremy, ed. 1982. *Policy Styles in Western Europe.* London: Allen and Unwin.

Richardson, Jeremy, Gunnel Gustafsson, and Grant Jordan. 1982. 'The Concept of Policy Style.' In Jeremy Richardson, ed., *Policy Styles in Western Europe.* London: Allen and Unwin, 1–16.

Richardson, M., J. Sherman, and M. Fismondi. 1993. *Winning Back the Words: Confronting Experts in an Environmental Public Hearing.* Toronto: Garamond Press.

Ricoeur, Paul. 1971. 'The Model of the Text: Meaningful Action Considered as a Text.' *Social Research* 38:529–62.

– 1973. 'Ethics and Culture: Habermas and Gadamer in Dialogue.' *Philosophy Today* 17:153–65.

– 1974. 'Psychoanalysis and the Movement of Contemporary Culture.' In his *The Conflict of Interpretations*, edited by Don Ihde. Evanston: Northwestern University Press, 121–59.

Riker, W.H. 1964. *Federalism.* Boston: Little, Brown.

Riker, William and Peter C. Ordeshook. 1973. *An Introduction to Positive Political Theory.* Toronto: Prentice-Hall.

Riley, Denise. 1988. *'Am I That Name?' Feminism and the Category of 'Women' in History.* Minneapolis: University of Minnesota.

Ritchie, Ronald S. 1971. *An Institute for Research on Public Policy.* Ottawa: Information Canada.

Rixecker, Stefanie S. 1994. 'Expanding the Discursive Context of Policy Design: A Matter of Feminist Standpoint Epistemology.' *Policy Sciences* 27:119–142.

Robichaud, Jean-Bernard and Claude Quiviger. 1991. *Active Communities.* Ottawa: Canadian Council on Social Development.

Robinson, Ian. 1993. *North American Trade As If Democracy Mattered.* Ottawa: Canadian Centre for Policy Alternatives.

Rhodes, R.A.W., D. Dargie and B. Tutt. 1995. 'The State of Public Administration: A Professional History, 1970–1995.' *Public Administration* 73, no. 1, 1–16.

Rorty, Richard. 1985. 'Habermas and Lyotard on Postmodernity.' In R.J. Bernstein, ed., *Habermas and Modernity.* Cambridge, Mass.: The M.I.T. Press, 161–75.

Rose, Richard. 1993. *Lesson-Drawing in Public Policy: A Guide to Learning across Space and Time.* Chatham, New Jersey: Chatham House.

Rosenau, James N. and Ernest-Otto Czempiel, eds. 1992. *Governance without Government: Order and Change in World Politics.* Cambridge: Cambridge University Press.

428   Policy Studies in Canada

Rosenau, P.V. 1993. 'Anticipating a Post-Modern Policy Current?' *Policy Currents* 3, no. 2, 1–4.
Ross, David and Peter J. Usher. 1986. *From the Roots Up: Economic Development As If Community Mattered.* Ottawa: Canadian Council on Social Development.
Rourke, Francis. 1984. *Bureaucracy, Politics and Public Policy*, 3rd ed. Toronto: Little, Brown.
Rowley, C.K. 1993. 'Introduction.' In Rowley, ed., *Public Choice Theory.* Aldershot: Elgar, ix–xxix.
Royal Commission on the Economic Union and Canada's Development Prospects. 1985. *Report.* Ottawa: Supply and Services.
Russell, Bob. 1990. *Back to Work? Labour, State and Industrial Relation in Canada.* Scarborough, Ont.: Nelson.
– 1991. 'Assault without Defeat: Contemporary Industrial Relations and the Canadian Labour Movement.' In L. Haiven, S. McBride, and J. Shield, eds., *Regulating Labour.* Toronto: Garamond.
Russell, Peter H. 1988. 'The Politics of Frustration: The Pursuit of Formal Constitutional Change in Australia and Canada.' *Australian-Canadian Studies* 6, 3–32.
– 1990. 'The Diffusion of Judicial Review: The Commonwealth, the United States, and the Canadian Case.' *Policy Studies Journal* 19 (Fall), 116–26.
– 1993. *Constitutional Odyssey: Can Canadians become a Sovereign People?* 2nd ed. Toronto: University of Toronto Press.
Rustow, Dankwart A. 1968. 'Modernization and Comparative Politics: Prospects in Research and Theory.' *Comparative Politics* 1:37–52.
Ryan, M. 1984. *Marxism and Deconstruction: A Critical Articulation.* Baltimore: Johns Hopkins University Press.
Ryerson, Stanley B. 1973. *Unequal Union: The Roots of Crisis in the Canadas, 1815–1873*, 2nd ed. Toronto: Progress Books.
Sabatier, P.A. 1987. 'Knowledge, Policy-Oriented Learning, and Policy Change: An Advocacy Coalition Approach.' *Knowledge* 8, no. 4, 649–92.
– 1988. 'An Advocacy Coalition Framework of Policy Change and the Role of Policy-Oriented Learning Therein.' *Policy Sciences* 21 (Fall), 129–68.
Sabatier, P.A. and M.C. Jenkins-Smith, eds. 1993. *Policy Change and Learning: An Advocacy Coalition Approach.* San Francisco: Westview Press.
Sabetti, F. 1980. 'Covenant Language in Canada.' Workshop on Covenant and Politics, Center for the Study of Federalism, Temple University.
Salisbury, Robert. 1984. 'Interest Representation: The Dominance of Institutions.' *American Political Science Review* 78:64–76.
Salter, L. and D. Salco. 1981. *Public Inquiries in Canada.* Ottawa: Science Council of Canada, Background Study 47.

Sapiro, Virginia. 1986. 'The Gender Basis of American Social Policy.' *Political Science Quarterly* 101, no. 2, 221–38.

Sarlo, Christopher A. 1992. *Poverty in Canada.* Vancouver: The Fraser Institute.

Saul, J.R. 1992. *Voltaire's Bastards: The Dictatorship of Reason in the West.* Toronto: Penguin.

Savoie, Donald J. 1990. *The Politics of Public Spending in Canada.* Toronto: University of Toronto Press.

– 1990. 'Studying Public Administration.' *Canadian Public Administration* 33, no. 3, 389–413.

– ed. 1993. *Taking Power: Managing Government Transitions.* Toronto: Institute of Public Administration in Canada.

– 1994. *Thatcher, Reagan, Mulroney: In Search of a New Bureaucracy.* Pittsburgh: Pittsburgh University Press.

Sawer, Marion. 1990. *Sisters in Suits: Women and Public Policy in Australia.* Sydney: Allen and Unwin

Scharpf, Fritz. 1988. 'The Joint-Decision Trap: Lessons from German Federalism and European Integration.' *Public Administration* 66:239–78.

– 1989. 'Decision Rules, Decision Styles and Policy Choices.' *Journal of Theoretical Politics* 1:149–76.

– 1990. 'Games Real Actors Could Play: The Problem of Connectedness.' Köln: Max-Planck-Institut für Gesellschaftsforschung, Paper 90/8.

Schelling, T.C. 1978. *Micromotives and Macrobehavior.* New York: Norton.

Schmidt, Manfred. 1983. 'The Welfare State and the Economy in Periods of Economic Crisis: A Comparative Study of Twenty-three OECD Nations.' *European Journal of Political Research* 11:1–26.

Schmitter, Phillippe C. 1979. 'Still the Century of Corporatism.' In Philippe C. Schmitter and Gerhard Lehmbruch, eds., *Trends toward Corporatist Intermediation.* Beverly Hills: Sage, 7–52.

– 1982. 'Reflections on Where the Theory of Neo-Corporatism Has Gone and Where the Praxis of Neo-Corporatism May Be Going.' In Gerhard Lehmbruch and Phillipe Schmitter, eds., *Patterns of Corporatist Policy-Making.* London: Sage.

Schneider, A. and H. Ingram. 1993. 'Social Construction of Target Populations: Implications for Politics and Policy.' *American Political Science Review* 87:334–48.

Schram, S.F. 1993. 'Postmodern Policy Analysis: Discourse and Identity in Welfare Policy.' *Policy Sciences* 26, no. 3, 249–70.

Schrecker, Ted. 1983. *The Conserver Society Revisited.* Science Council of Canada, Discussion Paper. Ottawa: Supply and Services Canada.

Schultz, Richard. 1988. 'Regulating Conservatively: The Mulroney Record, 1984–88.' In Andrew B. Gollner and Daniel Salée, eds., *Canada under Mulroney*. Montreal: Vehicule Press, 186–205.

Schutz, A. 1967. *The Phenomenology of the Social World*, trans. by G. Walsh and F. Lehnert. Evanston, Ill.: Northwestern University Press.

Schwartz, Mildred A. 1986. 'Comparing U.S. and Canadian Public Policy.' *Policy Studies Journal* 14 (June), 566–79. Reprinted in Robert J. Jackson, Doreen Jackson, and Nicolas Baxter-Moore, eds., *Contemporary Canadian Politics*. Scarborough: Prentice-Hall, 1987.

Science Council of Canada. 1977. *Canada as a Conserver Society: Resource Uncertainties and the Need for New Technologies*. Ottawa: Supply and Services Canada.

– 1979. *Forging the Links: A Technology Policy for Canada*. Report 29. Ottawa: Supply and Services Canada.

– 1981. *Hard Times, Hard Choices*. Committee Statement. Ottawa: Supply and Services Canada.

– 1989. *Annual Report, 1988–89*. Ottawa: Supply and Services Canada.

Scott, Joan W. 1988. 'Deconstructing Equality-versus-Difference: Or, the Uses of Poststructuralist Theory for Feminism.' *Feminist Studies* 14, no. 1 (Spring), 33–50.

Scott, W. Richard. 1991. 'Unpacking Institutional Arguments.' In Walter W. Powell and Paul J. DiMaggio, eds., *The New Institutionalism in Organizational Analysis*. Chicago: University of Chicago Press, 164–82.

Segal, Hugh D. 1981. 'A View from the Cabinet Office of Ontario.' In Daniel L. Bon, ed., *Lobbying: A Right? A Necessity? A Danger?* Ottawa: Conference Board of Canada.

Seidle, F. Leslie. 1993. 'Interest Advocacy through Parliamentary Channels: Representation and Accommodation.' Montreal: Institute for Research on Public Policy, 189–225.

– ed. 1993. *Rethinking Government: Reform Or Reinvention?* Montreal: Institute for Research on Public Policy.

– 1994. 'The Angry Citizenry: Examining Representation and Responsiveness in Government.' *Policy Options* (July–August).

– ed. 1994. *Equity and Community: The Charter, Interest Advocacy and Representation*. Montreal: Insitute for Research on Public Policy.

– ed. 1994. *Seeking a New Partnership: Asymmetrical and Confederal Options*. Montreal: Institute for Research on Public Policy.

Self, Peter. 1972. *Administrative Theories and Politics*. London: George Allen and Unwin.

Self, Peter and Herbert J. Storing. 1962. *The State and the Farmer: British Agricultural Policies and Politics*. Berkeley: University of California Press.

Sharman, G.C. 1990. 'Parliamentary Federations and United Government.'
Journal of Theoretical Politics 2:205–30.

Shepsle, Kenneth A. 1989. 'Studying Institutions: Lessons from the Rational
Choice Approach.' *Journal of Theoretical Politics* 1, no. 2, 131–47.

Shields, J. 1991. 'Building a New Hegemony in British Columbia: Can Neo-
Conservative Industrial Relations Succeed?' In L. Haiven, S. McBride, and J.
Shields, eds., *Regulating Labour: The State, Neo-Conservatism and Industrial
Relations*. Toronto: Garamond.

Shkilnyk, Anastasi. 1985. *A Poison Stronger than Love: The Destruction of an
Ojibwa Community*. New Haven: Yale University Press.

Shubik, Martin. 1983. *Game Theory and the Social Sciences*. Cambridge, Mass.:
The M.I.T. Press.

Siim, Birte. 1987. 'The Scandinavian Welfare States – Towards Sexual Equality or
a New Kind of Male Domination?' *Acta Sociologica* 30, no. 3–4, 255–70.

Simeon, Richard. 1976. 'Studying Public Policy.' *Canadian Journal of Political
Science* 9, no. 4 (December), 548–80.

– 1987. 'Inside the Macdonald Commission.' *Studies in Political Economy*
22:167–79.

– 1990. 'Globalization and the Canadian Nation State.' In Bruce Doern and Bryne
Purchase, eds., *Canada At Risk?* Toronto: C.D. Howe Institute, 46–58.

Simeon, Richard E.B. and David J. Elkins. 1974. 'Regional Political Cultures in
Canada.' *Canadian Journal of Political Science* 7:397–437.

Simms, Glenda. 1992. 'Beyond the White Veil.' In Constance Backhouse and
David H. Flaherty, eds., *Challenging Times: The Women's Movement in Canada
and the United States*. Montreal and Kingston: McGill-Queen's University
Press, 175–81.

Simon, Herbert A. 1947. *Administrative Behavior*, 2nd ed. New York: Macmillan.

– 1977. *The New Science of Management Decision*, rev. ed. Englewood Cliffs,
N.J.: Prentice-Hall.

Skocpol, Theda. 1986. 'Rediscovering the State: Strategies of Analysis in Current
Research.' In Peter B. Evans, D. Reuschemeyer, and Theda Skocpol, eds.,
Bringing the State Back In. Cambridge: Cambridge University Press, 3–37.

– 1992. *Protecting Soldiers and Mothers: The Political Origins of Social Policy
in the United States*. Cambridge: Harvard University Press.

Smiley, D.V. 1975. 'Canada and the Quest for a National Policy.' *Canadian
Journal of Political Science* 8:40–62.

Smircich, L. and C. Stubbart. 1985. 'Strategic Management in an Enacted World.'
Academy of Management Review 10, no. 4, 724–36.

Smith, Arthur J.R. 1980. 'The Economic Council of Canada.' In David C. Smith,
ed., *Economic Policy Advising in Canada: Essays in Honour of John Deutsch*.
Montreal: C.D. Howe Institute.

Smith, Dorothy. 1987. *The Everyday World as Problematic.* Toronto: University of Toronto Press.

Smith, James A. 1991. *The Idea Brokers: Think Tanks and the Rise of the New Policy Elite.* New York: The Free Press.

Spelman, Elizabeth. 1988. *Inessential Woman.* Boston: Beacon.

Sprague, Joey and Mary K. Zimmerman. 1993. 'Overcoming Dualisms: A Feminist Agenda for Sociological Methodology.' In Paula England, ed., *Theory on Gender: Feminism on Theory.* New York: Aldine de Gruyter, 255–80.

Sproule-Jones, M. 1975. *Public Choice and Federalism in Australia and Canada.* Canberra: Australian National University Press.

– 1981. *The Real World of Pollution Control.* Vancouver: Westwater Research Centre, UBC.

– 1982. 'Public Choice and Natural Resources.' *American Political Science Review* 76:790–804.

– 1983. 'Institutions, Constitutions and Public Policies.' In M.M. Atkinson and M.A. Chandler, eds., *Canadian Public Policy.* Toronto: University of Toronto Press.

– 1984. 'Methodological Individualism.' *American Behavioral Scientist* 28:167–83.

– 1984. 'The Enduring Colony.' *Publius* 14:93–108.

– 1989. 'Multiple Rules and the Nesting of Public Policies.' *Journal of Theoretical Politics* 1:459–77.

– 1993. *Governments at Work.* Toronto: University of Toronto Press.

– 1994. 'User Fees.' In A.M. Maslowe, ed., *Taxes as Instruments of Public Policy.* Toronto: University of Toronto Press.

– 1994. 'The Pragmatics of Special Purpose Bodies.' In D. Richmond and D. Siegel, eds., *Agencies, Boards and Commissions.* Toronto: Institute of Public Administration of Canada.

Sproule-Jones, M. and P.L. Richards. 1984. 'Towards a Theory of the Regulated Environment.' *Canadian Public Policy* 10:305–15.

Stabler, J.C. 1977. 'The Report of the Mackenzie Valley Pipeline Inquiry, Volume 1: A Socio-economic Critique.' *The Musk-Ox: A Journal of the North* 20:57–8.

Stanbury, W.T. 1977. *Business Interests and the Reform of Competition Policy.* Toronto: Methuen.

– 1986. *Business-Government Relations in Canada.* Toronto: Methuen.

– 1991. 'Controlling the Growth of Provincial Governments.' In M. McMillan, ed., *Provincial Public Finances.* Toronto: Canadian Tax Foundation, 371–402.

– 1993. 'A Sceptic's Guide to the Claims of So-called Public Interest Groups.' *Canadian Public Administration* 36, no. 4, 580–605.

– 1993. *Business-Government Relations in Canada,* 2nd ed. Toronto: Nelson.

Stark, Andrew. 1992. '"Political-Discourse" Analysis and the Debate over Canada's Lobbying Legislation.' *Canadian Journal of Political Science* 25 (September), 513–34.

Starling, Grover. 1982. *Managing the Public Sector*. Homewood, Ill.: The Dorsey Press.

Steiner, Peter O. 1969. *Public Expenditure Budgeting*. Washington: Brookings Institution.

Steinmo, Sveb, Kathleen Thelen, and Frank Longstreth, eds. 1992. *Structuring Politics: Historical Institutionalism in Comparative Analysis*. Cambridge: Cambridge University Press.

Stevenson, H. Michael, Eugene Vayda, and A. Paul Williams. 1987. 'Medical Politics after the Canada Health Act: Preliminary Results of the 1986 Physicians' Survey.' Paper delivered at the annual meeting of the Canadian Political Science Association, McMaster University, Hamilton, Ontario.

Stewart, J.D. 1958. *British Pressure Groups: Their Role in Relation to the House of Commons*. Oxford: Clarendon Press.

Stivers, Camilla. 1993. *Gender Images in Public Administration*. Newbury Park: Sage Publications.

Stone, Deborah A. 1988. *Policy Paradox and Political Reason*. New York: Harper Collins.

Straussman, Jeffrey D. 1985. *Public Administration*. New York: Holt, Rinehart and Winston.

Strick, John. 1990. *The Economics of Government Regulation: Theory and Canadian Practice*. Toronto: Thompson.

Sutherland, Sharon L. 1991. 'Responsible Government and Ministerial Responsibility: Every Reform Is Its Own Problem.' *Canadian Journal of Political Science* 24, no. 1, 91–120.

Sutherland, Sharon and Bruce Doern. 1986. *Bureaucracy in Canada: Control and Reform*. Toronto: University of Toronto Press.

Szablowski, G.J. 1977. 'The Optimal Policy-Making System: Implications for the Canadian Political Process.' In T. A. Hockin, ed., *Apex of Power: The Prime Minister and Political Leadership in Canada*, 2nd ed. Scarborough: Prentice-Hall, 197–210.

Taylor, Charles. 1971. 'Interpretation and the Sciences of Man.' *Review of Metaphysics* 25:3–51.

– 1985. 'Alternative Futures: Legitimacy, Identity and Alienation in Late 20th Centuty Canada.' In A. Cairns and C. Williams, eds., *Constitutionalism, Citizenship and Society in Canada*. Toronto: University of Toronto Press.

– 1990. 'A Free, Independent Quebec in a Strong, United Canada,' *Compass* 8:46–48.

- 1991. *The Malaise of Modernity*. Toronto: Anansi.
- 1992. *Multiculturalism and 'The Politics of Recognition.'* Princeton: Princeton University Press.
Teeple, Gary, ed. 1972. *Capitalism and the National Question in Canada*. Toronto: University of Toronto Press.
Teghtsoonian, Katherine. 1993. 'Neo-Conservative Ideology and Opposition to Federal Regulation of Child Care Services in the United States and Canada.' *Canadian Journal of Political Science* 26, no. 1, 97–121.
Tellier, Paul. 1993. *A Report on Progress*. Ottawa: Supply and Services.
Thelen, Kathleen and Sven Steinmo. 1992. 'Historical Institutionalism and Comparative Politics.' In Sven Steinmo, Kathleen Thelen, and Frank Longstreth, eds., *Structuring Politics: Historical Institutionalism in Comparative Analysis*. Cambridge: Cambridge University Press, 1–32.
Thomas, David. 1993. 'Introduction.' In David Thomas, ed., *Canada and the United States: Differences that Count*. Peterborough: Broadview Press, 9–18.
Thomas, Norman C. 1988. 'Public Policy and the Resurgence of Conservatism in Three Anglo-American Democracies.' In Barry Cooper et al., eds., *The Resurgence of Conservatism in Anglo-American Democracies*. Durham, N.C.: Duke University Press, 96–136.
Thomas, P.G. 1994. 'Central Agencies: Making a Mesh of Things.' In J.P. Bickerton and A.G. Gagnon, eds., *Canadian Politics*, 2nd ed. Peterborough: Broadview Press, 288–306.
Thompson, Fred and W.T. Stanbury. 1979. *The Political Economy of Interest Groups*. Montreal: Institute for Research on Public Policy.
Thorburn, H.G. 1964. 'Pressure Groups in Canadian Politics: Recent Revisions of the Anti-Combines Legislation.' *Canadian Journal of Economics and Political Science* 30, no. 2, 157–74.
- 1978. 'Canadian Pluralist Democracy in Crisis.' *Canadian Journal of Political Sciene* 11, no. 4, 723–38.
Throgmorton, J.A. 1991. 'Rhetorics of Policy Analysis.' *Policy Sciences* 24:153–79.
Tocqueville, A. de. 1960. *Democracy in America*, edited by P. Bradley. New York: Knopf.
Torgerson, Douglas. 1980. *Industrialization and Assessment: Social Impact Assessment as a Social Phenomenon*. Toronto: York University.
- 1985. 'Contextual Orientation in Policy Analysis: The Contribution of Harold D. Lasswell.' *Policy Sciences* 18:241–61.
- 1986. 'Between Knowledge and Politics: Three Faces of Policy Analysis.' *Policy Sciences* 19:33–59.
- 1986. 'Interpretive Policy Inquiry: A Response to Its Limitations.' *Policy Sciences* 19:397–405.

- 1990. 'Limits of the Administrative Mind: The Problem of Defining Environmental Problems.' In R. Paehlke and D. Torgerson, eds., *Managing Leviathan: Environmental Politics and the Administrative State*. Peterborough: Broadview Press, 115–61.
- 1990. 'Origins of the Policy Orientation: The Aesthetic Dimension in Lasswell's Political Vision.' *History of Political Thought* 11:339–51.
- 1992. 'Priest and Jester in the Policy Sciences: Developing the Focus of Inquiry.' *Policy Sciences* 25:225–35.
- 1992. 'Reuniting Theory and Practice.' *Policy Sciences* 25:211–24.
- 1993. 'The Paradox of Organizational Rationality: Uncertainty Absorption and the Technology of Foolishness.' Paper presented at the School of Business, Queen's University, Kingston, 2 April.
- 1994. 'Oppositional Knowledge: Policy Sciences and Transformative Politics.' Paper presented at the World Congress of the International Political Science Association, Berlin, 23 August.
- 1995. 'Policy Analysis and Public Life: The Restoration of *Phronesis*?' In J.S. Dryzek, J. Farr, and S. Leonard, eds., *Political Science in History: Research Programs and Political Traditions*. Cambridge: Cambridge University Press.
- 1995. 'The Uncertain Quest for Sustainability: Environmentalism and Public Discourse.' In F. Fischer and M. Black, eds., *Greening Environmental Policy: Toward a Politics of Sustainability*. London: Paul Chapman.
Trebilcock, Michael J. 1994. *The Limits of Freedom of Contract*. Cambridge, Mass.: Harvard University Press.
Trebilcock, M.J., D. Hartle, J.R.S. Prichard, and D. Dewes. 1982. *The Choice of Governing Instrument*. Ottawa: Economic Council of Canada.
Tribe, L.H. 1972. 'Policy Science: Analysis or Ideology?' *Philosophy and Public Affairs* 2:66–110.
- 1972/73. 'Technology Assessment and the Fourth Discontinuity: The Limits of Instrumental Rationality.' *Southern California Law Review* 46:617–60.
Tronto, Joan C. 1993. *Moral Boundaries: A Political Argument for an Ethic of Care*. New York: Routledge.
Truman, David. 1951. *The Governmental Process*. New York: Knopf.
Tullock, G. 1980. 'Why So Much Stability?' *Public Choice* 37:189–202.
Tuohy, Carolyn. 1988. 'Medicine and the State in Canada: The Extra-Billing Issue in Perspective.' *Canadian Journal of Political Science* 21:267–96.
- 1990. 'Interests and Institutions in the Occupational Health Arena: The Case of Quebec.' In William D. Coleman and Grace Skogstad, eds., *Policy Communities and Public Policy in Canada*. Toronto: Copp Clark Pitman, 238–65.
- 1992. *Policy and Politics in Canada: Institutionalized Ambivalence*. Philadelphia: Temple University Press.

436 Policy Studies in Canada

- 1994a. 'The Clinton Proposal: A Comparative Perspective.' *Journal of Health Politics, Policy and Law* 19, no. 1, 249–54.
- 1994b. 'Health Policy and Fiscal Federalism.' In Keith Banting, Douglas Brown, and Thomas Courchene, eds., *The Future of Fiscal Federalism*. Kingston: Queen's University School of Policy Studies, 189–212.
Tupper, Allan. 1993. 'Think Tanks, Public Debt, and the Politics of Expertise in Canada.' *Canadian Public Administration* 36, no. 4, 530–47.
Twight, Charlotte. 1988. 'Government Manipulation of Constitutional-Level Transaction Costs: A General Theory of Transaction-Costs, Augmentation and the Growth of Government.' *Public Choice* 56:131–52.
- 1992. 'Constitutional Renegotiation: Impediments to Consensual Revision.' *Constitutional Policy Economy* 3:89–112.
- 1994. 'Political Transaction-Cost Manipulation: An Integrating Theory.' *Journal of Theoretical Politics* 6, no. 2, 189–216.
Uslaner, Eric M. 1992. 'Energy Policy and Federalism in the United States and Canada.' In Jonathan Lemco, ed., *The Canada–United States Relationship: The Politics of Energy and Environmental Coordination*. Westport, Conn.: Praeger, 41–63.
Vaillancourt, François. 1992. 'An Economic Perspective on Language and Public Policy in Canada and the United States.' In Barry R. Chiswick, ed., *Immigration, Language, and Ethnicity: Canada and the United States*. Washington, D.C.: AEI Press, 179–228.
Van Loon, R.J. 1981. 'Kaleidoscope in Grey: The Policy Process in Ottawa.' In M. Whittington and G. Williams, eds., *Canadian Politics in the 1980s*. Toronto: Methuen.
van Waarden, Frans. 1985. 'Bureaucracy around the State: Varieties of Collective Self-Regulation in the Dutch Dairy Industry.' In Wolfgang Streeck and Philippe Schmitter, eds., *Private Interest Government*. London: Sage.
- 1992a. 'Dimensions and Types of Policy Networks.' *European Journal of Political Research* 21:29–52.
- 1992b. 'The Historical Institutionalization of Typical National Patterns in Policy Networks between State and Industry: A Comparison of the USA and the Netherlands.' *European Journal of Political Research* 21:131–62.
Veilleux, Gérard. 1989. 'Notes for an Address to the APEX Symposium.' Unpublished paper. Ottawa: Treasury Board Secretariat.
Veilleux, G. and D.J. Savoie. 1988. 'Kafka's Castle: The Treasury Board of Canada Revisited.' *Canadian Public Administration* 31, no. 4, 517–38.
Verba, Sydney. 1967. 'Some Dilemmas in Comparative Research.' *World Politics* 20:111–27.

Vickers, Jill, Pauline Rankin, and Christine Appelle. 1993. *Politics As If Women Mattered: A Political Analysis of the National Action Committee on the Status of Women*. Toronto: University of Toronto Press.

Vining, A. and A. Boardman. 1992. 'Ownership vs. Competition: Efficiency vs. Public Enterprise.' *Public Choice* 73:205–39.

Vogel, David. 1986. *National Styles of Regulation: Environmental Policy in Great Britain and the United States*. Ithaca, N.Y.: Cornell University Press.

Walker, Gillian. 1992. 'The Conceptual Politics of Struggle: Wife Battering, the Women's Movement, and the State.' In M. Patricia Connelly and Pat Armstrong, eds., *Feminism in Action: Studies in Political Economy*. Toronto: Canadian Scholars' Press, 317–42.

Walker, Jack. 1983. 'The Origin and Maintenance of Interest Groups in America.' *American Political Science Review* 77:390–406.

Walker, Michael, ed. 1988. *Freedom, Democracy and Economic Welfare*. Vancouver: The Fraser Institute.

Watkins, Melville et al. 1968. *Foreign Ownership and the Structure of Canadian Industry*. Ottawa: Privy Council.

Watkins, Mel. 1994. 'Foreign Ownership '94 – Buy, Bye Canada.' *This Magazine* (April/May), 30–2.

Watson, William G. 1994. 'The View from the Right.' In W.G. Watson, J. Richards, and D.M. Brown, *The Case for Change: Reinventing the Welfare State*. Toronto: C.D. Howe Institute.

Waylen, Georgina. 1986. 'Women and Neo-liberalism.' In Judith Evans et al., *Feminism and Political Theory*. London: Sage Publications, 85–102.

Weaver, R. Kent. 1985. *The Politics of Industrial Change: Railway Policy in North America*. Washington, D.C.: Brookings Institution.

– 1989. 'The Changing World of Think Tanks.' *PS: Political Science and Politics* 22, no. 3, 563–78.

– 1993. 'Through the One-Way Mirror: Research and Teaching on Canadian Politics in the United States.' Unpublished Paper. Washington D.C.: Brookings Institution.

Weaver, R. Kent and Bert A. Rockman, eds. 1993. *Do Institutions Matter? Government Capabilities in the United States and Abroad*. Washington, D.C.: Brookings Institution.

Webber, David J. 1992. 'The Distribution and Use of Policy Knowledge in the Policy Process.' In W.N. Dunn and R.M. Kelly, eds., *Advances in Policy Studies since 1950*. New Brunswick, N.J.: Transaction Books.

Weber, Max. 1946. 'Science as a Vocation.' In H.H. Gerth and C.W. Mills, eds., *From Max Weber: Essays in Sociology*. New York: Oxford University Press, 129–56.

– 1958. *The Protestant Ethic and the Spirit of Capitalism*, trans. by Talcott Parsons. New York: Charles Scribner's Sons.

– 1978. *Economy and Society*, 2 vols., edited by G. Roth and C. Wittich. Berkeley: University of California Press.

Weir, R.A. 1973. 'Federalism, Interest Groups and Parliamentary Government: The Canadian Medical Association.' *Journal of Comparative Political Studies* 10, no. 2, 159–75.

Weiss, Carol. 1980. 'Knowledge Creep and Decision Accretion.' *Knowledge* 3:381–404.

West, Edwin G. 1993. *Education and Competitiveness.* Discussion Paper 93–02. Government and Competitiveness Project, Queen's University School of Policy Studies.

Whitaker, Reginald. 1977. *The Government Party: Organizing and Financing the Liberal Party of Canada, 1930–58.* Toronto: University of Toronto Press.

White, S.K. 1991. *Political Theory and Postmodernism.* Cambridge: Cambridge University Press.

Whittington, Michael and Richard Van Loon. 1975. *The Canadian Political System.* Toronto: McGraw-Hill Ryerson.

Whitworth, Sandra. 1991. 'Planned Parenthood and the New Right: Onslaught *and* Opportunity?' *Studies in Political Economy* 35 (Summer), 73–101.

Wilcher, Marshall E. 1989. *The Politics of Acid Rain Policy in Canada, Great Britain and the United States.* Brookfield, Vt.: Gower Publishing Company.

Wildavsky, Aaron. 1979. *Speaking Truth to Power: The Art and Craft of Policy Analysis.* Boston: Little, Brown.

– 1984. *The Politics of the Budgetary Process*, 4th ed. Boston: Little, Brown.

– 1990. 'Introduction.' In A. Wildavsky et al., eds., *Public Administration: The State of the Discipline.* Chatham, N.J.: Chatham House.

– 1994. 'Why Self-Interest Means Less outside a Social Context.' *Journal of Theoretical Politics* 6:131–60.

Wilensky, Harold. 1975. *The Welfare State and Equality.* Berkeley: University of California Press.

Wilks, Stephen and Maurice Wright. 1987. 'Conclusion: Comparing Government-Industry Relations: States, Sectors, and Networks.' In Wilks and Wright, eds., *Comparative Government-Industry Relations.* Oxford: Oxford University Press.

Willer, David and Bo Anderson, eds. 1981. *Networks, Exchange and Coercion.* New York: Elsevier.

Williams, A.P. 1989. 'Access and Accommodation in the Canadian Welfare State: The Political Significance of Contacts between State, Labour and Business Leaders.' *Canadian Review of Sociology and Anthropology* 26, no. 2, 217–39.

Williams, Glen. 1986. *Not for Export: Toward a Political Economy of Canada's Arrested Industrialization.* Toronto: McClelland and Stewart.

Williamson, O.E. 1975. *Markets and Hierarchies, Analysis and Antitrust Implications: A Study in the Economics of Internal Organization.* New York: The Free Press.

– 1985. *The Economic Institutions of Capitalism.* New York: The Free Press.

– 1990. 'The Firm as a Nexus of Treaties.' In M. Aoki et al., eds., *The Firm as Nexus of Treaties.* Newbury Park: Sage Publications, 1–25.

Wilson, Elizabeth. 1977. *Women and the Welfare State.* London: Tavistock.

– 1987. 'Thatcherism and Women: After Seven Years.' *The Socialist Register,* 199–235.

Wilson, Harold. 1986. *Memoirs, 1916–1964: The Making of a Prime Minister.* London: Weidenfeld, Nicholson and Joseph.

Wilson, James Q. 1994. 'Reinventing Public Administration.' *PS: Political Science and Politics* 27, no. 4, 667–73.

Wilson, Jeremy. 1990. 'Wilderness Politics in B.C.: The Business Dominated State and the Containment of Environmentalism.' In W. Coleman and G. Skogstad, eds., *Policy Communities and Public Policy in Canada.* Toronto: Copp Clark Pitman.

Wilson, V. Seymour. 1981. *Canadian Public Policy: Theory and Environment.* Toronto: McGraw-Hill Ryerson.

Winch, P. 1963. *The Idea of a Social Science and Its Relation to Philosophy.* London: Routledge and Kegan Paul.

Winham, Gilbert. 1986. *International Trade and the Tokyo Round Negotiation.* Princeton: Princeton University Press.

Winner, L. 1969. 'Cybernetics and Political Language.' *Berkeley Journal of Sociology* 14:3–17.

Wolf, Charles, Jr. 1993. *Markets or Governments: Choosing between Imperfect Alternatives.* Cambridge, Mass.: The M.I.T. Press.

Wolfe, D. 1986. 'The Politics of the Deficit.' In G.B. Doern, ed., *The Politics of Economic Policy.* Toronto: University of Toronto Press.

Wolin, Sheldon S. 1960. *Politics and Vision.* Boston: Little, Brown.

– 1980. 'Political Theory and Political Commentary.' In M. Richter, ed., *Political Theory and Political Education.* Princeton: Princeton University Press.

Woodside, K. 1986. 'Policy Instruments and the Study of Public Policy.' *Canadian Journal of Political Science* 19, no. 4, 775–94.

Woolley, Frances R. 1993. 'The Feminist Challenge to Neoclassical Economics.' *Cambridge Journal of Economics* 17:485–500.

Woolley, Frances R. and Judith Marshall. 1992. 'Measuring Inequality within the Household.' Ottawa: Carleton University Economic Papers, August.

440   Policy Studies in Canada

Wright, Maurice. 1988. 'Policy Community, Policy Network and Comparative Industrial Policies.' *Political Studies* 36:593–612.

Yeatman, Anna. 1990. *Bureaucrats, Technocrats, Femocrats: Essays on the Contemporary Australian State.* Sydney: Allen and Unwin.

– 1994. *Postmodern Revisionings of the Political.* New York: Routledge.

Young, Brigitte. 1990. 'Does the American Dairy Industry Fit a Meso-Corporatism Model?' *Political Studies* 38:72–82.

Young, Iris Marion. 1990. *Justice and the Politics of Difference.* Princeton, N.J.: Princeton University Press.

– 1994. 'Gender as Seriality: Thinking about Women as a Social Collective.' *Signs* 19, no. 3, 713–38.

Young, R.A. 1991. 'Tectonic Policies and Political Competition.' In A. Breton et al., eds., *The Competitive State.* Kluwer, 129–45.

– 1994. 'The Political Economy of Secession: The Case of Quebec.' *Constitutional Political Economy* 5, no. 2, 221–46.

Zagare, Frank C. 1984. *Game Theory: Concepts and Applications.* Beverly Hills: Sage Publications.

Zeigler, Harmon. 1988. *Pluralism, Corporatism, and Confucianism: Political Association and Conflict Regulation in the United States, Europe and Taiwan.* Philadelphia: Temple University Press.

Zey, Mary. 1992. *Decision-Making: Alternatives to Rational Choice Models.* Newburry Park: Sage Publications.

Zolf, Dorothy. 1989. 'Comparisons of Multicultural Broadcasting in Canada and Four Other Countries.' *Canadian Ethnic Studies* 21:13–26.

Zussman, David and Jak Jabes. 1989. *The Vertical Solitude: Managing in the Public Sector.* Halifax: Institute for Research on Public Policy.

Contributors

Michael M. Atkinson is a member of the Department of Political Science, McMaster University.

Colin Bennett is a member of the Department of Political Science, University of Victoria.

Stephen Brooks is a member of the Department of Political Science, University of Windsor.

William D. Coleman is a member of the Department of Political Science, McMaster University.

Laurent Dobuzinskis is a member of the Department of Political Science, Simon Fraser University.

G. Bruce Doern is a member of the School of Public Administration, Carleton University.

Michael Howlett is a member of the Department of Political Science, Simon Fraser University.

Réjean Landry is a member of the Département de science politique, Université Laval.

David Laycock is a member of the Department of Political Science, Simon Fraser University.

Evert A. Lindquist is a member of the Department of Political Science, University of Toronto.

Stephen McBride is Chair of the Department of Political Science, Simon Fraser University.

Leslie A. Pal is a member of the School of Public Administration, Carleton University.

Richard W. Phidd is a member of the Department of Political Studies, University of Guelph.

Susan D. Phillips is a member of the School of Public Administration, Carleton University.

A. Paul Pross is Professor Emeritus in the Department of Political Science, Dalhousie University.

Donald J. Savoie holds the Clément-Cormier Chair in Economic Development at the Université de Moncton.

Mildred A. Schwartz is a member of the Department of Sociology, University of Illinois at Chicago.

Richard Simeon is a member of the Department of Political Science, University of Toronto.

Mark Sproule-Jones is a member of the Department of Political Science, McMaster University.

Douglas Torgerson is a member of the Department of Political Studies, Trent University.

Carolyn Hughes Tuohy is a member of the Department of Political Science, University of Toronto.